LANGUAGE LEARNING DISABILITIES IN SCHOOL-AGE CHILDREN AND ADOLESCENTS

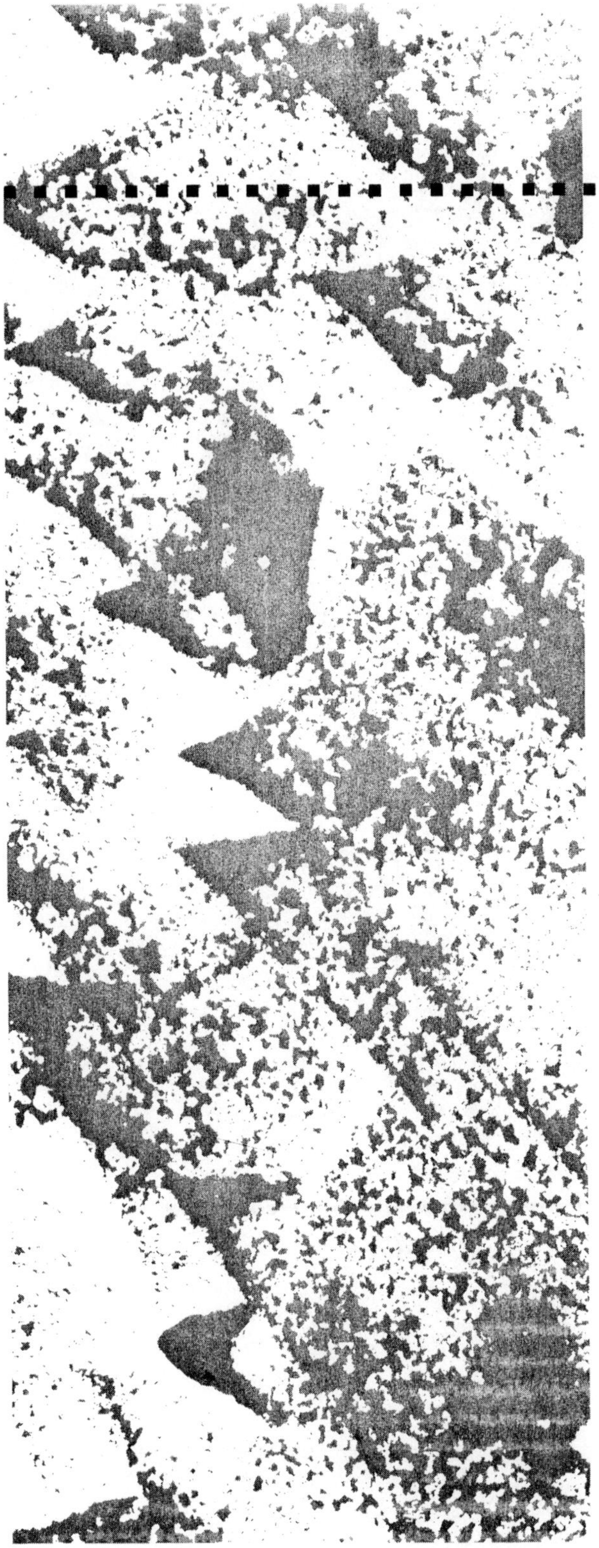

LANGUAGE LEARNING DISABILITIES IN SCHOOL-AGE CHILDREN AND ADOLESCENTS

Some Principles and Applications

GERALDINE P. WALLACH
Emerson College Los Angeles Center

KATHARINE G. BUTLER
Syracuse University

ALLYN AND BACON
Boston London Toronto Sydney Tokyo Singapore

About the cover:
The cover art was created by Melissa Hampe, an elementary school student in Terri Meade's profoundly mentally handicapped class at Corley Elementary School in Irmo, South Carolina. Melissa, who has cerebral palsy and a visual impairment, enjoys the class's "sensory art activities" such as the sponge painting session during which she produced this black and white tempera painting.

A Viacom Company
Needham Heights, Massachusetts 02194

Internet: www.abacon.com
America Online: keyword: College Online

ISBN 0-675-22153-6

Printed in the United States of America

10 9 8 01

PREFACE

One of the many advantages of a multiauthored text is that the reader is exposed to multiple perspectives on overlapping issues. As our wise readers know, when one begins to explore unfamiliar areas of knowledge, a term, a phrase, or a subheading may catch one's eye. Instinctively, if one is fresh to the topic, there is a tendency to hold fast to that term or phrase as the only "right stuff" and there may be a disinclination to challenge this partially rendered picture to closer examination or to explore other perspectives. Old-timers, defined here as anyone who has gone beyond the first reading of the text, may welcome the inevitable diversity of the subtle and not-so-subtle differences among authors. For example, Vygotsky's Zone of Proximal Development (ZPD) is addressed by a number of our authors in the chapters that follow. Readers will find that it is possible to view the ZPD through the sociocultural prism, through the assessment perspective, and through an instructional/intervention perspective, to name only three. Readers will also note the recasting of many themes and concepts throughout the text that integrate language proficiency, learning and academic success, and literacy development and growth. The editors have, in an effort to make several connections explicit, constructed a series of bridges between sections, attempting to clarify authors' intents as well as to reflect on what may be readers' questions and perceptions.

When an earlier version of this text was published in 1984, the preface contained the following:

> As professionals in the midst of a new decade of research and practice, we continue our quest by asking new and provocative questions about old and continuing problems. What cognitive and linguistic strategies underpin speaking and reading? What is literacy, and what level of inferencing does it require? What instructional variables may facilitate or deter classroom learning? What do we really mean by "developmental delay"? Does "dyslexia" really exist as an entity unto itself? Do language-disordered preschoolers ever catch up? Can early language programs make a difference? Who are these children we call "learning disabled"?

Language Learning Disabilities in School-Age Children and Adolescents: Some Principles and Applications brings us ahead ten years, to the present. Readers will, no doubt, recognize some familiar themes from the 1984 version that have become, in a sense, a trademark of the editors' ongoing self-questioning. Indeed, we wondered as we began to create the 1994 edition whether this excerpt, unless noted, would be recognized as over ten years old. Perhaps so, perhaps not. We also thought about what shape and form the 1994 edition—a "revision"—would take. How similar or how different would it be from the earlier version? Clearly, many issues raised in 1984 are raised now. The connections among language learning and literacy learning pervade both editions. The instructional variables that make and break academic learning remain a current focus of study. The quest for some answers to the ways that language disorders change over time continues and will, in all likelihood, be a topic of the next edition of this text. Likewise, the quest for productive alternatives to the ever-present deification of standardized tests and prepackaged programs continues; such tests and programs provide cookbook answers that cast their shadows on clinical and educational practice—often preventing practice from reaching a higher ground when practitioners unthinkingly accept them as true for all children in all settings and in all ways.

As the 1994 edition became a reality, that is, as we began to flesh out its topics and invite its authors, several observations struck us, and they became points of departure for versions one and two. First, there is much more common ground among our authors. Several theories and concepts that had been around for a while were revived and put into practice across many areas. The ZPD (Zone of Proximal Development) mentioned earlier is one example of a concept that several of our contributors included in their chapters. Likewise, several authors applied dynamic assessment and reciprocal teaching concepts to language-based intervention. Second, there is less separation between spoken and written language in the chapters. Further, there is more in-depth discussion of written language. As several authors note, *literacy* is a much broader concept than it was in 1984. Third, the reality of the educational reforms of the year 2000 appear to be influencing the way all of us think about school success and the delivery of services to students in trouble.

Many of the contributors from the first edition, including Blachman, Nelson, Silliman, van Kleeck, and Westby, are contributors to this edition. Readers who have access to the 1984 version of their work may find it most interesting to note the depth and scope with which the authors' research and thinking has evolved over the ten-year span. Some of the players may be the same but their work seems deeper and clearer. The new group of contributors brings an added freshness to the current edition. Blachowicz, Bloom, Brown, Campione, Catts, Ehren, Friel-Patti, German, Hoffman, Lahey, Milosky, Palincsar, Paratore, Scott, and Wilkinson all become threads of the new tapestry of ideas and suggestions we have woven.

The book is divided into four major sections: Part One: Introductory Considerations, Oral Language Connections to Literacy, and the Classroom; Part Two: Focus on Assessment: Potential and Progress; Part Three: A Closer Look: Discourse Across Ages, Stages, and Language Styles and Abilities; and Part Four: Special Issues: Understanding the Nature of Language Disorders Across Tasks and Time.

Part One sets the stage for the rest of the text. Readers are introduced to several themes, one of which is exemplified in this question: Why the focus on literacy in a text about language? Wallach and Butler answer the question in Chapter 1. Both the question and its suggested answers speak to an overriding theme of this text. Silliman and Wilkinson and van Kleeck provide some additional clarification in Chapters 2 and 3. Throughout the first section, the authors encourage readers to reexamine their beliefs about language learning and its connection to literacy learning. Wallach and Butler provide some specific examples of oral to literate acquisitions. They challenge some traditional notions about developmental sequences and take a hard look at content and form interactions, phonics and whole language arguments, and the labeling and categorizing of children.

Silliman and Wilkinson begin where Wallach and Butler end. They introduce the concept of discourse scaffolding and bring to the table the importance of oral language in the literacy and learning process. Through examples of classroom lessons they show how the instructional styles and the language choices teachers make help or hold back the students in their care.

Van Kleeck completes the section with a powerful chapter on metalinguistic development. She gives readers one of the most in-depth views available currently on aspects, models, and assessment and intervention practices of language awareness. Van Kleeck reminds readers to be ever cognizant of the theories that underlie clinical and educational assumptions and to be sensitive to adaptations one must make to bring children from literacy socialization, to pre-literacy to early literacy, and eventually to advanced reading and writing.

Part Two is focused a bit more specifically on assessment, although the authors and the editors note that the separation between assessment and intervention is an artificial one. The main thrust of the section involves two interrelated concepts: first, children and adolescents must be observed and assessed in the contexts in which they are having difficulty, and second, children's learning potential must also be assessed and understood. Nelson opens the section with a clear and readable message: go to the source of what students must master in school—the curriculum. She guides readers through several specific suggestions that speak to, albeit indirectly, some of the school reforms like inclusion, which proposes that special education students be educated in their home and community schools. Nelson outlines strategies across various grade levels for interviewing, observing, and scaffolding that will help diagnosticians and teachers understand their students' difficulties within the context of the school culture.

Palincsar, Brown, and Campione follow up with a discussion of dynamic assessment. They help readers understand the significant differences between more traditional assessment formats and the more dynamic formats that involve assessing a learner's potential. Vygotsky's Zone of Proximal Development (ZPD) becomes a center of the discussion. Palincsar and her colleagues also demonstrate how dynamic assessment principles are applied to intervention and remediation.

Silliman and Wilkinson round out the section with a chapter on several different types of observation. They provide us with a wonderful camera metaphor that demonstrates to readers how different "lenses" help us see (and sometimes, not see) what children can do. They remind us to think about what real progress might be and how to measure it.

Part Three is a potpourri of topics intersecting in many ways. We look across and into the continuum of communication success and difficulty through, to use Silliman and Wilkinson's metaphor, the author's different lenses. Westby and Scott take us through different aspects of oral and literate language. Westby gives readers an enhanced sensitivity to the multicultural nature of our society, helping us understand the danger of prejudging what children can and cannot do—particularly children from diverse cultures who are sometimes lost in mainstream American culture and its schools.

Westby provides very specific information about cultural differences across narrative and expository text, including some fascinating examples of how value systems affect what we comprehend as a metaphor for clinical and educational practice.

Scott takes professionals on a remarkable journey through a written language jungle and reveals a framework that cuts across modality and genre. Scott gives syntax its rightful place as she explores with readers the influence of written language on oral language, reiterating a theme that Wallach and Butler introduced in Chapter 1.

Blachman takes us back to basics with a look at one of the most basic of all literacy abilities—phonological awareness. She takes us through some seminal as well as some recent research and provides us with a concise, logical, and practical view of the early literacy acquisition. Blachman puts into perspective any doubts one might have about whole language as the only way and helps us see the impracticality of bypassing phonological awareness and other meta-activities in literacy programs.

Milosky follows and shifts to another aspect of language learning and literacy learning—figurative language. She reminds us of the richness of language and brings home to readers the notion that linguistic forms such as metaphors, similes, and idioms are far from being nice-to-have additions to language—a point van Kleeck also makes about metalinguistic abilities in Part One. Indeed, one might be hard-pressed to count the metaphors and other figurative devices used throughout this text, reflecting an aspect of language use that is very much a part of children's literature, television, and most conversations, as Milosky adeptly points out. She asks readers to think about figurative language and literacy connections and provides in-depth coverage of the seeds and the flowering of nonliteral language development, its assessment, and its intervention.

Blachowicz provides a highly readable excursion into another part of the language learning jungle as she speaks to LLD children and adolescents' problems with both problem solving and reading comprehension. Again, readers will see the importance of bringing together old and new information. Blachowicz uses the creative term "thoughtgetting" as she guides readers through many activities that will help children set purposes for reading, search their minds and memory for hypotheses, and make inferences and draw conclusions. Blachowicz's discussion shows how what educators view as vocabulary use is, in reality, only the surface of the jungle floor. Underneath that surface lies the reader's (and speaker's) prior knowledge. Her chapter closes with detailed suggestions on how one may assist children to consolidate word meanings and to capture these structures within a problem-solving context.

German also deals with words, their meanings, their presence, and their loss. She makes clear the pervasive nature of word-finding difficulties, defining their characteristics and their patterns of development. She also talks about the "disappearance" of words as children reach into memory to find them and the implications of such "disappearances" and other word-finding difficulties for children and youth with language learning disabilities. Assessment and programming suggestions conclude the chapter and Part Three.

Part Four addresses the nature of language disorders across tasks and times, eliciting from researchers and practitioners a series of seminars dealing with important questions of the '90s. The section begins with a discussion by Lahey and Bloom on the tremendous variability of language skills among children. Their chapter makes links between various aspects of information and language processing and production. Indeed, they question the value of attempting to measure processing as a variable (or a series of variables) apart from what is processed (i.e., language itself). They explore with readers the possibilities and difficulties that may be encountered when viewing human information processing and provide us with a provocative discussion of a limited capacity working memory. Lahey and Bloom postulate that children's performance on a variety of language tasks may be variable due to *how* processing components of the system interact with the task demands, revealing that each child may have a unique complex of factors that interfere with language performance. A careful reading of this chapter should see the demise of an assessment report that reads, "Jerry's language problem stems from poor memory."

Friel-Patti also looks at processing, but conceptualizes auditory linguistic processing with a matrix that calls into play various language theories, speech perception research, and current principles of language comprehension.She calls to readers' attention the fact that understanding auditory processing is no easy task. It requires that professionals traverse a number of disciplines in repeated attempts to find points of convergence as well as divergence. She offers six principles to help practitioners reflect on assessment and intervention with this imprecise entity clinicians and educators have called *auditory processing* or *central auditory processing*.

Ehren's contribution brings readers into the *blackboard jungle*, a term reflecting what it sometimes means to teach and be taught in urban secondary schools of today's large inner cities. She helps us take a hard look at the communication skills (and thus the psyches) of adolescents with language learning difficulties. Taking a realistic and at the same time positive view, Ehren notes that adolescence reflects that which has come before and that which will follow. Caught betwixt and between, adolescents' language learning needs could overwhelm them because the years of failure, or defeat, or discouragement, have a multiplying effect. Ehren reminds us that the manner in which language disabilities are reflected across time is reflected in adolescents' approach to academic tasks, to teachers, to parents, and to the community at large. To say the least, notes Ehren, language specialists pick up a heavy burden, the weight of the years that such children have been in the educational system. Language specialists in secondary schools must address the issues of children who are not on track for graduation from high school, must less on track for the demands of the twenty-first century. Ehren explores this LLD population, and illustrates the different ways that language disorders manifest themselves across time. She squarely faces the academic and social demands of secondary school settings and provides direct and immediate assistance to those practitioners who have elected to turn failure into success. Although there may be troubles aplenty, Ehren shows us a way out of the blackboard jungle. Using innovative delivery models, she concludes that a strategic orientation to language intervention can bring a measure of success to youth in middle and high schools, to those who have long gone down the up staircase.

Chapter 16 is presented by the co-editors with a series of contributors who respond to their questions. Our colleagues have provided us with an array of perspectives. They answer such questions as: What is the greatest misunderstanding that professionals may have about the "power" of standardized language tests? What are the best approaches to reading: whole language, direct instruction, or basal reading? What does phonemic awareness contribute to young children's learning to read and to write? How have collaborative/consultative models worked? How could professionals who might wish to incorporate a collaborative and consultative model into their practice begin?

The authors provide diverse perspectives, more than enough to fill any professional's language acquisition and disorders plate. *Language Learning Disabilities in School-Age Children and Adolescents: Some Principles and Applications* provides a current view of the questions, and offers some of the answers. Are these the final answers? Probably not. Are there final answers? Probably not. One of the most exciting opportunities offered to those who work in the area of child language acquisition and disorders is that there is much yet to be learned. Whether we are learning about the particular vulnerability of language-impaired children (von Berger et al., 1993) or the adaptive nature of cognitive vulnerability (Bjorklund & Green, 1992), we are engaged in exploring new and exciting frontiers that lead us ever onward into the dense jungle of the topic of language learning disabled children and their assessment and treatment. The only dangers we face are the dangers of looking in only one direction and failing to continue to ask questions.

Geraldine P. Wallach
Katharine G. Butler

References

Bjorklund, D. E., and Green, B. L. (1992). The adaptive nature of cognitive immaturity. *American Psychologist, 47*(1), 46–54.

von Berger, E., Wulfeck, B., Bates, E., and Fink, N. (1993). Developmental changes in real-time sentence processing. Technical report 9303, Center for Research in Language, University of California, San Diego.

ACKNOWLEDGMENTS

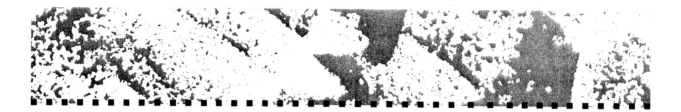

After four years of finding and fixing words in the process of preparing this text, it may be difficult to imagine that we might have trouble finding the appropriate words to thank the contributors to this text. Our co-writers worked with us over the course of this book's creation and re-creation with professionalism, patience, and, most importantly, good humor. We thank them for their superb contributions to the text, their commitment to excellence, and their overall support during the text's evolution. They became pieces to a complex puzzle—an overall picture we sometimes lost and then found again along the way. No longer puzzled, we are grateful to count them among our colleagues and friends. The world of language learning disabled students is made better each day by their presence, perseverance, and the products they have produced—the insightful chapters herein.

We would also like to acknowledge specific people who contributed to the completion of this project. The editors wish to thank their respective spouses, Walter Wallach and Joseph Butler, for living with the dawn-to-midnight faxes, the lost weekends, the last-minute panic attacks, and the "can't do that now" excuses among countless other creative crises for several years. Dr. Wallach would like to thank the Emerson College east and west coast contingents for their on-going support and encouragement, including Dr. Jacqueline W. Liebergott and Dr. Laurence Conner, who gave her the space, time, and confidence to succeed. She would also like to thank Janice Payne and Jay Faneuf who typed, retyped, copied, and "held down the fort" for many days and many long weeks and who endured the mood swings of an editor with a deadline long past. Dr. Butler wishes to thank her colleagues at Syracuse University, particularly Dr. Edward Conture and Dr. John Saxman, for their support of this and many other endeavors. Accolades also go to doctoral students Yancy Padget and Karen Nezelek for their involvement in multiple activities.

Dr. Lahey and Dr. Bloom wish to thank Toni Spiota, Elaine Fine, and Naomi Schiff-Myers for their thoughtful comments on the early drafts of their manuscript. Dr. Nelson would like to thank the graduate clinicians who assisted in gathering case examples for her chapter, including Janelle Carey, Barbara Clock, Sherra Layton, Juliane Licata, and Stephanie Walther. Dr. Silliman and Dr. Wilkinson express gratitude to the staff of the Communication Development Program of the South Metropolitan Association, Flossmoor, Illinois, for willingly giving them access to their classrooms. Silliman and Wilkinson give specific acknowledgment to Lauren Hoffman, Assistant Director and Supervisor of the Communication Development Program, and to Lisa Clark, Rebecca Einhorn, and Beth Miller, speech-language pathologists, whose creative approaches to discourse scaffolding for their language learning disabled students served as the substance for their chapters' development. In addition, Silliman and Wilkinson thank Joanie and Neil McKaig for their sharing of journal material and Tonya Daniels and Stephanie Lucenti, graduate assistants in the Department of Communication Sciences and Disorders, University of South Florida, and Jane Sherwood, administrative assistant at the Rutgers University Graduate School of Education, for manuscript preparation. Dr. van Kleeck thanks Rod Hart and Beth Schlechter for their helpful editorial suggestions regarding the writing of her chapter. She also thanks Ron Gillam and Alice Richardson for their very insightful input regarding the ideas presented. The contributors jointly thank their respective spouses, colleagues, friends, superiors, children, secretaries, and students who were always there with encouragement and support.

The authors also wish to thank the reviewers of this text: Marie E. Brittin, Ohio State University; Anthony B. DeFeo, University of Arizona; Marilyn K. Kertoy, University of Maine; Libby Kumin, Loyola College; Patricia B. Launer, San Diego State University; Marilyn A. Nippold, University of Oregon; and Elizabeth Skarakis-Doyle, Dalhousie University.

This text represents the best of what collaboration can be. We cut, we pasted, we computerized, and, yes, we negotiated. We agreed and we disagreed; we said the same things differently, and we said different things in similar ways. More often than not, we overlapped and restated each other's thoughts—a sometimes seemingly amazing result in the midst of such diversity. This text is a summary of our joint efforts. We offer it to readers for their use, enjoyment, and critical review. We trust that it will provide a comforting scaffold in the ongoing search to do the best for the students in our care.

G.P.W.

K.G.B.

BRIEF CONTENTS

CONTENTS

CHAPTER 9

Early Literacy Acquisition: The Role of Phonological Awareness 253

■ *Benita A. Blachman*

CHAPTER 10

Nonliteral Language Abilities: Seeing the Forest for the Trees 275

■ *Linda M. Milosky*

CHAPTER 11

Problem-Solving Strategies for Academic Success 304

■ *Camille L. Z. Blachowicz*

CHAPTER 12

Word Finding Difficulties in Children and Adolescents 323

■ *Diane J. German*

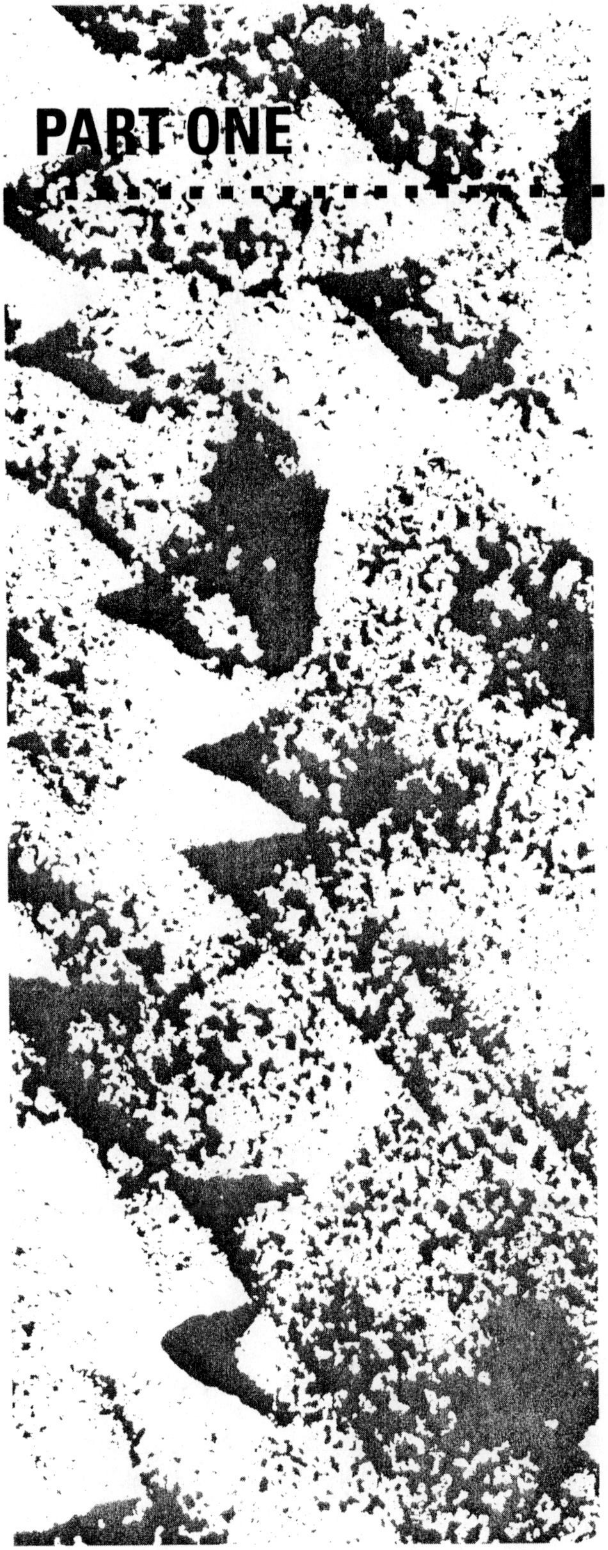

PART ONE

INTRODUCTORY CONSIDERATIONS, ORAL LANGUAGE CONNECTIONS TO LITERACY, AND THE CLASSROOM

CHAPTER 1 ■
Creating communication, literacy, and academic success

CHAPTER 2 ■
Discourse scaffolds for classroom intervention

CHAPTER 3 ■
Metalinguistic development

REFLECTIONS FOR PART ONE ■
School language and learning: Making scaffolding and metas matter

1

CREATING COMMUNICATION, LITERACY, AND ACADEMIC SUCCESS

■ Geraldine P. Wallach
Emerson College Los Angeles Center
■ Katharine G. Butler
Syracuse University

Many challenges face professionals involved in the business of facilitating communication and literacy in language learning disabled (LLD) individuals. A special challenge and a two-edged dilemma seems to have remained constant over several decades of research and practice. One side of this two-edged dilemma is the desire to find better ways to teach those in one's care, while the second is to maintain a cautiously optimistic view about the promises of new or reworked philosophies, tests, and intervention methods that pervade educational and clinical journals and conferences. Despite the prevalence of such "new" and "better" claims, academic success may be an elusive goal for many children for many reasons. This text addresses several of these reasons while keeping in mind the necessity for caution as well as optimism. Indeed, the answers to the "What do I *do* with language learning disabled children and adolescents?" questions now come from so many sources that professionals must do as much inferencing and reading between the lines as they expect their students to do when faced with complex topics in school texts.

An expanding body of research underpins some of the integrated language and literacy programs that are evolving (e.g., Silliman & Wilkinson, chaps. 2 & 6). Other programs and practices, to use Kamhi's words, "have little theoretical coherence" (Kamhi, 1993, p. 59). The greatest challenge still facing professionals, searching for answers to complex questions, is the translation of theoretical information into practice. The language development literature is just as rich as the literature in literacy learning. As the two fields grow, sometimes in parallel rather than intersecting fashions, professionals struggle to integrate the conceptual and practical ideas coming from the divergent frames of reference. Nevertheless, as information crosses over from one discipline to another, language practitioners learn more about not only what "works" but also what may not work in their settings.

Since the mid-1980s, when *Language Learning Disabilities in School-Age Children* (Wallach & Butler, 1984), was published, more information has become available about some of the theoretical and clinical connections between and among language proficiency, literacy, and academic success. Consequently, practice has moved further and further away from the 1960s and 1970s categorizations of children. Intervention programs of the 1990s have begun to stress the importance of each student's experience as a language learner and language user while recognizing some of the differences between social and academic contexts (Bashir, 1989; Lahey & Bloom, chap. 13; Silliman & Wilkinson, chap. 2; Wallach & Miller, 1988). One sees in the literature a rising tide of understanding of the drawbacks of standardized tests, particularly because they fall short in determining learner potential and they are often unconnected to the curriculum (e.g., Nelson, chap. 4; Palincsar, Brown, & Campione, chap. 5). Although more information is clearly available, school-based professionals are struck continually by the ever-increasing demands of their administrators to serve more students with more diverse problems in more efficient and cost-effective ways (e.g., Nelson, chap. 4; Westby, chap. 7). The same may be said for hospital and agency settings, where administrators may judge efficiency as "the greatest number of procedures completed" in the least amount of time. The complexity of speech-language services, particularly language assessment and intervention procedures, tends to be seen as unnecessarily intricate when compared with the apparent simplicity of procedures conducted by other allied health professionals. For example, the health-care worker who administers electrocardiogram procedures may see as many as twelve to fifteen patients an hour. Speech-language pathologists, on the other hand, work individually and more intensively over longer periods of time. Concerns about efficiency and cost-effectiveness vary from setting to setting but remain harsh realities for the 1990s and beyond.

Notwithstanding the pressures found in educational and clinical settings, the ultimate responsibility for professionals—as part of the responsibility of addressing the needs of the students and patients in their care—is to continue to ask themselves questions about their own biases and knowledge gaps. That responsibility includes recognizing that answers to questions such as "How do I measure real progress?" "What might I do to help students solve a problem or interpret a story?" and "Where do I begin?" will never be simple. It also includes thinking about why statements such as "Phonics is an inappropriate approach to early reading," "Oral language activities should always precede written language work," and "Encourage children to write the way they talk," reflect somewhat simplistic translations of complex concepts from the literature (Wallach, 1990).

This chapter introduces concepts about language, literacy, and academic learning that will be explored throughout the text. One basic question asked by graduate students and professionals alike and underpinning the core of many discussions is "Why focus on literacy in a book about language?" The first section responds to this question by outlining some of the broader definitions of literacy that will be entertained throughout the text. It also presents information about the advantages of being print literate. The second section focuses on some of the challenges facing LLD students attempting to make transitions to literacy. It takes a closer look at some of the theoretical constructs that drive clinical and educational practice. The third section addresses the ongoing nature of language disorders and the ever-present problem of labeling and categorizing children with communication and school problems. The final section highlights some of the principles that will be explored in upcoming chapters.

READING AND WRITING AS BRIDGES TO LEARNING

Access to Print Means Access to Learning and to One's Culture

Access to the written word, particularly in Western societies, provides its users with many things. Readers can learn new words and concepts, escape to exotic places, and hear what famous authors have to say when they are not present; writers can communicate with friends and co-workers through print, remind themselves of appointments, and store information for future use, both personal and impersonal—among many other things (Scott, chap. 8; Wallach, 1990). For children, literacy "marks the beginning of the ability to exist in a linguistically specified hypothetical world . . . and enables [them] . . . to live in the multifaceted world opened up by texts" (Wallach & Miller, 1988, p. 7). What would the 1990s' world be like without easy and frequent access to written text? How would people cope with the unreasonable demands placed on their auditory memories without the benefit of notebooks, handouts, and most of all, computers?

Gee (1990) points out that high technology cultures rely less on face-to-face interactions; they rely more and more on written—and therefore more formal—types of communication. Gee distinguishes between *pragmatic* and *syntactic modes* of communication. He says that pragmatic modes, reflected in oral cultures, have strong ties to face-to-face interactions; pragmatic modes force the listener to figure out what goes with what. The "what-goes-with-what" might include figuring out how a facial expression signals the true meaning of a statement and which referent goes with which gesture, and the like. Syntactic modes, on the other hand, are less personal than pragmatic modes. Syntactic modes, according to Gee, are like the communications in the "public sphere," such as memos, reports, proposals, etc. Hence, they are the predominant modes in highly literate and technically advanced cultures such as our own. Consequently, *print literacy,* being able to read and write, cannot be underestimated as an integral part of socialization, language learning, and life-long learning in general. Although people can and do obtain information from many sources other than written sources (e.g., radio, television, etc.), "only print provides opportunities for acquiring broad and deep knowledge of the world" (West, Stanovich, & Mitchell, 1993, p. 46).

The notion that literacy goes well beyond decoding the words and sentences of one's spoken language includes several perspectives that are also conveyed in chapters that follow. In his now classic book, *Cultural Literacy,* Hirsch (1987) points out that being literate includes being knowledgeable of the events of one's culture. He uses the "Grant and Lee" example that follows (only a portion is presented here) to show that understanding written text requires much more than being able to identify words or handle a text's syntactic or paragraph structure:

> ***Grant and Lee***
>
> When Ulysses S. Grant and Robert E. Lee met in the parlor of a modest house at Appomattox Courthouse, Virginia, on April 9, 1865, to work out the terms for the surrender of Lee's army in Northern Virginia, a great chapter in American life came to a close, and a great new chapter began.
>
> These men were bringing the Civil War to its virtual finish. To be sure, other armies had yet to surrender, and in a few days the fugitive Confederate government would struggle desperately and vainly, trying to find some way to go on living now that its chief support was gone. But in effect it was all over when Grant and Lee signed the papers. And the little room where they wrote out the terms was the scene of one of the poignant, dramatic contrasts in American history (Hirsch, 1987, p. 41). [The selection continues and describes the different backgrounds of the two generals.][1]

Hirsch (1987) says that "informationally deprived people," even people who can read the individual sentences and who can handle the vocabulary in the text, have difficulty making sense out of the selection. Drawing from the results of his research with different groups of college students, Hirsch (1987) reports that students who had limited knowledge of Grant, Lee, and the Civil War found the selection extremely difficult. They retained little information and had difficulty comprehending the passage. Hirsch says that readers who knew about the historical events surrounding the Civil War and who had some idea about who its players were found the passages relatively easy; that is, the Grant and Lee passages *added to knowledge they already had* (Wallach, 1990).

Consider the next example, in French, as the connection between cultural literacy and print literacy are explored further:

> "La lumière a un language, il faut la parler, il faut la faire chanter," s'éciait le peintre Eugene Boudin, ce Normand de Honfleur qui poussa Claude Monet hors de son atelier pour lui faire admirer la vaporeuse lumière qui mele grève et ciel dans un scintillement féerique.

The preceding passage is from a travel book for Normandy. It opens with a brief story of Eugene Boudin, the painter/sculptor who was from Honfleur in Normandy, talking to his friend Claude Monet and telling Monet how beautiful the coast of Normandy is. ("Light has a language. You have to make it speak, you have to make it sing.") He pushes Monet outdoors from his studio and makes him admire "the misty light, that light that merges sand and sky in a dreamlike shimmer of magic."

For those fluent in French, the passage might be relatively easy to decode and comprehend on some level. The "some level" implies that, although the French reader might demonstrate print literacy, it takes more than reading words and sentences to comprehend, interpret, and retain information. The more readers know about the subject, the better able they will be to handle the text while adding to their knowledge base of the subject. For example, readers who know that Boudin lived in Normandy have background information to draw on while reading the text. More importantly, readers who have traveled know where Normandy (or Honfleur) is and know that the rest of the text is about travel to Normandy (as opposed to being about the painters) may process and comprehend the text with little difficulty.

By contrast, English readers have a different task facing them when trying to decode and comprehend the "Normandy passage." They may know something about the subject (they may have read about or traveled extensively in the area) but have little opportunity to add to their knowledge base from this text without access to spoken French and without knowledge of its written counterparts. Adult speakers and writers of English, however, can apply strategies to the French text, demonstrating both cultural and print literacy ability. Some strategies will work; others will fail. For example, one could pull out familiar names from the text, such as Boudin and Monet, and

---

[1]Excerpt from *Cultural Literacy* by E. D. Hirsch. Copyright © 1987 by Houghton Mifflin Company. Reprinted by permission of Houghton Mifflin Company. All rights reserved.

infer that the passage is about art. Likewise, adults might note the quotations around certain words and recognize that someone is saying something to someone else. Rudimentary yet significant knowledge of print conventions—*conventions that are absent in spoken language*—such as knowledge about periods, spaces between words, and capital letters, provides adult English readers with some access to the French text. It is extremely difficult to remember and to simulate what it must be like to be a novice language learner and reader. Nevertheless, the French example may help English speakers appreciate that they know something about how print differs from speech. While the ultimate purpose of reading includes a different level of attention or focus, that is, *interpreting what is read,* proficient readers can and do shift their focus to the form and style of the printed material when necessary. This point will be returned to later in the chapter.

Access to Print Means Access to Academic Language

Definitions of literacy are broadened further when one is reminded, as in the chapter that follows, that "literacy transcends oral and written mediums" (Silliman & Wilkinson, chap. 2). Thus, one can add to the earlier discussion on the power of print the fact that spoken language, with its variety of discourse styles, genres, and purposes, may also be quite literate (Bloome, 1986; Guthrie & Greaney, 1991; Scott, chap. 8). As some authors of this text propose, oral language is as much a part of literacy learning and acquisition as written language. Indeed, although professionals may agree that oral language has a significant role in literacy acquisition, the primacy of printed language may override the primacy of oral language *at certain times and in certain situations.* Consider the following examples from Wallach (1990) that serve merely as a metaphor for the discussion:

1. "and then this guy here comes along from behind the building and he scares the kids . . . and then the good guys come along and save the kids."
2. "The man [who came from behind the building] scared the children. . . . However, the police came along and saved them. . . ."

The first example is more "oral" in style; the second example is more "literate." (As mentioned earlier, Gee, 1990, talked about this distinction in terms of pragmatic and syntactic modes of communication.) Technically speaking, both oral and literate styles are used in spoken and written language *depending on what the communicative situation demands.* However, some language forms are more likely to occur in oral language, and others are more likely to occur in written language, although there are some interesting crossovers (Scott, chap. 8). For example, the language style one would use for a conversation would differ from the style one would use for a formal college lecture, even though the conversation and the lecture both involve spoken language. Likewise, the language style for letters to close friends versus the style for a dissertation would differ markedly, even though the letters and the dissertation involve written language. Literate styles of communication such as the style of this text tend to be "syntactically heavy." Syntax and certain lexical choices provide explicit connections among thoughts. Embedded clauses, transitional phrases, active and passive sentence changes, conditional and causal conjunctions, among other structural devices, make meanings explicit in print and in formal oral language situations (Wallach, 1990). By contrast, "although speakers can choose any number of conjunctions, *and* or *and then,* accompanied by gesture and situation, usually work well to join thoughts and describe event sequences in oral exchanges" (Wallach & Miller, 1988, p. 7). Language specialists may be well aware that the need for language explicitness is reduced when speakers and listeners are face-to-face (Silliman & Wilkinson, chap. 2) but may increase dramatically when the author and reader "connect" only through the written word. Although merely introduced at this point, the complexity of language style differences across spoken and written mediums and situations is staggering, as readers will note in chapters that follow (e.g., see Scott, chap. 8 for an in-depth discussion). Nevertheless, whether professionals agree or disagree about the specifics, two questions might be posed to facilitate further reflection on this complex issue: "Which language styles are likely to be rewarded in school?" and "How do children learn that their oral language can take on more text-like and literate-like qualities?"

Children who *talk like books*—that is, students who use literate styles of communicating in oral language—tend to match teacher expectations more often than children who do not (Gee, 1988, 1990; Scott, chap. 8). While spoken demonstrations of literate language proficiency tend to be rewarded in school, *the most natural and common way of acquiring literate language is through print.* Therein lies the dilemma for children with and without language learning disabilities. Access to print means access not only to content knowledge and cultural literacy but also access to the language of academic success (Gilovich, 1991; Hayes & Ahrens, 1988).

As West et al. (1993) comment: "The distribution of language structures that people are exposed to in print are different from those encountered in speech" (p. 44). Print is "a source of exceptionally rich stimulation" for both vocabulary growth and the development of syntactic sophistication (p. 45). They point out that children who have little access to print are at a tremendous disadvantage because oral language may not have the same literate repertoire that is naturally part of written language. For example, children's books contain 50% more rare words than appear in prime-time television and in adult conversations; magazines contain about three times as many new words as prime-time television and adult conversations. Many moderate and low frequency words, which are part of the school curriculum, would be considered common in written material and rare in speech. Importantly, for vocabulary growth to occur after the middle grades, children must be exposed to words that would be considered rare in spoken language (West et al., 1993). In a similar way, more complex syntactic forms are also found in far greater numbers in written text (Biber, 1986). As Scott will show in her chapter (chap. 8), oral language certainly has highly literate aspects, but speech that is textlike (i.e., speech that is closer to the written word) occurs in instances that are uncommon in the average course of communication. For example, judicial proceedings, planned speeches at formal gatherings, and college lectures represent examples of printlike speech (West et al., 1993). Readers clearly have an advantage over nonreaders because they have more exposure to literate language; nonreaders must rely solely on those occasions in spoken language that are more formal to practice with literate forms. Children who are exposed to print early and who learn how to read have a two-tiered system at their disposal. Furthermore, because schools and school texts present themselves almost exclusively in literate/syntactic modes, students may be best served by learning as early as possible the value of print and its conventions.

Early learning of the value of print and its conventions means learning during the preschool years; learning means exposure to the printed word well before "real reading" begins, as van Kleeck also points out in Chapter 3. The beginnings of writing also appear in the preschool years when parents and teachers encourage early exposure to exploration of print (Butler, 1992; Chaney, 1992; Dickinson & McCabe, 1991; Temple, Nathan, & Burris, 1982).

Figure 1–1 provides an example of early writing. Janie, age 4:11, is the youngest of four girls. Her mother and father are teachers, and their house is filled with literate artifacts (books, magazines, and journals in the living room, notes and lists and clipped newspaper articles on the refrigerator in the kitchen, and several dictionaries in the dining room, where the children do their homework each evening). Janie's older sisters have played school with her on many rainy days. Janie has been scribbling since she was two years old and has engaged in "pretend writing" since she was three. By four, she was leaving messages for her mother, father, and sisters. But Janie was frequently disheartened about being left in the care of a baby-sitter. One day she decided to take matters into her own right hand. While the baby-sitter was involved in a long telephone call with a friend, Janie created the note reproduced in Figure 1–1.

Janie then packed a peanut butter and jam sandwich, her favorite book and teddy bear, and departed by way of the back gate. Only hunger and darkness drove her home, where the frantic baby sitter awaited her. If one had asked Janie to read her note, she would have said, "I wrote: 'Dear Mommy, I am running away because you don't take care of me. I am not lying, when you go to school. Love you.' [pause] Well, I wanted to tell her some more. This says 'You don't love me any more. All the things that you do to me were bad. Love you. Janie.'" Indeed, it should be obvious to all that Janie has begun to use her language skills to communicate via print and that she has some sophisticated knowledge of the value of print and its conventions.

As children enter school, they must respond to the academic demands of the classroom, which include ever more complex use of language and ever more decontextualized uses of communication in reading and writing. In Figure 1–2, a boy, John, aged 11:10, is completing a state-required test of his ability to generate written text. Only page 1 is provided.

FIGURE 1–1
An example of early writing:
Janie, age 4:11

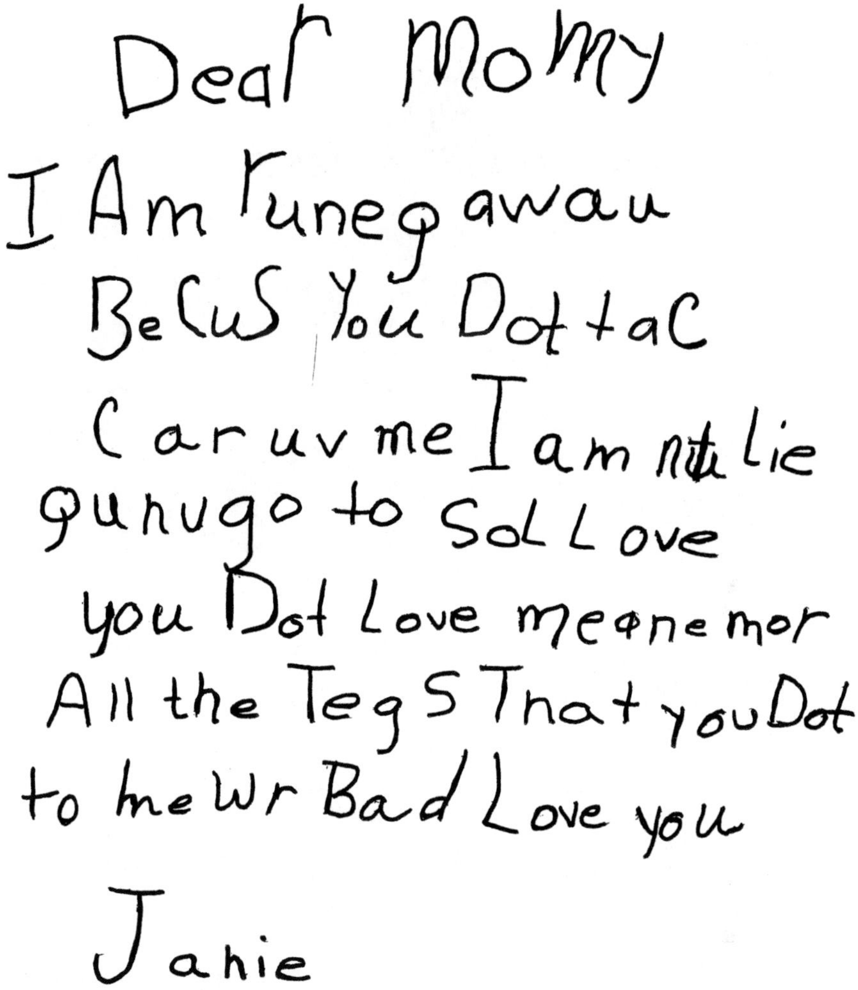
Dear Momy
I Am runegawau
BeCuS You DottaC
Caruv me I am nt lie
qunugo to SoL Love
you Dot Love meqnemor
All the TegS That you Dot
to me Wr Bad Love you
Janie

John was identified as LLD three years earlier. The reader will note that he is an enthusiastic, but difficult to read, author. When he reads his work aloud, the narrative states (spelling and punctuation corrected):

> My mom is special to me because she helps me with school and also she cleans. The good thing about it is she is always there for me. She takes me to hockey. She runs me all over. Takes walks with me. And she gives my allowance. She buys me stuff [unclear]. She gets school supplies.
>
> She took me to Florida. One time she took me to Niagara Falls. She takes me to grandma's house. She cooks good meals. She takes care of me even when I am. . . .

In contrast to Janie's efforts, John struggles with the conventions of print, with a generous sprinkling of periods and a lack of capitalization. When this piece of work was evaluated by his English teacher, she strongly suggested that he learn the "mechanics" of writing; when it was seen by his resource teacher, she wrote on the bottom of it, "You certainly have a nice Mom, John." John struggles with both reading and writing; his homework tends to take a back seat to his successful career on the ice as a goalie for the fifth grade team. John has some not-so-secret doubts about his ability to handle the rigors of middle school. He is joined by many other children, as they attempt to move along the oral-to-literate continuum.

FIGURE 1–2
A writing sample from an LLD student, age 11:10

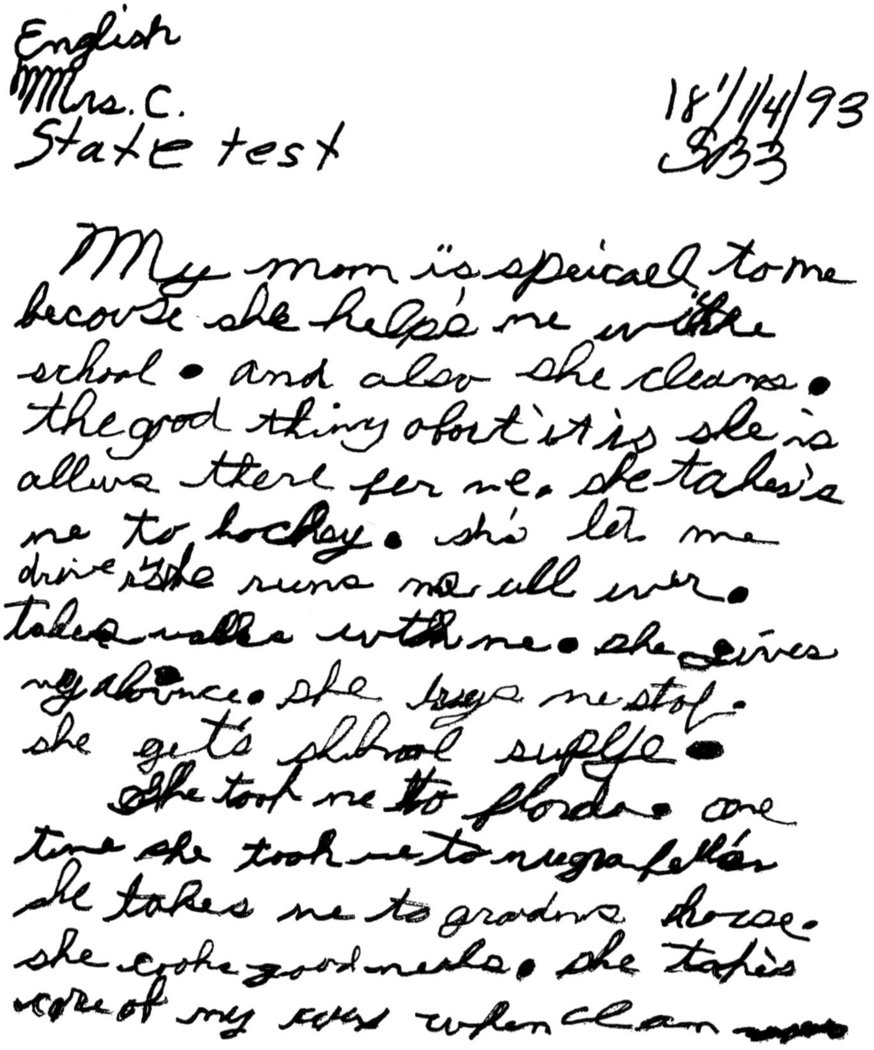

In summarizing the oral-to-literate balancing act of the school years, Silliman and Wallach (1991) propose three major interactions and provide descriptions from children's points of view. Figure 1–3 provides an abbreviated version of selected transitions to literacy.

Access to Print Means Access to Learning a "Meta Mode" and Vice Versa

Reading and writing encourage children to become linguists. As long as English remains an alphabetic system and as long as print maintains its conventions, young readers must do at least two related things: (1) They must come to terms with speech-to-print differences; and (2) they must bring their language knowledge to the surface by talking about language and analyzing it (Blachman, chap. 9; van Kleeck, chap. 3). "Beginning reading is the time when the implicit becomes explicit and the linguistic becomes metalinguistic" (Wallach, 1990, pp. 65–66). Additionally, reading and writing add to people's functional awareness of language by helping them develop an abstract and analytical sense about language (Roberts, 1992). Reading and writing also

1. Talking like Books
   - A great idea if you can read and write
   - Your talking starts to sound like books if you have been read to a lot and after you have learned how to read
   - Teachers might expect you to talk like books even if you do not read and write well
   - Comes in handy in class, with the principal, on job interviews, in speeches, broadcasts, and when talking is formal
   - Not the style of talk you have to use on the basketball court
2. Writing like Talking
   - You only write the way you talk in some situations, and writing is always different from talking
   - It is important to know when to use this style because writing like talking usually does not work well on the printed page
   - It is not allowed in school for too long
   - Writing like talking is great for the "personal stuff," when you are writing speeches for a character, when you are keeping a journal, and when you are reminding yourself about something
3. Writing like Books
   - A great idea if you have the books, you can read, and you know grammar
   - You will need to know how to write like books because it's the language of school, texts, and reports
   - Gets very formal and specific and a little impersonal
   - You have to plan ahead and make specific choices and really "know" your language
   - After grade 4, this ability is a must and stays that way for most of your life

FIGURE 1–3
Three aspects of oral-to-literate transitions written from students' points of view
Silliman and Wallach (1991).

involve more conscious and planful communication (Silliman & Wilkinson, chap. 2). This "planfulness" in communication, coupled with an abstract appreciation for language, provides a bridge to both literacy and academic success (Scott, chap. 8; Silliman & Wilkinson, chap. 2). As children progress through the early school years, print pushes them to analyze their language. Print teaches normally acquiring language users about language units. Being able to talk about language, pull its units apart and put them back together, compare and contrast words, reorganize paragraphs and topic sentences, change titles, and edit and correct spelling are among the school tasks that require an analytical and abstract understanding of language and its structures.

Children learn many new things about the structure of language when they encounter print. Some of the things they learn about language structure and form would be difficult to learn through spoken language alone. (A similar point was made earlier in the discussion about literate styles of communication.) Unlike spoken language, which is unsegmented, written language is segmented (Blachman, chap. 9; van Kleeck, chap. 3). The segmented nature of written language, characterized by spaces between words and letters representing phonemes, "helps the language user deliberately dissemble and reflect upon linguistic units" (Roberts, 1992, p. 126). Although it is possible to learn about linguistic units without print, and young children begin that way (as van Kleeck points out in chap. 3), it is very difficult to do so over extended periods of time. Indeed, written language makes sentence, phrase, word, and sound boundaries explicit. Roberts (1992) points out that written language is one of the ways that children really begin to understand what words are. Through written language, particularly through their own writing, "children come to learn that words are units of meaning which stand in a symbolic relationship to their referents" (Roberts, 1992, p. 125).

Interestingly, teachers and clinicians sometimes assume that children know more about words then they actually do. As van Kleeck points out in Chapter 3, young children's concepts about what words are differ from those of older children and adults (see van Kleeck's discussion, which covers several aspects of word awareness, chap. 3). While the current discussion focuses mainly on word structure knowledge, children's "word meaning" errors should not be underestimated. Very young children (ages three to five years) may not understand adult questioning but may appear to comprehend an adult's stated question by nodding or a brief verbal response.

For example, G. S. Goodman and Aman (1987, 1990) interviewed eighty young children regarding potentially abusive sexual acts. They asked such questions as "Did he touch your private parts?" (anatomically correct dolls and regular dolls were used in the interviews). A larger percentage of the three-year-olds than the five-year-olds said "yes." It later dawned on the researchers to ask the children where their private parts were. The children pointed to their ears, to their arms, to their hair, and to other not-so-private places. Abuse investigators call these *errors of commission.* Language specialists, however, might well say that such errors reflect naive language use by children who have only a partial understanding of word or phrase meanings. Three-, four-, and five-year-olds have many years of practice ahead of them before they master the multiple meanings of words and before they fully comprehend the intended meaning of phrases such as "private parts." Indeed, word meanings that are provided by adults who use phrases weighted with implicit, rather than explicit, terminology are later acquisitions (Milosky, chap. 10).

Returning to the discussion of word structure knowledge are examples that reflect—albeit a different level of metacomprehension than the previous example from the abuse research—children's unique concepts of what words are. Specifically, young children who are nonreaders often note that "thehouse" and "isrunning" are words (see van Kleeck, chap. 3); LLD students may write "stoppid" for "stop it" also demonstrating a misunderstanding of language segmentation (Wallach, 1990). Particularly noteworthy might be exploration of the differences in word awareness that exist between readers and nonreaders in the early elementary grades. It becomes interesting to think about ways in which print can facilitate word structure knowledge because one would be hard pressed to walk into any elementary school without observing all kinds of activities involving words—finding word roots, defining their meanings, supplying word opposites, and using words in sentences, among many others (Nelson, chap. 4).

In addition to presenting children with analytical challenges, written material also gives children a chance to practice with decontextualized language. In Chapter 3, van Kleeck helps language specialists see broader-based implications for the role of print in linguistic and metalinguistic development. She notes in Chapter 3 that "children . . . must learn to focus exclusively on the linguistic code, because it is often used in isolation from other communication channels in many academic tasks. . . ." Focusing on print is one way to focus exclusively on the linguistic code. Silent reading, report writing, formal oral presentations, and taking notes from teachers' lectures, among other school activities, require a similar focus. That is, the focus shifts from using and processing language in context—where pictures, gestures, facial expression and other nonlinguistic cues can and do disambiguate meanings—to focusing on the actual words and sentence structures to get the message. School learning, particularly by grade 4 and above, requires more and more attention to and understanding of decontextualized communication (Nelson, chap. 4). Early and frequent exposure to print, which begins in contextualized social situations similar to the beginnings of spoken language, may provide an early link to, and a familiarity with, decontextualized language. Furthermore, whereas the development of literacy may require a reflective or metalinguistic set, exposure to written language may facilitate this ability to reflect on language—providing an important two-way interaction, which will be discussed later (van Kleeck, chap. 3; Westby, chap. 7).

Language Learning and Literacy Learning: Summary Points

As Lahey and Bloom ask in Chapter 13, one might also be tempted to remark "So what?" How does theory really relate to practice? What will I do with my students Monday morning? Language specialists and teachers are challenged by broader definitions of literacy and language literacy connections on several fronts: One, implied in the first section of this chapter, is to recognize that cultural literacy, learning about and understanding the events of one's world, is difficult to attain without print literacy, being able to read and write the words of one's language. "Learning, both in school and beyond, is heavily dependent on acquiring information from . . . [written] text" (McKeown, Beck, Sinatra, & Loxterman, 1992, p. 79). A second front, also gleaned from the previous discussion, is that oral and written language, while connected, disconnect in interesting ways. Indeed, it may not be the case that "what is true for language in general is true for written language . . . [in all situations]" (Altwerger, Edelsky, & Flores, 1987, p. 145).

Speech is different from print. Children must understand the nature of these differences, as should educators and clinicians developing and implementing language programs. As implied at the beginning of this chapter, intervention is influenced by theory in uneven ways (Kamhi, 1993). Additionally, professionals' interpretations of what they read and hear will differ; those differences will be reflected in their assessment protocols, recommendations, and Individualized Education Plans (IEPs). Thus, the creation and implementation of language and literacy programs is as varied as the beliefs and theories that drive them. Key concepts relating to language literacy connections are summarized next. Examples of some of the different ways that interpretations might influence practice are also discussed.

MAKING TRANSITIONS TO PRINT AND TO LITERACY: HOW BELIEFS INFLUENCE LANGUAGE LITERACY PRACTICES

Converging and diverging points of view leave practitioners with several threads that are difficult to weave together. On the one hand, practitioners know that normal language learning and literacy learning are connected and *reciprocal* (Kamhi & Catts, 1989; Sawyer, 1991; Silliman, 1991; Silliman & Wilkinson, chap. 2). On the other hand, language specialists also understand that spoken and written language can be quite different (see Scott, chap. 8). How does one begin to sort out all of the possible continuities and discontinuities that exist on the literacy continuum? Three intersecting and overlapping themes, introduced earlier in this chapter, are considered next in an effort to explore ways in which theory translates into practice. The reciprocal relation between spoken and written language is discussed first, followed by a reconsideration of some of the differences between the two systems. The interaction between content knowledge and structure knowledge is presented in the third section.

The Reciprocal Nature of Spoken and Written Language: Recognizing the Caution Signs on the Two-Way Street

The connection between spoken language proficiency and the development of print literacy is well documented (e.g., see Kamhi & Catts, 1989, for an in-depth discussion). As part of the process of becoming literate, readers connect written language to oral language that is already known. Facility with spoken French provides the oral language base onto which the Normandy passage presented earlier is connected; some degree of explicit language knowledge, or metalinguistic ability, contributes to literacy learning. Whereas the specific nuances of all aspects of the spoken-to-written connection are unknown at this time, the notion that learning to read and write is part of, not separate from, learning to speak and comprehend language is generally accepted (Kamhi & Catts, 1989; Sawyer, 1991; Silliman & Wilkinson, chap. 2). To accurately understand the acquisition and development of written language requires understanding the acquisition and development of spoken language. One cannot talk accurately about reading disabilities without a discussion of its language-based nature. Thus, while language specialists and educators appear to be encouraged and excited by the language-based literacy philosophies that have reached school systems across the country, they are still faced with the reality that connections between the systems are more complex than were previously thought.

Reciprocal But Not Exactly the Same? The statements made in the previous paragraphs speak well for an oral language-to-written language sequence. Professionals have grown more comfortable with the notion that oral language "leads the way" to written language. One hears statements such as those presented at the beginning of this chapter, "Oral language intervention precedes written language intervention" and "Spoken language problems cause written language problems." Clearly, no one would suggest that discussions of reading problems are complete without a discussion of their oral language counterparts. However, the "one-way" influence of oral language on written language can be overemphasized in theory and in practice, particularly during the school-age period. The "one-way" notion represents a literal translation of a complex concept. Researchers in reading and writing present data suggesting that oral and written language relationships are bidirectional and multileveled.

Kamhi and Catts (1989) remind us that "the relationship between spoken and written language is dynamic. . . . [It] changes throughout the developmental period and the direction of causality can go both ways" (p. xiii). Two words, *dynamic* and *changes,* require emphasis. As noted earlier, professionals might consider ways that print influences both oral language and metalinguistic development at particular points in time (see van Kleeck, chap. 3; Scott, chap. 8). Indeed, children are socialized to print and literacy much earlier in development than was previously thought, as van Kleeck shows in Chapter 3. Children as young as three are already developing a mental set for analyzing language structure separate from language meaning (Chaney, 1992).

With these print-to-oral language connections in mind, language specialists might ask themselves several pertinent questions. How can print activities be incorporated into early language intervention programs? If written language influences and surpasses spoken language at certain points in time, as Scott demonstrates in Chapter 8, how might that concept influence what clinicians and teachers do in classrooms and resource rooms with LLD students? Have language specialists overloaded LLD students' auditory systems? Is heavy reliance on spoken language processing and production too much of a good thing?

Bashir (1988) takes the notion that spoken and written systems are dynamic and change in slightly different directions. He says that the differences that occur in both spoken and written language acquisition *over time* must be better understood. That understanding may result in language and reading intervention recommendations that not only reflect an age–stage perspective but also demonstrate an understanding of how the two systems interact. Consequently, professionals who take, for example, an "either/or" approach to reading, espousing "whole language" *or* phonics approaches, bypass the reality that what one does with children has more to do with what they are ready for rather than what a language or reading program promises (Bashir, 1988; Wallach, 1990).

The concept that spoken and written language systems interact with one another in a two-way fashion (spoken language influences written language and vice versa) is important and interesting. Professionals should be cautious, however, about taking the reciprocity idea too far when creating language and literacy programs. As the Bashir (1988) notion implies, decisions about "where to begin" and "what to do" can be oversimplified when programs or philosophies suggest that intervention methodologies that are appropriate for oral language, or first language acquisition, are always appropriate for written language (Moorman, Blanton, & McLaughlin, 1992). Moreover, reciprocity between systems may not translate into classroom recommendations that practitioners should follow the "same sequence of steps for facilitating written language as they followed for spoken language" (see also Blachman, chap. 9).

Spoken and Written Systems: Paying Attention to Differences

The proposal for a "same sequence" of developmental "steps" for both oral and written language represents an assumption that requires more careful consideration (Bashir, 1992; Thompson, 1992; Wallach, 1990). Indeed, many aspects of spoken and written language acquisition may overlap. There may also be some twists and turns. Language specialists and "whole language" proponents may become uncomfortable with some of the developmental twists and turns because they seem to contradict what appears to be intuitively correct; for example, language cannot be separated into its parts, one should teach only for meaning, readers scan and predict when reading, paying attention to phonemes disrupts comprehension, present new concepts in context, and the like. However, learning to read and write a language differs somewhat from learning to understand and speak it (see Scott, 1989; Scott, chap. 8). Beginning reading differs from proficient and adult reading. In sum, the auditory stream differs significantly from written text.

It may help to recall part of the discussion from a previous section addressing metalinguistic awareness and the importance of developing an analytical sense about language. Children who bring a metalinguistic sensitivity about words and sounds with them to school make smoother transitions to reading and writing (Adams, 1990; Wallach & Miller, 1988; Warren-Leubecker, 1987). Children who have a sense of syntactic and sound segments of language recognize how those units of language relate to print earlier than children who have little or no sense of language structure (Tunmer, Herman, & Nesdale, 1988). Tunmer et al. (1988), among other researchers and clinicians, believe that phonological and structural awareness may play a more important role in *beginning* reading than pragmatic awareness. Although focus on sounds, words, and sentence structures is never the ultimate goal of any reading program, structural awareness may be a means to an end at certain points in time. Remember, children cannot necessarily focus on two things at the same time—and do so automatically and simultaneously—the way adults can (Lahey & Bloom, chap. 13; van Kleeck, chap. 3). Focusing on meaning while one is focusing on form may be an unrealistic goal for young readers and readers with language learning disabilities. Children need some strategies for "getting into print" before they can apply inferencing, integration, and other discourse-level strategies to written text (Bashir, 1992; Blachman, chap. 9; Chall, 1983; Thompson, 1992; Wallach, 1990). As noted by Wallach (1990),

> In one sense, children may need to do the opposite of what they do in spoken language acquisition at the beginning stages of reading. That is, they may need to come to terms with the "smaller elements" initially, gaining some degree of automaticity with words and sounds, so that they are free to focus on the larger units of text two or three years later. (p. 67)

Chall's (1983) classic work reminds professionals that readers do different things at different stages of reading. She points out that some of the things children do, particularly in the early stages of reading, are not necessarily "true reading," as one might say about older children's and adult's reading. Nevertheless, children are engaged in and practicing with print, which is still part of the process of becoming literate. Chall (1983) points out that during the five- to seven-year-old period (stage 1), children learn about phoneme–grapheme correspondences. She reminds practitioners that understanding the nature of the letter–phoneme connection, unavoidable for readers of alphabetic systems, is a fundamental task facing beginning readers. Between seven and nine years of age (stage 2), young readers, according to Chall (1983), become "unglued from print." At this stage, children really use their decoding skills in addition to using other cues in language such as a story's organization, redundancies in sentence structure and word choices, and the like. Children break away from putting all their energies into decoding print in stage 2. They begin to read more fluently and attend to what the print means at this stage. Importantly, "the gradual automatization of decoding skills frees the child from the print and allows her or him to devote more attentional resources to focus on meaning" (Kamhi & Catts, 1989, p. 29; see Lahey & Bloom, chap. 13). It is not until subsequent stages (stages 3 to 5), beginning at the age of nine, that children and adolescents shift from "learning to read" to "reading to learn" strategies (Bashir, 1989). Only after some automatization with decoding has occurred do children read for meaning, make inferences about what they read, appreciate multiple viewpoints, and absorb most of the content areas of the curriculum through print (Chall, 1983; see Kamhi & Catts, 1989, for an excellent summary; see also Nelson, chap. 4). Thus, programs that bypass completely the two or three years that children need to practice with and be "glued to print," as Chall (1983) suggests, may do them a disservice in the long run.

Too Much "Alikeness" Assumed Between Spoken and Written Language? For proficient readers the written word is almost as natural as the spoken word. In fact, expert readers often think about spoken words as having the same characteristics as written words. One starts to think in terms of separated word units, and sentences' beginnings and ends as being marked in the auditory stream, when they are not. Interestingly, reading segments an unsegmented auditory stream (see Blachman, chap. 9). For young children learning language, however, understanding speech-to-print differences is an abstract concept that unravels after at least a few years of practice with spoken language and some practice with written language (van Kleeck, chap. 3). The example that follows highlights the importance of understanding spoken and written language process and form differences. It demonstrates an oversimplification about the ways in which oral and written language play off one another developmentally. Only part of the language intervention session is presented.

> A clinician is working with a three-year-old with a language disorder. One of Jane's difficulties includes asking questions in statement form and omitting auxiliary verbs (e.g., "We eating now?" "Go watch TV now?")
>
> The clinician has several blocks on the table. The blocks will be used to "teach" the child the correct sentence form. The clinician has indicated that the blocks will make the task more concrete. They will provide a tangible way for the child to think about language.
>
> The lesson goes something like this: After some preparation, the clinician points to the blocks and says, "We are eating snacks now." She exaggerates and slows down her speech, pointing to the blocks and stressing the words that Jane generally omits. Jane begins to do the task, omitting the auxiliary verb and not touching each block for each word. However, she seems to enjoy the task. Jane touches the blocks as she speaks, but not in a block-to-word correspondence. The clinician guides Jane's hand through several trials with different sentences.
>
> The task becomes more complex. The clinician continues the lesson. She now demonstrates the question form by using the blocks. The second block (second from the left for both clinician and child) is moved to the first position of the block sentence. The clinician says, "Now we'll say, 'Are we eating snacks now?'" The lesson continues. (Adapted from Wallach & Miller, 1988, p. 79)

One might have many reactions to the lesson. Certainly, one could question the aspect of language being taught. One would want to know more about the child and understand the nature of her language disorder, learn more about her life, and her abilities. Noteworthy for this discussion are several factors: (1) the assumption on the clinician's part that the auditory stream is segmented in the same way that written language is segmented (see Blachman, chap. 9); (2) the notion that blocks make the task "more concrete"; and (3) the decontextualized format of the lesson. Given the age, spoken language level, and nonreading status of the child in the preceding example, one could say that a lesson of this type (not necessarily the same lesson) might be more appropriate for an eight- or nine-year-old for the purpose of heightening written syntactic abilities (see Wallach and Miller, 1988, for additional discussions about this lesson and others).

Practitioners developing language-based literacy programs must remember that young children are generally nonanalytical (Roberts, 1992; Tunmer et al., 1988). Proficient English speakers are also nonanalytical when they hear French, Spanish, Japanese, and other languages they do not speak. That is, when processing a foreign language, particularly in the early stages of learning one, a listener has little time to focus on—to stop and analyze—the language's individual units. More often than not, the auditory stream sounds like an unending and *unsegmented* string of meaningless sounds to the naive listener (Wallach, 1990). Foreign languages once again point out speech-to-print differences to English speakers and readers who take them for granted. Learning that language consists of sentences, words, syllables, and especially, sounds is not necessarily an outgrowth of exposure to spoken language (van Kleeck, chap. 3). Early reading experiences—coupled with improving at language by the age of five or six years—may contribute to children's awareness of structural boundaries and help them come to terms with speech and print differences (Blachman, chap. 9).

"Successful reading requires some mastery of the alphabetic principle" (Raynor & Pollatsek, 1989, p. 354). Accessing print requires different strategies from accessing spoken text. Early literacy programs must come to terms with both the segmented nature of English and the metalinguistic and analytical bent of early reading. The suggestion that all children, including children with language learning disabilities, will do it on their own—will abstract word and sound segments of English without explicit instruction—may be another literal translation of a complex concept. For example, K. Goodman (1989) and others point out that "readiness" for reading is intrinsic when language is real. Indeed, the alphabet is as real as any other part of language. Creating literacy programs that are language based and meaningful is professionals' ultimate goal. Applying concepts to literacy acquisition that apply to adults and ignoring the realities of spoken and written language differences may do little to help them reach those goals.

Content Knowledge and Structure Knowledge: Not an Either/or Situation

Readers and listeners are constructive (Bransford & Johnson, 1973). They use what they know to help them interpret new incoming information (McNamara, Miller, & Bransford, 1991). Sometimes new information complements old information quite well. As demonstrated by Hirsch (1987), readers who had background knowledge of the Civil War read the Grant and Lee selection and learned more about the personal differences between the generals. Readers with prior knowledge of the topic picked up additional information about the war's last days. From Hirsch's point of view, new information has a better chance of being comprehended and retained when it is processed from within a larger context, or backdrop. The larger context includes a tremendous amount of *content knowledge*—knowledge about the topic of the text (Wallach, 1990; Winne, Graham, & Prock, 1993). Indeed, personal and academic experiences help people interpret what they see, hear, and read. The power of prior knowledge on comprehension and memory cannot be overestimated (Lahey & Bloom, chap. 13).

Information students bring with them to classroom lessons will certainly influence how they deal with new content in the curriculum. The more they know about a topic or subject area, the better they might be expected to do (McCormick, 1992). However, personal experience and knowledge, no matter how broad, can also be misleading and unrepresentative (Gilovich, 1991). At some point, listeners and readers must attend to the spoken or written text they are trying to process. Overreliance on prior knowledge—and the operative word is overreliance—can be as ineffective as trying to memorize everything in the text.

Research suggests a strong interaction between content knowledge and structure knowledge (e.g., Armbruster, Anderson, & Ostertag, 1987; Carver, 1992; Fincher-Kiefer, 1992; Foley, 1992; Meyer, 1984; Phillips, 1988; Richgels, McGee, Lomax, & Sheard, 1987; Roller, 1990; Spring & Prager, 1992). Proficient readers use linguistic clues in text to help them get and absorb critical points. Structural cues and the structural organization of text seem to be particularly facilitative to comprehension when content is moderately unfamiliar (Roller, 1990). "If the text is difficult, adults seem to attempt to use their structure schema [to deduce what the author is trying to say]. . . . If the text is well-structured . . . signaling appears to facilitate the ability of adults to activate and . . . focus on a content strategy" (Ohlhausen & Roller, 1988, p. 86). Reiterating Ohlhausen and Roller (1988), studies and observations of middle elementary school children suggest similar content–text "trade-offs." McKeown and her colleagues write:

> Background knowledge seems most useful if the text is coherent enough to allow the reader to see the connection between text information and previous knowledge so that the knowledge can be combined with the text information to create a meaningful representation. (McKeown et al., 1992, p. 91)

Beck, McKeown, Sinatra, and Loxterman (1991) point out that content-area textbooks assume an unrealistic amount of prior knowledge. For example, in a unit about the French and Indian War, they found that many fifth graders had vague and inaccurate knowledge about the topic. Assigned texts failed to provide much information about why the war occurred, how the colonies related to Britain, and how the French and Indian War related to the Revolutionary War. Numerous facts were presented, with few if any explanations of how the facts connected. The texts, in a sense, assumed that students would make inferences about relations from background knowledge acquired in class. Beck et al. (1991) added information to the texts that made the implicit explicit. They included facts such as (1) who fought the war, why was the war being fought, and what resulted, and (2) what was Britain's conflict with the American colonies. Text coherence was created by clarifying, elaborating on, explaining, and spelling out the important relations among the players of the French and Indian War. Beck et al. (1991) found that revising textbooks by filling in the missing pieces for students facilitated their comprehension and memory.

McKeown et al. (1992) also studied ways in which background knowledge plus text coherence contribute to improvements in comprehension. In another fifth-grade unit, this one covering the Revolutionary War, the authors found gaps in students' background knowledge. For instance, students were confused about the geographical locations involved in the war, the role Britain played, and the colonies' powers of self-government, among other topics. Thus, McKeown and colleagues created both knowledge modules and text revisions. One knowledge unit consisted of two parts: (1) a study of five geographic locations (North America, Britain, France, Massachusetts, and Boston) and (2) a discussion of identity issues. (The colonists were British, but grew to feel separate. How did this come about?) Texts were then created that made the concepts covered in the Revolutionary War more accessible to students. For example, in one section of the identity unit, a personalized text was substituted for a more formal expository text. The feelings expressed by the colonists are seen through the eyes of a teacher called Samantha Stevens:

> My name is Samantha Stevens. I spent many years of my life getting a school going in our town and helping to teach the children. . . . In Britain, only those who can afford it send their children to school. That used to seem fine to me. But here everyone goes to school—and I really think that is the way it should be. (McKeown et al., 1992, p. 82)

Ohlhausen and Roller (1988) also used social studies stimuli to study content/structure interactions in middle and later elementary grades. They showed, for example, that some social studies texts require a tremendous amount of internal structuring on the part of the reader (Wallach, 1990). In an abbreviated version of a complicated social studies text presented next, much information is provided about a little-known island called Melanesia. However, the text includes few explicit connections that would help the reader organize the information. Ohlhausen and Roller (1988) called this the "content version" because the text contains all the information needed about the topic.

> ***Melanesia (Content Version)***
>
> Each tribe exchanged goods with other tribes such as food, animals, clay and wooden bowls, woven mats, weapons, and even canoes. Religious ceremonies were often used to protect crops from harm or to increase their yields. Melanesia is a relatively unknown country. Some of the islands of Melanesia are large, single islands (New Britain and New Ireland) and some are made up of island groupings (The Solomon Islands and New Hebrides). Often villagers used magic to protect themselves from enemies or against villagers who failed to pay a debt or who broke a rule. (Ohlhausen & Roller, 1988, pp. 74–75)

Ohlhausen and Roller (1988) revised the passage to make the connections more explicit for fifth-, seventh-, and ninth-grade readers. The following example is the "content/structure" version; the content is better organized:

> ***Melanesia (Content/Structure Version)***
>
> Melanesia is a relatively unknown country. In order to learn more about Melanesia, *we will describe both the physical and cultural geography of the country. We will first describe the physical geography of Melanesia. Specifically, we will focus on its location, then the land forms, and finally the climate. First, we will look at the location as an aspect of physical geography* [emphasis added]. Melanesia is an island located in the Pacific Ocean, northeast of Australia. The curving chains of islands stretch from New Guinea to the Fiji Islands. (Ohlhausen & Roller, quoted in Wallach, 1990, pp. 76, 77)

Results showed that students below grade 7 performed better on comprehension activities when structural cues made content relations explicit, such as in the content/structure version of the Melanesia passage. Fifth graders were less experienced than seventh and ninth graders with social studies schema and expository text. *Social studies schema* means, for example, understanding what might be included in studying the characteristics of nations. Studying nations means studying their locations, land forms, climates, and so on. Students who had practice studying nations appeared able to reorganize incoming facts with that schema in mind. Ohlhausen and Roller (1988) noted that grade 7 and 9 students had a distinct advantage over their younger peers, not because they read better, but because they were absorbed in "nation schema" in their schoolwork. Thus, older students (with social studies schema on their minds) have an easier time imposing structure on content-oriented selections such as the "content version" of the Melanesia passage than their younger schoolmates. Younger students, perhaps being exposed to complex content for the first time, and LLD students may need the added textual coherence to help them develop a social studies schema and to make relations among facts more explicit.

Hennings (1993) talks about the importance of structural knowledge for history. She adds to some of the concepts that were discussed earlier in the American Revolution unit. She points out that students need to learn that dealing with history text may require a slightly different focus from dealing with English literature text (see also Scott's discussion of oral language differences across the curriculum in chap. 8). She writes:

> . . . if reading instruction is to be effective, it must take place across the curriculum as students read in a variety

of disciplines. Stress should be on learning the ways of knowing—the ways of reading, writing, and thinking about each of the major disciplines. (Hennings, 1993, p. 363)

Students faced with complex history texts that are filled with dates, people, and events must know how to do at least three major things: (1) they must know how to collect facts that are relevant to a topic; (2) they must organize those facts into a coherent pattern; and (3) they must process and interpret those facts. Indeed, as Hennings (1993) comments: "The key ideas that give structure to the study of history [are] . . . time, place, causation and ultimate meaning, change, and tenuousness of data" (p. 362). Thus, students of history, in addition to having general strategies for organizing incoming text, must organize events and people in a meaningful timetable and in a meaningful geographical framework, compare and contrast historical figures and cultures, interpret and hypothesize about cause–effect relations, generalize about the meaning of events, and assess the accuracy and validity of purported facts (Hennings, 1993).

Familiarity with history texts, along with knowledge modules such as the ones proposed by McKeown et al. (1992) for the American Revolution unit, combines structure knowledge and content knowledge. Hennings (1993) suggests that working on the text itself (i.e., analyzing an author's choice of words), as well as using diagrams and visual mapping aids, may facilitate comprehension and interpretation of history. For example, students should be alerted to key words and phrases in texts that signal important cause–effect, time, and other relationships. Phrases such as "as a result," "was caused by," "problems began when," "therefore," and "consequently," among others, tell students that cause–effect connections are being discussed. "First," "second, "for ten years," "not long after," "prewar," and "postwar," among countless other words and phrases, signal time relationships. Titles such as *Discovering Columbus: How History is Invented,* require nonliteral translations (Milosky, chap. 10) and alert readers to the fact that they might be examining historical facts for accuracy and validity. Finally, diagrams and mapping provide contextual support for otherwise very decontextualized information. Figures 1–4 and 1–5, both from Hennings (1993), provide examples of ways to help students collect and analyze causal relations and compare and contrast persons from the past.

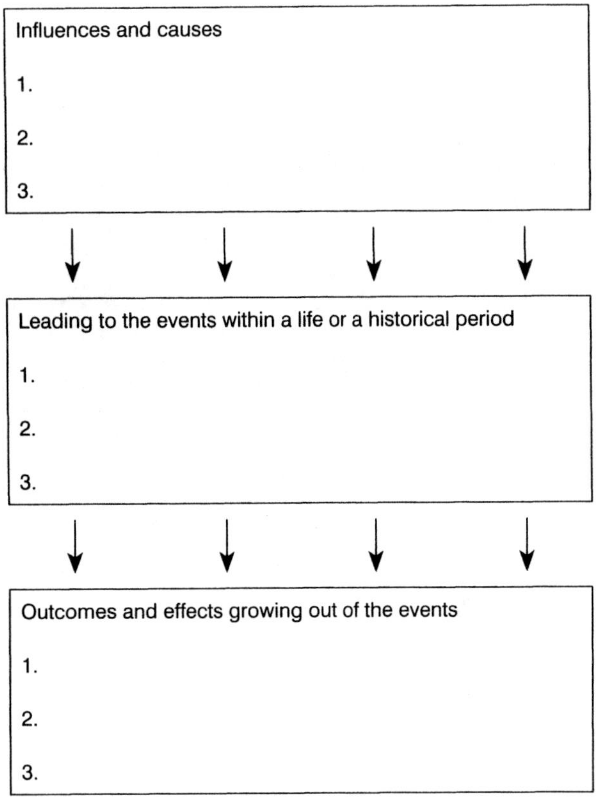

FIGURE 1–4
A visual map for causal relationships within the history curriculum

From "On Knowing and Reading History" by D. G. Hennings, 1993, *Journal of Reading, 36*(5), p. 367. Reprinted with permission of Dorothy Grant Hennings and the International Reading Association.

Although many skills are necessary for reading and absorbing the content of textbooks, several researcher–educators such as Hennings (1993) have suggested that graphic displays and visual mapping strategies can be useful when trying to help students express "what they know" (or may not know) about a subject. Visual maps, for example, help students organize information into a coherent form (Alvermann, 1991; Blachowicz, 1986; Blachowicz, chap. 11; Guzzetti, Snyder, & Glass, 1992). Guzzetti et al. (1992) noticed that misconceptions in science were prevalent among middle and junior high school students, even after classroom instruction and textbook readings. The authors used graphic discussion webs,

FIGURE 1–5
A visual map for comparing and contrasting events or persons from the past

From "On Knowing and Reading History" by D. G. Hennings, 1993, *Journal of Reading, 36*(5), p. 368. Reprinted with permission of Dorothy Grant Hennings and the International Reading Association.

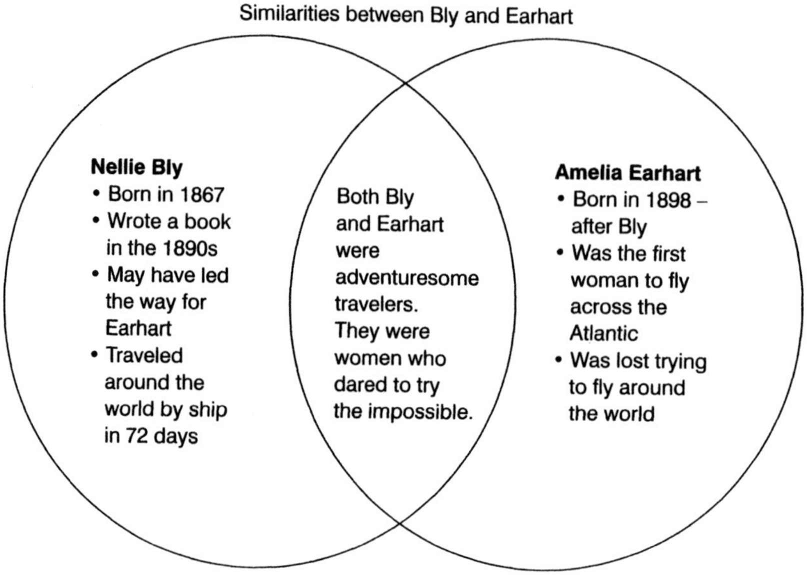

such as the one presented in Figure 1–6, to help students understand complex concepts, especially "when inaccurate prior knowledge gets in the way of what a text says" (Guzzetti et al., 1992, p. 642). They asked students to express their ideas about various topics. They then had students verify information by looking up the answers in their texts. Guzzetti et al. (1992) used questions or comments such as "What information in the text makes you think that?" and "Find places in the passage to support your ideas" to bring prior knowledge and text-based knowledge closer together.

Gillespie (1993) reminds practitioners that working on graphs and other visual mapping techniques may have additional benefits. Maps, charts, and graphs are among the dominant types of graphic displays that appear in most content-area textbooks. She points out that students who ignore graphs or have difficulty interpreting tables, maps, and other configurations in their texts may lose important information. Interestingly, language specialists might think about ways that graphs and maps form contextual supports for students with language learning disabilities, particularly when the text is complex and the topic is relatively unfamiliar.

The interaction between readers and text is a provocative piece of the literacy puzzle (Gee, 1990; Wallach, 1990). (See Westby, chap. 7 for an interesting discussion about how value judgments affect text comprehension.) Many fascinating studies are available that address some of the connections introduced in this chapter (see Yuill & Oakill, 1991, for a review). Additional research will say more about how prior knowledge, schooling, and text interact with one another. However, some of the implications for professionals working with LLD students are evident. For example, it seems clear that structural sensitivity

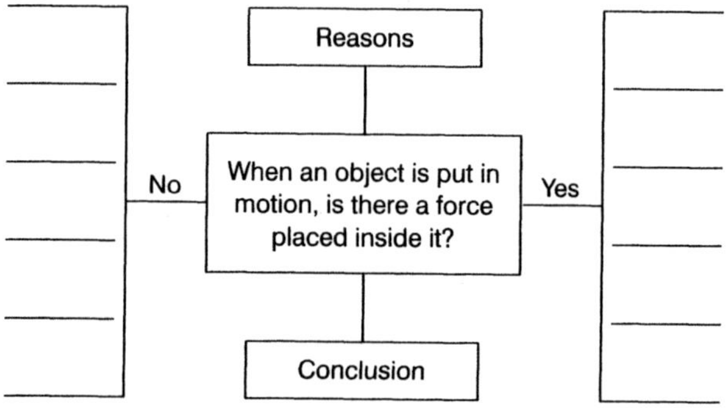

FIGURE 1–6
A graphic aid for a discussion web for science

From "Promoting Conceptual Change in Science: Can Texts Be Used Effectively" by B. J. Guzzetti, T. E. Snyder, & G. V. Glass, 1992, *Journal of Reading, 35*(8), p. 648. Reprinted with permission of Barbara J. Guzzetti and the International Reading Association.

can facilitate the memory and retention for new and difficult content. Additionally, presenting students with explicit instructions and feedback about how to make text-based inferences seems to help them understand how to integrate what they remember and know about a topic with what a text actually says (Winne et al., 1993). (Some ideas for facilitating structural awareness were presented in the previous sections; others will be presented later in the text; see Scott, chap. 8.)

Language specialists might also want to remember that practice with content schema (e.g., knowing the subtopics one might include in discussions about countries) may help students process text that is organized poorly (Wallach, 1990). Several authors, including Blachowicz (chap. 11), provide specific suggestions for improving students' use of background knowledge and text structure (e.g., Beyersdorfer & Schauer, 1992; Grant, 1993; Winne et al., 1993). Indeed, although intense discussions about topics through sequenced lessons provide sufficient background knowledge, background knowledge *and* coherent and explicit written texts apparently form a better partnership (Brannan, Bridge, & Winograd, 1986; McCormick, 1992).

The ability to deal with written text—to be able to decode it quickly and automatically—is a critical piece of academic success (Blachman, chap. 9). "Habituated patterns of skipping unknown words and guessing meanings are not going to help students develop reading mastery of their textbooks" (Thompson, 1992, p. 137). Strategies for using existing knowledge about topics, as Blachowicz shows in Chapter 11, as well as relating that knowledge to what a text says, are crucial for efficient and effective learning. Being "too text based" or "too reader based," terms that Tierney and Pearson (1981) used, is as ineffective as being "only whole language" or "only phonics" oriented.

LOOKING BACK TO LOOK FORWARD

Looking Back

The opening pages of Wallach and Butler's 1984 text, *Language Learning Disabilities in School-Age Children,* reviewed the problems attached to labeling and categorizing children based on the results of endless batteries of standardized tests and neuropsycho- or psychoneuro-babble. On page one, Wallach and Liebergott (1984) raised two questions about language learning disabled students that Stark raised in 1980: "Who are these children?" and "Why are they in trouble?" At that time, writers of the text reflected on twenty years of research in attempts to try to answer the questions. Ten years later, the questions are still relevant. However, they are answered, not necessarily in terms of finding new labels or new tests, but in terms of finding better ways of observing the contexts, materials, and instructional patterns of classrooms and clinics as well as observing the linguistic, cognitive, social, and academic patterns of children in those contexts (see Silliman & Wilkinson, chaps. 2 & 6).

In a classic fashion, Lahey reminded readers to recognize the circularity of reasoning involved in using labels such as "learning disabled":

> Question: Why are these children with normal intelligence having difficulty learning to read?
> Answer: Because they are "learning disabled."
> Question: How do you know that?
> Answer: Because they have normal intelligence and they are having difficulty learning to read.
> (Lahey, 1980, quoted in Wallach & Liebergott, 1984, p. 2)

In 1987, the Interagency Committee on Learning Disabilities (ICLD) recommended to Congress that the definition of learning disability be modified. The 1987 definition, which is being revised currently by committees such as the National Joint Committee on Learning Disabilities, included difficulties with social skills and attempted to make some causal aspects of LD more explicit. The changes are underlined:

> Learning disabilities is a generic term that refers to a heterogeneous group of disorders manifested by significant difficulties in the acquisition and use of listening, speaking, reading, writing, reasoning, mathematical abilities, <u>or of social skills.</u> These disorders are intrinsic to the individual and presumed to be due to central nervous system dysfunction. Even though learning disabilities may occur concomitantly with other handicapping conditions (e.g., sensory impairment, mental retardation, social and emotional disturbance), <u>with socio-</u>environmental influences (e.g., cultural differences, insufficient or inappropriate instruction, psychogenic factors) <u>and especially with attention deficit disorder, all of which may cause learning problems, a learning disability</u> is not a direct result of those conditions or influences (ICLD, 1987, p. 222).

In spite of the attempts by well-intentioned committees to clarify terminology, definitions and labels, as encouraged by federal, state, and local mandates, often bypass the developmental and intersecting nature of language learning and reading disabilities. Moreover, the overemphasis on issues of causality and exclusionary categorizations, as may be noted in the ICLD definition, wastes precious intervention time. As Lahey and Bloom note in Chapter 13, professionals may want to shift their focus from talking about causality per se to consider talking about processing demands and competing resources. Taking a slightly different approach by echoing some of the comments made in this chapter, Kamhi and Catts (1989) remind practitioners that the most effective assessment and intervention plans for language and literacy learning will grow out of "an appreciation for the specific relationships that exist between spoken and written language components and how these relationships change throughout development" (p. xiii). Indeed, searching for specific causes of language learning and reading disabilities is a complex business. Professionals are only beginning to understand some of the causal interactions that occur between aspects of spoken and written language, as demonstrated in this chapter and throughout this text. The search for neurological, genetic, and other medically based correlates, although useful for research purposes, does little to drive intervention at this time.

Christensen (1992) and Stanovich (1992) address some difficult issues surrounding the testing, labeling, and programming for "learning disabled" and "reading disabled" students. They question the usefulness of searching for defining features that make the two groups of children qualitatively different. Christensen (1992) asks whether "garden-variety poor readers" are really different from "learning disabled" students, who also tend to be poor readers. She comments:

> Thirty years of psychometric approaches have failed to provide satisfactory answers to the learning disabled dilemma. A continuation of such a quest should not be conducted without addressing the serious social, ethical, and moral issues involved in the pursuit of this select group. (Christensen, 1992, pp. 276–277)

Christensen (1992) asks professionals to take a hard look at the financial, educational, and intellectual resources that have been used to search for the "true" learning disabled student. She suggests that more time should be spent developing programs to meet the needs of students—regardless of their labels (see also Westby, chap. 7).

Stanovich (1992) responds to Christensen by saying that one may not want to discount the reality of neurological differences among children but rather question their interpretation in a causal sense. However, reiterating Christensen, Stanovich notes:

> It is indeed a national disgrace that United States social policies ensure that it is just those children who are at risk for school difficulty who are provided with meager educational resources. (Stanovich, 1992, p. 280, citing Kozol, 1991)

The position taken in this text is similar to the one taken in 1984: Children with language disorders, reading disabilities, and learning disabilities are not necessarily children from distinct populations. Consider the description presented next of a student with academic problems from Wallach and Butler (1984).

Bill has a language disorder *and* a learning disability. One could interpret this statement in several ways. It could mean: (1) Bill has two separate problems—one in language/communication and one in learning; (2) Bill is part of a subgroup of the larger learning disabled (LD) population, whose language problems are causing his learning disabilities; and (3) Bill's problems with language and learning are connected and overlapping and manifest themselves differently at different points in time. Interpretations that help professionals appreciate the *continuum* of language disorders, as suggested in the third interpretation, are the ones adapted, with variations, in this text. That the majority of learning disabilities are language disabilities at school-age levels whose label has changed to fit school contexts and the prevalence of written language problems is consistent with many of the views taken in this text and elsewhere (ASHA, 1982; Bashir, 1992; Ehren, chap. 15; Wallach & Butler, 1984; Wallach & Miller, 1988).

A case may exemplify the comments made about the continuum of language disorders:

Donald, age 9:3, and in the third grade, was referred by his teacher, who reported the following:

> Donald has made some good strides with fine motor, writing and sequencing. He is a very bright boy that couldn't organize his thoughts very well on paper. He also gets very lost with multiple directions. When he reads, he puts his face very close to the paper/book, but he had his eyes examined and nothing was detected. He has made a big breakthrough in fine motor controll [sic] and his reading/writing have also improved. He loves to sing, is a well coordinated athlete and likes school. I keep thinking there is something wrong with

his vision/tracking or maybe an unusual way that information is processed in the brain . . . ? Thanks, Helene, 3rd Grade Teacher.

A review of Donald's school folder revealed that in the first grade his performance in academic subjects varied from 95% (ninety-fifth percentile) in mathematics, to 46% in vocabulary, and 18% in reading comprehension. His performance in the second grade, as measured by the same standardized achievement battery, was reported to be at 99% in mathematics, 95% in social studies, and 91% in science. By contrast, vocabulary was now at 36%, "language mechanics" was at 78%, language expression at 25%, reading comprehension at 59%, and spelling, a low 10%.

During the language screening, when Donald was asked to read aloud a story he had brought from the classroom, he became very dysfluent. He announced, "It's better reading to myself. I pause when I do it out loud." However, when telling an original narrative, his dysfluencies disappeared. When asked to generate a written narrative and assigned the topic, "Write to me about a perfect day . . . a day that *you* think is perfect. Begin with when you get up and tell me about the whole day," he rapidly produced the product found in Figure 1–7. He then proudly displayed his "Dialogue Journal" and commented that he was supposed to write about "real people talking." The journal, in which he wrote every day, provided the examiner with additional insight into Donald's organizational and comprehension monitoring skills. His spoken language appeared to be free of difficulty.

Is Donald language learning disabled? Are the teacher's concerns valid? This child was referred for the first time for three things: (1) difficulty with multiple directions, (2) lack of "organizational" strategies, and (3) a continuing concern about visual perceptual skills despite an "eye examination" by an unspecified professional. The teacher's note closes with a tentative query about how information is being processed in Donald's brain.

Although the information provided by the screening is insufficient to answer the questions raised, and further evaluation is obviously required, a careful analysis of Donald's composition might lead one to consider the teacher's comments carefully. Observation in the classroom, continued collection of data regarding Donald's strengths and weaknesses in the academic context, consultation with his family, and a neurological examination may be appropriate. The school records include a commentary from Donald's mother that he is "active, independent, fantasizes mentally, has a short attention span and does not respond well to demands made by adults." In addition, she indicates that some of the developmental milestones were significantly delayed.

Donald represents a subgroup of children whose language learning problems are masked by their strengths in mathematics and science. His very jagged "profile" is submerged by standardized achievement tests, which give a final "percentile score" that falls in the average-to-above-average range. Donald's grades also mirror the achievement scores. In fact, his early elementary teachers were impressed with his "brightness." They had, until recently, ignored what are now seen as his emerging problems. Other children have gone beyond emergent spelling, while Donald's writing remains filled with more primitive attempts (e.g., Figure 1–7: radeo/radio; selebrat/celebrate; manchend/mansion; suplify/supply). One sees traces of late maturing phonological processing in Donald's written, but not spoken, performance. And while Donald has trouble deciphering multiple verbal directions, teachers and parents refer to his "short attention span" without considering the increasing demands of the school curriculum. As Donald is required to process more complex directions in an ever-more decontextualized and literate environment, the mask is slipping away. If his needs are left unattended, and school tasks become more complicated, moving from narrative to expository texts, from more concrete to more abstract, from a more conversational environment to an increasingly teacher instruction–student response–teacher evaluation mode, Donald may well be labeled dyslexic or learning disabled and his place on the continuum of language disorders identified.

It would not be an overstatement to say that "the sheer volume of research and clinical data should overwhelm the few remaining holdouts who still question whether reading disabilities is a language-based disorder" (Kamhi & Catts, 1989, p. 371). Indeed, despite the heterogeneity that exists within reading disabled and dyslexic populations, the majority of these children have language difficulties; specific reading disability or dyslexia may be a developmental language disorder (Kamhi & Catts, 1989). Many children who had language disorders in the preschool years have problems making the transition to literacy in their school years. Some of their early

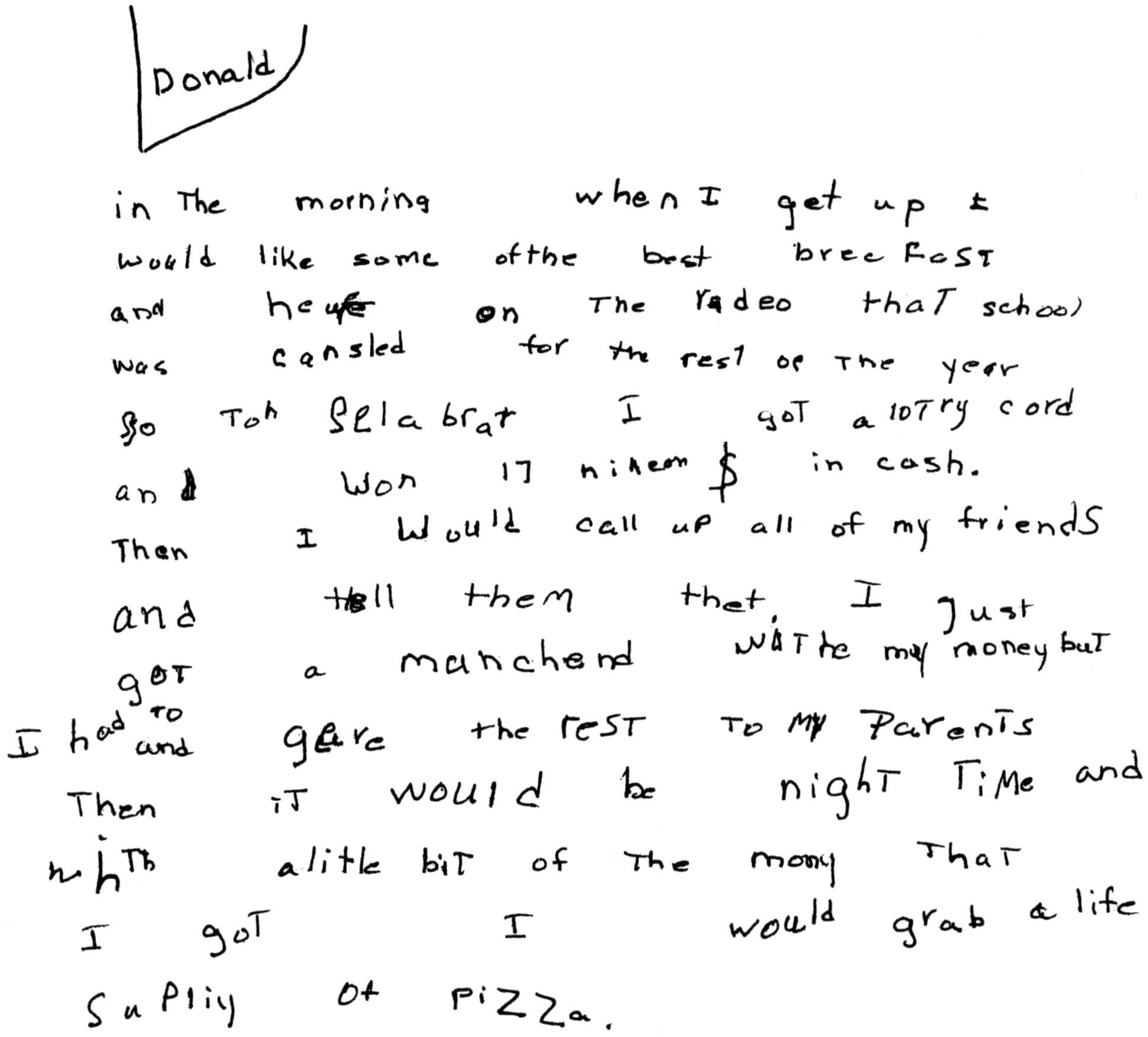
Donald

in The morning when I get up I
would like some of the best breeFaST
and he on The radeo that school
was cansled for the rest of the year
So Toh Selabrat I goT a loTry cord
and I Won 17 nileon $ in cash.
Then I Would call up all of my friends
and tell them that I just
got a manchend wiThe my money but
I had to and gave the rest To my Parents
Then iT would be night Time and
with alitle biT of The mony That
I goT I would grab a life
Supliy of PiZZa.

FIGURE 1–7
A writing sample from Donald, age 9:3

language disorders change over time, showing themselves in the school years as metalinguistic and written communication difficulties (Bashir & Scavuzzo, 1992). Language problems are life-long problems (see Ehren, chap. 15). They are dynamic and changing but rarely dismissed. As written so eloquently by Bashir and Scavuzzo (1992), the academic vulnerability of language disordered preschoolers who grow up to face challenges in school represents "a lifelong need to acquire language, to learn with language, and to apply language knowledge for academic learning and social development (p. 53)."

Looking Forward

In the chapters that follow, many examples are presented that further illuminate the issues outlined in this chapter. Additional questions are raised, and some answers are offered. Communication-based language and literacy programs provide a framework for the integration of oral and written language. The discourse scaffolding techniques presented by Silliman and Wilkinson in Chapter 2 give readers some specific guidelines for stimulating communication and academic learning through oral language supports, as do other authors throughout. Professionals might ask themselves how print might also be used as a *scaffold* for learning. Certainly, language specialists are beginning to come to terms with the idea that teaching oral language in isolation is an invalid concept—that is, not teaching language out of context but teaching spoken language separate from written language, especially in the school years. A variation of that theme, suggested by van Kleeck in Chapter 3, is that written language socialization and early reading experiences should be incorporated into language programming well before children enter school (see van Kleeck, chap. 3).

Practitioners have a long way to go before unraveling the most effective ways to help students make smoother transitions to literacy and to academic success. However, it is evident that language specialists and educators have become more sensitive to the ways in which oral communication styles influence children's reading and writing. They are also more cautious about the assumptions they make about why children do or do not "remember things" or why their students have difficulty generalizing from one day to the next, from resource room to classroom, or from class to class (see Lahey & Bloom, chap. 13). Nevertheless, all professionals must ethically reevaluate new programs and promises for quick "fixes." More importantly, they must continue to ask themselves what they mean by learning in general and literacy learning in particular (Gee, 1990; Wallach, 1990).

SUMMARY

The following are offered as part of the principles and possibilities that underpin many of the discussions throughout this text:

1. Children's "learning in classrooms critically depends on their communicative skills, because communication mediates learning" (Milosky, Wilkinson, Chiang, Lindow, & Salmon, 1986, p. 334).

2. Practical applications are drawn from more than one theory as "no [single] . . . theory of language learning could possibly encompass all of the areas that impact on the provision of effective clinical [and educational] . . . services" (Nelson quoted by Kamhi, 1993, p. 59).

3. The functions of literacy vary across societies and communities. The methods of learning literacy skills, as well as their consequences, vary considerably across societies (Heath, 1986; Westby, chap. 7). As minority children become the "majority" of children in many school settings, the abilities they possess and display in out-of-school contexts that are relevant to literacy should be exploited in schools (Heath, 1986).

4. The availability of two-way interactions along many language learning domains (e.g., spoken language facilitating written language and vice versa, content knowledge influencing structure knowledge and vice versa, etc.) provides students with a strong base for learning and school achievement (Wallach, 1990).

5. *Emergence* versus *mastery* are important concepts to keep in mind when observing and evaluating children's language learning and other abilities. As with intervention decisions, language learning and learning in general rarely involve an all or nothing phenomenon (Lahey & Bloom, chap. 13; Palincsar, Brown, & Campione, chap. 5; van Kleeck, chap. 3).

6. Learning and retaining information involve increasing efficiency (i.e., speed) and automaticity. Strategic learning is an outgrowth of practice and familiarity, and, in some cases, direct, explicit, and detailed instruction (Lahey & Bloom, chap. 13; Winne et al., 1993).

7. Scaffolding, both oral and written, facilitates the learning process throughout life. However, learners eventually must internalize their scaffolds and strategies, demonstrating increasing amounts of choice and control in their approaches to learning (Wyatt & Pickle, 1993).

8. Intervention rarely involves either/or choices. Emotionalism and irrational attachments to programs and procedures (Thompson, 1992) should give way to healthy skepticism. Research as well as clinical and educational data from several sources that illuminates professionals' understanding of the developmental continua attached to complex human behaviors and respect for individual variation among

children should drive intervention (Wallach, 1989; Wallach & Butler, 1984).

REFERENCES

American Speech-Language and Hearing Association Committee on Language learning Disabilities. (1982). The role of the speech-language pathologist in language learning disabilities. *ASHA, 24,* 937–944.

Adams, M. J. (1990). *Beginning to read: Thinking and learning about print.* Cambridge, MA: The MIT Press.

Altwerger, B., Edelsky, C., & Flores, B. (1987). Whole language: What's new? *Reading Teacher, 41,* 144–154.

Alvermann, D. E. (1991). The discussion web: a graphic aid for learning across the curriculum. *The Reading Teacher, 45,* 92–99.

Armbruster, B. B., Anderson, T. H., & Ostertag, J. (1987). Does text structure/summarizing instruction facilitate learning from expository text? *Reading Research Quarterly, 22,* 331–346.

Bashir, A. (1988, June). Language and literacy across the age and grade span: Clinical and educational implications. Workshop presented at the Emerson College Language Learning Disabilities Institute, Boston.

Bashir, A. (1989). Language intervention and the curriculum. *Seminars in Speech and Language, 10,* 181–191.

Bashir, A. (1992, June). *Historical perspectives and current knowledge: Language disorders from cradle to college, from spoken to written.* Workshop presented at the Emerson College Language Learning Disabilities Institute, Boston.

Bashir, A. S., & Scavuzzo, A. (1992). Children with language disorders: Natural history and academic success. *Journal of Learning Disabilities, 25*(1), 53–65.

Beck, I. I., McKeown, M. G., Sinatra, G. M., & Loxterman, J. A. (1991). Revised social studies text from a text-processing perspective: Evidence of improved comprehension. *Reading Research Quarterly, 26*(3), 251–276.

Beyersdorfer, J. M., & Schauer, D. K. (1992). Writing personality profiles: Conversations across the generation gap. *Journal of Reading, 35*(8), 612–616.

Biber, D. (1986). Spoken and written textual dimensions in English: Resolving contradictory findings. *Language, 62,* 384–414.

Blachowicz, C. (1986). Making connections: alternatives to the vocabulary notebook. *Journal of Reading, 29,* 643–649.

Bloome, D. (1986). *Literacy and schooling.* Norwood, NJ: Ablex.

Brannan, A. D., Bridge, C. A., & Winograd, P. N. (1986). The effects of structural variation on children's recall of basal reader stories. *Reading Research Quarterly, 21,* 91–104.

Bransford, J. D., & Johnson, M. (1973). Considerations of some problems in comprehension. In W. Chase (Ed.), *Visual information processing* (pp. 383–438). New York: Academic Press.

Butler, K. G. (1992). (Ed.). It's just talking, isn't it? In G. D. Kilburg, *Family-centered early intervention: Prevention and treatment of communication disorders* (pp. xi–xiii). Gaithersburg, MD: Aspen Publishers.

Carver, R. P. (1992). Effects of prediction activities, prior knowledge, and text type upon amount comprehended: Using rauding theory to critique schema theory research. *Reading Research Quarterly, 27*(2), 165–173.

Chall, J. S. (1983). *Stages of reading development.* New York: McGraw-Hill.

Chaney, C. (1992). Language development, metalinguistic skill, and print awareness in three year old children. *Applied Psycholinguistics, 13*(4), 485–514.

Christensen, C. A. (1992). Discrepancy definitions of reading disability: Has the quest led us astray? A response to Stanovich. *Reading Research Quarterly, 27*(3), 276–278.

Dickinson, D., & McCabe, A. (1991). The acquisition and development of language: A social interactionist account of language and literacy development. In J. F. Kavanagh (Ed.), *The language continuum: from infancy to literacy* (pp. 1–40). Parkton, MD: York Press.

Fincher-Kiefer, R. (1992). The role of prior knowledge in inferential processing. *Journal of Research in Reading, 15*(1), 12–27.

Foley, C. (1992). Evaluating the use of prediction: An experimental study with junior high and remedial readers in individualized small group settings. *Journal of Research in Reading, 15*(1), 28–38.

Gee, J. (1988, June). *Perspectives on literacy: Cultural and social diversity.* Workshop Presented at the Emerson College LLD Institute, Boston.

Gee, J. P. (1990). *Social linguistics and literacies. Ideology discourses.* London: Falmer Press.

Gillespie, C. S. (1993). Reading graphic displays: What teachers should know. *Journal of Reading, 36*(5), 350–354.

Gilovich, T. (1991). *How we know what isn't so.* New York: Free Press.

Goodman, G. S., & Aman, C. (1987, April). Children's use of anatomically detailed dolls to recount an event. In M. Stewart (Chair), *Anatomically detailed dolls: Developmental, clinical and legal implications.* Symposium conducted at the meeting of the Society for Research in Child Development, Baltimore, MD.

Goodman, G. S., & Aman, C. (1990). Children's use of anatomically detailed dolls to recount an event. *Child Development, 61,* 1859–1871.

Goodman, K. (1989). Roots of the whole-language movement. *The Elementary School Journal, 90*(2), 113–127.

Grant, R. (1993). Strategic training for using text headings to improve students' processing of content. *Journal of Reading, 36*(6), 482–488.

Guthrie, J. T., & Greaney, V. (1991). Literacy acts. In R. Barr, M. L. Kamil, P. Mosenthal, & P. D. Pearson (Eds.), *Handbook of reading research* (Vol. 2, pp. 68–96). New York: Longman.

Guzzetti, B. J., Snyder, T. E., & Glass, G. V. (1992). Promoting conceptual change in science: Can texts be used effectively. *Journal of Reading, 35*(8), 642–649.

Heath, S. B. (1986). The functions, and uses of literacy. In S. de Casteell, A. Luke, & K. Egan (Eds.), *Literacy, society, and schooling* (pp. 15–27). New York: Cambridge University Press.

Hayes, D. P., & Ahrens, M. (1988). Vocabulary simplification for children: A special case of "motherese." *Journal of Child Language, 15,* 395–410.

Hennings, D. G. (1993). On knowing and reading history. *Journal of Reading, 36*(5), 362–370.

Hirsch, E. D. (1987). *Cultural literacy.* Boston: Houghton-Mifflin.

Interagency Committee on Learning Disabilities, Department of Health and Human Services. (1987). Recommendation of the Committee. In *Learning Disabilities: A Report to the U.S. Congress* (pp. i–226).

Kamhi, A. G. (1993). Some problems with the marriage between theory and clinical practice. *Language, Speech, Hearing Services in Schools, 24,* 57–60.

Kamhi, A. G., & Catts, H. W. (1989). Reading disabilities: A developmental language perspective. Austin, TX: Pro-Ed.

Kozol, J. (1991). *Savage inequalities.* New York: Crown.

Lahey, M. (1980, May). *Learning disabilities: a puzzle without a cover picture?* Paper presented at the symposium on Language, Learning, and Reading Disabilities: A New Decade, City University of New York, New York.

McCormick, S. (1992). Disabled readers' erroneous responses to inferential comprehension questions: description and analysis. *Reading Research Quarterly, 27*(1), 55–77.

McKeown, M., Beck, I. I., Sinatra, G. M., & Loxterman, J. A. (1992). The contribution of prior knowledge and coherent text to comprehension. *Reading Research Quarterly, 27*(1), 79–93.

McNamara, T. P., Miller, D. I., & Bransford, J. D. (1991). Mental models and reading comprehension. In R. Barr, L. Kamil, P. B. Mosenthal, & P. D. Pearson (Eds.), *Handbook of reading research* (Vol. 2, pp. 230–245). New York: Longman.

Meyer, B. J. E. (1984). Text dimensions and cognitive processing. In H. Mandl, N. L. Stein, & T. Trabasso (Eds.), *Learning and the comprehension of text* (pp. 3–52). Hillsdale, NJ: Lawrence Erlbaum.

Milosky, L. M., Wilkinson, L. C., Chiang, C. P., Lindow, J., & Salmon, D. (1986). School-age children's understanding of explanation adequacy. *Journal of Educational Psychology, 78*(3), 334–340.

Moorman, G. B., Blanton, W. E., & McLaughlin, T. M. (1992). The rhetoric of whole language: Part one. *Reading Psychology, 13*(2), iii–xv.

Ohlhausen, M., & Roller, C. (1988). The operation of text structure and content schemata in isolation and interaction. *Reading Research Quarterly, 23,* 70–88.

Phillips, L. M. (1988). Young readers inferencing strategies in reading comprehension. *Cognition and Instruction, 5,* 193–222.

Raynor, K., & Pollatsek, A. (1989). *The psychology of reading.* Englewood Cliffs, NJ: Prentice-Hall.

Richgels, D., McGee, M., Lomax, R., & Sheard, C. (1987). Awareness of four text structures: Effects on recall of expository text. *Reading Research Quarterly, 22,* 177–196.

Roberts, B. (1992). The evolution of the young child's concept of "word" as a unit of spoken and written language. *Reading Research Quarterly, 27*(2), 125–138.

Roller, C. M. (1990). Commentary: The interaction of knowledge and structure variables in the processing of expository prose. *Reading Research Quarterly, 25*(2), 79–89.

Sawyer, D. J. (1991). Whole language in context: Insights into the current great debate. *Topics in Language Disorders, 11*(3), 1–13.

Scott, C. M. (1989). Problem writers: Nature, assessment, and intervention. In A. Kamhi & H. Catts (Eds.), *Reading disabilities: a developmental language perspective* (pp. 303–344). Austin, TX: Pro-Ed.

Silliman, E. R. (1991, June). *Observing is more than looking: The discourse scaffold of intervention.* Workshop presented at the Emerson College Institute in Language Learning Disabilities, Boston.

Silliman, E. R., & Wallach, G. P. (1991, November). *The communication process model for LLD children: Making it work.* Short course presented at the American Speech-Language-Hearing Association Convention, Atlanta, GA.

Spring, C., & Prager, J. (1992). Teaching community-college students to follow the train of thought in expository texts. *Reading and Writing: An Interdisciplinary Journal, 4,* 33–54.

Stanovich, K. E. (1992). Response to Christensen. *Reading Research Quarterly, 27*(3) 279–280.

Stark, J. (1980, May). *Some views from the back row.* Keynote speech presented at the symposium on Language, Learning, and Reading Disabilities: A New Decade, City University of New York.

Temple, C. A., Nathan, R. G., & Burris, N. A. (1982). *The beginnings of writing.* Boston: Allyn & Bacon.

Thompson, R. A. (1992). A critical perspective on whole language. *Reading Psychology, 13,* 131–155.

Tierney, R. J., & Pearson, P. D. (1981). Learning to learn from text: A framework for improving classroom practices. In E. Dishner, J. Readence, & T. Bean (Eds.), *Reading in the context area: Improving classroom instruction* (pp. 50–65). New York: Kendall Hunt.

Tunmer, W. E., Herman, M., & Nesdale, A. R. (1988). Metalinguistic ability & beginning reading. *Reading Research Quarterly, 23,* 134–158.

Wallach, G. P. (1989). Current research as a guide to meaningful language intervention programming for school-age students, *Seminars in Language, Speech, and Hearing, 10*(3), 205–217.

Wallach, G. P. (1990). "Magic buries Celtics": Looking for broader interpretations of language learning and literacy. *Topics in Language Disorders, 10*(2), 63–80.

Wallach, G. P., & Butler, K. G. (Eds.). (1984). *Language learning disabilities in school-age children.* Baltimore, MD: Williams & Wilkins.

Wallach, G. P., & Liebergott, J. W. (1984). Who shall be called "learning disabled": Some new directions. In G. P. Wallach & K. G. Butler (Eds.), *Language learning disabilities in school-age children* (pp. 1–14). Baltimore, MD: Williams & Wilkins.

Wallach, G. P., & Miller, L. (1988). *Language intervention and academic success.* Austin, TX: Pro-Ed.

Warren-Leubecker, A. (1987). Competence and performance factors in word awareness and early reading. *Journal of Experimental Child Psychology, 43,* 62–80.

West, R. F., Stanovich, K. E., & Mitchell, H. R. (1993). Reading in the real world and its correlates. *Reading Research Quarterly, 28*(1), 35–50.

Winne, P. H., Graham, L., & Prock, L. (1993). A model of poor readers' text-based inferences: Effects of explanatory feedback. *Reading Research Quarterly, 28*(1), 53–66.

Wyatt, M., & Pickle, M. (1993). "Good teaching is good teaching": Basic beliefs of college reading instruction. *Journal of Reading, 36*(5), 340–348.

Yuill, N., & Oakhill, J. (1991). *Children's problems with text comprehension.* Cambridge: Cambridge University Press.

2

DISCOURSE SCAFFOLDS FOR CLASSROOM INTERVENTION

■ Elaine R. Silliman
University of South Florida
■ Louise Cherry Wilkinson
Rutgers University

To a great extent within classrooms, the discourse created by teachers and students determines both what is learned and how learning takes place. The focus of this chapter is on oral language and literacy; it emphasizes the relationships between communication and the development of literacy. We discuss the importance of closely examining the actual language used by students and teachers to determine which aspects support and/or provide opportunities for students to develop and refine literacy skills. Special attention is directed to one such opportunity: scaffolding. *Scaffolding* refers to the guidance an adult or peer provides through verbal communication as a way of doing for the student what the student cannot do without assistance (Cazden, 1988). The application of scaffolds to classroom intervention for students with language learning disorders is developed by a discussion of three issues:

- An overall perspective for discourse scaffolding in relationship to the oral–literate continuum
- Some developmental and clinical issues related to the discourse continuum
- A comparison of the directive and supportive models of scaffolding for language learning disabled (LLD) students

LITERACY IS MORE THAN READING AND WRITING: THE IMPORTANCE OF COMMUNICATION AND ORAL LANGUAGE

Literacy is more than the acquisition of reading and writing (Wallach & Butler, chap. 1). Listening, speaking, reading, writing, and spelling are interrelated, because all are communicative processes (Westby, 1990; Westby, chap. 7). This chapter reiterates a broad notion of literacy that includes both oral and written communication. At one level, being literate is a confirmation of the social identity as a full participant in a community, as discussed in Chapter 1. In addition, because written language transcends immediate temporal and spatial constraints, it is a potentially powerful metacognitive tool for creating, understanding, and revising ideas about the world.

Integrated perspectives about the connections between language and learning share the view that the integration of communicative processes—listening, reading, speaking, and writing—is the pathway to literacy. This view undergirds the emergent literacy and whole language educational approaches that have been applied in the regular education settings (Goodman & Goodman, 1990; Mason & Stewart, 1990; Weaver, 1988, 1990, 1991) and in special education settings with students described as learning disabled (Rhodes & Dudley-Marling, 1988). This perspective is consistent with recent research on the writing-process or authoring approaches (e.g., Dyson, 1989; Harste, Short, & Burke, 1988; Raphael, Englert, & Kirschner, 1989; Shanklin, 1991; Sulzby, 1990), including integration into whole literacy programs involving cultural minority children (Au et al., 1990; Bloome, Harris, & Ludlum, 1991; Kawakami-Arakaki, Oshiro, & Farran, 1988; Pinnell, 1989; Shuy, 1988a; Staton, 1988b; Teale & Martinez, 1989). The communication process perspective in language learning disabilities is similar, with its emphasis on the integration of language intervention into regular and special education classrooms (Belkin & Hoffman, in Silliman & Wilkinson, 1991; Miller, 1990; Norris,

1991; Norris & Damico, 1990; Norris & Hoffman, 1990; Westby, 1990; Westby & Costlow, 1991).

Being literate can be seen as a continuum that transcends the oral and written mediums of communication, with different discourse styles overlapping both mediums (Biber, 1988; Horowitz & Samuels, 1987; Miller, 1990; Scott, 1988; Scott, chap. 8; Spiro & Taylor, 1987; Tannen, 1985; Westby, chap. 7; Wallach, 1990). For example, Tannen (1985) describes the overlap of communicative mediums according to the relative focus placed on interpersonal involvement in the discourse versus the relative focus placed on content.

Consider the following example. Across the oral and written mediums, one can select more literate styles—styles that are more linguistically explicit, content focused, and impersonal. Alternatively, one can use a more personal, communication-focused, and less explicit oral style, as Scott also points out in Chapter 8 and as Wallach and Butler note in Chapter 1. The selection of a style depends on several factors, including:

- The purposes for communicating
- The role relationships between discourse partners
- The temporal and spatial aspects of the discourse
- The medium of communication

Because communication is purposeful, the selection of a style is heavily influenced by the first factor—the goal or purpose.

The Purposes of Communication

It is interesting to note that the functional nature of classroom communication has not been a major focus in past research on literacy learning. Anders and Pearson (1987) describe this phenomenon in regular classrooms as follows:

> Consider the plight of students who are constantly barraged with assignment after assignment requiring them to find main ideas, underline verbs, correct spellings, distinguish facts from opinions, or write themes about a picture for an audience of one (the teacher). Students rarely are given opportunities in schools to perform literacy tasks for either personally satisfying reasons or for typically socially motivated reasons (e.g., publication). About the only reason we typically offer students for completing literacy tasks is, "because that's the assignment." And grades are virtually our only source of motivation. But what would literacy tasks look like, and how would performance change, if we set a requirement that we couldn't assign a task or teach a skill unless we could answer the question, "when and why should a student use it?" (p. 312)

Understanding the purpose of communication is relevant regardless of whether the task is one of comprehending or producing narrative and expository discourse in either the oral or written domain (Anders & Pearson, 1987; Baker & Brown, 1984a, 1984b; Brown & Palincsar, 1987; Cox, Shanahan, & Sulzby, 1990; Harste et al., 1988; Horowitz & Samuels, 1987; Meyer, 1985, 1987; Palincsar & Brown, 1984, 1987; Spiro & Taylor, 1987; Stein, 1983; Tierney, Lazansky, Raphael, & Cohen, 1987).

In the next section of this chapter, other important aspects of verbal communication are considered, including the relationships between speakers, constraints imposed by temporal and spatial elements, and the choice of the medium (oral versus written). Adequate understanding of these aspects of communication is necessary background for connecting literacy to learning.

Speakers' Roles

During conversations, speakers and listeners constantly monitor and negotiate the use of language as the interaction unfolds (Biber, 1988; Horowitz & Samuels, 1987). Social and cultural experiences influence the selection of discourse style and particular choices of words. Consider the following example of an individual presenting a lecture. In this situation, the speaker cannot assume that the audience is familiar with basic definitions and applications; thus, the speaker must organize discourse in a more linguistically explicit, or literate, manner. But, the speaker can still monitor whether listeners seem to understand and be interested in the topic and how it is being presented. As a result, the speaker has opportunities to clarify what is being said or revise how it is being said as these active feedback signals are processed and interpreted. The audience must also select more literate comprehension strategies because selective attention to essential information is crucial, as is continuous monitoring by each participant of her state of comprehension (Horowitz & Samuels, 1987; Sternberg, 1987).

Alternatively, when the relationship is one of reader–author, direct feedback is not possible, but variation does exist. Harste et al. (1988) and Meyer (1987) note that writing, during its production, involves speaking to a real or imagined audience. The actions of reading and listening, in turn, depend on inferring the speaker–author's plans, or underlying purposes, for communicating the message. Thus, identical to the speaker–listener role relationship, the author–reader relationship is foremost one of social interaction (Anders & Pearson, 1987; Meyer, 1987). It involves the construction of dialogue between the author and reader in which the reader acts as an interpreter of the author's purposes and meanings. The reader, in turn, becomes an interpreter of his own intentions and meanings when these are written down for others to interpret (Tierney et al., 1987).

Temporal and Spatial Aspects of Communication

Temporal and spatial factors affect communication to a great extent. For example, in the case of one family member writing another, a high degree of shared knowledge about family members is assumed. This familiarity forces the choice of a more oral and personal style of communication. Also, when communication takes place in a shared physical setting within the same temporal framework, the need for linguistic explicitness is reduced. In contrast, when the speaker gives a lecture and uses visual aids (e.g., transparencies and videotapes) as referents, the style becomes more literate. When communication is displaced in time and space, as is the case when the speaker is an author and the listener is a reader who is unfamiliar with the topic, then the entire communicative context of interaction must be reconstructed using verbal means alone. This reconstructive process is the recreation of what an audience needs to know to meet the purposes of communication (Cazden, 1988).

The Medium of Communication

Differences between the oral and written mediums influence comprehension and production. When discourse is written, it has permanency. Readers can work at understanding at their own rates and use different metacomprehension strategies (Anders & Pearson, 1987; Baker & Brown, 1984a, 1984b; Biber, 1988; Gavelek & Raphael, 1985). Metacomprehension strategies are concerned with how cognitive activity is modified to facilitate and monitor one's state of comprehension (Gavelek & Raphael, 1985; Palincsar & Brown, 1984; Paris, 1991). For example, the selection of metacomprehension strategies depends on how the purposes of reading are understood and the type and complexity of discourse structure, such as narrative versus expository structures. Comprehension breakdowns may be intentionally repaired by rereading, looking up unfamiliar words, self-questioning, or, even, asking another for assistance. Essential information may be identified by skimming content, underlining, outlining, or note taking for subsequent summarization.

Similar to the more skillful reader, the skillful author also can engage in a more controlled way in planning, organizing, editing, and revising the content to be communicated, as well as the linguistic forms of communication, over a period of time (Raphael et al., 1989). As a literate mode of communication, writing is more integrative than the oral mode. Large amounts of information can be condensed into the discourse through such linguistic devices as subordination, nominalization, development of adverbs (Biber, 1988; Scott, 1988, 1989a; Scott, chap. 8), and other cohesive devices that tie meaning together semantically within and across sentence boundaries (Hasan, 1984a). Hasan (1984b) has refined the notion of cohesion into one of cohesive harmony, the process by which chains of reference thematically unite semantic and syntactic information. A working knowledge of "cohesive harmony" influences knowledge of literacy, including children's developing metastrategies for becoming more effective speaker–authors or listener–readers of narrative and expository discourse (Cox, Shanahan, & Sulzby, 1990; DeStefano & Kantor, 1988; Eller, 1989).

Finally, regardless of the style of communication, the oral medium places a premium on "speed of production and comprehension" (Biber, 1988, p. 42). Speaking is bounded in time and is often fragmented in character because of transient breakdowns in planning or executing. False starts, silent and filled pauses, revisions, and word and phrase repetitions are common. As a consequence, listeners must also work under time pressure to understand what is said, as anyone knows who has ever sat in a classroom, trying to make sense of the vast array of information communicated.

In sum, this brief discussion has provided an expanded perspective on literacy, to include both oral and written domains. On the broadest level, being literate is a confirmation of the social identity as a full participant in a community. In addition, because written language can transcend immediate temporal and spatial constraints, it is a potentially powerful metacognitive tool for creating, understanding, and revising ideas about the world.

DEVELOPMENTAL AND CLINICAL ISSUES

Developmental Issues: The Origins of Learning Literacy

An important developmental issue in literacy concerns the origin of metacognition, which is embedded within the social activities in which students participate. Metacognition is the conscious awareness of thinking about thinking and a process that regulates how one goes about learning in purposeful ways, and transferring this learning flexibly (Silliman & Wilkinson, 1991). Its primary characteristics are choice and control (Garton & Pratt, 1989). *Choice* implies selectivity or deliberateness, while *control* implies directed attention.

One source stimulating metacognition is the set of materials available to support the development of literacy awareness (e.g., paper, pencil, and crayons to children's books, newspapers, cookbooks, videotapes, maps, etc.) (Stewart & Mason, 1989; van Kleeck, 1990; van Kleeck, chap. 3). Typically, these materials are used by students in interaction with others as well as by themselves.

A second source of metacognition knowledge arises from the social interactions between adults and children in which literacy is naturally embedded (Heath, 1983; Rogoff, 1990; Stewart & Mason, 1989; Taylor, 1983; van Kleeck, 1990). As discussed by van Kleeck in Chapter 3, some of these activities are highly visible, such as the joint reading of bedtime stories, newspaper comics, or recipes, or oral discussions about "literate things" (Taylor, 1983). Some activities, however, may be momentary and, therefore, less visible to adults. Taylor (1983), in a home-based study of values and beliefs on family literacy, describes an instance of unnoticed, momentary, literacy activity involving Steven (age 4 years, 10 months):

> Moving around the kitchen while we talked, I picked up a piece of yellow lined paper off a counter top. . . . I asked Jill (Steven's mother) if it was for my collection. She looked at it and said "No, I don't know where that came from." Steven walked into the kitchen and I asked him if he knew anything about the paper. He said, "Sure, I just did it." While we were talking Steven was drawing letters. No one was watching him, and no one had seen him put the paper on the counter top. (p. 58)

Other unnoticed momentary instances reported by Taylor (1983) included children's pretend (scribble) writing on scraps of paper or with a typewriter, making letters with plastic letter blocks, chalk drawing of letters on sidewalks, writing names on drawings and holiday cards, and reproducing written "messages" from books read previously. Thus, visible literacy activities can be seen as the interactional mechanism by which an adult "paints pictures with the sound of words" for the child (Farnsworth, 1978, cited in Taylor, 1983, p. 97). Less visible momentary events are those in which the child, with minimal adult assistance, uses language for its own sake as a way to practice (play) with the forms, content, and functions of these sound pictures (see also van Kleeck, chap. 3).

In effect, the precursors of metacognition—choice and control—or self-regulation do not reside in the child alone. Precursors of this skill emerge from verbal interactions between adults and children at home and at school (Rogoff, 1990).

Clinical Issue: The LLD Student as a Perpetual New Learner

Elsewhere, it has been argued that LLD students have difficulties in adequately participating in many classroom activities because of their problems with deciphering and managing oral language aspects of literacy learning (Silliman & Wilkinson, 1991). LLD students are neither particularly flexible nor efficient in dealing with all aspects of literacy learning, including the following:

- Phonological processing (Catts, 1989a, 1991; Kamhi, 1992; Kamhi & Catts, 1989a, 1989b; Snyder & Downey, 1991) and phonological planning (Blachman, chap. 9; Catts, 1989b)
- Lexical processing as manifested in word retrieval patterns (German, 1987; German, chap. 12; German & Simon, 1991; Kail & Leonard, 1986; Leonard, 1988)
- Verbal analogical reasoning (Kamhi, Gentry, Mauer, & Gholson, 1990)
- Narrative discourse processing and production (Liles, 1987; Merritt & Liles, 1987; Montague, Maddux, & Dereshiwsky, 1990; Roth & Spekman, 1986; Silliman, 1989; Snyder & Downey, 1991; Westby, 1989; Westby, Van Dongen, & Maggert, 1989)
- The understanding and production of written expository discourse structures, such as comparison–contrast, and problem solution (Scott, 1989a, 1989b; Scott, chap. 8)

Prior research also suggests that LLD students typically have difficulty in making transitions from novel to familiar information. In the next section, two patterns of behavior that are characteristic of LLD students are discussed. The discussion provides some insight into why LLD students are less successful in school.

The Pattern of Orality. LLD students typically produce narratives that are more oral in style than non-LLD students (e.g., Merritt & Liles, 1987). Researchers have suggested that metacognitive differences may underlie this pattern. One source may be a problem with perspective taking. LLD students may make false assumptions about what the listener needs to know. A second problem may originate from the problems encountered in organizing the linguistic elements of discourse, that is, in making the parts cohesively fit together. Silliman and Wilkinson (1991) suggest that these organizational problems may be related to both (1) less flexibility in retrieving narrative schemas that match the situation and (2) comprehension of chains of reference and their causal connectives. These connectives are the linguistic anchors for the narrative. A third problem may involve comprehension monitoring. Specifically, LLD students may not easily keep track of where they are in the narrative, so they may not be able to anticipate where they should be going to achieve their communicative goal. Lahey and Bloom's discussion about competing resources should be consulted for additional information along these lines (see chap. 13).

The Pattern of Automaticity. Lahey and Bloom's discussion in Chapter 13 and prior research also suggest that LLD students differ from non-LLD students in the adequacy of automatizing new information. In the transition from the novel to the familiar, performance tends to become automatized. For example, once one learns how to use a word processor, the mechanics of how to operate this technology do not have to be attended to during use. Sternberg (1987) has pointed out, as have Lahey and Bloom (chap. 13), that the individual no longer has to direct controlled attention to a task that previously placed a heavy demand on the allocation of cognitive resources. These cognitive resources include the following:

- Selective encoding (representation) of essential information in accord with the purposes for doing so
- Selective combination of the newly encoded information into an already existing knowledge structure to make sense of the new information
- Selective comparison of the old with the new to surpass current understanding by applying the newly integrated information to an appropriate situation

These controlled processes are viewed by Sternberg (1987) as interdependent: "Deciding what information to encode and how to combine it does not occur in a vacuum. Rather encoding and combination of new knowledge are guided by retrieval of old information" (p. 150). These controlled processes are also inferential activities that permit one to figure out "what works, when it works, and even why it works" (Sternberg, 1989, p. 125). For example, as a skilled, or expert reader, one no longer must think about the relations between speech and print unless unfamiliar words or ambiguous meanings are detected. If ambiguous or unfamiliar information is not sufficiently encoded, it will not be detected, much less integrated and compared for consistency in meaning (Baker & Brown, 1984a; Vosniadou, Pearson, & Rogers, 1988). As a result of inadequate encoding, LLD students may be unaware that a comprehension failure has occurred (Skarakis-Doyle & Mullin, 1990).

When information, including linguistic information, cannot be routinely managed through automatic modes of encoding, combination, and comparison, more resources need to be consciously allocated to master a new task (Snyder, 1984; Lahey & Bloom, chap. 13). From this perspective, LLD students may be described as perpetual new learners, rather than as delayed or disordered learners—an idea that will be returned to later in this text (e.g., Palincsar, Brown, & Campione, chap. 5). This analysis suggests that LLD students may have difficulty inferring and integrating connections between old and new information. As a result, they are continuously confronted with having to allocate more of their processing resources over longer periods of time to thinking deliberately about strategies for approaching each new task (Lahey & Bloom, chap. 13; Wallach & Miller, 1988). They become bogged down in trying to figure out what works, why it works, when it works, and how it works (Anders & Pearson, 1987; Sternberg, 1989). In sum, LLD students can be seen as inefficient problem solvers.

The dual problems of the orality of LLD students' communication and their apparent problems with automaticity suggest that classroom activities need to be designed to assist them in overcoming these problems. The application of one significant kind of assistance for LLD students, discourse scaffolds, is discussed next.

DISCOURSE SCAFFOLDS: TWO SCAFFOLDING MODELS

Scaffolding can be seen as a mechanism through which novice students are guided by a more knowledgeable adult or peer to achieve new levels of expertise. Both the directive and supportive scaffolds, and their associated discourse strategies, provide assistance to students who cannot learn to communicate adequately on their own. Each type of scaffold demonstrates something different about the purposes of communication. In the following section, two examples of classroom discourse are discussed and analyzed. The focus is on how discourse strategies enable or, unintentionally disable, LLD students' active participation in their own learning. Five components of each type of scaffold are compared:

- Scaffold structure
- Expectations for performance
- The teaching register
- Support of discourse planning
- Modeling strategies

Consider the following examples from two different classrooms for LLD students. The first activity was in a combined kindergarten–first grade, which had five children, ages five to seven years, all native English speakers. The speech-language clinician also served as the classroom teacher. The general curriculum goals are grounded within the language experience approach and are intended to facilitate oral communication and preliteracy skills. In this particular case, the clinician used the topic of "the school chef" as an example of a "community helper." The students sat in a semicircle of chairs facing the clinician/teacher, who stood near a table on which were placed various cooking tools and ingredients. The following verbal interaction occurred at the beginning of the lesson:

The Chef Lesson

1. Clinician/teacher: Boys and girls/ Remember this morning we went to visit this worker?/ (points to picture of a chef hanging on a bulletin board)
2. Mary: The chef/
3. Clinician/teacher: The chef (.) the chef/ And who can tell me what the chef's job is to do? Who remembers?

4a. Lori: [To cook] (simultaneous overlap of turns)
4b. Joey: [To make food]
5a. Clinician/teacher: To make food? What else?/ Remember when we went to the cafeteria and we saw the chefs in our cafeteria?/ They did a couple of [jobs]/
5b. Mary: [Made food]

6. Clinician/teacher: They made food/ And after they've made the food and you eat your food and you put your trays up/ What else do they do?/
7. Lori: They let us come in/ They let us eat/
8. Clinician/teacher: Right/ Right/ But let's look at it this way/ Let's think about it/

The second example is taken from a junior high classroom for six students, ages eleven to fourteen years, all native English speakers. The teacher, who is also a speech-language pathologist, has set the goal of assisting students to integrate newly acquired knowledge on healthy nutrition. Her approach in this lesson involves applying communicative strategies for identifying information resources, gathering information, and reporting it to others. The lesson is written on the board as (1) *review* of previous information gathering, (2) a *report* of information collection to date, and (3) *summarizing* of the lesson activity that will occur. The students were seated at desks arranged in a semicircle with the clinician/teacher standing at the head of the circle in front of the blackboard. The following verbal interaction occurred at the beginning of the lesson:

The Nutrition Lesson

1. Clinician/teacher: What comes first on our schedule, Frank?/ (pointing to word *review* on blackboard)
2. Frank: Review/
3. Clinician/teacher: Review/ Good/ What does review mean, Frank?/
4. Frank: Talk about things we did before/
5. Clinician/teacher: Talk about things we have *learned* before/ Why do we review, Karl?/
6. Karl: To get our brains going/
7. Clinician/teacher: (Gaze still directed to Karl) Good/ It gets our brains going/ I like that you are getting a lot of volume in your voice/ (smiling) [Note: a specified goal for Karl is to increase his volume to increase overall intelligibility.] (reorients gaze to whole group) It gets our brains going so that we are ready for what we are going to do today/ This is what is going

to be second on our schedule (pointing to the word *graphing* on the blackboard)/ Could someone read what this word says?/ Raise your hand please/ Diane/

8. Diane: Graphing/
9. Clinician/teacher: Graphing/ Good/ This is the last thing we are going to do today (pointing to word *summarize)* /Mike, can you read this word to me?/
10. Mike: Summarize/
11. Clinician/teacher: Summarize/ Good/ And what does summarize mean?/
12. Mike: It means that you summarize what you just said (.) a couple hours ago/

On the surface, the excerpts from the chef lesson and the nutrition lesson are similar, in terms of their use of the question–answer–evaluation sequence (Silliman & Wilkinson, 1991). Both also represent a type of expository discourse that has a general function of enumerating a series of points associated with a specific topic (Englert, Stewart, & Hiebert, 1988; Meyer, 1985; Meyer & Freedle, 1984). However, these two examples are very different in several important aspects. At the broadest level, both are examples of two models of discourse scaffolding for intervention: (1) The chef lesson represents the directive scaffold, and (2) the nutrition lesson represents the supportive scaffold.

This chapter proposes that supportive scaffolds may be more facilitative to communication and to learning than directive scaffolds. Some weaknesses of directive scaffolds are presented next. The positive aspects of supportive scaffolds are discussed for the remainder of the chapter. In several instances, examples of overlapping scaffolding techniques are noted (e.g., dialogue numbers 39 to 52).

Directive Scaffolds

Framework and Structure. The structure of directive scaffolds can be considered from several viewpoints, including the predominance of control mechanisms such as the use of IRE (initiation-response-evaluation) sequences. IRE sequences are the question–answer–evaluation sequences used frequently in classroom and clinical lesson discourse. IRE sequences have been the focus of the majority of previous studies in instructional language (e.g., Becker & Silverstein, 1984; Bloome & Theodorou, 1988; Bobkoff & Panagos, 1986; Cherry, 1978; Durkin, 1978–1979; Mehan, 1979; Panagos & Bliss, 1990; Ripich & Panagos, 1985; Silliman, 1984; Silliman & Wilkinson, 1991; Spinelli & Ripich, 1985). The IRE sequence appears in both special and regular education classrooms (Baker & Zigmond, 1990)—a finding that, by itself, suggests minimal sensitivity to the different learning needs of students in special education placements (Ysseldyke, Christenson, Thurlow, & Bakewell, 1989). In addition to the influence of IRE sequences, directive scaffolds are also better understood by observing teachers' instructional styles and their approaches to particular discourse and modeling techniques. Each of these areas are discussed in turn.

Expectations for Performance. Cazden (1988) identifies two key elements for directive scaffolds: (1) The IRE structure appears to reflect a "default pattern"; that is, the presumption is that the primary role of a teacher is to query and evaluate students' knowledge in accord with expectations for what is accurate and appropriate. (2) A major task for students is to learn to speak within the structure of the lesson. Students must match their discourse style to the teacher's style, to demonstrate that they know how to give accurate and appropriate responses in keeping with teacher expectations. These expectations often have to be inferred by students.

The following excerpts from the chef lesson demonstrate these elements of the default pattern and style matching:

20. Clinician/teacher: This week we've been talking about the chef and I have a picture of the chef up here (simultaneously pointing to the bulletin board)/ And I have on one of the tools on that a chef uses/ What's one of the tools that a chef uses that. Look at Mrs. Light (directs eye gaze to Larry)/ What do I have on that a chef uses/ (points to apron that she is wearing with right hand while simultaneously pointing with her left hand to Larry)
21. Larry: Apron/
22. Clinician/teacher: An apron/ And why do *I* wear this apron?/ (while walking to bulletin board and pointing at the picture of the chef)

23a. Sol: To get dirty [no bu]/

23b. Mary: [to get dirty]/

24. Clinician/teacher: To get dirty?/ (simultaneous with facial expression that communicates an incorrect reply) I use it so I can get dirty?/ (pointing to apron)

Teaching Register. A teaching register is a way of talking that marks a specific social role, in this case, the instructional role. A teaching register should be differentiated, however, from individual differences in the communicative style through which a register is actually expressed (Cazden, 1988). Stylistic variations tend to reflect personality differences. These variations in style can be communicated through (1) the verbal and nonverbal signals that convey caring, respect, support, and interest (Cazden, 1988); (2) the combination of grammatical structures selected to move the lesson along (Shuy, 1988b); and (3) how prosodic features are used (e.g., slower versus faster rate of speaking, loudness level, etc.).

A teaching register, on the other hand, functions as a management procedure for communicating attitudes (expectations) about the role students are to play in the teaching–learning process. Few studies on classroom or clinical discourse with LLD students have examined directly the underlying teaching register; thus, only inferences can be drawn from the results of existing studies. The evidence suggests that directive scaffolds are characterized by a high degree of control by the teacher. One can speculate that stylistic variations are overwhelmed by use of this register, because authority and an attitude of prescription about what is "proper" communication co-exist (Damico, 1990). Four features define this control register, all of which are reflected in the excerpt from the chef lesson and are discussed next.

Rigid Access to the Conversational Floor. The predominance of the IRE sequence co-occurs with a high demand for students to assume the responding role. Studies from regular education classrooms (e.g., Durkin, 1978–1979), special education classrooms (Baker & Zigmond, 1990; Ysseldyke, Christenson, Thurlow, & Bakewell, 1989), and language intervention settings (Becker & Silverstein, 1984; Letts, 1985; Prutting, Bagshaw, Goldstein, Juskowitz, & Umen, 1978; Silliman, 1984) provide evidence that teachers and clinicians do most of the talking.

Tight Topic Management. Prior studies show some variation in the degree to which clinicians allow students to digress on topics outside of the clinician's agenda. However, there is a pattern for clinicians not to permit students to initiate new topics unrelated to the immediate task at hand (Letts, 1984; Prutting et al., 1978; Ripich & Panagos, 1985; Ripich, Hambrecht, Panagos, & Prelock, 1984).

Clinicians' use of discourse markers, such as *okay, now, so,* and *well* to signal transitions within and between topical units also can indicate tight topic management. Kovarsky (1990) found that clinicians often used these markers to (1) control topic focus ("Okay we'll check it [the faucet] in just a second"; "So which one of these would you need?" [alternates pointing to teaspoon and tablespoon]); (2) evaluate the adequacy or inadequacy of students' response or actions ("Well, let's think about that and try it out"); and (3) direct students to reevaluate their own actions from the clinician's perspective ("Now do you know where to cut?") (Kovarsky, 1990, pp. 31–33).

Conduct Rules for Being a Listener and Speaker. The use of conduct regulators can mark the control register. From the clinician's perspective, conduct regulators may function solely as external monitors of children's attentional states. "Look at Mrs. Light" (see turn 20 in the chef lesson); "Don't interrupt"; "Wait for your turn"; and "Nice eye contact" are examples of these conduct regulators.

Directive scaffolds typically rely on prescriptions about appropriate listening and speaking behaviors (Spinelli & Ripich, 1985). Damico (1990) provides an example from a classroom activity in which the clinician/teacher and student (Bo, a male) are engaged in problem solving with a comparison of weights and pulleys. Bo provides the answer being sought, but his nonstandard use of the copula is the focus of evaluation, first negatively and then positively, after correction by the clinician:

1. Bo: Ain't nobody that can lift that (points to materials) without that (points to the pulley).
2. Clinician/teacher: (frowning) There isn't anyone who can lift that (points to the materials) without that (points to the pulley).
3. Bo: (tentatively) There isn't anyone who can lift that without that (no pointing).
4. Clinician/teacher: (smiling) Great Bo. I knew you could get it right. (Damico, 1990, p. 89)

Even requests to "Say the whole sentence" (Prutting et al., 1978) can be considered as serving a conduct function. In these instances, students are directed to suspend their natural knowledge of linguistic cohesion in which redundancy is reduced, through production of an elliptical reply. "Say it in a complete sentence" demands instead that the student substitute an artificial strategy for responding.

Procedural Display. Directive scaffolds are opportunities in which the unstated goal is often one of learning a conversational routine to complete the lesson for the lesson's sake. Conversational routines are highly predictable scripts for procedural display, a means by which teachers, clinicians, and students can "get through" the lesson together, creating the illusion that learning has occurred (Bloome, 1987). Value is placed on students' demonstration that they know how to speak within the structure of the particular lesson, most typically, by engaging in "fill-in-the-slot" responding. Students' roles are to provide minimal responses within the adult's frame of reference (McTear, 1985).

Conversational routines require that students take the teacher's perspective in the initiation and continuation of topics and assume the role of passive responder. The chef lesson is an example of procedural display (for further discussion, see Silliman & Wilkinson, 1991):

31. Clinician: Should I wear this apron to go to church?/ (looks at apron)
32a. Sol: [Nooo] [ ] indicates choral response
32b. Mary: [Nooo]
32c. Larry: [Nooo]
33d. Lori: [Nooo]
33e. Joey: [Nooo]
33. Clinician: Should I wear *this* to go swimming?/ (looks to the apron)

All five students again respond in unison, "Nooo," which is then followed by:

35. Clinician: Should I wear *this* if I'm gonna cook something?/

All students respond chorally with "Yeees," which the clinician evaluates positively. The clinician's goal was not to engage in procedural display but to engage students in language-rich experiences. The excerpt illustrates the disconnections that result when discourse practices are not clearly guided by a well-articulated set of assumptions about how students learn optimally to think and communicate (Bloome et al., 1991).

Ease of Planning Discourse. An important question about the use of discourse scaffolds is the degree to which they deliberately promote ease of planning. This issue is significant because discourse scaffolds create and sustain the communicative contexts for learning and influence how students and teachers understand the purposes of classroom activities, including lessons.

Discourse is planful (see Scott, chap. 8). However, the creation of discourse in particular communicative contexts can be more or less difficult, depending on several factors. To be planful as a speaker–author or listener–reader includes knowing the following: (1) The communications of ourselves and others are always purposeful because they are intended to accomplish goals; (2) others have multiple perspectives, which must be taken into account in formulating communicative plans; and (3) others, like ourselves, have internal states, such as intentions, thoughts, and emotions, which motivate the reasons for communicating (Gordon & Braun, 1985; Roth & Spekman, 1986; Stein & Glenn, 1979; Westby, 1989). Communication consists of choices for achieving these goals, such as the choice of requests for information versus requests for clarification versus acknowledgments. In addition, whether one is in the role of speaker or listener, communication is monitored constantly for trouble spots. Trouble spots, in turn, are subsequently repaired because speakers and listeners need to keep track of where they are in order to know where they are going. Finally, communication is evaluated for the effectiveness of outcomes. If the results are not effective, then either the goal or choices or both may be altered.

According to Ochs (1979) and Scott (chap. 8), when the particular purposes of face-to-face communication are found in highly familiar frames of reference, spontaneous construction of discourse becomes "relatively unplannable well in advance. . . . Rather, what will be said, the form in which it will be said, and who can say it can be anticipated for limited sequences only" (Ochs, 1979, p. 58). This type of discourse progressively evolves from the inferences made about the intentions of each conversational partner. It tends to be managed on a turn-by-turn basis. In other words, conversational partners are less able to anticipate in advance what will be said and what their contributions should be as a result. Ochs (1979) has identified some features of relatively unplanned discourse, which parallel more oral styles of communication. One feature is that speakers rely more on the immediate social situation to signal the interpretation of their meanings. The recovery of shared meaning is located in sources external to what is being said, and these language-external sources serve as the bases for the coherence of understanding (Hasan, 1984a).

The external recovery of meaning is a predominant feature in the chef lesson, reinforcing the students' existing orality. The clinician/teacher's intended plan is that students will first draw on their prior content knowledge about chefs (e.g., the visit to the school cafeteria) to identify cooking tools. This familiar knowledge will then be applied (transferred) to actual participation in making "tasty roll-ups" using some of the chef's tools. The content of discussion (the focus of discussion) is encased in a descriptive (expository) structure. The immediate task entails students' accurate retrieval of item names according to their functional attributes (tools a chef uses). Students' opportunity to be successful in retrieval is reduced, most likely because descriptive expository structures have the least amount of internal organization to aid retrieval (Lahey & Bloom, chap. 13; Meyer & Freedle, 1984; Westby, 1989). Because of how the discourse unfolds (local management), the clinician/teacher appears to expect that students' understanding of the activity's purpose will progressively emerge from a bottom–up process of discovering and comparing the functional relations among tools. Essentially, students need to infer the discourse structure (a descriptive structure) to understand what's going on.

One consequence of this pattern is that students are less able to predict what is going to happen, because the problem they are supposed to resolve remains ambiguous. The information sources for problem resolution are situated more in the multiple cues provided through the immediate temporal and physical context rather than residing more explicitly in the actual language used by the clinician/teacher to frame the activity. Most importantly, the shared purpose for communicating is lacking. Topical, or thematic, unity is absent as an overall plan by which students can make sense of what the problem is, why it is important, and how to resolve it.

Modeling. Modeling can take various forms: directive and nondynamic, directive and dynamic, and reciprocal and dynamic. The terms *directive* and *reciprocal* refer to the amount and kind of adult responsibility assumed for initial learning and subsequent transfer. The definition does not imply that *directive* is associated with *direct* or, conversely, with *indirect* (Lahey, 1988). *Indirect methods* are sometimes described as forms of incidental teaching. Directive and reciprocal modeling can function as direct or indirect methods for facilitation, depending on their actual implementation. Both categories of modeling represent choices made to affect how students use language and communication for specific purposes.

Directive and nondynamic modeling is most visible when the goal is to elicit immediate repetitions from the student, such as "Say the whole thing" or "Say I'm grating the onion." The chef lesson contained many examples of this form of nonconstructive modeling.

Modeling can also be directive and dynamic (reciprocal and dynamic strategies will be discussed shortly). The following conversational sequence from Brinton and Fujiki (1989) shows how the modeling choice can systematically serve to direct the child's attention to specific elements of the child's message in need of clarification:

1. Child: This big bear was chasing Donald down the road.
2. Clinician: What?
3. Child: This big bear was chasing Donald.
4. Clinician: What?
5. Child: (no response)
6. Clinician: The big bear was doing what?
7. Child: Chasing Donald along this road.
8. Clinician: Oh, now I get it, the bear was chasing Donald down the road.
9. Child: Yeah. (p. 179)

The selection of "The big bear was doing what?" was a modeled clarification strategy, more indirect in intent, but timed to direct the student to attend to the specific elements in his own message that the clinician wanted to have clarified. The student must subsequently infer (recover) those elements.

Modeling can facilitate transitions along the oral–literate discourse continuum and assist the novice to become more expert within various areas of the continuum. Several issues remain unresolved, however. One concerns the cognitive, communicative, and linguistic processes by which LLD students learn from the modeling of a scaffold to transfer this learning with increasing breadth of application (Fey & Cleave, 1990; Olswang, Bain, & Johnson, 1992). A second issue concerns the incorporation of modeling in the classroom as part of a communication process approach to intervention. Explicit and systematic distinctions are necessary for distinguishing modeling strategies that are directive/nondynamic/dynamic versus those that are reciprocal and dynamic. Without clear distinctions among these, clinicians may encounter difficulty in replicating modeling that meets criteria for educational and clinical effectiveness.

In summary, Figure 2–1 shows the assumptions underlying the directive scaffold. The clinician/teacher retains responsibility for what the student should be learning (Nelson, 1989). Dynamic and nondynamic modeling strategies are chosen for focusing students' attention on the details of curriculum content (Calfee, 1987). Students' progress is then typically defined in terms of the distance between previous baseline performance and the current level of performance. Progress is typically assessed through summative "what happened" evaluations, usually at the end of a lesson or unit (Howell & Morehead, 1987). With repeated exposure to the teaching procedures and content, the bottom–up expectation is that students will generalize and become increasingly capable of independently monitoring similar learning outcomes across comparable communicative contexts.

The assumptions underlying directive scaffolds, particularly those that are nondynamic, tend to be realized in teaching registers that emphasize three features:

- External regulation of the what, how, why, and when of learning
- Unintentional promotion of orality
- Learning activities in which a shared understanding of purpose is often missing

As a result of external control embedded in a simplified oral orientation, discourse planning may become more complex for some students. In addition, directive scaffolds, while often contributing to problem solving through students' active participation, typically involve indirect guidance. In directive scaffolds, exposure to a model is often equated with sufficient support for "making a leap" from novice to expert. Repeated failure to make this leap may then lead to the inaccurate conclusion that the student is context bound, less creative in strategy application, or even not exerting sufficient effort. In reality, *how* communicative processes are scaffolded creates the social and cognitive conditions for success or failure.

Supportive Scaffolds

The use of supportive scaffolds is an alternative that has the potential to increase the effectiveness of intervention. Before describing this alternative in detail, some of the notions underlying the approach are considered.

Framework. Vygotsky's (1962, 1983) theory underlines the view presented here about discourse scaffolds. Two essential organizational components for the development of higher level cognitive functions are (1) collaboration through discourse support and (2) gradual transfer of responsibility for one's own learning. The development of these metafunctions for organizing one's own learning activities is conceived of as a process of gradual internalization that proceeds from the social or collaborative plane to the individual or intrapersonal plane. Campione and Brown (1987) (see also Palincsar et al., chap. 5) describe how this internalization is gradually accomplished through supportive scaffolding:

FIGURE 2–1
The directive scaffold
From "The Instruction of Reading Comprehension" by P. D. Pearson and M. C. Gallagher, 1983, *Contemporary Educational Psychology, 8,* p. 337. Copyright 1983 by Academic Press. Adapted by permission.

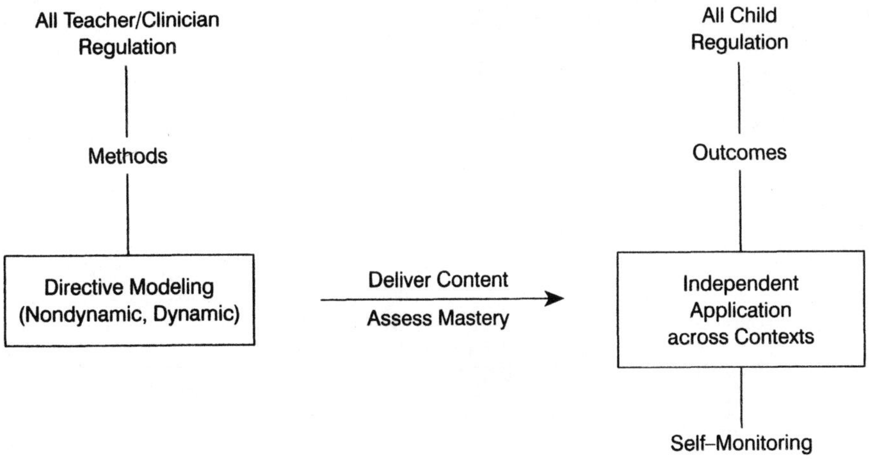

> At the outset, the child and adult work together, with the adult doing most of the work and serving as an expert model. As the child acquires some degree of skill, the adult cedes the child responsibility for part of the job and does less of the work. Gradually, the child takes more of the initiative, and the adult serves primarily to provide support and help when the child experiences problems. Eventually, the child internalizes the initially joint activities and becomes capable of carrying them out independently. At the outset, the adult is the model, critic, and interrogator, leading the child toward expertise; at the end, the child adopts these self-regulation and self-interrogation roles (p. 83).

This collaborative view of supportive scaffolds is illustrated in Figure 2–2.

From a developmental perspective, supportive scaffolds are considered as the process by which control is gradually transferred from the adult to the child for task planning, strategy selection, monitoring of effectiveness, and the evaluation of task outcomes. All four functions are the essence of self-regulation or proficiency in the flexible application of skills for strategic problem solving (Brown & Palincsar, 1987; Diaz, Neal, & Amaya-Williams, 1990; Palincsar et al., chap. 5; Paris, 1991). Thus, the continuous discovery, integration, and demonstration of connections among listening, speaking, reading, and writing can be viewed as a special kind of scaffolding process. This special scaffolding naturally "self-destructs . . . as the need lessens and the student's competence grows" (Cazden, 1988, p. 104). However, transfer of responsibility from other- to self-regulation is not an all-or-none phenomenon but a dynamic one. For example, marked differences in learning styles and preferences emerge with normally developing students in their speed of strategy learning and in the flexibility of strategy transfer. These variations are not fully accounted for by differences in general intelligence (Brown & Ferrara, 1985). Some students learn a strategy quickly and can apply it widely; others learn slowly but can then apply the strategy broadly; still others learn quickly but apply the strategy narrowly.

From the perspective of intervention, supportive scaffolds are considered as the discourse mechanism by which clinicians demonstrate their primary role as a working model for the elaboration of students' thinking (Staton, 1988a).

In the next section, aspects of the nutrition lesson illustrate how a communication process model may be used with LLD students to facilitate a literate style of communication and problem solving.

Collaborative Structure. The six students participating in the nutrition unit are part of a larger group of

FIGURE 2–2
The supportive scaffold
From "The Instruction of Reading Comprehension" by P. D. Pearson and M. D. Gallagher, 1983, *Contemporary Educational Psychology, 8*, p. 337. Copyright 1983 by Academic Press. Adapted by permission.

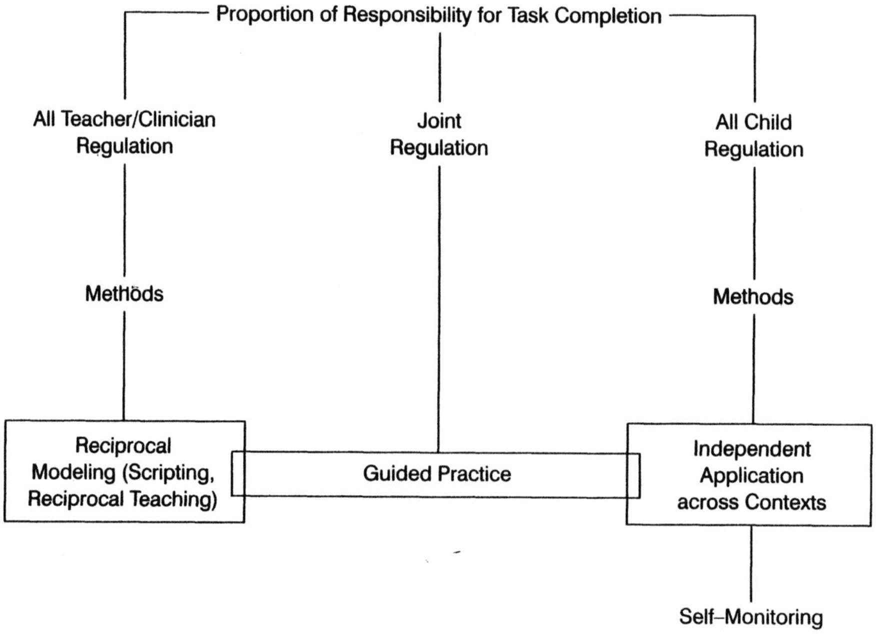

nineteen students in the class, which includes grades 5 to 7. Students are instructed by a team consisting of four members: two speech-language pathologists, who also function as classroom teachers; a teacher of the hearing impaired; and an aide. In addition, a social worker is a member of the team for one and one-half days a week. The team meets regularly to plan and to coordinate curriculum ideas, goals, activities, and procedures, to discuss individual students, and to evaluate outcomes at both programmatic and individual levels. Planning allows the opportunity to develop and sustain common frames of reference about students. In the classroom, responsibility is allocated among the three teachers, who jointly supervise the aide. Lessons are varied in structure but maintain a consistent theme. The structures follow:

- Whole class theme activities with emphasis on writing as a process
- Small group theme activities consisting of four to six children and emphasizing reading functions and strategies
- Small group theme activities in which spelling is addressed functionally and formally, depending on students' individual needs

The Theme as a Spiral Organizer. In terms of traditional academic areas, the Nutrition Unit is within the science content area, but implementation bridges other curriculum areas, including mathematics and language arts. Content difficulty is organized in a hierarchical manner; that is, "concepts are repeated at subsequent levels and are not necessarily expected to be completely mastered at a given level of the curriculum, since more difficult applications will appear at subsequent levels" (Idol, Nevin, & Paolucci-Whitcomb, 1986, p. vii).

Thematic unity is provided through the concept of nutrition, including its components and why it is important. Curriculum designers refer to this theme building as a "spiraling process" that

> makes use of recurring ideas and events that are common to the theme, and allows for multiple formats (art, pictures, play, literature, writing, drawing, storytelling, dance, snacks, discussion, and so forth) to be used to develop and express ideas related to the theme. (Norris & Damico, 1990, p. 216)

The building of a theme provides opportunities for developing both communicative competence and metacognitive skills (Harste et al., 1988; Nelson, 1989; Shuy, 1988b; Staton, 1988b). This is achieved in three ways: (1) by providing many multipurpose opportunities for using language in different ways; (2) by making every learning activity meaningful, motivating, and sufficiently challenging; and (3) by underscoring the value and importance of communication in mastering tasks.

Figure 2–3 provides an outline of the nutrition unit and includes examples of specific activities. Speaking, listening, reading, writing, and spelling are supported across implementation by integration of three foci:

- Facilitating literacy along the oral–literate continuum
- Promoting applications of metalinguistic skills
- Fostering more systematic use of metacognitive skills

Each of these is discussed in turn.

Literacy Functions. The elaboration of students' awareness of different communicative functions along the oral–literate continuum is reflected in three ways. One is the use of "brainstorming," an oral activity, which uses students' personal knowledge about foods and serves as a way to identify a nutrition lexicon that can be shared by all participants (see Figure 2–3, I.A, I.B).

A second function involves the written words as a permanent resource for storing and retrieving meaning, for example, developing semantic webs, word charts, and personal dictionaries (word banks) for words related to nutrition (see Figure 2–3, I.A, I.B, II.A).

A third function is the use of multiple formats for communicating information to others. Examples include the following:

1. Writing an accurate recipe for peanut butter and jelly sandwiches that others must follow (see Figure 2–3, II.B)
2. Writing food riddles containing sufficient clues for peers to resolve the riddle (see Figure 2–3, II.A.4)
3. Keeping a written food diary for all of the food eaten in one day (see Figure 2–3, III.A.3)
4. Using graphs to summarize and compare pertinent information (see Figure 2–3, III.A.3, III.B.2)
5. Collaborating with peers to review the steps in an experiment on the amount of fat and starch in food or in the preparation of a nutritional treat (see Figure 2–3, III.B.3, III.B.4)

I. Establish Shared Frame of Reference about Purposes and Sources of Nutrition
  A. What Is Nutrition?
    1. Develop semantic web for nutrition words (categorize words as nouns, verbs, adjectives; alphabetize; find hidden words, compound words, plurals, etc.); create individual word banks and word charts.
    2. Discuss vocabulary (semantic web list).
    3. Choose spelling words from the word bank and word charts; find definitions, opposites, synonyms, number of letters, number of syllables, practice writing words for familiarity.
  B. Where Do We Get Nutrition?
    1. Discuss sources (e.g., food, four basic food groups).
    2. Write the word *nutrition* vertically on a piece of paper, and find a word from your word bank that contains each of the letters in nutrition, e.g.:

Nuts	oaTmeal
bUtter	mIlk
toasT	Onions
Roast beef	freNch fries
fruIt	

II. The Four Basic Food Groups: How Nutrition Keeps Us Alive
  A. Fruits and Vegetables Group
    1. Brainstorm members of the fruit and vegetable group.
    2. Alphabetize items and categorize as fruit or vegetable.
    3. Discuss important attributes (e.g., size, shape, color, etc.).
    4. Combine and compare new information to existing information.
      a. With whole class, create fruit and vegetable riddles, stressing most critical attributes and how attributes function in words as adjectives, e.g., "I am round," "I am red," "I hang on a tree in bunches" (cherries).
      b. Individually write down own fruit and vegetable riddles; in small oral report groups, evaluate clues given and revise work based on peer feedback.
      c. Following revision, read riddles to whole class; final riddle is then typed and posted in classroom.
  B. Protein Group
    1. Brainstorm members of the protein group (meat, fish, chicken, nuts, etc.; students preferred to call this group *proteins*).
    2. Discuss nutrient value of peanut butter and jelly sandwiches and how to make them.

FIGURE 2–3
Integrated unit for LLD students at the junior high level—the nutrition theme
From Communication Development Program, South Metropolitan Association, Flossmoor, IL.

3. Combine and compare new information to existing information.
    a. Each student writes own recipes on how to make peanut butter and jelly sandwiches.
    b. One student orally reads his or her directions while the other five follow them exactly.
    c. Accuracy of written directions is then evaluated by each student and revised, if necessary.

(Similar procedures are followed for the dairy and bread and cereal groups.)

III. The Six Basic Nutrients and Their Relationship to the Food Groups
  A. Basic Nutrients
    1. Select nutrients (fats, carbohydrates, water, minerals, vitamins, and proteins) from a prepared word search.
    2. Introduce analogies for understanding of relevance (e.g., "Gas is to car as food is to body").
    3. Combine and compare new information to old information.
        a. Each student keeps a written food diary of the foods consumed during an entire day and labels each food according to the food group to which it belongs.
        b. Discuss the number of servings necessary from each food group to meet daily nutritional requirements; using a worksheet showing the number of necessary servings, students graph their own food consumption to determine whether "appropriate" amounts of food have been eaten (see Figure 2–4).
  B. Other Applications on the Importance of Nutrients
    1. Program nurse discusses anorexia, bulemia, and fat consumption (e.g., why it is important to eat healthy food).
    2. Program nurse weighs and measures each student in the classroom; each student's height and weight is then graphed on a growth chart.
    3. Students conduct experiments to determine the amount of fat and starches in different foods; assess materials needed and their order of use; predict possible outcomes of experiment and compare to actual outcomes, e.g., for fat content, smear a variety of foods on a paper bag and allow smears to dry.
    4. Students make nutritional treats (e.g., trailmix) from written recipe in groups of four; each student is given one ingredient and then works together to follow the directions, including how to obtain necessary other ingredients from other partners; evaluate outcomes.

Metalinguistic Skills. The metalinguistic focus is found in several topic areas and tasks and emphasizes the interrelationships among reading, writing, and spelling at two levels, word recognition and manipulation of word meaning.

Many LLD students have problems with encoding new phonological information into memory (Blachman, chap. 9; Kamhi, Catts, & Mauer, 1990; Snyder & Downey, 1991). The semantic webs and personal word banks can serve as external supports for encoding and, as a result, may guide students' retrieval of specific lexical information from the mental lexicon for word recognition purposes. At the same time, the notion is naturally reinforced that written words, similar to orally produced words, also consist of a sequence of phonemes that must be recorded from print to speech forms, as well as from speech to print (Ehri, 1989a, 1989b; Juel, 1990; Kamhi & Catts, 1989a). Of the students in the group, Aaron, age 14 years, still needed the most practice with manipulating syllable and phoneme segments. As a consequence, the clinician/teacher seized on different opportunities for him to practice this skill. For example, the following exchange occurred during review of the nutrient categories, which were being written on the board:

81. Clinician/teacher: Aaron, what's another one that begins with a vee?/
82. Aaron: Um—vitamins/
83. Clinician/teacher: Good/ Vitamins/ How many syllables, Aaron?/
84. Aaron: Three/
85. Clinician/teacher: Good—good!/

Word recognition also plays a role in choosing words to spell (see Figure 2–3, I.A). In learning how to spell a word, connections must be made between word meaning, word pronunciation, and the visual form of these connections represented by spelling (Ehri, 1989b). Two sources of information must be drawn on from the mental lexicon (Ehri, 1989a). One source refers to specific knowledge of how words are spelled, that is, that the graphemes (letters) represent phonemes in the conventional spelling of the word. When specific knowledge of connections is not automatic, as is the case when Aaron spells vitamins, then the second source, general knowledge of how the spelling system works, must be recalled. General knowledge supports plausible predictions about connections, for example, Aaron's subsequent phonetic spelling of the word as *vitmans.*

The second metalinguistic aspect involves more directed control of known word meanings, as exemplified by play with the word *nutrition* in the form of a crossword puzzle (see Figure 2–3, I.B.2), an activity that requires cross referencing with the personal word banks. Food riddles are another example of focused manipulation, at a somewhat more complex level. A more challenging example concerns managing the category knowledge necessary for linking and manipulating relations between basic nutrients and food groups (see Figure 2–3, III.A).

Metacognitive Skills. An important aspect of metacognition is planning, which will be discussed in a later section of the chapter.

Expectations for Performance. Further analysis of the nutrition lesson provides us with additional information. In the following excerpt, students combine and compare relationships between the daily need for the basic nutrients and individual students' personal state of health (see Figure 2–3, III.A.3.a, b). The students had been working with the nutrition theme for approximately 3 weeks before this activity. Over the weekend, they had completed "food diaries," which required that they write down all the food they had eaten during one day. These personal diaries were the information sources used in class on the previous day for categorizing the foods eaten according to the four basic food groups. The session was a follow-up consisting of three segments written on the blackboard: (1) review of the basic food groups and basic nutrient categories, a procedure for assessing the accuracy of information retrieval similar to the demands of a "typical test"; (2) as shown in Figure 2–4, demonstration by the teacher/clinician

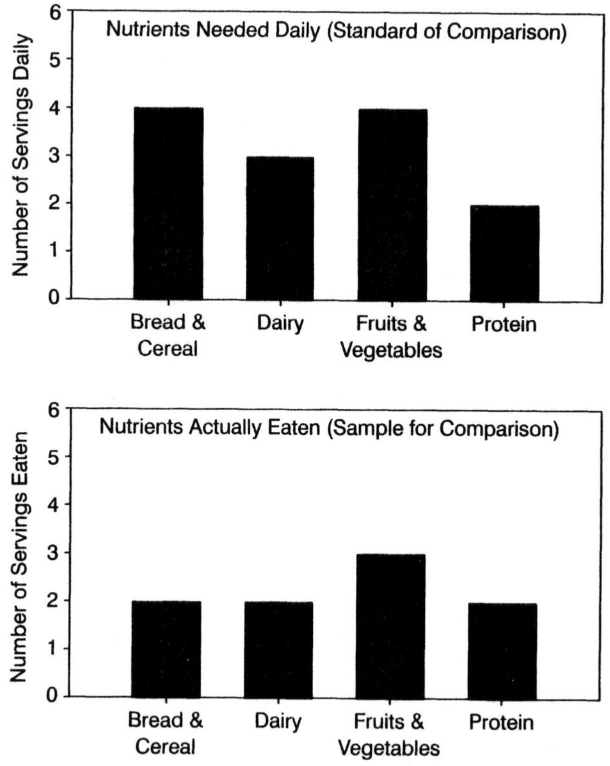

FIGURE 2–4
Graphing activity for comparing nutrients needed versus those actually eaten

and an independent application by students on the use of a graph as a means for summarizing and evaluating information about nutrients needed (the standard of comparison) versus nutrients actually eaten (sample for comparison, based on information collected through the food diaries); and (3) student summaries of the main points of what was learned and how it was learned.

The purpose of each segment was understood by the students. For example, the specific objective of the review segment (an expository task) was to maximize students' success in retrieving factual information (a descriptive schema) under a condition of speed consistent with the requirements of a typical test (all students eventually took a written test). Elements of the IRE default pattern and speaking within the lesson structure dominate during this segment, for example:

39. Clinician/teacher: We have been talking about nutrition/ And what are some of the things we have learned about nutrition, Terry?/
40. Terry: About how we eat and what we eat like the four basic food groups/
41. Clinician/teacher: OK/ Let's start with that, the four basic food groups/ Who can tell me what one of the food groups is?/ Raise your hand please/ (Terry and Diane raise their hands) Someone over here/ (directing gaze and head orientation to the four males who are seated next to each other) How come it's the girls that always have their hands up/ (rhetorical statement accompanied by a smile) Mike/
42. Mike: (Looking at diary) Uh—veg—fruit and vegetables/ (self-correction)
43. Clinician/teacher: Good/ Fruits and vegetables/ (writes category on blackboard) Karl, give me an example of fruits and vegetables/
44. Karl: (Looking at diary) Green beans/
45. Clinician/teacher: Green beans/ Excellent!/ OK/ What's another food group, Terry?/
46. Terry: (Not looking at diary) Dairy/
47. Clinician/teacher: (Back turned to group while writing the category on the board) Dairy/
48. Terry: Ice cream/(two-second gap) Vanilla ice cream/
49. Mike: Mmmmm/ (backchannel comment on the preceding example)
50. Clinician/teacher: Aaron, give me an example of something from the dairy group/
51. Aaron: Yogurt/
52. Clinician/teacher: Yogurt/ Excellent, good remembering/

One observation from these IRE sequences is that, for this task involving familiar information, students demonstrated the independent ability to access and quickly execute effective strategies for accurate retrieval. Referral to their written food diaries (Mike in turn 42, Karl in turn 44) was one strategy used. When the clinician/teacher evaluated a possible trouble spot, a general prompt was provided immediately to guide retrieval (e.g., "Something you eat for breakfast").

A second observation concerns the conflicting demands imposed by the supportive scaffold and "school survival skills" (Rhodes & Dudley-Marling, 1988). For example, the rapid recall of factual bits of information typical of a test is a "school survival skill." One consequence of the least restrictive requirement of Public Law (PL) 94–142 is that some LLD students will enter regular education classrooms where learning scaffolds are more directive (e.g., Baker & Zigmond, 1990; Ysseldyke et al., 1989). An unresolved issue for many LLD students is whether supportive scaffolds in the special education setting may constitute the least restrictive education environment for them.

Teaching Register: Supporting Aaron, Mike, and Karl. In supportive scaffolds, the teacher, as a higher status individual, shares power with students in getting things done in the classroom (Staton, 1988b). The role of the student is that of an active participant in accomplishing goals. Another issue that arises is the extent to which the needs of individual LLD students can be reconciled with this joint responsibility for teaching and learning.

For example, despite his placement in an environment with supportive scaffolds for two years, Aaron showed general problems with impulsive decision making. His impulsivity was reflected in his selection of inappropriate strategies for group participation, including his choice of language forms that communicated respect for his peers and teachers. He seemed to be less willing to accept his limitations; this attitude influenced his self-esteem and motivation to learn. The other students in his group increased their capacity and motivation to engage in joint responsibility. The clinician/teacher's use of supportive scaffolds may appear to be excessively controlling, depending on how the clinician/teacher and students conduct their work together.

Fluid Access to the Conversation and Topic Management. The previous analysis of the nutrition lesson focused exclusively on directed activities. Emphasis was placed on predictable rules for turn taking and topic management. These rules are integral to this lesson format and are necessary to keep the lesson "on track," such as attending to the talking rights of others and the relevance of staying on topic. In the two examples that follow, the clinician/teacher monitors these rules with Aaron, as shown in the ways she deals with momentary violations, including positive recognition of his appropriate rule use (turns 29 and 36).

Turn Interruption. Mike has the conversational floor and is explaining what *summarize* means.

17a. Mike: It means that you summarize what you just said a couple (hours ago)/
17b. Aaron: (It's called summarizing)/
18. Clinician/teacher: Ooops-oops you're interrupting, Aaron/ Who was talking?/ (pointing at Mike while simultaneously looking at Aaron, who offers no response) Who was talking?/
19. Aaron: Mike/
20. Clinician/teacher: You need to apologize to Mike/
21. Aaron: Sorry/ (while turning to Mike)
(Off-topic digression)
29. Clinician/teacher: Aaron, I like the way you kept your hand raised/
30. Aaron: Um—tomorrow if like when we do read[ing]/
31. Clinician/teacher: [OK]/ What are we talking about right now?/
32. Aaron: I don't know/
33. Diane: You're off topic/
34. Clinician/teacher: So you're off topic, and if you don't know what the topic is then you can ask now/
35. Aaron: OK/
36. Clinician/teacher: You need to wait until we are done with this lesson, and then you can ask about your topic/ OK?/ (Aaron shakes head positively) Good, I'm glad/ I liked the way you raised your hand, too/

Access to the conversational floor can become more fluid when students request clarification, offer to provide clarification for others, or introduce new information that extends the topic. In these instances, students understand that they may select the role of speaker themselves. For example, in the following dialogue, when Karl has difficulty rapidly retrieving the word *protein,* Mike, who is familiar with the strategy of phonetic cuing, helps Karl. His action is positively acknowledged by the clinician/teacher, at which time, Diane requests clarification about the meaning of *cue:*

87. Clinician/teacher: Karl, can you think of the last one?/ I can't even think of it/ (No response from Karl)
88. Mike: (Turning to Karl) What's the word that starts with pee?/
89. Fred: I know (.) minerals/
90. Karl: Proteins/
91. Clinician/teacher: (To Mike) Nice cuing—nice cuing!/Did you guys hear that?/
92. Group: No/
93. Clinician/teacher: Go ahead, Mike/ Say it again/
94. Mike: What's the word that starts with pee?/
95. Clinician/teacher: That was a good cue/
96. Diane: Well, what's it mean and what's a cue?/
97. Clinician/teacher: A cue is when you give someone a strategy/ A cue is when you give someone a hint/ He gave him a hint—he said it begins with a pee and Karl said proteins right away/ Kinda what we do to one another/
98. Diane: We help each other/

Self-Management of Attention. A function of regulation of students' behaviors as speakers and listeners, such as "Look at me" or "You must listen carefully," is to direct students to demonstrate visibly their attention to the teacher (Cazden, 1988). The emphases of supportive scaffolds differ. One aspect is aimed at assisting students to direct attention toward solving a particular problem. A second is enhancing students' self-esteem so that students will recognize the affective benefits of paying attention. Both goals may be communicated through a teaching register, in which individual and collective instances of self-management are continuously valued and interpreted, as for example in the following interchange:

191. Clinician/teacher: (To group) I like the way you're sitting quietly and I've got all your eyes up here/ That's excellent/
278. Clinician/teacher: Frank—you are working so hard/ Good for you/ Karl is doing nice reading, too/
287. Clinician/teacher: (Asking students to put pencils down) Thank you, Karl—you stopped right away/ Excellent/ I can tell it makes you feel good, Karl/ Nice smile/

Ease of Planning Discourse. In comparison to the chef lesson, the nutrition lesson contains more advanced planning. The nutrition theme acts as a spiral organizer of comprehension. Students more readily engage in plannable discourse behaviors for problem solving (Ochs, 1979). In a metacognitive sense, *plannable* means that the intentions underlying communication have been organized in more deliberate ways before their actual execution. Advanced planning is reflected in three ways. First, less of the discourse structure needs to be inferred, because the problem to be resolved is explicitly framed as one of comparison. Second, students are systematically guided in applying the necessary tools for successful execution of a comparative discourse structure. Third, literate strategies for communicating are supported by the clinician/teacher.

Successfully executing the plan independently for an activity depends on how adequately the plan, including its details, are remembered (the features of the task) and how the context for performance is understood (Gauvin, 1989). Because these students planned in advance by reviewing meaningful activities (see Figure 2–3), the potential for integrating the goals of planning via expository means was increased. A further benefit of advance planning is a social one. When students are provided with multiple opportunities to collaborate in advance planning activities, they are also provided with "opportunities to reflect on a process that is difficult for them to do on their own, thereby influencing their developing planning skills" (Gauvin, 1989, p. 97).

The graphed segment of the nutrition lesson illustrates the progressive process of removing a scaffold. Removal occurs from the point of joint responsibility for plan execution, to more independent responsibility for execution, with the latter serving as an instance of near transfer. The task involved combining information about nutrients and food groups needed daily for comparison with what each student actually ate during one day (see Figure 2–4). Demonstration preceded the application to the task.

Demonstration Phase. The shift from the review of category information to integration of knowledge of categories was marked by the clinician/teacher's drawing of a graph on the board as a hypothetical example of what she ate (the bottom graph in Figure 2–4). She asked the students "How many servings from each food group did I actually eat, and how do these servings compare with the number of servings I needed?" (the top graph in Figure 2–4). Students were guided through the steps of determining the number of necessary servings from each food group, as seen in the following example:

160. Clinician/teacher: Terry, why don't you pick one (food group)/
161. Terry: I know there is—there is—like a (two-second-plus silent pause) four of—um—of—um—fruits/ (the phrase repetitions combined with the filled and silent pauses suggest that the decision-making process requires controlled attention; it is not yet automatic)
162. Clinician/teacher: Fruits and vegetables/ Four 1 2 3 4/I'm going to draw a line right there (pointing to four servings in the column) so I know what (.) Terry—what's that line mean?/
163. Terry: That's—that's how many we eat—that we need/(self-corrects word choice)

The students were guided in determining how many portions they ate in comparison to the standard portions. Demonstration of strategies focused on modeling questions on the written worksheet and coordinating reading questions with "reading" the sample graph, for example, "How many servings from the bread and cereal group do you need each day? Did you get enough servings from the bread and cereal group? How do you know?"

Independent Application. In this last phase of the lesson, the teacher/clinician transferred responsibility for comparison to the students. The teacher/clinician returned graphs filled out on the previous day by the students based on their food diaries and distributed worksheet questions. The clinician/teacher continued to be involved, by offering reassurance or guidance only when requested by students. With the exception of Aaron, who continued to need extensive external support, all of the students rapidly and successfully completed the task.

Other examples of advance planning can be found in the peer-directed activities in Figure 2–3. Each activity shared in common the need to predict outcomes, selection of the appropriate strategies for achieving those outcomes (including material selection), monitoring of strategy effectiveness, revising these strategies when necessary, and finally, evaluation of the results.

Modeling. Recall that *modeling* was defined as the amount and kind of discourse responsibility assumed by the adult for initial learning and follow-up instances of transfer. Directive/nondynamic modeling strategies are incompatible with a supportive scaffold of intervention, because they are prescriptive. In contrast, directive/dynamic and reciprocal/dynamic are characteristic of supportive scaffolds.

Directive/Dynamic Modeling. Directive/dynamic modeling is a choice. Typically, this choice is made for one of two purposes. One aim is clarification; students' attention is specifically directed to elements of their message that the clinician/teacher has not understood, for example, requests for repetition, such as "What?" or requests for specification, such as "Four of what?" (for a broader discussion of systematic clarification strategies, see Brinton & Fujiki, 1989). Another purpose is to minimize the potential for breakdowns in the retrieval of specific lexical information. Cues related to the topic focus may be offered as external memory aids for directing successful retrieval of a requested item. Often these cues are a form of a cloze procedure where the child fills in an object slot in a main or subordinate clause, such as "Instead of reading words you are going to have to read __________ [a graph]." Alternatively, cues may be circumscribed as a phonemic cue, as in "Mike, give me another nutrient." [A gap occurs in responding.] "What's a long one that begins with a /k/?" [carbohydrates].

At a minimum, cloze procedures in the oral domain indicate students' ability to use familiar linguistic information to make a "best fit" prediction about meaning (Rhodes & Dudley-Marling, 1988). An important issue for the frequency and sequencing of directive/dynamic modeling—such as the use of cloze procedures to facilitate the ease of prediction—concerns the consideration of certain tradeoffs. For example, the clinician/teacher's goal for students to succeed in tasks that may be genuinely challenging for them may result in unnecessary external regulation. The goal of success must be balanced with allowing students sufficient opportunities to take on some degree of responsibility for self-evaluating of when they, or others, are experiencing trouble spots in recall. Further, students must learn which cuing strategies might be effective in resolving these trouble points. Despite the fact that Mike could not readily recall all of the phonological segments of carbohydrates, as noted earlier, he spontaneously evaluated Karl's difficulty in recalling proteins and assisted him in successful retrieval with a phonemic cue.

Reciprocal/Dynamic Modeling. Modeling strategies can also be reciprocal and dynamic. They can probably approximate everyday interaction more closely than other modeling strategies because the focus is on communication. This kind of modeling forms the core of many whole language approaches in the regular education setting, although the specifics often are unelaborated.

One version of a reciprocal/dynamic modeling can be found in shared reading experiences in the lower elementary grades (Weaver, 1990). The teacher prepares highly predictable material for students to read (or write about) in a group (rhyme, story, song, etc.); then, together, they "master" it, for example, through repetition. The same material is "read" as a group, followed by students being invited to locate and read certain lines and, later, to locate certain sounds, words, and word endings. This kind of modeling strategy has several purposes. It invites students to concentrate more deliberately on language forms and cultivates opportunities to recognize and analyze metalinguistic connections among word meaning, word pronunciation, and spelling.

Reciprocal teaching is another version of reciprocal/dynamic modeling but one that has a more systematic research base (Brown & Palincsar, 1987; Palincsar & Brown, 1984, 1986). As noted by Palincsar and her colleagues in Chapter 5, on the broadest level, the reciprocal teaching approach is specifically crafted to scaffold a novice-to-expert transition for students (Wertsch, 1990). The approach is intended to assist students who are at educational risk as a result of language and learning differences to learn how to facilitate and monitor their strategies for oral and reading comprehension within the classroom setting.

Brown and Palincsar (1987) and Palincsar et al. (chap. 5) define *reciprocal teaching* as an instructional procedure in which a collaborative dialogue (discussion) between the teacher and students is gradually structured by four metacomprehension strategies.

1. Summarizing, or self-review of essential information to determine that comprehension and retention have occurred (Palincsar, 1989)
2. Question generating, practiced as an ongoing activity within the larger theme of the lesson and predicated on what a teacher or a test might reasonably ask

3. Clarification of ambiguous or inconsistent interpretations of oral narrative or written expository discourse when gaps in comprehension are detected
4. Prediction of what an author might say next as the method for validating, disconfirming, or modifying how that content fits with previous understanding

These strategies are task specific in the sense that they are regarded as critical for discourse processing of narrative and expository structures across curriculum areas in both the oral and written mediums of communication.

Grant and Elias (1989) note that regular classroom teachers do not engage routinely in the explicit teaching of comprehension strategies similar to reciprocal teaching. Supportive scaffolds with LLD students require the kind of systematic approach afforded through the dynamic procedures of reciprocal teaching. In practice, as shown in Figure 2–5, the nutrition lesson contains elements of reciprocal teaching, but these elements are not integrated.

A major aim of the modeling strategies used by the clinician/teacher in this lesson was to enable students to monitor the level and depth of their understanding. However, the efficacy of a communication process approach for LLD students depends, in part, on the adequacy with which they can be guided from other- to self-regulation of their own understanding, remembering, and being understood.

SUMMARY

The goal of supportive scaffolds is the gradual transfer of responsibility for learning from the teacher to

1. Soliciting Specific Clarification Strategies
   - What do we need to do if you have a question?
   - What do we do if we don't understand?
   - If we didn't understand something that went on today, what can we do?
2. Soliciting Collaborative Assistance for Clarification
   - Who can tell him what that line means?
   - Fred just asked what he has to do now. Can someone tell Fred?
3. Supporting Transfer of Strategy Selection to Others
   - Aaron is using a good strategy. Aaron, tell Terry what you are doing.
4. Checking Understanding
   - What have we been talking about?
   - Show me how you know that. I want to be sure you understand.
   - Make sure that you can read the graphs, that you understand them, and that you've got your lines in the right place.
   - How did you goof up? (follow-up to student's awareness that he had "goofed up on the fruits and vegetables because I didn't get enough")
5. Supporting Question Generation
   - But what is my question?
   - I don't have a pencil here. You are going to have to ask someone else.
   - What is the question? (for student to ask of self)
6. Supporting Prediction
   - Can someone predict what we're going to do on this worksheet?
   - What do you need to do? (to be ready to initiate the graph comparisons)
   - What are you going to have to read? (referring to the graph vs. words)

FIGURE 2–5
Examples of reciprocal/dynamic modeling strategies in the nutrition lesson

the student. Supportive scaffolds can occur within and across thematically meaningful learning activities, and they emphasize collaboration among teachers, clinicians, and students. Success involves facilitating the structure for communication, and providing the social support for students to reach beyond current levels of competence. A major benefit of the supportive scaffolds is its function as a kind of "communication safety net." Risk taking is reduced, until an adequate level of skill develops for the students to feel confident to test out new skills on their own.

The problems of transfer and maintenance of new skills demonstrated by LLD students exemplify the transfer of responsibility. Within one of the classrooms discussed here, the passage from less to more competent was seen as a "spiral," because the new level of competence became the lower edge of learning. Students were challenged to go beyond that lower level to maximize learning. Individual differences did not appear in the rate of progress. Some students progressed to the point where, depending on learning styles and preferences, they functioned independently, with no or minimal support. Other students in the same class did not progress very far and continued to need a high degree of support. In both cases, evaluating progress depends in large part on the clinician/teacher's skill in assessing adequately the level of support needed by students to attain specific levels of learning and to apply that learning in new situations.

REFERENCES

Anders, P. H., & Pearson, P. D. (1987). Instructional research on literacy and reading: Parameters, perspective, and predictors. In R. J. Tierney, P. L. Andes, & J. N. Mitchell (Eds.), *Understanding readers' understanding: Theory and practice* (pp. 307–319). Hillsdale, NJ: Lawrence Erlbaum.

Au, K. H., Scheu, J. A., Kawakami, A. J., & Herman, P. A. (1990). Assessment and accountability in a whole literacy curriculum. *Reading Teacher, 43,* 574–578.

Baker, J. M., & Zigmond, N. (1990). Are regular education classes equipped to accommodate students with learning disabilities? *Exceptional Children, 56*, 515–526.

Baker, L., & Brown, A. L. (1984a). Cognitive monitoring in reading. In J. Flood (Ed.), *Understanding reading comprehension* (pp. 21–24). Newark, DE: International Reading Association.

Baker, L., & Brown, A. L. (1984b). Metacognitive skills and reading. In P. D. Pearson (Ed.), *Handbook of reading research* (pp. 353–394). New York: Longman.

Bashir, A. S., & Scavuzzo, A. (1992). Children with language disorders: Natural history and academic success. *Journal of Learning Disabilities, 25,* 53–65.

Becker, L. B., & Silverstein, J. E. (1984). Clinician–child discourse: A replication study. *Journal of Speech and Hearing Disorders, 49,* 104–106.

Biber, D. (1988). *Variation across speech and writing.* New York: Cambridge University Press.

Bloome, D. (1987). Reading as a social process in a middle school classroom. In D. Bloome (Ed.), *Literacy and schooling* (pp. 123–149). Norwood, NJ: Ablex.

Bloome, D., & Theodorou, E. (1988). Analyzing teacher–student and student–student discourse. In J. L. Green & J. O. Harker (Eds.), *Multiple perspective analysis of classroom discourse* (pp. 217–248). Norwood, NJ: Ablex.

Bloome, D., Harris, O. L. H., & Ludlum, D. E. (1991). Reading and writing as sociocultural activities: Politics and pedagogy in the classroom. *Topics in Language Disorders, 11*(3), 14–27.

Bobkoff, K., & Panagos, J. M. (1986). The "point" of language interaction. *Child Language Teaching and Therapy, 2,* 50–62.

Brinton, B., & Fujiki, M. (1989). *Conversational management with language impaired children.* Rockville, MD: Aspen Publishers.

Brown, A. L., & Ferrara, R. A. (1985). Diagnosing zones of proximal development. In J. V. Wertsch (Ed.), *Culture, communication, and cognition* (pp. 275–305). New York: Cambridge University Press.

Brown, A. L., & Palincsar, A. S. (1987). Reciprocal teaching of comprehension strategies. In J. O. Day & J. G. Borkowski (Eds.), *Intelligence and exceptionality: New directions for theory, assessment, and instructional practice* (pp. 81–132). Norwood, NJ: Ablex.

Calfee, R. C. (1987). The school as a context for the assessment of literacy. *The Reading Teacher, 40,* 738–743.

Campione, J. C., & Brown, A. L. (1987). Linking dynamic assessment with school achievement. In C. S. Lidz (Ed.), *Dynamic assessment: An integrated approach to evaluating learning potential* (pp. 82–115). New York: Guilford Press.

Catts, H. W. (1989a). Phonological processing deficits and reading deficits and reading disabilities. In A. G. Kamhi & H. W. Catts (Eds.), *Reading disabilities: A developmental approach to evaluating learning potential* (pp. 101–132). Boston: College-Hill Press.

Catts, H. W. (1989b). Speech production deficits in developmental dyslexia. *Journal of Speech and Hearing Disorders, 54,* 422–428.

Catts, H. W. (1991). Early identification of reading disabilities. *Topics in Language Disorders, 12*(1), 1–16.

Cazden, C. B. (1988). *Classroom discourse: The language of teaching and learning.* Portsmouth, NH: Heinemann.

Cherry, L. (1978). Teacher–student interaction and teachers' expectations of students' communicative competence. In R. Shuy & M. Griffin (Eds.), *The study of children's functional language and education in the early years* (Final report to the Carnegie Corporation, New York). Arlington, VA: Center for Applied Linguistics.

Cox, B. E., Shanahan, T., & Sulzby, E. (1990). Good and poor elementary readers' use of cohesion in writing. *Reading Research Quarterly, 25,* 47–65.

Damico, J. S. (1990). Prescriptionism as a motivating mechanism: An ethnographic study in the public schools. *Journal of Childhood Communication Disorders, 13,* 85–92.

DeStefano, J. S., & Kantor, R. (1988). Cohesion in spoken and written dialogue: An investigation of cultural and textual constraint. *Linguistics and Education, 1,* 105–124.

Diaz, R. M., Neal, C. J., & Amaya-Williams, M. (1990). The social origin of self-regulation. In L. C. Moll (Ed.), *Vygotsky and education: Instructional implications and applications of sociohistorical psychology* (pp. 127–154). New York: Cambridge University Press.

Durkin, D. (1978–1979). What classroom observations reveal about reading comprehension instruction. *Reading Research Quarterly, 14,* 481–533.

Dyson, A. H. (1989). *Multiple worlds of child writers: Friends learning to write.* New York: Teachers College Press.

Ehri, L. C. (1989a). The development of spelling knowledge and its role in reading acquisition and reading disability. *Journal of Learning Disabilities, 6,* 356–365.

Ehri, L. C. (1989b). Movements into word reading and spelling: How spelling contributes to reading. In J. M. Mason (Ed.), *Reading and writing connections* (pp. 65–81). Boston: Allyn & Bacon.

Eller, R. G. (1989). Ways of meaning: Exploring cultural differences in students' written compositions. *Linguistics and Education, 1,* 341–358.

Englert, C. S., Stewart, S. R., & Hiebert, E. H. (1988). Young writers' use of text structure in expository text generation. *Journal of Educational Psychology, 80,* 143–151.

Fey, M. E., & Cleave, P. L. (1990). Early language intervention. *Seminars in Speech and Language, 11,* 165–181.

Garton, A., & Pratt, C. (1989). *Learning to be literate.* New York: Basil Blackwell.

Gauvin, M. (1989). Children's planning in social contexts: An observational study of kindergarten's planning in the classroom. In L. T. Winegar (Ed.), *Social interaction and the development of children's understanding* (pp. 95–117). Norwood, NJ: Ablex.

Gavelek, J. R., & Raphael, T. E. (1985). Metacognition, instruction, and the role of questioning activities. In D. L. Forrest-Pressley, G. E. MacKinnon, & T. G. Waller (Eds.), *Metacognition, cognition, and human performance* (Vol. 2, pp. 103–136). New York: Academic Press.

German, D. J. (1987). Spontaneous language profiles of children with word finding problems. *Language, Speech, and Hearing Services in Schools, 18,* 217–230.

German, D. J., & Simon, E. (1991). Analysis of children's word finding skills in discourse. *Journal of Speech and Hearing Research, 34,* 309–316.

Goodman, Y. M., & Goodman, K. S. (1990). Vygotsky in a whole-language perspective. In L. C. Moll (Ed.), *Vygotsky and education: Instructional implications and applications of sociohistorical psychology* (pp. 223–250). New York: Cambridge University Press.

Gordon, C. J., & Braun, C. (1985). Metacognitive processes: Reading and writing narrative discourse. In D. L. Forrest-Pressley, G. E. MacKinnon, & T. G. Waller (Eds.), *Metacognition, cognition, and human performance* (Vol. 2, pp. 1–75). New York: Academic Press.

Grant, J., & Elias, G. (1989). An application of Palincsar and Brown's comprehension instruction paradigm to listening. *Contemporary Educational Psychology, 14,* 164–172.

Halliday, M. A. K. (1984). Language as code and language as behavior: A systematic-functional interpretation of the nature and ontogenesis of dialogue. In R. P. Fawcett, M. A. K. Halliday, S. M. Lamb, & A. Makka (Eds.), *The semiotics of culture and language* (Vol. 1, pp. 3–35). Dover, NH: Frances Pinker.

Harste, J. C., Short, K. G., & Burke, C. (1988). *Creating classrooms for authors.* Portsmouth, NH: Heinemann Educational Books.

Hasan, R. (1984a). Coherence and cohesive harmony. In J. Flood (Ed.), *Understanding reading comprehension* (pp. 181–219). Newark, DE: International Reading Association.

Hasan, R. (1984b). Ways of saying; ways of meaning. In R. P. Fawcett, M. A. K. Halliday, S. Lamb, & A. Makka (Eds.), *The semiotics of culture and language* (pp. 105–162). Dover, NH: Frances Pinter.

Heath, S. B. (1983). *Ways with words.* New York: Cambridge University Press.

Horowitz, R., & Samuels, S. J. (1987). Comprehending oral and written language: Critical contrasts for literacy and schooling. In R. Horowitz & S. J. Samuels (Eds.), *Comprehending oral and written language* (pp. 1–52). New York: Academic Press.

Howell, K. W., & Morehead, M. K. (1987). *Curriculum-based evaluation for special and remedial education.* New York: Merrill/Macmillan.

Idol, L., Nevin, A., & Paolucci-Whitcomb, P. (1986). *Models of curriculum-based assessment.* Rockville, MD: Aspen Publishers.

Juel, C. (1990). The role of decoding in early literacy instruction and assessment. In L. M. Morrow & J. K. Smith (Eds.), *Assessment for instruction in early literacy* (pp. 135–154). Englewood Cliffs, NJ: Prentice-Hall.

Kail, R., & Leonard, L. B. (1986). *Word-finding abilities of language-impaired children* (ASHA Monographs, No. 25). Rockville, MD: American Speech-Language-Hearing Association.

Kamhi, A. G. (1992). Response to historical perspective: A developmental language perspective. *Journal of Learning Disabilities, 25,* 48–52.

Kamhi, A. G., & Catts, H. W. (1989a). Language and reading: Convergences, divergences, and development. In A. G.

Kamhi & H. W. Catts (Eds.), *Reading disabilities: A developmental language perspective* (pp. 1–34). Boston: College-Hill Press.

Kamhi, A. G., & Catts, H. W. (1989b). Reading disabilities: Terminology, definitions, and subtyping issues. In A. G. Kamhi & H. W. Catts (Eds.), *Reading disabilities: A developmental language perspective* (pp. 35–66). Boston: College-Hill Press.

Kamhi, A. G., Catts, H. W., & Mauer, D. (1990). Examining speech production deficits in poor readers. *Journal of Learning Disabilities, 23,* 632–636.

Kamhi, A. G., Gentry, B., Mauer, D., & Gholson, B. (1990). Analogical learning and transfer in language impaired children. *Journal of Speech and Hearing Disorders, 55,* 140–148.

Kawakami-Arakaki, A. J., Oshiro, M. E., & Farran, D. C. (1988). Integrating reading and writing in a kindergarten curriculum. In J. M. Mason (Ed.), *Reading and writing connections* (pp. 199–218). Boston: Allyn & Bacon.

Kovarsky, D. (1990). Discourse markers in adult-controlled therapy: Implications for child-centered intervention. *Journal of Childhood Communication Disorders, 13,* 29–41.

Kronick, D. (1988). *New approaches to learning disabilities: Cognitive, metacognitive, and holistic.* New York: Grune & Stratton.

Lahey, M. (1988). *Language disorders and language development.* New York: Macmillan.

Leonard, L. B. (1988). Lexical development and processing in specific language impairment. In R. L. Schiefelbusch & L. L. Lloyd (Eds.), *Language perspectives: Acquisition, retardation, and intervention* (pp. 69–87). Austin, TX: Pro-Ed.

Letts, C. (1985). Linguistic interaction in the clinic—how do therapists do therapy? *Child Language Teaching and Therapy, 8*(1), 321–331.

Liles, B. Z. (1987). Episode organization and cohesive conjunctions in narratives of children with and without language disorder. *Journal of Speech and Hearing Research, 30,* 185–196.

Mason, J. M., & Stewart, J. P. (1990). *Emergent literacy assessment for instruction in early literacy* (pp. 155–175). Englewood Cliffs, NJ: Prentice-Hall.

McTear, M. (1985). *Children's conversation.* New York: Basil Blackwell.

Mehan, H. (1979). *Learning lessons.* Cambridge, MA: Harvard University Press.

Merritt, D. D., & Liles, B. Z. (1987). Story grammar ability in children with and without language disorders: Story generation, story retelling, and story comprehension. *Journal of Speech and Hearing Research, 30,* 536–552.

Meyer, B. J. F. (1985). Prose analysis: Purposes, procedures, and problems. In B. K. Britton & J. B. Black (Eds.), *Understanding expository text: A theoretical and practical handbook for analyzing explanatory text* (pp. 11–64). Hillsdale, NJ: Lawrence Erlbaum.

Meyer, B. J. F. (1987). Following the author's top-level organization: An important skill for reading comprehension. In R. J. Tierney, P. L. Anders, & J. N. Mitchell (Eds.), *Understanding readers' understanding: Theory and practice* (pp. 59–76). Hillsdale, NJ: Lawrence Erlbaum.

Meyer, B. J. F., & Freedle, R. O. (1984). The effects of discourse types on recall. *American Educational Research Journal, 21,* 121–143.

Miller, L. (1990). The roles of language and learning in the development of literacy. *Topics in Language Disorders, 10*(2), 1–24.

Montague, M., Maddux, C. D., & Dereshiwsky, M. I. (1990). Story grammar and comprehension and production of narrative prose by students with learning disabilities. *Journal of Learning Disabilities, 23,* 190–197.

Nelson, K. E. (1989). Strategies for first language teaching. In M. L. Rice & R. L. Schiefelbusch (Eds.), *The teachability of language* (pp. 263–310). Baltimore: Paul H. Brookes.

Norris, J. A. (1991). From frog to prince: Using written language as a context for language learning. *Topics in Language Disorders, 12*(1), 66–81.

Norris, J. A., & Damico, J. S. (1990). Whole language in theory and practice: Implications for language intervention. *Language, Speech, and Hearing Services in Schools, 21,* 212–220.

Norris, J. A., & Hoffman, P. R. (1990). Language intervention within naturalistic environments. *Language, Speech, and Hearing Services in Schools, 21,* 72–84.

Ochs, E. (1979). Planned and unplanned discourse. In T. Givon (Ed.), *Syntax and semantics, Vol. 12: Discourse and syntax* (pp. 51–80). New York: Academic Press.

Olswang, L. B., Bain, B. A., & Johnson, G. A. (1992). Using dynamic assessment with children with language disorders. In S. F. Warren & J. Reichle (Eds.), *Causes and effects in communication and language intervention* (pp. 187–215). Baltimore, MD: Paul H. Brookes.

Palincsar, A. S. (1989). Roles of the speech-language pathologist in disadvantaged children's pursuit of literacy. *Partnerships in education: Toward a literate America* (ASHA Reports No. 17, pp. 34–40). Rockville, MD: American Speech-Language-Hearing Association.

Palincsar, A. S., & Brown, A. L. (1984). Reciprocal teaching of comprehension fostering and comprehension monitoring activities. *Cognition and Instruction, 1,* 117–175.

Palincsar, A. S., & Brown, A. L. (1986). Interactive teaching to promote independent learning from text. *The Reading Teacher, 38,* 771–777.

Palincsar, A. S., & Brown, D. A. (1987). Enhancing instructional time through attention to metacognition. *Journal of Learning Disabilities, 20,* 66–75.

Panagos, J. M., & Bliss, L. S. (1990). Clinical presuppositions for speech therapy lessons. *Journal of Childhood Communication Disorders, 13,* 19–28.

Panagos, J. M., Bobkoff, K., & Scott, C. M. (1986). Discourse analysis of language intervention. *Child Language Teaching and Therapy, 2,* 211–229.

Paris, S. G. (1991). Assessment and remediation of metacognitive aspects of children's reading comprehension. *Topics in Language Disorders, 12*(1), 32–50.

Pinnell, G. S. (1989). Success of at-risk children in a program that combines reading and writing. In J. M. Mason (Ed.), *Reading and writing connections* (pp. 237–259). Boston: Allyn & Bacon.

Prutting, C. A., Bagshaw, N., Goldstein, H., Juskowitz, S., & Umen, I. (1978). Clinician–child discourse: Some preliminary questions. *Journal of Speech and Hearing Disorders, 43,* 123–139.

Raphael, T. E., Englert, C. S., & Kirschner, B. W. (1989). Acquisition of expository writing skills. In J. M. Mason (Ed.), *Reading and writing connection* (pp. 261–290). Boston, MA: Allyn & Bacon.

Rhodes, L. K., & Dudley-Marling, C. (1988). *Readers and writers with a difference: A holistic approach to teaching learning disabled and remedial students.* Portsmouth, NH: Heinemann.

Ripich, D. N., Hambrecht, G., Panagos, J. M., & Prelock, P. (1984). An analysis of articulation and language disorder patterns. *Journal of Childhood Communication Disorders, 7,* 17–26.

Ripich, D. N., & Panagos, J. M. (1985). Accessing children's knowledge of sociolinguistic rules for speech therapy lessons. *Journal of Speech and Hearing Disorders, 50,* 335–346.

Rogoff, B. (1990). *Apprenticeship in thinking.* New York: Oxford University Press.

Roth, F. P., & Spekman, N. J. (1986). Narrative discourse: Spontaneously generated stories of learning disabled and normally achieving children. *Journal of Speech and Hearing Disorders, 51,* 8–23.

Scott, C. M. (1988). Spoken and written syntax. In M. A. Nippold (Ed.), *Later language development* (pp. 49–95). Boston, MA: College-Hill Press.

Scott, C. M. (1989a). Learning to write: Context, form and process. In A. G. Kamhi & H. W. Catts (Eds.), *Reading disabilities: A developmental language perspective* (pp. 261–302). Boston: College-Hill Press.

Scott, C. M. (1989b). Problem writers: Nature, assessment, and intervention. In A. G. Kamhi & H. W. Catts (Eds.), *Reading disabilities: A developmental language perspective* (pp. 303–344). Boston: College-Hill Press.

Shanklin, N. L. (1991). Whole language and writing process: One movement or two? *Topics in Language Disorders, 11*(3), 45–57.

Shuy, R. (1988a). Identifying dimensions of classroom language. In J. L. Green & J. O. Harker (Eds.), *Multiple perspective analysis of classroom discourse* (Vol. 28, pp. 115–134). Norwood, NJ: Ablex.

Shuy, R. (1988b). The oral language basis for dialogue journals. In J. Straton, R. W. Shuy, J. K. Peyton, & L. Reed (Eds.), *Dialogue journal communication* (pp. 73–87). Norwood, NJ: Ablex.

Sidner, C. L. (1983). Focusing and discourse. *Discourse Processes, 6,* 107–130.

Silliman, E. R. (1984). Interactional competencies in the instructional context: The role of teaching discourse in learning. In G. P. Wallach & K. G. Butler (Eds.), *Language learning disabilities in school-age children* (pp. 288–317). Baltimore, MD: Williams & Wilkins.

Silliman, E. R. (1989). Narratives: A window on the oral substance of written language disabilities. *Annals of Dyslexia, 39,* 125–139.

Silliman, E. R., & Wilkinson, L. C. (1991). *Communicating for learning: Classroom collaboration and observation.* Gaithersburg, MD: Aspen Publishers.

Skarakis-Doyle, E., & Mullin, K. (1990). Comprehension monitoring in language-disordered children: A preliminary investigation of cognitive and linguistic factors. *Journal of Speech and Hearing Disorders, 55,* 700–705.

Snyder, L. S. (1984). Cognition and language development. In R. C. Naremore (Ed.), *Language science* (pp. 107–145). San Diego, CA: College-Hill Press.

Snyder, L., & Downey, D. M. (1991). The language reading relationship in normal and reading disabled children. *Journal of Speech and Hearing Research, 34,* 129–140.

Spinelli, F. M., & Ripich, D. N. (1985). A comparison of classroom and clinical discourse. In D. N. Ripich & J. M. Spinelli (Eds.), *School discourse problems* (pp. 179–196). San Diego, CA: College-Hill Press.

Spiro, R. J., & Taylor, B. M. (1987). On investigating children's transition from narrative to expository discourse: The multidimensional nature of psychological text classification. In J. Tierney, P. L. Anders, & J. N. Mitchell (Eds.), *Understanding readers' understanding* (pp. 77–93). Hillsdale, NJ: Lawrence Erlbaum.

Staton, J. (1988a). Contributions of dialogue journal research to communicating, thinking, and learning. In J. Staton, R. W. Shuy, J. K. Peyton, & L. Reed (Eds.), *Dialogue journal communication: Classroom, linguistic, social and cognitive views* (pp. 312–321). Norwood, NJ: Ablex.

Staton, J. (1988b). An introduction to dialogue journal communication. In J. Staton, R. W. Shuy, J. K. Peyton, & L. Reed (Eds.), *Dialogue journal communication: Classroom, linguistic, and social and cognitive views* (pp. 1–32). Norwood, NJ: Ablex.

Stein, N. L. (1983). On the goals, functions, and knowledge of reading and writing. *Contemporary Educational Psychology, 8,* 261–292.

Stein, N. L., & Glenn, C. G. (1979). An analysis of story comprehension in school children. In R. O. Freedle (Ed.), *New directions in discourse processing* (pp. 53–120). Norwood, NJ: Ablex.

Sternberg, R. J. (1987). A unified theory of intelligence and exceptionality. In J. D. Day & J. G. Barkowski (Eds.), *Intelligence and exceptionality* (pp. 135–172). Norwood, NJ: Ablex.

Sternberg, R. J. (1989). Domain-generality versus domain-specificity: The life and impending death of false dichotomy. *Merrill-Palmer Quarterly, 35,* 115–130.

Stewart, J., & Mason, J. M. (1989). Preschool children's reading and writing awareness. In J. M. Mason (Ed.), *Reading and writing connections* (pp. 219–236). Boston: Allyn & Bacon.

Sulzby, E. (1990). Assessment of emergent writing and children's language while writing. In L. M. Morrow & J. K. Smith (Eds.), *Assessment for instruction in early literacy* (pp. 83–109). Englewood Cliffs, NJ: Prentice-Hall.

Tannen, D. (1985). Relative focus on involvement in oral and written discourse. In D. R. Olson, N. Torrance, & A. Hildyard (Eds.), *Literacy, language, and learning* (pp. 124–147). London: Cambridge University Press.

Taylor, D. (1983). *Family literacy: Young children learning to read and write*. Exeter, NH: Heinemann.

Teale, W. H., & Martinez, M. G. (1989). Connecting writing: Fostering emergent literacy in kindergarten children. In J. M. Mason (Ed.), *Reading and writing connections* (pp. 177–198). Boston: Allyn & Bacon.

Tierney, R. J., Lazansky, J., Raphael, T., & Cohen, P. (1987). Author's intentions and readers' interpretations. In R. J. Tierney, P. L. Amders, & J. N. Mitchell (Eds.), *Understanding readers' understanding: Theory and practice* (pp. 205–226). Hillsdale, NJ: Lawrence Erlbaum.

van Kleeck, A. (1990). Emergent literacy: Learning about print before learning to read. *Topics in Language Disorders, 10*(2), 63–80.

Vosniadou, S., Pearson, P. D., & Rogers, T. (1988). What causes children's failures to detect inconsistencies in text: Representation versus comparison difficulties. *Journal of Educational Psychology, 80,* 27–39.

Vygotsky, L. S. (1962). *Thought and language.* Cambridge, MA: MIT Press.

Vygotsky, L. S. (1983). School instruction and mental development. In M. Donaldson, R. Grieve, & C. Pratt (Eds.), *Early childhood development and education* (pp. 263–269). New York: Guilford Press.

Wallach, G. P. (1990). Magic buries Celtics: Looking for broader interpretations of language learning and literacy. *Topics in Language Disorders, 10*(2), 63–80.

Wallach, G. P., & Miller, L. M. (1988). *Language intervention and academic success.* Boston: College-Hill Press.

Weaver, C. (1988). *Reading process and practice.* Portsmouth, NH: Heinemann.

Weaver, C. (1990). *Understanding whole language: From principles to practice.* Portsmouth, NH: Heinemann.

Weaver, C. (1991). Whole language and its potential for developing readers. *Topics in Language Disorders, 11*(3), 28–44.

Wertsch, J. V. (1990). The voice of rationality in a sociocultural approach to mind. In L. C. Moll (Ed.), *Vygotsky and education: Instructional implications and applications of sociohistorical psychology* (pp. 111–126). New York: Cambridge University Press.

Westby, C. E. (1989). Assessing and remediating text comprehension problems. In A. G. Kamhi & H. W. Catts (Eds.), *Reading disabilities: A developmental language perspective* (pp. 199–259). Boston: College-Hill Press.

Westby, C. E. (1990). The role of the speech-language pathologist in whole language. *Language, Speech, and Hearing Services in Schools, 21,* 228–237.

Westby, C. E., & Costlow, L. (1991). Whole language in special education. *Topics in Language Disorders, 11*(3), 69–84.

Westby, C. E., Van Dongen, R., & Maggert, Z. (1989). Assessing narrative competence. *Seminars in Speech and Language, 10,* 63–76.

Ysseldyke, J. E., Christenson, S. L., Thurlow, M. L., & Bakewell, D. (1989). Are different kinds of instructional tasks used by different categories of students in different settings? *School Psychology Review, 18,* 98–111.

3

METALINGUISTIC DEVELOPMENT

■ Anne van Kleeck
University of Texas at Austin

At age 2;4 (years;months), Zachary muses, "Ukelele. That's hard to say." Three months later (aged 2;7), he says, "Noodle and boodle. That matches!" And one month after that (at 2;8), he comments while pointing to his own back, "See my back back there. See my back back there. That means different things." (Examples from van Kleeck & Bryant, 1983.) What do these comments have in common? They all reflect budding metalinguistic ability. In each case, the child has focused his thoughts on the linguistic code itself. He has temporarily shifted attention from using language to convey a message to considering the formal features of language. He has noted that, regardless of meaning, sound sequences can be difficult to produce or they can sound similar. Zachary has also discovered that an identical sound sequence can have different meanings. *Metalinguistic skill,* or language awareness, refers to this ability to reflect consciously on the nature and properties of language.

One might reasonably wonder if such insights are all that important. They seem like "frosting on the cake," especially for children who find using language for very basic communication fraught with difficulty. Far from being mere "frosting," research conducted during the last several years underscores the integral relationship between metalinguistic skill and success in school. Many researchers believe metalinguistic skill is crucial to achieving print literacy. Linguistic awareness has also been tied to a child's ability to gradually disembed language from the immediate, concrete, personal contexts in which it is initially learned and used. This frees both language and thought from immediate social contexts and fosters the development of abstract, decontextualized thought (see also, Lahey & Bloom, chap. 13). Metalinguistic skill is also considered important to further development of the linguistic code itself. All of these functions of metalinguistic skill combine to make it a most salient factor in a child's early academic success, which in turn is the foundation for all later academic, and often lifelong, success.

Those who work with language delayed and disordered preschoolers know full well that language problems do not end when these children have achieved competence in using language as a social-interactive tool. Instead, their problems later manifest in the classroom, where they experience difficulty with a new set of language demands, as addressed by other authors in this text (e.g., Nelson, chap. 4; Silliman & Wilkinson, chap. 2). Many of these new language demands rest on various metalinguistic skills. As such, an understanding of metalinguistic skills—what they are and how they develop—provides a link for moving children from social to increasingly instructional uses of language.

This chapter first explores the realm of metalinguistic ability by comparing and contrasting it with other areas of language and cognitive ability. Theories attempting to explain the developmental unfolding of metalinguistic ability are then offered. The various focuses of language awareness are organized according to a definition of language, and the development of skills within each focus is discussed next. Finally, several assessment and intervention ideas are presented.

LANGUAGE AWARENESS DEFINED

One helpful approach to defining metalinguistic ability is to consider how it relates to several other similar and often overlapping areas of study. In the following pages, the terms *pragmatics, metacommunication,*

Some of the ideas and organizing frameworks in this chapter are taken from two earlier chapters (van Kleeck, 1984a, 1984b). However, the majority of this information is new, and many of the ideas differ from those earlier works.

metapragmatics, and *metacognition* are defined. A more careful consideration of the boundaries of each domain helps define metalinguistics.

Pragmatics

To understand more fully the notion of language awareness, it is helpful to distinguish it from the practical skill of using language in a social context (i.e., pragmatics). In most social conversation, language serves to transmit thought. In these instances, both the speaker and the listener are attuned to the meaning of the message. The specific language being used (i.e., the actual sounds, how they are arranged, the order of words within a sentence) remains below the level of conscious awareness. That is, neither the listener nor the speaker particularly notices or attends to how the message is being conveyed until something unexpected occurs during the conversation.

For example, listeners may notice a particular word because it was incorrectly produced or produced with an unfamiliar accent, because its meaning was not known to them, or because the speaker played with its meaning (e.g., in creating a pun) or used its meaning metaphorically. In all of these cases, language takes on a metalinguistic character. There is a temporary shift in one's attention from what is being said to the language used to say it. The mere activity of reflecting on the word entails thought, and as such, language itself temporarily becomes the object of a person's thoughts. A listener may, for example, get "caught up" in a foreign speaker's accent or in the lisper's lisp at the cost of missing some or most of the messages conveyed.

Unexpected events within a conversation may serve as catalysts for both adults and children to shift their focus from the messages conveyed by language to the language itself. Children also sometimes spontaneously ask questions or make comments about the linguistic code. Some examples include their questions or comments about pronunciation, grammar, or the meanings of words. At age 2;11, Casey stops her mother as they are singing "Santa Claus is coming to town" and asks, "What's 'for goodness sake' mean?" Two months later they are singing "Did you ever see a laddie?," in which Casey's mother substituted the word "lassie" for "laddie." Casey interrupts this song as well to inquire about meaning. She asks, "Mama, what's a lassie?" (van Kleeck & Bryant, 1983).

Children may also occasionally delight in playfully manipulating language for no apparent utilitarian purpose. They simply derive joy from the activity itself, verbal play being its own reward. One witnesses them playing with sounds and words. They create strings of highly inflected jargon, nonsense words, rhymes, and alliteration, all often framed with giggles of pleasure and mischief. And so, a two-year-old utters, "Bee bee, bo bo, boo boo, ba ba. Pee pee, po po, pa pa," and so on for the sheer fun of it (van Kleeck & Bryant, 1984). In a somewhat related vein, the older child will gleefully join in playground chants and ritualized insults, where language itself is the object of the game.

In all of these cases, the children are focusing on language as an object having its own existence. Like all other objects, language is a potential item of play. Unlike concrete objects, however, language can always be "conjured up" by the resourceful child. And indeed, it is often in just those contexts where the child has little or nothing tangible to play with that language play is likely to occur, such as in the crib at bedtime (Kuczaj, 1983; Weir, 1962) or in the backseat of a car (Iwamura, 1980).

While all of the previously addressed examples of language awareness occur more or less spontaneously, numerous tasks are also presented to the child (often by educators or researchers) designed to intentionally elicit "metalinguistic reflections" (or thought about language) from the child. For example, one metalinguistic task is the prereading exercise that requires the child to circle all the pictures on a page that depict words beginning with a certain sound. These tasks require the child to focus primarily on the *form* of language. Psycholinguistic researchers have devised numerous experimental tasks that likewise require a shift from the child's habitual focus on messages conveyed by language to some aspect of either the form or meaning of the language itself. For example, they might ask a child to judge the grammaticality of a sentence, to segment a sentence into its component words, or to consider alternate meanings for a multiple-meaning word, such as "bat."

Such examples point out situations in which the distinction between pragmatic or practical linguistic skills and metalinguistic skills become apparent. Cazden (1974) captures the general distinction metaphorically. She discusses how we normally "hear through" language to its intended message and thus treat language forms transparently. In attending to the language itself, it becomes, in a sense, temporarily opaque. Many academic tasks require that the child treat language in this "opaque" manner.

Several catalysts that might potentially promote language awareness can be isolated. *Communication failure* (real or potential) serves as one such catalyst. Here, awareness is reflected by efforts to avert or rectify the failure or breakdown. For example, I might correct a mispronunciation quite automatically to this end. On a far more conscious level, I might dramatically alter my vocabulary in attempting to explain my research to my mother as opposed to explaining it to another language development scholar.

Having fun or *entertaining oneself* seems to be another catalyst revealed in early language play. Later, having fun with language may take on a more social nature, as manifested in ritualized forms of language play among peer groups, such as telling riddles and using secret languages. The need for creative, verbal *self-expression* might serve as a catalyst for the creation of figurative language.

Kenneth Koch (1973), for example, offers splendid examples of children acting as budding poets in his book, *Rose, Where Did You Get that Red?* Koch taught New York City public school third through sixth graders poetry by masters such as Blake, Donne, Shakespeare, and Lorca. He then had them write poems that were in some way like those of the poet they were studying. After reading Whitman's "Song of Myself," sixth grader Vivian Tuft wrote:

> Come with me and I'll show you my heart. I know where it is. I know all about it.
> Come with me to a place I know. It's a very mysterious place. I get there through the back roads of my mind.
> Come with me, I'll take you to a world, not a world that you know. Not a world that I know. But a world that nobody knows, not me or you. It's a world of our own to live the way we want.
> To do the things we want.
> To know the things we want.
> There's no way to get there.
> It's ourselves that takes us there. (Koch, 1973, pp. 106–107)

Yet another catalyst, *curiosity,* invokes various types of questions about the linguistic code and language use. Finally, awareness can be provoked by adults questioning the child about language.

These same catalysts can move any automatically regulated activity into conscious awareness. Consider, as an example, the sensorimotor activity of walking. Most people rarely consciously think about walking until one of these same catalysts provokes their awareness. When there is a breakdown—as a temporary tripping or more permanent leg break—the act of walking might become very conscious indeed. In a related vein, people might become aware of walking when they need to adapt this habitual activity to markedly different terrain, such as a steep hill or loose sand. From yet another perspective, the dancer becomes aware of walking in order to enhance that movement. In this case, walking becomes a means of creative self-expression. Finally, awareness of the act of walking may constitute a professional, lifelong area of conscious study, as it does for a physical therapist.

This discussion is not intended as a request to abandon or even de-emphasize our continuing efforts to acknowledge, describe, and explain the nature and development of the ability to use language as a pragmatic tool. Rather, the purpose is to consider another aspect of the language development process—namely, how children learn to treat language as a focus of cognitive reflection. The importance of pragmatic skill is evident; language is the fundamental means for participating in and managing human relationships. Language awareness is important as the crux of early reading, writing, and spelling skills. These print literacy skills are crucial to success in our academic institutions and in our highly literate society in general.

Metacommunication

So far the prefix *meta-* has been discussed in relation to reflecting specifically on language itself. This prefix has also been used in a different sense with communication (e.g., Bateson, 1972; Goffman, 1974; Hymes, 1974; Jakobson, 1960; Watzlawick, Beavin, & Jackson, 1967). The term *metacommunication* defines a domain (although it is not synonymous for all who use it) that is distinct from metalinguistics.

Metacommunication refers to communication that "goes along with" language. This is quite different from metalinguistic reflections on language itself. Metacommunicative messages serve to negotiate both the flow of conversation and the context in which a particular utterance is to be interpreted. As a speaker talks, much more than words are exchanged. Messages accompanying language communicate how speakers feel about their messages and about their listener. They also communicate how to interpret the message (e.g., as a joke, seriously, ironically), whether the speaker would like to continue talking some more before the listener takes a turn, and so forth.

All of these messages can be said in words, but none of them has to be communicated in the actual talk. They are often conveyed simultaneously with (hence, *meta-* in the sense of "along with") a linguistic message by nonlinguistic means. These nonlinguistic devices include kinesics (eye contact, facial and body gesture, touching); proxemics (use of distance and space); paralanguage (e.g., suprasegmentals of intonation, pitch, loudness); and artifactual devices (e.g., clothing, badges, hairstyle).

In contrast to metalanguage, which decontextualizes language to make it an object of thought, metacommunicative messages are intrinsic parts of using language in context. As such, metacommunication is in the realm of pragmatics, because it addresses what is communicated in social interactions and how this occurs. The development of a child's ability to both interpret and produce metacommunicative cues—such as gaining access to a conversation and taking turns—is of utmost importance but is outside the realm of metalinguistics and hence beyond the scope of the present chapter. It will be covered in later chapters (e.g., Nelson, chap. 4; Palincsar, Brown, & Campione, chap. 5; see also Silliman & Wilkinson, chap. 2).

Metapragmatics

Yet another *meta-* term that is used in the literature is *metapragmatics* (e.g., Bates, 1976). Pragmatic skills allow the effective use of language in context. The use of pragmatic rules for carrying out an interaction generally remains below the level of consciousness. Furthermore, the flow of a conversation is generally maintained implicitly through nonverbal channels. At times, however, a child's conscious awareness of the social rules for language use is reflected in explicit comments the child makes. With this conscious reflection on the use of language, pragmatics enters the realm of metapragmatics. Such comments might focus on what is socially acceptable behavior in using language. For example, the child may make statements such as "You're not supposed to interrupt," "Let her finish talking," "Don't use your loud voice in the classroom," or "You're not supposed to talk about other people." These types of comments focus on the social use of language and stand in contrast to spontaneous metalinguistic comments, which focus on the language itself (i.e., its elements, grammar, and meaning).

Relationship between Metalanguage and Metacognition

Metacognitive skills involve insights one can have regarding internal mental actions or cognitive processes. The goals of such processing are numerous and include memory, comprehension, learning, attention, and using language. Metalinguistic skills therefore are sometimes thought of as a subset of the broader domain of metacognitive skills (Brown & DeLoache, 1978; Flavell, 1981; Tunmer & Bowey, 1984).

However, there is one clear distinction between the other metacognitive skills mentioned previously and metalinguistic skills. Most of these skills have mental goals (e.g., to remember, to learn, to attend, to comprehend) but no observable products. For example, people can be conscious of what types of things they tend to remember best and thus can engage in metacognition. However, there is no observable, quantifiable entity called "remember" that can be recorded and analyzed (see Lahey & Bloom, chap. 13, for additional information).

Language also requires cognitive processing to be understood and produced. Language is also, however, an external product (the acoustic energy in orally produced language or visual display in signed or written language) that can be observed, recorded, and analyzed. So, if awareness is focused on the internal cognitive processing of language (which rarely seems to be the case), metalinguistic and metacognitive skills do indeed overlap. They do not overlap when language is reflected on as an external object comprised of various elements and having certain characteristics.

In summary, metalinguistics is defined in this chapter as having some differences as well as some overlap with both pragmatic and metacognitive skills. In contrast, it rarely overlaps with the domains of metacommunication or metapragmatics. This definition addresses at least two boundaries that are important for clinicians and teachers to keep in mind when constructing language experiences. One boundary lies between using language and other communication channels as communicative tools (i.e., metacommunication and pragmatics) and focusing on language consciously. At least initially, the child should not be asked to perform both of these tasks at once. If the task is to communicate meaning, as in reading a story, the adult should avoid shifting to a conscious focus on language form by, for example, pointing out a particular letter. Each task is important, but they should be dealt with separately at the outset, with flexible movement across this "boundary" being a later goal.

A second boundary in the definition offered here is between language and other communication channels. Of course, it might be helpful for a child to consciously understand how language and other communicative channels interact to make communication effective (i.e., metapragmatic skill). But other channels of communication (e.g., gesture, intonation) cannot be decontextualized in the same way language can. Hence, it is important that the child learn to focus exclusively on the linguistic code, because it is often used in isolation from other communication channels in one critical academic activity: reading independently.

THEORIES ON THE DEVELOPMENT OF METALINGUISTIC SKILLS

It has always been far easier to examine and report what skills children have at various ages or developmental levels than to uncover the mysteries of how such learning occurs. In child language development, many theories of how development unfolds continue to be debated in the literature (see also Friel-Patti, chap. 14). On a very basic level, such theories can be divided into two broad camps: those that view a child's mental endowments, either innate or developed, as having primary importance versus those that believe that social interaction with significant others in the child's environment is the most critical element in development.

Theories of metalinguistic development can likewise be broadly divided into those that emphasize children's mental endowments (cognitive models) and those that emphasize the role of parental guidance, particularly in relation to metalinguistic skills tied to early reading (social constructivist models).

The Cognitive Models

Two theories posit that cognitive abilities are the crux of metalinguistic abilities, although they are quite different in one critical respect. One theory views metalinguistic stages as being tied to the age-related global stages of cognitive development proposed by Piaget (see Hakes, 1980; van Kleeck, 1982). As such, all normally developing children at a particular stage of cognitive development will function in a certain characteristic manner on a multitude of metalinguistic tasks. This first approach is identified here as the cognitive stage model. The other theory uses the term *phase* to highlight that metalinguistic development is not age related. "Rather, phases are recurrent cycles of processes which take place again and again as different aspects of the linguistic system develop" (Karmiloff-Smith, 1986, p. 104). Each particular aspect of the linguistic system passes through a series of phases in terms of how it is mentally organized or represented. At any given age, some earlier learned linguistic knowledge may be organized mentally at a much higher level and hence may even be available for conscious reflection. Later learned aspects of language may be at a much earlier phase of mental organization and not yet available for conscious reflection. This second approach, which was forwarded by Karmiloff-Smith (1986), is identified here as the cognitive phase model.

Cognitive Stage Model. In two works just before his death, Piaget (1976, 1978) provided a model that captured the essence of the process of moving inward (i.e., the ability to reflect). Although this model was developed to look at the growth in awareness of sensorimotor actions (e.g., crawling on all fours), it provides a helpful framework for considering growth of awareness in language as well (see van Kleeck, 1982). The model considers the child, the objects in the child's environment, and the practical actions resulting from the interactions between them. Awareness can be aimed at any of these three aspects of a given activity—the actor, the action, or the objects employed in the action. It begins with the child's awareness of the goals and results of the child's practical actions. In a sense, this awareness is peripheral to both the child and the object used in carrying out the action. Later, the child becomes aware of the object, notes its special properties, and so forth. Finally, the child's own part in the action can potentially become a focus of awareness. That is, the child might consciously consider what kind of mental manipulations she did to carry out the action.

In extending Piaget's model to consider language awareness specifically, the notion of "types of awareness" can be used to clarify the diverse skills considered by researchers to be metalinguistic. In Figure 3–1, the practical sensorimotor action in Piaget's model is replaced by another practical skill—language. At this level, the focus is on the instrumental use of language in context. As a practical skill, language is a utilitarian, pragmatic tool. Its goal is to convey meaning. Awareness at this point focuses on the success or failure of language in achieving that goal. One asks if the message was successful; in other words, was the meaning conveyed? Only the end product needs to be considered to make this judgment. For example, if the child gives a command that is subsequently carried out, the message is judged successful according to such criteria.

Moving from a focus on the practical action where the child considers *what* is said, the child can focus on the language itself and consider *how* the message was phrased. Here, the focus is on the observable elements of language—the sounds, words, and surface aspects of the morphologic and syntactic structures.

Finally, the child can consider the cognitive processes he uses when producing and interpreting messages. Even more abstract than these processes are the general rules systems underlying language processing. It is frequently suggested that the grammars of language remain inaccessible to conscious awareness (e.g., Read, 1978; Seuren, 1978; Sinclair, 1978). Indeed, explaining the internal processing mechanisms and the rules of grammar is the type of awareness that the linguist or psycholinguist seeks (assuming one believes it is even necessary to postulate rules, a stance questioned by recent connectionist theorists, e.g., Rumelhart & McClelland, 1987).

Stage 1 of Language Awareness: The Preoperational Child. According to the cognitive stage model, stage 1 of metalinguistic development occurs between the onset of language and approximately 6 years of age, corresponding with Piaget's preoperational stage of cognitive development. From the perspective of the cognitive stage model, the metalinguistic skills demonstrated by children in this age range can be explained by looking at the general cognitive skills they typically possess. According to Piagetian theory, two interrelated characteristics of children's thought in this stage are centration and irreversibility. *Centration* refers to children's tendency to concentrate on one aspect of a situation at a time. *Irreversibility* refers to their inability to shift back and forth easily between aspects of a situation.

These limitations in the reasoning capacity of preoperational children are viewed as influencing their metalinguistic skills. Many aspects of metalinguistic performance in the preoperational stage do indeed appear to reflect the child's tendency to focus on only one aspect of a situation at a time. Generally, children in this stage seem capable of focusing on language either as a communicative tool designed to convey meaning or as an object of play divorced from use in a meaningful communication context. Thus, one sees two separate threads of development in this first stage. These threads are depicted in Figure 3–2 by the separation of language use from language itself.

In stage 1, therefore, children's nascent metalinguistic skills tied to language use include being able

FIGURE 3–1
The application of Piagetian notions on awareness to considering three focuses of language awareness

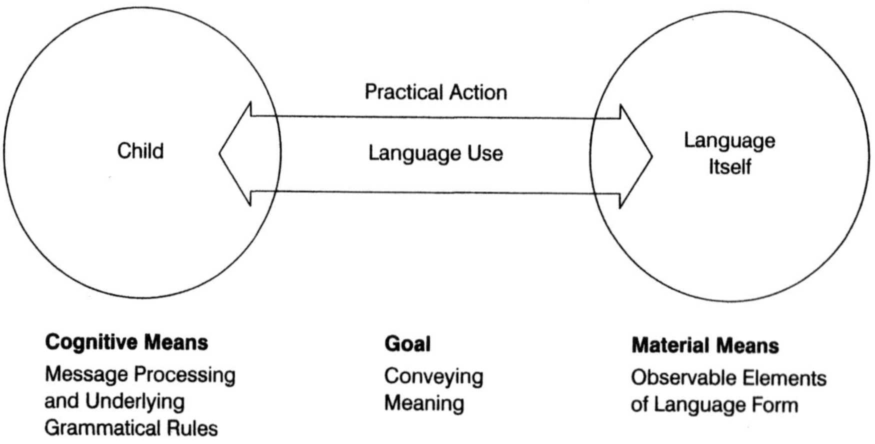

FIGURE 3–2
Stage 1 of the cognitive stage model of language awareness

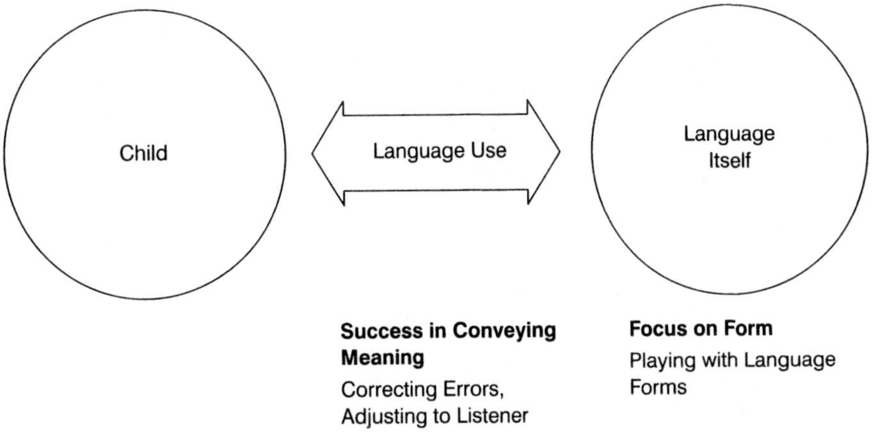

to make corrections to form or meaning to facilitate ongoing interaction and beginning to learn to adapt to their listeners. As discussed in a later section, both of these skills emerge during the preschool years. Additionally, on many experimental tasks that have been designed to elicit a metalinguistic response, stage-1 children will often (although not always) manifest a tendency to remain focused on the message conveyed. Correspondingly, children exhibit a general inability to shift their attention to language form.

Stage-1 children, however, can and do sometimes focus on linguistic form when conveying meaningful messages is not their primary goal. One sees this in children's language play, where form component of language becomes an object of play rather than a medium for a message. Here, the meaning has been abandoned or at least relegated to lesser importance. Stage-1 (preoperational) children's performance on numerous experimental tasks discussed next underscores their tendency to remain focused on message meaning. They can shift focus to language form only when the forms are either not meaningful or their meaning is not of paramount importance.

Stage-1 children cannot separate words from their meanings; words remain tied to the things they represent. Because referents for physical objects have more obvious meaning, they are more readily considered to be words by the preoperational child. So, a child says, "strawberry is a word because it grows in the garden" (Berthoud-Papandropoulou, 1978). In effect, this child is reflecting the belief, "Because I can locate the physical referent for you, what it is called is indeed a word." When asked for a long, short, or difficult word, the physical properties of the object denoted and not the linguistic elements of the word itself are again focused on. Thus, a child might offer "train" when asked for a long word. Likewise, in segmenting sentences into words, functor words (e.g., *the* and *is*) are often not identified as words because they have little or no independent semantic status (as per additional examples presented later in this chapter).

Some metalinguistic tasks tap the native intuitions a child has regarding whether a sentence presented to them is acceptable or not. Grammaticality judgments can focus on the acceptability of phonological, morphological, syntactic, or semantic properties of language. Preoperational children can succeed in making such judgments if the unit to be judged is not in itself meaningful, as when a phoneme in a word is inaccurate (e.g., "Fix this sentence: Close the lindow"). They are also quite adept at detecting semantic violations, as they are requested to do in judging semantic selection restriction violations (e.g., "Can chairs dance?" or "Do bicycles eat?"). Once again, the examples reflect children's "meaning of the message" orientation at this age.

Given this general "meaning" orientation, one wonders about the nursery rhymes so popular with young stage-1 children. Clearly, these rhymes direct attention to language form—the sound component in particular—because they contain a lot of rhyming. Rhyming requires segmentation of initial consonants or consonant clusters, but these sounds by themselves are not meaningful. Are the nursery rhymes themselves all that meaningful? There often seems to be little that would actually be in the preschooler's grasp (e.g., "sat on a tuffet," about which the *Webster's New Twentieth Century Dictionary Unabridged* edition says, "in the nursery rhyme, *tuffet* is of doubtful meaning"). Perhaps there is a reason for the somewhat nonsensical nature of many nursery rhymes. Preschoolers might find it quite difficult to deal with attending to language form and having meaningful messages conveyed simultaneously. Yet they seem to love the rhythm and sounds of these classic "baby" rhymes.

In summary, preoperational children seem to demonstrate that they can handle form alone, or meaning alone, and can even adjust form if their goal is to convey more effective messages. However, they have trouble focusing on form consciously when meaning competes for their attention. Piaget believes that preoperational children focus on the most salient perceptual aspect of a given situation. Extending this notion beyond perception to language, one might say that the most salient aspect is the meaning of the message. Form can be focused on, but only when meaning is somehow made less salient, or when the unit of form that is being focused on does not itself carry meaning (as with a phoneme).

If one were to adopt a cognitive stage model to guide classroom or intervention activities with a stage-1 child, there are several skills an adult might model and encourage children to attempt themselves. For example, the adult might occasionally, (a) mispronounce a word and then correct it; (b) engage in language play by making up words (e.g., "Let's call this hat a zorget!") or by playing with "foreign accents"; (c) encourage word awareness by commenting on a word that is very long or short (e.g., "Encyclopedia—what a long word!"); (d) encourage awareness of the sounds of language by reading or creating rhymes (e.g., Dr. Suess books), alliteration (e.g., "Big Billy bounces the blue ball beautifully"), or other sound play (e.g., "Listen to the popcorn. P-p-p-popcorn").

Stage 2 of Language Awareness: The Concrete Operational Child. In Piagetian theory, the limitations of the preoperational child's thought are overcome in the transition to concrete operations, a stage that spans from approximately 7 to 11 years of age. Whereas the preoperational child's thought is characterized by centration and irreversibility, the concrete operational child's thought is characterized by decentration and reversibility. *Decentration* refers to the ability to hold in mind and relate more than one aspect of a situation at a time. Related to this, *reversibility* allows thought to shift back and forth between aspects of the situation. Stage 2 of language awareness reflects these changes in children's reasoning ability.

Because of their ability to decentrate, concrete operational children can now simultaneously think of language in two ways. They can consider language as a medium for conveying meaning and as an object in its own right. In other words, language communicates, but it is also simultaneously an entity that can be acted on. This integration of awareness of the goal of language use with language itself is depicted in Figure 3–3.

The metalinguistic skills that emerge during stage 2 of language awareness can be divided into two broad categories. First, children in this stage can focus on and compare two meanings of one particular linguistic form at a time. Hence, they can deal with ambiguity. Second, they can manipulate the linguistic form while retaining the semantic content of the message and are as such successful in syntactic judgments.

FIGURE 3–3
Stage 2 of the cognitive stage model of language awareness: The integration of goals and material means

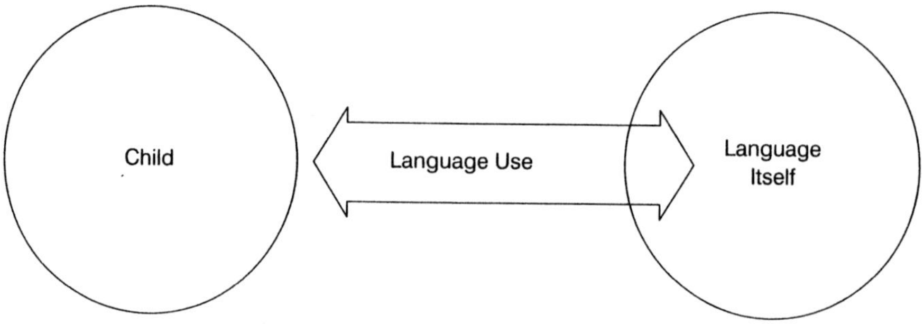

The cognitive model appears to explain children's performance across a wide range of metalinguistic skills. However, two research projects presented next suggest that although a child's general stage of cognitive development is a powerful correlate of metalinguistic development, it does not alone fully explain metalinguistic development.

The first study employed a cross-sectional experimental design to look at the relationship between metalinguistic and cognitive ability in children from 4;6 to 7;0 (van Kleeck & Reddick, 1982). The specific cognitive skill assessed was the ability to conserve. A child can conserve length, for example, when she knows that a string is just as long when formed into a circle as it is when straightened into a line. The thirty children in this study each completed a *Peabody Picture Vocabulary Test* (Dunn & Dunn, 1981) and a test that tapped a range of metalinguistic skills (adapted from Saywitz & Wilkinson, 1982). They were also administered a verbal test of conservation abilities called the *Goldschmid-Bentler Concept Assessment Kit* (Goldschmid & Bentler, 1968) and a less verbal test of conservation adapted from the work of several researchers (Brainerd, 1974; Brainerd & Hooper, 1975; Miller, 1976; Saywitz & Wilkinson, 1982). The less verbal cognitive conservation task was included because the researchers suspected that the more verbal conservation tasks may require some metalinguistic ability. That is, the child's verbal responses given to explicate her reasoning may involve consciously focusing on language divorced from its social context.

The results of this study showed a significant correlation between both the verbal and less verbal measures of conservation skill and metalinguistic performance ($r = .65$ and $r = .60$, respectively, both being significant at the .001 confidence level). Although correlations do not address causality (i.e., which variable influenced which), the findings did not negate the hypothesis forwarded by the cognitive stage model (i.e., that metalinguistic abilities are constrained by the child's general level of cognitive development).

Closer scrutiny of the data indicated that age was the best predictor of metalinguistic performance, suggesting that other age-related variables have an even greater impact on metalinguistic performance than does conservation ability. While conservation skill was also a significant predicator, it accounted for less variance than age. Even more compelling evidence weakening the claims of the cognitive stage model was found in the raw data. The authors noted that a subgroup of six children performed quite well on the metalinguistic tasks although they did very poorly on the conservation tasks. This indicates that although conservation skill may facilitate metalinguistic performance, it is clearly not a necessary prerequisite. Thus, teachers and clinicians should be aware that a child's cognitive level, at least as measured by Piagetian tasks, will not always predict a child's potential level of metalinguistic ability. The cognitive phase and social constructivist models discussed in later sections offer other possible explanations for metalinguistic performance in children.

The second study involved ongoing naturalistic observations made by parents trained to keep diary data over a twelve-month period (van Kleeck & Bryant, 1983). The children's ages at the onset of the study ranged from 1;6 to 2;4. The eight children in this study, although far from being at the concrete operational stage of development, exhibited some metalinguistic behaviors that would have required such cognitive ability according to the cognitive stage model.

Some examples included the ability to deal with dual-meaning words (e.g., an example mentioned earlier, "See my back back there. See my back back there. That means different things."); focusing on properties of linguistic form rather than properties of the referents of words (e.g., "William is a long name" and "This one has a long name," said as the child scribbled all the way across the page); and using figurative language ("I love you as much as an elephant's nose is long").

Although these studies call into question the notion that cognitive advances are *necessary* for certain kinds of metalinguistic skill to emerge, it is still possible that a somewhat weaker version of the cognitive stage model may have validity. Children may indeed experience a "flowering" of metalinguistic skill across a wide range of linguistic content as they emerge into the concrete operational stage. In other words, although children may occasionally exhibit some more precocious metalinguistic skills as preschoolers, as they advance into concrete operations, they may be able to be "metalinguistic" more broadly and more consistently.

A recent study by Tunmer (1991) lends further support to this weaker version of the cognitive stage model. Tunmer measured the decentration abilities of preliterate children entering school. Those with above-average abilities made significantly greater progress in phonological awareness (one aspect of metalinguistic ability) than those with below-average ability.

The Cognitive Phase Model. In an article published in 1986, Karmiloff-Smith proposed an account of children's metalinguistic development based on phases rather than the global stages espoused by the cognitive stage model. She defined *phases* as the cycles of processes that recur again and again as different aspects of the linguistic system develop. This concept is important for teachers and clinicians because it reminds them to be alert to the possibility that a child may be at rather different stages of linguistic awareness, not only broadly for different components of language (e.g., syntax, phonology, morphology), but also for different specific language forms. As such, a child may be able to consciously reflect on a sound that has been in his sound repertoire for some time but not be able to do so with a recently mastered sound.

Via the three phases she proposed, Karmiloff-Smith refined the thinking found in the previously held notion that metalinguistic development is a dichotomous phenomenon—knowledge is either conscious or unconscious, tacit or explicit. She discusses the nature of the changes in internal representation as the child unconsciously reorganizes mental content to the end of creating ever greater cognitive flexibility (as Lahey & Bloom do in chap. 13). And, importantly, she does not restrict the term *meta-* to conscious accessibility.

In phase 1, Karmiloff-Smith (1986) views the expression of any particular linguistic form as resulting primarily from the child's reaction to events in the environment. Language use at this stage, in other words, is driven by stimuli external to the child. Also, if a particular form (e.g., a particular word) is used in different contexts, the child will mentally store two separate representations of that form. So, "juice" uttered as part of the breakfast routine is mentally stored separately from the "juice" uttered when looking at a picture book.

At this phase, then, there is a one-to-one mapping of specific linguistic forms to particular extralinguistic/pragmatic contexts. The goal in using forms is behavioral success in a particular context. Mental procedures run in their entirety. Their components cannot be accessed or operated on separately. Numerous researchers who have studied early lexical development likewise make the case that early attempts to use words are tied to specific contexts or routinized experiences (e.g., Bates, Benigni, Bretherton, Camaioni, & Volterra, 1979; Chapman, 1988; Nelson, 1985; Snyder, Bates, & Bretherton, 1981; Werner & Kaplan, 1963). Lahey and Bloom also discuss the connection between mental models, linguistic form, and context in Chapter 13.

As children move into the second phase proposed by Karmiloff-Smith (1986), they enter a period in which they tend to ignore aspects of external stimuli as they concentrate on gaining control over internal representations (see also Lahey & Bloom, chap. 13). The cognitive reorganization at this juncture involves scanning operations that are sensitive to identical forms that have been paired with different functions. Conversely, the mental operations are also sensitive to identical functions that have been paired with different forms. As the child unconsciously makes these links, a single form becomes plurifunctional (so "juice", as a single mental entry, can be used to get juice at breakfast and to name a picture), and a single function can be achieved by multiple forms (possession may be signalled by a possessive pronoun or by the final -s morpheme).

Karmiloff-Smith (1986) posits that for the linguistic content in phase 2, children are basically impermeable to external correction. Hence, the classic example of the temporarily inexorable overgeneralized past-tense marker, as in "goed" or "wented." In Karmiloff-Smith's phase 3, children incorporate into their representations the external stimuli that were ignored during phase 2 and can make numerous corrections to the system.

The cognitive phase model proposed by Karmiloff-Smith (1986) offers some important refinements over the cognitive stage model discussed earlier. First of all, as mentioned earlier, it not only allows for a gradual unfolding of conscious awareness, but actually hypothesizes the steps of mental reorganization that must occur before such conscious access. (Lahey & Bloom also provide information in this area in chap. 13.) Second, the major difference in Karmiloff-Smith's approach lies in the view that specific linguistic forms enter the system at different times and hence pass through the phases at different times. The duration of this progression is likely somewhat different for different forms, depending on their inherent complexity, frequency of usage, and so forth. As such, at any given time, a child would have linguistic knowledge at each phase of representation. This notion is supported by recent empirical research on children's grammaticality judgments of verb forms (Sutter & Johnson, 1990). The children in this study found it harder to detect ungrammatical presentations of later acquired than earlier acquired verb forms.

The cognitive phase model brings clarity to the processes, particularly during the early stages of language development, that underlie later conscious reflection. It also illuminates why some aspects of the linguistic system may be available for conscious reflection at a much younger age than others, because consciousness is not viewed as an across-the-board process. Academically and clinically, the cognitive phase model provides a reminder that children cannot simply jump to awareness; much foundation needs to be laid. Furthermore, when teachers or clinicians attempt to help children achieve awareness, this model is a reminder to make sure that the forms to be focused on are well established in the child's language system.

The Social Constructivist Model

Social constructivists consider meaning to be socially created by "the joint intentional actions of minded creatures" (Harre, 1984, p. 8). This philosophical orientation is inherent in the approach to children's psychological development proposed by the Russian psychologist Vygotsky. He claimed that "Every function in the child's cultural development appears twice: first, on the social level, and later, on the individual level; first, *between* people *(interpsychological),* and then *inside* the child *(intrapsychological)*" (emphasis in original) (1978, p. 57). Applications of Vygotskian theory have often focused on the role of adult guidance in fostering various aspects of a child's development (as discussed in chaps. 2 & 5), although his ideas clearly extended into the realm of the child's internal cognitive restructurings as well.

In the 1980s, the role of adult guidance, in particular parental guidance, in children's early metalinguistic development evolved not in language acquisition research per se, but in reading acquisition research. Previously, reading acquisition was believed to automatically unfold as a result of brain maturation (e.g., Gessell, 1925, 1928). Alternatively, reading acquisition was viewed as a primarily visual and motor skill that could be enhanced by formal instruction in "reading readiness" skills such as auditory and visual discrimination and memory. Neither of these approaches viewed the preschool years as particularly important to subsequent reading achievement.

More recent research poses a substantial challenge to the claim that the preschool years are basically irrelevant to later reading development. This work focuses on foundational knowledge that children acquire about print in the years before they learn how to read. Some of this knowledge would clearly be considered metalinguistic in nature (e.g., rhyming and other sound segmentation skills). Researchers engaged in this work have often used the term *emergent literacy* to underscore the fact that becoming print literate is a gradual process (e.g., Clay, 1966; Hall, 1987; Mason & Allen, 1986; Teale & Sulzby, 1986).

Many of these studies have focused on the role of the family environment in fostering children's nascent awareness of what print is, what it is used for, and how it works. Three types of research have been particularly illuminating. First, ethnographic studies, involving intensive observations of both individual families or preschools in various communities have provided insight into the literacy experiences of preschoolers from a variety of cultures and backgrounds (e.g., Cochran-Smith, 1984; Heath, 1983; Westby, chap. 7). Second, descriptive studies have looked in more detail at the nature of the adult–child interaction that occurs during literacy events (e.g., Snow, 1983). Finally, researchers have attempted to determine the specific aspects of preschool literacy experience that predict or correlate with later reading achievement (e.g., Blachman, chap. 9; Share, Jorm, MacLean, & Matthews, 1984).

From the plethora of research accumulating in this area, it can be concluded that literacy experiences during the preschool years are (a) embedded naturally in ongoing social interactions as part of everyday life (with the exception of the all-important book reading routine) and (b) guided by a literate member of the culture. This guidance occurs for book reading (e.g., Cochran-Smith, 1984; DeLoache & Mendoza, 1986; Harkness & Miller, 1982; Ninio & Bruner, 1978; Pelligrini, Brody, & Sigel, 1985; Snow & Goldfield, 1981, 1983) and for various kinds of environmental print (Dewitz, Stammer, & Jenson, 1980; Hiebert, 1978).

Hiebert (1986) captured the critical nature of adult guidance when she stated,

> While research supports the idea that print-related learning results from informal experiences rather than didac-

> tic or highly structured ones, the process is not one of children acquiring information about print via osmosis from a print saturated environment. In one manner or another, children's attention needs to be directed to the print in these informal experiences. (1986, p. 151)

The role of parental guidance has led many researchers to adopt Vygotskian theory to explain the process of emergent literacy (e.g., Cochran-Smith, 1984; Heath, 1983; Ninio & Bruner, 1978; Scollon & Scollon, 1981; Teale, 1984; Wells, 1985). As noted earlier, according to Vygotskian theory, children learn all psychological functioning in social interaction with a more competent, experienced member of their culture. Initially, the adult (or more competent child) provides a great deal of support to ensure the child's successful participation at whatever level she can participate. Over time, the adult gradually relinquishes control of the interaction to the child, who can eventually perform the task independently. Vygotsky refers to this shift as movement from other-regulation to self-regulation or, as mentioned earlier, interpsychological to intrapsychological functioning (Vygotsky, 1978). Bruner (1978) refers to this kind of adult support as *scaffolding* (a concept introduced by Silliman and Wilkinson in chap. 2 and also discussed in Nelson, chap. 4.; Palincsar et al., chap. 5).

Tunmer and Bowey (1984) discuss one kind of knowledge that children gain via exposure to print during their first few years as "general awareness." This entails the fundamental insight, often arising from being read to, "that what the adult says somehow depends upon those mysterious marks on the page in front of him" (p. 153). Preliteracy experiences also facilitate the development of numerous metalinguistic skills. For example, phonological awareness, which will be discussed later as critical to early reading, is fostered as parents read nursery rhymes to their children (e.g., Blachman, chap. 9; Bryant, Bradley, MacLean, Crossland, 1989; MacLean, Bryant, & Bradley, 1987). Research such as this clearly demonstrates that the people in a child's environment are indeed influential in the child's development of metalinguistic skills.

An Integration of Constructivist and Cognitivist Theories

In discussing how to explain children's literacy development, Olson (1984) asks

> Do we look into the mental activities of children, an essentially piagetian undertaking, or do we look into the tutorial practices of parents, an essentially durkheimian, vygotskian, or brunerian undertaking? . . . We may note, however, that these two systems are not fully commensurate. They involve different levels of description—the psychological and the social. (p. 185)

It is possible to go a step beyond Olson's (1984) important insight that both psychological and social contributions to development are important. One might consider the possibility that these positions (i.e., the social and the psychological) represent different emphases at different points along a developmental continuum. The model shown in Figure 3–4 suggests that social constructivist notions are most explanatory for the initial stages of learning. The behaviors or skills a child is learning are embedded in meaningful activities. Initially, the adult must take major responsibility for the activity's unfolding. Adult input and direct scaffolding are necessary until the child has formed a rather comprehensive mental representation of the event or activity. Beyond that point, children can begin the process of internal cognitive reorganizations as their mental representations go through the phases outlined by Karmiloff-Smith (1986). (Recall Silliman & Wilkinson's discussion in chap. 2.)

As such, social transmission, it is suggested, is critical to early stages of learning, whereas internal cognitive reorganization is emphasized later. This conceptualization is not entirely new. Vygotsky (1978), as well as both K. Nelson (1986) and Karmiloff-Smith (1986), imply a progression from socially to cognitively constructed mental representation (see also Lahey & Bloom, chap. 13). The model in Figure 3–4 integrates the social constructivist and cognitivist perspectives far more explicitly.

The general framework suggested by this theoretical integration of the constructivist and cognitivist views allows for consideration of when and to what extent adult intervention is possible in fostering metalinguistic skill development. The adult cannot conduct the actual cognitive reorganizations, or the "covert metacognitive processes," as Karmiloff-Smith (1986) calls them, for the child. However, being aware that any content must hypothetically go through such reorganization before conscious access will be possible should caution adults to first provide the input needed for these metacognitive processes to work on in the context of a meaningful activity. Then, adults must allow the time for mental reorganization to covertly take place before using the language in the earlier input in a more decontextualized context.

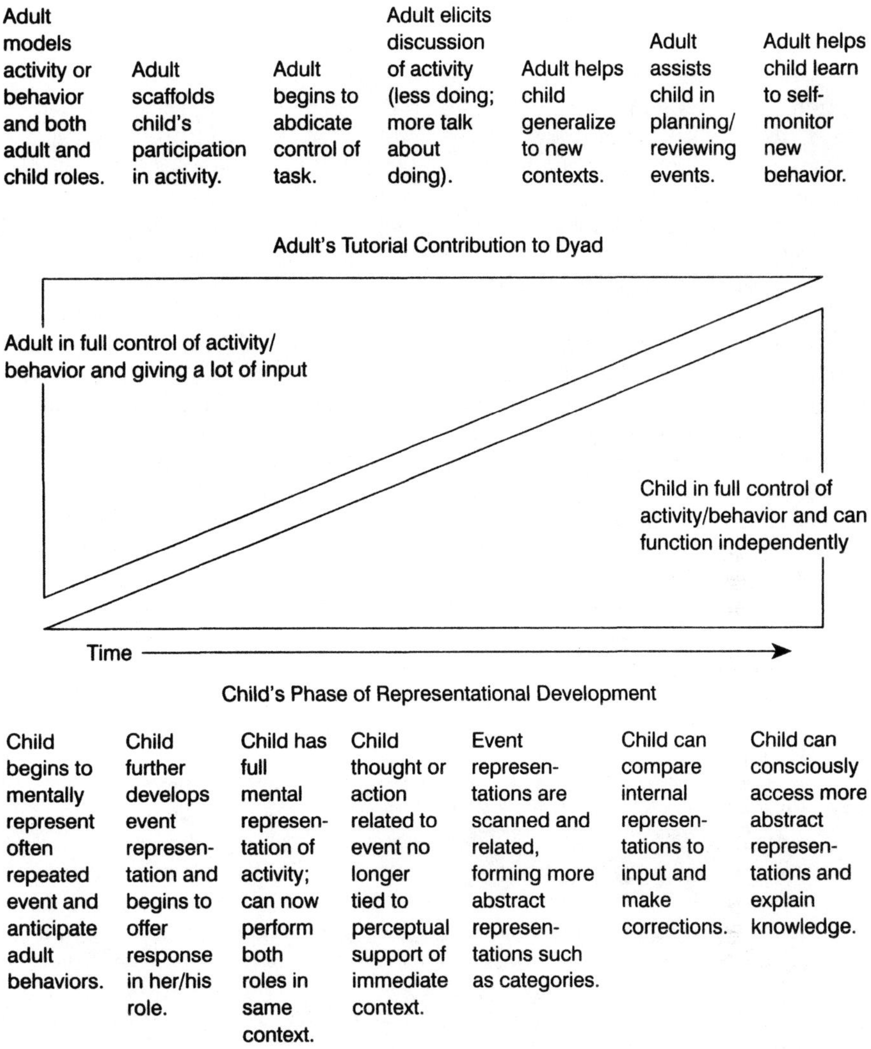
Adult models activity or behavior and both adult and child roles.
Adult scaffolds child's participation in activity.
Adult begins to abdicate control of task.
Adult elicits discussion of activity (less doing; more talk about doing).
Adult helps child generalize to new contexts.
Adult assists child in planning/ reviewing events.
Adult helps child learn to self-monitor new behavior.
Adult's Tutorial Contribution to Dyad
Adult in full control of activity/ behavior and giving a lot of input
Child in full control of activity/behavior and can function independently
Time
Child's Phase of Representational Development
Child begins to mentally represent often repeated event and anticipate adult behaviors.
Child further develops event representation and begins to offer response in her/his role.
Child has full mental representation of activity; can now perform both roles in same context.
Child thought or action related to event no longer tied to perceptual support of immediate context.
Event representations are scanned and related, forming more abstract representations such as categories.
Child can compare internal representations to input and make corrections.
Child can consciously access more abstract representations and explain knowledge.

FIGURE 3–4
Model representing process over time of learning a skill or behavior as the adult's role decreases and the child's role increases

FOCUSES AND FUNCTIONS OF LANGUAGE AWARENESS

The question of what behaviors constitute evidence of awareness is a difficult one. A person can demonstrate awareness of language via a tremendous range of behaviors. It extends from the playful manipulations of sounds in words by the toddler to the sophisticated and subtle manipulations of language meanings by the poet or novelist, the intentional and skillful switching between languages of the professional translator, and the esoteric ruminations of the linguist attempting to explain the nature of language itself. The common thread uniting such diverse skills seems elusive at best. One helpful approach to organizing this domain, however, is to consider the variety of specific focuses language awareness can take.

Because any property of language can potentially be consciously thought about, a system for categorizing metalinguistic skills should be based on a clear and consistent definition of language. Bloom and Lahey (1978, p. 4; see also Bloom, 1988, p. 2; Lahey & Bloom, chap. 13) define language as "a code whereby ideas about the world are represented through a conventional system of arbitrary signals for communication." Using this definition, one can conceive of metalinguistic skills as falling into two broad categories, (a) those that reflect an awareness that language is an arbitrary, conventional code and (b) those manifesting an awareness that language is a system of elements that are combined in systematic ways. Although Bloom and Lahey's definition also includes the notion of language being used for communication, the child's awareness of the rules for using language in communicative contexts is considered to be in the realm of metapragmatics rather than metalinguistics, as discussed earlier.

In the next section, the two broad aspects of the Bloom and Lahey definition of language—that it is arbitrary and systematic—will be used to provide an organizational framework for considering the various focuses language awareness can take. The skills each of these focuses gives rise to and the uses to which those skills can be put will be examined. Some developmental trends will be briefly explored. It should be noted that some of the functions that metalinguistic skills can serve incorporate a number of focuses—not one single aspect of language. For example, beginning reading incorporates several skills such as word consciousness, the ability to segment words into sentences, and phonological awareness—skills that, as will be discussed in the next sections, cut across numerous focuses of language awareness.

Language as an Arbitrary Conventional Code

The human capacity to represent—to have one thing stand for another absent thing—is manifested in many ways. Some forms of representation are iconic; they attempt to reproduce directly the perceptual properties of the things they represent. A picture, for example, looks like the objects and persons it represents, although it is most often smaller. Road maps are somewhat less iconic in that they use arbitrary symbols to denote some things, such as types of roads (e.g., blue, red, or black lines) or points of interest (triangles, squares). However, they still have iconic properties in that they attempt to accurately reproduce locations and distances on a proportional scale.

Although language is also used to represent things that are not perceptually present, it differs from the picture and the road map in having an arbitrary, as opposed to iconic, relationship with the things it represents. There is no systematic relationship between words and the objects, events, and relationships they encode (with the rare exception of the acoustic correspondence of onomatopoeic expressions). The particular sound sequence that constitutes any given word does not have any perceptual or otherwise meaningful correspondence to that which it denotes. The very different sound sequences in *gift, cadeau,* and *regalo* refer to the same thing in English, French, and Spanish, respectively.

Arbitrary symbols are effective for communicating only because their meanings are shared by the linguistic community; that is, they are conventional. Because of the arbitrary quality of linguistic symbols, words are separable from the things they represent. This leads to several properties of language that become potential focuses for linguistic awareness. Figure 3–5 shows that awareness of the arbitrary nature of language gives rise to word consciousness and an ability to deal with synonymy, ambiguity, and figurative language. The practical uses or real-life manifestations of each focus of awareness are also shown in Figure 3–5. The framework depicted in Figure 3–5 will be used to organize the ensuing discussion of all of these areas of metalinguistic development and their uses. As such, it may be helpful to the reader to refer back to Figure 3–5 frequently to see how the smaller pieces to be discussed fit into this larger framework.

Word Consciousness. Knowledge of the arbitrary nature of words and hence their separability from their referents is known as *word consciousness.* As can be seen in Figure 3–5, word consciousness is sometimes demonstrated in language play and second-language development, and is believed important to early reading. In addition, researchers attempt to directly assess word consciousness via "word-referent differentiation" tasks. These various manifestations of word consciousness are discussed next.

Word-Referent Differentiation Tasks. Word consciousness has often been explored using experimental procedures that are referred to as *word-referent differentiation tasks.* These tasks typically require a child to define words; give examples of words with certain properties (e.g., long, short, or difficult words); make judgments about whether sound sequences qualify as words (e.g., is *the* a word? is *boat* a word? is *tiv* a word?); and ask about characteristics of objects when the conventional names are changed to either related words or nonsense words (e.g., Bowey & Tunmer, 1984; Osherson & Markman, 1975; Berthoud-Papandropoulou & Sinclair, 1974; C. Smith & Tager-Flusberg, 1982; Vygotsky, 1962). Figure 3–6 gives examples of such procedures.

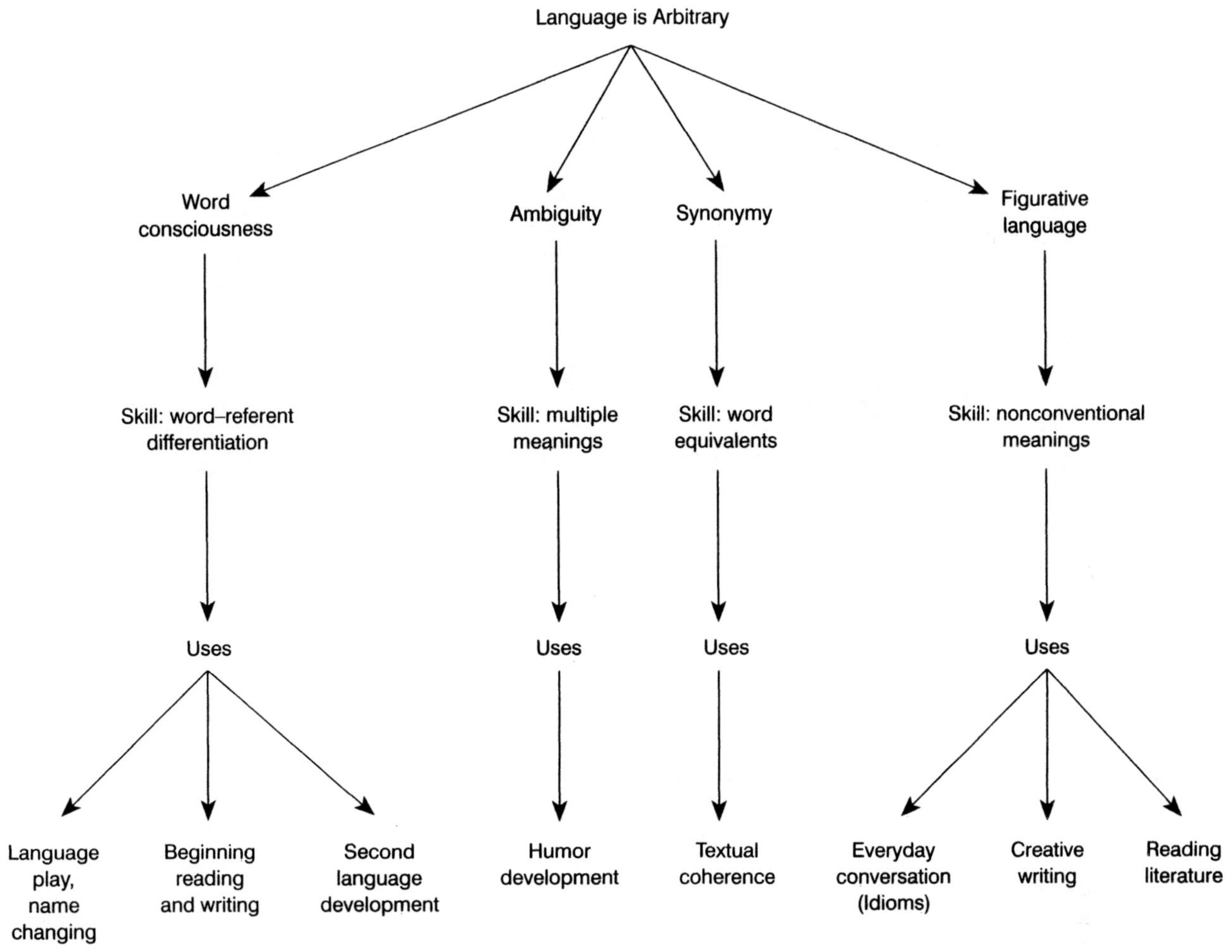

FIGURE 3–5
Awareness that language is arbitrary, the skills such knowledge supports, and the uses to which these skills can be put

As noted earlier in discussing the cognitive stage model, preschool children often display word realism in responding to all of these tasks designed to reflect word consciousness. They perceive the word as "co-substantial with the thing" or as "an invisible quality of the object" (Piaget, 1929). Vygotsky (1962, p. 128) likewise noted that "the word, to the child, is an integral part of the object it denotes." The following examples of preschool children's responses to a variety of word consciousness tasks demonstrate how language has not yet emerged as an object in its own right, separate from the physical reality it represents.

When asked to define the term *word,* preschool children often suggest that words are words because they refer to concrete things. They define words as the act of speaking itself, often giving as examples an entire sentence (Berthoud-Papandropoulou, 1978). In judging which words are words, the criterion of needing to have a physical referent in order to be a word is again demonstrated. (Recall the previous example "strawberry is a word because it is grown in the garden," Berthoud-Papandropoulou, 1978.) For the same reason, children will more readily identify concrete nouns and adjectives as words

1. Interview questions
   A. Tell me a long word. Why is it long? ______________________
   B. Tell me a short word. Why is it short? ______________________
   C. Tell me a difficult word. Why is it difficult? ______________________
   D. Tell me an easy word. Why is it easy? ______________________
   E. I'm going to say some sentences and I want you to tell me how many words are in each.
      (1) The cat climbed the tree. How many words? ______________
          What are they? ______________________
      (2) Six children are playing. How many words? ______________
          What are they? ______________________
2. Word identification: I'm going to say some things and I want you to tell me whether or not they are words. If child says no, ask why.

   house ______________________

   bink ______________________

   a ______________________

   cat ______________________

   the ______________________

   my ______________________

   mup ______________________

   boy ______________________

   ptib ______________________

   and ______________________

FIGURE 3–6
Informal procedures for assessing word–referent differentiation skills
From "Assessment and Intervention: Does 'Meta' Matter?" by A. van Kleeck in *Language Learning Disabilities in School-Agė Children* edited by G. Wallach and K. Butler, 1984, Baltimore: Williams & Wilkins. Reprinted by permission of the author.

than they will prepositions, conjunctions, possessive pronouns, and other types of function words (Berthoud-Papandropoulou & Sinclair, 1974; Ehri, 1975, 1976; Fox & Routh, 1976; Holden & McGinitie, 1972; Huttenlocher, 1964; Karpova, 1966). Indeed, children do not consistently count articles and other functors as words until age eleven (Berthoud-Papandropoulou, 1978).

Word realism is once again demonstrated when children are asked to provide examples of words having certain characteristics such as being long, short, or difficult. Preschool children typically focus on the

3. Word length versus referent length: I'm going to say some words and I want you to tell me if they are long words or short words. Then I want you to tell me why.

crocodile (long word; long referent) ______________________

spaghetti (long word; long referent) ______________________

train (short word; long referent) ______________________

fly (short word; small referent) ______________________

banana (long word; long referent) ______________________

hose (short word; long referent) ______________________

toe (short word; small referent) ______________________

real-world referent, as indicated in the example presented earlier, providing *train* when asked for a long word (Berthoud-Papandropoulou, 1978). A preschooler might also explain that *chair* is a short word because "you sit on it, and the person that is sitting on it is taller than it" (Spencer, 1986).

Another task might ask children if the name of an object could be arbitrarily changed. For example, one might be asked "Could you call a cat a dog?" Studies show that preschool children will play this game and agree that you can indeed change names. However, the attributes of the animal cling to the word. In the example just mentioned, these children might insist that a cat called a dog could now also bark (Osherson & Markman, 1975; Vygotsky, 1962).

Language Play. Experimental studies support the notion that children initially have a proclivity to view words as an integral part of the objects they represent, just as the perceptual and functional properties are a part of the object. Even very young children, however, manifest a rudimentary level of word consciousness in their spontaneous language play and in their comments and questions about language. For example, two- and three-year-olds will spontaneously and very playfully change the names of objects to a nonsense word or another alternate name (e.g., calling *butter* "sish," van Kleeck & Bryant, 1984). Additional anecdotal evidence of children spontaneously and playfully changing the names of objects has been reported (Horgan, 1979).

This apparent discrepancy regarding the age of onset of a particular skill between evidence garnered in experimental settings versus that observed in naturally occurring spontaneous behavior is to be expected. Experimental studies generally shed light on when a skill is demonstrated by a large number of children in a rather artificial, decontextualized setting. Spontaneous behavior, on the contrary, often captures the very earliest emergence (rather than mastery) of a behavior in a supporting context where it has been generated by a particular child. Standardized tests are constructed much like experimental studies. Both attempt to provide a controlled setting in which every child is treated identically. Most often, the adult administering the experimental task or the standardized test avoids giving the child any type of assistance or cues. Standardized tests therefore often assess a child's mastery of a skill that might begin emerging much earlier in spontaneous behavior.

Beginning Reading. In addition to underlying some types of language play, word consciousness is believed important to beginning reading. Here children must focus on words in isolation and attend to their form in both recognizing sight words and decoding words. To accomplish this focus on the formal features of words, it might be helpful to have the ability to dissociate words from their meaning. Although it is often suggested that metalinguistic skills such as word consciousness facilitate the acquisition of reading, the exact nature of the relationship between reading and metalinguistic skill is far from clear (Bereiter & Engelmann, 1966; Blachman, chap. 9; Ehri, 1979; Francis, 1973; Ryan, 1980).

Second Language Development. Because sound sequences are arbitrary and therefore separable from their referents, totally different sound sequences can refer to the same thing, as long as that sequence is shared by a community of speakers. Hence, different languages can and do have different ways of saying the same thing—*mushroom* in English becomes the very different sequence of sounds, *champignon,* in French.

If a child lives in an otherwise growth-stimulating environment, it is logical that exposure to two languages in childhood could provide an advantage in revealing that different sound sequences can be used to refer to the same thing (Cazden, 1974). Indeed, numerous researchers have demonstrated that bilingual children are in advance of their monolingual counterparts in realizing that words are arbitrary (Ben Zeev, 1977; Bialystok, 1986, 1987, 1988; Diaz, 1985; Feldman & Shen, 1971; Ianco-Worral, 1972). These researchers contend that early word awareness is a natural consequence of learning the vocabularies of two languages simultaneously. Because bilingual children are exposed to two different phonological representations for the same referent, they are forced at an earlier age to appreciate the arbitrary relationship between words and their referents.

Children might spontaneously demonstrate such an awareness by asking for the second-language equivalents of English words (e.g., Slobin, 1978). They may just pretend to speak another language, as when a child aged 2;8 pointed to objects depicted on a bib and said, "I'm doing Spanish. This is mindo, dindo, findo, lindo" (van Kleeck & Schuele, 1987, p. 21).

From a different perspective, Tervoort (1979) discusses how, between the ages of 5;0 and 9;0, his Dutch-speaking daughter spontaneously learned some French by noting in particular the arbitrary nature of language. She discovered that similar sound sequences had totally different meanings in French compared with Dutch. For example, at the age of 5;0, she stated that one could get ice cream in a French cafe by saying the Dutch word for glass (these two words are pronounced the same in the two different languages). This child eventually built up an entire vocabulary through the strategy of establishing the alternate meanings of Dutch–French homonyms.

As discussed in this section, word consciousness is one metalinguistic ability related to an awareness that language is arbitrary. Word-referent differentiation tasks have been used to tap this ability experimentally. Rudiments are observed in early spontaneous language play; it has also been spontaneously evoked in children learning second languages. The importance of word consciousness lies in the connection to early reading. If word consciousness is learned through exposure to print (as Ehri, 1976,

1979; Lomax & McGee, 1987; Spencer, 1986, and others suggest), it may be best facilitated in just that manner—by exposure to print. Early language play that involves word consciousness may also smooth the transition to early reading.

In addition to allowing word consciousness, children's awareness that language is arbitrary enhances their facility with three semantic properties of language—ambiguity, synonymy, and figurative language (see Figure 3–5). These areas are discussed next.

Ambiguity. Because language is arbitrary, the same sound sequence can have very different meanings both across and within languages. Within a language, the French word *avocat* refers both to an avocado and an attorney. The English word *bark* refers to a noise emitted by a dog and the outer layer of a tree. Likewise, the sentence, "The mayor ordered the police to stop drinking" (Kessel, 1970) has two different interpretations. In one case, the police themselves—and in the other case the people they serve—have developed an excessive habit that concerns the mayor. Linguistic ambiguity occurs when identical (or similar) forms have more than one meaning within a language. Most often, the context disambiguates the meaning. For example, if a group was discussing the mayor's tendency to infringe on the private lives of the police force, the interpretation of the preceding sentence would be clarified by the context.

Children will sometimes exploit the fact that context disambiguates potentially ambiguous linguistic forms to create humor. Through contextual cues, the humor based on linguistic ambiguity first biases the listener toward one interpretation of a particular word or sentence and then uses an alternate interpretation in the punch line. The expectancy violation created by shifting to the alternate meaning is the basis for the humor. The following riddle provides an example:

> Question: Why can't your nose be twelve inches long?
> Answer: Because then it would be a foot.

Here the alternate meaning of the word *foot* as a unit of measurement or as a body part are responsible for the humor. Indeed, the development of the ability to deal with ambiguity in language has most often been studied in the context of humor development.

Humor Development. Ambiguity can occur at several levels of linguistic form. The various types include (1) lexical, (2) phonological, (3) deep structure, (4) surface structure, and (5) morpheme boundary. Children's ability to resolve the various types of ambiguity in humor emerges over a number of years. The ability to resolve lexical ambiguity emerges earliest, at around six or seven years. This form of ambiguity results when a single phonological sequence (spelling may or may not be identical) identifies two separate words that have different meanings. In the following example, the resolution rests on the dual meaning of the word *club* as either a social organization or a large stick:

> Question: Do you believe in clubs for young people?
> Answer: Only when kindness fails. (Shultz, 1974, from W. C. Fields)

At around eight or nine years of age, children begin to comprehend humorous ambiguity by relying on alternate interpretations of deep or underlying structure. The ambiguity results when a single sequence of words has two transformational sources identifying different sentence meanings. In other words, two deep structures can be projected into a single surface structure. An example follows:

> Question: Will you join me in a bowl of soup?
> Answer: Do you think there is enough room for both of us? (Hirsh-Pasek, Gleitman, & Gleitman, 1978)

The remaining three types of ambiguity—phonological, surface structure, and morpheme boundary—all require the child to combine awareness of *two* aspects of language. First, as with the other forms of ambiguity, the child must have some awareness of the arbitrariness of language. In addition, the child needs to become aware of the fact that language consists of elements that are combined in systematic ways. Knowledge of this latter aspect underlies the ability to "manipulate" the elements of language. In phonological ambiguity, for example, two similar phonetic sequences (which differ only in a single sound segment) identify two separate words, which have different meanings. The child must be able to focus on the single sound segment, as in the following example where the joke "turns" on the initial sound segment of "crackers" as opposed to "quackers."

> Question: If you put three ducks in a box, what do you have?
> Answer: A box of quackers. (Hirsh-Pasek et al., 1978)

The ability to resolve all three of these types of ambiguity humor emerges latest, when children are approximately twelve years of age.

Synonymy. The same basic semantic notions can be coded in language in a variety of ways, a property of language referred to as *synonymy* (although differences in form always signal some difference in meaning, according to E. Clark's Principle of Contrast, 1987). For example, the following sentences result in basically the same semantic representation (although subtle semantic and pragmatic distinctions are implicit in the various choices):

John kissed Mary.
Mary was kissed by John.
It was Mary whom John kissed.

In synonymy tasks, one must determine first that the linguistic forms differ. The preceding example has form differences in word order and the inclusion or exclusion of functor words. Furthermore, the meaning must be essentially the same. Hakes (1980) studied developmental changes in children's performance on synonymy judgments. When younger than six years, children made judgments on the basis of form alone. Several strategies were observed in his research. For example, a "different form equals different meaning" response strategy resulted in correct responses when the sentences were in fact nonsynonymous and in incorrect responses when they were synonymous.

The younger children in Hakes' study did in fact demonstrate a tendency to base their responses on the similarity of form alone, while discounting meaning. "Their judgments of nonsynonymous pairs were correct significantly more often than chance, but their judgments of synonymous pairs were incorrect significantly more often than chance" (1980, p. 86). Children older than six judged on the basis of both form and meaning, yielding many more successful responses on this type of task.

As a "disembedded" skill exhibited on a task such as that devised by Hakes (1980), synonymy may seem of little relevance to a child's general ability to function well with language in the classroom or elsewhere. However, as children learn to string sentences together to create either oral narratives or written text, the use of synonymy is seen as critical to achieving coherence within the text (this practical use of synonymy is depicted in Figure 3–5).

Textual Coherence. Halliday and Hasan (1976) define the word *text* as "any passage, spoken or written, of whatever length, that does form a unified whole" (p. 1). (Scott uses a similar definition in chap. 8.) Their classic book on the topic discusses the devices used in English to create coherence within a text. They identified five major categories of such devices, which they refer to as *cohesive ties.* One of these five, lexical ties, is achieved by linking a word used earlier in a text by subsequently using the same word, a synonym, a superordinate word, a general word (e.g., *stuff, thing, creature, person, place*), a complement *(boy/girl),* an opposite *(wet/dry),* another member of an ordered series *(January, February, March),* or a co-hyponym—a member of the same general class *(chair/table).*

Synonyms, as such, are only one device available for achieving coherence in texts. Although some research has been conducted on the development of cohesive ties in children's early conversations and narratives (e.g., Dore, 1985; McCutchen & Perfetti, 1982; Pelligrini, 1984; Peterson & Dodsworth, 1991), researchers have not focused on the use of synonyms separate from the more general category of lexical cohesion. We therefore have little specific information on the development of this practical application of synonymy. Nonetheless, clinicians and teachers might foster the development of synonymy within the context of enhancing the written narrative abilities of children.

Indeed, a more conscious application of synonymy undoubtedly occurs when children begin polishing their efforts at producing written text, as Scott discusses in Chapter 8. At this juncture, the mere repetition of lexical items is discouraged, and students may even consult a reference that provides synonyms and antonyms—the thesaurus—to aid in effective use of this particular cohesive device.

Figurative Language. Because words are not directly tied to things, they can be used in new domains only indirectly (and sometimes remotely) related to their literal meanings. Such figurative language, as it is called, takes a clear step beyond literal, conventional meaning. A complete chapter about figurative language is presented in Part 3 (Milosky, chap. 10). The topic is introduced here to place it within the larger context of language awareness; specifically, because language is arbitrary, new meaning can be "added to" the conventional meaning of an existing word or phrase.

As long as a recognizable fiber of the original meaning is retained, conventional meaning can be "stretched." Thus, the language user becomes the language creator. The process of using conventional forms in new contexts to convey subtle variations or extensions of meaning underlies the creation of literary devices such as metaphor, simile, proverbs, and personification. Besides resting on ambiguity, humor also occasionally rests on figurative uses of language, as in

Question: Why did the girl throw a clock out the window?
Answer: Because she wanted to see time fly.

An iconic representational system would lack this flexibility to create subtle modification of meaning, because nonarbitrary terms could not be so easily transferred to different but somehow related contexts. As such, the richness of nuances in meaning that can potentially be achieved in language derives from its arbitrary nature. To some extent, conventional meanings must be adhered to in order to make communication possible. And yet, as the phrase "poetic license" suggests, the linguistic community united by the conventions at the same time allows deviations from these conventions—whether for aesthetic purposes or to obfuscate meaning.

Gardner and his colleagues, who have studied the development of figurative language in children, focus on its potential rewards when they state, "We gain pleasure, inspiration, and often deep insight from instances of figures of speech" (Gardner, Winner, Bechofer, & Wolf, 1978, p. 30). From this perspective, language enters the realm of art. Like other art forms, figurative language use serves to communicate on an intensely personal, if often highly abstract, plane.

Figurative language, however, also sometimes has a more insidious quality. For better or worse, conventionalized metaphors of our culture can and do unconsciously shape our attitudes and beliefs. Because metaphors can be extended in some ways but not in others, their unconscious use correspondingly structures "how we perceive, how we think, and what we do" (Lakoff & Johnson, 1980, p. 4). Metaphor's ability to veil meaning was witnessed in 1991 when a war waged in the Persian Gulf was referred to as a "storm" (i.e., "Operation Desert Storm"). Although both wars and storms often cause human casualties and other massive destruction, the latter is an act of nature while the former clearly is not. But by calling a war a "storm," people are perhaps less reminded of its volitional nature and hence more accepting of it (Verrillo, 1991).

Winner (1988) discusses an additional function of metaphoric ability, one that extends far beyond being able to produce aesthetically pleasing prose. "Metaphoric thinking is important in ordinary cognitive tasks as well as in scientific discovery. It may well be the primary route by which we acquire new information" (Winner, 1988, p. 117). Winner reviews research conducted with adults supporting the role of metaphor in reasoning and acquiring new knowledge. In one developmental study she discusses, children ages 6;0 to 8;0 were better able to both understand and recall texts that contained analogies (Vosniadou & Ortony, 1983). In another study, both preschoolers and ten- and eleven-year-olds were able to make use of nonexplicit analogies presented in stories in a subsequent problem-solving task (Holyoak, Junn, & Billman, 1984).

While clearly important developmentally, figures of speech, even the idioms common to everyday parlance, can elude young language learners. When a child named Jessica was 2;8, her mother was helping her with her bedtime prayers and said, "And thanks for all the new friends I've made this year at school." Jessica interrupted immediately. "I didn't make them with glue," she protested, "Their mamas brought them" (from van Kleeck & Bryant, 1983). Another child, Megan, was 3;0 when the following interchange took place with her mother. Megan was building a train by lining up wooden blocks on a table. She then took a bubble wand and explained, "I'm gonna catch the train," as she placed one of the blocks on the bubble wand. Her mother was a bit confused and replied, "Oh, you mean *cut* the train." Megan adamantly stuck to her original literal meaning and said, "No, *catch* the train." And she had in fact caught the block in the bubble wand, just as one would catch a bubble in a bubble wand.

While Jessica and Megan demonstrate the difficulties a preschooler may have with idiom comprehension, numerous researchers believe that metaphor production is within the purview of the very young preschool child (Billow, 1981; Bloom, 1973; Carlson & Anisfeld, 1969; Hudson & Nelson, 1984; Nelson, Rescorla, Gruendel, & Benedict, 1978; Thomson & Chapman, 1977; Winner, 1979). These researchers suggest that some instances of children's early overextensions may in fact be metaphoric. Winner (1988) provides the example of a child who called skywriting a "scar" after seeing a scar on her mother. In examples such as this, "the child may deliberately stretch the reference of a word in order to point out some perceived resemblance" (Winner, 1988, p. 91).

Not all agree on the metaphoric nature of these early productions (see Milosky, chap. 10). Hakes (1982) suggests that these seemingly creative productions of young children "result from their not knowing enough not to be creative" (p. 196). His position is supported by the fact that such productions begin to wane after six years of age. Some young children, however, do create a very intentional match between the emotional and visual domains in crating a simile. For example, Casey, aged 3;0, told her mother, "I love you as much as an elephant's nose is long; as much as that light is tall; as much as that truck is red; as much as that building is big" (van Kleeck & Bryant, 1983). So while Hakes' criticism may be valid for early overextensions, it is apparently not universally true regarding the figurative language abilities of preschoolers.

In general, while the "figurative-like" language productions discussed previously decline after the preschool years, comprehension improves over the next several years. In their early school years, children seem to have little flair for figurative language. The six- to eight-year-old will interpret idioms and proverbs literally, slowly becoming increasingly accurate in making figurative interpretations over the next several years into adolescence (Gibbs, 1987; Nippold & Martin, 1989; Nippold, Martin, & Erskine, 1988). This ability, however, is not yet complete even at eighteen years of age (Gibbs, 1987; Nippold & Martin, 1989; Prinz, 1983; Thorum, 1980).

In the early elementary years, children are consolidating literal meanings and are reluctant to allow violations of these recent acquisitions. Their literalness is exemplified in responses obtained by Winner and her colleagues (1976). The children were asked to paraphrase metaphoric sentences such as "After many years of working in a jail, the prison guard had become a hard rock that could not be moved." Six- and seven-year-olds used a magical approach. One child responded, "A witch turned the guard to rock." Eight- and nine-year-olds focused on the concrete physical feature. One responded, "The guard was like a rock because he had hard muscles." Only by ten to eleven years were children able to appreciate the metaphors and explain the psychological meaning of a phrase such as "hard as a rock" (Winner, Rosentiel, & Gardner, 1976).

The protracted development of figurative language has been tied to several variables. Figurative language comprehension is strongly correlated with receptive vocabulary (Nippold & Sullivan, 1987). Adolescents are better able to interpret figurative expressions in context than in isolation (Strand & Fraser, 1979). And idioms that have closely related literal and figurative meaning (e.g., "hold your tongue") are easier than those less closely related (Gibbs, 1987).

Earlier researchers, such as Elkind (1969) and Inhelder and Piaget (1958), suggested that a flowering of metaphoric skill requires the onset of Piaget's formal operational stage, which begins somewhere between ten and twelve years of age. As children advance to formal operations, they are able to deal cognitively with possibilities. Correspondingly, comprehending and producing figurative language involves stretching meaning into hypothetical realms. Winner (1988), however, calls this Piagetian explanation into question:

> In brief, given that there is no pure measure of metaphor comprehension, and given the questionable status of Piagetian stages, investigations of the relationship between metaphor comprehension and Piagetian stages are in my view, limited. (p. 115)

The work of Nippold and her colleagues demonstrates an alternate cognitive ability in proverb comprehension, namely, perceptual analogical reasoning (Nippold et al., 1988). The ability of the "A is to B as C is to D" format does, indeed, seem logically related to being able to understand the underlying relationship between a proverb and its context.

In this section, awareness of the arbitrary nature of language has been implicated in metalinguistic skills dealing with word consciousness, synonymy, ambiguity, and figurative language. The practical uses of these skills in developing literacy are manifold. Word consciousness may either precede or follow closely on the heels of the earliest stages of decoding text. As children progress in their skill with print literacy, skill with synonymy may help in achieving coherent written (and spoken) texts. Finally, figurative language may be incorporated by making the transition from merely coherent to more creative texts, as Milosky also suggests in Chapter 10.

Both synonymy and figurative language might be fostered from a very early age by reading to children, because both would be modeled frequently in stories.

The more input of this nature, the more likely children will be to use such devices in their own productions.

Language as a System

Language contains a finite set of elements. The elements include words, which are themselves composed of elements—the sounds of a particular language. These elements are combined in predictable ways by phonological, syntactic, morphologic, and semantic rules to yield a potentially infinite number of sentences. As mentioned earlier, not all current theorists believe that people unconsciously consult rules in using language (e.g., Rumelhart & McClelland, 1987). All do agree, however, that language is a structured system. The idea of rules is nonetheless useful for describing the systematic nature of language and will as such be used in this chapter.

A child's growing awareness that language consists of elements that are combined in systematic ways is the crux of many metalinguistic skills. In Figure 3–7, the elements and rules of language and the skills that demonstrate an awareness of them are

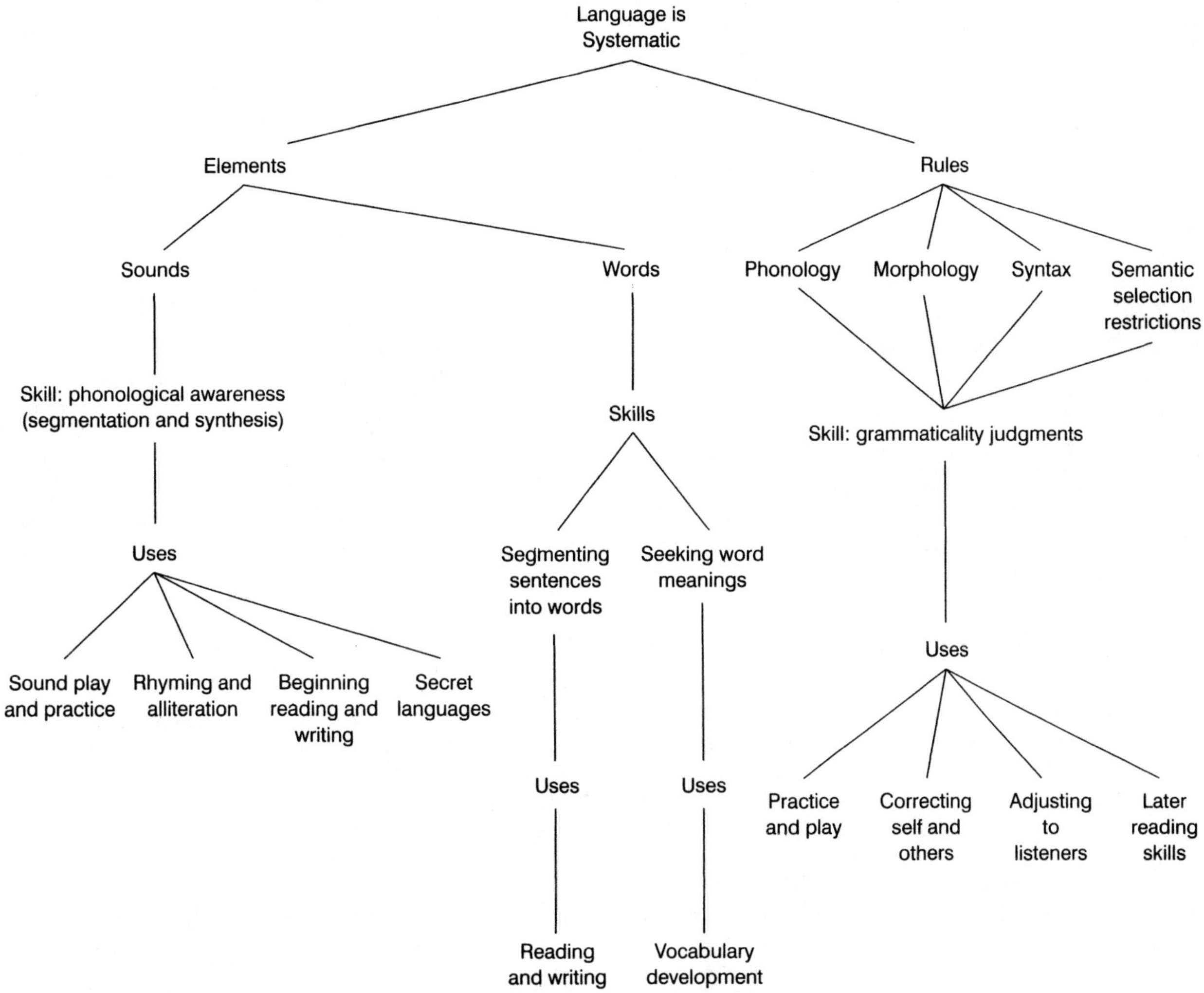

FIGURE 3–7
Awareness that language is systematic gives rise to numerous metalinguistic skills that can be used for a variety of purposes

shown. The practical applications of those skills are also noted. Once again, the reader may wish to refer back to Figure 3–7 frequently to relate the overall framework it depicts to the pieces of that framework discussed in this section.

Knowledge of Elements

Phonological Awareness. The ability to segment language into sounds requires a far more conscious focus on the acoustic signal than is required for understanding and producing connected discourse for the purposes of communication. Children's awareness that words in language are composed of a variety of units of sound (syllables, the subsyllabic units of onset and rime, and phonemes) is referred to as *phonological awareness.* It is integral to producing rhymes and alliteration. Phonological awareness is also involved in mastering the complexities of play languages such as "Pig Latin," in which the sounds are often rearranged and additional sounds or syllables added to words. Perhaps the most important application of phonological awareness is its role in the early stages of reading acquisition, which will be discussed later (and by Blachman in chap. 9).

Not all the various units of sound are equally accessible in the speech that children hear. As Blachman also points out (chap. 9), while syllable boundaries can be detected in the acoustic signal (A. Liberman, Cooper, Shankweiler, & Studdert-Kennedy, 1967), there are usually no equally discrete acoustic boundaries for individual words or sounds. That is, "the speech that children hear consists of a steady stream of sound with overlapping acoustic features" (Chaney, 1989). Words and phonemes are, as such, abstract entities with no simple physical correlate.

I. Liberman and Shankweiler (1991) discuss the advantages and disadvantages of this phenomenon of overlapping sounds, or *coarticulation*. As an advantage, they note that coarticulation allows speech to proceed at a pace that matches our perceptual mechanism for understanding it (A. Liberman et al., 1967). The disadvantage accrues for the reader because of the lack of direct correspondence between the sounds one hears and the underlying phonological structure of the word. Learning that language consists of words, and particularly of phonemic units, is therefore not necessarily a natural outgrowth of exposure to spoken language. Indeed, studies of illiterate adults find that fluent speakers cannot even segment the first sound segment of a word by omitting it (Morais, Cary, Alegria, & Bertelson, 1979), as Blachman (chap. 9) also points out.

Combining the results of several experimental studies, one can derive a developmental sequence processing from an ability to segment sentences into propositions or phrases and then into words. Next, the child can segment words—first into syllables, then into subsyllabic units called the *onset* and *rime,* and finally into individual phonemes (e.g., Chaney, 1989; Ehri, 1975; Treiman, 1983, 1985, 1986, 1992; Tunmer, Bowey, & Grieve, 1983).

Some of the youngest of the subjects in a group aged 3;6 to 7;0 studied by Karpova (1966) divided sentences into semantic propositions. One child in this study indicated that the sentence, "Galya and Vova went walking" had two words, explaining that these two words were, "Galya went walking and Vova went walking."

Younger children will sometimes isolate semantically important words but not functor words, such as *the, is, and,* and *on,* thereby offering phrases when asked to segment sentences into words. Functors serve primarily syntactic rather than semantic functions. In fact, researchers have found that some functors are more difficult to segment than others, and the amount of semantic information seems to differentiate those that are easier from those that are more difficult. For example, *the, a, is,* and *to* (used as an infinitive) appear to be more difficult than functor words such as *my, many,* (Chaney, 1989), *his,* and *her* (Tunmer et al., 1983).

Segmenting sentences into words is a skill that might be considered partly semantic, because words are individual units of meaning, and partly phonologic, because this skill requires that the child separate out individual words in the acoustic stream of speech. On experimental tasks, it follows developmentally after the ability to segment sentences into phrases. More specific aspects of word segmentation will be discussed in the section on word awareness and in Blachman, Chapter 9. It is mentioned here as part of a proposed (and recently questioned) developmental sequence that ultimately leads to the ability to segment words into their component sounds.

On experimental tasks, the ability to segment words into syllables emerges next, being competently executed by about half of preschoolers and kindergartners and the vast majority (90%) of first graders (I. Liberman, Shankweiler, Fischer, & Carter, 1974). This might be considered the first segmentation ability (demonstrated in structured experimental tasks, at any rate) to emerge that is based solely on phonological awareness, because syllables do not by themselves carry meaning (unless, of course, they are single syllable words or compound words composed of single syllable words).

Next follows the ability to segment words into subsyllabic units known as the *onset* and *rime.* The onset is the initial consonant or consonant cluster of a syllable. It is optional. The rime is the remainder of the syllable, containing a vowel nucleus and an optional final consonant or consonant cluster. So, a child might divide the word *train* into the onset "tr" plus the rime "ain." In like fashion, numerous researchers have found the initial phonemes are easier for children to segment than final phonemes (Rosner & Simon, 1971; Stanovich, Cunningham, & Cramer, 1984; Trieman & Baron, 1981), perhaps because the initial phoneme, if it is a consonant, is also the onset of the syllable it occurs in.

On experimental tasks, the ability to segment words into their component phonemes is the latest to emerge (I. Liberman et al., 1974). It is not surprising that phoneme segmentation is the hardest, because individual sounds are not perceptually available in the acoustic signal of speech. As such, isolating sounds in a word is a cognitive activity imposed on speech. In learning an alphabetic print system, "children actually must learn to ignore what they hear (a syllable) and begin to think of words as if they are composed of strings of phonemes" (Sawyer, 1987, p. 36).

The path to phoneme segmentation suggested by the research reviewed previously (and considered in more detail in Blachman, chap. 9) moves stepwise from larger to smaller units—from propositions, to words, to syllables, to the subsyllabic units of onset and rime, and finally to individual phonemes. Although this hierarchy makes intuitive sense, it may not have psychological reality. The possibility of an alternate route to phoneme awareness will be discussed in the upcoming sections on rhyming and alliteration and beginning reading.

Sound Play and Practice. Van Kleeck and Schuele (1987) presented numerous examples of phonological awareness found in children's play with language. One example, "tri ya ya ya yangle," was produced by a child aged 2;5 (van Kleeck & Bryant, 1984). "Cow go moo, mommy go mamoo, daddy go dadoo" was produced by a child aged 1;8 (Horgan, 1979). Another child, aged 3;6, playfully pronounced the word "yes" several different ways in the span of thirteen utterances of conversation. She said, "yeah," "yes," "yup," "yippie," and "yuppie."

Kuczaj suggests that early in acquisition, "language play serves a practice function and thereby facilitates the acquisition of form" (1983, p. 14). Children's focus on the sound system can sometimes seem less like play and more like deliberate practice. The famous presleep monologues of Ruth Weir's son Anthony provide an example. At age 2;10, he said to himself "Berries/ not barries/ barries, barries/ not barries/ berries/ ba ba" (1962, p. 108).

Cazden (1974) hypothesized a connection between language play and later print literacy development, in that play makes literacy "easier to achieve because the child's attention has been focused on the means, the forms of language, whereas in normal communicative contexts, his attention is focused on the end" (p. 11). It should be noted, however, that this early play and practice progresses to the level of the subsyllabic onset and rime units. It does not appear to progress to the level of isolating all individual phonemes in a word—a level of development that may not occur until a child begins to read. This possibility will be discussed in the upcoming section on beginning reading.

Rhyming and Alliteration. Rhyming and alliteration constitute other evidence of children's awareness of the sound system that is manifested in their spontaneous play with language. Both rhyming and alliterative words share some component sounds but not others. In the most common and basic type of rhyme, the onset is changed in the two words, while the rime remains the same. For example, in forming a word that rhymes with *make,* the child must isolate and then delete the onset /m/ and then replace it with another onset, perhaps /t/. The rime is retained to then form *take.*

Van Kleeck and Bryant's (1984) data revealed rhyming play in subjects as young as 1;6. So, one hears, "daddy, naddy, faddy," from a child aged 2;5 and "David is a Shavid," from a child aged 2;7. Spontaneous examples of alliteration were also noted. The following sequence was produced by a three-year-old, "Beebee, bo bo, boo boo, ba ba, pee pee, po po, pa pa, dee dee, do do. . . ." Both rhyming and alliteration are employed in the following nonsense poem produced during a bedtime soliloquy of Weir's son Anthony: "Bink. Let Bobo bink. Bink ben bink. Blue kink" (1962, p. 105). Others, as well, have found that producing rhymes and alliteration is clearly within the purview of many preschool children (Chukovsky, 1963; Dowker, 1989; Rogers, 1979; Weir, 1962).

Van Kleeck and Bryant (1984) furthermore found that some of the children they studied began indicating conscious awareness of the rhyming process as young as 2;8. This was witnessed in "Annie, Mannie. That's the same" (by a child aged 2;8) and "Newspaper, bewspaper. That rhymes" (by a child aged 3;1). MacLean et al. (1987) used an experimental task that asked children to identify which one of three words did not rhyme. Using this method, they found that their three-year-old subjects could detect rhyming and alliteration at this conscious level. Furthermore, MacLean et al. found a high correlation between knowledge of nursery rhymes (and hence exposure to rhyming) and success on phonological awareness tasks. Both of these abilities were related to early reading skills at age 4;6. Their findings suggest that "adults play a direct role in fostering the growth of phonological awareness in children with the help of formal linguistic routines" (p. 280).

As with most complex behaviors, however, additional research is required before connections between rhyming and alliteration and segmentation skills are completely understood (see, e.g., Lundberg, Frost, & Petersen, 1988; Morais, Bertelson, Cary, & Alegria, 1986; Stanovich et al., 1984).

Beginning Reading. One very important application of the phonological awareness skills is their critical role in learning to read (refer to Figure 3–7). Phonological awareness is believed necessary to success in beginning reading because, in an alphabetical writing system such as English, individual sound segments correspond (more or less) to letters in the alphabet. But in addition to knowing the sounds that correspond to letters, the child must also grasp the fact that these sounds make up spoken words. This is called the *alphabetic principle.* This allows the child to then analyze words into their component sounds and synthesize sounds together to form words (see Blachman, chap. 9; Golinkoff, 1978; Wagner & Torgesen, 1987, for reviews of phonological awareness in beginning reading).

As implied earlier, the nature of the relationship between phonological awareness and reading remains unresolved. Is it a precursor to or a result of learning to read, or is the relationship a reciprocal one? Some researchers believe that it is prerequisite to reading (Bryant, Bradley, MacLean, & Crossland, 1989; Elkonin, 1973; Fox & Routh, 1976; I. Liberman & Shankweiler, 1977); others believe it is a consequence of learning to read (I. Liberman et al., 1974; I. Liberman, Rubin, Duques, & Carlisle, 1985; Morais et al., 1979; Read, Zhang, Nie, & Ding, 1986). Two other positions take the middle ground regarding the relationship of reading and metaphonologic knowledge. One suggests that metaphonologic skills and reading *interact,* that is, that the relationship is a reciprocal one (e.g., Blachman, chap. 9; Bryant & Goswami, 1987; Ehri, 1979; Perfetti, Beck, Bell, & Hughs, 1987; Vygotsky, 1962). The other middle position considers the possibility that these skills correlate not because one causes the other but because both rely on a common underlying cognitive ability (Hakes, 1980).

Recently, some researchers have suggested that the controversy can be resolved not by positing reciprocal causation, but by treating phonological awareness as a construct consisting of two (or perhaps three) distinct levels. The hypothesis has been forwarded that sensitivity to syllabic and subsyllabic (also referred to as intrasyllabic) units (i.e., onset and rime) may emerge before alphabetic instruction. Awareness at the phonemic level, however, may be the result of such instruction. Two recent studies provide convincing support for this hypothesis (Bowey & Francis, 1991; Swank, 1991). Indeed, Bowey and Francis found "no nonreader sensitive to the phonemic structure of words" (p. 115).

Goswami and Bryant (1990) suggest that there are two ways to view this more refined look at phonological awareness and beginning reading. One view posits that sound awareness at the subsyllabic level is an important foundational step to becoming aware of individual phonemes. The second view is that awareness at the subsyllabic level may make a contribution to early reading that is independent of phonemic awareness. The second position is supported by the stronger relationship found in two studies between rhyme and alliteration tasks and beginning reading than between phonemic awareness and beginning reading (Bowey & Francis, 1991; Bryant, MacLean, & Bradley, 1990).

From the results of the Bryant et al. (1990) study (also discussed by Blachman, chap. 9), it appears that both of these positions may be true. In the longitudinal research by Bryant et al., rhyme scores were strongly related to later phoneme awareness task scores. Rhyme scores, however, still predicted success in early reading when phoneme awareness ability had been controlled. The second finding points to an independent role of phonological awareness of onset and rime in early reading achievement (see also Ellis & Large, 1987).

One might ask whether traditional phonics programs are adequate for such training, because they entail phoneme awareness by emphasizing individual letters and the sounds that correspond with them. Considering the letter–sound correspondence carefully, one sees that it rests on three component skills, (a) the recognition of the visual symbols (i.e., letters); (b) knowledge of the names of the letters (without which one sacrifices referential clarity in instruction; see Adams, 1990); and (c) awareness that spoken words comprise individual sounds. These skills combine to lead to the alphabetic principle (i.e., that letters in the alphabet correspond to sounds in spoken words).

The importance of phonological awareness in achieving insight into the alphabetic principle seems to provide unequivocal support for a phonics approach to early reading instruction. If only it were that simple! One question looms large in the instructional method controversy. Do children achieve the alphabetic insight spontaneously, or does it always require outside intervention?

I. Liberman and Shankweiler (1991) note that 75% of children learn to read regardless of the method. That is, they pick up the alphabetic principle on their own. However, one might question how "on their own" these children truly learn to read. Many may have had considerable assistance at home and arrive at school with the component strands of the alphabetic principle already established. They may as such appear to learn on their own, when in fact they have had a great deal of environmental support. Gough and Hillinger (1980) suggest that learning to read is an "unnatural act" that almost always requires outside guidance to learn.

On the other hand, the "unnatural act" conclusion is questioned by the recent discovery of a group of children who may have learned to read very much on their own. These children are autistic. Their unexpected literacy skills have been tapped by facilitated communication—a physically and emotionally supported method of typing messages (see Biklen, 1990). Before their success with facilitated communication, these children could not communicate and were thought to be retarded. If they had any oral language at all, it was echoed words or phrases. And yet Biklen and his colleagues report that of forty-three such children, all but one over the age of five could type out messages (Biklen, Morton, Gold, Berrigan, & Swaminathan, 1992). *Most had never been taught to read!* Other similar reports are accruing (see Crossely, 1992; Donnellan, Sabin, & Majure, 1992).

There is clearly a need for further research on such autistic individuals. Their unexpected literacy, however, may potentially provide insight into factors that account for the spontaneous acquisition of the alphabetic principle. Donnellan and her colleagues (1992) speculate that higher than average performance of autistic individuals in the areas of visual-spatial, perceptual, and memory abilities may partly explain their literacy achievements. At the very least, their independently acquired print literacy accomplishments (assuming the reports are accurate in this respect) seriously question the "unnatural act" view of learning to read and, hence, the need for structured phonics training for every child.

As many of these autistic children have apparently done, some normal children may also "crack the code" on their own. Others may crack the code with considerable guidance from parents, siblings, or other literate persons in their lives. Yet other children may have the component skills in place (knowledge of the alphabet and phonological awareness) and need very little assistance in "putting it all together" once they reach school. Certainly, for children who can already read and perhaps for those poised and ready to learn, a typical phonics program may be an unconscionable waste of time (these programs can spend up to two weeks on each sound–letter correspondence, according to Adams, 1990). (See also Catts's response in chap. 16.)

What of the children who do not come to school equipped with phonological awareness and knowledge of the alphabet? And what of the children who may for other reasons experience a great deal of difficulty in cracking the code? Is a phonics approach—in other words, a structured approach to teaching the alphabetic principle—best for these children? And if so, are some alterations warranted in light of current research and thinking? To these hotly debated questions, I offer my own answers: yes and yes.

A structured approach seems warranted in light of research showing that phonological awareness skills can be systematically trained and that such training improves reading ability (see Blachman, chap. 9, for a review of this work). However, alterations to phonics approaches as they are currently structured also seems warranted for reasons discussed next.

Adams believes that children should have a "solid visual familiarity with individual letters" (1990, p. 255) before phonics instruction begins. The research just reviewed also suggests that phonics programs (with their sound–letter correspondence emphasis) might be preceded by or supplemented with instruction on onsets and rimes. This approach may be a key to unlocking phonemic awareness (as Adams, 1990; Treiman, 1991, 1992, suggest). However, it may also be important to early reading independent of phonemic awareness (Goswami & Bryant, 1990).

Including training at the subsyllabic onset and rime level may address one pervasive criticism of the phonics approach. Because sound–letter correspondences are rather markedly inconsistent, critics of the phonics method argue that children must undoubtedly discover the overwhelming majority of them on their own (e.g., F. Smith, 1973, 1988). Vowels, in particular, are "rampantly inconsistent" (Adams, 1990, p. 246). However, "the representation of rimes by sequences of letters is certainly a great deal more reliable than the representation of phonemes by single letters" (Goswami & Bryant, 1990, p. 147). Vowel sounds are also far more predictable in the context of rimes (Adams, 1990, p. 320). Perhaps this consistency explains the stronger relationship of rhyme tasks than phoneme awareness tasks to beginning reading. That is, children may be using onset and rime knowledge to read even though they are not explicitly taught to do so.

Criticism of phonics methods also arises when phonics is used in isolation and not supplemented with activities in which print is used in ways that are meaningful and important to children. The research on emergent literacy discussed earlier clearly supports a facilitative role of key activities such as reading to children and allowing them to explore writing (even before they can do so conventionally) in laying the foundation for early reading. From these activities, children learn the functions of print and the practical utility it holds for them. This "larger picture" of print may be important both motivationally and cognitively. Cognitively, it exposes children to the higher order dimensions of print and allows them to use these top–down insights as they approach print (see also Adams, 1990, in press). Hence, a focus on sound awareness gives bottom–up strategies introduced separately from, but ultimately coordinated with, top–down strategies developed by exposure to meaningful print. The bottom–up and top–down strands for beginning reading and writing are depicted in Figure 3–8. The bottom–up strand most closely corresponds with phonics approaches and the top–down strand with whole language (e.g., C. Weaver, 1990) approaches.

The cognitive stage model of metalinguistic development presented earlier supports the strands of development posited in Figure 3–8. Recall that in the earliest stage of metalinguistic development (stage 1), the child has a definite preference for focusing on meaning. Form can be attended to at this stage, but only when meaning is de-emphasized or absent. As such, the top–down approach described here may best be emphasized initially, because it introduces the goal of print—to convey meaning. The individual sounds of words and of letters are presented during stage 1 without being tied to meaning. The alphabetic insight that those individual sounds of letters correspond to sounds in meaningful words would be expected to occur at stage 2. Now the child can integrate form and meaning simultaneously.

Some researchers believe that problems in learning to read may for some children lie in difficulties at

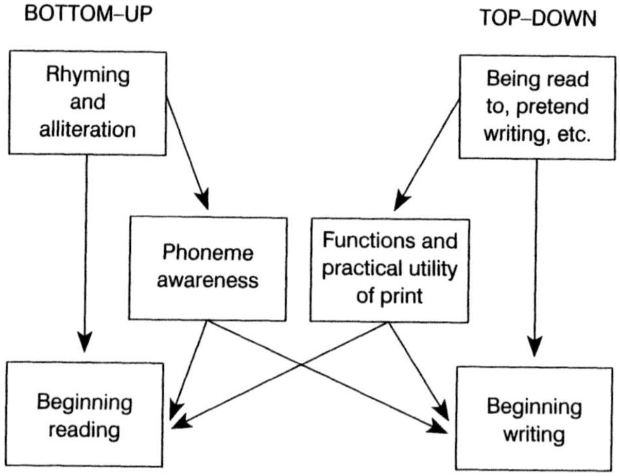

FIGURE 3–8
Bottom–up and top–down contributions to early reading ability

the phonological rather than the metaphonological (i.e., phonological awareness) level of representation. I. Liberman and Shankweiler, for example, note that

> evidence of various kinds has led us to consider seriously the possibility that the problems of the disabled reader may not be limited to metalinguistic deficits but may reflect a more general deficiency in the phonological domain. (1991, p. 9) (see also Blachman, chap. 9; Catts, 1989; Wagner & Torgesen, 1987)

Secret Languages. Secret languages are perhaps the capstone of children's language play in general and of phonological awareness specifically. They are also the crowning achievement of a variety of types of language play that are used by the childhood culture to perpetuate its own lore (Opie & Opie, 1959). In addition to secret languages, this language play includes playground chants, jump-rope rhymes, hand-clap songs, puns, and ritualized insults, such as, "I'm the king of the castle and you're a dirty rascal" (Sanches & Kirshenblatt-Gimblett, 1976, p. 72). These various forms of linguistic play are distinctive in that they do not represent linguistic creations by individual children (as have other examples of language play provided previously) but are instead traditions transmitted within the childhood culture. Children essentially socialize each other in these traditions of language play.

Bernstein (1960) discusses the interrelated social functions served by these "public" forms of language play—public in that they "continuously signal the normative arrangements of the group rather than the individual experiences of its members" (p. 179). Because it is public language in the child culture, speech play serves to (a) insulate the child from full responsibility for what she or he says, (b) reinforce group solidarity, and (c) make the child "sensitive to role and status and also to the customary relationships connecting and legitimizing the social positions within his peer groups" (p. 179). Regarding secret languages specifically, "a common function of [these] play languages is concealment and a corresponding delineation of social groups and subgroups" (Sherzer, 1976, p. 34). Facility with these various forms of language play, as such, allows the child access to and membership in the childhood culture (see also Nelson, chap. 4, on school culture, particularly the "underground curriculum").

The phonological segmentation skills that underlie secret languages are often rather substantial, because they must be accomplished "on-line" as the child also attempts to produce and comprehend meaningful messages. Pig Latin is probably one of the best known and easiest secret languages to learn, and yet even it requires a fair amount of phonological awareness. To produce Pig Latin, one must move the onset (whether a single consonant or a consonant cluster) to the end of the word and then add the syllable ay. If the word starts with a vowel, one simply adds way to the end of the word.

Secret languages seem to be most popular in late childhood before children reach their teen years (e.g., Conklin, 1956; Haas, 1957; Kirshenblatt-Gimblett, 1976). In informal interviews conducted by the author with elementary schoolchildren a few years ago, nearly all who knew a secret language indicated that they had learned it in the fifth grade (when most of them would have been around ten to eleven years of age). Cowan (1989) followed a kindergarten child learning Pig Latin, indicating that it is certainly possible to embark on learning this secret language earlier than fifth grade. Indeed, in their studies of an extremely sophisticated type of language play—talking backward— Cowan and Leavitt (1982) note that the majority of their subjects remembered that they began to do so between seven and twelve years of age, while the remainder reported having begun in their early teens. The subjects who learned as young as seven to nine years of age were undoubtedly very precocious metalinguistically.

Word Awareness

Segmenting Sentences into Words. As children become aware that spoken language consists of individual words, they begin to be able to break sentences down into their constituent words. This skill may be related to word consciousness discussed earlier, but it is also different in one important respect. Word consciousness focuses a child on the fact that words are separate from their referents. This does not necessarily ensure the ability to segment the acoustic stream of speech in a sentence into its component words—a skill requiring phonological awareness.

Children's ability to segment sentences into words on experimental tasks was discussed earlier (and in Blachman, chap. 9), where it was viewed (by some at least) as a step in developing phonological awareness. In addition to their performance on the experimental tasks discussed earlier, one also sees examples of children's word awareness in their spontaneous comments, practice, and play with language.

Many young children have been observed spontaneously engaging in a word substitution exercise that very much resembles drills often used in teaching adults a second language. The child will repeat a sentence numerous times, substituting a new word (often the last word of the sentence) with each production. So, a child aged 2;6 in van Kleeck and Bryant's study (1984) substituted words in a familiar verse, saying, "Dog ran away with the spoon. Dog ran away with dog. Dog ran away with dish." And, a child aged 3;6 offered the following as she rode along in the car with her mother, "That drives me bananas. That drives me nuts. That drives me gas stations. That drives me trees. That drives me cars. That drives me signs. . . ." All fourteen children Kuczaj (1983) followed during the period that they produced bedtime monologues (from approximately 1;6 to 3;0 years) gave examples of such word substitutions.

Besides word substitutions, children will sometimes comment on word boundaries. One delightful example of word boundary confusion was provided by a child aged 4;0. The child asked, "Mommy, is it AN A-dult or A Nuh-dult?" (Gleitman, Gleitman, & Shipley, 1972, p. 139). Chaney (1989) asked children to segment The Pledge of Allegiance by asking them to say just one word at a time so she could write it down. Some of the amusing word boundary confusions she observed were, "for witches stand" (for which it stands), "to three the pug lit" (to the republic), and "night of steaks/stakes" (United States).

Beginning Reading. The ability to segment sentences into their component words is deemed necessary to early reading because, to associate spoken and written words, the child must realize that one spoken word corresponds to one written word (Bialystok & Ryan, 1985; Biemiller, 1970). And indeed, children's awareness of aural word boundaries has been found to be a significant predictor of beginning reading achievement in first graders (Evans, Taylor, & Blum, 1979; McNinch, 1974; Morris, 1980).

Seeking Word Meaning. In children's earliest uses of words, those words are tied to communicative functions such as requesting objects. At some point during the single-word phase of development, children arrive at what has been called the "naming insight" (McShane, 1979, 1980). That is, they come to an awareness that words represent concepts independent of the communicative functions they can serve. Words become symbols (Nelson, 1983) in addition to serving as a means to an end. And, not surprisingly, the child experiences a rapid increase in vocabulary at this juncture.

On the advent of the naming insight, children may begin asking "what's that?" for countless items they encounter. In this way, this insight about language provides a strategy for learning more language—in this case, more vocabulary. This insight is undoubtedly a far cry from conscious knowledge about language and hence cannot reasonably be considered a metalinguistic skill. However, a corollary behavior in older children is more explicit and correspondingly reflects a more conscious awareness of the nature of language.

For example, at age 3;1, Slobin's daughter Heida broke down an utterance into individual words or parts of words and asked for their meanings. She asked, "Are these little petal things? What's 'are these'? What's 'are'? What's 'me' mean?" On another occasion, Heida (aged 3;8) seemed confused about the meanings of *before* and *after* and asked, "What does 'before' mean?" (Slobin, 1978). Chaney and Estrin (1987) report similar examples for children under the age of three. In one instance, after hearing, "The ducks were beginning to molt," a child asked, "What's 'molt'?" In another, after hearing, "Humpty Dumpty sat on a wall," a child responded, "Satona, Sa . . . do . . . na. What's satona?"

Knowledge of Rules (or Linguistic Regularities). The rule systems of English, as mentioned earlier, are generally divided into those governing phonology (rules governing the sound system); morphology (rules for combining free and bound morphemes); syntax (rules governing word order, among other things); and semantics (rules governing the semantic roles of words and word co-occurrence—the latter being known as semantic selection restrictions). Knowledge of linguistic rules remains, for the most part, largely unconscious. And indeed, even the most brilliant linguist falls short in being able to make all linguistic knowledge conscious—knowledge that we so blithely apply in our day-to-day use of language. If, as mentioned earlier, some current scholars are correct and rules turn out not to have psychological reality but only descriptive utility, the word *rules* in this section could be replaced with the word *regularities* (because the fact of systematicity in language is not debated).

Children, as well, converse freely if somewhat less effectively than adults, while remaining quite oblivious to the underlying linguistic rules governing verbal behavior. And yet, becoming at least somewhat conscious of the rule-governed nature of language is believed to underlie abilities that either can make a communicator more effective (e.g., making on-line corrections of linguistic errors or adjusting to one's listener) or can enhance a child's more advanced abilities in dealing with print.

Researchers have attempted to directly tap children's knowledge of the rule systems by having them make judgments about the grammatical correctness—or grammaticality—of sentences presented to them. And, once again, spontaneous evidence of children's nascent awareness of rule systems is found in their play and practice with language (see Figure 3–7).

Grammaticality Judgments. In grammaticality judgment tasks, researchers present children with either grammatically acceptable or unacceptable sentences and ask them to judge them. Children might be asked, for example, if a given sentence is either "good" or "silly." Sometimes they are simply given a sentence and asked, "Is that right?" Emerson (1980) used clown and teacher puppets to help children make "sensible" and "silly" judgments. Sentences offered may be either accurately produced, or they may violate phonological rules (e.g., could you say, "Read the mook?"); morphological rules (could you say, "Their parents wented to work?"); syntactic rules (could you say, "boy the ball kicks"); or semantic selection restriction rules (could you say, "That plate drove the car?").

The norms from a test called the Analysis of the Language of Learning: The Practical Test of Metalinguistics perhaps provides one of the best developmental comparisons of the various types of grammaticality judgments (Blodgett & Cooper, 1987). A subtest entitled Repairing Sentences has children correct a total of twenty-four sentences, six each in the categories of word order, semantics, grammar (specifically, morphology), and phonology. From their norming sample of six hundred children (approximately one hundred each at one-year intervals from ages 4;0 through 9;11), a distinct developmental progression for these metalinguistic judgments emerges.

The clearest developmental trends in these data emerged from ages 4;0 to 6;0. Beyond that age, performance was quite high on all the tasks. The pattern that emerged for the younger children was that phonological repairs were the easiest. Semantic selection restriction violations and morphological errors were somewhat harder, and performance on these two types of repairs was quite similar. Word order corrections were the most difficult.

Previous research supports aspects of the data. Several studies have found that by age 4;0, children can accurately judge sentences that present selection restriction rule violations (Carr, 1979; Howe & Hillman, 1973; James & Miller, 1973). These young children, however, are unsuccessful on syntactic acceptability judgments. At this age, they appear to judge the truth value or assertion of these utterances rather than focusing on whether the linguistic form is acceptable (Bohannon, 1975; deVilliers & deVilliers, 1974; Gleitman et al., 1972; Hakes, 1980; James & Miller, 1973; Leonard, Bolders, & Curtis, 1977). Gleitman and her colleagues (1972) provide an excellent example of this. The suburbanite children in their study judged the syntactically correct utterance "The men wait for the bus" to be inaccurate on the grounds that only children wait for buses.

Practice and Play. Besides grammaticality judgment tasks posed by researchers and testers, children's knowledge of the rule systems of language is often revealed in their play and practice with language (although Kuczaj, 1982, notes that it is often quite difficult to distinguish between practice and play). Modifications that occur in language play have been categorized as buildups, breakdowns, completions, and substitutions (Kuczaj, 1983; Weir, 1962). Kuczaj provides examples of each:

- Buildup: Block. Yellow Block. Look at all the yellow blocks.
- Breakdown: Clock off. Clock. Off.
- Completion: Anthony take the (pause), take the box.
- Substitution: Heather's bad. I'm bad. You bad. (1983, pp. 3–4)

The earliest modifications focus on the sound system (e.g., Garvey, 1977; Weeks, 1979). Kuczaj (1983) notes, however, that manipulations of syntax and morphology begin quite early and are most common from ages 1;6 to 3;6 (Braine, 1971, 1974; Britton, 1970; Craig & Gallagher, 1979; Scollon, 1976; Snyder, 1914; Weeks, 1979; Weir, 1962).

As with other early emerging behaviors, practice and play that involve the rule systems of language do not constitute strong evidence for conscious awareness of those rules. They are included in a discussion of metalinguistic development, however, because they involve a focus on language form, and the ability to consciously focus on language form is the crux of many later developing skills that are more clearly metalinguistic in nature.

Correcting Self and Others. Several investigators suggest that detecting and repairing errors made in conversation is metalinguistic because "conscious intervention is [then] required and the language user is—momentarily at least—in some fashion aware of the linguistic entity that causes the problem" (Levelt, Sinclair, & Jarvella, 1978, p. 9). In natural conversations, repairs can involve correcting oneself or others. Self-corrections can be either spontaneous or elicited by others (e.g., after a request for clarification).

To the extent that such repairs are carried out to aid the listener's understanding, they serve the goal of facilitating the success of communication. However, although children's repairs are often viewed as motivated by attempts to help the listener understand, E. Clark and Andersen (1979) argue that they are often not needed to help understanding. Instead, children's repairs often seem to function as repairs to the children's own growing system of knowledge regarding language. Indeed, such repairs often reflect monitoring of "just those parts of the system the child is in the process of acquiring" (p. 7). Clark and Andersen plot the growth of such repairs as moving from being primarily focused on phonology, to morphology, to the lexicon, and finally to syntax. Note that this is basically the same developmental progression witnessed for grammaticality judgments and (although more generally) for language practice and play as well.

As with practice and play, ample evidence indicates that corrections or repairs occur from the very earliest stages of language development. Regarding elicited repairs, Gallagher (1977) provided evidence that in the earliest stages of language development, children either repeat, or more frequently attempt to revise or correct their own speech after an indication of communication failure (e.g., in response to an adult asking, "What?").

Children will also monitor others. A common manifestation of this begins around the age of 4;0, when children sometimes comment on or correct the mistakes of younger siblings. Weir (1962) provides an example:

> Michael (2;4): Record 'top. Mine.
> Anthony (5;4): Mike says only top instead of stop.

Another type of repair occurs as children self-monitor their own speech. Scollon (1976) reports examples of a child aged 1;6 repeating words several times, often changing a subsequent production to more closely match the adult pronunciation. E. Clark and Andersen's (1979) longitudinal study of the spontaneous repairs in three children (whose ages ranged from 2;2 to 3;7) extends beyond Scollon's findings. Like Scollon, they note that children's earliest repairs tend to be phonological. The proportion of phonological repairs subsequently decreases with age, and lexical and syntactic repairs increase. Finally, they note that an older group of children (ages 4;0 to 7;0) made repairs or adjustments to the speech style register when role playing a father, mother, child, doctor, and nurse.

Adjusting to One's Listener. Children often adjust their language in response to various characteristics of their listener. This is reflected in the various general speech styles (or registers) a speaker can adopt to promote effective, appropriate communication in a particular social setting. These are considered metalinguistic skills because the speaker presumably chooses (and therefore to an extent focuses on) the specific language forms—the syntactic structures and vocabulary—that are most appropriate to the situation. And the child may be quite aware (or at least quite explicitly reminded) that certain language forms or manners of speaking are or are not appropriate to a given social situation. Admonitions to say "thank you" to the adult proffering a compliment provide an example of such context-sensitive reminders. Children undoubtedly sometimes internalize some of these "rules" without explicit teaching, as they might when monitoring (and subsequently mitigating) playground expletives in the presence of authority-wielding adults.

Some rules for altering language content and form to fit social situations are explicitly taught and consciously executed. Furthermore, much listener adaptation undoubtedly is not determined by sociocultural norms and occurs automatically and unconsciously. Indeed, a large body of research on adult's communicative behavior indicates that participants in conversations (who like each other) often begin communicating similarly. That is, they converge on each other's rate, intensity, pitch, accent, linguistic structure, and so forth. Furthermore, these adjustments may be enacted automatically with little or no conscious awareness (e.g., Berger, 1980).

Similarly, preschool children adjust numerous aspects of language form automatically and unconsciously when speaking to a two-year-old versus an adult (Shatz & Gelman, 1973), to a sighted person versus one they are told is blind (Maratsos, 1973), or to developmentally delayed peers (Guralnick & Paul-Brown, 1977). For example, four-year-olds' utterances to a two-year-old or to a developmentally delayed peer were shorter and syntactically less complex than their utterances to an adult. When speaking to someone they were told was blind, children in this age range gave more explicit messages, hence adjusting their language semantically.

Another manifestation of speech style adjustments is evidenced in the dialogue used by children as they take on various roles in their play. Andersen (1977) had children aged 4;0 to 7;0 enact the dialogue of a puppet in the roles of a father, mother, and baby and in the roles of a doctor, nurse, and child patient. She found that even her youngest subjects adjusted their speech to differentiate among the three family roles. For example, in assuming the father role, the content of the children's talk centered on business-oriented issues. The style was straightforward, unqualified, and forceful. In assuming the mother role, the content revolved around issues of family care. The style was more talkative, polite, qualified, and softer. The pronunciation contained more "baby-talk" forms.

That these types of adjustments are not the result of explicit socialization or even modeling is suggested by the Shatz and Gelman study (1973). In their study, four-year-olds with and without two-year-old siblings made similar kinds of adjustments in their language addressed to two-year-olds. Even more convincing evidence that many such adjustments are not consciously carried out comes from a study demonstrating that babies use a higher fundamental frequency on average in their babbling to an adult female than when babbling to an adult male, and their very highest average frequency occurs in solitary babbling (Lieberman, 1966). Quite possibly, even these more automatic kinds of listener adaptations might eventually come under more conscious control. In this sense, metalinguistic skill might enhance the speaker's facility in using language as a social-interactive tool.

Piaget (1976) discusses how, without awareness, success in practical skills is achieved by trial and error. In the process of becoming aware of the action, the child comes to understand all the possibilities in the situation. This allows deliberate choice of the most effective means to replace the less efficient trial and error solutions. Extending this notion into the language domain specifically, one sees how awareness of language form and meaning might potentially enhance the instrumental use of language in context.

As children eventually become able not only to make such modifications but also to consciously judge appropriateness, more awareness can be assumed. At this point, these skills would be considered both metalinguistic (because form is consciously manipulated) and metapragmatic (because the form adjustments are sensitive to the use of language in context). Children demonstrate an ability to make linguistic adjustments as a function of listener characteristics very early in their careers as communicators. Not surprisingly, the ability to make judgments about situational appropriateness emerges at a developmentally later time.

Later Reading Skills. The roles of word consciousness and phonological awareness were discussed earlier as critical skills in the early stages of reading acquisition. One of the child's tasks in learning to read is to discover that written words correspond to spoken words by noting the systematic correspondences between their respective subunits of graphemes (letters) and phonemes (represented by sounds). At this juncture, the child begins to recognize printed words—one-by-one—but still may not be able to comprehend the overall meaning being conveyed at the sentence or text level (P. Weaver & Shonkoff, 1978). This led some researchers to claim that the ability to decode is necessary but not sufficient for reading comprehension (Cromer, 1970; Goodman, 1973).

Tunmer and Bowey (1984) contrast the early stage of learning to read, or decoding, with the later stage, in which comprehension takes precedence, by considering the shift in metalinguistic focus at these two stages (note, however, that advocates of a whole language approach would not view decoding as an initial stage of reading) (see also Wallach & Butler, chap. 1). They suggest that awareness shifts from a primary focus on phonemes and words in the first stage to a focus on structural aspects of language (generated by the rules systems) in the later stage.

> In the early reading acquisition process, the child must *ignore* information that is not relevant to the task at hand. He must separate the word from its sentential context . . . and focus his attention on discovering systematic correspondences between the units of written and spoken *words*.

> But as soon as the child has fairly well mastered the grapheme–phoneme correspondence rules, he must change his strategy and put humpty-dumpty back together again. He must consciously begin to organize the text into higher-order *syntactic* groupings, since the structures of sentences are crucial to their understanding. He must therefore bring his syntactic knowledge of the spoken language to bear upon the written language, which again requires the metalinguistic ability to reflect upon the structural features of spoken language. (p. 163)

Other researchers have taken a somewhat different tack in conceptualizing later reading by suggesting that it integrates a variety of skills. From this view, efficient reading is considered to require the ability to simultaneously process phonology, syntax, and semantics with contextual knowledge to infer meaning (e.g., M. Clark, 1978; Goodman & Goodman, 1977; Nelson, chap. 4; Silliman & Wilkinson, chap. 6). Some who espouse the whole language approach would argue that this integration need not be conceived of as a later stage of reading. Instead, they would propose that this integration can happen earlier if the environment *allows* it (e.g., C. Weaver, 1990).

APPLICATIONS TO LANGUAGE ASSESSMENT AND INTERVENTION

The realm of metalinguistic development is obviously broad. It affects a wide variety of skills children need to both effectively use the linguistic code in ongoing social interaction and to achieve success in the highly verbal and print-literate environment of our schools. Even in work with language delayed toddlers and preschoolers, clinicians and teachers must begin preparing them for the more sophisticated uses of language that require a more conscious focus on the linguistic code that will dominate their later classroom experience. Such efforts may help avoid the classroom failure that awaits far too many of these children who, as discussed in the next section, often have difficulties with metalinguistic skills.

Metalinguistic Skills in Language Disordered Children

Keen observers of language delayed children have been aware of their difficulties with metalinguistic skills for many years, long before the term *metalinguistics* was widely used. As early as 1976, for example, Wiig and Semel discussed numerous language deficits in language-learning disabled children that are metalinguistic in nature.

Of the kindergartner, Wiig and Semel stated, "He is not able to sit through a story, learn the alphabet, word rhyming, finger plays or songs, or make one-to-one correspondences between sounds and letters" (1976, p. 5). In the first grade, "they may have problems in same–different discriminations of sounds, in analyzing and synthesizing phoneme sequences, in segmenting words into smaller grammatical units, and in forming stable sound–symbol associations. These deficits may result in limited or slow academic achievement in spelling, reading, and math, among others" (p. 5).

Elsewhere, Wiig and Semel (1976) noted other deficits in skills now considered to be metalinguistic. These include interpreting ambiguous sentences, idioms, puns (p. 27), multiple-meaning words, metaphors (p. 31), synonyms (p. 33), verbal opposites, and verbal analogies (p. 35). Corroborating Wiig and Semel's clinical and classroom observations, Blue (1981) discussed five uses of language that are particularly problematic for language disordered children. Three require metalinguistic ability: understanding idioms, ambiguous statements, and words with multiple meanings. Blue suggested avoiding these uses of language with language delayed children, which is probably not the best solution. Clearly, however, Blue also repeatedly noticed metalinguistic skill deficits in the language disordered children with whom he worked.

Subsequent empirical research has supported many of these clinical and classroom observations. Regarding the arbitrary nature of language, for example, language disordered children have difficulty producing and comprehending metaphor (Lee & Kamhi, 1985; Nippold & Fey, 1983). Their difficulty in dealing with language as a system is reflected in problems in segmenting language into its component units (Kamhi, Lee, & Nelson, 1985) and in making syntactic and morphologic grammaticality judgments (Dunton, Fujiki & Brinton, 1984; Kamhi & Koenig, 1985; Liles, Shulman, & Bartlett, 1977; Perry, Newhoff, & Buday, 1983). Joffe and Shapiro (1991) found that the six-year-old language-impaired children they studied were unable to successfully engage in sound-based language play. Kamhi (1987) reviews additional research on the metalinguistic task difficulties encountered by many language disordered children.

Recent research has revealed an interesting finding regarding a most important metalinguistic skill—learning to read—and phonologically impaired children. Although many language delayed children have problems learning to read, this is not true of most children with phonological disorders who have no concomitant language disorder. Three studies have independently revealed that children exhibiting phonological disorders in preschool are not likely to have later reading and spelling deficits (Bishop & Adams, 1990; Lewis & Freebairn, 1992; Shriberg & Kwiatkowski, 1988).

Metalinguistic tasks are likely to also be difficult for some children who are not language delayed. Some children may not have been exposed to language play, rhyming, or books and as such may not have had the opportunity to develop a metalinguistic orientation to language. Others may simply lack talent with language, just as some children may lack musical or athletic talent. To guide the teacher or language specialist in working with any children experiencing difficulties with metalinguistic skills, the next sections focus on assessment and intervention issues.

Metalinguistic Assessment

As with any area of language, metalinguistic assessment is undoubtedly best accomplished informally by observing children in contexts that are as naturalistic as possible. One could efficiently determine a great deal about a child's metalinguistic skills, for example, by creating a small book designed to probe those skills. The adult tells the child that, rather than reading this book like one reads stories, they will talk about lots of different things in the book. The book could, for example, contain some rhymes that inspired a discussion about rhyming and an opportunity to see if the child could rhyme. The adult could also easily assess letter knowledge, the child's grasp of sound–letter correspondences, and segmentation abilities (at the word, syllable, onset and rime, and phoneme levels) by first providing some models from the book and then seeing what the child can do. Some long objects denoted by short words (e.g., *train*) and vice-versa, or a common object given a nonsense or foreign-language name, might effectively elicit word–referent differentiation skills (see Figure 3–6, page 68). The story could contain some idioms, metaphors, and multiple-meaning words to assess how the child copes with both figurative and ambiguous language. And it could also contain dialogue from a "very young child" with some grammatical, morphological, and phonological errors. These could be used to probe the child's ability to make grammaticality judgments and to correct and explain them. Emerging print concepts, such as knowing that English print goes from left to right, could also easily be ascertained.

Alternatively, one could use standardized tests to tap metalinguistic abilities, although not many are designed explicitly to do so. One test that has been published assesses 4;6- to 7;0-year-old children's segmentation abilities at the word, syllable, and sound levels (Sawyer, 1987). Unfortunately, this test does not tap subsyllabic segmentation on onset and rime, either directly or through rhyming ability.

Another test, called Analysis of the Language of Learning: The Practical Test of Metalinguistics, was developed for children ages 4;0 to 9;11 (Blodgett & Cooper, 1987). In addition to assessing select segmentation abilities (sentences into words and words into sounds), it also assesses the child's ability to correct grammatical errors (of word order, phonology, semantics, and morphology) and to recognize, generate examples of, and define language concepts such as *letter, word, rhyming word, spelling, sentence,* and *story.* This test has norms generated from a sample of 1,324 children and, as such, may be useful when a standardized test score is mandatory. However, the information could be obtained informally, which would likely be both more efficient and ecologically valid (also see Blachman, chap. 9, for ideas on assessing phonological awareness).

Numerous tests of emergent literacy have been developed in the last few years. They often assess such concepts as awareness of environmental print, the alphabet and its functions, conventions of written language, functions of print, story grammar, and early writing concepts (see van Kleeck, 1990; van Kleeck & Richardson, 1990, for specific tests). Although the norms provided for many of these tests are helpful when standardized test scores are necessary, the information these tests provide can more easily and efficiently be obtained informally.

One can glean further information about a child's metalinguistic skills from bits and pieces of other commercially available language tests. Two examples follow. A subtest of the Clinical Evaluation of Language Functions (CELF) has items assessing idiom, metaphor, and proverb comprehension (Semel & Wiig, 1980). One item testing idiom comprehension provides an example of the format used on this test: "Vanessa was struck by the point. Does it mean Vanessa was hit by the point of a sharp instrument?" The Word Test (Jorgensen, Barrett, Huisingh, & Zachman, 1981) contains a subtest designed to determine the child's ability to understand dual- or multiple-meaning words. One learns if the child can relate several meanings of, for example, the word *block* (as a shape, a portion of a neighborhood, and an action found in the game of football).

In addition to these tests designed to assess language abilities that have metalinguistic components, intelligence tests also often contain subtests that are metalinguistic in nature. For example, on these tests children may be asked to give definitions, complete verbal analogies, rhyme, crack secret codes, and solve anagrams. All of these skills require that the child consciously focus on and, in some cases, manipulate language.

In some respects, all formal language tests may be considered to be somewhat metalinguistic, even if they do not contain explicitly metalinguistic components. Formal tests measure language skills by taking them out of the interactive contexts in which they are typically used. Furthermore, they often require that the child focus on language in ways that would be inappropriate in a social context (e.g., a child might be asked to repeat verbatim semantically unrelated sentences presented by the examiner). Indeed, this requires children to ignore their knowledge about the social uses of language! As such, formal language tests may reveal more about how children deal with decontextualized language than how they can use language in the social-interactive contexts.

Formal tests also reflect children's ability to focus on language independently. That is, most formal tests do not allow examiner support once the initial task demonstration items have been completed. In this sense, formal tests provide information about the latest emerging phases of representational development depicted in Figure 3–4. At this point, children are in full control of the behavior and can function independently. As stated in Figure 3–4, children can now consciously access more abstract representations and explain their knowledge. Formal tests, as such, capture a mastery of a skill. Informal assessments, especially when the examiner freely supports children's efforts, are far more likely to tap skills that are just emerging or are in the process of being acquired.

Intervention

In language intervention, a distinction is made between goals (*what* one wishes to facilitate) and procedures (*how* such facilitation will, it is hoped, be accomplished). The notion of language awareness can potentially influence the clinical or classroom treatment of language disorders in both of these respects. First, it is relevant to the procedures used in intervention. Even when the broad goal is to enhance the child's communicative uses of language, the procedures may sometimes involve making the child consciously aware of language, particularly if the child is school-aged or older. This would constitute a metalinguistic approach to facilitating social-interactive uses of language. Second, metalinguistic skills might themselves constitute the goals of language intervention.

Metalinguistic Procedures. In general, language development specialists have shifted away from metalinguistic procedures for facilitating language as the need for pragmatically relevant intervention contexts has been increasingly acknowledged during the last decade. Few would currently advocate a metalinguistic approach to teaching a nonverbal child, for example, although there have been such programs historically (e.g., Carrier, 1974). Such a practice is contrary to the normal developmental progression; children often use language forms for years before they can consciously reflect on and make judgments about them.

The picture might change with older children who have a great deal of language, but who nonetheless still lag substantially behind their peers. If the cognitive stage model discussed earlier is valid, children in the concrete operational stage of cognitive development may have the ability to consciously reflect on language forms they have not yet mastered. If therapy is focused on a particularly entrenched grammatical inaccuracy, a child might benefit from explicit discussion and demonstration of the "rule" being violated. It seems unlikely, however, that a well-practiced behavior would change just from discussing it. As such, one would suspect that such explicit procedures would be most efficacious if used in conjunction with other, more naturalistic, procedures that allowed plenty of practice in real-life contexts.

Metalinguistic Goals. Social-interactive uses of language are always foundational in language intervention. If a child has problems interacting, intervention starts there. The social-interactive uses of language retain paramount importance throughout life. As such, using language as a social tool remains very important to the language disordered child's overall development. After a child enters school, however, other uses of language are also essential to the child's success. It is no longer enough for children to be good at using language to interact socially. To succeed in the educational system, children must learn "to turn language and thought in upon themselves" (Donaldson, 1978, p. 90). Language "turned in upon itself" is the very definition of metalinguistic ability. All of the skills discussed in this chapter therefore become viable goals for intervention. But why wait until the child experiences school failure to consider facilitating a child's ability to consciously focus on language?

Introducing Metalinguistic Skills to Preschoolers. The shift to a metalinguistic focus once in school may be rather abrupt for some children, particularly those with a history of language learning difficulties. Such abruptness might be alleviated if language specialists working with preschoolers plan a gradual transition between early social and these later metalinguistic uses of language used in a classroom. Constable and van Kleeck proposed just such a conceptual framework for working with language delayed preschoolers (1985). They conceived of language intervention as involving the therapist's manipulation of three aspects of the context: nonlinguistic, linguistic, and metalinguistic. Over time during the preschool years, the relative emphasis shifts from being first on the nonlinguistic component, to later being on the linguistic component, to finally being on the linguistic and metalinguistic components of the context. A rather simplified portrayal of this shift in clinical focus over time is presented in Figure 3–9.

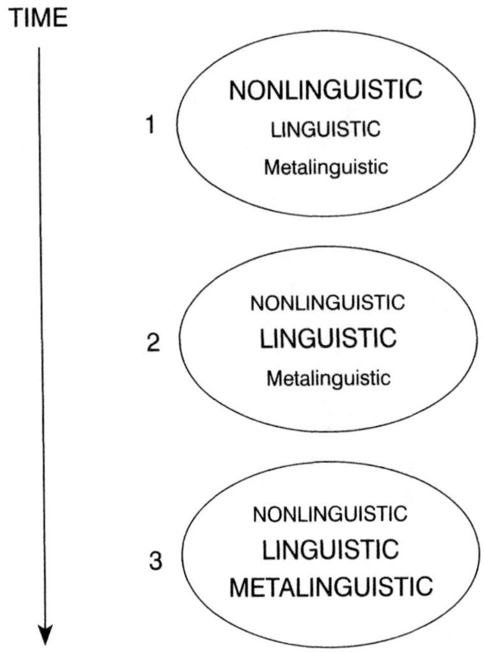

FIGURE 3–9
The changing emphasis on the nonlinguistic, linguistic, and metalinguistic components of the intervention context over time during the preschool years

In Figure 3–9, time 1 depicts the earliest stages of intervention. At this point, the nonlinguistic context is emphasized. Time is devoted to doing a practical, concrete activity to establish a cognitive context (a routine event) to support the expression of early language forms. Language at this stage is about the practical action, or it is used to negotiate the practical action (e.g., allocating turns at the practical action).

Rudiments of metalinguistic skill are introduced occasionally at time 1, primarily by modeling them and encouraging the child to attempt them. They are embedded as naturally as possible in established routines, such as making popcorn or reading a story. Some examples might include playing with sound devoid of meaning (particularly rhyme and alliteration); making up new names for objects the child can already name; exchanging words in well-known sequences such as nursery rhymes ("Humpty Dumpty sat on a chair"); commenting on words that are hard to say (e.g., "tyrannosaurus rex"); and having the child participate in various activities that involve the adult using print (making a list of things you'll need to make popcorn tomorrow, referring out loud to a recipe while making something, reading a story, writing a birthday card, etc.).

Time 2 in Figure 3–9 represents the gradual increase in emphasis on the linguistic input that coordinates with the nonlinguistic activity. Because the structure for the nonverbal event is by now well-known, violations in the expected script can be used to stimulate more linguistic initiations (especially of protests and directives) and more complex language from the child. Violations might involve skipping a child's turn, performing parts of the activity in the wrong order (e.g., trying to pour the milk before the lid has been opened), having the wrong object, not being able to find needed objects, having several choices for needed objects, using the wrong object for the task, and so forth. These violations can foster big negotiations (and hence lots of talk) over little issues (e.g., which spoon to use in mixing the pudding).

Also at time 2, the adult can begin making the transition from doing the activity to talking about the activity. This retelling is an important precursor to the language of discussion characteristic of classroom settings. Adults can continue to model and encourage the metalinguistic focuses discussed for time 1. Metalinguistic words—words used to talk about aspects of language—might also be introduced (e.g., *word, story, sentence,* and *letter*).

As indicated in Figure 3–9, by time 3 the focus on physically doing the activity is decreased, while the linguistic and metalinguistic emphases are increased. Hence the child is increasing his or her ability to attend to proportionately more language constituted activity. Violations of the routine event are also further increased, setting the child up for the "what is the correct answer" game so familiar in the elementary classroom.

The primary catalyst for the changes proposed by Constable and van Kleeck (1985) for time 3 is an "activity board"—a large pad of paper placed on an easel. This is used to help the child make the transition to representing the routine activity with print. Before actual print is introduced in isolation, however, first pictures and then line drawings with print under them can be used. The pictures and drawings can be gradually faded out.

In sum, Constable and van Kleeck (1985) suggest moving the child over time from doing an activity, to talking about the activity, to finally representing the activity with print. Furthermore, a metalinguistic focus on language is naturally introduced throughout, beginning with the earliest stages of intervention.

The teacher or clinician might also facilitate rudimentary language awareness in preschoolers outside of the context of meaningful activities proposed by Constable and van Kleeck. Language games that foster metalinguistic ability can constitute activities in themselves. Many ideas for language games to play with children from birth through the elementary school grades are offered by McCabe (1987) and Geller (1985).

Emphasizing Phonological Awareness among Kindergartners and First Graders. The gradual transition to more metalinguistic uses of language previously suggested for preschoolers might also be helpful, if the transition were less protracted, with kindergartners and even first graders. While focus on the sound system with preschoolers is done informally in play, some children may need more guidance than is offered in informal play. These children may benefit from a more structured approach to phonological awareness once they are in school. As mentioned earlier in this chapter, there have been numerous successful attempts to train phonological awareness in children at this level. Suggestions for such training are offered by Blachman (chap. 9) and by Catts (1991). Ideas can also be gleaned from the earlier section on phonological awareness in this chapter.

Facilitating Later Emerging Metalinguistic Skills. For the somewhat older school-aged child, the reader is referred to two texts that offer myriad suggestions for facilitating various aspects of metalinguistic ability. These are *Language Intervention and Academic Success* (Wallach & Miller, 1988) and *Steps to Language Competence: Developing Metalinguistic Strategies* (Wiig, 1989). The authors of each of the books construe the term *metalinguistic* somewhat differently from each other and from the perspective offered in this chapter. Nonetheless, there are concrete suggestions for facilitating many of the areas of metalinguistic skill development that were discussed here, including multiple-meaning words, figurative language, and text cohesion.

SUMMARY

Metalinguistic skills cover a vast territory of language abilities. They vary considerably in different children and in different adults. Some people are naturally talented with language. One of the most stunning "metalinguists" is perhaps Lewis Carroll. His language play was so intricate that it has kept scholars busy exploring it for over a century. In fact, an entire scholarly journal, *Jabberwocky,* published by the Lewis Carroll Society, is devoted to the language play in his works.

A recent discovery regarding *Alice's Adventures in Wonderland* was made by two high school seniors from New Jersey. The "Mouse's Tale" they studied contains numerous well-known puns. In the text, the "tale" is typed in the visual form of a mouse's tail, hence the tail includes the tale. The tale is also told in a form known as a tail-rhyme. These two students uncovered yet another layer of Carrollian word play. When the tail-shaped tale was straightened out into traditional stanza form, each stanza took the form of a mouse. The first two lines were shorter and of roughly equal length, forming the body of the mouse. The third line was much longer, forming the mouse's tail ("Tale in Tail(s)," 1991). These two young men are quite precocious "metalinguists" themselves!

And so, metalinguistics need not be equated with classroom drudgery. Language play can be great fun. Adults who inspire children to experience this fun not only foster children's academic success. They also guide children into a world of limitless capacity—the world of language!

REFERENCES

Adams, M. (in press). Why not phonics *and* whole language? In W. Ellis (Ed.), *All language and the creation of literacy.* Baltimore: Orton Dyslexia Society.

Adams, M. (1990). *Beginning to read: Thinking and learning about print.* Cambridge, MA: MIT Press.

Andersen, E. (1977). Young children's knowledge of role-related speech differences: a mommy is not a daddy is not a baby. *Papers Reports Child Language Development, 13,* 83–90.

Bates, E. (1976). *Language and context: The acquisition of pragmatics.* New York: Academic Press.

Bates, E., Benigni, L., Bretherton, I., Camaioni, L., & Volterra, V. (1979). *The emergence of symbols: Cognition and communication in infancy.* New York: Academic.

Bateson, G. (1972). *Steps to an ecology of mind.* San Francisco: Chandler.

Ben Zeev, S. (1977). The influence of bilingualism on cognitive strategy and cognitive development. *Child Development, 48,* 1009–1018.

Bereiter, C., & Engelmann, S. (1966). *Teaching disadvantaged children in preschool.* Englewood Cliffs, NJ: Prentice-Hall.

Berger, C. (1980). Self-consciousness and the study of interpersonal attraction. In H. Giles, P. Robinson, & P. Smith (Eds.), *Language: Social Psychological Perspectives.* Oxford: Pergamon Press.

Bernstein, B. (1960). Review of "The lore and language of school children" by I. Opie and P. Opie. *British Journal of Sociology, 11,* 178–181.

Berthoud-Papandropoulou, I. (1978). An experimental study of children's ideas about language. In A. Sinclair, R. Jarvella, & W. Levelt (Eds.), *The child's conception of language.* (pp. 55–64). New York: Springer-Verlag.

Berthoud-Papandropoulou, I., & Sinclair, H. (1974). What is a word? Experimental study of children's ideas on grammar. *Human Development, 17,* 241–258.

Bialystok, E. (1986). Children's concept of word. *Journal of Psycholinguistic Research, 16,* 13–32.

Bialystok, E. (1987). Words as things: Development of word concept by bilingual children. *Studies in Second Language Acquisition, 9,* 133–140.

Bialystok, E. (1988). Levels of bilingualism and levels of linguistic awareness. *Developmental Psychology, 24,* 560–567.

Bialystok, E., & Ryan, E. (1985). A metacognitive framework for the development of first and second language skills. In D. Forrest-Pressley, G. MacKinnon, & T. Waller (Eds.), *Meta-cognition, cognition, and human performance.* New York: Academic Press.

Biemiller, A. (1970). The development of the use of graphic and contextual information as children learn to read. *Reading Research Quarterly, 6,* 75–96.

Biklen, D. (1990). Communication unbound. *Harvard Educational Review, 60,* 291–314.

Biklen, D., Morton, M., Gold, D., Berrigan, C., & Swaminathan, S. (1992). Facilitated communication: Implications for individuals with autism. *Topics in Language Disorders, 12*(3), 1–28.

Billow, R. (1981). Observing spontaneous metaphor in children. *Journal of Experimental Child Psychology, 31,* 430–445.

Bishop, D., & Adams, C. (1990). A prospective study of the relationship between specific language impairment, phonological disorders, and reading retardation. *Journal of Child Psychology and Psychiatry, 31,* 1027–1050.

Blodgett, E., & Cooper, E. (1987). *Analysis of the language of learning: The practical test of metalinguistics.* Moline, IL: LinguiSystems.

Bloom, L. (1973). *One word at a time: The use of single-word utterances before syntax.* The Hague, The Netherlands: Mouton.

Bloom, L. (1988). What is language? In M. Lahey, *Language disorders and language development.* New York: Macmillan.

Bloom, L., & Lahey, M. (1978). *Language development and language disorders.* New York: John Wiley & Sons.

Blue, M. (1981). Types of utterances to avoid when speaking to language-delayed children. *Language, Speech, and Hearing Services in Schools, 12,* 120–124.

Bohannon, J. (1975). The relationship between syntax discrimination and sentence imitation in children. *Child Development, 46,* 444–451.

Bowey, J., & Francis, J. (1991). Phonological analysis as a function of age and exposure to reading instruction. *Applied Psycholinguistics, 12,* 91–121.

Bowey, J., & Tunmer, W. (1984). Word awareness in children. In W. Tunmer, C. Pratl, & M. Herriman (Eds.), *Metalinguistic awareness in children: Theory, research, and implications.* Berlin: Springer-Verlag.

Braine, M. (1971). The acquisition of language in infant and child. In C. Reed (Ed.), *The learning of language.* Norwalk, CT: Appleton-Century-Crofts.

Braine, M. (1974). Length constraints, reduction rules, and holophrastic processes in children's word combinations. *Journal of Verbal Learning and Verbal Behavior, 13,* 448–456.

Brainerd, C. (1974). Training and transfer of transitivity, conservation, and class inclusion of length. *Child Development, 45,* 324–334.

Brainerd, C., & Hooper, F. (1975). A methodological analysis of developmental studies of identity conservation and equivalence conservation. *Psychological Bulletin, 82,* 725–737.

Britton, J. (1970). *Language and learning.* London: Penguin Books.

Brown, A., & DeLoache, J. (1978). Skills, plans, and self-regulation. In R. Sielger (Ed.), *Children's thinking: What develops.* Hillsdale, NJ: Lawrence Erlbaum.

Bruner, J. (1978). How to do things with words. In J. Bruner & A. Garton (Eds.), *Human growth and development.* Oxford, UK: Oxford University Press.

Bryant, P., Bradley, L., MacLean, M., & Crossland, J. (1989). Nursery rhymes, phonological skills and reading. *Journal of Child Language, 16* (2), 407–428.

Bryant, P., & Goswami, U. (1987). Phonological awareness and learning to read. In J. Beech & A. Colley (Eds.), *Cognitive approaches to reading.* Chichester, UK: Wiley.

Bryant, P., MacLean, M., & Bradley, L. (1990). Rhyme, language and children's reading. *Applied Psycholinguistics, 11,* 237–252.

Carlson, P., & Anisfeld, M. (1969). Some observations on the linguistic competence of a two-year-old child. *Child Development, 40,* 565–575.

Carr, D. (1979). The development of young children's capacity to judge anomalous sentences. *Journal of Child Language, 6,* 227–241.

Carrier, J. (1974). Application of functional analysis and non-speech response mode to teaching language. In L. McReynolds (Ed.), *Developing systematic procedures for training children's language. ASHA Monograph 18.* Rockville, MD: American Speech-Language-Hearing Association.

Catts, H. (1989). Phonological processing deficits and reading disabilities. In A. Kamhi & H. Catts (Eds.), *Reading disabilities: A developmental language perspective.* Boston: Little, Brown.

Catts, H. (1991). Facilitating phonological awareness: Role of speech-language pathologists. *Language, Speech, and Hearing Services in Schools, 22*(4), 196–203.

Cazden, C. (1974). Play with language and metalinguistic awareness: one dimension of language experience. *Urban Review, 7,* 28–39.

Chaney, C. (1989). I pledge allegiance to the flag: Three studies in word segmentation. *Applied Psycholinguistics, 10* (3), 261–281.

Chaney, C., & Estrin, E. (1987, November). *Metalinguistic awareness.* Miniseminar presented at the American Speech-Language-Hearing Association, New Orleans.

Chapman, R. (1988, June). *Child talk: Assumptions of a developmental process model for early language learning.* Invited address, Wisconsin Child Language Disorders Symposium, Madison.

Chukovsky, K. (1963). *From two to five.* Berkeley: University of California Press.

Clark, E. (1987). The principle of contrast: A constraint on language acquisition. In B. MacWhinney (Ed.), *Mechanisms of language acquisition.* Hillsdale, NJ: Lawrence Erlbaum.

Clark, E. V., & Andersen, E. (1979). Spontaneous repairs: Awareness in the process of acquiring language. *Papers and Reports on Child Language Development, 16,* 1–12.

Clark, M. (1978). The short-circuit hypothesis of second-language reading—or when language competence interferes with reading performance. *The Modern Language Journal, 64,* 311–317.

Clay, M. (1966). *Emergent reading behavior.* Unpublished doctoral dissertation, University of Auckland, New Zealand.

Cochran-Smith, M. (1984). *The making of a reader.* Norwood, NJ: Ablex.

Conklin, H. (1956). Tagalog speech disguise. *Language, 32,* 136–139.

Constable, C., & van Kleeck, A. (1985, November). *From social to instructional uses of language: Bridging the gap.* Short course presented at the annual convention of the American-Speech-Language-Hearing Association, Washington, DC.

Cowan, N. (1989). The acquisition of Pig Latin: A case study. *Journal of Child Language, 16,* 365–386.

Cowan, N., & Leavitt, L. (1982). Talking backward: exceptional speech play in late childhood. *Journal of Child Language, 9,* 481–495.

Craig, H., & Gallagher, T. (1979). The structural characteristics of monologues in the speech of normal children: Syntactic nonconversational aspects. *Journal of Speech and Hearing Research, 22,* 46–62.

Cromer, W. (1970). A different model: A new explanation for some reading difficulties. *Journal of Educational Psychology, 61,* 471–483.

Crossely, R. (1992). Getting the words out: Case studies in facilitated communication training. *Topics in Language Disorders, 12*(4), 46–59.

DeLoache, J., & Mendoza, O. (1986). *Joint picture book reading of children.* Champaign, IL: University of Illinois.

deVilliers, J., & deVilliers, P. (1974). Competence and performance in child language: Are children really competent to judge? *Child Language, 1,* 11–22.

Dewitz, P., Stammer, J., & Jenson, J. (1980, December). *The development of linguistic awareness in young children from label reading to word recognition.* Paper presented at the annual meeting of the National Reading Conference, San Diego, CA.

Diaz, R. (1985). Bilingual cognitive development: Addressing three gaps in current research. *Child Development, 56,* 1376–1388.

Donaldson, M. (1978). *Children's minds.* New York: W. W. Norton.

Donnellan, A., Sabin, L., & Majure, L. A. (1992). Facilitated communication: Beyond the quandary to the questions. *Topics in Language Disorders, 12*(4), 69–82.

Dore, J. (1985). Children's conversations. In T. van Dijk (Ed.), *Handbook of discourse analysis, Vol. 3: Discourse and dialogue* (pp. 47–65). London: Academic Press.

Dowker, A. (1989). Rhyme and alliteration in poems elicited from young children. *Journal of Child Language, 16,* 181–202.

Dunn, L., & Dunn, L. (1981). *Peabody Picture Vocabulary Test (Revised).* Circle Pines, MN: American Guidance Service.

Dunton, S., Fujiki, M., & Brinton, B. (1984, November). *Metalinguistic judgment skills in normal and language-disordered children.* Paper presented at the annual convention of the American Speech-Language-Hearing Association, San Francisco.

Ehri, L. (1975). Word consciousness in readers and prereaders. *Journal of Educational Psychology, 67,* 204–212.

Ehri, L. (1976). Word learning in beginning readers and prereaders: Effects of form class and defining contexts. *Journal of Educational Psychology, 68,* 832–842.

Ehri, L. (1979). Linguistic insight: threshold of reading acquisition. In T. Waller & G. MacKinnon (Eds.), *Reading research.* New York: Academic Press.

Elkind, D. (1969). Piagetian and psychometric conceptions of intelligence. *Harvard Educational Review, 39,* 319–337.

Elkonin, D. (1973). USSR. In J. Downing (Ed.), *Comparative reading: Cross-national studies of behavior and processes in reading and writing.* New York: Macmillan.

Ellis, N., & Large, B. (1987). The development of reading: As you seek so shall you find. *British Journal of Developmental Psychology, 78,* 1–28.

Emerson, H. (1980). Children's judgments of correct and reversed sentences with if. *Journal of Child Language, 7,* 137–155.

Evans, M., Taylor, N., & Blum, I. (1979). Children's written language awareness and its relation to reading acquisition. *Journal of Reading Behavior, 11,* 7–19.

Feldman, C., & Shen, M. (1971). Some language-related cognitive advantages of bilingual five year olds. *Journal of Genetic Psychology, 118,* 235–244.

Flavell, J. (1981). Cognitive monitoring. In W. Dickson (Ed.), *Children's oral communication skills.* New York: Academic Press.

Fox, B., & Routh, D. (1976). Analyzing spoken language into words, syllables, and phonemes. A developmental study. *Journal of Psycholinguistic Research, 4,* 331–342.

Francis, H. (1973). Children's experience of reading and notions of units in language. *British Journal of Educational Psychology, 43,* 17–23.

Gallagher, T. (1977). Revision behaviors in the speech of normal children developing language. *Journal of Speech and Hearing Research, 20,* 303–318.

Gardner, H., Winner, E., Bechofer, R., & Wolf, D. (1978). The development of figurative language. In K. E. Nelson (Ed.), *Children's language* (Vol. 1). New York: Gardner Press.

Garvey, C. (1977). *Play.* Cambridge, MA: Harvard University Press.

Geller, L. (1985). *Word play and language learning for children.* Urbana, IL: National Council for Teachers of English.

Gessell, A. (1925). *The mental growth of the pre-school child.* New York: Macmillan.

Gessell, A. (1928). *Infancy and human growth.* New York: Macmillan.

Gibbs, R. (1987). Linguistic factors in children's understanding of idioms. *Journal of Child Language, 14,* 569–586.

Gleitman, L., Gleitman, H., & Shipley, E. (1972). The emergence of the child as grammarian. *Cognition, 1,* 137–164.

Goffman, E. (1974). *Frame analysis.* New York: Harper.

Goldschmid, M., & Bentler, P. (1968). *Goldschmid-Bentler concept assessment kit.* San Diego: Educational and Industrial Testing Service.

Golinkoff, R. (1978). Critique: Phonemic awareness and reading achievement. In F. Murray & J. Pikulski (Eds.), *The acquisition of reading: Cognitive, linguistic, and perceptual prerequisites.* Baltimore: University Park Press.

Goodman, K. (1973). The 13th easy way to make learning to read difficult: A reaction to Gleitman and Rozin. *Reading Research Quarterly, 8,* 484–493.

Goodman, K., & Goodman, Y. (1977). Learning about psycholinguistic process by analyzing oral reading. *Harvard Educational Review, 47,* 317–333.

Goswami, U., & Bryant, P. (1990). *Phonological skills and learning to read.* East Sussex, UK: Lawrence Erlbaum.

Gough, P., & Hillinger, M. (1980). Learning to read: An unnatural act. *Bulletin of the Orton Society, 30,* 179–196.

Guralnick, M., & Paul-Brown, D. (1977). The nature of verbal interactions among handicapped and nonhandicapped preschool children. *Child Development, 48,* 254–260.

Haas, M. (1957). Thai word-games. *Journal of American Folklore, 70,* 173–175.

Hakes, D. (1980). *The development of metalinguistic abilities in children.* New York: Springer-Verlag.

Hakes, D. (1982). The development of metalinguistic abilities: What develops? In S. Kuczaj (ed.), *Language development: Vol. 2. Language, thought and culture.* Hillsdale, NJ: Lawrence Erlbaum.

Hall, N. (1987). *The emergence of literacy.* Portsmouth, NH: Heinemann.

Halliday, M. A. K., & Hasan, R. (1976). *Cohesion in English.* London: Longman.

Harkness, F., & Miller, L. (1982, October). *A description of the interaction among mother, child, and books in a bedtime reading situation.* Paper presented at the 7th annual Boston University conference on language development, Boston.

Harre, R. (1984). *Personal being.* Cambridge, MA: Harvard University Press.

Heath, S. B. (1983). *Ways with words: Language, life, and work in communities and classrooms.* New York: Cambridge University Press.

Hiebert, E. (1978). Preschool children's understanding of written language. *Child Development, 49,* 1231–1234.

Hiebert, E. (1986). Issues related to home influences on young children's print-related development. In D. Yaden & S. Templeton (Eds.), *Metalinguistic awareness and beginning literacy.* Portsmouth, NH: Heinemann.

Hirsh-Pasek, K., Gleitman, L., & Gleitman, H. (1978). What did the brain say to the mind? A study of the detection and report of ambiguity by young children. In A. Sinclair, R. Jarvella, & W. Levelt (Eds.), *The child's conception of language.* New York: Springer-Verlag.

Holden, M., & McGinitie, W. (1972). Children's conception of word boundaries in speech and print. *Journal of Educational Psychology, 63,* 551–557.

Holyoak, K., Junn, E., & Billman, D. (1984). Development of analogical problem solving skill. *Child Development, 55,* 2042–2055.

Horgan, D. (August, 1979). *The emergence of Kelly as comedienne: a case study of metalinguistic abilities.* Presented at the Second International Conference on Humor.

Howe, H., & Hillman, D. (1973). The acquisition of semantic restrictions in children. *Journal of Verbal Learning and Verbal Behavior, 2,* 132–139.

Hudson, J., & Nelson, K. (1984). Play with language: Overextensions as analogies. *Journal of Child Language, 11,* 337–346.

Huttenlocher, J. (1964). Children's language: word–phrase relationship. *Science, 143,* 264–265.

Hymes, D. (1974). *Foundations in sociolinguistics: An ethnographic approach.* Philadelphia: University of Pennsylvania Press.

Ianco-Worral, A. (1972). Bilingualism and cognitive development. *Child Development, 43,* 1390.

Inhelder, B., & Piaget, J. (1958). *The growth of logical thinking from childhood to adolescence.* New York: Basic Books.

Iwamura, S. (1980). *The verbal games of pre-school children.* New York: St. Martin's Press.

Jakobson, R. (1960). Linguistics and poetics. In J. Seboek (Ed.), *Style and language.* Cambridge, MA: MIT Press.

James, S., & Miller, J. (1973). Children's awareness of semantic constraints in sentences. *Child Development, 44,* 69–76.

Joffe, V., & Shapiro, G. (1991). Sound based language play in four language-impaired subjects. *The South African Journal of Communication Disorders, 38,* 119–128.

Jorgensen, C., Barrett, M., Huisingh, R., & Zachman, L. (1981). *The word test.* Moline, IL: Linguisystems.

Kamhi, A. (1987). Metalinguistic abilities in language-impaired children. *Topics in Language Disorders, 7*(2), 1–12.

Kamhi, A., & Koenig, L. (1985). Metalinguistic awareness in language-disordered children. *Language, Speech, and Hearing Services in Schools,* 16, 199–210.

Kamhi, A., Lee, R. F., & Nelson, L. K. (1985). Word, syllable, and sound awareness in language disordered children. *Journal of Speech and Hearing Disorders, 50,* 207–212.

Karmiloff-Smith, A. (1986). From meta-processes to conscious access: Evidence from children's metalinguistic and repair data. *Cognition, 23,* 95–147.

Karpova, S. (1966). The preschooler's realization of the lexical structure of speech. Abstracted by D. Slobin in F. Smith & G. A. Miller (Eds.), *The genesis of language.* Cambridge, MA: MIT Press.

Kessell, F. (1970). The role of syntax in children's comprehension from ages six to twelve. *Monographs of the Society for Research in Child Development, 35,* 1–59.

Kirshenblatt-Gimblett, B. (1976). *Speech play.* University of Pennsylvania Press.

Koch, K. (1973). *Rose, where did you get that red? Teaching great poetry to children.* New York: Random House.

Kuczaj, S. (1982). Language play and language acquisition. In H. Reese (Ed.), *Advances in child development and behavior.* New York: Academic Press.

Kuczaj, S. (1983). *Crib speech and language play.* New York: Springer-Verlag.

Lakoff, G., & Johnson, M. (1980). *Metaphors we live by.* Chicago: The University of Chicago Press.

Lee, R., & Kamhi, A. (1985, November). *Verbal metaphor performance in learning disabled children.* Paper presented at the American Speech-Language-Hearing Association, Washington, DC.

Leonard L., Bolders, J., & Curtis, R. (1977). On the nature of children's judgments of linguistic features: semantic relations and grammatical morphemes. *Journal of Psycholinguistic Research, 6,* 233–244.

Levelt, W., Sinclair, A., & Jarvella, R. (1978). Causes and functions of linguistic awareness in language acquisition: Some introductory remarks. In A. Sinclair, R. Jarvella, & W. Levelt (Eds.), *The child's conception of language.* New York: Springer-Verlag.

Lewis, B., & Freebairn, L. (1992). Residual effects of preschool phonology disorders in grade school, adolescence, and adulthood. *Journal of Speech and Hearing Research,* 35, 819–831.

Liberman, I., Cooper, F., Shankweiler, D., & Studdert-Kennedy, M. (1967). Perception of the speech code. *Psychological Review, 74,* 431–461.

Liberman, I., Rubin, H., Duques, S., & Carlisle, J. (1985). Linguistic abilities and spelling proficiency in kindergartners and adult poor spellers. In D. Gray & J. Kavanagh (eds.), *Biobehavioral measures of dyslexia.* Parkton, MD: York Press.

Liberman, I., & Shankweiler, D. (1977). Speech, the alphabet and teaching children to read. In L. Resnick & P. Weaver (Eds.), *Theory and practice of early reading.* Hillsdale, NJ: Lawrence Erlbaum Associates.

Liberman, I., & Shankweiler, D. (1991). Phonology and beginning reading: A tutorial. In L. Rieben & C. Perfetti (Eds.), *Learning to read: Basic research and its implications.* Hillsdale, NJ: Lawrence Erlbaum.

Liberman, I., Shankweiler, D., Fischer, M., & Carter, B. (1974). Explicit syllable and phoneme segmentation in the young child. *Journal of Experimental Child Psychology, 18,* 201–212.

Lieberman, P. (1966). *Intonation, perception and language.* Cambridge, MA: MIT Press.

Liles, B., Shulman, M., & Bartlett, S. (1977). Judgments of grammaticality in normal and language-disordered children. *Journal of Speech and Hearing Disorders, 42,* 199–210.

Lomax, R., & McGee, L. (1987). Young children's concepts about print and reading: Toward a model of word reading acquisition. *Reading Research Quarterly, 22,* 237–256.

Lundberg, I., Frost, J., & Petersen, O-P. (1988). Effects of an extensive program for stimulating phonological awareness in preschool children. *Reading Research Quarterly, 23,* 264–284.

MacLean, M., Bryant, P., & Bradley, L. (1987). Rhymes, nursery rhymes, and reading in early childhood. *Merrill-Palmer Quarterly, 33*(3), 255–281.

Maratsos, M. (1973). Nonegocentric communication abilities in preschool children. *Child Development, 44,* 697–700.

Mason, J., & Allen, J. (1986). A review of emergent literacy with implications for research and practice in reading. In C. Rothkopt (Ed.), *Review of research in education* (Vol. 13). Washington, DC: American Educational Research Association.

McCabe, A. (1987). *Language games to play with your child.* New York: Fawcett Columbine.

McCutchen, D., & Perfetti, C. (1982). Coherence and connectedness in the development of discourse production. *Text, 2,* 113–139.

McNinch, G. (1974). Awareness of aural and visual word boundary within a sample of first graders. *Perceptual and Motor Skills, 38,* 1127–1134.

McShane, J. (1979). The development of naming. *Linguistics, 17,* 879–905.

McShane, J. (1980). *Learning to talk.* Cambridge, UK: Cambridge University Press.

Miller, S. (1976). Nonverbal assessment of Piagetian concepts. *Psychological Bulletin, 83,* 405–430.

Morais, J., Bertelson, P., Cary, L., & Alegria, J. (1986). Literacy training and speech segmentation. *Cognition, 24,* 45–64.

Morais, J., Cary, L., Alegria, J., & Bertelson, P. (1979). Does awareness of speech as a sequence of phones arise spontaneously? *Cognition, 7,* 323–331.

Morris, D. (1980). Beginning reader's concept of word. In E. Henderson & J. Beers (Eds.), *Development and cognitive aspects of learning to spell: A reflection of word knowledge.* Newark, DE: International Reading Association.

Nelson, K. (1983). The conceptual basis for language. In T. Seiler & W. Wannemacher (Eds.), *Concept development and the development of word meaning.* New York: Springer-Verlag.

Nelson, K. (1985). *Making sense: Development of meaning in early childhood.* New York: Academic.

Nelson, K. (1986). *Event knowledge: Structure and function in development.* Hillsdale, NJ: Lawrence Erlbaum.

Nelson, K., Rescorla, L., Gruendel, J., & Benedict, H. (1978). Early lexicons: What do they mean? *Child Development, 49,* 960–968.

Ninio, A., & Bruner, J. (1978). The achievements and antecedents of labelling. *Journal of Child Language, 5,* 1–15.

Nippold, M., & Fey, M. (1983). Metaphoric understanding in preadolescents having a history of language acquisition difficulties. *Language, Speech, and Hearing Services in Schools, 14,* 171–181.

Nippold, M., & Martin, S. (1989). Idiom interpretation in isolation versus context: A developmental study with adolescents. *Journal of Speech and Hearing Research, 32,* 59–66.

Nippold, M., Martin, S., & Erskine, B. (1988). Proverb comprehension in context: A developmental study with children and adolescents. *Journal of Speech and Hearing Research, 31,* 19–28.

Nippold, M., & Sullivan, M. (1987). Verbal and perceptual analogical reasoning and proportional metaphor comprehension in young children. *Journal of Speech and Hearing Research, 30,* 367–376.

Olson, D. (1984). "See! Jumping!" Some oral antecedents of literacy. In H. Goelman, A. Oberg, & F. Smith (Eds.), *Awakening to literacy.* Portsmouth, NH: Heinemann.

Opie, I., & Opie, P. (1959). *The lore and language of school children.* Oxford, UK: Clarendon Press.

Osherson, D., & Markman, E. (1975). Language and the ability to evaluate contradictions and tautologies. *Cognition, 3,* 213–226.

Pelligrini, A. (1984). The effect of dramatic play on children's generation of cohesive text. *Discourse Processes, 7,* 57–67.

Pelligrini, A., Brody, G., & Sigel, I. (1985). Parents' bookreading habits with their children. *Journal of Educational Psychology, 77,* 332–340.

Perfetti, C., Beck, I., Bell, L., & Hughs, C. (1987). Phonemic knowledge and learning to read are reciprocal: A longitudinal study of first-grade children. *Merrill-Palmer Quarterly, 33,* 283–319.

Perry, B., Newhoff, M., & Buday, E. (1983, November). *Normal and language disordered children's metalinguistic awareness of the -s morpheme.* Paper presented at the annual convention of the American Speech-Language-Hearing Association, Cincinnati.

Peterson, C., & Dodsworth, P. (1991). A longitudinal analysis of young children's cohesion and noun specification in narratives. *Journal of Child Language, 18*(2), 397–416.

Piaget, J. (1929). *The child's conception of the world.* New York: Harcourt, Brace & World.

Piaget, J. (1976). *The grasp of consciousness.* Cambridge, MA: Harvard University Press.

Piaget, J. (1978). *Success and understanding.* Cambridge, MA: Harvard University Press.

Prinz, P. (1983). The development of idiomatic meaning in children. *Language and Speech, 26,* 263–272.

Read, C. (1978). Children's awareness of language, with emphasis on sound systems. In A. Sinclair, R. Jarvella & W. Levelt (Eds.), *The child's conception of language.* New York: Springer-Verlag.

Read, C., Zhang, Y., Nie, H., & Ding, B. (1986). The ability to manipulate speech sounds depends on knowing alphabetic spelling. *Cognition, 24,* 31–44.

Rogers, T. (1979). *Those first affections: An anthology of poems composed between the ages of two and eight.* London: Routledge & Kegan Paul.

Rosner, J., & Simon, D. (1971). The Auditory Analysis Test: An initial report. *Journal of Learning Disabilities, 4,* 384–392.

Rumelhart, D., & McClelland, J. (1987). Learning the past tenses of English verbs: Implicit rules or parallel distributed processing. In B. MacWhinney (Ed.), *Mechanisms of language acquisition.* Hillsdale, NJ: Lawrence Erlbaum.

Ryan, E. (1980). Metalinguistic development and reading. In F. B. Murray (Ed.), *Language awareness and reading.* Newark, DE: International Reading Association.

Sanches, M., & Kirshenblatt-Gimblett, B. (1976). Children's traditional speech play and child language. In B. Kirshenblatt-Gimblett (Ed.), *Speech play.* Philadelphia: University of Pennsylvania Press.

Sawyer, D. (1987). *Test of awareness of language segments (TALS).* Austin, TX: PRO-ED.

Saywitz, K., & Wilkinson, L. (1982). Age-related differences in metalinguistic awareness. In S. Kuczaj (Ed.), *Language development: Vol. 2. Language, thought and culture.* Hillsdale, NJ: Erlbaum.

Scollon, R. (1976). *Conversations with a one-year-old.* Honolulu: University Press of Hawaii.

Scollon, R., & Scollon, S. (1981). *Narrative, literacy and face in interethnic communication.* Norwood, NJ: Ablex.

Semel, E., & Wiig, E. (1980). *Clinical evaluation of language functions.* New York: Merrill/Macmillan.

Seuren, P. (1978). Grammar as an underground process. In A. Sinclair, R. Jarvella, & W. Levelt (Eds.), *The child's conception of language.* New York: Springer-Verlag.

Share, D., Jorm, A., MacLean, R., & Matthews, R. (1984). Sources of individual differences in reading acquisition. *Journal of Experimental Psychology, 76,* 1309–1324.

Shatz, M., & Gelman, R. (1973). The development of communication skills: modifications in the speech of young children as a function of the listener. *Monographs of the Society for Research in Child Development, 38,* 1–37.

Sherzer, J. (1976). Play languages: implications for (socio) linguistics. In B. Kirshenblatt-Gimblett (Ed.), *Speech play.* Philadelphia: University of Pennsylvania Press.

Shriberg, L., & Kwiatkowski, J. (1988). A follow-up study of children with phonological disorders of unknown origin. *Journal of Speech and Hearing Disorders, 53,* 144–155.

Shultz, T. (1974). Development of the appreciation of riddles. *Child Development, 45,* 100–105.

Sinclair, H. (1978). Conceptualization and awareness in Piaget's theory and its relevance to the child's conception of language. In A. Sinclair, R. Jarvella, & W. Levelt (Eds.), *The child's conception of language.* New York: Springer-Verlag.

Slobin, D. (1978). A case study of early language awareness. In A. Sinclair, R. Jarvella, & W. Levelt (Eds.), *The child's conception of language.* New York: Springer-Verlag.

Smith, C., & Tager-Flusberg, H. (1982). Metalinguistic awareness and language development. *Journal of Experimental Child Psychology, 34,* 449–468.

Smith, F. (1973). *Psycholinguistics and reading.* New York: Holt, Rinehart, and Winston.

Smith, F. (1988). *Understanding reading* (4th ed.). New York: Holt, Rinehart, and Winston.

Snow, C. (1983). Literacy and language: Relationships during the preschool years. *Harvard Educational Review, 53*(2), 165–189.

Snow, C., & Goldfield, B. (1981). Building stories; The emergence of information structures from conversation. In D. Tannen (Ed.), *Analyzing discourse: Text and talk.* Washington, DC: Georgetown University Round Table on Language and Linguistics, Georgetown University Press.

Snow, C., & Goldfield, B. (1983). Turn the page please: Situation-specific language acquisition. *Journal of Child Language, 10,* 551–569.

Snyder, A. (1914). Notes on the talk of a two-and-a-half year old boy. *Pedagogical Seminary, 21,* 412–424.

Snyder, L., Bates, E., & Bretherton, I. (1981). Content and context in early lexical development. *Journal of Child Language, 8,* 565–582.

Spencer, B. (1986). The concept of *word* in young children: Tacit and explicit awareness of children at different operational levels. In J. Niles & R. Lalik (Eds.), *Solving problems in literacy: Learners, teachers, and researchers* (pp. 271–280). 35th Yearbook of the National Reading Conference. Rochester, NY: National Reading Conference.

Stanovich, K., Cunningham, A., & Cramer, B. (1984). Assessing phonological awareness in kindergarten children: Issues of task comparability. *Journal of Experimental Child Psychology, 38,* 175–190.

Strand, K., & Fraser, B. (1979). *The comprehension of verbal idioms by young children.* Unpublished paper, Boston University.

Sutter, J., & Johnson, C. (1990). School-age children's metalinguistic awareness of grammaticality in verb form. *Journal of Speech and Hearing Research, 33*(1), 84–95.

Swank, L. (1991). *A two level hypothesis of phonological awareness* (Working Papers in Language Development, Vol. 6, No. 2). Lawrence, KS: University of Kansas Child Language Program.

Tale in Tail(s): A study worthy of Alice's friends. (1991, May 1). *New York Times,* p. 21.

Teale, W. (1984). Reading to young children: Its significance for literacy development. In H. Goelman, A. Oberg, & F. Smith (Eds.), *Awakening to literacy.* Exeter, NH: Heinemann.

Teale, W., & Sulzby, E. (Eds.). (1986). *Emergent literacy: Writing and reading.* Norwood, NJ: Ablex.

Tervoort, B. (1979). Foreign language awareness in a five-to-nine year-old lexicographer. *Journal of Child Language, 6,* 159–166.

Thomson, J., & Chapman, R. (1977). Who is "Daddy" revisited: The status of two-year-olds' overextended words in use and comprehension. *Journal of Child Language, 4,* 359–375.

Thorum, A. (1980). *The Fullerton language test for adolescents: Experimental edition.* Palo Alto, CA: Consulting Psychologists Press.

Trieman, R. (1983). The structure of spoken syllables: Evidence from novel word games. *Cognition, 15,* 49–74.

Trieman, R. (1985). Onsets and rimes as units of spoken language: Evidence from children. *Journal of Experimental Child Psychology, 39,* 161–181.

Trieman, R. (1986). The division between onset and rimes in English syllables. *Journal of Memory and Language, 25,* 476–491.

Trieman, R. (1991). The role of intrasyllabic units in learning to read. In L. Rieben & C. Perfetti (Eds.), *Learning to read: Basic research and its implications.* Hillsdale, NJ: Lawrence Erlbaum.

Trieman, R. (1992). The role of intrasyllabic units in learning to read and spell. In P. Gough, L. Ehri, & R. Treiman (Eds.), *Reading acquisition.* Hillsdale, NJ: Lawrence Erlbaum.

Trieman, R., & Baron, J. (1981). Segmental analysis ability: Development and relation to reading ability. In G. Mackinnon & T. Waller (Eds.), *Reading research: Advances in theory and practice* (Vol. 3, pp. 159–198). New York: Academic Press.

Tunmer, W. (1991). Phonological awareness and literacy acquisition. In L. Rieben & C. Perfetti (Eds.), *Learning to read: Basic research and its implications.* Hillsdale, NJ: Lawrence Erlbaum.

Tunmer, W., & Bowey, J. (1984). Metalinguistic awareness and reading acquisition. In W. Tunmer, C. Pratl, & M. Herriman (Eds.), *Metalinguistic awareness in children: Theory, research and implications.* Berlin: Springer-Verlag.

Tunmer, W., Bowey, J., & Grieve, R. (1983). The development of young children's awareness of the word as a unit of spoken language. *Journal of Psycholinguistic Research, 12,* 567–594.

van Kleeck, A. (1982). The emergence of linguistic awareness: A cognitive framework. *Merrill-Palmer Quarterly, 28,* 237–265.

van Kleeck, A. (1984a). Assessment and intervention: Does "meta" matter? In G. Wallach & K. Butler (Eds.), *Language learning disabilities in school-age children.* Baltimore: Williams & Wilkins.

van Kleeck, A. (1984b). Metalinguistic skills. Cutting across spoken and written language and problem solving abilities. In G. Wallach & K. Butler (Eds.), *Language learning disabilities in school-age children.* Baltimore: Williams & Wilkins.

van Kleeck, A. (1990). Emergent literacy: Learning about print before learning to read. *Topics in Language Disorders, 10*(2), 25–45.

van Kleeck, A., & Bryant, D. (1983, October). *A diary study of very early emerging metalinguistic skills.* Paper presented at the Eighth Annual Boston University Conference on Language Development, Boston.

van Kleeck, A., & Bryant, D. (1984, November). *Learning that language is arbitrary: Evidence from early lexical changes.* Paper presented at the Annual Convention of the American Speech-Language-Hearing Association, San Francisco.

van Kleeck, A., & Reddick, C. (1982, October). *The relationship between concrete operational thought and the development of metalinguistic skill.* Paper presented at the Seventh Annual Boston University Conference on Language Development, Boston.

van Kleeck, A., & Richardson, A. (1990). Assessment of speech and language development. In J. Johnson & J. Goldman (Eds.), *Developmental assessment in clinical child psychology: A Handbook.* New York: Pergamon Press.

van Kleeck, A., & Schuele, M. (1987). Precursors to literacy: Normal development. *Topics in Language Disorders, 7*(2), 13–31.

Verrillo, E. (1991, February). *Metaphors, myths, and messages: Figurative language in war propaganda.* Presented at a conference on Media and the Gulf War, University of Texas at Austin.

Vosniadou, S., & Ortony, A. (1983). The influence of analogy in children's acquisition of new information from text: An exploratory study. In J. Niles (Ed.), *Searches for meaning in reading, language processing, and instruction,* Rochester, NY: National Reading Conference.

Vygotsky, L. (1962). *Language and thought.* Cambridge, MA: MIT Press.

Vygotsky, L. (1978). In M. Cole, V. John-Steiner, S. Scribner, & E. Souberman (Eds.), *Mind in society: The development of higher psychological processes.* Cambridge, MA: Harvard University Press.

Wagner, R., & Torgesen, J. (1987). The nature of phonological processing and its causal role in the acquisition of reading skills. *Psychological Bulletin, 101,* 192–212.

Wallach, G., & Miller, L. (1988). *Language intervention and academic success.* Boston: Little, Brown.

Watzlawick, P., Beavin, J., & Jackson, D. (1967). *Pragmatics of human communication.* New York: W. W. Norton.

Weaver, C. (1990). *Understanding whole language: From principles to practice.* Portsmouth, NH: Heinemann Educational Books.

Weaver, P., & Shonkoff, P. (1978). *Research within research: A research-guided response to concerns of reading educators.* St. Louis, CEMREL.

Weeks, T. (1979). *Born to talk.* Rowley, MA: Newbury.

Weir, R. (1962). *Language in the crib.* The Hague, The Netherlands: Mouton.

Wells, G. (1985). Preschool literacy related activities and success in school. In D. Olson, N. Torrance, & A. Hildyard (Eds.), *Literacy, language and learning: the nature and consequences of reading and writing.* New York: Cambridge University Press.

Werner, H., & Kaplan, B. (1963). *Symbol formation.* New York: John Wiley.

Wiig, E. (1989). *Steps to language competence: Developing metalinguistic strategies.* San Antonio, TX: The Psychological Corporation.

Wiig, E., & Semel, E. (1976). *Language disabilities in children and adolescents.* New York: Merrill/Macmillan.

Winner, E. (1979). New names for old things: The emergence of metaphoric language. *Journal of Child Language, 6,* 469–491.

Winner, E. (1988). *Points of words: Children's understanding of metaphor and irony.* Cambridge, MA: Harvard University Press.

Winner, E., Rosentiel, A., & Gardner, H. (1976). The development of metaphoric understanding. *Developmental Psychology, 12,* 289–297.

REFLECTIONS FOR PART ONE: CHAPTERS 1–3

SCHOOL LANGUAGE AND LEARNING

Making Scaffolding and Metas Matter

All three of the previous chapters discuss various aspects of metalinguistic and metacognitive ability as they relate to language learning, literacy learning, and learning in general. Silliman and Wilkinson stress the importance of thinking about ways in which supportive scaffolds help children plan, make choices, and gain control over their own decision-making processes as learners. Both Wallach and Butler and Silliman and Wilkinson make a case for the role of written language as a scaffold.

Indeed, Silliman and Wilkinson's discussion of discourse scaffolds in Chapter 2 points out that because language in its written and read form can transcend time and space, "it is a potentially powerful metacognitive tool for creating, understanding, and revising ideas about the world." These authors stress that to be metacognitive means that children can make deliberate choices and control their attentional resources—a point that Lahey and Bloom make in Chapter 13. At the same time, Silliman and Wilkinson point out that language learning disabled children have difficulties with making choices and managing their comprehension activities. Silliman and Wilkinson's discussion of directive and supportive scaffolds provides readers with a framework for assessment and intervention procedures that are identified by other authors. Whereas Silliman and Wilkinson remind readers that directive scaffolds can be too controlling, professionals should keep an open mind regarding the varying degrees of adult–teacher control that may be required for certain children at certain points in time. Most importantly, the Silliman and Wilkinson discussion focuses readers' attention on a recurring theme discussed in the text: adults (and other children at times) can provide support through verbal communication (scaffolding), thereby assisting the language learning disabled child to move along the language and literacy continuum, achieving new and higher levels of language comprehension and use. As also noted by Wallach and Butler, adults can assist children through nonverbal and printed supportive contexts, that is, by presenting information in a carefully orchestrated fashion. For example, clinicians and teachers who use highly structured materials with children (e.g., semantic categories represented by pictured and/or written examples of food groups, animals, clothing, etc.) make them more aware of organizational principles and assist them in remembering such categories through metacomprehension and metacognitive strategies (Best, 1993; Best & Ornstein, 1986; Butler, 1986; Nelson, chap. 4; Palincsar, Brown, & Campione, chap. 5; Rabinowitz, 1988; Scott, chap. 8; Silliman & Wilkinson, chaps. 2, 6).

In Chapter 3, van Kleeck gives readers a very careful definition of what is and what is not metalinguistic in her view. Although some authors may take a broader and some a narrower view, her analysis of the components of this critical skill(s) will be of direct assistance in constructing appropriate clinical assessment and intervention procedures, several of which van Kleeck provides. Equally important is van Kleeck's discussion of the cognitive models on which an understanding of metalinguistic development may be constructed. While the bases for communication is viewed within a social-interaction framework, a view also taken by Silliman and Wilkinson (and Palincsar et al., chap. 5), van Kleeck stresses the importance of *thinking about language* to use *language to think.* She cleverly brings readers back to the importance of helping children manage language in school-based tasks in addition to its use in the social domain. Indeed, children, parents, teachers, and clinicians in almost all parts of American society value academic success. Thinking "academically" requires metacognitive and metalinguistic skills—choice, control, and planning—if literacy is to be achieved. Many definitions of literacy abound, but the simple truth is that literacy is defined as language use (Bleich, 1989).

In discussing age-dependent factors of great importance to metalinguistic performance, van Kleeck joins many authors of this text who also provide information on factors that appear to depend more on developmental age than on piagetian stages. Readers will encounter this dilemma more than once in this book. Research does not yet hold all the answers to the questions raised by Wallach and Butler in Chapter 1. Although the focus on oral language and written language connections remains a predominant theme throughout this text, the authors recognize that much remains to be learned about linguistic precocity, early reading, and emergent literacy (Crain-Thoreson & Dale, 1992). For example, in a longitudinal study of twenty-five children, from ages twenty months to four-and-a-half-years old, Crain-Thoreson and Dale (1992) found that talking alone, verbal precociousness, did not necessarily translate to precocious reading. Rather, exposure to and instruction in letter names and sounds, coupled with story reading, had a significant influence on both overall language ability and knowledge of print conventions at two and a half and four and a half years of age, respectively (Crain-Thoreson & Dale, 1992).

Indeed, there is much to learn. Readers of this text will find that it is often necessary to hold two opposing viewpoints in mind while perusing the contents of this book. Although that does not simplify the readers' task, it reflects the real world of both research and practice. It is well to remind ourselves that certainty is only a sometime thing. Clinicians and educators must live, as do we all, with some uncertainty.

One certainty is that competency in language enhances school learning and learning enhances language. All authors in this book have identified the language–learning connection as a priority area of interest and concern. Their focus on the *metas-* and other cognitive enterprises are reinforced in a recently reported study by Wang, Haertel, and Walberg (in press), who reviewed fifty years of research on approaches to school learning. The accumulated evidence is based on 11,000 statistical findings. Wang et al. indicated that the most powerful variable influencing learning was metacognition (defined here as the child's executive capacity to plan, monitor, and if necessary, replan learning strategies). Included in this metacognitive ability is students' understanding of and ability to discuss what they "know" as well as what they "do not know" about various subjects and topics. Again, a cautionary note applies. As Garner and Alexander (1989) have noted, researchers in metacognition should probably describe metacognition as "telling more than one can know" as well as "knowing more than one can tell" (p. 167). They point out that professionals do not yet know with any consistent accuracy how children and adults can report on what they think about thinking and what they truly know about persons, tasks, and strategy variables. Garner and Alexander also note that young children may have great difficulty in specifying what they may understand about their cognitions, because verbal facility (or lack thereof) may be a problem. A well-researched exemplar, however, has been reported by Palincsar and her colleagues (chap. 5) and cited by Wang et al. (in press). *Reciprocal teaching,* is, in the editors' view, an example of a teaching strategy that is also good language intervention. Reciprocal teaching assists children and adolescents in developing awareness and self-monitoring skills through repeated and shared dialogues, as discussed in some detail in Chapter 5 by Palincsar and co-workers; also see Chapter 2 by Silliman and Wilkinson.

As authors will ask throughout this text, reflecting in a sense on the findings of Wang et al. (in press), how do children become active and competent learners? Metastrategies, both linguistic and cognitive, are an outgrowth of many years of practice and instruction. Children, particularly children with language difficulties, may not necessarily "grow into" metastrategies; similarly, they may not "grow into" reading and writing. Many areas of cognitive and linguistic processing, from nonmeta- and meta-points of view, will be discussed in the chapters that follow. In summary, if both metalinguistic and metacognition are vital to children's learning and their success in school, as suggested by the meta-analyses conducted by Wang et al. and the authors throughout this text, clinicians and teachers may have the beginnings of a framework to apply to daily practice. As it turns out, there may be a few things that professionals may be certain of, after all.

REFERENCES

Best, D. L. (1993). Inducing children to generate mnemonic organizational strategies: An examination of long-term retention and materials. *Developmental Psychology, 29*(2), 334–336.

Best, D. L., & Ornstein, P. A. (1986). Children's generation and communication of mnemonic organizational strategies. *Developmental Psychology, 22,* 845–853.

Bleich, D. (1989). Reconceiving literacy; Language used and social relations. In C. M. Anson (Ed.), *Writing and response, theory, practice, and research* (pp. 15–36). Urbana, IL: National Council of Teachers of English.

Butler, K. G. (1986). *Childhood language disorders.* Austin, TX: Pro-Ed.

Crain-Thoreson, C., & Dale, P. S. (1992). Do early talkers become early readers? Linguistic precocity, preschool language, and emergent literacy. *Developmental Psychology, 28*(3), 421–429.

Garner, R., & Alexander, P. A. (1989). Metacognition: Answered and unanswered questions. *Educational Psychologist, 24*(2), 142–158.

Rabinowitz, M. (1988). On teaching cognitive strategies: The influence of accessibility of conceptual knowledge. *Contemporary Educational Psychology, 13,* 229–235.

Wang, M. C., Haertel, G. D., & Walberg, H. J. (in press). Improving school learning: An evaluation of approaches. *Educational Leadership.*

PART TWO

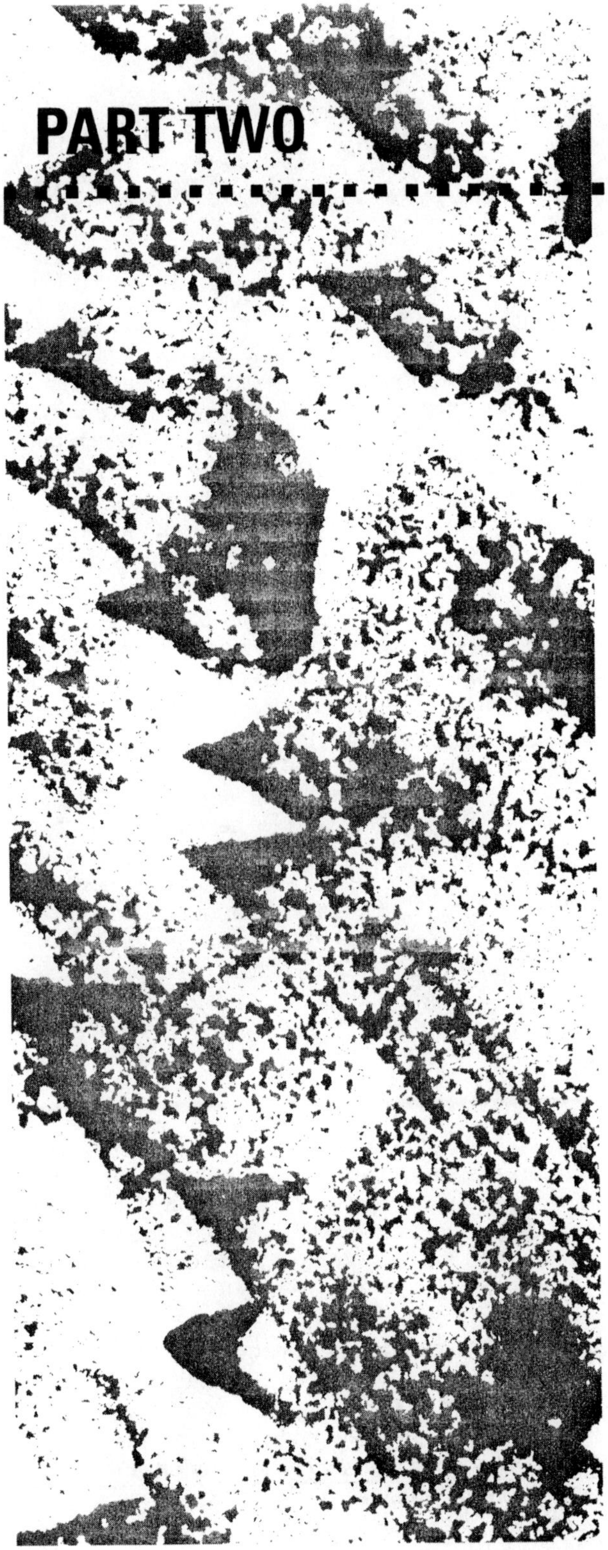

FOCUS ON ASSESSMENT: POTENTIAL AND PROGRESS

4

CURRICULUM-BASED LANGUAGE ASSESSMENT AND INTERVENTION ACROSS THE GRADES

■ Nickola Wolf Nelson
Western Michigan University

Children and adolescents with language learning disabilities are at risk for failing to meet the demands of the regular school curriculum in a number of areas. The traditional special education response has been to remove youngsters from the contexts in which they are unable to achieve so they can receive services in alternative learning contexts, usually with separate and different curricular expectations. The extent to which children are removed from regular classrooms (and the regular curriculum) generally depends on the nature and degree of impairments identified through individualized formal testing. Such approaches, however, too often focus on splinter skills rather than functional outcomes that can foster success when children return to their regular classrooms.

In this book, several authors describe alternative assessment strategies (see Palincsar, Brown, & Campione, chap. 5; Silliman & Wilkinson, chap. 6) that are more relevant to students' everyday needs. Such approaches are compatible with the framework and philosophy described in this chapter for organizing informal activities of curriculum-based language assessment and intervention to foster students' opportunities to participate successfully in regular classroom settings across the grades.

PROBLEMS STEMMING FROM TRADITIONAL "SOLUTIONS"

In elementary school, the frequent pattern for many children with milder impairments is to be "pulled out" of their regular classrooms for isolated practice on specific skills, often twice a week for half-hour sessions with a speech-language pathologist. Children with slightly more severe impairments might receive, in addition, the services of a specialist in learning disabilities for several hours a week in a resource room. Some children in the United States with language learning problems, but no identifiable disabilities, qualify for "Chapter One" services, federally funded remedial and compensatory education programs designed to help children who are economically disadvantaged and educationally deficient. Other children, who have identifiable disabilities, spend increasing proportions of their school days in special education settings, perhaps participating in regular classrooms only for such activities as "homeroom," art, music, and physical education. Children with the most severe deficits are sometimes placed in "self-contained" classroom programs, which may be located in separate school buildings or even separate school districts.

At adolescence, secondary school programs generally include modifications to meet revised scheduling demands (see Ehren, chap. 15). For some individuals, departmentalization involves moving from class to class, in a combination of regular and special education environments. If traditional approaches were working to keep students involved in regular classroom settings, one might expect fewer children to need special services at each grade level, but the data do not support such a conclusion. They show instead that the proportion of children enrolled in remedial and compensatory programs increases from 25% in second grade to 38% by seventh grade (Anderson & Pellicer, 1990). For many secondary students with diagnosed language learning disabilities, resource rooms and self-contained classrooms continue to serve as primary placement settings.

Practices that involve removing students from the regular curriculum have been based on the assumption that failure can be prevented if children are removed from the contexts that are giving them difficulty. A second assumption is that children's impairments can be remediated only if they are taught by approaches that differ radically from those used in regular classrooms.

A third is that working on basic skills that are deficient can fix academic problems, so that young people might eventually go back into regular classrooms or might make the transition to regular job settings successfully (see also Lahey & Bloom, chap. 13).

The trouble is that this kind of "fix-it" strategy has not worked for many children and adolescents. Rather than catching up, many fall farther and farther behind, with increased risk for dropping out of school prematurely, or never achieving complete independence. In some cases, the special curriculum even seems to ensure that children will never meet the standards expected of their same-age peers. The following statement, which was written primarily for students in compensatory and remedial programs, could easily apply to many students in special education programs as well:

> Students in compensatory and remedial programs have very high success rates (in terms of the percentage of correct responses to classroom questions and the percentage of correct answers or solutions to exercises included on worksheets or other written assignments). Unfortunately, however, the demands placed on these students by the academic content that is the basis for these questions and worksheets are often far lower than those typically included on the state or national tests they may have to pass to exit from the programs. (Anderson & Pellicer, 1990, p. 13)

KEEPING STUDENTS IN THE REGULAR CURRICULUM

A basic value underlying this chapter is that, to the extent possible, children with language learning disabilities should receive services aimed at keeping them in the regular curriculum. This goal is not the same as saying that all students should be mainstreamed full-time, certainly not in the way that mainstreaming has been implemented traditionally. Returning students, without additional support, into situations where they have already failed and then asking them to meet the standards expected of students who do not have language learning disabilities is a sure recipe for further failure and frustration. The alternatives of pulling students out of the regular curriculum entirely or expecting them to learn more than one curriculum also have long-term implications for limiting youngsters' future options in school and in life.

Keeping students in the regular curriculum is not the same as giving them more of the same, and it does not mean making their regular education teachers totally responsible for teaching them. Rather, it requires the commitment of both regular and special educators (including speech-language pathologists) to engage in the ongoing process of analyzing the language and communication expectations of the regular curriculum deliberately, to identify points of match and mismatch between the curriculum and the abilities of the target student, and to design intervention strategies that support students' attempts to make sense of what is going on, to communicate competently, and to learn. Even when a special curriculum is clearly required for a student to progress, it is a basic premise of the curriculum-based language intervention approach that professionals responsible for teaching the alternative curriculum should keep their eyes on the regular curriculum. They should use pieces of the regular curriculum in the intervention process, and they should maintain the goal to assist students to gain increasing access to it and to regular classroom activities.

Some professionals who have concerns about the current state of the regular education curriculum might object to this rather strong statement of purpose. They would point out the many things that are wrong with curricular outlines and textbook series currently used in many regular education classrooms (as per Scott in chap. 8, this volume). Although it may be true that many curriculum plans could use revisions in goals, materials, and methods, it is the premise of this chapter that, in most cases, the value of keeping students in the regular curriculum of their own school far outweighs potential disadvantages associated with any particular curriculum. When professionals have concerns about the curriculum used in their school districts, they might work toward two different goals simultaneously: (1) to keep students in the regular curriculum whenever possible, and (2) to collaborate with others in modifying the regular curriculum so that it is more appropriate for all students (e.g., by volunteering to serve on the district's curriculum committee and by reading the literature on educational reform).

What is the regular curriculum? A broad definition of *curriculum* has been suggested to encompass the variety of things children are expected to learn in school to become successful, independent citizens (see Nelson, 1989, 1990, 1993). The broad definition includes five or six different kinds of curricula. Some are official and clearly evident; others are more subtle to all involved, both students and school officials. Six kinds of curricula are summarized in Figure 4–1.

FIGURE 4–1
A summary of the kinds of curricula children must learn to succeed in school

From *Childhood Language Disorders in Context: Infancy through Adolescence* (p. 416) by N. W. Nelson, 1993, New York: Merrill/Macmillan. Copyright 1992 by N. W. Nelson. Shared by permission of the author.

Official Curriculum	The outline produced by curriculum committees in many school districts. May or may not have major influence in a particular classroom. To find out, ask the teacher to show you a copy.
Cultural Curriculum	The unspoken expectations for students to know enough about the mainstream culture to use it as background context in understanding various aspects of the official curriculum.
De facto Curriculum	The use of textbook selections rather than an official outline to determine the curriculum. Classrooms in the same district often vary in the degree to which "teacher manual teaching" occurs.
School Culture Curriculum	The set of spoken and unspoken rules about communication and behavior in classroom interactions. Includes expectations for metapragmatic awareness of rules about such things as when to talk, when not to talk, and how to request a turn.
Hidden Curriculum	The subtle expectations that teachers have for determining who the "good students" are in the classrooms. They vary with the value systems of individual teachers. Even students who are insensitive to the rules of the school culture curriculum usually know where they fall on a classroom continuum of "good" and "problem" students.
Underground Curriculum	The rules for social interaction among peers that determine who will be accepted and who not. Includes expectations for using the latest slang and pragmatic rules of social interaction discourse as diverse as bragging and peer tutoring.

Curriculum-based language intervention for students with language learning disabilities involves starting with an inventory of areas where change is needed most. This is the primary distinction between traditional approaches and curriculum-based language assessment and intervention. Traditional approaches use isolated language processing tasks to probe suspected areas of deficit and to identify specific skills that are deficient. Similar isolated tasks provide the context and content of both assessment and intervention, with only late efforts to transfer the new skills to more natural contexts. In contrast, curriculum-based language assessment and intervention activities start with an identification of curricular contexts where language-related problems are evident and draw on those contexts to provide the content and contexts for both language assessment and intervention.

It also helps to understand what curriculum-based language intervention is *not.* It is not tutoring.

Although a speech-language pathologist or other language specialist may work with a student in the context of studying for a specific exam to help the student acquire new vocabulary and strategies for organizing, remembering, and recalling semantic concepts, this professional cannot assume responsibility for teaching the entire content of the curriculum or testing for its acquisition. The student's Individualized Education Plan (IEP) Committee must consider the student's need for tutoring or other support needed to pass courses. They should build opportunities for consultation into the IEP to help the tutor acquire the mediating and scaffolding strategies of curriculum-based language intervention when tutoring is necessary. As advocated throughout this text (e.g., by Wallach & Butler, chap. 1; Ehren, chap. 15; Silliman & Wilkinson, chap. 2), the goal for all students is to facilitate learning, while assisting students to acquire the communicative skills and strategies to become as independent in school as they can.

Table 4–1 provides an example of the way that a team of professionals mapped out expectations for one high school student named Tim. Tim's case is discussed further in the section on secondary school later in this chapter. Briefly, Tim was a 17-year-old who had been identified as having a severe language learning disability when he was a preschooler and who had been receiving special services since that time. Table 4–1 was constructed during a group interview arranged by the school principal with the author as consultant during a 10-minute session early one morning before school in Tim's sophomore year.

Sometimes, mapping out the current status of a student's program in this manner can lead to collaborative efforts to redefine areas where the student might function relatively more independently. That is what happened in Tim's case. Before consultation, Tim had identified himself as a nonreader, as had most of the important adults in his environment. Based on this assumption, Tim was supported almost entirely in meeting regular classroom requirements by his resource room special education teacher (who was experiencing burnout from this immense responsibility). During the brief interview session, it became clear that Tim's regular education teachers saw him as capable of meeting more of the curricular demands of their classrooms independently (previously, he had been completing all written assignments and examinations in the resource room with his special education teacher). Collaborating to construct the outline shown in Table 4–1 allowed the team of regular and special educators to redefine Tim's program. The team outlined areas where Tim could meet regular classroom requirements without special support, where he could meet regular class-

TABLE 4–1
Summary of curricular expectations and educational support needs for Tim, a high school student with a history of severe speech-language impairment and reading–writing disability

Independent	Assisted	Special Curriculum
Phys. ed.	Some written tests	
Metal fab. (projects; some note taking)*	All major written tests	
Health (some notes)	All homework and tests	
History (some notes) (some interactive homework)	All homework and tests	
		Language (literature and composition) thinking skill—using instrumental enrichment

*Parenthetical statements represent possible need for minor assistance.

This table was generated in a brief meeting with Tim's teachers. "Assisted" activities were completed with the assistance of a teacher of students with learning disabilities in the resource room. "Independent" activities were completed in the regular classroom, with the student meeting regular curriculum standards. Tim's Individualized Education Plan included a stipulation that his English credit would be earned entirely in the special education classroom using a special curriculum.

room demands with special support, and where he needed to be in a special and separate curriculum. In this way, the team moved beyond the common problem in traditional "mainstreaming," in which regular education teachers do not consider themselves responsible for the special education students in their classrooms but view them more as extra bodies. Following the collaborative meeting, Tim's status as a full member of the regular classroom was more clearly established, along with a format for encouraging him to gain even greater independence in the future.

Curriculum-based *language* assessment is distinguished from more general types of "curriculum-based assessment" or "curriculum-based measurement" by differences in its scope of purpose. Curriculum-based assessment is defined, in general, as use of the local curriculum for determining a student's instructional needs and progress (Tucker, 1985). It addresses such questions as "Has the student learned the regular curriculum?" In contrast, curriculum-based *language* assessment addresses such questions as "Does this student have the language skills and strategies for processing the *language* of the regular curriculum?" (Nelson, 1990, emphasis added). Differences of purpose lead professionals who use curriculum-based language assessment and intervention to adopt special kinds of assessment and intervention techniques and strategies.

IDENTIFYING ZONES OF SIGNIFICANCE

When conducting curriculum-based language assessment, a team of professionals cannot thoroughly investigate a student's functioning in every aspect of the curriculum. Spending so much time on assessment would delay intervention, and when intervention finally began, the student's curricular-based needs would likely have altered. The first step, therefore, in the process of conducting curriculum-based language assessment is to zero in on the areas of greatest significance for a particular student.

"Zones of significance" are contextually based areas that two or more informants identify as being of primary concern to the target child and significant others. Their relevance may be due to a variety of factors, such as the following:

- Emotional and/or social importance
- Academic importance
- Functional importance
- Relative degree of impairment or strength
- Frequency or intensity of contextually based need

Such factors can be identified only in collaboration with others. Therefore, specialists in language learning disabilities must collaborate with parents, teachers, and students to identify areas of the curriculum (defined broadly) that should be addressed in the intervention process. The advantage of the collaborative process is that "the outcome is enhanced, altered, and produces solutions that are different from those that the individual team members would produce individually" (Idol, Paolucci-Whitcomb, & Nevin, 1986, p. 1). A variety of techniques, many of which are ethnographic and borrowed from linguistic anthropologists, may be used (Katz, 1990; Nelson, 1990; Westby, 1990). These include participant interviews, artifact analysis, onlooker observation, and participant observation (see also Westby, chap. 7).

Participant Interviews

Participant interviews are used to view the problem through the eyes of its primary participants (Spradley, 1979; Westby, 1990). Effective interviews are conducted by professionals who adopt phenomenological acceptance of the participants' varied viewpoints. Phenomenology is the philosophical stance that "truth" is relative and that the actual nature of the phenomena being observed may vary according to the ways in which they are observed and the perspectives of the observers. There is no one true version or description of a phenomenon but potentially a number of different versions, all of which may be "true" to those who hold them.

Interviewers also adopt views of their own. They may ultimately decide it is worthwhile to help other participants to move closer to that viewpoint through the intervention process. However, it is important initially to attempt to view the "problem" as each of the participants does, as suggested by Westby in Chapter 7. This involves asking accepting and open-ended questions of the major participants. Usual participants include teachers, parents, and the students themselves. Interviews are carried out in such a way that participants are encouraged to talk about issues of importance to them, while covering matters of importance to the interviewer, "in a way that allows participants to use their own concepts and terms" (Stainback & Stainback, 1988, p. 52).

Interviews should be conducted as conversational interactions, not as tasks aimed at filling out forms. Therefore, it might be well worth resisting the development of sets of predetermined questions to guide interviews for fear that, at some point, the list might be turned into a form to be handed to teachers or parents to fill out on their own. Valuable information can be obtained from written communication, particularly when participants write open-ended summaries of reasons for referrals. However, the dynamic interaction of a face-to-face interview is advantageous, not only for its value in information gathering, but also because it sets a tone and initiates the intervention process.

Assessment blends into intervention in several ways. As informants attempt to answer questions about a student's most noticeable difficulties and strengths, they begin to analyze how the student's problems might be minimized and assets emphasized by modifying current contextual demands and opportunities. As they do so, many participants begin to see the process of change, and their potential role in it, in a new light.

Every interview is a unique and living entity. Some work better than others. When an interview is not working, one possibility to consider is whether the interviewer may be acting inappropriately according to some unrecognized cultural standard of the interviewee. For example, Westby (1990; chap. 7) reported an incident in which two male staff members in a Southwestern city were unsuccessful in attempting to interview mothers recently arrived from Mexico about their children. The interviewers ultimately discovered that, in the families' culture, it was inappropriate for males to interview women alone.

In ethnographic interviewing, questions are not predetermined. Rather, "both questions and answers must be discovered from the people being interviewed" (Westby, 1990, p. 105). Nevertheless, for someone inexperienced with the process, it may help to have some ideas about where to start. Therefore, Table 4–2 includes starter questions and key areas to probe with participants. In curriculum-based language assessment, interviewers might begin each interview with broad, open-ended prompts for interviewees to tell about what has been happening in the classroom (or classrooms). More specific questions may be asked as needed.

Although the focus of curriculum-based language assessment is communication in the classroom, it is usually best not to limit the domain of interviews to areas that participants perceive as being relevant to language specialists only or to classroom issues only. The professional should convey to interviewees that every aspect of living involves communication and language. In school settings, to a large extent, education *is* language, but communication is a key to success in social and vocational realms as well. Therefore, when parents and teachers ask whether or not they should talk about their greatest concerns only in the area of communication, language, or reading, they should be told, "No, if you were to consider any area of this child's life, tell me the things that concern you most and those things that make you most happy."

Interviews may be used to elicit two kinds of description from participants using two kinds of discourse: *expository* and *narrative* (Nelson, 1990). Questions that ask participants to talk about priorities and to list behaviors elicit forms of expository discourse. As noted by Scott (chap. 8), expository discourse conveys information. In interviews, it is usually organized as a prioritized list or as a hierarchy labeling categorical areas of strength, disability, and need. For example, a teacher might report hierarchically that a target child has considerable trouble with attention, which affects the student's ability to understand the teacher's directions and to stay on task in the classroom. Once such areas have been identified, further insights might be gained by asking interviewees to provide anecdotes that exemplify what they mean by their labels and lists. Requests for anecdotes tend to elicit stories that are framed more often as *narrative discourse*. For example, the teacher might list difficulty understanding directions as a major problem for a student. When probed for an anecdote of a recent event where this problem was observed, the teacher might tell a story about how the student needed direct assistance earlier that day to perform workstation activities involving number drills.

When answers are framed as *expository discourse,* it is helpful to pay attention to the order in which topics arise. It is generally safe to assume that areas of greatest significance to the interviewee are named first, although some participants withhold significant concerns until more trust in the interviewer is established. Nonverbal and paralinguistic cues (e.g., intonation and vocal stress patterns) can also signal the relative significance of a topic to the participant. However, all communicative signals must be inter-

TABLE 4–2
Starter questions to be asked of the key participants in the curriculum-based language assessment process

From *Childhood Language Disorders in Context: Infancy through Adolescence* (p. 410) by N. W. Nelson, 1993, New York: Merrill/Macmillan. Copyright 1992 N. W. Nelson. Shared by permission of the author.

Teacher Interviews	Parent Interviews	Student Interviews
Objective information about the student's academic performance, both from achievement tests and classroom levels of performance Descriptions of the student's classroom strengths A prioritized review of the problems the teacher identifies as most important Anecdotal descriptions of recent classroom events with which the student has experienced difficulty Descriptions of aspects of the curriculum that present the greatest difficulties to the student and the most concern to the teacher The teacher's view of the student's potential within the current school year and in the future	Early development (Did they suspect a problem early?) Medical history (especially middle ear problems) Educational history When did problems first show up at school? Did decoding problems show up early? Or did the problems show up in third or fourth grade, when it became more important to read longer texts for meaning? Anecdotal evidence of specific problems within the past year or so A prioritized review of the problems the parents view as most critical The parents' goals for their child's future	The student's description of what is hardest about school The student's description of what is best about school The student's prioritized list of changes to be made Anecdotal evidence—accounts of recent classroom events that made the student feel really bad The student's ideas about the future

preted according to the culture of the participants. For the most part, when parents, teachers, or students mention topics without hesitation and with strong emotion, the language specialist may infer that those areas need attention and should be represented in the intervention plan.

Although labels and lists provide insights into multiple views of a situation, they are insufficient by themselves. *Narratives* round out the picture. When participants retell anecdotes of recent or highly significant events, language specialists may interpret situations from their own professional and personal perspectives and begin to plan how to improve them. It is not uncommon for multiple participants to recall voluntarily the same event (e.g., a term paper gone wrong, a Boy Scout project that was highly successful), but to tell it from different perspectives. When that happens, particularly rich insights might be stimulated by the multiple perspectives. This form of validation, in which similar zones of significance are noted independently in more than one interview, is similar to what ethnographers called *triangulation*.

Artifacts

School contexts offer many more opportunities for written language communication than for oral language communication by students (see Scott, chap. 8). Not only the curriculum, but the nature of large group interactions dictates this. As Scott reminds us in Chapter 8, when children do get the opportunity to participate orally in whole classroom interactions, they are generally expected to honor unspoken rules for classroom discourse that involve taking short turns, producing few words per utterance, and sharing less than 25% of the formal classroom talking time with fellow students (Sturm, 1990).

In spite of the fact that students do very little talking in formal classroom interactions, it is not true that children spend little time communicating in school. Most of what happens in school involves some sort of communication. Much of it leaves artifacts in the form of written assignments, workbook pages, writing journals, test scores, and records of homework completed. Artifacts are particularly helpful because they provide a built-in, culturally appropriate, local sample for normative comparison of the work of a target child with that of classmates completed under similar conditions. This is important because more mature written language samples are not necessarily more "error free" (Weaver, 1982). By comparing samples within classrooms and cultural groups, educational team members may sort out areas developing normally from those requiring special intervention without penalizing students for culturally based variants or normal "errors" resulting from positive risk taking. The disadvantage of reviewing artifacts to gain insight into a student's abilities and needs is that when professionals are not present while artifacts are created, they cannot adequately consider potential influences of contextual variables. Remote observers can only guess about such variables as timing, strategies, and support that might have influenced the creation of a product.

Onlooker Observation

Another technique for identifying zones of significance involves "onlooker observation," which is conducted in such a way that the observer tries to learn from a situation while not participating directly in it. The observer may sit in the back of a classroom with notepaper and some type of recording device (usually an audiotape recorder but sometimes a videotape recorder), writing observational field notes about the target student's participation in some fairly typical classroom activity. Many different observational systems and recording techniques may be selected to guide classroom observations, depending on the goals of the process. Silliman and Wilkinson describe several observational systems in Chapter 6 as well as in their 1991 text (Silliman & Wilkinson, 1991). When onlooker observation is used as part of curriculum-based language assessment, it is best if several different activities can be watched, preferably at several points in the school day. Time constraints, however, probably will limit this possibility. It may be necessary to narrow observational times to those identified through the interview process as being especially significant for a particular student.

While conducting onlooker observation, the observer records two kinds of information. First, the observer identifies linguistic, communicative, and cognitive demands of the curriculum that seem to give the target student particular difficulty. Second, the professional observes evidence of the student's current knowledge, skills, and strategies when attempting those curricular tasks. Because much of the processing in classrooms is internal, it is not easily observed with onlooker observation. Therefore, the majority of onlooker observation data gathering is aimed at meeting the first objective. The second objective is addressed mostly by noting outward signs of attention, comprehension, note taking, and peer interaction. Observing such behaviors can help the examiner to infer something about the degree to which the student may be successfully processing the language of the curriculum and to hypothesize about the possible variables that may be particularly facilitative or distracting.

The "lens" metaphor, suggested by Silliman and Wilkinson (chap. 6), may be used to guide decision making about when onlooker observation is the best choice and when it is too limited. The concept of using different lenses for different observational purposes reminds us that focusing on one aspect of the student's performance, such as the context, may obscure other important aspects of the interaction, which may only be understood with a closer look.

Participant Observation

To gain full insight into a student's internalized language-based activity and other information processing strategies, participant observation is required. This procedure involves an interaction between the student and professional as the student attempts to complete curricular tasks. Onlooker and participant observation exist along a continuum rather than as discrete end points. The continuum is characterized by increasing degrees of involvement by the professional in the curriculum-based activities of the student.

In the purest forms of *onlooker* observation, the professional might observe from across the room, or even from a videotape recorded by someone else. No interaction occurs between the professional and the student (although the student might be aware of the observer's or the camera's presence and be influenced by it in that sense). At the other extreme of most intense participation, the professional might sit side-by-side with the student as the student attempts to complete some curricular task. At this extreme, the adult works closely with the student, perhaps asking the student to "think aloud" to permit glimpses of internalized processing. The adult may also model strategies such as self-questioning to mediate the activity, as suggested by Palincsar et al., Chapter 5, and Silliman and Wilkinson, Chapter 2.

Participant observation involves more than just observing the current status of the situation. It involves deliberate modifications of tasks to assess supports needed to enable students to recognize relationships, comprehend language of curricular activities, and formulate appropriate responses to them. Adults in such situations act not as traditional teachers, but as co-conspirators or co-learners, attempting to figure out the demands of activities *with the student,* and probing how much assistance the student needs to meet them. The attitude is one of participation more than evaluation. Between the two extremes along the onlooker–participant continuum are varying degrees of participation that may be adjusted depending on the needs of particular students and the opportunities of varied situations.

The setting of participant observation depends on a number of variables as well. Generally speaking, the younger the student, the more appropriate it is to conduct participant observation activities in the regular classroom. As students advance in grade level, they tend to be increasingly sensitive about receiving individualized attention that is "special" within the classroom (Jenkins & Heinen, 1989). That is, the same level of classroom participation that might be perceived as positive attention by a first grader might be perceived as highly embarrassing by a seventh grader. Fortunately, higher grade levels are also associated with more expectations for work to be done outside of the regular classroom. For older elementary to secondary level students, therefore, it may be most appropriate for them to bring curricular tasks to a special room that is set apart from their regular classrooms. The interaction that takes place there still might be called participant observation.

Although onlooker observation can be arranged in some higher grade level classrooms, a better approach for observing the oral language of the curriculum at the secondary level might involve remote observation strategies. For example, a speech-language pathologist might ask a teacher to record classroom discourse by placing an audio recorder in a strategic spot in the classroom so that the language specialist can listen to the tape later to get a better idea of classroom language expectations. For older students, heavier reliance might also need to be placed on interview data rather than direct observation to identify zones of significance to be targeted in intervention, especially because secondary students may have as many as six or seven different teachers.

TARGETS AND STRATEGIES

Guiding Questions

Language specialists bring to the collaborative process of curriculum-based language assessment and intervention an ability to analyze the interface between the communicative and linguistic demands of contexts and the communicative and linguistic abilities of students. Four questions guide the process (Nelson, 1989). The first and the last serve as "outside–in" questions. That is, they address the effects of context on the performance of students (these are related to Silliman and Wilkinson's "wide-angle lens" discussed in chap. 6). The two middle questions serve as "inside–out" questions. That is, they address the knowledge, abilities, and strategies that students bring to particular curricular tasks. The questions follow:

1. What are the language and communication demands of the curriculum?
2. What are the student's current inner resources for meeting those demands?
3. What additional abilities and strategies might the student acquire that would make processing more effective and efficient?

4. What changes might be made in the curriculum, or in the way it is taught to this particular student, that would make it more accessible?

Although the first two questions are aimed relatively more at assessment, and the last two are aimed relatively more at intervention, their relationship is not a simple sequential one. The four questions of curriculum-based language assessment and intervention are all asked continuously in rotation over a period of time. They guide the process of ongoing change.

An assessment process that begins by asking what an individual *needs* to do to succeed in a given context leads rather directly to selection of intervention targets that are defined functionally rather than as discrete linguistic and communicative behaviors to be acquired. What it does not do is lead directly to diagnostic labels, to normative quantifications, or to decisions about whether individuals qualify for service. Other assessment approaches are more appropriate for those purposes.

When looking at interfaces between contexts and individuals, it is natural for lines between assessment and intervention processes to become blurred. That is because the underpinnings of dynamic assessment, as conceptualized by Vygotsky (1934/1962) and later operationalized by Feuerstein (1979), involve viewing inner resources such as intelligence to be malleable properties that may be influenced by contextual factors, as discussed by Palincsar and her colleagues in the next chapter.

A key ingredient in dynamic assessment is not only to look at what a person has learned but also at what that individual can learn when the proper scaffolding and mediation are provided. As discussed in Chapter 5, what is being assessed is not so much the amount of knowledge, skill, and strategy that the person brings to the task, but the potential for the individual to modify the approach to a task when guided to do so. Intervention then becomes an integral part of the assessment process (guided by such questions as "What happens if I ask the student to focus on this part of the message?"), and assessment is never abandoned, even when the primary focus appears to be intervention.

Mediation and Scaffolding

As both Palincsar et al. (chap. 5) and Silliman and Wilkinson (chap. 2) comment, the tools used in participant observation, *mediation* and *scaffolding*, are also primary tools of intervention. Mediating processes of framing and focusing (Feuerstein, 1979) that teachers and language specialists use with school-age children are similar to the "scaffolding" techniques that parents use with infants and toddlers to help them make sense of the world. Bruner (1975) described the earliest interactions of parents and babies as "joint referencing," and he credited them as forming the basis for further language development. Joint referencing behavior, as described by Bruner (1975, 1978), involves parents' use of language and gestures to segment ongoing experiences into meaningful elements that are appropriate to their child's range of understanding. For scaffolding to work, adults must enter the world of the child at the child's level.

Building a scaffold to reach higher levels of understanding involves systematic focusing on elements that are just a little higher than the child can currently reach. Increasingly, teachers are being encouraged to see their jobs not only as telling children about the world, and then measuring what they know, but also as leading students systematically to higher stages of comprehension (see, e.g., Cazden, 1988; Muth, 1989; Wallach & Miller, 1988). As in constructing a scaffold to paint a building, when children demonstrate increased competence at a new level, additional increments are added. However, it cannot be too strongly emphasized (see also Silliman & Wilkinson, chap. 2) that, to be effective, interventionists not only must build the scaffold but also must systematically take it down. Allowing an individual to become dependent on the process of scaffolding does a disservice to the individual. True scaffolding, like true mediated learning, leads to further development by the child. Its hallmark is that the child becomes increasingly independent and capable of functioning successfully in multiple contexts. A symptom of maladaptive, or false scaffolding, is that the child cannot function effectively without the presence of a particular adult. That is what happened for Tim, the high school student whose case is discussed later in this chapter (and in Table 4–1), before the team modified his program.

Applying Mediation, Scaffolding, and Miscue Analysis

How does a language specialist assess what goes on inside a student's head? How is it possible to "know" when a student has internalized a rule or concept? This is where the techniques of participant observation come in. They are used to assess the output of a student's attempts to make sense of a particular communicative event. Two kinds of information provide evidence of internal processing. One is more direct and the other more indirect.

Relatively Direct Evidence of Internalized Processing. Relatively direct evidence may be gathered simply by asking individuals to report what they are doing or thinking while performing a task. For example, in social studies, a student's internal report while attempting to answer questions at the end of a chapter might go something like this:

> First, I have to read the directions. Then I read the first question. [Reads question aloud.] Now I have to find the part of the chapter that talks about this. Here it is. [And so forth.]

When completing a page of math computational problems, an internal report might involve "reading" the numerical problems, for example:

> 72 divided by 13 is . . . Let me see. I have to figure out how many times 13 goes into 72.

When students are encouraged to label internal reporting as "thinking aloud" or "thinking language," the labels may be used in other contexts by various adults (e.g., teachers, parents, and speech-language pathologists) to prompt students to use questions and comments that their adult facilitators have modeled to mediate their own thinking.

Mature communicators often use their mature language skills to formulate questions for themselves for guiding thinking and organizing their approaches to problem solving. Emphasizing top–down influences of question asking even on low-level perceptual processes, Smith (1975) commented that "attention is perhaps best conceptualized as questions being asked by the brain, and our perceptions are what the brain decides must be the answers" (p. 28). Although, as van Kleeck reminds readers in Chapter 3, metacognitive strategies are later acquisitions, Smith's comment might even apply to babies whose "brain questions" might be said to organize their behavior. That is, as a baby learns which stimuli hold meaning and which can be safely ignored, the brain may be guiding the process with question-like mechanisms. For example, when a door in the home slams, the baby's cognitive experience might orient the child to look expectantly in the direction of the door. Infantile attempts to make sense out of seemingly chaotic sensory stimulation might be characterized as protoquestions designed to turn noise into information. In this example, it is as if the child's brain is asking, "What is that? Is that my daddy?"

Despite early precursors of metacognitive behavior, reporting one's own thoughts makes considerable metacognitive and linguistic demands. In fact, the demands may be so great as to preclude some children with language-learning disabilities from being able to do so, at least initially and without special training. Even normally developing children do not use inner speech to direct their actions spontaneously in the early years of school, although they may use externalized self-talk.

In his classic discussion of "inner speech" as a way of supporting mature thought, Vygotsky (1934/1962) contrasted his own views about how inner speech develops with those of Piaget. Piaget viewed the self-talk of young children as immature "egocentric speech" that must be eliminated as thought becomes mature. In contrast, Vygotsky explained the value of inner speech to mediate thinking this way:

> Our experimental results indicate that the function of egocentric speech is similar to that of inner speech: It does not merely accompany a child's activity; it serves mental orientation, conscious understanding; it helps in overcoming difficulties; it is speech for oneself, intimately and usefully connected with the child's thinking. Its fate is very different from that described by Piaget. Egocentric speech develops along a rising, not a declining, curve; it goes through an evolution, not an involution. In the end, it becomes inner speech. (p. 133)

When Bivens and Berk (1990) studied the development of externalized "private speech" in a three-year longitudinal study of first, second, and third graders, they found that, in accordance with Vygotsky's theory, private speech moved from externalized to more internalized task-relevant forms as the children worked on math seatwork across the three grades. Apparently, improvements in the ability to use private speech and other metacognitive strategies are associated with greater proficiency as well as with older children. When Forrest-Pressley and Waller (1984) studied third and sixth graders who were poor, average, and good readers, they found that only the older and better readers were able effectively to employ metacognitive strategies to monitor their own comprehension.

If, during curriculum-based language assessment, a student seems to have no idea how to "think aloud" or how to report internalized activity, the strategy should be modeled for the child by the adult participant observer (as per Palincsar et al., chap. 5). When a student has difficulty learning to use thinking language even after it is modeled, the finding is significant for determining prognosis to benefit from strategy-based instruction.

Students who have difficulty acquiring self-questioning and related strategies on their own may need to have fairly direct instruction in how to use them (see Ehren, chap. 15). Perhaps they are asking few questions; perhaps they are asking the wrong questions; perhaps they are asking inefficient questions. Unless professionals attempt to access what children may be thinking, there is no way to know. When the adult mediator does begin to get an idea of how the student is currently approaching the problem-solving process through participant observation, an appropriate scaffold of questions may be provided to help the child move from current simplistic understandings to more complex ones. The process of intervention in such cases involves modeling effective questioning for the student and then getting the student to ask similar questions without direct guidance. Moving the questions from the mind of the facilitator to the mind of the student in this way may be thought of as a "question transplant."

Support for the effectiveness of strategy-based intervention comes from research on approaches that use "talking about talking" (metalinguistics) and "thinking about thinking" (metacognition) to modify how children approach problems (see Palincsar et al., chap. 5). The evidence suggests that it is indeed possible to change such things as problem solving, memory, and abstraction by focusing consciously on how one goes about them (Chipman, Segal, & Glaser, 1984). As Feuerstein suggested (1979, p. 179), what is required is the presence of an "experienced, intentioned adult," who initially provides the language of mediated learning and then systematically assists children to acquire the mediating function for themselves (see also Butler and Wallach's statements in the reflection after Part 1).

Relatively Indirect Evidence of Internalized Processing. In addition to the relatively direct pathway of self-report, examiners might obtain indirect evidence about internal processing from observed behavior.

Some evidence of this sort may be inferred through onlooker observation. As noted previously in this chapter, however, onlooker observation has limitations. When a child is talking to a friend, it is fairly safe to assume that he is not listening to the teacher. When another child, who is looking intently at the teacher during instruction, finds the appropriate place in a textbook when asked to read aloud, it is more likely that she is effectively receiving and processing instructional communication. However, it is dangerous to equate outward signs of orientation and attending with inward processes of listening and comprehension. Many critical aspects of internalized processing are simply inaccessible from an onlooker observation viewpoint.

Participant observation, therefore, is necessary to obtain a clearer picture of internalized processing. In participant observation, as described previously in this chapter, the clinician uses curricular contexts and content to ask systematic questions about areas of the student's language and cognitive processing system that are working well and those that are not. As the professional sits beside the student while the student attempts to work on a particular curricular task, the professional gathers evidence about internalized processing based on what the student asks, says, writes, reads aloud, or reports having thought. The professional uses this evidence to assess how effectively the student is able to call on linguistic knowledge, pragmatic understandings, and metacognitive strategies while using memory and attentional processes to perform the task.

Perhaps, in some cases, key pieces of linguistic knowledge may simply be unavailable to the student. For example, one student may not know what sound a given symbol makes. Another may be unaware pragmatically that remote audiences for written language need more background context than immediately present oral language partners do. Still another may not understand the logical meaning of certain grammatical connectives. In any of these cases, investigative probes may help to identify areas where direct instruction could help. When a student has begun to form weak concepts in an area but is not yet able to integrate them with other ways of processing, mediated learning may provide the boost to assist the child to step up to the next level. When sufficient information has been gathered about multiple kinds of knowledge and skills and the contextual influences that affect them, observational findings may be turned into objectives for IEPs and strategies for implementing them.

One way to operationalize indirect assessment of internalized processes is to adopt some strategies for assessing reading that Kenneth Goodman (1973) called "miscue analysis." The basic premise of miscue analysis is that nothing a person does while reading aloud is accidental. As Goodman expressed it:

> In every act of reading, the reader draws on the sum total of prior experience and learning. Every response results from the interaction of the reader with the graphic display. Responses which correspond to expected responses mask the process by which they are produced. But observed responses [ORs] which do not correspond to expected responses [ERs] are generated through the same process as expected ones. By comparing the ways these miscues differ from the expected responses, we can get direct insights into how the reading process is functioning in a particular reader at a particular point in time. Such insights reveal not only weaknesses, but strengths as well, because the miscues are not simply errors, but the results of the reading process having miscarried in some minor or major ways. (p. 160)

A thorough explanation of miscue analysis techniques in both detailed and abbreviated versions has been provided by Yetta Goodman and her colleagues (Goodman, Watson, & Burke, 1987). They define a miscue as "an observed response (the OR), that does not match what the person listening to the reading expects to hear (the ER)" (p. 37). To conduct miscue analysis using procedures suggested by these authors, reading material is selected that is appropriately challenging, unfamiliar, and unpracticed. When using miscue analysis as part of curriculum-based language assessment, reading material is selected from the regular curriculum, often including both narrative and expository texts, guided by information about zones of significance.

Students are then asked to read directly from the original source as the professional follows along on a photocopy of the text (or a typescript prepared to match the original text as closely as possible) marking miscues as the student reads (it pays also to make an audio recording). When using traditional miscue analysis procedures, students are asked to read aloud as if they were reading alone. They are told that they will not receive help while they are reading and that they should try to understand what they read because they will be expected to retell it or answer questions about it when they are done. Methods for marking transcripts are summarized in Figure 4–2.

Alternative systems may be used for analyzing the miscues (Y. Goodman et al., 1987; Weaver, 1988). Some focus on individual miscues at the word level, but it is generally more helpful to focus on how children use information from larger units of text. That is, after all, the goal of mature reading. Miscue analysis techniques are designed to determine which cuing systems are activated when an individual reads, and which are not, possibly because they are unavailable or ignored. A set of questions to guide analysis at the level of the sentence may be summarized as follows:

1. Syntactic acceptability: Does the miscue occur in a structure that is syntactically acceptable in the reader's dialect? Miscues that maintain acceptability with preceding text may be taken as evidence that the reader is using syntactic knowledge to make logical predictions about what might come next. When such miscues fail to make sense with text that follows, attempts to self-correct generally signal that a reader is using syntactic cuing strategies. Lack of self-correction may indicate that the reader is not engaging in effective ongoing self-monitoring for syntactic acceptability and meaning.

2. Semantic acceptability: Does the miscue occur in a structure that is semantically acceptable in the reader's dialect? Semantic acceptability cannot be coded higher than syntactic acceptability. It is often not possible to separate syntactic and semantic cuing strategies, however, because both contribute to the construction of grammatical, meaningful sentences that make sense within the context of larger units of discourse.

3. Meaning change: Does the miscue result in a change in meaning of the overall text? This question is asked only if the miscues are both syntactically and semantically acceptable. When miscues make sense but vary from the author's words and message, the reader may be overusing top–down strategies to construct meaning, but with minimal attention to graphophonemic details that express the author's intended message. Such readers may need to practice monitoring their predictions to make sure they are consistent with graphophonemic, initial letter, and final morpheme cues.

4. Correction: Is the miscue corrected? As noted previously, self-correction suggests that the reader is engaging in ongoing monitoring of meaning using all cuing systems available. Correction is usually a positive sign, which can be pointed out to the reader as evidence of strategy use; readers who self-correct all miscues, including those that make no difference, e.g., "father said," for "said father," may be too glued

FIGURE 4–2
Codes for marking miscues on oral reading transcripts

Adapted from "Analysis of Oral Reading Miscues: Applied Psycholinguistics" by K. S. Goodman in *Psycholinguistics and Reading* (pp. 158–176) edited by F. Smith, 1973, New York: Holt, Rinehart & Winston. And from *Reading Miscue Inventory: Alternative Procedures* by Y. M. Goodman, D. J. Watson, and C. L. Burke, 1987, New York: Richard C. Owen.

Omissions (circled)	Jill said, "When I get (to) the farm, . . ."
Substitutions	
1. Text item substitutions.	owl An ^oak tree cannot grow from . . .
2. Involving reversals.	"This bus is slow," said Jill.
3. Involving bound morphemes.	ing Soon the bus stopped for a wagon.
4. Involving nonwords.	Chakers or /tʃækɚz/ Chickens lay eggs too.
5. Misarticulations.	/ʃeɪkɪŋ/ Mutt started shaking cold water from the lake.
6. Intonation shifts.	The dog hopped into the wagon.
7. Split syllables.	That cold water will be good after sit|ting on this hot, slow bus.
8. Pauses	15 sec. Fish/lay eggs.
Insertions (indicate with a ^)	in Jill looked at^the wagon.
Repetitions and **regressions**	I'll give you a ride to the house.
Corrections	(c) was I wish I did not have to ride on a hot bus . . .
Dialect and other language variations	(d) The tiny cell is call(ed) a sperm.
Assistance from the examiner	Chakers [Chickens] lay eggs too.

to text and might benefit from strategies to help them judge which miscues are critical so that they may learn to read faster and more fluently, while still maintaining the author's original meaning.

5. Graphic similarity: How much does the miscue look like the text? When an OR looks like an ER in print, but the miscue does not maintain syntactic or semantic meaning, the reader may be showing the effects of past reading instruction that emphasized memorization of sight word vocabulary, with words out of context; such readers need assistance to appreciate that printed text is supposed to make sense; they also may need to be encouraged to risk skipping unknown words, expecting that such words may "pop" as the reader reads on, or that the reader may even be able to make sense without a word undecoded here or there.

6. Sound similarity: How much does the miscue sound like the expected response? Miscues that sound like the word on the page generally also have some graphic similarity; a reader who produces phonemic miscues that violate syntactic and semantic cuing systems may have learned to view reading as a process of sounding out the words; such readers may need to be taught to use predictive cues first, to continually ask themselves, "Does this make sense?" and only to check graphophonemic cues to confirm their predictions.

The first four questions in this series are answered yes (Y), no (N), or partial (P), depending on the degree of acceptability. The last two questions are answered high (H), some (S), or none (N), depending on the degree of similarity. When using a formal miscue analysis system, sentences may be numbered and entered on a form that allows the examiner to check off the characteristics that apply to each sentence. Weaver (1988) suggested a miscue analysis format that is particularly useful for language specialists seeking to understand connections between oral language and written language difficulties and strengths because it recognizes that miscues of various types often occur in combination. Her form included columns for listing the original text and the reader's response to it, followed by five additional columns with subdivisions for checking *yes, no,* or *partially,* addressing the questions: (1) Did the miscue go with the preceding context? (2) Did the miscue go with the following context? (3) Did the miscue preserve essential meaning? (4) Was the miscue corrected? (5) Was the miscue either meaning preserving or corrected? (referring back to columns 3 and 4).

The primary rationale for using miscue analysis with students who have language-learning disabilities is to investigate their ability to integrate information from a mixture of cognitive-linguistic systems (graphophonemic, semantic, syntactic, discourse, pragmatic, and world/prior knowledge) while reading aloud and attempting to comprehend what they read. Miscues of various types are viewed as positive evidence that a reader is engaging a part of that system, although evidence from another part might be ignored or unavailable. For example, a "syntactic miscue" represents a positive sign that the reader is using syntactic knowledge to guide the process, even though it is inconsistent with the graphophonemic information available in print. When youngsters violate syntactic acceptability, professionals should consider whether this observation is consistent with evidence from oral communication that the student's knowledge of syntactic structure is weak or immature. If not, perhaps the student has a faulty concept of the reading process and could benefit from strategies for actively engaging syntactic knowledge to make sense while reading.

Professionals using miscue analysis as part of curriculum-based language assessment expand the technique beyond oral reading. They use it to investigate how students integrate linguistic knowledge with processing abilities and metacognitive strategies to solve varied language-based problems from the regular curriculum. This may include, for example, adaptation of miscue analysis techniques to a situation in which a student makes no miscues at all while reading a passage from the social studies text aloud but clearly demonstrates faulty language comprehension when attempting to answer questions at the end of the chapter. As another example, miscue strategies might illuminate that a child who reads the math "sentence" $13\overline{)72}$, as "13 divided by 72," could be adopting a strictly left-to-right strategy because the numeral 13 appears on the left of 72. Such a child might need mediation to be able to frame such problems appropriately and to approach them with an appropriate set of questions, such as "What number is in the 'box'? What number might go into the other one?" The desired outcome of curriculum-based language assessment is a qualitative description of language processing in real-life curricular contexts rather than a set of quantitative scores. Thus, smaller samples and informal analysis techniques may be appropriate in lieu of the elaborate record-keeping methods suggested by developers of standard miscue analysis procedures (Y. Goodman et al., 1987).

Another distinction associated with using miscue techniques for curriculum-based language assessment is that language specialists using miscue analysis may act as active participants (as well as active observers) with students during curriculum-based language assessment. During traditional miscue analysis, any active involvement by the adult is discouraged (Y. Goodman et al., 1987; Weaver, 1988). During curriculum-based language assessment, a participant observer can learn more about a student's underlying processing system and can begin to influence it, by occasionally inserting questions and observations. It requires delicate timing to know when to stop a student reading aloud to ask the student to explain meaning, to identify the referent for a personal pronoun (e.g., *he, she, they*) or a relative pronoun (e.g., *who*), or to point out significant mismatches between expected and observed responses. Such timing comes with experience. The best way to acquire it is to stay in the role of co-learner with the student, attempting to work with the student to make sense of a piece of text that is important in the child's curriculum. It also may be helpful to consider Cazden's (1988) review of literature, which showed that, all too frequently and consistently, the usual pattern is for teachers to interrupt poorer readers more immediately and to correct them more frequently than better readers. Better readers tend to be given more "wait time" for self-correction and are allowed to finish phrases and sentences before corrections are made.

The special form of scaffolding that is used in conjunction with miscue analysis is known as *mediated reading.* It is not simply a form of testing, and it is not a way of feeding students the answers, thus making them dependent on the adult. Rather, it involves framing and focusing the student's attention on three aspects of reading in top–down order: first, whether or not the words make sense within sentences; second, whether or not they make sense in the context of the larger text; and third, whether or not they match the printed page. This can be done by an adult who repeats a piece of text the child has just read with the child's miscues intact and asking the child to reflect on one or more aspects of the mismatch between what is written and what was read. Questions include, for example:

- Does this make sense?
- Does this fit with what we have been reading?
- Does it fit what we see on the page?

In some cases, the mediating procedure may involve a bottom–up strategy of helping the child focus on a particular word and showing the mismatch between the data on the page and what the child said. For older children, it may mean helping them to learn to syllabicate multisyllabic words and to recognize the correspondence between syllables and frequently occurring morphemes like *-tion* and *-ly.*

Procedures associated with miscue analysis and mediated reading are consistent with other activities of curriculum-based language assessment and intervention. In all cases, the goal is to *facilitate the student's use of language and communicative skills and strategies for real purposes, in meaningful, functional contexts, and, as much as possible, to keep the student in the regular curriculum.* Within this broad purpose, of course, individual variations in objectives and techniques must be based on students' individualized needs. Nevertheless, the long-term goal should be aimed at facilitating the development of a person who can function independently and effectively in all kinds of communicative contexts, including those of the academic setting.

GRADE-LEVEL EXPECTATIONS AND CASE EXAMPLES

The lives of most students with language learning disabilities are affected across several domains. Interviews and other assessment activities are used to narrow down potential zones of significance for a particular individual. Beyond individual differences, some expectations may be associated with predictable changes in grade-level curricular expectations.

To a greater or less degree, the following expectations may arise in curricular contexts across grade levels. Many make appropriate contexts for curriculum-based language assessment and intervention, either in their original form within the regular classroom or in simulated form as part of specialized assessment activities:

- Understanding and complying with metapragmatic rules of school culture curriculum, showing awareness of the teacher's everyday expectations for appropriate classroom communication (thus limiting the need to attend to redundant oral and written directions, freeing up attention for specific unique instructions for novel tasks).
- Reading narrative texts, retelling stories read by selves or others, and answering comprehension questions about them–both product (factual) and process (inferential).
- Reading and comprehending expository texts, completing written assignments based on text content, and demonstrating metacognitive strategies for recognizing text organization and looking for key information.
- Writing personal narratives or completing other varied written classroom assignments.
- Completing mathematical computations and reading, setting up, and solving written story problems.
- Participating in the "underground" curriculum of social interaction with peers, in social conversation as well as in cooperative learning activities.

Within this general outline, variations may be expected according to different grade levels as well as for individual students. Some general expectations are outlined in the sections that follow.

The Early Years (Kindergarten to Second Grade): Learning the Basics

When children start school, they enter a whole new world of communicative expectations. For the first time (except perhaps in preschool), many children are "on their own" communicatively. Before children start school, primary care givers usually mediate communicative events, make repairs and facilitate successful communicative events. When they enter school, young children must understand the language of an unfamiliar adult, usually in the context of group communication, talking about topics that may be remote or metalinguistic (topics such as *sounds* and *letters*). For example, the following sample of classroom discourse was gathered in a first-grade classroom by Sturm (1990). It illustrates how choral "group" speaking occurs in early grade classrooms as well as responses by individual students:

> Teacher: Today, I'm going to introduce you to a new word. When you have two letters together and they blend one sound, it is called a blend. The word is "prize" [exaggerates "pr"].
> Student: "Prize."
> Teacher: And if you blend it together it goes "prrr."
> Group: "Prrr."
> Teacher: Let's try it.
> Group: "Prrr."

To succeed in the new communicative context of the early grades, children must learn to process language that is more complex and decontextualized than at home. They must recognize on their own when repairs are needed and how to make them. They must also learn new rules of communicative interaction that involve expectations for making formal requests to take communicative turns (e.g., by raising their hands) and for keeping their turns short, to the point, and responsive to topics raised by the teacher rather than initiating turns of their own.

The curriculum and atmosphere in individual early grade classrooms may differ considerably depending on the philosophy of the child's school system or building staff. In many traditional kindergarten and first-grade classrooms, a major proportion of the day may be spent learning to recognize and name letter and number symbols, to sound out words, and to perform simple mathematical computations. Often, teachers use worksheets and isolated tasks to target components of the processes of learning to read, write, and do arithmetic. In other curricula, designed more around the "whole language" model, more time may be spent listening to literature being read aloud, doing personal reading or looking at wordless picture books, writing, talking about personal experiences, and developing conscious awareness of reading and writing processes. Teachers in whole language classrooms tend to view their roles more as facilitators than as instructors (K. Goodman, 1986; Norris & Damico, 1990). However, children with language learning disabilities may be disadvantaged in any type of curriculum if their individualized needs are not considered.

In most early grade classrooms, relatively little time is spent learning about content in the areas of science or social studies, and new information is conveyed primarily through oral means rather than through written texts. Some early grade classrooms, however, especially those built on the whole language model, do integrate expository texts experiences into the curriculum. For younger children, such experiences may be most successful in expressive modes, using self-generated topics, rather than in comprehension modes about other-generated topics. This is because of the different demands the two modes make on children's prior knowledge.

Between the two relative extremes of traditional and whole language classrooms, many curricular variations may be found on the theme of helping children move toward literacy. When conducting curriculum-based language assessment with young school-age children in the early grades, professionals need to understand the processes involved in learning to read and write, the interactions of a student's current oral and written language abilities with task expectations, and the theories, methods, strategies, and vocabulary used by a particular child's teacher and school system.

Curriculum-based language assessment for an individual child involves asking questions about the child's ability to function within the particular instructional model used with the child. It may also involve experimenting with procedures designed to help the child acquire concepts that might not be addressed directly enough within the regular instructional model implemented in the child's classroom. For example, children with speech-language impairments in whole language classrooms may not get enough direct instruction about sound–symbol relationships to be successful written language decoders. Conversely, children in classrooms that use highly structured behaviorist programs to teach decoding with an imitative format may need more literacy experiences before they can understand that sense making is what reading and writing are all about. They also may need more explicit instruction in how to use prior knowledge and multiple kinds of cues to make sense in their own reading and writing.

Case Example from the Early Elementary Years: Nancy Nancy's situation illustrates issues that arise as a part of curriculum-based language assessment for a child in the early grades. Nancy was in kindergarten and age 5;9 when brought by her mother to the university-based clinic for an evaluation. Nancy was referred by a psychologist who has been seeing her for learning difficulties and emotional problems. The emotional problems seemed to stem at least partially from earlier childhood experiences with a violent father, who was no longer in the home. Nancy's mother, who was a registered nurse, reported having had learning problems in school herself, as had her brother (Nancy's maternal uncle), who had epilepsy and concomitant learning problems.

Nancy's mother at first reported her greatest concerns to be Nancy's delayed articulation and language skills, particularly problems with direction following and occasional frustration when Nancy could not think of a word she wanted to say (she knew we were interested in these kinds of things). When prompted to report more broadly, Nancy's mother stated that her highest life priorities for Nancy were related to Nancy's fear about visitations with her father and her school anxiety, which was expressed as morning stomachaches and reports that "I don't like school; it's too hard."

Nancy's developmental history included normal birth and normal developmental milestones except in the area of language development. She reportedly babbled normally but then produced speech that was largely unintelligible until the age of three. Nancy's mother reported no serious injuries or illnesses except for three middle ear infections, at six months, one year, and fifteen months. Nancy's fine and gross motor skills were age appropriate. She had only recently begun to use her right hand for drawing and writing, previously having used both hands with equal preference. Her mother reported that Nancy liked and excelled at drawing and ballet.

Nancy's kindergarten teacher confirmed her mother's concern about performance of such academic tasks as recognition and naming of letters, numbers, shapes, and colors, as well as other early reading experiences. Nancy had been tested during the second semester of her kindergarten year and was found to qualify for services as a child with learning disabilities in the area of mathematical computation. Since that time, Nancy had been placed in a special education classroom in the morning and had continued to attend her regular kindergarten classroom in the afternoon. In spite of ongoing emotional problems, Nancy was demonstrating relatively normal socialization in the kindergarten classroom with her peers. This was viewed as an improvement over her preschool experiences, where she was reported to interact well with adults but poorly with other children.

Nancy probably could have benefitted more from a holistic approach to early literacy learning and a more deliberate teaching of sound–symbol relationships. However, she was placed in a kindergarten classroom that used a highly structured curriculum that focused on recognizing isolated "simple" little words. Being expected to remember and recall isolated symbols without meaning is difficult for any child, but it was particularly difficult for Nancy. She and her mother had spent numerous frustrating evenings with Nancy attempting to recognize a sight word vocabulary made up of function words such as, *it, in, is, the, and, we, will, I, a,* and *to.* On the other hand, Nancy showed a curiosity about the names of things in her world and questioned freely when she did not understand something. In fact, her teacher reported that Nancy had managed to recruit a classmate on her own to help her when she was not sure of classroom directions (the teacher was now discouraging this).

Modifying aspects of the current curriculum was clearly an important feature of Nancy's intervention program. However, helping Nancy stay in the curriculum also meant that she would have to learn to process phonological sequences more accurately and to perform tasks of sound–symbol recognition and recall. Even though such tasks tapped an area of specific disability for Nancy, they were an important part of the official curriculum in her classroom. The mismatch was glaring because of the highly structured and segmentalized nature of the instructional methods used in that classroom. However, Nancy would likely have had similar needs for specialized intervention even if she had been in a classroom where meaningfulness was emphasized more. Then, her problems probably would have appeared as too much guessing about textual meaning and delayed ability to connect spoken sounds, syllables, and words with print. Nancy was not likely to infer the relationships between sounds and syllables unless she had some fairly deliberate help.

Nancy's team began to explore some intervention techniques that might work with Nancy. Side-by-side participant observation showed that some of her difficulty in encoding, storing, and retrieving information about sound–symbol relationships was related to difficulty maintaining stable concepts of words in multiple modalities. This problem appeared not just in reading but auditorily and in speaking, a problem identified frequently among children with reading disabilities (Blachman, chap. 9; Kamhi & Catts, 1989). For example, distortions of phonological patterns were apparent in Nancy's misarticulation of words with complex shapes (and in her history of unintelligible speech). Her word finding difficulties also may have been exacerbated by this problem (see German, chap. 12). In cases like Nancy's, residual phonological processing problems tend to show up as misarticulation of phonologically complex words rather than as consistent single phoneme substitutions. In fact, some (but not all) of Nancy's word distortions demanded oral motor behaviors that were actually as complex or more so than the target words they replaced. For example, *school* was produced /skruel/, and *rabbit* was produced /braebit/.

The mediated learning process for Nancy involved helping her develop concepts of written symbols that were more concrete than were her current wobbly concepts. This involved sitting side-by-side with her and helping her to focus on distinguishing features of the written, auditory, and articulatory patterns that she was attempting to learn. The strategy was designed to show Nancy and her mother that she could learn to make stable connections between sounds and symbols. Indeed, she could learn to recognize those little connector words that were also important, but she needed more than just drill.

Like many children, Nancy demonstrated confusion between letter *sounds* and letter *names.* Thus, it might have been preferable if Nancy's curriculum had avoided the use of letter names, at least until she began to demonstrate some automatic sound–symbol association ability. However, because letter names were used in the regular curriculum in Nancy's classroom, her teachers carefully contrasted requests to say a letter's name from requests to say the sound that it usually makes in words. First, however, Nancy was shown how to carefully articulate the sounds /t/, /d/, /n/, and /s/. The sounds were introduced one-by-one and associated with their printed symbols on little squares of card stock that could be moved around and produced alternatively. First, the cards were moved around with a great deal of support, and later, with almost none. Nancy learned to attend the distinctive visual perceptual features of each letter when scaffolding instructions were provided for printing them while she produced their sounds. Nancy's printing was done on lined paper with verbal mediation about where to draw lines and curves, and where to cross "t's." With brief practice, Nancy could point reliably to each symbol when its sound was produced, using prompts such as, "Show me /t/." She was also able to make each sound when asked, "What sound does this letter make?" Finally, she was able to write letters to correspond with each sound following prompts like, "Write /t/." At this point, she was shown how to blend the sounds into different sequences by moving the little paper squares with symbols on them around to form different examples of real words and pretend words suggested by the examiner. Following this practice, the words, *in, it, is,* and *and,* were printed as whole words on other note cards (like the drill cards she had at home). At this point, Nancy was shown how to use the newly practiced knowledge to "sound out" those words. When she produced a miscue, such as reading the word *it* as *to,* the mismatch was pointed out to her, "When you call this word [pointing to "it"] *to,* you're telling me you see a /t/ sound at the beginning; is that what you see?" When Nancy responded "no," the question would be asked, "What sound do you see there first?" Always the attempt was to get Nancy to connect what she said with what she saw with as little assistance as possible.

It was important for Nancy and her mother to be shown in early sessions that Nancy could identify the difficult little words if she learned some new strategies. However, Nancy's intervention program needed to involve comprehensive aspects of language processing; not just a limited focus on graphophonemic processing. Consultation with Nancy's teacher was used to identify areas of the regular curriculum where Nancy could experience success. For example, Nancy could listen to her teacher reading selections from real children's literature that had a strong narrative structure. Her relatively high world knowledge and dramatic streak would aid comprehension, and she could lead her classmates in acting out the characters. Literature contexts could also help Nancy develop an inner language sense for the structure of written language. This meaningful exposure could enhance her receptive vocabulary and expressive word recall. Because of Nancy's legitimate impairment in processing and remembering oral directions (especially lengthy ones), a plan could be devised in collaboration with Nancy's teacher to allow her to call on her friend for help when needed. The teacher could also be encouraged to check Nancy's comprehension when possible and to praise her whenever she was working appropriately on her own. Nancy's metapragmatic awareness of classroom expectations could be enhanced by encouraging her to play school with her special friend and others in the class who seemed to have a better grasp on it. Because independence in direction following was important to Nancy's teacher (for good reason), the collaborative process should be used to generate a mutual goal for Nancy to become increasingly independent in varied classroom settings. Such a plan would address concerns of all involved, Nancy, her mother, and her teachers.

The Transition Years (Third to Fourth Grade): Using Language to Learn

By the time children reach third or fourth grade, they experience fairly dramatic shifts in the purposes for which they read and write. It is commonly said that, in the early grades children *learn to read,* whereas in the later elementary grades they begin to *read to learn.* In fact, "reading to learn" is the identifying feature of the stage reached by nine-year-olds in Chall's stage theory of reading development (1983), as also noted by Wallach and Butler in Chapter 1. Although that theory is now considered controversial by some whole language theorists (e.g., Taylor, 1989), few would argue that children in their later elementary years are expected to learn new information from increasingly decontextualized written language texts as they advance into the third and fourth grade levels.

In many third-grade classrooms, science and social studies textbooks are introduced for the first time. Children also may begin to use nonfiction sources to read and write expository reports about things and events that they have never experienced first hand. For example, as part of her ethnographic study of children learning to write, Calkins (1983) reported watching fourth grader Susie constructing a report about glaciers. The report was written to meet the official/cultural fourth-grade curricular requirement for "New Hampshire State Reports" that were required to be written every spring in Susie's school:

> I remember one morning watching Susie "read" about glaciers. She began by scanning five pages of notes she'd collected. Each of the pages represented a different subtopic:
> Where do glaciers come from?
> Are they going to be around a lot again?
> How many are left?
> Where did they start forming?
> Other?
>
> Susie put down her notes and headed to the bookshelf at the back of the classroom. She found a reference book, searched through it, then returned that book to the shelf. She located a second book, and this time Susie returned with it to her desk. Putting on her newly acquired glasses, Susie began to look over the book. Page 268 must have contained what she was looking for—Susie read the entire page, slowly. Then she added to her notes:
>
> Piedmont glaciers are rare. They are valley glaciers that move onto a plain. Alaska has a piedmont. (Calkins, 1983, pp. 163–164)

Susie's use of metacognitive strategies to approach this learning task may appear to be somewhat unusual for a fourth grader. They had grown as she worked with her fellow classmates on writing as a process involving reading, discussing, editing, and revising of their texts in cooperation with one another. The example demonstrates the potential that children have during the transition years to take increasing control over their own learning in classrooms where active learning is encouraged. Knowing how expository texts are organized is an expectation that most children face as they enter the transition years (see related discussions in this text by Scott, chap. 8; Silliman & Wilkinson, chap. 2; Westby, chap. 7). From middle elementary years on, students may be expected to complete academic assignments that involve comprehension of complex texts and searching for information using tools such as book indices, glossaries, or appendices. They also begin to be aware of devices such as boldface print or italics that may be used to identify words that are especially important.

Case Example from the Middle Elementary Years: Andrew. Andrew provides an example of a third grader who needed curriculum-based language assessment and intervention. Andrew had been receiving services for remediation of a speech-language impairment from the time he was a preschooler. Even so, in third grade Andrew was still having difficulty articulating multisyllabic words, particularly in running speech, and he was unable to produce any of the allophones of /r/ in any context. Occasionally, his spontaneous language included morphological and syntactic immaturities. The biggest problem for Andrew, however, involved a conflict between Andrew's parents and the staff at his school about whether he had a learning disability or not.

In second grade, Andrew had been in the lowest reading group. Andrew's third-grade teacher did not believe in grouping students by ability level. His parents believed that he had a specific reading disability, but the school personnel viewed Andrew's parents, particularly his mother, as being too hard on him and expecting too much. Indeed, there was anecdotal evidence that Andrew would sabotage his own work, crumpling an assignment and throwing it in the trash, rather than ask for help with his homework after school. When asked what subject Andrew was best at, his mother reported that he did not have a best subject—that before this year it had been math, but that with the introduction of more story problems, that was no longer true.

Andrew's third-grade teacher reported that he was performing adequately for his grade level in most subjects, with his best subject being math. She concurred that his weakest skills were in reading and writing, and she reported that he avoided written language activities when possible, preferring instead to answer verbally. She disagreed with the assertion of Andrew's parents that he was unable to read. The teacher reported that Andrew posed no disciplinary problems in the classroom and that she had seen major improvements in his academic abilities during the school year.

Andrew's case was complicated by the fact that his teachers and parents were locked in a competitive goal setting struggle (Nelson, 1990). That is, one faction could win only if the other lost. With consultation, Andrew's parents and teachers began to refocus on aspects of his reading "problems," which both could agree he had, rather than the battle over whether he could read or not. As parents and teachers began to set mutual goals, they collaborated to decide how best to help Andrew use language to learn. Gradually, they moved closer to a cooperative goal setting mode.

Eventually, it was found that Andrew did qualify for help from the school as a student with learning disabilities. His parents decided to stop spending every day after school in a different tutoring or clinical environment and to work instead with the regular and special education staff at his school. Andrew's school speech-language pathologist began redefining her role with Andrew as well. In particular, she agreed to use what she knew about Andrew's relatively better (and self-preferred) oral language abilities to help him make sense of what he read. Andrew also expressed some of his own feelings about his reading difficulties. He noted, that although reading was not easy for him in third grade, he liked working at the same level as the rest of the third grade class as opposed to being in a separate low-reading group, as he was in the second grade. Andrew indicated that he did not know how to feel about his upcoming special education placement because, "I've never been in there."

Miscue analysis was used to assess Andrew's difficulties when solving math story problems. The particular curriculum-based language assessment activity was conducted using math story problems that Andrew's class had completed together earlier in the day. One problem was particularly difficult for Andrew. He was unable to solve it after one and one-half minutes. The problem, as written, follows:

> ***Painter***
> Estimate for job was $185.
> Actual cost was $208.
> How much less was the estimate?

Andrew produced two critical miscues when reading the problem aloud. He misread the printed word *actual* as "amount," and he misread the sequence of numbers in the numeral *$208* as "280." The observed response (OR) *amount* for the expected response (ER) *actual* maintained both semantic and syntactic sense fairly well, but it lost something of the essential textual sense. To fully comprehend the nature of this problem, Andrew had to understand the rather abstract vocabulary words, *estimate* and *actual,* and he needed some world knowledge about how businesses operate. Children with good school language strategies might make a pretty good guess about how to solve this sort of problem by noting the key word *less* and subtracting the smaller number from the larger one even without the corresponding world knowledge. Andrew was, in fact, able to state correctly that the problem involved subtraction, which he called "minus."

Andrew corrected the OR miscue of *280* for the ER of *$208* when he wrote the numbers in a computational format. However, during the setup, he inverted the subtraction problem, putting the smaller number on top. When the examiner pointed this out, Andrew stated, "I know, but look, the smaller number's on top so you have to borrow [pause] duh!" Even as a third grader, Andrew had begun to express his self-deprecation and discomfort in academic activities with both linguistic and nonlinguistic means, such as slumped body posture and eye rolling. For many students with language learning disabilities, such behaviors appear more commonly at the beginning of adolescence. For Andrew, they were already present.

As Andrew proceeded to attempt to solve the problem, it was apparent that he was focusing on subtracting numbers by columns, one at a time. His calculations for the ones and tens columns were correct as he set them up. He borrowed to subtract 8 from 15 to get 7 in the ones column; then subtracted 0 from 7 to get 7 in the tens column. When he got to the hundreds column, he simply subtracted the 1 from the 2, even though he had written the problem with the 1 on top. In this small sample, Andrew's bit-by-bit focus was counterproductive for him. He needed a more holistic focus on the meaning of the problem. He also needed to adopt some verbal mediation strategies to help him in setting up problems, to self-monitor for sequencing transpositions (which he tended to produce in multiple modalities), and to guide him as he performed the computations.

Top–down strategies were fairly productive for Andrew. For example, in reading a sample from his social studies textbook earlier, Andrew had been able to explain that a "hydrologist" is a person who studies water, even though he was unable to pronounce the word after repeated attempts and some assistance. He needed to learn how to apply similar world knowledge strengths in other areas.

In Andrew's case, keeping him in the regular curriculum, at least during the current school year, would be relatively easy. It had been his teacher's opinion that this was entirely possible, and she maintained a classroom atmosphere that encouraged acceptance of students at different instructional levels in the same group. On the other hand, Andrew's sequencing problems were fairly severe. He clearly needed additional work on phonological analysis and sequencing in both written and oral language contexts. Without it, he would likely fall farther and farther behind. He was at risk to withdraw increasingly from academic participation emotionally and possibly, eventually, to drop out of school literally. Andrew also needed to be encouraged to remember to use his relatively higher world knowledge when he ran into decoding problems, without becoming overreliant on it. The revised cooperative goal setting mode established facilitative school and home contexts where that work could begin.

Middle School (Fifth to Eighth Grade): Coping with New Expectations

The middle school years are defined differently in different school systems. Some systems include a middle school and junior high school. Others include all of these grades in a middle school. Still others maintain elementary school classes up through sixth grade and a junior high school for grades 7 through 9. Such confusion mirrors appropriately the general confusion of the preadolescent and early adolescent years. It is a time when two children of exactly the same chronological age may have entirely different bodies, as well as entirely different social and intellectual needs and interests.

The middle school and junior high school years involve combined forces of the dramatic physiological changes of puberty and beginning movement toward independence. It is a time of tension between parents and children, and between teachers and students, as all seek to negotiate the paired concerns of autonomy and responsibility. Meanwhile, adolescents must construct new ways of relating to peers who are members of the same and opposite sexes. Cooper and Anderson-Inman (1988) noted that linguistic resources acquired by the time children reach adolescence help them to situate themselves in the social world, commenting:

> Whether children talk with their friends, initiate a romantic conversation, or make a delicate request of their parents, competent use of language skills is required. (p. 243)

Many students begin to cope for the first time during the middle school years with the expectations of moving each class period to different classrooms and teachers. Along with such changes, they are expected to organize their own study time and to complete assignments outside of class. They experience more lecture-style classroom communication, with beginning expectations for note taking and outlining, plus the need to understand ideas that are increasingly abstract and couched in more complex language than ever before.

Systematic increments in the grammatical complexity of teachers' instructional discourse have been found from third- to fifth- or sixth-grade levels (Cuda, 1976; Sturm, 1990), when no significant increments appeared from first to third grade (speaking rate increments, however, were observed from first to third grade by Cuda, 1976). Such evidence supports impressions of increased linguistic demands in later elementary and middle school classrooms. Accompanying the increases in contextual demands, students in the middle school years make gains in the ability to understand complex and abstract meanings. Nippold's (1988) review of the research on language acquisition during the years from nine to nineteen showed increments in full acquisition of subtle lexical meanings. She also found evidence of increased verbal reasoning ability and increased ability to process figurative language and linguistic ambiguity. Scott (1988; chap. 8) found similar advances in the ability to process complex spoken and written syntax during the years from nine to nineteen.

Much of the language learning during the middle school years is, in fact, facilitated by experiences with the written form, as Scott (chap. 8) also notes. Chall (1983) noted that two separate but related substages of reading development usually spanned the grades from fourth to sixth and seventh to ninth. In the first, children begin to use reading to gain conventional information about the world from sources that usually do not require special prior knowledge. In the second, they begin to use reading to acquire knowledge that is truly new to them. By the end of this period, adolescents can read local newspapers, popular adult fiction, and popular magazines such as *The Reader's Digest.*

Students who continue to have difficulty with abstract meanings and complex syntax may be overwhelmed by increased linguistic demands of school discourse at this stage. When complexity factors are compounded by social-interaction and self-esteem issues, the challenges are multiplied.

Case Example from the Middle School Years: Larry. Larry had particular difficulty with the social interaction demands of the "underground curriculum." Larry was aged 13 years 5 months when his mother brought him to the university clinic. Her main concerns were related to Larry's speech problems and his lack of positive social interactions, particularly at school. She described the video game Nintendo as Larry's "best friend." Larry had been receiving special education services since he was in the first grade. His current IEP involved special education services during the first, fifth, and sixth periods, with regular seventh-grade classes the rest of the day.

Larry's own greatest concern was being teased by the other students. The following excerpt of language interaction with a clinician represents Larry's anecdotal account of how school felt to him:

Clinician: Well, tell us the last time that someone teased you that made you feel real bad. Tell us about that specific time, okay?

Larry: Yesterday. But they didn't really tease me. They somebody / uhm / like somebody named Robby. He / uh / sp spit in mm my face face. And I got mad.

Clinician: Where were you?

Larry: At lunch.

Clinician: And were you sitting at the same table?

Larry: No, no I wasn't sitting at the same table 'cuz they tease me too much. So I get to sit / in the lunch / in the cafeteria where they fix the food in the back.

Clinician: So you sit back there with the cafeteria lady?

Larry: With the cafeteria ladies. They / I / uh / where they store store store the food and stuff. I sit back there.

Clinician: How do you feel about that?

Larry: Uh / I had / I don't really like it. Some sometimes I don't like sitting / I sit back there sometimes. It's just . . .

Clinician: It's what?

Larry: I like sitting / sometimes I like sitting at the tables when I came.

Clinician: Is there anybody that treats you nice, Larry?

Larry: Uhmm, not really. There there're a few but but they're not really / not really nice to me.

Larry's language sample could be analyzed on multiple levels. The fluency problems and grammatical formulation difficulties are quite apparent. What is not observable from this written transcription is Larry's consistent substitution of labiodentals for all bilabial consonants (which turned out to be related to a marked oral-motor apraxia that made it impossible for him to protrude and maneuver his tongue, or to simulate blowing or whistling). Although none of these issues should be ignored (all contributed to the problem as a whole), they were not as centrally located in a zone of significance for Larry as was the content of the message. Here was a youngster whose social life at school was miserable, and something had to change.

When a communication sample was analyzed for Larry using Damico's (1985) "clinical discourse analysis" procedures, he was found to demonstrate a total of 47 discourse problem behaviors in 14 of 23 utterances (60.1%). These included numerous linguistic nonfluencies in the "manner" category, several problems with nonspecific vocabulary in the "quantity" category, and fewer problems in the "quality" (message inaccuracy) and "relation" (topic maintenance and relevance) categories. Certainly, such behaviors would need to be targeted in social conversational contexts in Larry's IEP (perhaps using something such as Hoskins' (1987) *Conversations* program). That was the "inside–out" part of Larry's intervention program.

Larry's situation, however, also called for a heavy dose of "outside–in" intervention, with attempts to modify a most unfriendly environment. Getting a group of adolescents to accept an outsider voluntarily is not an easy task. The team approached the situation by calling on the expertise of the school social worker. When contacted, she was anxious to be involved. Larry was already on her caseload. As the team talked about possibly finding one or more boys in the school's "in" group who might be convinced to consider a supportive "friendship" with Larry as a special project, it became apparent that, at first, the social worker was thinking only in terms of modifying the curriculum for the special education social interaction group in which Larry was included. The other special education students in that group had as many "underground curriculum" problems as Larry did. As the school social worker became open to the idea of collaborating with regular education teachers, she and the seventh-grade "Skills for Living" teacher decided to work together. They worked on a thematic unit about individual differences of all kinds, emphasizing acceptance of people with disabilities even when the problems appeared to be relatively mild. The effort was designed to bring out into the open some elements of the underground curriculum that had become quite damaging for one young man. It was hoped that the school staff and students would begin to pull together to make some changes that would benefit all of them.

Secondary School (Ninth to Twelfth Grade): Strategies for Success

The steady march toward independent learning and living continues during the secondary school years. Both oral and written language demands increase as students enter high school. It has been estimated that secondary school students spend as much as 90% of their school days listening to teachers talk (Griffin & Hannah, 1960; Scott, chap. 8). Students with inadequate language comprehension skills may be left in the position of "dropping out," either literally or figuratively. The problem is compounded for many of these students because the note-taking skills they have begun to develop during their junior high school years become essential for survival during high school. Inefficient, inaccurate, and disorganized approaches to note taking pose significant risks for students who have trouble listening, recognizing discourse organization, transposing words they hear or read from the chalkboard to their notes, abbreviating or omitting redundant or nonessential words, comprehending as they listen and write, and asking questions appropriately when they fail to understand or get behind in their note taking. Students also must learn to budget their own time better, often being expected to complete long reading and writing assignments outside of school time.

While all of these organizational shifts in responsibility are occurring, the content of instruction shifts as well. In her stage theory of literacy development, Chall (1983) identified the high school years as one of "multiple viewpoints." Secondary students are expected to develop the ability to consider more than one point of view as they read and learn. Textbooks at the high school level reflect this shift by providing greater depth and more viewpoints. Students may be expected to go to original references when they do expository writing (recall that Susie could do some of this even at the fourth-grade level), and they may have to reconcile divergent points of view.

Students at the high school level also encounter more abstract language and the need to interpret texts on multiple levels as they read narrative works and poetry. They are expected to construct more mature texts when they write. They also may acquire more formal discourse skills of oral debate and group discussion, particularly as they work together in cooperative learning or peer tutoring contexts (also discussed by Scott in chap. 8).

The social lives of adolescents continue to undergo dramatic shifts as well. Learning to drive, dating, and first jobs all create immense pressures for young people (and their parents). Deciding which peer group to identify with, both within school and out, remains a major task of the underground curriculum during the years of later adolescence. Certainly, these developmental needs make demands on more than language and communication skills, but without adequate communicative abilities, young people can face real disadvantages in other important areas of their lives (see Ehren's discussion in chap. 15).

Case Example from the Secondary School Years: Tim. Tim was introduced earlier in this chapter as the high school sophomore whose special education teacher had been providing a scaffolding that was supporting his ability to pass his courses with high grades but no independence. She was experiencing "burnout" in the process. Unlike Larry, Tim was well accepted by his peers. As a star athlete on the football and track teams, he was quite popular. Tim's teachers all recognized his communicative strengths for interacting socially with both peers and adults (although he often dropped his eyes and mumbled with adults), for demonstrating strong elements of executive control (he cared about his grades and academic future), for asking clarification questions when he did not understand, and for grasping concepts that were presented auditorily in class.

Tim, his mother, and his special education teacher all identified greater independence in reading as their primary goal. To achieve this goal, Tim agreed that he would need to spend more time reading, writing, and talking about things he was interested in, both in school and out. At first, the team thought he might be able to read the magazine *Sports Illustrated for Kids* relatively independently, but that proved to be too challenging. He started out reading baseball cards, moved to comic books, then started reading the newspaper (particularly captions for pictures), and finally, began to read novels independently.

The other change in Tim's program was to implement conscious efforts to reduce the amount of scaffolding in his special education classroom. This plan included revision in strategies to be used both by the learning disabilities resource room teacher (Mrs. L.) and the speech-language pathologist (Mrs. P.). Alternative methods were discussed for accomplishing this objective in these excerpts from a consultation report regarding Tim:

1. Across the board modifications might include: (a) more paraphrasing of questions and text material by Tim before attempting to write answers; (b) encouraging Tim to show greater independence in analyzing text structure of new chapters when they are first introduced; (c) expecting Tim to use that knowledge to recall major topics of chapters when searching for answers; (d) to the extent that time allows, expecting Tim to formulate answers orally to questions himself, and to rely on Mrs. L. primarily for spelling difficult words; (e) support from the speech-language pathologist, Mrs. P., regarding attention to frequently appearing organizing words in the history discussion questions (e.g., *include, discuss*), focus on word analysis skills involving syllabication, recognition of prefixes and suffixes, and pronunciation for words found in Tim's history and social studies texts.
2. More dramatic modifications might be implemented on a more limited basis. These include: (a) expecting Tim to answer at least one question completely independently before asking for help; (b) encouraging him to analyze for himself what he can and cannot do without help; (c) allowing Tim time to use and describe the strategies Mrs. L. has modeled while he attempts to work independently; (d) timing how long it takes him to answer a single question independently, adding more problems to his independent processing load as he gets faster.

The result was a modification of all of these suggestions. Mrs. L. worked with several special education resource room students who shared the same history class. They formed a cooperative learning group to work on their history discussion questions together in the resource room with gradually decreasing dependence on her intervention.

Several months later, repeat interviews with Tim and his mother showed that Tim had become "a different kid." He was taking charge of his own life and no longer needing reminders about his schedule and other responsibilities. Tim's mother reported that for the first few days after the original consultation visit, Tim thought Mrs. L. might be mad at him because she was not helping as much as she did before. After the first few days, however, Tim's mother no longer heard those kinds of comments. When interviewed about how he felt about what was happening, Tim commented, "I like it." When asked what he meant by "it," he said that he liked doing more things by himself. He was also glowing from the experience of having successfully organized and implemented a project to earn his Eagle Scout badge by building new steps over the Lake Michigan sand dunes for a camp for children with disabilities. That project had even included public speaking before the local Lions Club and American Legion Post to raise money to pay for lumber and other supplies. (Tim's mother reported that he had asked them to "borrow" him some money, but he made the request himself, without assistance from anyone, and the clubs readily donated the money.) The ultimate badge of communicative independence for Tim was driving on his own to visit his brother many miles away at college, something his parents had forbidden before because they feared that he would not be able to read the road signs. Not only did Tim make the trip successfully, he changed a flat tire in the process, leaving a nervous mother waiting for a phone call, but delighted to recognize the more independent abilities of her son when the call finally came.

The Postsecondary Years: Developing Independence

It has been traditional for discussions of children with language learning disabilities to address the needs of children only during their school-age years, and that indeed is the scope of this book, as defined by its title. Increasingly, however, professionals understand that the success of intervention during the school-age years can be measured only in terms of long-term outcomes. Whether a student with language learning disabilities can attain a goal of participating in postsecondary education or holding down a job depends, to a large extent, on the independent skills, coping mechanisms, and strategies that the individual acquires during the many years of schooling. The new federal requirement that "transition plans" be included in the IEPs of students with disabilities from the time they are sixteen years old is based in part on acknowledgment of the importance of the past in determining the future. As they mature, however, some individuals become "ready" to see things about themselves that they have not recognized before. In their late adolescent and young adult years, they may be more open than ever before to the kind of mediated learning discussed here.

MEASURING PROGRESS

Designing ways to measure progress should be part of any intervention plan. Advantages of curriculum-based language assessment and intervention activities are that assessment is ongoing and that progress can be measured in terms of "functional outcomes," as Silliman and Wilkinson also note in Chapter 6. When a student's language learning disability interferes with the student's ability to benefit from educational experiences, measures of improvement should include evidence that areas previously affected by the disorder are functioning more smoothly. This can be accomplished by comparing evidence of baseline levels of functioning with evidence of improved functioning following intervention.

Both qualitative and quantitative evidence of progress should be gathered (as discussed by Lahey and Bloom in chap. 13). Quantitative data may be gathered using relatively naturalistic observational activities, not just by counting correct and incorrect responses in structured activities. For example, the number of appropriate bids for the teacher's attention might be tallied in similar situations both before and after a period of intervention designed to help the student learn how and when to ask questions in the classroom. Another possibility is that counts may be made of the proportion of reading miscues to which a student appropriately returns when the miscues fail to maintain syntactic sense. Later, progress might be measured for the same student when the number of miscues drops from baseline levels. For a student who has trouble understanding pronoun reference, IEP objectives may be written with criteria for improvements to be measured in the context of real classroom communicative events. For example, the student might be asked to identify pronoun referents when reading stories in the classroom reading series or a library book, and successful proportions of attempts might be reported.

The unique aspect of accountability in curriculum-based language intervention is its reliance on measurement using materials drawn from a student's actual classroom curriculum. For criterion-referenced approaches such as this, intervention is considered complete when the student meets classroom criteria established in collaboration with the classroom teacher. This differs from norm-referenced accountability approaches, in which a set of standardized assessment tasks are administered and then re-administered in prescribed fashion to measure acquisition of new knowledge.

The primary advantages of using curriculum-based approaches over using formal test–retest approaches to measure progress relate to their greater sensitivity to small increments in learning and to their greater functional relevance. Especially relevant is evidence in the form of follow-up interviews and observational data that changes have occurred in the situations that were identified as significant during initial interviews and observations. It takes more than one perspective and more than one type of evidence to build a multidimensional picture of the "true" state of affairs for a particular student. It also takes more than one person and a good deal of collaboration for problem situations to improve. Alternative approaches such as these are discussed further by Palincsar and her colleagues (chap. 5) and Silliman and Wilkinson (chap. 6). They can make links between assessment and intervention more direct.

SUMMARY

This chapter has focused on the philosophy and methods of curriculum-based language assessment and intervention. It has been argued that such methods can build greater relevance into programs for school-age children and adolescents with language learning disabilities by tying assessment and intervention directly to communicative expectations that advance with grade level. Keeping students in the regular curriculum as much as possible has been advocated as a primary goal. It has also been emphasized that keeping students in the regular curriculum does not mean keeping them in a regular classroom without special help. It does mean being sensitive to general curricular expectations (with curriculum being defined in the broad sense, as all of the things students need to learn in school) and conducting careful analyses of mismatches between what is expected and what is observed. Along with onlooker observation, participant observation is a primary technique of curriculum-based language assessment and intervention. It involves participating with students as they attempt curricular tasks that have been identified as zones of significance for them through the collaborative process.

At the beginning of this chapter, several service delivery models were associated with isolation from the regular curriculum. This may have led the reader to infer that all curriculum-based language intervention should take place within the walls of the regular classroom. Some intervention activities are best conducted in one-to-one interactions or in small group settings away from the distractions of the regular classroom, at least initially as the student acquires new abilities and strategies. Instead of moving therapy into the classroom, curriculum-based language intervention sometimes involves moving aspects of the regular classroom curriculum into the therapy room. Classroom carryover happens when regular education teachers, special education teachers, and speech-language pathologists collaborate to provide similar kinds of mediational assistance. They do this through mutual goal setting, the use of coordinated methods and terminology to facilitate learning for the student, taking advantage of the student's current strengths and building new ones, and communicating with each other frequently. The service delivery model may involve a combination of approaches and placement options. No one service delivery model is associated with the practices of curriculum-based language assessment and intervention. It can take place in a variety of settings as long as the regular curriculum is the guiding blueprint.

Inability to process the regular curriculum without help is what makes students eligible for special education services. No one wants to give them more of the same. Therefore, part of the curriculum-based language intervention process involves modifying the regular curriculum or the way it is taught to a particular student. Professionals may be required to balance sometimes conflicting needs to keep classroom events within a student's communicative reach without diluting the regular curriculum so much that the student will be farther and farther removed from it.

In this chapter, four case examples were used to illustrate the flexibility that can occur in the goals, methods, and strategies that accompany this type of assessment and intervention. To a certain extent, the case examples have been selected to illustrate how grade-level differences influence the kinds of choices made. However, the individual differences represented among this sample should illustrate far more than variation with age. They illustrate the variation that appears when anyone scratches the surface of complex human lives.

REFERENCES

Anderson, L. W., & Pellicer, L. O. (1990). Synthesis of research on compensatory and remedial education. *Educational Leadership, 48*(1), 10–16.

Applebee, A. N., & Langer, J. A. (1983). Instructional scaffolding: Reading and writing as natural language activities. *Language Arts, 60,* 168–175.

Bivens, J. A., & Berk, L. E. (1990). A longitudinal study of the development of elementary school children's private speech. *Merrill–Palmer Quarterly, 36,* 443–463.

Bruner, J. (1975). The ontogenesis of speech acts. *Journal of Child Language, 2,* 1–19.

Bruner, J. (1978). *The role of dialogue in language acquisition.* In A. Sinclair, R. J. Jarvella, & W. J. M. Levelt (Eds.), *The child's conception of language: Springer series in language and communication* (pp. 242–256). New York: Springer–Verlag.

Calkins, L. M. (1983). *Lessons from a child: On the teaching and learning of writing.* Portsmouth, NH: Heinemann.

Cazden, C. B. (1988). *Classroom discourse: The language of teaching and learning.* Portsmouth, NH: Heinemann.

Chall, J. S. (1983). *Stages of reading development.* New York: McGraw–Hill.

Chipman, S., Segal, J., & Glaser, R. E. (Eds.). (1984). *Thinking and learning skills (Volume II): Current research and open questions.* Hillsdale, NJ: Lawrence Erlbaum.

Cooper, D. C., & Anderson-Inman, L. (1988). Language and socialization. In M. A. Nippold (Ed.), *Later language development: Ages nine through nineteen* (pp. 225–245). Austin, TX: Pro–Ed.

Cuda, R. A. (1976). *Analysis of speaking rate, syntactic complexity, and speaking style of public school teachers.* Unpublished master's thesis, Wichita State University, Wichita, KS.

Damico, J. S. (1985). Clinical discourse analysis: A functional approach to language assessment. In C. S. Simon (Ed.) *Communication Skills and Classroom Success: The Assessment of Language-Learning Disabled Students* (pp. 165–203). San Diego: College-Hill Press.

Feuerstein, R. (1979). *The dynamic assessment of retarded performers.* Baltimore, MD: University Park Press.

Forrest–Pressley, D. L., & Waller, T. G. (1984). *Cognition, metacognition, and reading.* New York: Springer–Verlag.

Goodman, K. S. (1973). Analysis of oral reading miscues: Applied psycholinguistics. In F. Smith (Ed.), *Psycholinguistics and reading* (pp. 158–176). New York: Holt, Rinehart & Winston, Inc.

Goodman, K. S. (1986). *What's whole in whole language?* Portsmouth, NH: Heinemann.

Goodman, Y. M., Watson, D. J., & Burke, C. L. (1987). *Reading miscue inventory: Alternative procedures.* New York: Richard C. Owen Publishers.

Griffin, K., & Hannah, L. (1960). A study of the results of an extremely short instructional unit in reading. *Journal of Communication, 10,* 135–139.

Hoskins, B. (1987). *Conversations: Language intervention for adolescents.* Allen, TX: Developmental Learning Materials.

Idol, L., Paolucci–Whitcomb, P., & Nevin, A. (1986). *Collaborative consultation.* Rockville, MD: Aspen.

Jenkins, J. R., & Heinen, A. (1989). Students' preferences for service delivery: Pull-out, in-class, or integrated models. *Exceptional Children, 52,* 7–17.

Kamhi, A. G., & Catts, H. W. (Eds.). (1989). *Reading disabilities: A developmental language perspective.* Austin, TX: Pro–Ed.

Katz, K. B. (1990). Clinical decision making as an ethnographic process. *Journal of Childhood Communication Disorders, 13,* 93–99.

Muth, K. D. (1989). *Children's comprehension of text.* Newark, DE: International Reading Association.

Nelson, N. W. (1989). Curriculum-based language assessment and intervention. *Language, Speech, and Hearing Services in Schools, 20,* 170–184.

Nelson, N. W. (1990). Only relevant practices can be best. *Best Practices in School Speech-Language Pathology, 1,* 15–27.

Nelson, N. W. (1993). *Childhood language disorders in context: Infancy through adolescence.* New York: Merrill/Macmillan.

Nippold, M. A. (Ed.). (1988). *Later language development: Ages nine through nineteen.* Austin, TX: Pro–Ed.

Norris, J. A., & Damico, J. S. (1990). Whole language in theory and practice: Implications for language intervention. *Language, Speech, and Hearing Services in Schools, 21,* 212–220.

Scott, C. M. (1988). Spoken and written syntax. In M. A. Nippold (Ed.), *Later language development: Ages nine through nineteen* (pp. 49–95). Austin, TX: Pro–Ed.

Silliman, E. R., & Wilkinson, L. C. (1991). *Communicating for learning: Classroom observation and collaboration.* Gaithersburg, MD: Aspen Publishers.

Smith, F. (1975). *Comprehension and learning: A conceptual framework for teachers.* New York: Holt, Rinehart & Winston.

Spradley, J. (1979). *The ethnographic interview.* New York: Holt, Rinehart & Winston.

Stainback, S., & Stainback, W. (1988). *Understanding and conducting qualitative research.* Reston, VA: The Council for Exceptional Children.

Sturm, J. M. (1990). *Teacher and student discourse variables in academic communication.* Unpublished master's thesis, Western Michigan University, Kalamazoo, MI.

Taylor, D. (1989). Toward a unified theory of literacy learning and instructional practices. *Phi Delta Kappan, 71,* 184–193.

Tucker, J. A. (1985). Curriculum-based assessment: An introduction. *Exceptional Children, 52,* 199–204.

Vygotsky, L. S. (1962). In E. Hanfmann & G. Vakar (Eds. & Trans.), *Thought and language.* Cambridge, MA: MIT Press. (Original work published 1934)

Wallach, G. P., & Miller, L. (1988). *Language intervention and academic success.* Austin, TX: Pro–Ed.

Weaver, C. (1982). Welcoming errors as signs of growth. *Language Arts, 59,* 438–444.

Weaver, C. (1988). *Reading process and practice: From socio-psycholinguistics to whole language.* Portsmouth, NH: Heinemann.

Westby, C. E. (1990). Ethnographic interviewing: Asking the right questions to the right people in the right ways. *Journal of Childhood Communication Disorders, 13,* 101–111.

5

MODELS AND PRACTICES OF DYNAMIC ASSESSMENT

■ Annemarie Sullivan Palincsar
University of Michigan
■ Ann L. Brown
University of California at Berkeley
■ Joseph C. Campione
University of California at Berkeley

Few practices in education have been challenged to the same extent as traditional assessment procedures and instruments (cf. Cannell, 1987; Frederickson, 1984; Shepard, 1989). Concern about the nature of "high stakes" testing has led to a burgeoning of interest in alternative, more meaningful, and more useful assessment practices. One of these alternative conceptions of assessment, introduced in Nelson, Chapter 4, is dynamic assessment.

This chapter defines dynamic assessment. It describes various approaches to dynamic assessment, presents examples of the application of the principles of dynamic assessment to assessment/instruction in reading and writing, and discusses the implications of dynamic assessment for research and practice.

THE DEFINITION OF DYNAMIC ASSESSMENT

Dynamic assessment is a term used to identify a number of distinct approaches that are characterized by guided learning for the purpose of determining a learner's potential for change. In contrast to more traditional and static procedures that focus on the products of assessment, dynamic assessment is concerned with the different ways in which individuals who earned the same score achieved that score. In contrast to static measures, which reveal only those abilities that are completely developed, dynamic measures are concerned with how well a child performs once given assistance. Hence, dynamic assessment provides a prospective measure of performance, indicating those abilities that are in the process of developing. The nature and extent of the assistance the child requires may be predictive of how the child will perform independently in the future. The response the child makes to the assistance that is provided aids in recommending effective instruction (Brown, Campione, Weber, & McGilly, in press 1992; Lidz, 1987).

With these shared goals in mind, the chapter explores several approaches to dynamic assessment, focusing on distinguishing features of each. (See Lidz, 1987, for a comprehensive review of contemporary dynamic assessment programs.) It begins with the work of Feuerstein, because he is generally acknowledged to have coined the term *dynamic assessment* and is one of its chief proponents.

MODELS OF DYNAMIC ASSESSMENT

Feuerstein

Feuerstein suggested that cognitive growth is the result of incidental and mediated learning. Whereas incidental learning is a consequence of the child's exposure to the changing environment, it is mediated learning to which Feuerstein attributed greater importance. "Mediated learning is the training given to the human organism by an experienced adult who frames, selects, focuses, and feeds back an environmental experience in such a way as to create appropriate learning sets" (Feuerstein, 1969, p. 6). Through interactions in which supportive others (parents, teachers, siblings, peers) guide problem-solving

---

Portions of this chapter are adapted from a chapter entitled "Dynamic Assessment," by A. S. Palincsar, A. L. Brown, and J. C. Campione in *Handbook on the Assessment of Learning Disabilities* (pp. 75–94) edited by L. Swanson, 1991, Austin, TX: Pro-Ed.

activity and structure the learning environment, children gradually internalize structuring and regulatory activities of their own. The literature on language development is rich with examples of the ways in which language acquisition is mediated by care givers. For example, Ninio and Bruner (1978) describe how one mother mediated her eight-month-old child's engagement in "reading" activities. Initially, the mother treated all vocalizations on the part of the child as meaningful verbalizations while looking at picture books, while the mother supplied the actual words. Over time, as the child began to use words, the mother no longer accepted mere vocalizations on the part of the youngster but rather approached the reading activity with the expectation that the child would supply words in response to questions. With each reading, the mother, attending to the growing inventory of words that the child had previously understood, would mediate the child's use of these words and build on this growing language base.

Feuerstein maintained that different learners have different capacities to profit from mediated experience. He suggests that the poor performance of many disadvantaged adolescents can be explained in terms of the absence of consistent mediated learning experiences in their earlier developmental histories. This deprivation results in poor performance on a broad array of academic tasks; however, Feuerstein submitted that, provided intensive mediated learning experiences, these same learners will show improvement. In contrast, students whose poor academic profile is the result of organic brain damage or retardation would be expected to profit less from these remediation experiences.

Driven by the belief that traditional psychometric devices could not tap the child's ability to acquire knowledge, Feuerstein developed the Learning Potential Assessment Device (LPAD) to measure low-achieving students' ability to profit from instruction. The goal of the LPAD is to "produce changes in the very structural nature of the cognitive processes that directly determine cognitive functioning" (Feuerstein, 1979, p. 42). Hence, the LPAD was designed as an intervention to serve two functions: (1) to produce changes in the child's performance to assess the child's degree of modifiability; and (2) to remediate problems in problem solving and thus serve as the basis for remediation following assessment.

To achieve this dual purpose, Feuerstein selected tasks that he suggested require higher mental processes that are accessible to change and that permit the detection of minimal change. The LPAD is constructed around such tasks as matrix problems, span tests, and embedded figure tasks. In this respect, the LPAD bears a strong resemblance to numerous traditional and static measures of IQ. However, Feuerstein substantially modifies the testing situation.

When administering the LPAD, the examiner assumes the roles of teacher–observer while the examinee becomes learner–performer. In this role, the examiner is interacting in a flexible and individualized manner with the examinee. "The examiner constantly intervenes, makes remarks, requires and gives explanations, whenever and wherever they are necessary, asks for repetition, sums up experiences, anticipates difficulties and warns the child about them, and creates insightful reflective thinking in the child . . ." (Feuerstein, 1979, p. 102).

Because the purpose of the assessment is not to predict future performance based on a score but rather to depict the modifiability of cognitive structures and the source of difficulties in learning, the results are to be considered in terms of a *cognitive map* (see Lahey & Bloom, chap. 13; Silliman & Wilkinson, chaps. 2, 6). Features of the cognitive map that are to guide analysis of the interactions and results include the following:

1. *Content*—Examinee's familiarity with content.
2. *Modality*—Verbal, pictorial, numerical, etc.
3. *Phase*—A mental act can be divided into three phases: input, elaboration, and output. Failure may occur during any or all phases.
4. *Operations*—Strategies or sets of rules that facilitate problem solving.
5. *Level of complexity*—Quantity and quality of information.
6. *Level of abstraction*—"The distance between the mental act and the object or events upon which it operates" (Feuerstein, 1979, p. 124).
7. *Level of efficiency*—For example, a high level of complexity attributable to a lack of familiarity may lead to relatively inefficient handling of the task. Factors such as fatigue and anxiety can also lead to inefficiency.

Guided by this cognitive map, the examiner seeks to specify the nature of the child's problem, asking questions about (for example), the role that familiarity of content plays in the child's success or failure, the phase(es) with which the child experiences difficulty, the strategies the child employs, and the efficiency of learning. In this assessment process, the primary indication that structural change has occurred is the decreased dependence on the examiner's help. This help can be described both in terms of amount and type. Improvement in the examinee is the goal of assessment in this model of dynamic assessment, because this improvement permits one to make a statement regarding modifiability of the learner.

There are several criticisms of LPAD as an assessment procedure. One is related to the need for clarification regarding such constructs as "cognitive structure." It is unclear what it means to modify "the structural nature of cognitive functioning" (Brown et al., 1992; Lidz, 1987). A second concern is related to the clinical and, in many respects, intuitive nature of assessment using the LPAD. The open-ended flexibility of this procedure suggests that its success is largely a reflection of the skill of the examiner. A final concern is that the emphasis on very general skills leads to a significant problem with regard to transfer (Bransford, Delos, Vye, Burns, & Hasselbring, 1987; Brown et al., 1992). The tasks and materials used in the LPAD intentionally bear little resemblance to school-like activities. It is quite possible for children to show improvement in their ability to deal with these activities without showing concurrent gains on academic tasks. In contrast to the recent trends toward curriculum-based assessment (cf. "Curriculum Based Assessment," 1985; Nelson, chap. 4), Feuerstein's (1979) procedure is divorced from the content and context of classrooms. Despite these criticisms, Feuerstein is to be acknowledged for the impetus he has provided in the reexamination of special education assessment and placement practices in this country. Approaches to dynamic assessment that have been informed by the work of Vygotsky are considered next.

Vygotsky

Central to Vygotsky's theory of development is the zone of proximal development, or " . . . the distance between the actual developmental level as determined by independent problem solving and the level of potential development as determined through problem solving under adult guidance, or in collaboration with more capable peers" (Vygotsky, 1978, p. 86). Hence, Vygotsky argued that one cannot understand the child's developmental level without considering both the actual level of development as well as the potential level of development.

The static tests of development that are typically in use today, at best, inform us regarding the child's level of development. Such an approach, in the words of Vygotsky, means that

> We focus on what the child has and knows today. Using this approach, we can establish only what has already matured, we can determine only the level of the child's actual development. To determine the state of the child's development on this basis alone, however, is insufficient. The state of development is never defined only by what has matured. If the gardener decides only to evaluate the matured or harvested fruits of the apple tree, he cannot determine the state of his orchard. The maturing trees must also be taken into consideration. Correspondingly, the psychologist must not limit his analysis to functions that have matured; he must consider those that are in the process of maturation. . . . the zone of proximal development. How can this be accomplished?
>
> When we determine the level of actual development, we use tasks that require independent resolution. These tasks function as indices of fully formed or fully matured functions. How then do we apply this new method? Assume that we have determined the mental age of two children to be eight years. However, we do not stop with this. Rather, we attempt to determine how each of these children solve tasks that were meant for older children. We assist each child through demonstration, through leading questions, and by introducing the initial elements of the task's solution. With this help or collaboration from the adult, one of these children solves problems characteristic of a twelve year old while the other solves problems only at a level typical of a nine year old. This difference between the child's mental ages, this difference between the child's actual level of development and the level of performance that he achieves in collaboration with the adult, defines the zone of proximal development. In this example, the zone can be expressed by the number 4 for one child and by the number 1 for the other. Can we assume that these children stand at identical levels of mental development, that the state of their development coincides? Obviously not. (Vygotsky, 1934/1986, pp. 203–204)[1]

Several research programs in this country have been informed by Vygotsky's theory. Two considered in this chapter have been conducted by Carlson and colleagues and by Campione and Brown and their

[1]From L. S. Vygotsky in *Thought and language* (pp. 204-204) by A. Kosulin (Ed.), 1934/1986, Cambridge, MA: MIT Press. Copyright 1986 by MIT Press.

colleagues. Each of these programs employs an approach that can be characterized as "test-train-test," to the extent that some form of guided learning occurs between the administration of a pretest and posttest. They differ in terms of what that guidance entails and what the goal of the assessment procedure is. (For a more comprehensive analysis of these programs, see Brown et al., 1992.)

Carlson and Colleagues

Distinguishing the model of Carlson and his colleagues (Bethge, Carlson, & Wiedl, 1982; Carlson & Widaman, 1986; Carlson & Wiedl, 1978, 1988) is the integration of specific interventions within the testing procedure. By modifying the testing procedures, they attempt to determine which procedures are better estimates of the upper limits of competence. Theirs is an interactive approach to assessment in which they analyze the effects of *personal factors* (e.g., motivation, cognitive factors), *task requirements,* and *diagnostic approaches* (e.g., strategy use) on the problem-solving process. The procedures that guide the assessment process are designed to test the limits of children's ability and include the following: (1) Children are provided simple feedback regarding whether or not they have correctly solved the problem. (2) Children are prompted to verbalize how they attempted to achieve a solution. (3) Children are encouraged to verbalize while attempting to solve the problem. (4) Children are provided with an explanation regarding why a particular solution is correct or incorrect, including the principles involved in task completion. (5) Completion of the task is modeled for the children with a verbal explanation.

Carlson and his colleagues report that these "Testing the Limits" procedures yield higher estimates of ability than do standardized test results and that the more intrusive procedures inducing children to reflect, explain, and elaborate on their responses (3, 4, and 5) increase test performance (Carlson & Wiedl, 1988). An additional outcome of this procedure worth noting is the reduction of test anxiety among children (Bethge et al., 1982). Bethge et al. suggest that changes in such affective variables may well contribute to differences in cognitive performance. This last observation is perhaps best understood by considering what is known about the relationships between motivation, attributions, and achievement. The research of Borkowski and his colleagues (Borkowski, Weyhing, & Carr, 1988), Dweck (1985), and Weinstein (1986) suggests that students who experience difficulty in school are often inclined to attribute success with a task to "luck," while they attribute failure to their own lack of abilities. By appraising these students of the merits of combining effort with strategic ingenuity, and by calling students' attention to the processes in which they are engaged, during problem-solving activity, as is the case in this dynamic assessment process, these students can make more constructive attributions and assume a more active and fruitful role in their learning activity.

A second research program, influenced in part by interpretations of Vygotsky's writings and driven, in large measure, by questions regarding learning and transfer processes, has been conducted by Campione and Brown and their colleagues. Their approach is discussed next.

Campione and Brown

The principal purpose of the assessment model delineated by Campione and Brown and their research group (Brown & Ferrara, 1985; Brown & French, 1979; Bryant, Brown, & Campione, 1983; Campione & Brown, 1984; Campione, Brown, & Ferrara, 1982; Campione, Brown, Ferrara, & Bryant, 1984; Campione, Brown, Ferrara, Jones, & Steinburg, 1985; Ferrara, 1987; Ferrara, Brown, & Campione, 1986) is to determine the facility with which students learn from others and the flexibility with which they use what they have learned. Hence, their procedure assumes the following form. Students are first pretested to plan the match between the students and the task they are presented so that they are successful with easier tasks but do not perform well on the harder tasks. As the students attempt each problem, the examiner/teacher provides a series of hints until they successfully solve the problem. The early hints are general, metacognitive prompts encouraging the student to, for example, "think of similar problems," "plan ahead," while later hints are more specific to the demands of the task. For example, one of the final hints in a series completion problem is to provide the student a template that illustrates the relationship between the various letters in the sequence while the examiner verbalizes this relationship. This phase of the assessment process continues until the child can solve an array of target problems with no help. The amount of help each student needs is interpreted to be an estimate of learning efficiency within that domain at that particular time.

After achieving independent learning, students are then given a series of transfer problems that vary in terms of their similarity to the items originally learned. The purpose at this point in the assessment is to determine the extent of lateral transfer (Gagne, 1965) students can achieve. These transfer problems are classified as "near," "far," or "very far" depending on the number of transformations performed on the initial learning problem. For example, in the series completion problems, the transformations include repetitions and alphabetical ordering of the letters.

Once again, the student is provided help, but only the help necessary to solve the transfer problem. The amount of help needed is used to estimate students' "transfer propensity" in the specific domain, which, in turn, is regarded as a measure of the extent to which students understand the procedures they have been taught during the prompted assessment phase. The question addressed is the extent to which they can access and modify the problem-solving procedures in flexible ways.

To summarize the principal results of investigations of the Brown and Campione dynamic assessment model: There is evidence of concurrent validity to the extent that grade school children of higher academic ability required less help to learn rules and principles and transferred use of these rules to novel problems more readily than did students of lower academic ability. In addition, differences between ability groups were greater on transfer measures than on the initial learning problems; that is, higher ability students showed greater degrees of lateral transfer, whereas students who were academically weak had difficulty applying what they learned to the novel but related situations (Campione et al., 1985; Ferrara et al., 1986).

Studies examining the predictive validity of these procedures were conducted with preschool children using either series completion or matrix problems (Bryant, 1982; Bryant et al., 1983). The children were first given a series of pretests measuring both general ability using the Wechsler Preschool and Primary Scale of Intelligence (WPPSI) (Wechsler, 1967) and Raven's (Raven, 1938, 1977) as well as task-specific competence (unaided performance on the problem types to be included in the dynamic assessment phase). The children then participated in the dynamic assessment sessions, including the prompted learning, maintenance, near transfer and far transfer problems described earlier. The principal question in this investigation was related to the change from pretest to posttest performance. What were the best predictors of this gain score: (a) the static scores derived from the general ability measures and measures of entering competence, or (b) the dynamic scores (i.e., the learning and transfer measures)?

The results indicated that the initial unaided performance of the children was a significant underestimate of what the children could achieve with minimal assistance. There were sizable differences in the gain scores. Regression analyses conducted to determine the best predictors of this gain score indicated that the estimated IQ score and Raven score were related to the gain score, accounting together for about 36% of their variance. The learning and transfer scores, however, still accounted for an additional 39% of the variance in the matrices task. In summary, the learning and transfer measures provided further significant diagnostic information regarding the children. Furthermore, if one considers the simple correlations, the assisted learning and transfer scores were better predictors of gain than were either of the static measures. Finally, the results of these investigations supported earlier studies indicating that, despite the fact that children had learned the same problem to the same criterion, they differed dramatically in terms of how flexibly they could apply this new knowledge. Children achieving lower scores on the ability measures demonstrated less flexible knowledge use than children scoring higher on these measures.

It is important to emphasize that in this research program the goal of quantifying learning potential has been for theoretical and empirical purposes, not for the purpose of identifying children in terms of their initial learning and transfer ability. To suggest that the measures arising from this research suggest stable learning characteristics would be to repeat the error of reifying test scores as cognitive entities. In addition, it would imply a belief in very general learning factors, wherein the problem of transfer once again rears. It is because of these issues that Brown and Campione and their research team explored the principles of dynamic assessment within academic contexts. The ways in which the principles informing dynamic assessment might be applied to intervention with students experiencing difficulty with reading comprehension and with the acquisition of writing are presented next.

DYNAMIC READING ASSESSMENT AND INSTRUCTION

The domain of reading is a particularly appropriate one in which to examine the themes of dynamic assessment and the links between assessment and instruction. Recent reading theory and research emphasize the highly interactive nature of reading performance; as reflected throughout this text, "Reading is the process of constructing meaning through the interaction among the reader, the text, and the context of the reading situation" (Wixson & Lipson, 1986, p. 132).

This interaction has been found to vary as a function of numerous factors: the reader's prior knowledge (Anderson, Reynolds, Schallert, & Goetz, 1977; Milosky, chap. 10), the structure of the text (Stein & Glenn, 1979; Scott, chap. 8), motivation (Butkowsky & Willows, 1980), and the difficulty of the text (Lipson, Irwin, & Poth, 1986; Scott, chap. 8). Such an understanding of reading suggests an agenda quite different from the traditional assessment agenda applied to the case of reading disability. Rather than administering an array of aptitude, achievement, and diagnostic measures to determine the deficits displayed by the child, assessment is focused on determining the conditions under which the child can and does experience reading success (Wixson & Lipson, 1986).

Because this is a fairly new perspective on reading and reading disability, few assessment models have been investigated from this perspective. Illustrative, however, is the work of Paratore and Indrisano (1987). Rather than assessing a series of subskills in reading, they assessed students' ability and inclination to use such strategies as activating background knowledge, building relationships among ideas presented in text, and using text structure to organize and recall text. The materials used in the assessment are representative of the kinds of materials used in classrooms. The assessment itself follows a test-teach-test paradigm. For example, to assess the student's use of text structure to organize and recall information, the student is presented a passage to read. The student is then asked to retell the story. The number of idea units recalled as well as the organization of the recall are evaluated. The student is then shown a "map" that depicts the structure of the text (e.g., comparison–contrast, problem solution, cause–effect). The student is then asked to reread the story, focusing on the events outlined on the map. Following this reading, the student is once again asked to retell the story. If the student continues to display limited recall, he is guided to use the map for the purpose of note taking. This step is followed by another recall measure. The results of this assessment procedure can be used to identify the strategies the reader currently deploys, to identify strategies that would assist the reader, and to determine responsiveness to strategy instruction.

The assessment model designed by Paratore and Indrisano (1987) is nicely complemented by a second model of dynamic assessment that is receiving considerable attention; that is, the use of anecdotal records as a tool for dynamic assessment. Anecdotal recording refers to the process of carefully observing and writing about the processes and outcomes of the learner's activity (Genishi & Dyson, 1984; Goodman, 1985; Johnston, 1992; Silliman & Wilkinson, chap. 6). Anecdotal recording is not, of course, a novel assessment procedure. Thorndike and Hagen in 1977 suggested guidelines for maintaining anecdotal records including the following: (1) Describe a specific event or product; (2) report rather than evaluate or interpret; and (3) relate the observations to other information about the child. What renders anecdotal recording dynamic is the extent to which the observations are used as a vehicle for drawing inferences about students' reading, identifying and confirming patterns in students' responses to reading tasks, and using the results of such analyses to plan instruction so that it supports and extends learning. A recent year-long case study conducted by Klenk (in press) of an eight-year-old with serious language difficulty reveals how anecdotal records provided evidence regarding this child's understanding of herself as a reader and writer, use of phonemic awareness, construction of story, and acquisition of sight words.

A model of instruction is presented next that has grown out of the tenets of dynamic assessment: reciprocal teaching. Similar to much of the dynamic assessment research discussed in this chapter, the design of reciprocal teaching was informed by Vygotsky's theory that a zone of proximal development is created, sustained, and extended in a social situation (Brown & Palincsar, 1989; Palincsar & Brown, 1984; 1989). Vygotsky argued that thinking is a social activity, initially shared between people but gradually internalized to reappear again as individualized achievement (Vygotsky, 1978; Wertsch, 1980). Indeed, Vygotsky proposed that through social dialogue, it is possible for children to participate in strategic activity without understanding it completely. Through repeated and shared dialogues, as suggested by several authors of this text, children come to discover the import of the more knowledgeable participant's utterances and their own responses.

Reciprocal teaching then, assumes the form of a dialogue in which teachers and students take turns leading discussions about shared text. The discussions are structured by the use of four activities, also described toward the end of Silliman and Wilkinson (chap. 2), that are practiced as strategies in the dialogues: predicting, questioning, summarizing, and clarifying (see also Blachowicz, chap. 11). Generally, these four activities are used to structure the discussion in the following manner: The person who is serving as the discussion leader for a portion of text begins by asking questions pertinent to the material read. Other members of the group respond to the questions and suggest additional questions, which are also answered. The discussion leader then summarizes the same portion of text, and other members of the group are invited to comment or elaborate on the summary. If there were points in the text that were unclear (e.g., concepts, vocabulary, references), these are discussed to achieve clarity. Finally, the group determines if there are clues as to upcoming content, and these predictions are discussed. While these particular strategies are useful for supporting the dialogues, it is the teacher who supports the students' participation in the dialogues. This support varies according to the ability of the students and the difficulty of the text, similar to the scaffolds proposed by Silliman and Wilkinson in Chapter 2.

The effectiveness of reciprocal teaching has been investigated in a number of studies conducted since the early 1980s. In each study (1) the intervention period occurred over a relatively extensive period (between 20 and 60 days); (2) the older students (middle school) were at least two years behind on standardized measures of reading comprehension, and the younger students (primary) were identified as "at risk" for academic difficulty; (3) progress was measured, not only by evaluating students' participation in the dialogues, but also by assessments of comprehension of novel text and strategy use; and (4) measures of long-term maintenance and generalization were included.

Focusing on the independent tests of comprehension, students typically scored approximately 30% on these measures before intervention. If one regards criterion performance as achieving a score of 75 to 80% correct on four-out-of-five consecutive days, approximately 80% of the students across ages attained criterion performance. Furthermore, with the older population, maintenance was demonstrated for up to a year following instruction (Brown & Palincsar, 1982); progress generalized to other classroom activities, specifically science and social studies; and the students improved approximately two years on standardized measures of comprehension (Palincsar & Brown, 1984). The young students demonstrated comparable gains on the criterion-referenced measures but not on the standardized measures. We believe that this is an artifact of the nature of standardized measures at the early grades. Tests of reading are primarily tests of decoding skills, practiced out of context. Tests of listening tap primarily ability to follow directions, auditory sequencing, and rote recall of facts. Because of this mismatch between instruction (in comprehension) and assessment (of decoding, rote recall, etc.), the improvement indicated on the other measures employed in these studies has not been demonstrated on the standardized tests.

How is reciprocal teaching an assessment procedure? First, the strategies themselves provide the students the opportunity to self-test their understanding of the text. If the student is unable to summarize the text, this may well be an indication that the student has difficulty understanding the text and remedial action is called for. This self-monitoring is, of course, not only useful in the context of the group discussions but, more importantly, is useful to independent reading of text. The strategies induce the reader to engage in the kinds of activities (i.e., reviewing and integrating content, anticipating information, resolving confusion) in which skilled readers engage (Bereiter & Bird, 1987).

Second, the dialogues provide a window on the manner in which the children approach text for the purpose of making sense of it. As the discussion leader frames the summary and other participants comment on the summary, the teacher is privy to the decisions the children have made with regard to what was important in the text. As the group generates predictions, the teacher acquires some sense of the extent, accuracy, and organization of the knowledge the children have regarding the content at hand. The clarifications the children request inform the teacher about the features of text to which they attend. For example, when the dialogues first begin, the children generally request clarification of "hard words" (even if they are unimportant to understanding the text). As instruction proceeds, the children begin to discriminate among words that are important to understanding the text, and clarifications are more frequently focused on ideas in the text.

Third, the dialogues provide the opportunity to assess the children's responsiveness to instruction and to adjust instruction as needed. In these dialogues, the teacher monitors the engagement of each student in the discussions, provides feedback tailored to the individual's participation, and provides the assistance needed for the child to successfully join the discussion. Because reciprocal teaching usually occurs in small but heterogeneous groups, the teacher's involvement in the instruction varies with each child and changes over the course of instruction. The teacher's goal is to transfer responsibility for the comprehension activity to the students as soon as they are able to assume this responsibility. Because the teacher is focused on this transfer, he is engaged in ongoing diagnosis and adjustment of instruction in response to students' needs.

RECIPROCAL TEACHING WITH LANGUAGE LEARNING DISABLED STUDENTS

This section illustrates the use of reciprocal teaching dialogues with a student experiencing serious comprehension difficulty. Specifically, the transcript that follows depicts a reciprocal teaching session with Sara, a first grader whom the teacher had identified as at risk for academic difficulty. Sara was later placed in a self-contained setting for students with serious language-related problems. The group was reading a story about aquanauts and the work that they do under water. It was Sara's turn to lead the discussion.

Teacher: [Reading] One thing you need is an air tank. The air tank gives you air to breathe underwater. You wear the tank on your back. A short hose from the tank brings the air to your mouth. Before you dive, a lot of air is pumped into your tank. The tank can hold enough air for you to breathe under water for about an hour. Your hour is almost over. It's time to go up. As you swim slowly to the top, the pressure gets lighter. The water is warmer too. The top of the water looks like a wavy mirror. At last your head comes out. You can breathe the air around you.

Teacher: [Clarifying] When it says "you" who are they talking about?

Students: The aquanauts.

Teacher: Yes, now Sara think about that section and a question you might ask us. [The teacher then paused, when Sara made no response the teacher changed the nature of the task] Well, maybe you could first think of a summary. What did this paragraph tell us about?

Sara: About whenever that tank is not filled up, he has to come up.

Teacher: Yes! [Building on Sara's idea, the teacher then models generating a question about this information] Now, we could make a question about that, couldn't we? We might ask, "Why does the aquanaut have to come up?" Would you like to ask that question?

Sara: Why does the aquanaut come up? [calling on another child] Candy?

Candy: Because it didn't have enough air?

Sara: That's right.

Teacher: [Continuing to scaffold Sara in the activity of question generating] Sara has already summarized. . . . Let's try for another question. Let me read this part of this again [Rereads the second paragraph]
Can you think of a question?

Sara: I know. They can see themselves.

Teacher: Hmmm. You could ask a question about that couldn't you? [She then supports Sara by suggesting how she might begin her question] Start the question with "how."

Sara: How can the

Teacher: aquanauts

Sara: see themselves in the mirror?

Teacher: O.K. You answered your own question. What is the mirror?

Sara: The water.

Teacher: So, you might ask, "How could the aquanauts see themselves?" or "What was the water like?" Let's go on now. What do you suppose, Sara, we will learn about next in the story? [eliciting a prediction]

Sara: More about breathing in the water?

Teacher: Fine! Let's go on and see.

As this transcript illustrates, the teacher used an array of instructional moves to support Sara's engagement in the dialogue, including changing the nature of the demands on Sara, working from the contributions that Sara has made to the discussion, modeling the activities, prompting, and requesting that Sara repeat what the teacher has modeled. This particular discussion occurred on the fourteenth day of instruction in reciprocal teaching; at a point when the majority of children in Sara's group needed fairly little support to sustain their involvement. Sara continued to require considerable support for the duration of instruction. In addition, the teacher noted that the topic of the text played a significant role in Sara's engagement in the dialogue. She required much less support when working with topics that were familiar to her. (See Lahey and Bloom's discussion about "competing resources" in chap. 13.) Sara participated in a second phase of intervention when the texts that were discussed were all related thematically, as in the communication-based lesson described by Silliman and Wilkinson (chap. 2). Sara was much more successful in this phase of instruction because the related texts provided a rich array of concepts and coherent information from which she could draw. In the next portion, the application of these principles to the teaching of writing with students with serious language difficulties is illustrated.

DYNAMIC WRITING ASSESSMENT AND INSTRUCTION

Recently, Palincsar and Klenk (1992a, 1992b) conducted research with special educators in self-contained classrooms for students identified as learning disabled and emotionally impaired. Work with these teachers began with the researchers making extensive observations in classrooms to determine the kinds of literacy activities in which these students were engaged. The observations suggested that the children experienced only low-level activity, such as copying poems from the board, copying their spelling words, and practicing the printing of their names. As a consequence of these kinds of experiences, the students had extremely limited concepts of the nature and purposes of writing. For example, the children reported that writing was "drawing," "holding your pencil right," and "developing strong muscles so that you could learn cursive." As the implications of these observations were considered in planning "remediation," the observers/researchers confronted an interesting dilemma: one of the tenets of the zone of proximal development is that children are active and seek to make sense of their world. However, there was little evidence that these children sought to make sense or demand meaning of what they were doing. In addition, working in zones of proximal development is predicated on some joint understanding of the nature of the activity; but little was shared in terms of the children's and teachers' understandings of the nature and purposes of written language. How could instruction proceed in a dynamic fashion so that one met the children where they were but at the same time engaged them in new levels of understanding and activity in writing?

In collaboration with the special education teachers, the following remedial program was designed: The cornerstone was a developmental approach to writing instruction in which a wide range of writing activities would be acknowledged and treated as communication, reiterating several concepts expressed throughout this text. The children were encouraged to write "their own way," accepting all preconventional forms of literacy as equally legitimate and meaningful. From this emergent literacy perspective, teachers' conceptions of children's zones were modified to admit a broad range of problem-solving activity by each child, for example, the use of drawing and rebuses to represent words, as well as their emergent spellings (Gentry, 1987; Henderson & Beers, 1980; Read, 1986; Teale & Sulzby, 1986; Temple, Nathan, & Burris, 1982; van Kleeck, chap. 3). Instruction was essential to introducing the children to this concept of writing. Teachers and researchers modeled the use of invented spellings; the teacher thought aloud while writing about choices of letters, based on sounds as well as known spellings.

In addition, an emergent literacy perspective suggested multiple, alternative forms of scaffolding of children's efforts: holding children's ideas in mind as they struggled to translate them on paper, sounding out words for the children as they wrote, or prompting the children to "sound out the words" as they wrote, and reminding them to incorporate sight words into their writing (to cite a few examples). Palincsar and Klenk (1992a, 1992b) predicted that this approach, as contrasted with copying words from the chalkboard, or practicing isolated letter formation would enable the children to experience the whole enterprise of written language—perhaps, in turn, influencing their understandings of this enterprise and providing opportunities for the children to bring useful strategies to bear in the engagement of this activity.

In addition to the use of an emergent literacy perspective, there were other changes, including changing the context in which the children used written language. Given that oral and written language develop as students are engaged in authentic experiences in which they see the need to communicate, story time was modified by selecting themes that would guide the choice of literature and provide topics for writing. Whereas before there was little interaction during the reading of stories, there were now multiple opportunities for children to engage in interactions before, during, and after story reading, using many of the same activities described in reciprocal teaching. The teachers also provided books and magazines for the children and encouraged them to talk about what they were learning from their emergent readings of these texts. For example, strategies such as using their background knowledge, looking at illustrations, discussing with peers, identifying their sight words, and employing their "sounding out" skills to figure out what the text was about were encouraged. The children were asked to share their written responses to these books and magazines with other members of the class. In time, the children's writings were published.

One child, whose case is presented next, illustrates the outcomes of these efforts. Ben was eight years old when, after attending a year of first grade, he was transferred from the general education program into the special education class. Ben had a history of fluctuating hearing loss, which accompanied frequent ear infections and high absenteeism from school. (Ben missed fifty-eight days of school during first grade.) He attained a full-scale IQ of 82 on the Wechsler Intelligence Scale for Children (WISC) (Wechsler, 1974) when he was in kindergarten. He was a white child who lived with his mother and infant brother.

Ben's first attempt, in February, to "write his own way" was an emotional and difficult event for this youngster as well as for those of us working with him. Following the group reading of a book about Clifford, a big red dog, the children were asked to write about their favorite part of the story. Ben's favorite part was when Clifford joins the family on vacation by riding in the bed of a huge truck. He indicated that he would write, "Clifford rides in a truck." Ben cried silently as a teacher sat at his side, sounding out "K–l" and encouraging him to "write what you hear." As Ben continued to cry, the teacher suggested that perhaps Ben would like to draw his favorite part of the story. This drew more tears as Ben explained that he didn't know how to draw a dog. The teacher gently nudged, "Well, let's see, maybe we should begin with the legs. How many legs does a dog have?" We were now at a place in the zone where Ben could—or would—participate. He drew an illustration of Clifford the Big Red Dog on the back of a truck and, indeed, went on to label his drawing, without any prompting or assistance, GilClSHe, which he read back as "Clifford was on the truck."

One month later, following the reading of a story about a young boy who wished he were something else, namely an animal of some sort, the children were writing about what kind of animal they would like to be. At this time the novelty of writing your own way had begun to wear off, and Ben had gained some confidence in his ability to compose text. In the following sample, which Ben generated independently and without tears, he demonstrated much greater knowledge of spelling: I (I) YAd (want) do (to) bi (be) A (a) dog z (they) can KtBks (catch burglars). In this example, one could see to a greater degree the influence of Ben's phonetic knowledge as he used close phonetic approximations for matching sounds and letters (Gentry, 1987). In addition, one can see his knowledge of conventional print as he used conventional spellings for some words and spacing between some words. His invented spellings had become more complex, for example he used beginning, medial, and final consonants as well as vowels.

Between March and April, a new level of scaffolding was introduced. The children's writing was transcribed into conventional print, and transcripts were attached to their original writings. The children were then given the opportunity to read from whichever form of print they chose. Ben, who spoke extremely softly and was painfully shy, embraced these opportunities to read from his writings. He practiced his reading a number of times in preparation for his presentation to the class. He was delighted with the praise that he received from the teacher and his peers.

In early April, in a letter to a friend, Ben wrote: "Kom and see Micke. My mom HaS a Presant for You.Ben" Perhaps as a consequence of using a new genre, interpersonal communication, in hand with the exposure to the conventional presentation of print, Ben showed an understanding of the need for punctuation and capitalization. His use of vowels and sight words showed continuing progress toward more conventional writing.

In May, writing his contribution to the chapter on rules for the class book, Ben wrote:

Doyourbesteveryday
DoDfit (Don't fight)
Dodcs (Don't cuss)
BeeGDAVreDay (Be good every day)
Kown AnD ST n (Come in and sit down)
I Lik HwM Sk (I like Holmes School)

In some conventional respects, this writing appears to show regression and is an excellent illustration of Vygotsky's (1978) observation that "the developmental history of written language among children is full of discontinuities" (p. 106). For example, this sample does not show the conventional use of spacing observed in earlier samples. As evidenced by the conventional and invented spellings of *every*, he was not consistently holding the conventional spellings in memory. However, at the same time, he had generated considerably more writing than seen previously. One can speculate that, for Ben, communicating his message had begun to assume priority over careful attention to the mechanics of writing. Again, the reader is directed to Lahey and Bloom's hypotheses about "trade-offs" when resources compete with one another (see Lahey & Bloom, chap. 13). Ben's confidence in himself as a writer continued to grow. For example, nine months later, he wrote this final example with minimal assistance:

My babybrother is 1 yer lod
he growls
I gif him a ride on my gotcrt (go-cart) wth my wagn.
he sit on hss corsete (car seat).
et has a huc (hook) on it

Here one can see that Ben is using not only his phonetic knowledge to invent spellings, but he is using as well his knowledge of conventional spellings. In addition, he is also using writing to convey complete thoughts, and there is a coherence to his story as well.

In the fall of 1990, Ben was asked "Do you know any good writers?" He named his mother and his teacher. In the spring of 1991, when asked the same question, Ben identified himself, noting that he was better than all of his classmates. When asked "How does one become a good writer?" Ben responded in 1990, "By doing morning news and stuff. By copying stuff." In spring of 1991, he advised, "Let them write all the time and write stories for their friends and stuff."

SUMMARY

There have been numerous and sustained calls for changes in assessment practices, particularly those assessment practices that lead to the identification and placement of children with special needs (Meisels, 1987; Meyers, Pfeffer, & Erlbaum, 1985; Shepard & Smith, 1988; Swanson, 1984). Often, the concerns voiced are couched in terms of the technical adequacy of the instruments and procedures that have historically been used for these purposes. One might argue that underlying these concerns are questions of an ethical nature. In what procedures can professionals have the confidence to make the "educational career decisions" (Mehan, Hertwech, & Meihls, 1986) that assessment typically leads to? In a time of increased financial constraints, how can educators justify the costs associated with assessment, which frequently exceed the costs associated with instruction (Shepard & Glass, 1981)?

Although dynamic assessment research, for the purpose of translating this model of assessment into assessment procedures, is still in its infancy in many respects, the tenets of dynamic assessment offer considerable promise in guiding contemporary assessment decisions. These tenets include the following: (1) The social contexts in which learning occurs significantly influence the learning process. (2) Learners can learn to be more efficient, and assessment should measure this flexibility. (3) The real value in assessment lies in the ability to prescribe rather than to predict.

Research identifying the most critical components of dynamic assessment, as well as research defining the specificity of the domain in which dynamic assessment must be conducted to be instructionally useful, is extremely important at this juncture. Perhaps most complementary to these efforts will be research focused on the integration of instruction and assessment.

REFERENCES

Anderson, R. C., Reynolds, R. E., Schallert, D. L., & Goetz, E. T. (1977). Frameworks for comprehending discourse. *American Educational Research Journal, 14,* 367–381.

Bereiter, C., & Bird, M. (1987). Use of thinking aloud in identification and teaching of reading comprehension strategies. *Cognition & Instruction, 2*(2) 131–156.

Bethge, H., Carlson, J. S., & Wiedl, K. H. (1982). The effects of dynamic assessment procedures on Raven matrices performance, visual search behavior, text anxiety and test orientation. *Intelligence, 6,* 89–97.

Borkowski, J. G., Weyhing, R. S., & Carr, M. (1988). Effects of attributional retraining on strategy-based reading comprehension in learning disabled students. *Journal of Educational Psychology, 80,* 46–53.

Bransford, J. D., Delos, V. R., Vye, N. J., Burns, M. S., & Hasselbring, T. S. (1987). Approaches to dynamic assessment: Issues, data and future directions. In C. S. Lidz (Ed.), *Dynamic assessment: Foundations and fundamentals.* New York: Guilford Press.

Brown, A. L., Campione, J. C., Weber, L. S., & McGilly, K. (1992). *Interactive learning environments: A new look at assessment and instruction.* Berkeley: University of California, Commission on Testing and Public Policy.

Brown, A. L., & Ferrara, R. A. (1985). Diagnosing zones of proximal development: An alternative to standardized testing? In J. Wertsch (Ed.), *Culture, communication and cognition: Vygotskian perspectives* (pp. 273–305). New York: Cambridge University Press.

Brown, A. L., & French, L. A. (1979). The cognitive consequences of education: School experts or general problem solvers. Commentary on "Education and cognitive development: The evidence from experimental research." *Monographs of the Society of Research in Child Development, 44,* (1–2, Serial No. 178).

Brown, A. L., & Palincsar, A. S. (1982). Inducing strategic learning from texts by means of informed, self-controlled training. *Topics in Learning Disabilities, 2*(1), 1–17.

Brown, A. L., & Palincsar, A. S. (1989). Guided cooperative learning and individual knowledge acquisition. In L. Resnick (Ed.), *Knowing, learning and instruction: Essays in honor of Robert Glaser.* Hillsdale, NJ: Lawrence Erlbaum.

Bryant, N. (1982). *Preschool children's learning and transfer of matrices problems: A study of proximal development.* Unpublished master's thesis, University of Illinois.

Bryant, N. R., Brown, A. L., & Campione, J. C. (April, 1983). *Preschool children's learning and transfer of matrices problems: Potential for improvement.* Paper presented at the Society for Research in Child Development meetings, Detroit, MI.

Butkowsky, S., & Willows, D. (1980). Cognitive-motivational characteristics of children varying in reading ability: Evidence for learned helplessness in poor readers. *Journal of Educational Psychology, 72,* 408–422.

Campione, J. C., & Brown, A. L. (1984). Learning ability and transfer propensity as sources of individual differences in intelligence. In P. H. Brooks, R. Sperber, & C. McCauley (Eds.), *Learning and cognition in the mentally retarded* (pp. 137–150). Baltimore: University Park Press.

Campione, J. C., Brown, A. L., & Ferrara, R. A. (1982). Mental retardation and intelligence. In R. J. Sternberg (Ed.), *Handbook of human intelligence.* New York: Cambridge University Press.

Campione, J. C., Brown, A. L., Ferrara, R. A., & Bryant, N. R. (1984). The zone of proximal development: Implications for individual differences and learning. In B. Rogoff & J. Wertsch (Eds.), *New directions for cognitive development: The zone of proximal development* (pp. 77–91). San Francisco: Jossey-Bass.

Campione, J. C., Brown, A. L., Ferrara, R. A., Jones, R. S., & Steinburg, E. (1985). Breakdown in flexible use of information: Intelligence-related differences in transfer following equivalent learning performance. *Intelligence, 9,* 297–315.

Cannell, J. (1987). *Nationally normed elementary achievement testing in America's public schools: How all fifty states are above the national average.* Daniels, WV: Friends for Education.

Carlson, J. S., & Widaman, K. F. (1979). Toward a differential testing approach: Testing-the-limits employing the Raven matrices. *Intelligence, 3,* 323–344.

Carlson, J. S., & Widaman, K. F. (1986). Eysenck on intelligence: A critical perspective. In S. Modgil & C. Modgil (Eds.), *Hans Eysenck: Consensus and controversy* (pp. 103–132). Philadelphia: Falmer Press.

Carlson, J. S., & Wiedl, K. H. (1978). The use of testing-the-limits procedures in the assessment of intellectual capabilities in children with learning difficulties. *American Journal of Mental Deficiency, 82,* 559–564.

Carlson, J. S., & Wiedl, K. H. (1988). The dynamic assessment of intelligence. In H. C. Haywood & D. Tzuriel (Eds.), *Interactive assessment.* Hillsdale, NJ: Lawrence Erlbaum.

Curriculum based assessment [Special issue]. (1985). *Exceptional Children, 52*(3).

Dweck, C. (1985). Intrinsic motivation, perceived control, and self-evaluation maintenance: An achievement goal analysis. In C. Ames & R. Ames (Eds.), *Research on motivation in education* (vol. 2), 289–305.

Ferrara, R. A. (1987). *Learning mathematics in the zone of proximal development: The importance of flexible use of knowledge.* Doctoral dissertation, Department of Psychology, University of Illinois at Urbana-Champaign.

Ferrara, R. A., Brown, A. L., & Campione, J. C. (1986). Children's learning and transfer of inductive reasoning rules: Studies in proximal development. *Child Development, 57*(5), 1087–1099.

Feuerstein, R. (1969). *The instrumental enrichment method: An outline of theory and technique.* Jerusalem, Israel: Hadassah-Wizo-Canada Research Institute.

Feuerstein, R. (1979). *The dynamic assessment of retarded performers: The learning potential assessment devise, theory, instruments, and techniques.* Baltimore: University Park Press.

Feuerstein, R. (1980). *Instrumental enrichment: An intervention program for cognitive modifiability.* Baltimore: University Park Press.

Frederickson, N. (1984). The real test bias. *American Psychologist, 39,* 193–202.

Gagne, R. M. (1965). *The conditions of learning.* New York: Holt, Rinehart & Winston.

Genishi, C., & Dyson, A. (1984). *Language assessment in the early years.* Norwood, NJ: Ablex.

Gentry, J. R. (1987). *Spel . . . is a four letter word.* Ontario: Heineman.

Goodman, Y. (1985). Kidwatching. In A. Jaggar & M. T. Smith-Burke (Eds.), *Observing the language learner.* Newark, DE: International Reading Association.

Henderson, E. H., & Beers, J. W. (1980). *Developmental and cognitive aspects of learning to spell: A reflection of word knowledge.* Newark, DE: International Reading Association.

Johnston, P. (1992). *Constructive evaluation of literate activity.* White Plains, NY: Longman.

Klenk, L. (in press). Case study in reading disability: An emergent literacy perspective. *Learning Disability Quarterly.*

Lidz, C. S. (Ed.). (1987). *Dynamic assessment: Foundations and fundamentals.* New York: Guilford Press.

Lipson, M. Y., Irwin, M., & Poth, E. (1986). The relationship between metacognitive self-reports and strategic reading behavior. In J. Niles & R. Lalik (Eds.), *Solving problems in literacy: Learners, teachers, and researchers* (pp. 214–221). Thirty-fifth Yearbook of the National Reading Conference. Rochester, NY: National Reading Conference.

Mehan, M., Hertwech, A., & Meihls, J. L. (1986). *Handicapping the handicapped: Decision making in students' educational careers.* Stanford, CA: Stanford University Press.

Meisels, S. J. (1987). Uses and abuses of developmental screening and school readiness testing. *Young Children, 42*(2), 4–73.

Meyers, J., Pfeffer, J., & Erlbaum, V. (1985). Process assessment: A model for broadening assessment. *The Journal of Special Education, 19*(1), 73–89.

Ninio, A., & Bruner, J. S. (1978). The achievement and antecedents of labeling. *Journal of Child Language, 5,* 1–15.

Palincsar, A. S., & Brown, A. L. (1984). Reciprocal teaching of comprehension fostering and comprehension-monitoring activities. *Cognition and Instruction, 1*(2), 117–175.

Palincsar, A. S., & Brown, A. L. (1989). Classroom dialogues to promote self-regulated comprehension. In J. Brophy (Ed.), *Teaching for understanding and self-regulated learning* (vol. 1). Greenwich, CT: JAI Press.

Palincsar, A. S., & Klenk, L. (1992a). Examining and influencing contexts for intentional literacy learning. In C. Collins & J. Mangieri (Eds.), *Teaching thinking: An agenda for the 21st century.* Hillsdale, NJ: Lawrence Erlbaum.

Palincsar, A. S., & Klenk, L. (1992b). Fostering literacy learning in supportive contexts. *Journal of Learning Disabilities, 25*(4), 211–225, 229.

Paratore, J. R., & Indrisano, R. (1987). Intervention assessment of reading comprehension. *The Reading Teacher, 40*(8), 778–782.

Raven, J. C. (1938, 1977). *The Raven Progressive Matrices.* Cleveland: Psychological Corporation.

Read, C. (1986). *Children's creative spelling.* London: Routledge & Kegan Paul.

Shepard, L. (1989). Why we need better assessments. *Educational Leadership, 46*(7), 4–9.

Shepard, L. A., & Glass, M. L. (1981). *The identification, assessment, placement, and remediation of perceptual and communication disordered children.* Boulder, CO: Laboratory of Educational Research, University of Colorado.

Shepard, L. A., & Smith, M. L. (1988). Escalating academic demand in kindergarten: Counter-productive policies. *The Elementary School Journal, 89*(2), 135–145.

Stein, N. L., & Glenn, C. G. (1979). An analysis of story comprehension in elementary school children. In R. O. Freedle (Ed.), *Advances in discourse processes. Vol. 2: New directions in discourse processing.* Norwood, NJ: Ablex.

Swanson, H. L. (1984). Process assessment of intelligence in learning disabled and mentally retarded children: A multidirectional model. *Educational Psychologist, 19*(3), 149–162.

Teale, W. H., & Sulzby, E. (1986). *Emergent literacy: Writing and reading.* Norwood, NJ: Ablex.

Temple, C. A., Nathan, R. G., & Burris, N. A. (1982). *The beginnings of writing.* Boston: Allyn & Bacon.

Thorndike, R. L., & Hagen, E. P. (1977). *Measurement and evaluation in psychology and education* (4th ed.). New York: John Wiley & Sons.

Vygotsky, L. S. (1978). In M. Cole, V. John-Steiner, S. Scribner, & E. Souberman (Eds.), *Mind in society: The development of higher psychological processes.* Cambridge: Harvard University Press.

Vygotsky, L. S. (1986). In A. Kozulin (Ed.), *Thought and language.* Cambridge, MA: MIT Press. (Original work published 1934)

Wechsler, D. (1967). *Wechsler Preschool and Primary Scale of Intelligence.* Cleveland: Psychological Corporation.

Wechsler, D. (1974). *Wechsler Intelligence Scale for Children—Revised.* Cleveland: Psychological Corporation.

Weinstein, R. S. (1986). Teaching reading: Children's awareness of teacher expectations. In T. Raphael (Ed.), *The contexts of school-based literacy* (pp. 233–252). New York: Random House.

Wertsch, J. V. (1980). The significance of dialogue in Vygotsky's account of social, egocentric, and inner speech. *Contemporary Educational Psychology, 5,* 150–162.

Wixson, K. K., & Lipson, M. Y. (1986). Reading (dis)abilities: An interactionist perspective. In T. E. Raphael (Ed.), *Contexts of school-based literacy* (pp. 131–148). New York: Random House.

6

OBSERVATION IS MORE THAN LOOKING

■ Elaine R. Silliman
University of South Florida
■ Louise Cherry Wilkinson
Rutgers University

The field of communication disorders has changed dramatically since the mid-1980s, demanding new roles for speech-language clinicians who work in communication-centered classrooms. Clinicians now need to know how to select and integrate methods for careful observation of students' actual language usage. Comprehensive knowledge of these methods allows clinicians: (1) to assess students' performance along the continuum of classroom discourse and (2) to evaluate the efficacy of their model of intervention. Efficacy includes the validity of the intervention (Olswang, 1990). It also includes the transfer and maintenance of skills, as shown by the significance, scope, flexibility, and durability of intervention effects over time (Bain & Dollaghan, 1991; Fey & Cleve, 1990; Olswang, 1990).

The chapter includes a discussion of how to organize systematic observation in classrooms and use observation as a method for assessment of students' progress in developing speech, language, and communication skills. It expands on the assessment concepts discussed in the two previous chapters by Nelson and Palincsar and her colleagues. A model for observing in classrooms is described that allows speech-language clinicians to work with other educational professionals to address several issues: (1) the issue of effectiveness—"Does a communication process approach work?"—and (2) the issue of efficacy—"How and why it works (or does not work)."

It may be pertinent to consider Kavale's (1990) caution about research on intervention. He notes that intervention research oriented to effectiveness tends to assume that an approach consists only of a set of instructional techniques. Often, the result of traditional effectiveness research is the collection of fragmented findings that are difficult to interpret because they are disconnected from an explanatory framework. In contrast, research that addresses efficacy is theoretically based on assumptions that may best explain how or why a particular communication process approach works to achieve functional changes. These changes may be defined in terms of criteria for authenticity, significance, and their overall impact on the student's everyday communication (Bain & Dollaghan, 1991; Olswang & Bain, 1991). In this way, theory and practice mutually inform the other. Rather than making the evidence conform to the framework, refinements to a model occur naturally as a result of the integration of new evidence (Kuhn, 1970, cited in Warren & Reichle, 1992).

SUMMATIVE AND FORMATIVE ASSESSMENT OF STUDENTS' PROGRESS

Assessing individual progress in communication and language is vital for addressing efficacy and effectiveness. Assessment can be viewed as a way of collecting information about a student when that information is closely connected with (1) the actual instructional practices in which the student participates; (2) the teaching and learning contexts that constitute the student's school experience; and (3) individual differences among students (Lahey & Bloom, chap. 13; Wilkinson & Silliman, 1990).

Summative Assessment

Traditional procedures for documenting students' progress in educational and clinical settings have relied on summative evaluations. Summative evaluations are static assessments oriented almost exclusively toward the products, or outcomes, of learning (Campione, 1990). Summative forms of documentation portray the degree of overall progress within a particular domain after specific instructional/intervention activities have taken place (Howell & Morehead, 1987). For example, gain scores from norm-referenced or criterion-referenced measures of language performance may be used as indices of progress.

Gain scores derived from norm-referenced language measures have been criticized on psychometric grounds (Lahey, 1988, 1990; Lahey & Bloom, chap. 13; McCauley & Swisher, 1984). One argument is that language tests assess relatively gross and stable behaviors, and negative gain scores can underestimate progress because the tests lack sensitivity to subtle changes in specific behaviors for individuals. A second argument is that positive gains scores may overestimate progress when the standard error of measurement and the possibilities of teaching to the test are not considered routinely.

Criterion-referenced measures, in contrast, are directed to individual or group performance in relationship to particular tasks or goals (Idol, Nevin, & Paolucci-Whitcomb, 1986; Lahey, 1988). Their use as a measure of gain requires that the standard of performance be specified in advance, for example, the number or percentage of skills that a student completes to a criterion level in relation to an initial baseline. A problem with criterion referencing is defining how many instances of a behavior and under what circumstances denote mastery.

Criterion- and norm-referenced measures of progress also share two other limitations. First, the underlying assumption of both is that change is linear. In practice, changes may be discontinuous, more like a cycle of "peaks and valleys" (Bain & Dollaghan, 1991, p. 267). Second, both typically exclude the student as an active participant in the evaluation of progress (Bigge, 1988). The clinician (or teacher) remains the decision maker in determining the purposes of learning, specific learning objectives, the content to be mastered, and the time line for reaching objectives. As a result, summative approaches communicate what counts as achievement according to the adult's perspective (Archbald & Newmann, 1988).

Formative Assessment

Campione (1990), Campione and Brown (1987), and Palincsar et al. (chap. 5) reject the summative orientation. Alternatively, they propose that the documentation of progress should be dynamic, not static. As Palincsar, Brown, and Campione also note in Chapter 5, in dynamic assessment, one can observe the degree of support needed by a student to achieve a specific level of learning and its flexible application to new problem-solving situations (formal or practical). In this definition, the concept of achievement is combined with the concept of transfer of responsibility. The progressive transfer of responsibility is defined as the degree to which adult–child collaboration in a specific learning context promotes the child's transition from being a novice learner (external regulation by the adult) to a more expert learner (the self-regulation of learning) within a specific domain (Campione, 1990).

The concept of flexibility also can be extended. From a sociocultural perspective, summative approaches to assessing what has been learned reinforce the traditional belief that learning equals the student's ability to reproduce, or implement, the products of knowledge transmitted by others (Archbald & Newmann, 1988). This belief is also reflected in the use of directive discourse scaffolds of traditional classroom and clinical discourse (see Silliman & Wilkinson, chap. 2); therefore, schooling often socializes students into the "implementor style" of problem solving. Consequently, students are routinely assessed by the degree of progress made as an implementor (Sternberg, 1990). Although implementation represents one style preference for problem solving, it is not an exclusive style. Creative and analytic thinking represent other style preferences more closely linked to critical thinking (Smith, 1990). Sternberg (1990) proposes that more flexible use of one's problem-solving abilities can be considered as the more balanced use of one's creative, analytic, and implementation resources. Selection of the style depends on the particular interpretation of events. For example, the individual's understanding of the situations in which tasks are embedded and of the purposes of these tasks influences the selection of a problem-solving style.

SAMPLING ISSUES AND DEFINING PROGRESS

With repeated opportunities for elaboration of old information in the context of new information, behavior culminates in a new and flexible knowledge structure (Lahey & Bloom, chap. 13; Shuell, 1988). Within the same framework of modification, elaboration, and adaptation, progress can also be considered as synonymous with a student's zone of instructional sensitivity, also discussed by Nelson and Palincsar et al. in the two preceding chapters (Brown & Ferrara, 1985). As Palincsar et al. pointed out in Chapter 5, understanding this zone provides direction about the boundaries between a student's readiness to learn and the speed and scope of learning that occur within challenging tasks. A challenging task is one that the student cannot solve independently but may be able to solve with supportive discourse guidance.

The width of this zone is defined by the communicative strategies and skills a student currently uses without supportive adult assistance (the lower boundary of competence within a task domain) and her potential for attaining an advanced level of competence with particular communicative strategies and skills given optimal adult assistance (the upper boundary of competence within a task domain). The greater the zone width, the greater is the flexibility between that student's current developmental level (the lower boundary) and her potential for a higher level of development (the upper boundary). Features such as the degree to which it is necessary to make each step of a task explicit, and for how long, are indicators of an individual student's zone width (Brown & Ferrara, 1985). Hence, the broader the zone width and the greater the speed of learning, the greater is the probability that the student can play an active role in successfully learning from instruction (Shuell, 1988). Conversely, the narrower the zone for any learning activity, the less likely is the potential that rapid, efficient, and successful learning from instruction will occur. In other words, given maximum discourse scaffolding, a narrow zone means a reduced potential for the progressive transfer of responsibility and adaptation that defines the transition from novice to expert (Brown & Ferrara, 1985; Palincsar et al., chap. 5).

An important qualification is in order. Subtle within-student differences exist for zone widths (Campione & Brown, 1987; Feuerstein, 1990). For one student engaged in a particular learning activity, such as peer collaboration in completing a task, the zone width may be wide. For example, one child (A) assumes responsibility with a minimal degree of adult assistance for guiding another (B) in completing her counting task, including asking her (B) why it was important to count to 19. His (A) pattern of performance indicated that he had attained some "expertise" in this role when numbers were the focus of joint attention. The same student (A) involved in another learning activity, such as explaining why his own effort was being rewarded, may manifest a narrower zone of developmental readiness because of the complexity of relating psychological cause (motivation to learn) with its effects (receiving an award). In this case, student A could be characterized as a novice although less of one than other students in the class. Thus, it should not be expected that zone widths are equivalent within students across all of the many learning activities in which they participate.

REPRESENTATIVE SAMPLES OF PROGRESS

Obtaining a representative sample of students' language is the most important aspect governing the assessment of progress. Guidelines for the representativeness of a sample are directed to description of a student's current level of development (e.g., Gallagher, 1983; Bain, Olswang, & Johnson, 1992; Miller, Freiberg, Rolland, & Reeves, 1992). In the framework presented here, the transition from novice to expert reflects a "spiral" in which the upper boundary of an achievement within a domain becomes the lower boundary against which the student is challenged next. The lower boundary can be viewed as most typical behavior, what the student is currently doing in terms of existing schemas. However, because optimal behavior may or may not be accessible at a given point in time as a demonstration of the upper boundary of a zone width, it would be better to substitute multiple instances of a student's most effective demonstrations of understanding and expression. These demonstrations can be seen as indicators of the student's potential capacity for modifying or elaborating existing schemas during a period of intervention. In a communication-process model of intervention, the definition of most effective should emerge as a joint decision made by clinicians and other team members about those discourse contexts that support the most successful participation by the student. Note that *typical* and *most effective* are not synonymous. In either case, for the purposes of sampling progress, the meaning of *typical* and *most effective* should be agreed on collaboratively if the range and depth of a student's repertoire is to be reflected accurately.

Furthermore, the contexts for assessing progress must be carefully scrutinized so that relevant and appropriate ones will be selected (Wilkinson, 1982). The relevancy and appropriateness of multiple contexts is an essential consideration for allowing students sufficient opportunities to demonstrate their most effective performances as they travel the spiral path from novice to expert. These opportunities may arise momentarily, as when a student suddenly reveals understanding of a more efficient strategy in a particular task, or may be planned more formally, as illustrated by the end-of-unit assessment for the pond theme later in this chapter.

Two basic kinds of sampling can be employed: *time sampling* and *event sampling*. When correctly used, each procedure will capture representative samples of changes in students' communicative competencies. These samples can then be analyzed to determine whether these changes in the "look" of an individual student's communicative profile can be attributed to the contexts of intervention, including particular discourse strategies that serve as samples from which to learn (Cazden, 1988).

Time sampling is used when the interest is the occurrence or nonoccurrence of a particular action or behavior within a specified time period. Time-sampling procedures are often applied to classroom and clinical observation (e.g., Brunson & Haynes, 1991; Hegde, 1987; McReynolds & Kearns, 1983; Repp, Karsh, Van Acker, Felce, & Harman, 1989). Time-sampling allows extensive control over the focus of observation, and the information gathered can be used for both quantitative and qualitative purposes. The disadvantages of time sampling are significant, however. For example, because samples are taken out of context and out of sequence, the natural stream of interaction is arbitrarily broken, which then affects the validity of interpretations. Moreover, time sampling is most effective for observing behaviors or actions that occur frequently. Finally, the information collected seldom reveals any cause–effect relationships; it can be noted that a student responded inappropriately, but the reasons for inappropriateness remain unknown.

Event sampling allows the recording of a particular behavior or category of behavior each time it spontaneously occurs. The main advantage of event sampling is that it allows one to observe the multifaceted layering of events as they occur. A major disadvantage is that the information gathered may not be so readily quantifiable as time-sampling information; thus, more time may be needed to analyze what has been recorded in order to answer the questions posed.

FORMATIVE ASSESSMENT AND OBSERVATION

Observation is a type of nonformal assessment that involves the sampling of information in a somewhat informal, but systematic, manner (Wilkinson & Silliman, 1990). Observation is also consistent with formative assessment approaches, as Nelson also points out (see chap. 4). In contrast with the product orientation of summative assessments, a formative approach to the assessment of progress serves as a tool for teaching. It is directed to the ongoing evaluation of an individual student's process of learning while this learning occurs (Howell & Morehead, 1987).

Formative evaluation approaches have not been adequately studied (Howell & Morehead, 1987). They remain subject to the same technical criticisms about reliability and validity directed to summative evaluation systems (Lahey, 1990). Formative evaluation tied to observation, however, has been identified as a key aspect of effective teaching in the regular education classroom (Hiebert & Calfee, 1989, p. 50):

> When . . . teachers are asked about a student's comprehension strategies, for example, they talk in specific terms about the student's ability to infer characters' motives or to connect the plots of different novels. They call on a wealth of observations stored in their memories and on rich documentation of their students' writing performances. Some teachers keep checklists; more rely on portfolios containing samples of student work along with their own comments and interpretations. . . . [S]tudents keep data on books they have read, including their personal reactions, summaries of key themes, and new vocabulary. These teachers can explain in detail how this information serves them in planning instruction—for the class as a whole, as well as in guiding individual students.

Proficiency as an Observer and Formative Assessment

If valid decisions are to be made about an individual student's learning, a major task is to acquire proficiency as a skilled and systematic observer of that learning, as it occurs within classrooms (Hiebert & Calfee, 1989; Stiggins, 1990). Proficiency in the systematic observation of classroom interactions is a powerful tool for understanding how classroom interaction supports students' learning and development. Most importantly, because the student is "the informant" (Harste & Burke, 1989), skillfulness in the use of observational tools can integrate five aspects of decision making about a student's progress: (1) selecting intervention strategies best oriented to student's individual communicative needs and learning style; (2) identifying sources of student's abilities as they make transitions in classroom activities; (3)

monitoring the effectiveness and utility of specific intervention strategies on changes in performance; (4) modifying teaching–learning strategies; and (5) determining whether a change in performance is significant because not every difference is meaningful or obvious (Howell & Morehead, 1987).

OBSERVING THE CONTEXT OF COMMUNICATION

The context of classroom communication has many levels. It consists of (1) the channel for communication, whether spoken, written, gestural, or paralinguistic; (2) the physical setting, including its spatial and temporal aspects; (3) the participants engaged in communication, their role relationships, and the degree of cultural, social, and world knowledge they have in common (Nelson, 1985); (4) the activities shared by participants and the goals of these activities; and (5) the familiarity or novelty of the topics being talked about. Context, therefore, is not a fixed set of features but is dynamic. The adequacy of teachers' and students' understanding of each other varies according to interpretations about who can talk, when they can talk, and the ways in which talk occurs in particular places. Hence, observation cannot be separated from context, because all forms of human interaction, whether spoken or written, are embedded in a context.

THE OBSERVATIONAL LENS MODEL

Observing in classrooms is more than looking at what is going on. Observation is a method of inquiry about children, the instructional practices in which they participate, the classrooms in which they learn, and the social situations within which teaching and learning take place. Classroom observation is conceptualized as a series of "snapshots" that depict different views of events and behaviors of both teachers and children. The observational lens model (Silliman & Wilkinson, 1991) is a conceptual model—a metaphor—for the particular approach to assessment presented here.

Careful observation can capture and clarify classroom realities. These descriptions, in turn, can serve as the basis for teachers and other educational professionals to make informed judgments about children's progress in the development of language and literacy skills and about teachers' effectiveness in promoting this development (e.g., instructional effectiveness). However, like the filtering effect of the camera lens, human observers also alter the reality of what they view. The lenses through which information is filtered are those cognitive mechanisms that allow interpretation of human actions relative to the context and purposes of interaction. Because different observational lenses filter information in different ways, only selected factors may be seen through the lens selected. The outcome is that any set of data represents a reduced version of an event, not a copy of the total event (Mishler, 1991; Ochs, 1979; Zukow, 1982).

Observation is a method for revealing particular classroom events and behaviors more clearly, including children's usage of key language and literacy skills. Selection of the most appropriate lens for observing students' learning depends on the questions asked about the purposes of observation. Purposes regulate how events will be interpreted; therefore, the importance of specifying goals in advance cannot be overstated, because "To observe without knowing at least fairly well what and why one is observing is usually to blunder" (Dollaghan & Miller, 1986, p. 108). A brief discussion of the details of the observational lens model, including a definition of the four lenses, or level of detail (Figure 6–1), is presented next.

The Wide-Angle Lens

Figure 6–1 shows that a wide-angled observational lens is best suited to capturing an overview of learning across the different activities that constitute the classroom. Checklists and rating scales are observational tools that typically yield a wide-angled perspective of learning in classrooms. Reliable use presumes teachers agree on the foci of the observation, that is, which specific skills are to be assessed.

For example, a modification of the Rating Scale for Literacy Development (Heald-Taylor, 1987), reproduced in Figure 6–2, is used to assess general progress across four areas: (1) degrees of print awareness, (2) changes in reading strategies, (3) changes in the contexts for application of reading strategies, and (4) development of spelling and writing conventions and purposes. This instrument scale is used as a summative or formative instrument, depending on how its application is viewed. Because frequency of occurrence is included as part of the rating judgment, numerical weights can be assigned to the outcomes.

FIGURE 6–1
The observational lens model
From *Communicating for Learning: Classroom Observation and Collaboration* (p. 9) by E. R. Silliman and L. C. Wilkinson, 1991, Gaithersburg, MD: Aspen. Copyright 1991 by Aspen Publishers, Inc. Adapted by permission.

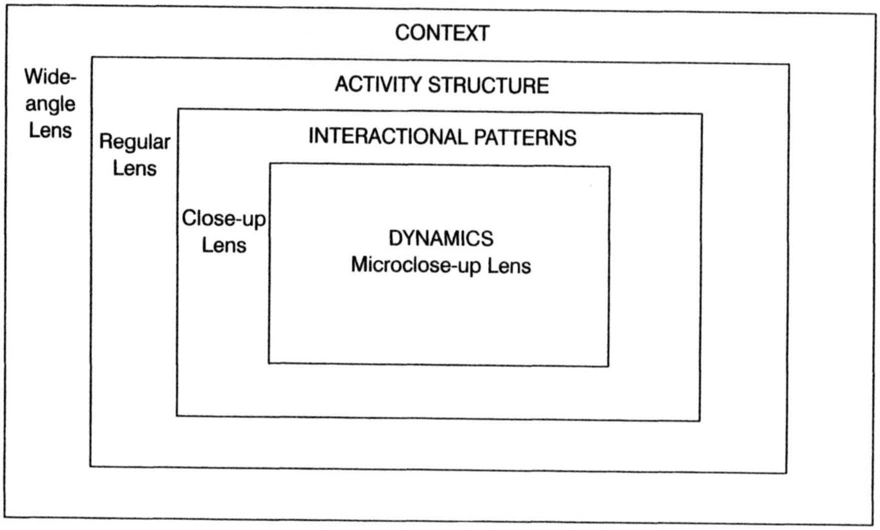

The Regular Lens

The regular lens provides more detailed insight into how effectively an individual child understands the structure of a particular classroom activity. The structure of classroom activities includes information on (1) the physical aspects in which an activity takes place; (2) the task and purposes (the goal and subgoals to be achieved); (3) the expectations for participation, including the social organization of participation, such as collaborative versus independent performance or both; and (4) discourse strategies for forming and sustaining interaction (Wilkinson & Silliman, 1990).

The Close-up Lens

The close-up lens permits a more detailed picture of patterns involving teachers and children within a specific activity at a given point in time. For example, a close-up view can illuminate critical behaviors that demonstrate a child's need for discourse scaffolding within a particular task.

The Micro-close-up Lens

If observation needs to be magnified to a greater degree, then use of the micro-close-up lens is recommended. At this most detailed level, this lens is used to reveal, in fine detail, the dynamics of interaction over time to address specific questions about particular children's communicative behavior, including their language usage.

An important issue concerning the selection of which observational lens to use concerns the distinction between qualitative and quantitative methods. Quantitative methods can be distinguished by neutral scientific language that is free from the context-bound everyday use of language. In using quantitative methods, clinicians, teachers, and researchers seek the objective of the reporting of facts as separate from their values. The goal is to describe, explain, and predict relationships among a succession of objects and events that occur, for example, within classrooms.

In contrast, qualitative methods are characterized by the everyday use of language—what is unique and true at that point in time and place. Values are reflected within the reporting, and there can be no facts without particular values reflected within them. Clinicians, teachers, and researchers using qualitative methods also seek an understanding of what goes on in classrooms. They believe that understanding is obtained by knowing and experiencing what happens to others within that unique and particular context.

All observational lenses share the same set of common elements, as shown in Table 6–1 (page 153).

In selecting the specific instrument, each of these elements needs to be carefully considered.

OBSERVATIONAL TOOLS

The relationship between the filtering effects of different observational lenses and the perspectives they allow has been treated extensively elsewhere

(Silliman & Wilkinson, 1991). In this section, an overview of categories of specific observational tools is presented, with an emphasis on their application to formative assessment. Recall that the lens model is a conceptual model; this discussion now turns to specific observational tools that can be used. Following is an examination of three types of tools based on the classification system developed by Evertson and Green (1986): (1) *categorical tools;* (2) *narrative tools;* and (3) *descriptive tools.* The relationships between tools and the observational view they offer are presented in Table 6–2 (page 154).

Categorical Tools

Categorical tools are closed systems that have definite preset categories into which all events and behaviors are coded during the observation. The coded categories are then summed, so that observation can be described quantitatively. These tools consist of recordings of selective behaviors that are writ-

Student____

Rating Scale

1 = not observed
2 = observed occasionally with teacher cues
3 = observed frequently with teacher cues
4 = observed occasionally without teacher cues in structured situations
5 = observed frequently without teacher cues in structured situations
6 = master across subject areas
N/A = not applicable

PRINT AWARENESS	Date	Date	Date
Attends to reading			
Shares reading with others			
Begins to look at print independently (books, calendars, labels, tags)			
Attends to pictures			
Enjoys having stories/information read to him/her			
Handles printed materials appropriately			
Turns pages from right to left			
Recognizes where print begins			
Recognizes where print ends			
Tracks print appropriately			
Comments on characteristics of print (i.e., long words, short words)			

READING STRATEGIES	Date	Date	Date
Pretends to read using pictures as a cue			
Pretends to read using text as a memory cue			
Focuses on print while retelling a story/information			
Reads familiar sight words			
Uses sound cues			
Uses picture cues			
Uses grammar cues			
Uses sentence meaning cues			

FIGURE 6–2
Behavior inventory for literacy development

(continued)

READING STRATEGIES *continued*			
Uses word structure cues (e.g. word length, configuration, suffixes, prefixes, root words)			
Uses knowledge of topic and content			
Monitors reading rate			
Monitors understanding of content			
Asks questions about content			
Rereads for clarification			
Uses a variety of strategies together			
Explains own use of reading strategies			
Reads smoothly from left to right without pausing between words			

CONTEXTS FOR APPLICATION OF READING STRATEGIES	Date	Date	Date
Material which he/she has dictated			
Familiar material written by others			
Unfamiliar material written by others			
Material with a predictable pattern			
Material without a predictable pattern			
Material important for daily living			

WRITING	Date	Date	Date
Uses random letters to express ideas (A R X for "I went to school")			
Uses first consonant letter sound ("I x t sk." for "I went to school.")			
Uses increased consonant sounds/letters ("I wit tu skul." for "I went to school.")			
Uses mostly correct spelling			
Writes for a variety of purposes			
Uses mechanics of writing			

FIGURE 6–2, *continued*
From Communication Development Program, South Metropolitan Association, Flossmoor, Il. With permission of L. Hoffman. From Heald-Taylor, G. (1987). "Predictable Literature Selections and Activities for Language Arts Instructions" by G. Heald-Taylor, 1987, *The Reading Teacher, 41*(1), pp. 6–12. Adapted by permission.

ten on a specifically devised format or transcribed into computer files (e.g., Miller et al., 1992). These behaviors may be summarized in a numerical representation, such as an overall rating, summary score, ranking, frequency count, or percentage.

Categorical tools are often directed to providing information about many students, as a method for understanding general communicative patterns. One result is diminished attention to individuals and their communication. These tools, therefore, may be of limited value, if the purpose of observation is to delineate changes for individual children. Three types of categorical tools are discussed: (1) checklist systems, (2) rating systems, and (3) category systems. The choice among these tools depends on several factors, including the availability of information, the amount of time and other resources that need to be expended on observation, and the goals of observation.

Checklists. Checklists are used to obtain a relatively large amount of information in a numerical form that will be able to address general questions of interest. Because the purpose of checklists is to note the occurrence or nonoccurrence of a behavior, they typically yield a wide-angled view of behavior. For example, they may be used to answer questions such as the following:

How often did students request information from the clinicians?
How often did they independently request information from each other?
How often did they initiate (or maintain) a topic without high levels of adult support?
How often did they present evidence of phonological awareness in what communicative modes of expression (oral alone, oral integrated with reading, oral integrated with writing, oral integrated with drawing, etc.)?

TABLE 6–1
Six features shared in common by all observational tools

Feature	Questions to Ask
1. A *purpose* (why)	Why is this observation taking place (to evaluate a child's current level of development, to assess effects of scaffolding with individual children, to evaluate program effectiveness, to implement a research project, etc.)?
2. A *focus* of observation (who)	Who is to be looked at or listened to (clinician or teacher alone, child alone, clinician/teacher-child or children, child-child, etc.)? What activities, materials, and environmental factors are to be recorded with these participants?
3. A *content* focus (what)	What aspect is to be learned about (phonological awareness, semantic development, speed of word retrieval, topic maintenance, integrating information from oral, written, and graphic domains, etc.)?
4. A *coding* unit (how)	What unit should be chosen to describe behaviors (T-units vs. total number of grammar categories vs. propositions, types of discourse functions, etc.)? How long should observation take place before recording and what should be the duration of observation?
5. A *means* to record data (how)	How should observational data be recorded (video recording, audio recording, paper and pencil)?
6. A *setting* (where)	Where should recording occur (classroom, cafeteria, playground, home)?

TABLE 6–2
Types of observational tools and the view of behavior allowed

Tool	Lens
1. *Categorical* (closed systems)	
Checklists	Wide angled
Rating scales	Wide angled
Classification systems	Regular or close-up
2. *Narrative* (open systems)	
Anecdotal notes	Wide angled or regular
Running records	Regular
Critical incidents	Close-up
Portfolios	Regular, close-up, or micro-close-up
3. *Descriptive* (open systems)	
Transcriptions	Close-up or micro-close-up

These questions are considered wide angled, because a broad focus of attention is placed on what happened.

Checklists are usually employed "on the spot" to record events. They can be completed after the fact by reviewing an audiotape or videotape as long as the behaviors of interest have been recorded. Typically, observers are not participants, and they need to be trained to use the checklist before observation. Decisions about what to check need to be made with split-second timing during the observation. Finally, Irwin and Bushnell (1980) note that checklists (1) need to be carefully developed and tested beforehand; (2) should have the specific behaviors of interest listed separately rather than collapsing them into categories; (3) should be logically organized; and (4) should meet all of the stated purposes of the observation. Advantages of checklists are their ease of use and minimal time needed to interpret findings. Checklists alone, however, are not sensitive to subtle changes in individual students' communicative repertoires.

Rating Scales. Rating systems are another method for recording observations in which preselected behaviors are identified. In this case, judgments are made about the quality of the behavior, such as its dynamic versus static nature or quality. Rating systems are used typically at the end of an observation to summarize the cumulative effect of direct observations. In comparison, checklist systems, as well as category systems, can be coded one by one "on the spot." Rating systems are most often used to assess global constructs, such as the modification of the Heald-Taylor (1987) inventory reproduced in Figure 6–2 or the system developed by Campbell and Dollaghan (1992) to rate the amount of information brain-injured students produce in a narrative task. Rating scales can offer only a wide-angled perspective on the nature of change. (For further discussion on the types of rating scales and common errors in their use, see Silliman & Wilkinson, 1991.)

Categorical Systems. Categorical systems are the third type of categorical tool consisting of preset categories into which all behaviors are recorded. They are classification systems used as the events under observation unfold. These events may be collected during live, on-line observation or from audio and video recordings.

Category systems work well when a low degree of inference is required in classifying behavior. These systems are most effective when the observer sees a close relationship between behavior as it actually occurs in a particular context and the coding system being used. For example, one can use Fujiki and Brinton's (1991) classification system to note changes in interactions with different conversational partners (other individual students, with a clinician, with the entire class, etc.) along the following dimensions: (1) the amount of talk (total number of utterances); (2) the type of discourse functions (requests, assertions, responses); (3) the types of turn initiations (smooth exchange without overlaps, overlaps, etc.); and (4) conversational sequences in which the topic was maintained (either by duplicating portions of what just had been said versus incorporating new information). Because of the enhanced specificity afforded by a classification system, a regular lens perspective is likely. Depending on the degree of detail in the construction of a classification system, a close-up analysis may be possible.

Westby (1990) provides examples of the application of category systems within a communication process model to the close-up tracking of students' progress in semantic, syntactic, and graphophonemic domains. Similar to checklist and rating systems, effective use of category systems requires preparation and training. Observers need to carefully define the various behaviors to reliably recognize instances.

Advantages and Disadvantages of Categorical Tools. Categorical tools have three obvious advantages. First, they are relatively easy and inexpensive to use, although these systems do take effort to develop, modify, and apply in reliable and effective ways. Second, a comparatively wide range of behaviors and larger numbers of students can be observed when necessary. Third, categorical tools can be used on-line or with prerecorded information. The quality of behavior can be inferred from the use of category systems but not from checklists or rating scales. Another disadvantage for checklists and rating scales is that without adequate training and preparation before observation, use of these tools is unreliable.

Narrative Tools

Compared to the closed nature of categorical tools, narrative tools are open systems that do not have predetermined categories. Narrative tools are used by observers to record broad segments of events or behaviors such as those that occur in the classroom. These tools consist of systematic and detailed written descriptions of an individual's speech and actions.

The period of observation can vary for narrative descriptions; it can be of longer duration during a period of several hours, a day, or, in the case of the assessment of progress, weeks, months, or years. Single or multiple incidents may be observed. Observers typically record events and behaviors as they unfold, most preferably from video or audio recordings or other forms of permanent documentation, and the natural order of events is preserved in the written record. The choice of a narrative tool will depend on the same factors operating for selection of categorical tools. Although there are several types of narrative tools, three kinds of narrative descriptions will be highlighted because of their pertinence for the formative assessment of progress: (1) running records, (2) critical incidents, and (3) portfolios.

Running Records. One type of running record, developed by Clay (1985), is specific to children's oral book reading and records everything ". . . that a child says and does as he tries to read the book you have chosen" (Clay, 1985, p. 17). This running record can then serve as a method for analyzing a student's reading miscues and self-correction strategies.

Running records as defined here have a broader function. They are used to record all significant behavior regarding a child or group, in sequence. The observer does not select out or evaluate what he thinks is important but, rather, writes in everyday language the complete stream of behavior as it unfolds during the observational period. Because the running record provides a systematic, intensive, and chronological account of behaviors within events, it provides a regular lens perspective into the activity structure.

Although running records are more complete in preserving a specific period of time and context, they are not inherently longitudinal documentation and do not preserve the sense of recurring behaviors and events over time that is evident in portfolios. On the other hand, running records tend to be more detailed and occur over a longer duration of observation than do critical incidents, which will be discussed next. Thus, running records tend to be more extended than critical incidents but do not encompass as long a period of time as portfolios.

Running records form the backbone of case studies because extensive training in recording techniques is not required for appropriate use of this tool. Some degree of training, however, is necessary for focusing on the basic elements of a running record. In addition, because observers do filter information differently, it is important for observers to reconcile any conflicting perspectives on events or the chronological sequence.

Critical Incidents. The critical incident is used to obtain a relatively small amount of detailed information in a narrative form that addresses a specific question of interest arising from the running record. Critical incidents can vary in duration from lengthy sequences of interaction to a brief one. They may be recorded as they occur, or, most preferably for the purposes of reliability and validity, should be reconstructed after the fact from video or audio recordings. Before identifying a critical incident, observers need to be clear about the question being asked and the focus of observation. Other necessary requirements involve agreement on when a critical incident happens, including when it begins and ends, and agreement that all of the relevant behaviors are included in the incident.

Portfolios. Portfolios are permanent collections of the most effective samples of students' achievements. They have two general purposes (Paulson, Paulson, & Meyer, 1991): (1) to document the long-term evolution of works in progress and (2) to monitor individual students' self-assessment of the learning process. Because portfolios contain performance samples from real-time communicative contexts, they become a comprehensive and longitudinal method for documenting the process and outcomes of communication-centered learning. The value of portfolio documentation as a narrative tool for formative assessment is their potential to ". . . offer multiple authentic indicators of achievement" (Archbald & Newmann, 1988, p. 29). Furthermore, portfolios have the added advantage of incorporating students' own perspectives on their developing strengths as learners, including their emerging abilities to elaborate creative and evaluative approaches to problem solving (Smith, 1990; Sternberg, 1990). Depending on the purposes of analysis, portfolio information can provide a regular, close-up or, even a micro-close-up, view of progress.

A portfolio can consist of a variety of samples of a student's adaptive efforts along the classroom discourse continuum. The same samples can also demonstrate how a child is progressing in integrating the formal conventions underlying reading and writing, such as punctuation, capitalization, and spelling, with their appropriate use. As Rhodes and Dudley-Marling (1988) comment, knowing the formal rules for punctuation, capitalization, or spelling is not the same as knowing how to apply these rules flexibly, depending on the purpose of their use (a job application vs. a personal note passed in class); the potential audience (a prospective employer vs. one's friend); and the topic (getting a job vs. going to a party). Three different kinds of samples follow to illustrate the potential of the portfolio as a longitudinal narrative tool: (1) journal writing, (2) dialogue journals, and (3) the video portfolio.

Journal Writing. Journal writing is a narrative tool. It is also an individualized expression of the narrative genre of discourse, as noted by Scott (chap. 8). Events of significance to the author are recounted within a temporal–causal organizational structure to clarify beliefs or values or to work through social problem solving. While fictional and personal experience narratives are generally familiar forms, less well-known is the personal fiction, a mixture of fact and fiction (Sutton-Smith, 1986). Tales are based on aspects of factual experiences that become embellished with the teller's imaginings and, perhaps, partial role assumption of the main character.

An illustration of this creative embroidery can be found in the "turkey journals" (Figure 6–3) of an urban third-grade class in Florida where journals are a tool of the writing process approach (Englert, 1990). In this particular situation, journal writing was used as a means for merging fictional and personal experience to develop a creative plan about saving the turkey from becoming the centerpiece of the Thanksgiving holiday dinner. Students made turkeys from pine cones as a whole class activity. Each student owned her turkey, decided on a name, and was responsible for it. Individual journal writing as a creative activity began the next day and continued daily over a one-week period. Students were asked to "hold your turkey up to your ear so that the turkey can tell you what went on at night while you were home" and to write in their turkey's voice in their personal journal. Each day, if students chose to do so, they orally reported on the adventures of their turkeys. As Thanksgiving approached, the children brainstormed on possible escape plans for their turkeys and then recorded a particular plan in their journal.

The regular lens allows monitoring of the developing themes and structure of the narrative form, such as the turkey journals. For example, the narrative structure of Jimmy's turkey journal might be described as one in which planning is missing but can be inferred based on the subheading of "The Escape." The narrative evolves as a series of action and reactive sequences in which the character's actions are chained together in time but are not yet causally related (see Lahey & Bloom, chap. 13).

A purely structural focus for the regular lens may obscure some of the narrative's functional relevance and expressive qualities. Refocusing to the close-up lens could make more visible Jimmy's experimentation with new ways of expressing his involvement, which is central to more literate forms of communication (Rowe, Harste, & Short, 1988). According to Tannen (1989), joint and active involvement of speakers with listeners and authors with readers is the *primary* motivation for interaction across spoken and written

FIGURE 6–3
Jimmy's turkey journal about Charlie (original spellings and punctuations are retained)

November 14
I feel happy because I'm small.

Nov. 15
I went flying with the other turkey. I crashed oene. Then I went to the lunchroom. Thare having pizza. Isn't it great. Yum! Yum!

Nov. 16
Ouch! I said! Man! Last night was the wourst! Somebody like your teacher picked me up. She thought I was a rock. Wait till I get my hand on your teacher.

Sat
Nov 17
We went to Daytona and it was fun.

Sun.
Nov. 18
Nice tent. We went camping in a indoor tent.

Nov. 19 (No entry)

Nov. 20
Yo Miami here I come. Oh no. I'm getting out of here. Can you here. This is real. Put me in the closet. Help I hope you heard that. Here they come. Uh oh.

Nov. 20
The Escape
Wire cutters please. Not that monkey wrench. Ouch! Here we go again. Whoe. What in the world. There's a tennage mutant ninja turtle poster down here.

Nov 21
The last time Bye Bye world! Bye Bart Simpson. I'll see you in Miami. I'm coming Mom + Dad. Where the spoon & fork Bye Duede. See you in Miami.

mediums of communication. Involvement entails "an internal, even emotional connection individuals feel which binds them to other people as well as to places, things, activities, ideas, memories, and words" (Tannen, 1989, p. 12). This emotional connection is the basis by which discourse participants make sense of each other's meanings. In Jimmy's account of Charlie, two discourse devices contribute to involvement. One is the richness of detail drawn from Jimmy's personal experience that allows the reader to connect emotionally with the events and feelings being described; the other strategy is one of "speaking through" the character of Charlie. This perspective-taking strategy creates a sense of audience participation in the events happening to Charlie and in his emotional reactions to these events (Tannen, 1989).

Dialogue Journals. In contrast to journal writing, Staton (1988b) defines dialogue writing as an activity in which a journal is used "for the purpose of carrying out a written conversation between two persons, in this case a student and a teacher, on a regular, continuous basis" (p. 4). Dialogue writing is a communicative tool that goes beyond "telling stories." It provides multipurpose opportunities to develop and practice the ability to give reasons for beliefs, describe events more explicitly, and craft persuasive arguments (Scott, chap. 8; Staton, 1988a). Dialogue journals therefore may serve as a tool for cultivating an evaluative orientation to problem solving. Because it draws on students' existing competence as oral communicators, dialogue journal communication can also serve as a conversational scaffold for the generation of things to say to a real audience (Staton, 1988b). A natural transition to expository writing is offered through this tool as well, one that also maintains interactional involvement as central to meaningful communication.

Shuy's (1988) analysis of complaints illustrates the varied functions of dialogue writing as the development of these functions is captured through the close-up lens of observation. Complaints are communicative acts that may be true or false in terms of their truth value but that must be sincere in intent (Searle, 1969, cited in Shuy, 1988). The speaker–author (complainer) believes the complaint to be true, has evidence for the validity of what is being complained about, and believes this evidence. The goal to be accomplished is to cause the listener–reader to mitigate her behavior in such a way that the less valid aspects of the event will be decreased or abolished; hence, the complaint is a prototype for the persuasive form of expository discourse.

When complaints are accepted by teachers and clinicians as valid concerns through the mechanism of dialogue writing, they become a formative means for tracking the perspectives of individual students on events in learning activities and on the reshaping of their beliefs about themselves as learners (Harste & Burke, 1989). Shuy (1988) comments that the sharing of complaints as one function of written dialogue communication supports students' role in their own learning. Shuy adds that such activity can also cultivate a sense of involvement and empowerment and provide multiple opportunities to compare, contrast, and practice discourse strategies for resolving practical problems in the settings where, traditionally, student complaints are less acceptable.

Two examples follow of early dialogue writing with Annette, an educationally at-risk student at the upper primary level. One excerpt deals with interpersonal conflict, and the other involves an implied academic complaint (Shuy, 1988, p. 151):

> Annette: At lunch recess, Sam and Gordon were cheating and so the other team lost.
>
> Teacher: We'll be electing new team captains soon—remember who the people are who can be fair and play for the benefit of all.
>
> Annette: I thought what we did today was boring . . .
>
> Teacher: You felt that our science was boring or that all the time was wasted in discipline was boring. Having boys and girls from other classes come in takes time to get going, doesn't it?

In the first example, Annette gave new information but does not provide a complete accounting of the event in terms of evidence for the "lack of fair play" complaint. The teacher acknowledged Annette's feelings and suggested a longer term resolution by which this specific kind of conflict can be diminished in the future. The teacher's strategy differed in the second example. Here, the intent was to guide Annette in evaluating more precisely the evidence for her feeling of academic boredom as represented in the complaint. Shuy (1988) suggests that developing competence in learning how to complain more effectively can be assessed along three observational dimensions, all of which are accessible to the close-up lens: (1) how the student in the role of author demonstrates over time that a conflict event is prejudicial to him, for example, from formulating inferred complaints to formulating explicitly stated complaints; (2) the extent to which the account of the complaint becomes elaborated, which provides fuller support for the validity of the complaint; and (3) the degree to which the implied complaint is made obvious through the linguistic integration of a clear conflict statement with new information encased in an account that contains more complete information.

Video Portfolios. As defined here, a video portfolio (e.g., the end-of-unit pond assessment, presented later), is a permanent longitudinal record of events that were designated for the formative assessment. These events may include whole class and small group events, as well as the recording of vignettes that sample individual students' performance within the larger theme.

Video portfolios integrated with other narrative tools, such as the systematic written recording of daily, on-line observations, running records of a video taped session, and related critical incidents, have three major advantages. First, they allow individual behavioral patterns to be selected for refined examination at the close-up and micro-close-up foci. Second, based on their integration with other narrative tools, discourse strategies can be modified and students' communicative needs and goals can be altered on systematic grounds. A third advantage of video portfolios is that real change, as opposed to spurious claims of "improvement," can be determined (Bain & Dollaghan, 1991; Fey & Cleave, 1990). Recordings may be made at the beginning of a thematic unit as a means for determining students' current or typical levels (the novice level or lower boundary of competence), midway through a unit, and at the end of a unit when assessing most effective behaviors is an objective (the upper level of competence). This sequence of sampling is consistent with the collection of multiple measures, an important procedure for reducing the potential for clinician bias in sampling and analysis. Without multiple measures, one would not know that bias is present and affecting apparent gains (Fey & Cleave, 1990). Because of the flexibility now offered by camcorders, one can alternate as necessary within a recording session between group interactions and a tighter focus on one student's sequences of efforts. By comparing these recording points within and across sessions, it is possible to track, over time, and in more reliable and objective ways, new behaviors, including their integration and scope of application. Depending on other technological support available, individual portfolios can be created for each student by editing the running record of each session into a unified record of critical incidents.

Video portfolios, as well as portfolios in general, provide a longitudinal record of progress. As longitudinal documentation of a wide range of behaviors, they allow in depth case studies to be developed for individual students (Fujiki & Brinton, 1991). Portfolios also overcome some of the difficulties associated with the traditional case study, such as the "snapshot" of a student's current level of performance produced by an analysis at a single point in time (McTear & Conti-Ramsden, 1992).

Furthermore, portfolios may be constructed to reflect a form of within-subject design where children serve as their own controls. McReynolds and Kearns (1983) note that an assumption for use of a within-subject case study design in the treatment of communication disorders is that individual variability in behavior is the norm: ". . . therefore, effective treatment programs can be developed only when the variables responsible for client variations are understood and brought under control" (p. 9). While structured control (manipulation) of independent and dependent variables is antithetical to a communication process approach, a more compatible tenet is that the locus of control is not the child. Rather, the locus of control resides in the reliability and validity of the methodology selected for the continuous sampling and interpretation of data in real communicative contexts (McReynolds & Kearns, 1983). When designed as qualitative research, within-subject designs can afford more rigorous opportunities to begin identifying how and in what ways the intended effects of a supportive discourse scaffold match its actual effects over time. Only then can more refined questions be asked to examine specific cause-effect relationships about intervention effectiveness and efficacy.

Advantages and Disadvantages of Narrative Tools. The narrative tools discussed have both collective and individual advantages. (1) Most allow clinicians and colleagues to record events in everyday language and, in the case of portfolios, in the students' own use of language. (2) Observers can recount what they see as it occurs in a particular environment, and these written and technological records can be reviewed again and again; as a result, observers are aided in the reliable collection of multiple measures and in making more valid inferences about the authenticity of progress. (3) The focus of narrative tools can be on the individual student, a group within a particular event, or it can be on the event itself, such as students' public performances of what they have learned in a unit. (4) Because portfolios are longitudinal records, students' perspective on their learning experiences with different communicative activities become an integral part of the formative assessment process. (5) Narrative accounts, such as running records, critical incidents, journals, and dialogue journals, can be generated with a minimum use of technological equipment and, therefore, are not costly.

These advantages of simplicity are offset, to some extent, by two disadvantages. First, because of the filtering effect, new observers may find it difficult to decide what is important, thus, compromising the reliability of observations. Second, it is sometimes difficult to analyze completely what has been either written down by the observer or student or recorded electronically. The length of time it takes to read through or look at narrative records may result in problems in determining what is most germane and how to summarize it. For example, if a running record is insufficiently detailed, critical incidents may be obscured; if, on the other hand, a running record is too detailed, then what is most relevant may be equally obscured. Because of these potential disadvantages, observers need in-depth preparation and experience with the use of narrative tools if standards for reliability and validity are to be met.

Descriptive Tools

Descriptive tools are used to obtain a verbatim account of the language used, along with a detailed description of the context within which language use occurs. Observers typically are concerned with identifying a developing process or pattern of behavior that occurs across situations. A focus of description might be students' developing process of understanding how the purpose for a learning activity relates to the outcomes of learning (e.g., see the following description of the "pond unit:" "Why did you earn this special award?" in the next section, entitled "The Observational Lens Model and Guide to Formative Assessment"). Descriptive tools could also function as a micro-close-up lens in revealing possible sources for breakdowns in students' comprehension during lessons (see the "pond unit").

Although there are many kinds of descriptive tools, a key element among them is the use of transcriptions of discourse from video or audio recordings. Thus, by necessity, descriptive tools depend on the use of some technology for the production of a transcription. The transcribed discourse may then be supplemented by notations to designate other behaviors found to be important for interpreting the interaction, such as accompanying nonverbal actions, prosodic features, verbal overlaps, silent pauses, revisions, and the like. Analysis of these transcriptions occurs retrospectively, not live or online. Descriptive tools also incorporate a knowledge of the dynamics of the context within which recordings are made so that interpretation can be as complete and accurate as possible.

When to use a descriptive tool, such as a transcription, depends on its purpose and the view of the student within particular communicative contexts that one chooses to see. The pathway taken for analysis will depend on the purposes of analysis. If the purpose is to determine whether observed changes are authentic advancements, defined as more effective demonstrations of the transfer of responsibility for learning from the clinician to the student, then a good starting point for analysis might be the integration of narrative and descriptive tools. For example, running records of video- or audiotaped events or of a specific video portfolio, can be used as the basis for identifying whether critical incidents are present and may be especially indicative of real advancement. A descriptive tool, such as transcription, may then be applied to critical incidents to allow narrow scrutiny of the interactional processes supporting progress or its absence.

On the other hand, if the purpose is to assess the stability and scope of real changes in the transfer of responsibility, for example, in a student's use of the semantic–syntactic system, then a different process of tool integration may be more efficacious. Because stability and scope need to be examined as a function of interactional demands along the oral–literate continuum, as a first step, a fine-grained analysis available only through transcription may be necessary. Based on this transcription, the decision could be made to integrate a categorical tool into interpretation, such as a system for classifying the kinds and instances of semantic–syntactic strategies that increase the density and cohesiveness of clauses and, thus, increase verbal productivity in both the oral and written domains (e.g., see Strong & Shaver, 1991). Using the same classification system, the stability and breadth of these strategies could be analyzed across different types of discourse structures (narrative vs. expository); modes of expression (e.g., the oral retellings of personal experiences vs. dialogue journal writing); and communicative functions (creating an oral autobiography vs. evaluating interpersonal conflict).

Advantages and Disadvantages of Descriptive Tools. In using descriptive tools, observers focus on and record exactly what is said as it unfolds in a particular situation. These original records, on video or audio recordings, are permanent, can be reviewed indefinitely by multiple observers, and are transcribed into everyday language. Their primary advantages are a completely accurate record of what language was produced in a particular interactional event and the careful analysis that can accrue from detailed examination of the record.

The advantages of the completeness and infinite retrievability of information are offset to some degree by three disadvantages: (1) New observers need training to gain proficiency in the use of descriptive tools; without such training, reliability of transcription and the validity of interpretations are seriously compromised. (2) It is often difficult to analyze an audiovisual record and transcribe it because of inadequate camera positioning, noise, or other flaws within the technological record. (3) It is time-consuming and expensive to make audiovisual records, to transcribe the data, and to code them—a major disadvantage in school settings, where clinicians' caseloads, even in the collaborative structure of a communication process model, are often large.

THE OBSERVATIONAL LENS MODEL AND GUIDE TO FORMATIVE ASSESSMENT

To illustrate the use of the observational tools to guide formative assessment, an end-of-unit assessment conducted by two speech-language pathologists, who also served as the teachers in a combined first grade–kindergarten, is presented. The unit involved learning about pond life. This theme was carried out over a six-week period in this lower primary classroom for nine students with severe language learning disabilities. These students ranged in age from five years and eight months to seven years and three months. Their classroom, team taught by the two speech-language pathologists, was part of a larger collaborative program, the Communication Development (CD) Program of the South Metropolitan Association (SMA), located in suburban South Cook County, Illinois. This public school program serves students with severe language learning disabilities at five levels from kindergarten through high school. Eligible students are sent from fifty-five school districts, who fund various aspects of the SMA services.

A communication process philosophy guides the program and functions as the basis for integrating educational and clinical goals and practices. Communication goals and intervention procedures are mediated through the use of *supportive discourse scaffolds.* Supportive scaffolds assist students to discover, integrate, and apply the multiple connections between listening, speaking, reading, writing, and spelling as communicative tools for interpreting, remembering, and expressing meaning (for further elaboration see Hoffman, 1990; Silliman & Wilkinson, 1991; also, see chap. 2, the discussion on the nutrition lesson).

Students Studied

Of the five girls studied, three were white and two were black; one of the four boys was black and three were white. Durations varied for their placements in the program. Some students were transferred from the early childhood program connected with SMA; others were referred from their sending school districts and determined to be eligible for placement at the beginning of the school year. According to initial assessment findings, students' proficiency varied in linguistic, social-interactional, cognitive, and academic domains. Most had serious difficulties with planning and were delayed significantly in emerging literacy awareness. Several were described as having severe comprehension problems (Trina, Nancy, Charles, Clark), including problems in word retrieval ranging from moderate (Abbey) to severe (Alan). An additional factor for one student, Nancy, was a high frequency hearing loss. Although she was fitted with hearing aids, a trial period of use did not significantly alter her classroom performance. Two other students, John and Shanzi, had severe phonological process disruptions as the primary symptoms. Another, Kim, was considered as a potential slow learner. Finally, two students, Trina and Clark, displayed hyperlexic tendencies; they were superior at decoding but had minimal comprehension of what they read, and in many circumstances, what they heard. Clark also tended to repeat portions of what had just been said and frequently interacted with inappropriate facial expressions and prosody.

Finally, nearly all of the students entered the program with low self-esteem, an affective quality generally reflected through a variety of behaviors that influenced their motivation to learn. These behaviors ranged from passive participation to inattention to acting out. For example, Charles, who was receiving 10 mg of methylphenidate hydrochloride (Ritalin) in the mornings only, tended to handle interpersonal conflicts with angry confrontations; Nancy often experienced difficulties in attending to the relevance of various classroom activities; Clark often withdrew from participation because, when confronted with tasks he could not easily manage, he became frustrated; Abbey often acted with uncertainty because she tended to interpret competence as giving the "right" answer; John frequently acted before considering his actions; and Alan, who could not function well when speed of information retrieval was a factor, frequently withdrew into nonresponsiveness.

Instructional Theme of the Lesson

The unit was organized around a book from the big-book series *Jump, Frog, Jump* (by R. Kalan, 1981). Over a five-week period from early November to early December, the nine children engaged in building and elaborating this theme. Consistent with a communication process approach, the theme cut across traditional curriculum content areas, such as reading, mathematics, science, and language arts. A major emphasis was assisting students to learn that ways of meaning could be created and expressed through alternate communication modes.

Reading. In reading, a big-book activity was read together daily as a whole-group activity. Students were divided into two small groups for experiences with a variety of related communicative functions, for example:

- Read charts that categorize information on pond life (chart titles included flowers, plants, water, pond animals, fish, boats, and birds).
- Draw pictures of their favorite part of the big-book story.
- Construct a story grammar chart, and then discuss the important components of the story (setting, characters, problem, actions, solution).
- Choose sight words to hang up.
- Make puppets to act out the story.
- Illustrate their own version of the story and then alternate turns retelling it.
- Order the story sequence using actual pages from the book.

Mathematics. To practice the coordination of number recognition with a basic understanding of ordinal relations, students were involved in two activities:

- A number was written on paper frogs or fish, and students "fed" these objects the specific number of pennies.
- Alternating turns during reading to problem solve which page numbers came before or after other page numbers.

Science. Students were introduced to books about pond life. "Information charts" were collaboratively written about fish, turtles, snakes, and frogs. Additionally, a pet newt was purchased to compare and contrast similarities and differences between frogs and newts. Students also talked about the meaning of *amphibian.*

Language Time. Cooperative and independent activities included the following:

- Paint and stuff a large fish.
- Write a word from *Jump, Frog, Jump,* and display it in the pond museum.
- Sing songs about *Jump, Frog, Jump.*
- Follow rules to play *Go Fish.*
- Listen to *Jump, Frog, Jump* using books the students individually illustrated.
- Construct a snake from socks.

Independent Choice Centers. During this daily afternoon activity, students made their own decision about what they wanted to do based on a menu of choices, such as:

- Play *Go Fish.*
- Play *Memory* with colored fish.
- Write the word *green,* or a similar attribute, inside a fish.
- Play a number fishing game or a wind-up fishing game.
- Listen to *Jump, Frog, Jump* on an audiotape.
- Connect dot-to-dot pictures of various pond animals.
- Color pond animals to decorate the class "Pond Bulletin Board."
- Color three specific turtles from a sheet of fifteen turtles.

Data Collection

The end-of-unit activity, one hour and seven minutes in duration, was videotaped. The purpose of this activity, as defined by the clinicians, was to assess progress in three areas: (1) planning and problem solving (the metacognitive domain); (2) manipulating units of language (the metalinguistic domain); and (3) communication selected to express meaning (the domain of literacy functions). The use of an analysis based on the regular lens allowed a more detailed description of how the activity was organized. The analysis included phases of the lesson, expectations for demonstrating what had been learned, how interactional sequences unfolded, and the roles that students assumed in participating in the lesson.

Physical Aspects of the Lesson

The lesson took place in the students' classroom on December 14 in the late morning. Different print tools are highly visible throughout the room (word charts, number charts, the students' authored books, pictures, etc.). Students were seated at five circular tables, either in small groups or individually. The physical arrangement facilitated ease in adapting head orientation to maintain face-to-face-communication with peers and with the clinicians. In certain instances, the physical arrangement allowed peers to assist one another during implementation of the activity. Students were also free to move around the room when their teacher allowed them to do so. In this activity, clinician 1 stood near a chart taped to the blackboard; clinician 2 held a camcorder toward the rear of the room (the students were familiar with being videotaped in this particular classroom).

Organization of the Lesson

The pond unit was the second unit of the school year. It was organized to reveal what students had learned from this thematic unit. The activity was structured by three phases, each of which was marked by different interactional sequences: (1) an opening phase, (2) a demonstration phase, and (3) a closing phase.

Orientation Phase. In the orientation phase, which was six minutes and thirty seconds in duration, clinician 1 began by (1) defining the shared purpose of the event (showing what had been learned); (2) focusing attention on the communicative choices available to demonstrate learning; and (3) encouraging students with higher levels of print comprehension to try out different choices other than reading or counting aloud. Referring to the chart taped on the blackboard, clinician 1 read the title, and reviewed the five choices: (1) reading *Jump, Frog, Jump,* a book collaboratively drawn and written by all nine students; (2) singing a "pond" song that they had learned; (3) feeding a fish pennies, which involved number sets; (4) using a written science chart about animal and insect life in ponds to "tell us what you learned"; and (5) from the perspective of bodily kinesthetic communication, "using your body" to act out the book or song with props or through pantomime.

After one and one-half minutes, students began evaluating the "choice menu." Of the nine students, five (Trina, John, Abbey, Kim, and Nancy) made their selections without any need for clinician assistance; however, Trina, Abbey, and Nancy chose modes that they preferred (i.e., "were good at" or "did best"), such as reading aloud (Trina) and counting (Abbey and Nancy). Their decisions were accepted; however, clinician 2 challenged them to expand their display of understanding. For example, Trina was asked to consider whether she might "answer some questions" about the *Jump, Frog, Jump* story once she finished reading it.

The remaining four students (Alan, Shanzi, Clark, and Charles) needed guidance in selecting a preferred mode of communication for demonstrating their knowledge to others. Shanzi and Charles needed oral repetition of choices only ("Do you need to hear the choices again?") or to be redirected to "Look at the choice menu, and tell us what you've learned." Alan's decision making (acting out) needed more support. Not responding to oral repetition of the five choices, he was able to select when given three choices. Clark, on the other hand, had focused on clinician 1's comment at the beginning of the orientation that, following the selection of choices, he could introduce the demonstration phase. He chose "introducing." Acknowledging that Clark could introduce at the appropriate time, clinician 1 had to combine repetition with a set of limited choices to support Clark's attending to the immediate task. Clark selected reading the story, also a mode of communication that he preferred.

Demonstration Phase. This phase was forty-eight minutes and thirty-six seconds in duration. The transition from the opening phase was communicated by Clark's standing up, facing the video camera, and announcing his name, the room number, the unit to be presented, and why it was being presented. He needed extensive verbal support from clinician 1 to formulate the linguistic elements of the announcement. Students then communicated what they had learned; this information is summarized as follows.

Trina, six years and seven months old, was the first to demonstrate (over the past two months, she had demonstrated an increasing ability to retain and apply comprehension strategies). Asked to initiate her role by sitting on the floor, over the next four minutes and forty-five seconds, she fluently and expressively read the *Jump, Frog, Jump* story to her audience, both peers and clinicians. Because of the predictability of the content, the students spontaneously joined in and "read along" with her for the final thirty-seven seconds. Following completion of the story, Trina answered some questions about what a question mark means in the story and about the characters in the story and the problem to be solved. Assistance was provided about the meaning of a question mark, when she stated "Cause it comes at the end". Trina was also assisted when she seemed to misinterpret the meaning of "characters" in the context of the story. With this guidance, she was able to manage successfully the series of questions about the communicative function of the question form of punctuation as well as basic story structure.

Abbey, seven years and one month old, next demonstrated her counting proficiency in "feeding" a fish puppet seventeen pennies, a number she had selected. She smiled broadly on completion. The clinicians were somewhat confused, however, about the accuracy of her count. She was asked to recount with some guidance from clinician 1. Needing several trials, she accurately deposited seventeen pennies; then, clinician 2 asked Abbey if she was ready for "the million dollar question." She smiled and said "yes." She successfully answered what came after and before seventeen.

Charles, age seven years and one month, was next. Strongest in rote math skills, he chose to read several science charts about animal life in ponds. He stood and walked to one wall chart and faced it. Clinician 1 immediately suggested different aspects that he could talk about, such as what happened in the pond, what pond animals ate, or "something interesting" about a snake or turtles. Charles then offered what pond animals eat and pointed to a picture of a duck, identified it as a duck, and responded with grass when asked what ducks like to eat. The clinician next asked Charles if he could read any other words from the chart. Charles spelled *plants* aloud in a soft voice and then spelled *worms.* Clinician 2 asked him what word said *worms* and then provided him with a prompt, focusing on the initial grapheme (What word starts with "w"?). Charles accurately pointed to the word and spelled it aloud. With guidance, he then answered questions about attributes and actions of turtles and performed a physical demonstration of how a turtle walks.

Shanzi, age five years and eight months, using props, acted out a series of actions from another story, *In the Pond,* collaboratively authored by the children. She provided a simultaneous comment on the actions she was performing.

At twenty-four minutes and thirty-six seconds into the demonstration phase, Clark, six years and eight months old, began to read the story about *Jump, Frog, Jump.* As Clark read the story, the students again joined in and participated in a chorus in the story reading. At twenty-eight minutes and two seconds, Trina stated "The end", which was challenged by Charles. He was then asked by clinician 2 how he knew whether the end had been reached. He responded with "Cause there are a few more pages left." The clinician then stated that Clark should be allowed to read by himself, which he did, in a fluent and expressive manner, to the end of the story.

Kim, age seven years and three months, selected to tell about the information on the science charts. She walked to a pond chart, pointed to a word, and stated "This is a shrimp." Clinician 1 suggested that she first point to the question "What is in the pond?". Guided by the clinician's questions, Kim listed some fish and insects found in ponds and then was able to elaborate on what turtles eat. Asked by clinician 1 where turtles live, Kim returned her gaze to the wall chart and answered that they live in a shell in a pond. She was reminded to continue looking at the wall chart that contained the information she described and to ask other students when she was uncertain about particular information, such as "What do turtles like to do during the day?".

Alan, age seven, was asked to pantomime the *Jump, Frog, Jump* book that he made. Shanzi held his book and verbalized pictorial content as Alan began pantomiming actions. When Shanzi encountered some difficulty recreating the story, clinician 2 suggested to Shanzi that clinician 1 read the story, because it was Alan's turn to show what he knew. Alan smiled, looked at clinician 1, and appeared to monitor the clinician's speaking rate and stress patterns in timing his gestures with her formulation of the story's actions. He was further supported in the story events and actions by the other students, who orally read along with the clinician. He then showed a book for which he said "I do the pictures." Asked by clinician 2 whether the appropriate word was "do the pictures" or "draw the pictures," he selected "draw" and repeated it five times, as a good strategy to help him "remember."

Nancy, age seven years and two months, walked to the number chart and seemed to be indecisive about what number to pick for feeding the fish pennies. Because one of Charles's strengths was counting, he was asked to help Nancy. He took her hand, stated "Come on over," walked to the number chart with her, and stated "See what number you would like to pick." Clinician 2 then suggested to Charles that he show Nancy two possible choices, a big number and a small number. He selected nineteen and six. Nancy then picked nineteen as the number of pennies to count for feeding the fish. As she approached nineteen, she began to look at the number chart to check when she has reached nineteen. Charles spontaneously tapped Nancy and asked "Why do we stop at nineteen?" Attending to clinician 1, Nancy did not answer; but a few seconds later, Charles was asked by clinician 2 to provide the reason. He stated "Because she counted out nineteen pennies," while simultaneously pointing to 19 on the number chart. Nancy was then requested to determine how she would check that she was accurate. She dumped the pennies out, and Charles assisted her by verbally counting along with her in a soft voice. Nancy stopped counting at seventeen, and Charles added two additional pennies to her pile.

John, age six years and five months, elected to sing a pond song; however, when his turn arrived, he started to sing a Christmas song. Clinician 1 interrupted him and asked if his choice was a Christmas song or the pond song. John replied the "pond song" and was asked if he needed the book to help him sing along. He retrieved the book and then proceeded to sing with other students also singing. The students were reminded that it was John's turn. Because John had severe phonological problems, clinician 1 helped him to monitor the pronunciation of *ducks* and *swoops.*

This phase ended with John assigned responsibility for leading all of the students in singing several stanzas of *Jump, Frog, Jump.* Clinician 1 guided the students in selecting the stanzas and then asked "How can we end it?" Students acted out frog jumping, as a finale.

The Closing Phase. The shift from the demonstration to closing phase (seven minutes and five seconds) was signaled by clinician 2's indirect directive "Could everyone sit down, please?" Students returned to their chairs. The general purpose of this phase was to recognize individual accomplishment in the choices made to communicate what was learned. Each student received an award on which was written "I learned a lot about the pond"; however, a critical goal was to assess students' self-awareness about motivations for learning. One aspect involved the status of students' understanding of their individual strengths as participants in the pond unit. The other aspect concerned the degree to which students could see relationships between the reason for the award and the award itself. For example, six weeks earlier, in a similar end-of-unit assessment, students provided reasons for receiving awards that focused on their good behavior. Hence, the closing phase has an evaluative function in addition to recognition of students' accomplishments.

Clinician 1 was seated at the front of the room holding the awards. Each of the nine students was called separately to receive their award, which Abbey creatively named "The Frog Award." Clapping was heard as each student was called on. Each student was also asked variations of four questions: (1) "What did you like (or enjoy) best about the pond unit?" or, alternately, "What was your favorite thing you did?" (2) "Was it easy or hard for you?" (3) "What did you learn?" (4) "Why did you get (or earn) the award?"

With minimal assistance, most of the students identified what they enjoyed best and its ease or difficulty. However, inferring causal links between the psychological purpose of the "pond theme" and the reason for the award was elusive for many. For example, Abbey, who six weeks earlier explained her award as one for good behavior, was now able to express the reason partially as "Fur-fur-doin'-fur-fur-fur working hard." Charles formulated "Because I was participating." Even with prompting from the clinicians to focus on "learning a lot," the majority of others' explanations centered on components of conduct, such as good behavior (Nancy), being good (Alan), and listening and doing what the teacher tells me (John).

Students' Language Usage

Taking this analysis further, the regular lens (appropriately focused for formative assessment of progress) focuses on particular aspects of students' language usage, including (1) access to the floor, (2) managing topics, (3) self-regulating attention, and (4) planning the discourse.

Access to the Floor. Students understood that equity of opportunity in "having a turn" was an operative rule. This was manifested in the orientation phase, where each student was allocated the opportunity to choose a way to express what had been learned. Equity of access was a feature of the demonstration phase. In this latter phase, students waited for their turn without interruption and attended to the contributions of the student in the conversational spotlight.

Students also seemed to understand the conditions in which more fluid access to the conversational floor was permissible. Conditions for self-selection as a speaker included awareness of a need for clarification about task procedures or word meaning. Self-selection also occurred when it was assessed that another's student's contribution was not appropriate for completion of the task. One example comes from Clark's oral reading turn. Charles issued a challenge to Trina that the end of the story had not been reached. This challenge suggested that Charles was in the process of developing socially appropriate communicative strategies for questioning others' judgments.

When the role of a student shifted from that of listener (audience) to active collaborator, for example, when one student was directed to ask another for factual information about pond animals, some students could rapidly produce accurate information for the questioner. Others were still less skilled. While they were able to retrieve topically related content, the content was not yet accurately recalled. On the other hand, Charles, when asked to assume the role of "teacher," proficiently assisted Nancy in the counting task, including guiding her to an appropriate evaluative question to ask about task outcome ("Why do we stop counting at nineteen?").

Topic Management. A majority of the students demonstrated that they could manage a limited set of choices, with varying levels of external support, about how they preferred to communicate their shared learning experiences. However, choice entailed comparison and contrast relative to an anticipated outcome. It was not clear that, for any individual student, a process of planned comparison was involved.

From this analysis, one can conclude that the pond theme functioned as a holistic schema for topic management as a social activity (Nelson, 1985; chap. 4). That is, as a group, students could not yet analyze the process of making choices into its component parts and relations. They could approach it on a more global level, as a particular kind of event that consisted of certain expectations and ways of getting things done and attending to the topic at hand.

Self-Regulating Attention. With further analysis, the degree to which students self-regulated the focus of attention was revealed by using the regular lens correctly. Despite the length of the activity, students were attending to the unfolding of events. Clinicians directed a student to "pay attention" to the immediate task only once during the sixty-seven-minute session. This occurred during John's turn in the closing phase when he became focused on his award and appeared not to be attending to clinician 1's question regarding the reason for obtaining the award.

The clinicians intervened only when it became obvious that students' natural collaboration in a student's turn might be counterproductive. Only three instances of this form of intervention occurred: (1) during Clark's oral reading when the other students began to "read" chorally with him; (2) during Alan's turn, when Shanzi had problems reconstructing the story for him to pantomime; and (3) when John initiated his turn with a "Christmas" song rather than the "pond" song.

Planning Discourse. All students were successful in the choices they made about how to participate. The discourse demands underlying students' communicative choices varied. A high degree of predictability appeared to be important for regulating the ease of discourse planning for those students who chose a narrative form of expression, such as reading, singing, or acting out a familiar story in which action sequences predominated. The predictability of a routine varied for those who selected counting, which required formulating a more expository type of discourse where a number set was highlighted. A question concerned whether Trina and Clark processed linguistic information in chunks or as unanalyzed wholes. Clinician 2 sought to assess Trina's success in continuing to move beyond superficial processing by posing questions about the meaning of question marks and certain story components. When directed to focus on specific elements, Trina's responses indicated that she had encoded information on, for example, the main characters and the obstacles they encountered. Trina had not, however, necessarily integrated the information into a basic story schema. Clark, on the other hand, produced no evidence that he could manage active manipulation of story meaning.

The two students who recounted the science charts (Charles and Kim) needed to engage in more advance planning to summarize essential information in expository form, based on their inferences about what others needed to know. Neither student was highly successful in accomplishing the goals, although both attempted to go beyond what they perceived themselves to be currently capable of doing. In taking a risk, however, Charles showed some momentary attempts to apply a metalinguistic approach for word recognition. Kim, in contrast, displayed only a trial and error approach to the task. Charles invoked a spelling approach, which suggested an effort to relate graphemes (the visual representation of the word) to their phonemic counterparts (phonemic representation of the word). Later, when given the cue of the initial grapheme in *worm,* he was able to recognize the word within the functional setting of the chart.

Modeling. Finally, the data generated by using an analysis based on the regular lens can point to, but not necessarily explain, specific effects of the clinicians' discourse strategies in supporting the students' successful participation in the pond activity. The clinicians' modeling can be characterized as directive and dynamic because of the high frequency of two types of discourse devices: (1) providing limited choices from which to select an answer and (2) cloze, or fill-in, procedures. Both types of devices derived from the clinicians' experiences with students' retrieval difficulties. Modeling was aimed at helping students to focus their attention on best-fit predictions about what could be said next, based on what just had been said. Reciprocal and dynamic modeling occurred less often but still with some regularity, for example, inviting a student to ask another for assistance or shifting the "teacher" role to a student.

A third type of modeling, acknowledgment of effort through elaboration, is more evaluative. Evaluation through elaboration drew students' explicit attention to the cognitive and affective dimensions of communication. For example, as a general pattern, the clinicians drew students' attention to the manner in which their cognitive approach to the task influenced successful participation. In these instances, mental state words referring to internal processes were often invoked, such as "You know, Abbey, you counted nice and slowly"; (to John) "I think you really learned so much about the animals in the pond. I'd like to thank you because you always listened during all of our science lessons"; and (to Trina) "You did that really well [reading] because you like reading best." At the same time, these evaluations through elaboration were interpretations for students that their communicative efforts had value for them and were also valued by others.

Continuing with the analysis at a greater level of detail with the close-up lens permits a more detailed account of patterns involving student(s) within a specific activity at a given point in time. For example, a close-up view can reveal critical behaviors that demonstrate a student's need for scaffolding within a particular task domain.

Returning to the pond unit, the close-up lens can be applied to the demonstrations created by individual students. The tighter focus of this lens allows assessment of the extent to which students' choices were implemented with various degrees of support from the clinicians. Consider the following example with Abbey. Recall that she chose feeding the fish pennies to show how, during the course of this unit, she had partially mastered the notion of one-to-one correspondences. This served as a basic concept for understanding the numerical equivalence between two sets (Piaget, 1965). The major question concerned the adequacy of the self-monitoring that Abbey used to achieve her goal of mapping between the written numerical representation of seventeen and the actual "feeding" of seventeen pennies to the fish puppet.

Abbey began by counting the pennies aloud and putting them on the table. Clinician 2 asked whether Abbey wanted to place them in the fish puppet, and Abbey indicated yes. She then began to drop the pennies when clinician 1 recognized that the pennies were being placed in the wrong end of the paper puppet. The clinician requested that Abbey start over. First, she is asked how many pennies she has counted so far. Replying "two," Abbey dumped the pennies over and began again. She monitored her counting from one to seventeen. She said each number as she simultaneously dropped a penny into the fish puppet. Although Abbey was counting slowly, it appears that she may have been counting aloud faster than the actual correspondence of the oral counting with each penny. Asked by clinician 1 how she would make certain that seventeen pennies had been counted, Abbey replied "Count." She was then directed to take the pennies out and to check her outcome by recounting. Abbey then started counting aloud from one, glancing at clinician 2. This time, however, rather than dropping the pennies into the puppet, Abbey counted by touching each penny on the table and moving it toward herself. She stopped counting at fourteen and said "Wrong." Clinician 1 then suggested that Abbey "start again if you get a little mixed up." Once more, Abbey began recounting but this time touched each penny as she counted. She ended at fourteen.

Clinician 1 then invited Abbey to drop the pennies "back in (the puppet) after we count them." On this fifth trial, Abbey counted to eleven when clinician 1 cautioned her not to count a penny until she actually picked it up. Abbey next said "twelve" (indicating twelve pennies were already counted), which was corrected to "eleven" by clinician 1. Abbey then picked up the count at twelve and continued to seventeen. Finally, clinician 2 asked Abbey "How do we write the number seventeen?". Abbey replied, with a smile, "A one and a seven." Asked if she was ready for the million dollar question, Abbey, still smiling, said yes. She was asked what comes after seventeen. Glancing at the number chart, she replied "eighteen". The follow-up was "What comes before seventeen?" and Abbey without looking at the chart answered "sixteen." Her smile continued.

It seems reasonable to conclude that Abbey remains in the preoperational stage, albeit in a transitional phase, in relation to her understanding of number as an equivalence (Piaget, 1965). She is still bounded by perceptual comparison of correspondences, which may partially account for descriptions of her as good at rote counting. On the other hand, the picture that emerges from the close-up lens portrays a different view than the one offered through the regular lens. By examining Abbey with a tighter focus, her strategies for keeping track of the task and where she is in the task may continue to progress with guided practice.

Evidence of her monitoring appeared when she picked each penny up and said the corresponding number (trials 1 and 2). Guided by the clinician to recheck her outcome (which may or may not have been correct initially), trial 3 was characterized by an integration of more deliberate movement with oral tracking of amount. Abbey first touched each penny and moved it toward her, as contrasted with using the puppet as a container; however, she did not slow her rate of counting as a means for coordinating it with the rate of movement. The outcome was incorrect but, for the first time, Abbey verbalized her recognition of error with the evaluative "Wrong." On trial 4, she attempted to correct her approach, this time by shifting to the procedures initially used in trials 1 and 2. The end result was still incorrect. Trial 5 indicated that Abbey has to refine coordination of deliberate movement (picking up each penny) with a deliberately timed rate of oral counting. Given the reminder to time the verbal actions of counting with the actual movement of picking up a penny, Abbey finally reached her objective.

If observation needs to be magnified to a greater degree, then use of the micro-close-up lens is recommended. At this most detailed level, this lens is used to better perceive the actual dynamics of interaction in detail and over time, so that specific questions about particular students can be answered.

An illustration of the use of this lens is taken from the closing phase of the pond unit. In this example, students were asked why they received an award. It became apparent that students' understanding of the motivations for the award differed from the clinicians' motivations despite nearly four months of emphasis on learning as an activity having intrinsic rewards. Only two students, Abbey and Charles (see following dialogue), were able to express responses that revealed some understanding of these reasons. Their responses are contrasted from the first end-of-unit assessment in early November on a nursery rhyme theme, to the second pond unit assessment five weeks later, in mid-December.

Charles

November 2

Clinician 1: Charles, why are you getting this special award?/ (Charles is the fifth child to obtain the award)

Charles: Because I participated/ (said with a slowed rate and equal stress on each syllable)

Clinician 1: You participated/ Did you learn anything about Mother Goose?/ (Charles nods head indicating agreement) We think you did, Charles/

December 14

Clinician 1: Charles, what did you like about our pond lesson?/ (Charles is the seventh child to be given the award)

Charles: Um-hum/ I liked about our pond unit is/

Clinician 1: Did you like it when we talked about math and fed the fish?/ Or did you like our science charts?/

Charles: Science charts/

Clinician 1: Oh really/ I thought you would say math, Charles/ Do you like math or science better?/

Charles: Science/

Clinician 1: Oh really/ OK/ Well, why did you earn this award?/

Charles: Because—because I was participating/

Clinician 1: You participated and tried your hardest/ I think you learned a lot also/ Thank you/

Charles: Can I put this (the award) in my mail box?/

Abbey

November 2

Clinician 1: Abbey knows why she earned this

special award/ (Abbey is the sixth to receive the award; she follows Charles)
Abbey: For good behavior/
Clinician 1: For good behavior?/
Abbey: No/ For good listening/
Clinician 1: For good listening/ And what else, Abbey?/
Abbey: And to participate/
Clinician 1: Participating and learning/

December 14

Clinician 1: Abbey, why did you get a frog award?/ (Abbey had just named the award, the "frog award" and was acknowledged for her creativity; she is the first to receive the award)
Abbey: That says "Charles"/ (pointing to the award the clinician is holding)
Clinician 1: Sorry/ I should have found the one with your name, shouldn't I?/ Why did you get a frog award?/
Abbey: Fur—fur—doin'—fur—fur—working hard/ (repetitions and revision suggest more intentional deliberation on what is to be said)
Clinician 1: And what else?/ You're right/ You worked really hard/ And you ______ (implied fill-in)/
Clinician 2: What did you do?/
(No response)
Clinician 1: Do you think you learned anything?/ (Abbey nods her head in acknowledgment) You did/
Clinician 2: You just showed us/
Abbey: (reading the award) I learned a lot/
Clinician 1: You learned a lot about pond life/

This analysis suggests a gap between the clinicians' definition of learning as a purposeful process and the students' understanding of that process. Several explanations for this apparent discrepancy are offered. First, sociocultural patterns governing child rearing and educational practices are a powerful influence on the ways students learn to understand the world. Heath's (1983) and Westby's (chap. 7) work indicates that certain socialization practices linked to particular cultural orientations influence how students come to interpret the meaning of learning. One orientation is that school learning means being quiet (pay attention to the teacher), work hard to learn lessons (do them right), and be good (stay out of trouble). This orientation may be inadvertently reinforced through traditional classroom and clinical discourse (see discussion in chap. 2). The potential discontinuity between home practices and the practices of a communication process approach may need to be recognized as a factor affecting students' progress.

A second possible source for the discrepancy may lie in those metacognitive and metalinguistic processes by which communicative activities in the physical world (e.g., telling, writing, reading, drawing, acting, singing, counting, etc.) are related to interpreting the mental world of motivations or intentions (Feldman, Bruner, Renderer, & Spitzer, 1990). The interpretations of intent always incorporate the dual perspectives of self ("In what ways do I think [feel, believe] this activity is relevant for me?") and of others ("In what ways might I think [feel, believe] this activity is relevant for you?"). Inferring and integrating how others, much less oneself, are supposed to think, feel, or believe is an aspect of a language learning disability that appears to persist over time. This persistence is often attributed, in part, to difficulty in the flexible use of analytic metastrategies for these purposes and may be a major factor affecting progress, depending on how progress is defined (for a review, see Silliman & Wilkinson, 1991).

For example, the regular and close-up lens revealed progress for Charles and Abbey in their initial use of metastrategies to achieve specific task purposes. The view afforded by the micro-close-up lens suggested that their interpretations of purpose (i.e., participating or working hard) was still focused on the social world of generalized actions, or "What I am doing." This social interpretation composed their meaning of "participating" or "working hard."

A third possibility for discrepancy of purpose with process lies with the specific communications among students and teachers. For example, consider the clinicians' use of language to maintain topical continuity; it was marked linguistically by structural parallelism or topical redundancy (Bennett-Kastor, 1986; Gee, 1986). Similar syntactic structures recur within and across students' speaking turns with the lexical content varied (Lahey, 1988), for example, "Why are you getting this special award?" "Why did you earn this award?" "Why did you get a frog award?" "Do you like *X* or *Y* better?" "And you [fill in]."

The use of structural parallelism as a strategy for topic maintenance produces a predictable pattern within which students can "slot in" their discourse participation. This usage limits the introduction of new information. Alternately, as Gee (1986) suggests, this tactic slows down the pace of topic development, while simultaneously guiding students from a more general topic focus ("Why did you . . . ?") to a progressively more specific one ("And you [fill in]"). Various effects of this pattern on the students can be seen through the micro-close-up lens. Some students "filled in the slot" with words and phrases, such as participating, only on a transient basis. By observing the unfolding of the communicative context of interaction, they may have been able to infer that saying these words were the "right" words to say. Saying and understanding were not connected, because children easily reverted to conduct explanations the next time around.

By December 14, only Charles and Abbey were able to select more preferred responses, such as "I was participating" or "for working hard." They did this with minimal assistance from the clinicians and some conscious effort on Abbey's part in formulating what to mean. But this recasting of learning as "participating" or "working hard" is far from being more stable or flexible. To illustrate, just two minutes and forty-three seconds after Charles spontaneously equated participating with the reason for his award, he was asked by Shanzi why she earned her award. Charles replied without hesitation that Shanzi earned the award "Because she was good."

Several important questions emerge from this analysis. Does the separation between action and intention remain, or is it eventually bridged? If so, at what rate and in what domains does the effect occur? Another issue is the extent to which modeling where recurrence and redundancy predominate helps to move students along in their development. It may be that these types of modeling contribute to reinforcing student's existing preferences for a high degree of predictability.

SUMMARY OF OBSERVATIONAL LENS MODEL AND IMPLICATIONS

Observation applied to the assessment of progress has been described as a series of mental lenses. The lenses are capable of providing increasingly refined pictures of variations in interaction along the continuum of context, from a broad picture to the finer details of discourse. Depending on the reasons for observation, each lens can be used by itself or in combination with the others. Thus, the purposes for observing determine which of the lenses should be selected, when they should be selected, and how they should be focused.

Systematic observation of students' progress is tied to formative assessment. Teaching and learning are seen as opportunities for authentic assessment (Calfee, 1987; Weaver, 1990). The formative assessment approach is similar to the concept of dynamic assessment (Campione, 1990; Olswang, Bain, & Johnson, 1992; Palincsar et al., chap. 5). It is also consistent with performance assessment systems that are being developed in a number of states for evaluating educational achievement (Roeber, 1990). The shift from an almost exclusive emphasis on formal summative approaches to the functional assessment of progress may be a result of changes in responsibility for educational performance. If school-based decision making is the unit for accountability, then the locus of assessment should be the classroom. While all professionals, including speech-language specialists, may be required to demonstrate a command of observational tools for sampling, analyzing, and reporting the results of observation, the communication process approach with language learning disabled students makes such proficiency essential.

SUMMARY

Perhaps no topic is more complicated than that of the efficacy of the communication process model for students with language learning disabilities. However, the complications inherent to the evaluation of efficacy should not obscure the need to design programs in which the dimensions of efficacy are explicitly taken into account. In conclusion, three important aspects need be considered.

First, beliefs about how students learn best need to be carefully considered with discourse practices that reflect those beliefs. Otherwise, a gap between theory and practice will result, and neither will be able to support the other in revising aspects of either the model or its procedures.

Second, the significant effects to be generated as a result of these beliefs, principles, and practices must be agreed on and refined periodically through the use of observational tools. The systematic observation of the multiple levels of the classroom as a communicative context is essential if clinicians and other educators are to develop and maintain shared understanding of why, how, when, and what is observed in their students. Through the mental lenses of observation, from the wide-angled to the micro-close-up, relationships between variations in practices and their differential effects are seen. Understanding what is meant by progress in individual students and determining overall programmatic integrity also depend on the reliable and valid determination of the relationship between practices and outcomes.

Finally, observational systems for the assessment of effectiveness need to be sufficiently robust, if they are to serve as functional and flexible tools for dynamic evaluation. For us, *dynamic evaluation* means that the sampling procedures and observational tools selected for assessing progress must have the capacity to allow clinicians to discern, for example, how a discourse scaffold works. In the end, the primary goal of intervention remains one of assisting students to assume increasingly greater responsibility for maximizing themselves as competent communicators.

REFERENCES

Archbald, D. A., & Newmann, F. M. (1988). *Beyond standardized testing.* Reston, VA: National Association of Secondary School Principals.

Bain, B. A., & Dollaghan, C. A. (1991). The notion of clinically significant change. *Language, Speech, and Hearing Services in Schools, 22,* 264–270.

Bain, B. A., Olswang, L. B., & Johnson, G. A. (1992). Language sampling for repeated measures with language-impaired preschoolers: Comparison of two procedures. *Topics in Language Disorders, 12*(2), 13–27.

Bennett-Kastor, T. (1986). Cohesion and predication in child narrative. *Journal of Child Language, 13,* 353–370.

Biber, D. (1988). *Variation across speech and writing.* New York: Cambridge University Press.

Bigge, J. (1988). *Curriculum based instruction for special education students.* Mountain View: Mayfield Publishing.

Brown, A. L., & Ferrara, R. A. (1985). Diagnosing zones of proximal development. In J. V. Wertsch (Ed.), *Culture, communication, and cognition* (pp. 275–305). New York: Cambridge University Press.

Brunson, K. W., & Haynes, W. O. (1991). Profiling teacher/child classroom communication: Reliability of an alternating time sampling procedure. *Child Language Teaching and Therapy, 7,* 192–211.

Calfee, R. C. (1987). The school as a context for assessment of literacy. *The Reading Teacher, 40,* 738–743.

Calfee, R., & Hiebert, E. (1988). The teacher's role in using assessments to improve learning. In E. E. Freeman (Ed.), *Assessment in the service of learning: Proceedings of the 1987 ETS Invitational Conference* (pp. 45–61). Princeton, NJ: Educational Testing Service.

Campbell, T. F., & Dollaghan, C. A. (1992). A method for obtaining listener judgments of spontaneously produced language: Social validation through direct magnitude estimation. *Topics in Language Disorders, 12*(2), 42–55.

Campione, J. C. (1990). Assisted assessment: A taxonomy of approaches and an outline of strengths and weaknesses. In J. K. Torgesen (Ed.), *Cognitive and behavioral characteristics of children with learning disabilities* (pp. 179–212). Austin, TX: Pro-Ed.

Campione, J. C., & Brown, A. L. (1987). Linking dynamic assessment with school achievement. In C. S. Lidz (Ed.), *Dynamic assessment: An interactional approach to evaluating learning potential* (pp. 82–115). New York: Guilford Press.

Cazden, C. B. (1988). *Classroom discourse: The language of teaching and learning.* Portsmouth, NH: Heinemann.

Clay, M. M. (1985). *The early detection of reading difficulties* (3rd ed.). Portsmouth, NH: Heinemann.

Dollaghan, C., & Miller, J. (1986). Observational methods in the study of communicative competence. In R. Schiefelbush (Ed.), *Language competence: Assessment and intervention* (pp. 101–129). New York: Academic Press.

Englert, C. S. (1990). Unraveling the mysteries of writing through strategy instruction. In T. E. Scruggs & B. Y. L. Wong (Eds.), *Intervention research in learning disabilities* (pp. 186–223). New York: Springer-Verlag.

Evertson, C., & Green, J. (1986). Observation as inquiry and method. In M. Wittrock (Ed.), *Handbook of research on teaching* (pp. 119–161). Washington, DC: American Educational Research Association.

Feldman, C. F., Bruner, J., Renderer, B., & Spitzer, S. (1990). Narrative comprehension. In B. K. Brittion & A. D. Pellegrini (Eds.), *Narrative thought and narrative language* (pp. 1–78). Hillsdale, NJ: Lawrence Erlbaum.

Feuerstein, R. (1990). The theory of structural cognitive modifiability. In B. Z. Presseisen, R. J. Sternberg, K. W. Fischer, C. C. Knight, & R. Feuerstein, *Learning and thinking styles: Classroom interaction* (pp. 68–134). Washington, DC: National Education Association.

Fey, M. E., & Cleave, P. L. (1990). Early language intervention. *Seminars in Speech and Language, 11,* 165–181.

Fujiki, M., & Brinton, B. (1991). The verbal noncommunicator: A case study. *Language, Speech, and Hearing Services in Schools, 22,* 322–333.

Gallagher, T. (1983). Pre-assessment: A procedure for accommodating language use variability. In T. M. Gallagher & C. A. Prutting (Eds.), *Pragmatic assessment and intervention issues in language* (pp. 1–28). San Diego: College-Hill Press.

Gee, J. P. (1986). Units in the production of narrative discourse. *Discourse Processes, 9,* 391–422.

Harste, J. C., & Burke, C. L. (1989). Examining instructional assumptions: The child as informant. In G. Manning & M. Manning (Eds.), *Whole language: Beliefs and practices* (pp. 33–47). Washington, DC: National Education Association.

Heald-Taylor, G. (1987). Predictable literature selections and activities for language arts instructions. *The Reading Teacher, 41*(1), 6–12.

Heath, S. B. (1983). *Ways with words.* New York: Cambridge University Press.

Hegde, M. N. (1987). *Clinical research in communicative disorders.* Boston: Little, Brown.

Hiebert, E. H., & Calfee, R. C. (1989). Advancing academic literacy through teachers' assessments. *Educational Leadership, 46*(7), 50–54.

Hoffman, L. P. (1990). The development of literacy in a school-based program. *Topics in Language Disorders, 10*(2), 81–92.

Howell, K. W., & Morehead, M. K. (1987). *Curriculum-based evaluation for special and remedial education.* New York: Merrill/Macmillan.

Idol, L., Nevin, A., & Paolucci-Whitcomb, P. (1986). *Models of curriculum-based assessment.* Rockville, MD: Aspen Publishers.

Irwin, D., & Bushnell, D. (1980). *Observational strategies for child study.* New York: Holt, Rinehart & Winston.

Kalan, R. (1981). *Jump, Frog, Jump.* New York: Greenwillow Books.

Kavale, K. A. (1990). Variances and verities in learning disability intervention. In T. E. Scruggs & B. Y. L. Wong (Eds.), *Intervention research in learning disabilities* (pp. 3–33). New York: Springer-Verlag.

Kerlinger, F. (1973). *Foundations of behavioral research.* New York: Holt, Rinehart & Winston.

Kuhn, T. S. (1970). *The structure of scientific revolutions.* Chicago: University of Chicago Press.

Lahey, M. (1988). *Language disorders and language development.* New York: Macmillan.

Lahey, M. (1990). Who shall be called language disordered? Some reflections and one perspective. *Journal of Speech and Hearing Disorders, 55,* 612–620.

McCauley, R. J., & Swisher, L. (1984). Use and misuse of norm-referenced tests in clinical assessment: A hypothetical case. *Journal of Speech and Hearing Disorders, 49,* 338–348.

McReynolds, L. V., & Kearns, K. P. (1983). *Single-subject experimental designs in communication disorders.* Baltimore, MD: University Park Press.

McTear, M. F., & Conti-Ramsden, G. (1992). *Pragmatic disability in children.* San Diego, CA: Singular Publishing Group.

Miller, J. F., Freiberg, C., Rolland, M., & Reeves, M. A. (1992). Implementing computerized language sample analysis in the public school. *Topics in Language Disorders, 12*(2), 69–82.

Mishler, E. G. (1991). Representing discourse: The rhetoric of transcription. *Journal of Narrative and Life History, 1,* 255–280.

Nelson, K. (1985). *Making sense: The acquisition of shared meaning.* New York: Academic Press.

Ochs, E. (1979). Transcription as theory. In E. Ochs & B. B. Schiefflin (Eds.), *Developmental pragmatics* (pp. 43–72). New York: Academic Press.

Olswang, L. B. (1990). Treatment efficacy research: A path to quality assurance. *ASHA, 32,* 45–47.

Olswang, L. B., & Bain, B. A. (1991). Treatment efficacy: When to recommend intervention. *Language, Speech, and Hearing Services in Schools, 22,* 255–263.

Olswang, L. B., Bain, B. A., & Johnson, G. A. (1992). Using dynamic assessment with children with language disorders. In S. F. Warren & J. Reichle (Eds.), *Causes and effects in communication and language intervention* (pp. 187–215). Baltimore, MD: Paul H. Brookes.

Paulson, F. L., Paulson, P. R., & Meyer, C. A. (1991). What makes a portfolio a portfolio? *Educational Leadership, 48,* 60–63.

Piaget, J. (1965). *The child's conception of number.* New York: W. W. Norton.

Repp, A. C., Karsh, K. G., Van Acker, R., Felce, D., & Harman, M. (1989). A computer-based system for collecting and analyzing observational data. *Journal of Special Education Technology, 9*(4), 207–217.

Rhodes, L. K., & Dudley-Marling, C. (1988). *Readers and writers with a difference: A holistic approach to teaching learning disabled and remedial students.* Portsmouth, NH: Heinemann.

Roeber, E. D. (1990). Performance assessment: A national perspective. *Policy Briefs of the North Central Regional Educational Laboratory, 10, 11,* 1–2.

Rowe, D. W., Harste, J. C., & Short, K. G. (1988). The authoring cycle: A theoretical and practical overview. In J. C. Harste, K. G. Short, & C. Burke, *Creating classrooms for authors* (pp. 3–37). Portsmouth, NH: Heinemann.

Shuell, T. J. (1988). The role of the student in learning from instruction. *Contemporary Educational Psychology, 13,* 276–295.

Shuy, R. W. (1988). Discourse level language functions: Complaining. In J. Staton, R. W. Shuy, J. K. Peyton, & L. Reed, *Dialogue journal communication: Classroom, linguistic, social, and cognitive views* (pp. 143–161). Norwood, NJ: Ablex.

Silliman, E. R., & Wilkinson, L. C. (1991). *Communicating for learning: Classroom observation and collaboration.* Gaithersburg, MD: Aspen.

Smith, F. (1990). *To think.* New York: Teachers College Press.

Staton, J. (1988a). Contributions of dialogue journal research to communicating, thinking, and learning. In J.

Staton, R. W. Shuy, J. K. Peyton, & L. Reed, *Dialogue journal communication: Classroom, linguistic, social, and cognitive views* (pp. 312–321). Norwood, NJ: Ablex.

Staton, J. (1988b). An introduction to dialogue journal communication. In J. Staton, R. W. Shuy, J. K. Peyton, & L. Reed, *Dialogue journal communication: Classroom, linguistic, social, and cognitive views* (pp. 1–32). Norwood, NJ: Ablex.

Sternberg, R. F. (1990). Intellectual styles: Theory and classroom implications. In B. Z. Presseisen, R. J. Sternberg, K. W. Fischer, C. C. Knight, & R. Feuerstein (Eds.), *Learning and thinking styles: Classroom interaction* (pp. 18–42). Washington, DC: National Education Association.

Stiggins, R. J. (1990). Relevant assessment training for educators. *Newsletter for Educational Psychologists of the American Psychological Association, 13*(1), 3–4.

Strong, C. J., & Shaver, J. P. (1991). Stability in cohesion in the spoken narratives of language-impaired and normally developing school-aged children. *Journal of Speech and Hearing Research, 34,* 95–111.

Sutton-Smith, B. (1986). The development of fictional narrative performances. *Topics in Language Disorders, 7*(1), 1–10.

Tannen, D. (1989). *Talking voices: Repetition, dialogue, and imagery in conversational discourse.* New York: Cambridge University Press.

Warren, S. F., & Reichle, J. (1992). The emerging field of communication and language intervention. In S. F. Warren & J. Reichle (Eds.), *Causes and effects in communication and language intervention* (pp. 1–8). Baltimore, MD: Paul H. Brookes.

Weaver, C. (1990). *Understanding whole language: From principles to practice.* Portsmouth, NH: Heinemann.

Westby, C. E. (1990). The role of the speech-language pathologist in whole language. *Language, Speech, and Hearing Services in Schools, 21,* 228–237.

Wilkinson, L. C. (1982). Introduction: A sociolinguistic approach to communicating in the classroom. In L. C. Wilkinson (Ed.), *Communicating in the classroom* (pp. 3–11). New York: Academic Press.

Wilkinson, L. C., & Silliman, E. R. (1990). Sociolinguistic analysis: Nonformal assessment of children's language and literacy skills. *Linguistics and Education, 2,* 109–125.

Zukow, P. (1982). Transcription systems for videotaped interactions: Some advantages and limitations of manual and computer rendering techniques. *Applied Psycholinguistics, 3,* 61–79.

REFLECTIONS FOR PART TWO: CHAPTERS 4–6

ON BEING OBSERVANT AND DYNAMIC IN SCHOOL-BASED CONTEXTS AND ELSEWHERE

As language specialists in the schools are caught up in a tidal wave of changes in the educational milieu, the importance of finding more appropriate assessment procedures that are relevant to children's lives in and out of school contexts arises. Clinicians and teachers alike, whether they practice their profession in or outside of the school doors, are beginning to recognize that in a postindustrial society where high technology will reign supreme, today's children, and especially those with language learning disabilities, must be prepared to attain a level of literacy unequaled in our country's past. Thus, even if language specialists work with children in noneducational contexts such as hospitals or rehabilitation settings, there remains a need to understand many aspects of school and to collaborate with its key participants (teachers, resource room specialists, etc.). Indeed, school remains the primary source of instruction in language, learning, and literacy. Professionals who work with school-age children must continually ask themselves: How does this test, assessment tool, and/or observational strategy connect with "Monday morning in the classroom"?

Nelson (chap. 4) makes the Monday-morning classroom connections explicit. She speaks eloquently to the problems and profit that may be gained from curriculum-based language assessment and intervention. As she points out, examiners and interventionists should be able to identify the curricular contexts where language-related problems are evident. Readers whose professional lives are outside the educational system or its classrooms may wonder how it is possible to practice what Nelson preaches. Fortunately, some solutions become apparent as readers move through the chapters in this section (i.e., Nelson, chap. 4; Palincsar, Brown, & Campione, chap. 5; Silliman & Wilkinson, chap. 6). These authors provide a perspective on observation and assessment that can be adapted to both educational and rehabilitation contexts. However, application of the Palincsar et al. and Silliman and Wilkinson concepts does require that school-based and clinic-based professionals understand how schools work in general and how an individual child's school works in particular (as expressed in Nelson's multitiered curriculum described in chap. 4). (Ehren asks a similar question in Chapter 15.)

Readers who have progressed through Parts 1 and 2 now have a perspective on how oral language connects with academic learning to and through discourse scaffolds. They also know how metalinguistic development occurs throughout the preschool and school years. Building on that base, Nelson reminds speech-language pathologists and other language specialists that they are *not* to play the role of teachers or tutors. Similarly, language specialists cannot assume responsibility for teaching the curriculum or testing for its acquisition. However, language specialists should be asking another critical question that echos the Monday-morning classroom question: "Does this [child] have the language skills and strategies for processing the language of the regular curriculum?" (Nelson, chap. 4).

Among other techniques, Nelson recommends artifact analysis, onlooker observation, and ethnographic techniques to help practitioners find answers to the question she poses. In daily assessment practices, Nelson's suggestions translate in any number of ways. For example, one might ask the mother, teacher, or child to provide the examiner with the appropriate "artifacts": bringing textbooks and dialogue journals to the assessment session(s), asking the school to forward the results of standardized and nonstandardized testing, communicating with the teacher regarding observed classroom behaviors, and so forth. Nelson also shows how direct observation both in and out of the classroom can provide information about a student's various information processing strategies across curricular areas. While language specialists might agree that actual observation in the classroom is the preferred strategy, they also know that reality does not always permit in-class observation to occur. As one of many alternatives, Nelson reminds practitioners that student interviews can give them much to observe and interpret. She notes that each interview is a unique and living entity that can provide language specialists with uniquely individualized information. Seeing the school or classroom through the child's eyes provides a special "lens" for the examiner—a lens, albeit, which is shaded by the child's self-concept, the perceived nature and requirements of the school, and the ability to describe the multiple interactions that occur in school settings.

Readers may be reminded of some of the earlier work of Creaghead and Tattershall (1985). They provide an excellent sequence of diagnostic questions along these lines. For example, they suggest interviewing students to obtain information about their knowledge of the routines and rules of their classrooms. Their questionnaire includes the following self-assessment targets: (1) What does your teacher do or say when he or she is angry with the class? (2) What really makes your teacher mad or angry? (3) What is the most important thing that you should always do in class? (4) What is the most important thing that you should never do in class? (5) How do you know when it is time to go inside after recess? (6) What is the first thing you should do when class begins? (7) What does your teacher do or say when she is going to say something really important? (8) What is the last thing that you should do before you go home at the end of the day? (9) When is it OK to talk out without raising your hand at school? (10) How do you know when your teacher is joking or teasing? (11) What does your teacher do when it is time for a lesson to begin? (12) When is it right to ask a question in class? Indeed, as seen in these examples and as discussed in the next paragraph, one's self-awareness is measured, yet again, by one's ability to express that awareness through language.

Nelson also introduces in some detail the concept of dynamic assessment, mediation, and indirect assessment of internalized processes, including miscue analysis, both as produced in the classroom or obtained in simulated form as part of a specialized assessment. Palincsar et al. (chap. 5) bring to their discussion of the models and practices of dynamic assessment a wealth of experience in application of such models in the areas of reading, writing and mathematics. As readers will readily note, most of the techniques suggested or reported by van Kleeck in Chapter 3 require the child to use language to talk about language in a problem-solving manner. *Thus, spoken language is the hallmark of dynamic assessment.* It rests on the examiner's ability to estimate not only the upper limits of competence but also to explore the linguistic and cognitive components of the zone of proximal development, that is, the glimpse of the child's potential uncovered as the child works through problems in collaboration with an adult (or, at times, more capable peers). For readers who are now or who will be involved in the assessment of children with language, learning, and literacy difficulties, dynamic assessment holds special meaning and requires special cautions. Two important points spring to mind. First, the use of language to discern potential language achievements within the supportive context of dynamic assessment may hold great promise on the one hand; on the other hand, it is typically the disordered language itself that has brought the child to the assessment process. Nevertheless, it is a strength of dynamic assessment that it leads to outcomes beyond those anticipated when static instruments are used. Using norm-based tests leads the examiner to discontinue evaluation when a specified number of full or partial "failures" occur. Children are led to believe that only "the answer, the whole answer, and nothing but the [teacher's] answer is correct." Yet, as readers of this text well know, learning does not occur in this fashion, nor does language. No one expects a two-year-old to have a fully developed semantic map for "dog," when the toddler points to a St. Bernard and says "doggie, doggie." Nor do examiners expect adults who have not traveled in Mexico to be able to define "Potocatapetal" or any individual who is not familiar with Mary Poppins to explain "supercalafrajalisticexpialidocious." It is in the zone of proximal development (ZPD) that the emerging landscape of language first appears.

As seen in Part 1, language, learning, and literacy become intertwined as children move into and through the school years. When moving from *learning language* to *using language to learn* in the academic context, children's efforts to comprehend and produce written text are critical to their school success. As stressed throughout this text and in line with many of Nelson's suggestions, written language assessment is as important as spoken language assessment. Comparing a student's performance in reading from well-known texts from school or home and providing new, unknown texts (books, newspapers, and magazines at the appropriate age-grade level) to be read during the assessment may provide comparative data about access to and recall from written text. Reviewing the dialogue journals or other samples of handwritten school assignments (not computer-generated stories or artifacts) with written samples completed by the child with the examiner observing may offer additional insight into the child's linguistic and academic skills. In particular, language specialists will also find it useful to attend to Palincsar and her colleagues comments on the work of Paratore and Indrisano. Several points are made about the importance of story reading and verbal retelling, the use of anecdotal records as a tool for examiner inferencing, and the Vygotskian notion of social dialogue, as seen through the authors' work in reciprocal teaching. These activities, among others, as suggested by authors in the remainder of this volume, provide a framework for viewing a language learning disabled child's ability to respond to the demands of the academic context.

A decade of research precedes the discussion that Palincsar et al. provide about how reciprocal teaching can also be used as an assessment procedure. Children's ability to self-monitor during reciprocal teaching matches closely with how language specialists view metacomprehension and metacognitive strategy use in spoken language. Indeed, readers are referred to van Kleeck's Figure 3–4 for a review of adults' responsibilities in social dialogue. Reciprocal teaching also permits teacher/clinician modeling, prompting, requesting, scaffolding, and dialoging. Palincsar and her colleagues conclude by bringing readers back to the written word and providing insight into how dynamic writing and assessment and instruction may take place. This discussion sets the stage for much that readers will encounter in the following chapters that deal with phonological awareness (Blachman, chap. 9) and the continuum of discourse (Scott, chap. 8), as children move further along the language continuum (or fail to do so).

Silliman and Wilkinson are even better the second time around. In Chapter 6, they tackle the tough topic of establishing the efficacy of their model of language, hoping, as it were, that readers would feel called on to do likewise. The call for efficacy and for efficiency is not new but has become even more essential. More than hope and a hospitable environment are required, as Wallach and Butler imply very early in Chapter 1. Language specialists know, as they have always known, that they must require much of themselves. Indeed, what they do with individuals with language learning disabilities must make a difference—a difference to the child, adolescent, or adult who is the subject of assessment or intervention. The pervasive and continuing nature of language disorders across time, as reflected in Chapter 1, coupled with pressures to make progress happen efficiently, make for a formidable challenge.

Indeed, assessing progress, presuming that viable instruction/intervention has been undertaken, means that the clinician must incorporate a procedure that measures transfer—transfer of the learned material to similar *and* new settings. In an interesting discussion of transfer, Salomon and Perkins (1989) present their notion that there is both a "low road" and a "high road" of transfer. Low-road transfer depends on practice and occurs when automatic triggering of well-learned behavior occurs in a new context. High-road transfer may happen when an individual intentionally is mindful of what has been learned and is able to abstract from an old context to a new context. The authors maintain that certain conditions are required for either low- or high-road transfer and note their applicability to what occurs when experience, therapy, or tutoring assist in transferring old information to new contexts and situations. Low-road transfer requires only automaticity of an "old" response, for example, moving from driving a car for a long time to driving a truck for the first time. The transition, they say, is relatively painless, with old skills requiring only fine tuning (Salomon & Perkins, 1989, p. 117). Conversely, high transfer requires that one explicitly know and apply prior experience in an explicit way to a new situation. An example of high transfer is recalling counting to ten as a young child after having been told to "hold your temper," and applying that recollection to an adult situation that involves volitional control of behavior, which does not relate to highly volatile emotional reactions. Readers are referred to Salomon and Perkins (1989) for an illuminating discussion of how, why, and what transfers one may anticipate can and will occur. Lahey and Bloom pick up the discussion of automaticity and transfer in Chapter 13 in Part 4. This theoretical formulation deals directly with both Chapters 2 and 6, by Silliman and Wilkinson, which cover the effectiveness of how the "communication process works" and "how and why it works." The occurrence of functional changes (or transfer) is central to their discussion and to their claim that assessment is a way of collecting information about the actual instructional practices used, the teaching and learning contexts that constitute the child's experiences, and the individual experiences among students. Silliman and Wilkinson reference the work of Palincsar, Brown, and Campione and bring to bear a sociocultural perspective, which is an underlying girder of Silliman and Wilkinson's work and of Westby's work (chap. 7) with children from many cultural and socioeconomic strata. Silliman and Wilkinson's perspective in Chapter 6 draws readers further into the possibilities inherent in determining what is a "representative sample of progress." Calling into play the "novice-to-expert" paradigm, Silliman and Wilkinson point out the need to provide multiple instances of a student's most effective demonstration of understanding and comprehension, to which many an experienced clinician would provide a hearty "amen." One is reminded of Milosky (chap. 10), by this metaphor for testing and assessment, "One swallow does not a summer make."

One of Silliman and Wilkinson's major contributions to the field of language intervention is their conceptualization of the observational lens model (chap. 6). They reinforce an important notion: *observation is not haphazard; rather, it is a systematic approach.* A careful perusal of their concept of how "lenses" may be best placed by the beholder of the classroom context yields demonstrably more significant evaluations of the classroom and the students' activities within that setting. They provide a commendable service to the field by analyzing the relative importance of the observational and categorical tools and systems, that is, the "tools of the trade" professionals must use. Their discussion of categorical tools versus narrative tools is worthy of inspection, as is the comparison between open and closed systems. Also informative is their contrasting of running records, critical incidents, portfolios, journal writing, dialogue journals, and video portfolios. (Should one ever doubt that high technology has come to, or will come to the schools, let the reader beware. It is here, it is now, but it is not yet everywhere.)

Functional (formative) assessment is seen, as is dynamic assessment, as a procedure available today, and although it might be enhanced by technological advancement, it essentially relies on the skills and abilities of the language specialist willing to undertake it. As Silliman and Wilkinson conclude, although the topic is complicated, its demands can be met through measuring how students learn best, how observational tools can assist in that measurement, and how such tools can help clinicians discern how it is that students with language learning disabilities can be assisted in taking on responsibility for becoming competent communicators.

To summarize, education in the United States today is in a state of flux. With this fluctuating environment, it is requisite that decisions regarding children, particularly language learning disabled children, be made on scientific and ethical grounds. That statement not only implies, but demands, that language specialists use their background and training to offer the most efficacious assessment and intervention possible. The preceding chapters have brought to the fore some of the most recent and scientifically substantiated suggestions for intervention and assessment. The chapters to come do the same. Armored with today's knowledge, the language specialist sets off into the future. May the armor be a bulwark against failure and a sign of success on the battlefield against multiple disabilities that can, and do, affect children with language, learning, and literacy difficulties.

REFERENCES

Creaghead, N., & Tattershall, S. (1985). Observation and assessment of classroom pragmatic skills. In C. S. Simon (Ed.), *Communication skills and classroom success: assessing language-learning disabled students* (pp. 105–134). Austin, TX: Pro-Ed.

Salomon, G., & Perkins, D. N. (1989). Rocky roads to transfer: Rethinking mechanisms of a neglected phenomenon, *Educational Psychologist, 24*(2), 113–142.

PART THREE

A CLOSER LOOK

Discourse Across Ages, Stages, and Language Styles and Abilities

7

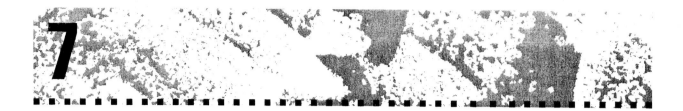

THE EFFECTS OF CULTURE ON GENRE, STRUCTURE, AND STYLE OF ORAL AND WRITTEN TEXTS

■ Carol E. Westby
University of New Mexico

CHANGING TIMES

Changing Approaches to Language Assessment

Since the middle of this century, each decade has witnessed significant changes in our understanding of language development—both *what* develops and *how* it develops. As language acquisition data accumulated, professionals became increasingly aware of the variations in what children acquired and how they acquired it (Bates, 1988; Nelson, 1981; Peters, 1983; Schieffelin & Ochs, 1986). Although a number of theories have been proposed to explain language acquisition, no single theory explains all the elements of language acquisition—phonology, syntax, semantics, and pragmatics (Bohannon & Warren-Leubecker, 1993; Friel-Patti, chap. 14).

The *What* of Language Development. The first half of the century saw the documentation of children's age-related changes in vocabulary size and sentence length (Davis, 1937; McCarthy, 1954; Templin, 1957). The 1960s witnessed an expanding understanding that sentence length evolved through children's acquisition of syntactic rule systems (Bellugi & Klima, 1966; R. Brown & Fraser, 1963; McNeill, 1970). In the 1970s semantics and the emergence of pragmatics provided an understanding that syntax was used to convey semantic meaning for a variety of pragmatic functions (Bates, 1976; Bloom, 1970). The 1980s witnessed the development of text and discourse length analysis and an increasing focus on the ways language varied in different contexts (G. Brown & Yule, 1983; Stubbs, 1983; Tannen, 1982b, 1984a; Westby, 1986).

Integration of syntax, semantics, and pragmatics in the 1980s resulted in a move away from discrete point approaches of language evaluation, that is, away from viewing each aspect of language as a separate entity and assuming that if the parts of students' language were adequate their discourse would be adequate (Oller, 1979). Discourse analysis provided a broader view of communicative competence. Language evaluation now considered children's ability to use phonological, syntactic, and semantic knowledge to formulate discourse length material that was appropriate to the context, that is, appropriate to the person being communicated with and to the setting in which the communication occurred (Nelson, chap. 4; Ripich & Spinelli, 1985; Silliman & Wilkinson, 1991; chap. 2; Westby, 1984).

The *How* of Language Development. As researchers realized the increasing complexity of what children had to learn about language, they began to realize that the paradigms they used to explain the *how* of acquisition were inadequate. Through the 1950s and early 1960s, the behaviorist philosophy was used to explain language development (Skinner, 1957; Staats & Staats, 1957). Children learned to speak by hearing words and sentences and being reinforced for appropriately repeating what they heard. Clearly, however, children said things they had never heard. Chomsky (1965) explained this production of novel utterances by postulating an innate language acquisition device (LAD) that sensitized children to underlying transformational grammar rules. Chomsky claimed that language acquisition was relatively independent of a child's intelligence or experience. Others, as van Kleeck discusses in Chapter 3, suggested a cognitive–interactionist view of language acquisition (Bruner, 1974; Vygotsky, 1962; 1978), asserting that a child had an active role in language learning. Children began to be seen as active participants with others around them; both social and maturational factors were seen as influencing development. The fields of anthropology, social psychology, and sociology have contributed significantly to our understanding of how the nature of interactions of children with significant others in their environment results in children's communicative competence (Heath, 1983; Schieffelin & Ochs, 1986). Through this work professionals have gained an understanding of how the context in which language is spoken and the sociocultural identities of the persons speaking influences what is said and how it is said (Gee & Michaels, 1989; see also Friel-Patti, chap. 14).

Integrating the *What* and *How*. As researchers and practitioners have gained awareness of the *how* of language acquisition, they are becoming increasingly aware of the variations in the *what* of language acquisition. Although nearly all children do learn language, they do not all acquire the same language in the same ways. These changes in the understanding of the *what* and *how* of language development have resulted in changes in the ways professionals assess language skills. Language evaluation requires understanding of the experiences children have had in language learning. Isolated measures of a child's phonology, syntax, and semantic abilities are less often made under the artificial conditions of an isolated therapy room, as pointed out in the previous section of this text. Instead, children's discourse is evaluated in seminaturalistic and naturalistic situations. For preschool children, this involves evaluation of children during care-giving activities and play with siblings and peers. For school-age children, this involves evaluation of language use in the home and classroom (as Nelson, chap. 4, and other authors of this text have discussed). Classroom language involves both a *social text,* which refers to information about expectations for participation (who can talk, when, where, in what ways, with whom, for what purposes), and *academic text,* which refers to the content of the lesson and the structure of that content (Green, Weade, & Graham, 1988; Nelson, chap. 4; Scott, chap. 8). Investigation of social text and academic text has resulted in study of the interactive discourse styles of teachers and students and the nature of both oral and written text-length discourse (Scott, chap. 8; Silliman & Wilkinson, chap. 2). Research is documenting the contributions of differences in care-giver–child, peer–peer, and student–teacher interaction patterns; the types and varieties of language genres used; and the structure, content, and style of these genres to students' success or lack of success in the academic school environment (Scott, chap. 8).

The variations in the *what* and *how* of language acquisition are highlighted in the distinction between oral and written language and in the acquisition of language in primarily oral cultures and primarily literate cultures. Oral and written narratives have been the focus of much discourse and text analyses. Gradually, the analyses are extending to a variety of expository text genres (Britton & Black, 1985; Connor & Kaplan, 1987). Narratives are a major genre for primary oral cultures to high literary and electronic information processing cultures (Ong, 1982). Many other genres are culture specific and require varying degrees of literacy, as Scott discusses in Chapter 8. Narratives have been of particular interest because they are a universal genre, a primary mode of thought (Bruner, 1985); because they are the earliest extended monologue texts produced by children (Nelson, 1989); and because their comprehension and production is essential for academic success (Feagans & Short, 1984; Merritt & Liles, 1987; Roth & Spekman, 1986; Westby, 1985; Westby, Maggart, & Van Dongen, 1984). Narratives have a central place in the lives of humans.

Story telling is a panhuman ability; it is "a primary act of mind" (Hardy, 1977). Story telling serves a variety of functions—to entertain, to teach, to explain where people have come from and where they are going, and to reflect on our own experiences and the experiences of others. Although cultures share some common functions of narration, major differences or contrasts exist between narratives arising from oral traditions (e.g., the Homeric epics, the stories of Native American storytellers, or the "rappin' and stylin' out" of African American teenagers) and narratives from literate traditions that were generated in written form (e.g., *Winnie-the-Pooh,* the mysteries of Poe, or the novels of Dickens or Michener). Oral and literate narrative traditions differ in why and how narratives are used, how they are remembered, how they are organized, and the focus of their content.

Although differences exist in oral and literate story telling, narratives can function as a transition between oral and literate language styles. Story-telling activities in school can be varied along several dimensions: (1) degree of contextualization or decontextualization, that is, how much contextual support is available to interpret the story; (2) syntactic/semantic redundancy and complexity, that is, how familiar is the content and structure and how frequently is information repeated; (3) the degree of audience support in the narration; that is, whether the audience assists the narrator in telling the story; and (4) the action or psychological focus, that is, is attention given to physical or psychological events? Narratives can be told about immediate, familiar events (as in oral language) or unfamiliar, decontextualized events (as in literate language). They may use the simple, repetitive syntax and style of oral language or the complex, concise syntax and style of literate text. Narratives may be produced using the support of listeners (as in oral conversation) or as an individual monologue (as in literate or written language). Interpretation may be readily determined from explicit textual explanations of character actions (as in oral folktales) or may only be inferred from implicit hints at characters' values, beliefs, and emotional and psychological characteristics (as in modern novels).

Narrative understanding and production in schools require children to integrate their language skills into a coherent, independent, literate language production—a monologue produced without the assistance or support of others. Such monologue language is essential for reading and writing text-length materials. The content and structural development of narrative abilities in mainstream, middle-class, primarily white students has been documented (Ames, 1966; Applebee, 1978; Botvin & Sutton-Smith, 1977; Lystad, 1974; C. Peterson & McCabe, 1983; Pitcher & Prelinger, 1963; Stein & Glenn, 1979). Failure to comprehend or produce narratives significantly limits individuals' participation in their culture. Language learning disabled students produce narratives that are shorter, less complex, less coherent, and more disorganized than the narratives produced by their normal age-matched controls. Students who may pass traditional intellectual and language tests but who experience academic difficulties in school may produce significantly less complex narratives than students not experiencing academic difficulties (Westby et al., 1984). Narrative assessment appears to be more sensitive to the language requirements of school than more traditional, standardized discrete-point tests. In educational systems, expository texts become important at advancing levels (Black, 1985; Heath, 1987). Educational programs must assess and facilitate students' textual language abilities, not simply their knowledge of discrete aspects of syntax, semantics, and pragmatics, as Scott also discusses in Chapter 8.

Changing Demographics

Because data on the development of narrative texts in normal mainstream students are available, because narrative development has been related to school success, and because language learning disabled students have been shown to have deficits in narrative skills, it is tempting to use narrative assessment to identify learning disabilities in students. This may be appropriate for mainstream children from highly literate environments, but at this time, it is not appropriate for students from nonmainstream and nonliterate backgrounds. Discourse level skills are more susceptible to the influence of culture than are sentence level phonological, semantic, and syntactic skills. Children from different sociocultural groups develop different discourse genres and different communicative strategies for text production. Not all discourse genres are present in all cultures. Although all cultures have narrative genres, narration varies across cultures in terms of the functions and genres of narratives that are used, the content and thematic emphasis of narratives, the structural organization and style of narratives, who has the privilege to tell narratives, and how children are socialized into the understanding and production of narratives. As mentioned earlier, the ability to produce narratives is a panhuman capability; however, the specific nature of narrative production depends on cultural practices. Types, uses, and organization of expository texts is even more variable than narrative texts.

Most of the data on the narrative development are based on white, middle-class children from two-parent homes; yet an increasing percentage of students are not from this background. By the year 2000, one third of the population will be from nondominant cultural groups (American Council on Education, 1988). In 1986, 17% of whites, 27.3% of Hispanics, and 31.1% of African Americans had incomes below the poverty level. Rates are higher for preschool children: 18% for whites, 41% for Hispanics, and 47% for African Americans. Fifty-nine percent of children born in 1983 will live with only one parent before reaching the age of 18.

Language evaluation of students from these culturally diverse backgrounds is difficult, because little data are available on normal language development of these children. Without such data, how can schools determine if a student exhibits a language difference or a language deficit? Schools walk a tightrope in evaluating and placing students from nondominant cultural groups in programs for the learning disabled. Many states continue to have overrepresentation of culturally different students in classes for the learning disabled. Other states have responded to this overrepresentation by refusing to place any culturally different students in classes for the learning disabled. What is the right solution? How can diagnosticians make a determination of language learning disability in students from nondominant cultural groups? Perhaps they cannot. A primary language activity in one culture may be nonexistent in another culture. Language use that may represent a language disorder in one culture may be a common language pattern in another culture.

Of what use, then, are the data that are available, and how can these data be used to understand the discourse of the schools and the discourse of students from nondominant cultural groups? One would not want to inappropriately label culturally different students as language learning disabled, but at the same time, a teacher or clinician would not want to withhold information that would help these children integrate into the mainstream. Success in mainstream schools depends on learning the social and academic texts of the schools. Students must learn the appropriate ways to interact with peers and teachers in the school setting (Silliman & Wilkinson, 1991; chap. 2). They must learn when to talk and when not to talk—how they are to initiate, maintain, and terminate a conversation (Brinton & Fujiki, 1989). They must learn to comprehend and produce texts that vary in structure and content; they must learn to think in different ways for different academic disciplines (Clarke, 1990; Scott, chap. 8). Both students who have true language learning disabilities and students who have language learning differences must acquire the social and academic texts of school.

VARIATIONS IN TEXT GENRES AND SOCIALIZATION

Types of Text Genres

Discourse has a wide variety of genres and functions. A *genre* is a map or plan for a discourse or text. Specific genres may have a variety of functions. For example, narratives are used to entertain, to display knowledge or skill, to teach, or to organize and plan (regulate) behavior. Consider the following examples of narrative genres:

- Did you hear what happened to George last night?
- Tell Daddy about our trip to the zoo.
- I'm loading the van, and then I'll put the soda in the ice chest so we'll have plenty to drink on the trip.
- Once upon a time there were three billy goats, and their name was Gruff.

Each of these sentences represents a different narrative genre and consequently has a different function and organization. The first example, "Did you hear what happened to George last night?" serves to capture the floor so the speaker can give an account of something that happened and that the listener did not experience with the speaker. The second statement, "Tell Daddy about our trip to the zoo," is a request for a *recount,* a retelling of an event that had been shared with the person asking for the recount. In this case, the storyteller does not have to gain the floor himself and, in fact, the storyteller is assisted in telling the story. The person who has requested the recount often provides scaffolding assistance for the teller by asking questions about specific aspects of the story. The third statement, "I'm loading the van, and then I'll put the soda in the ice chest so we'll have plenty to drink on the trip," is an *eventcast,* a description of ongoing activity and planning for the future. The fourth statement, "Once upon a time there were three billy goats, and their name was Gruff," is the introduction to an *imaginative story.*

All of these types of narratives are highly familiar to children and adults from mainstream, middle-class families. Other sociocultural groups vary in the frequency of use of each of these narrative types, in who has the privilege of producing these narratives, and in how children are socialized for each type of narrative production. In addition, cultures vary in the general reason or purpose for narrating. For many mainstream Americans, the major purpose of story telling is to entertain, whereas for some cultures the general purpose is to teach (Heath, 1982b, 1983; Indrasuta, 1988; Tseng & Hsu, 1972). For example, Basso (1987) described three general functions for speech in the Apache culture: ordinary talk, prayer, and narrative or story. Narratives have major functions in preserving Apache culture. They can be categorized into four major genres that differ in the time of the events they report and the purposes for telling the narrative. *Myths* talk about "in the beginning" and are used to enlighten or instruct. They are performed only by medicine men and medicine women. *Historical tales* talk about "long ago" and are told to criticize or warn individuals who are not following social norms. Apaches talk about "shooting" these tales like arrows. The stories are intended to "stalk" individuals by reminding them of the undesirability of their behavior. *Sagas* are told about events in "modern times" and function to entertain or engross. *Gossip* involves stories of "now" and are used to inform, or to malign, or simply to keep people informed of community events. More information is needed regarding the types and uses of narratives in different cultures.

Expository genres are less universal than narrative genres but are of greater importance in technological, informational societies. Expository genres have been categorized according to their topical content (natural science, social science, humanities, journalism) and their structure/function (descriptive/enumerative, persuasive, comparison–contrast, procedural, problem–solution, and cause–effect) (Connor & McCogg, 1987). Acquisition of expository text structures depends primarily on exposure to formal schooling. (See Scott, chap. 8 for a more detailed discussion of school/formal texts.)

Participating in Genres

Children are socialized to comprehend and produce the texts of their cultures. Cultures vary in how they produce narrative and expository texts and how children are socialized to these texts. Particularly important in narrative genres are the variations in the roles the storyteller and audience have in story production. In mainstream American culture, most narrative genres eventually involve a monologue production. Individuals are expected to carry out the narrative without assistance. In other cultural groups, the production of narratives may be a negotiated and cooperative activity with members of the audience, and the contributions of the members may overlap. Although a single individual may begin a story, other speakers and members of the audience contribute to the story development. Cooperative story telling is a major attribute of Hawaiian conversations called talk story (Boggs, 1985). In talk story, the story is co-narrated by more than one person, and the speech of the narrators is also overlapped by audience responses.

Audience participation is also a feature of Athabaskan Indian story telling (Scollon & Scollon, 1981, 1984). Listeners are expected to respond with at least *ehe* (*yes*) at the end of each verse. In many cases, the listeners expand on the verse and even complete the verses and story. Scollon and Scollon (1984) use the term *nonfocused situation* to refer to communication involving active negotiation between participants; they use *focused situation* to refer to communication that limits this negotiation. They reported that because of this audience participation, the storyteller need not be explicit and need not conclude the story. Such stories would appear confusing and unsatisfying to those unfamiliar with this particular narrative style.

Children are socialized early into narrative genres and their roles in narrative activities. School programs particularly value focused communication such as monologue recounting and eventcasting for assessment procedures. Traditionally in schools, cooperative discourse has been viewed, at best, as disruptive, and at worst, as cheating behavior. Children are expected to recount what they have read or done and they are expected to give eventcasts to explain activities they are carrying out. Unsolicited accounts are seldom valued and are usually actively discouraged. Mainstream families begin early to provide opportunities to learn eventcasting and recounting. They model eventcasts (e.g., "Push the car to Mommy. Good boy, you're pushing the car. Here it comes. Oh, you're pushing it sooo fast"), and they scaffold interaction with infants that will facilitate children's abilities to produce extended monologue narratives (Cazden, 1983). They read their children many stories and encourage them to participate in the retelling. Snow and Goldfield (1981) reported the type of conversations that a mainstream mother engaged in around books with her child. The mother first gave information and then asked the child questions about the information. When the child was between two years five months to three years four months old, the mother asked and answered the following types of scaffolding questions:

(labeling)	What is this?
(item elaboration)	What kind of airplane is this? What color is it?
(event description)	What happened?
	What is _____ doing?
(reason/cause)	Why is _____ doing that?
(reaction)	Isn't that silly?
	How does _____ feel?
(real world relevance)	Remember when we went swimming?

Mainstream families engage in similar vertical scaffolding with children daily. A vertical scaffolding generally consists of a minimal spontaneous utterance from the child and a subsequent request by the adult for more information followed by additional information from the child. The following is an example of such vertical scaffolding:

Child: kitty's gone
Adult: Where's the kitty?
Child: in the tree
Adult: The kitty's in the tree? How did it get in the tree?
Child: The dog scared her.
Adult: Who let the dog loose?

By asking questions, the parent has provided the child with the structure to produce a coherent narrative—a narrative that contains the elements associated with story grammars. The scaffolding provides guidance as to what to talk about but not the specifics of what to say and how to say it.

Scollon and Scollon (1981) suggested that the literate language style characteristic of storybook narratives depends on this vertical scaffolding. Not all cultural groups, however, engage in this type of scaffolding conversation. For example, Scollon and Scollon noted that such scaffolding conversations did not occur in Athabaskan Indian interactions. In its place they observed what they called *glossing.* The child speaks, and then the care giver glosses what the child says. The meaning appears to be something like, "What you said can be taken as *X*." Glosses may be paraphrases, translations into English or another language, or a somewhat involved explanation, for example, "He said that because of X, Y, Z." Unlike vertical scaffolding, glosses do not add new information. Instead, they signal understanding or interpretation of the child's utterance. No attempt is made to make the child say anything else or different, only to understand it for what it is. Scollon and Scollon propose that this glossing prepares the child for the negotiated adult interactions. The story-telling patterns of the elders is foreshadowed in adults' responses to children's utterances. The children are being trained to indicate appreciation or understanding of a narrative.

Vertical scaffolding tends to be uncommon in cultures that rely on oral language rather than print for transition of information. Heath (1982a, 1982b) reported that working-class families in the Piedmont Carolinas also did not engage in narrative scaffolding. In addition, a University of New Mexico student from a Pueblo Indian tribe who was analyzing children's stories for a language development course also reported that in her tribe narrative scaffolding did not occur with young children (J. Enote, personal communication, 1987). In her community, children are not assisted in describing the events of their day. In addition, she noted that although story telling has an important place in her tribe, story telling is the prerogative of the older men. Children watch and listen to story telling for many years. As boys grow older, they are given story-telling opportunities that are not given to girls.

Watching and listening appear to be predominant means of language learning in many cultures. The narrative scaffolding of mainstream families in the United States is, in fact, rare in most other cultures (Schieffelin & Ochs, 1986). Many cultures use prompting to socialize children to the language patterns of the cultures. With prompting, children are told exactly what to say in specific contexts.

As part of language socialization, children learn the roles they are to play in discourse with peers and adults; that is, they learn who they are to talk to, about what, how, and when. American schools expect a particular form of adult–child (teacher–child) interaction that is not necessarily the case in other countries (Cazden, 1988; Mehan, 1979). As the preceding examples demonstrate, cultural attitudes toward children participating in discourse with adults and telling stories vary. In some cultures, children are expected to be seen and not heard. They might not be expected to have information (Heath, 1983); they may be viewed as incapable of conversing (Scollon & Scollon, 1984); giving a recount or account might be regarded as inappropriate showing off or attempting to appear better than others (Philips, 1983); or such a story-telling performance might be viewed as dangerous to the child's spiritual, mental, and psychological well-being (Scollon & Scollon, 1981). Children may not be encouraged to attempt to gain the floor to give an account, and in fact, may be actively discouraged from doing so in adult company. In these same cultures, within their peer groups children may learn a variety of appropriate strategies to gain the floor, and giving accounts and producing imaginative stories may be a highly valued activity (Boggs, 1985; Brady, 1984; Heath, 1983; Labov, 1972). Cultural groups differ in the degree to which they demand literal or creative accounts. Some groups view any variation or elaboration on the original experience as a lie, whereas others value such variation as a sign of creativity and verbal skill. In cultures that rely on prompting to teach language, children may not respond to scaffolding questions and may be hesitant to contribute unless given specific models for what to say. These differences across cultures should be kept in mind when incorporating many of the scaffolding suggestions described throughout this text (e.g., Nelson, chap. 4; Palincsar et al., chap. 5; Silliman & Wilkinson, chap. 2).

Socialization to Genre Types

Knowing what genres students have been socialized to and *how* they have been socialized can facilitate our understanding of why students may experience difficulties participating in the social and academic texts of schools (Scott, chap. 8). Heath (1983, 1986a, 1986b) has reported on the use of narrative genres of Chinese Americans and Mexican Americans in the San Francisco area and of African American and white working-class families and African American and white mainstream families in the Carolina Piedmont. See a summary of these data in Table 7–1. Heath was particularly interested in the role of narrative socialization in children's school success. A number of investigators have observed that children who have been socialized into the narrative functions, organization, and style of the school during the preschool years adapt more easily to the academic tasks of school (Heath, 1982b; Michaels & Collins, 1984; Scollon & Scollon, 1984). Chinese American families in the San Francisco area requested few recounts from their children. At home, children were asked to give accounts of their day, but outside the home or when strangers were present, they were expected to listen to adult conversation without interrupting and to be quiet unless addressed by adults. Accounts might also focus on inappropriate behaviors ("Where have you been? You're not supposed to leave the yard"), and follow-up comments might focus on the appropriateness of the behavior for the role ("You're too old for that" or "Girls don't do that"). Eventcasts were also relatively common, with mothers providing eventcasts as they modeled everyday activities for their children. Story telling occurred during book reading and in tales about historical events and people and generally functioned to teach values. Talk around books might include analogous stories in which a character or a set of events was similar to that in the story just read. Adults did not, however, model meaning interpretations based on emotions; for example, parents were not likely to comment that a character was sad or angry because of an event in the story.

In Mexican American families who were recent migrants from Mexico, requests for recounts were extremely rare. Recounts might occur only when children were asked to tell an unknowing third party about an event. For example, a mother might ask her son to tell a visiting aunt about his sister's birthday party. Accounts were requested more often, especially in family gatherings. Eventcasts almost never occurred. Teaching in the home involved modeling and close observation but not verbal descriptions or explanations. Cooperative eventcasts did occur when the family planned future events such as a trip to Mexico or plans to bring a relative from Mexico to live. These eventcasts were not, however, produced and delivered as mandates from a single individual. Story telling was common. Both young and old told *bruja* (witch) tales, as well as stories about real events. Storybooks, however, were uncommon. In Mexico, children's literature has not been promoted as a literary genre, and children generally have not had experiences interacting with adults around books.

In the white working-class community in the Carolina Piedmont studied by Heath (1986b), care givers modeled eventcasts during play with young children and while planning family projects with older children. In contrast to the eventcasting of mainstream families, however, they did not talk about steps and procedures of how to do things, instead they demonstrated, "Do it like this." Invitations to give accounts did not begin until children were in school, and even then they were rare. Recounts were frequent during the preschool years. They were, however, tightly scaffolded, with the adults seeking specific responses from the child, and adults' questioning might continue until the child produced a specific, desired response. Stories were rare at all ages and when told were generally the prerogative of those with status in the community or family. Stories were to be truthful, and any variation or exaggeration was viewed as lying. Consequently, children were actively discouraged from making up imaginative, creative stories. Books available to the children at home emphasized nursery rhymes, the alphabet, and Bible stories. In children's first three years, care givers engaged in some scaffolding around books, asking children to describe actions and events in the books. They did not however, pursue discussion of feelings or explanations about events in books, nor did they relate information in books to real-life experiences.

TABLE 7–1
Cultural variations in narrative genres

Genre	Mainstream	Mexican American	Chinese American	White Working Class	Black Working Class
Recounts (Tell Daddy about our trip to . . . .)	Common with young children Open-ended scaffolding Invitations to recount decrease with age	Rare	Rare	Predominant genre Tightly scaffolded	Rare
Accounts (Did you hear what happened to . . .?)	Begun before 2 years Adults request further explanation Adults suggest alternative outcomes Adults assess attitudes and actions of actor	Frequent Occur especially in family gatherings	At home; asked about events of day Not outside the home or with strangers	Not until school Must be accurate Privilege of older adults	Frequent in response to teasing Exaggeration values May be produced cooperatively
Eventcasts (I'm putting the soda in the chest, and then I'll load the car).	Begun with preverbal children Continue throughout the preschool	Almost never in daily events Family may cooperatively plan future events	Occur during ongoing activities at home More frequent for girls than boys	In play with young children In planning family projects with older children	Rare
Stories (Once upon a time . . .)	Frequent story reading Story comprehension negotiated Produce own imaginative stories	Bruja tales Stories about real events embellished with new details and about historical figures and events Children's literature absent	Tales about historical people and events Prefer informational rather than fictional books	Listen to stories read Comprehension not negotiated	No children's story books

In an African American working-class community in the same region, children had few, if any experiences with recounts before entering school. Their most frequent experiences were with accounts with peers and adults, if they could get the floor. Accounts and stories often emerged in teasing encounters with adults or older children and resulted in exaggerated stories that were cooperatively produced. During these accounts, children invited the audience to respond and participate. Children seldom heard "Once upon a time"-type stories until they entered school.

These patterns of genre socialization differed significantly from the experience of mainstream children. Mainstream children were given opportunities to recount from the time they began to talk. Adults provided open-ended scaffolding and were accepting of a variety of responses. Accounts were also accepted. Adults requested further information about accounts and were particularly interested in attitudes and actions of the actors in the account, and they suggested possible alternative outcomes to the story. Their comments functioned as indirect scaffolds to cue children as to the significance of feelings and intentions in stories and additional information that could be included in the account to explain the events. Eventcasts were begun with infants and continued throughout the preschool years. Children were encouraged to talk aloud as they performed routine and unfamiliar activities. Reading of storybooks was also common and for many children began shortly after birth. Adults used scaffolding questions to encourage the children to participate in the story reading. They were asked to label pictures in the stories, describe events, comment on character's feelings and intentions, and explain reasons for actions. Their attempts to produce their own imaginative stories were encouraged as long as the fictional nature of the story was clearly identified. With this exposure to narrative genres in the preschool years, mainstream students came to school with the texts that were to be valued and assessed in that setting. They knew how to participate in both the social and academic texts of school: They knew how to answer the types of questions teachers asked about texts, they knew what types of texts were acceptable, and they knew how to organize texts so they were comprehensible to the teachers.

The differences in narrative functions and genres and socialization for these functions and genres result in differences in story structural organization, story content, and story style. Although less information is available on expository genres and their socialization, research has determined that structure, content, and style of expository texts are also affected by cultural influences (Connor & Kaplan, 1987; Purvis, 1988). Differences in the areas of text structure, content, and style will be described in the remaining sections.

VARIATION IN TEXT STRUCTURE

Logical Global Structure

The study of contrastive linguistics in second language learning has described differences in text structures across languages and cultures. Kaplan (1966) was one of the first to investigate cultural variation in discourse structure. He explored the writing styles of foreign students writing in English. Although these students had mastered the vocabulary and grammar of English, their writing appeared disorganized and not to the point. Kaplan hypothesized that different cultures had developed different logical systems and, consequently, different organization formats for texts. In his first article on the topic, which he called his "doodles paper," he presented diagrams for text organization in several cultures. He did not mean to imply that these were the only text organizations that appeared in a culture. In fact, he stated that one might find all examples within each culture, but that one type of text structure predominates (Kaplan, 1987). See Figure 7–1.

FIGURE 7–1
Patterns of discourse organization
From "Cultural Thought Patterns in Intercultural Education" by R. Kaplan, 1966, *Language Learning, 16* (1, 2), p. 15. Copyright 1966 by Language Learning. Reprinted by permission.

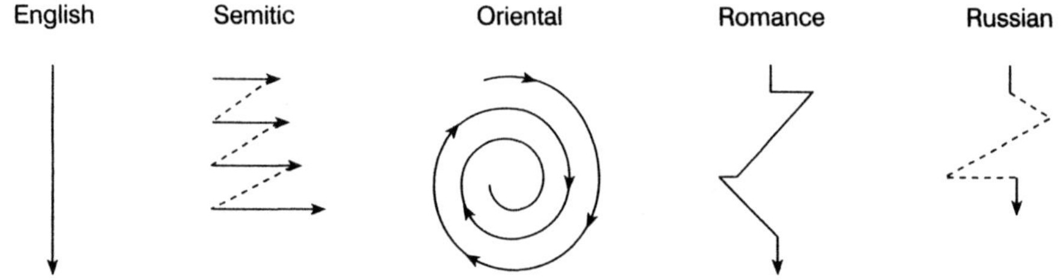

Kaplan proposed that English texts are direct and straightforward, with one point following logically from the preceding, and with minimal digressions. Semitic texts (e.g., Arabic and Hebrew) are based on a series of parallel constructions. This construction is particularly obvious in the King James version of the Bible. Semitic texts tend to rely on coordinate constructions (use of *and, therefore, but*), whereas maturity in English texts is measured by increasing subordination (use of *when, that, because, if*). This lack of subordination in Semitic texts makes it difficult for English speakers to realize the interrelationships among the elements of the text. Asian texts are indirect. Kaplan viewed Asian texts as developing in a widening gyre. The circles or gyres turn around the topic and show it from a variety of tangential views, but the topic is never looked at directly. Ideas are developed in terms of what they are not, rather than in terms of what they are. To comprehend Asian texts, one must have additional shared knowledge with the speaker/writer. In the romance languages, such as French and Spanish, it is permissible to introduce what appears to be extraneous or superfluous material. For listeners or readers unfamiliar with this style, the digressions lead them away from the main point of the story, and they have difficulty following the story line. To the writer or speaker, however, these apparent digressions are a means to elaborate on aspects of the text and to provide greater contextualization for the reader or listener. Russian texts appear to operate on a dialectic model of thesis and antithesis. Speakers begin presenting information to substantiate their point but then give information contradictory to the point—in effect giving both sides of the picture. If one is unfamiliar with this type of text, however, one is not certain if the speaker is supporting or opposing a position. An audience member attending a workshop on intercultural communication suggested this type of miscommunication may have occurred at the Reagan and Gorbachev summit meeting in Reykjavik, Iceland. Reagan exited the meeting and reported that agreement had been reached on several issues. When Reagan's comments were translated, Gorbachev insisted that agreement had not been reached on those matters. Perhaps the confusion arose because Reagan and his translators were not aware of the dialectic nature of Russian text. They expected that a text lists either a series of agreements or a series of opposing ideas, but they did not anticipate that a text would alternate between the two views. When Reagan thought Gorbachev was agreeing on positions, Gorbachev may have been indicating his disagreements. The relatively rapid and frequent switches between the two viewpoints would be difficult for an American to follow, even if the text had been in English.

The author of this chapter has struggled with interpreting texts of Native American students. When discussing this matter with a Native American faculty member, she was told, "Navajo thought is like Indian fry bread [deep-fried pastry]. An idea bubbles up here, then another idea over there, and another idea there" (L. Benally, personal communication, 1989). In Navajo thought, there is no need to indicate the relationships among the ideas.

Text structures vary, but the nature of the variation is in the eyes of the beholder. A Korean woman attending a workshop taught by the author of this chapter commented, "I thought he [Kaplan] wasn't Korean. I always thought it was we Koreans who talked in a straightforward manner and it was you Americans who talked in circles." The text organization pattern that a particular cultural group uses is the most logical and straightforward to them.

These global organization patterns affect all text genres, and the organization of texts can affect memory for texts. Eggington (1987) had Korean students read expository texts written using a Korean organization and expository texts using an English organization. Students were tested for memory of the texts immediately after reading and two weeks later. Although the content of the texts was the same, the students remembered significantly more of the texts written using a Korean organizational structure.

Episodic Structures

Episodic structures of stories have been the most widely studied aspect of texts. Stories vary in terms of the favored number of episodes, actions, or repetitions of behavior. Western cultures prefer their narratives in three parts or three episodes. Many Native American cultures prefer four-part stories. Northwest Coast Indians and some Chinese use series of five episodes, while some other Asian cultures prefer repetitions of two (Dundes, 1980; Jacobs, 1959; Scollon & Scollon, 1981). Listeners and readers come to expect certain structures in narrative. When that structure is violated, one may unconsciously reorganize the story to fit expectations. Kintch and Green (1978) reported that when Anglo (non-Native American, non-Hispanic) students read and retold four-part Indian stories, they omitted one part or condensed two of the parts into one. In contrast, Scollon and Scollon (1981) reported that when Athabaskan Indians retold three-part Anglo stories they added an additional episode.

Variation in episode structure extends to the emphasis placed on the components of stories as reflected in their story grammars. Story grammars represent the text structures of narratives (Stein & Glenn, 1979). According to story grammars, stories are composed of a *setting* or *orientation,* which introduces the characters, place, time, and circumstances of the story and which allows the rest of the story to happen. The plots of stories begin with some *initiating event* or *complicating action,* which is disequilibrating—a change of state or an action that initiates a character's reaction or response. Although the theme of a story is rarely stated explicitly, the initiating event should present information necessary for the listener/reader to recognize the underlying theme of the story. The character's reaction to the initiating events can be an *internal response* such as emotional feelings and cognitions or overt, goal-directed reactions such as physical attempts to cope with the initiating event. For a story to be perceived as a "good story" to mainstream Americans, there must be some *consequence* or *outcome* of the character's attempts. In addition, there may be a *resolution* or *reaction* that relates to the character's thoughts, feelings, or action in relation to the consequence. There may also be an *ending* or *coda,* which may be as simple as "that's all" or "the end," or which in some way addresses the overall theme of the story or gives a summary or a moral.

Different cultural groups vary in the emphasis they place on various components of the story structure, and the goal-directed basis of character action in the most commonly used story grammars is not applicable to stories from primarily oral and some non-Western cultures (Matsuyama, 1983; Ong, 1982). Soter (1988) asked English, Arabic, and Vietnamese students in sixth and eleventh grade in Australia to write a bedtime story for a child. English students immediately began the story and focused on the plot, producing a series of actions carried out by the characters. Vietnamese students never got to the actual task, but instead produced a lengthy introductory description (a story within a story) and did not complete the actual story; for example, they spent time discussing putting the child to bed or the parents choice of a story before beginning the actual story. They appeared intent on providing a contextual framework for their stories. Arabic writers emphasized detailed description of the settings for their stories.

Indrasuta (1988) compared the narratives of high school seniors in Urbana, Illinois, and Bangkok, Thailand. The students were asked to write a personal narrative on the topic, "I Succeeded, At Last" and "I Made a Hard Decision." Thai students wrote two narratives, one in English and one in Thai. The English and Thai narratives produced from Thai speakers were more similar to each other than either was to the American English narratives. Like Soter's Vietnamese writers, Thai writers devoted more attention to background contextual information in their narratives than did the American writers. They also used more verbs of mental states and descriptions of mental states to express the writers' thoughts as opposed to the higher use of settings and verbs of action in the stories of American students. Thai students' narratives were more likely to include a moral coda. Thai students used more highly figurative language such as metaphor, similes, and personification because, according to Indrasuta, analogy appears to be a preferred way of describing things in Thai.

Indrasuta explained these differences in narratives by referring to differences in beliefs. The author noted that Thai narratives may be influenced by Buddhism, which enhances the belief that people do not have control over their lives. Because of these beliefs, the events per se of the story are not as important as how those events affect peoples' lives. This contributes to the focus on internal rather than external struggles, as reflected in frequent reference to mental states and background information. Americans, on the other hand, perceive that they have control over their lives and stories. Consequently, they emphasized settings and initiating events to which they reacted with a goal-directed plan involving a series of attempts that led to consequences. Indrasuta suggested that some of this structural variation may also have been related to the writers' goals in writing the stories. Thai writers reported that they sought to teach, whereas American writers reported that they sought to interest readers.

Matsuyama (1983) observed similar patterns when applying story grammar analysis to Japanese folktales. Eighty percent of the Japanese folktales studied did not have a goal structure for the main character. Thus, the stories lacked attempts and consequences and consisted primarily of initiating events and resolutions. Matsuyama also attributed this folktale structure to the effects of Buddhism because Buddhism emphasized the importance of having no desires. It discourages aggressiveness and usually does not encourage goal-directed behavior.

Native American story structure may be farthest removed from typical story grammar structure (Highwater, 1981). Worth and Adair (1972) observed that Navajos devoted more attention to background and setting information than to the initiating events and consequences. In most Navajo stories, the storytellers spend much of their time describing walking, the landscape, and the places they pass, talking only briefly about what to us are the plot lines. To mainstream Americans, these stories do not seem to be stories. Highwater (1981) proposed that Native American narratives represent a different view of space, time, and motion than narratives of people from Western cultures. Unlike peoples from Western thought backgrounds, Native Americans do not view events, which are the basis of most stories, as involving sequence, causality, and succession. Consequently, the structure and organization of ideas in many Native American narratives is markedly different from narratives based on the Western worldview. The content of Native American narratives significantly affects the structure of the narratives. All story content, however, impacts on story structure.

Expository Structures

Narratives within a culture all have similar episodic structures. Figure 7–2 shows the classic episodic structure in mainstream American and Western European narratives.

Expository texts, however, have varied structures depending on their function:

1. Descriptive texts tell what something is.
2. Enumerative texts give a list related to a topic.
3. Sequential/procedural texts tell what happened or how to do something.
4. Comparison–contrast texts show how two or more things are the same or different.
5. Problem-solution texts state a problem and offer solutions.
6. Persuasive texts take a position on some issue and justify it.
7. Cause–effect texts give reasons for why something happened.

Figure 7–3 shows the structure of the major types of expository texts used in American textbooks. Table 7–2 (page 194) summarizes the attributes of expository texts. Cultures differ in the specific nature

FIGURE 7–2
Story text structure in mainstream American and Western European narratives

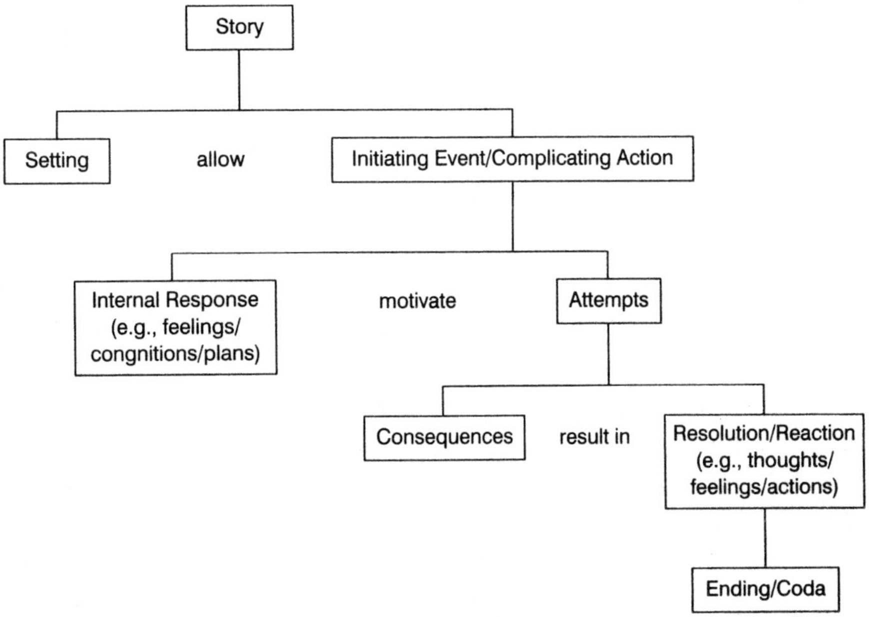

FIGURE 7–3
Structure of expository texts

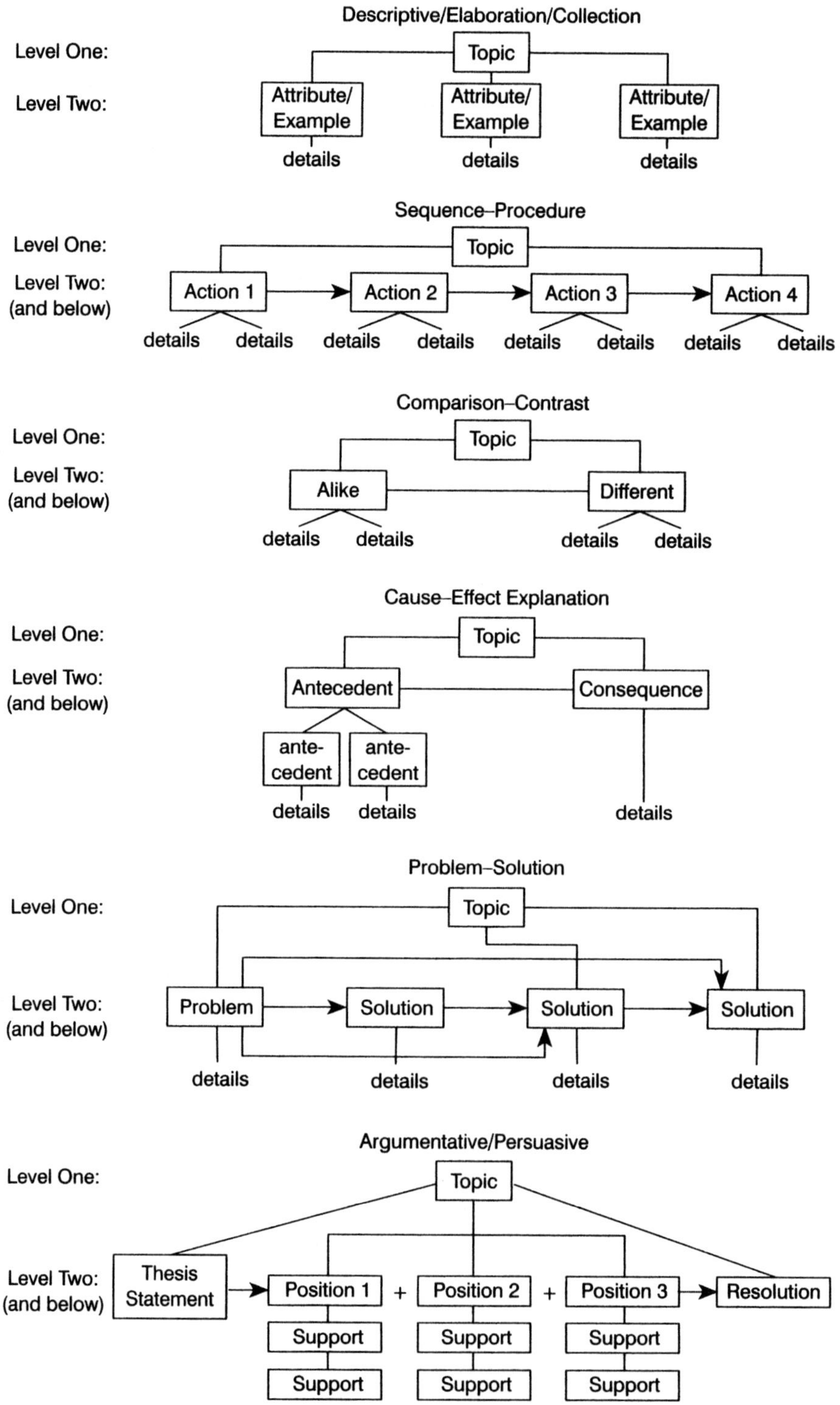

of these structures for each of these expository functions (Connor, 1987). It is common for language learning disabled students and students from nondominant cultural groups to transition out of special support programs in the early grades with, apparently, the language necessary for classroom success. These same students, however, are frequently referred in later elementary school or junior high for learning problems. A likely explanation for this is that the children acquired the few text structures that were essential in the early grades but did not have the variety of text structures that are essential for handling course content at higher levels. Each class subject is likely to use a different text structure, and if more than one book is used in a course, each book may have a different structure. Even a single book may use a variety of expository text structures within a chapter. Scott expands on the discussion of expository texts in Chapter 8.

VARIATION IN TEXT THEMES

Narrative Themes

Because people are human, they all share certain experiences. Consequently, one would anticipate that some story content and themes would be universal. Botvin and Sutton-Smith (1977) reported that the earliest two themes to emerge in young children's narratives by age four are villainy and lack or loss. These themes represent events that disrupt normal equilibrium. All cultures also have trickster tales, suggesting that deception is also a cultural universal (Basso, 1987; Radin, 1956). Children develop the ability to recognize deception and to deceive others intentionally and successfully between eight to ten years of age (D. M. Abrams & Sutton-Smith, 1977; DePaulo & Jordan, 1982). Many cultures present trickster characters in animal forms, for example, the spider of African folktales, the raven of Northwest Coast Indians, the coyote of Southwest Indians. Children's television cartoons in the United States often employ animals engaged in trickery, such as *The Pink Panther, Tom and Jerry, Bugs Bunny.* Characters in trickster tales, however, are not limited to animals. In fact, the vast majority of stories have characters who engage in some degree of deception. Villainy, lack, loss, and trickery or deceit are universal themes that appear in stories. The values, belief systems, and specific experiences of each culture differ, however. Consequently, one would expect to find some differences in plots, or working out of universal themes and concepts presented in stories and some differences in the themes that are emphasized.

Qualitative and quantitative content analysis systems have been developed and applied to texts to reveal the values and beliefs of an individual, culture, society, and nation (Berelson, 1971; Go, 1984; C. Peterson & Seligman, 1984; Polanyi, 1985; Starosta, 1984). Stewart (1972), applying Kluckhohn and Strodtbeck's value orientation framework (1961) to American culture, reported valuing of individualism, activity, responsibility, and control of one's environment. These themes were reflected in the stories Polanyi (1985) analyzed that were told by middle-class, urban women. She reported that their story themes focused on individuals, their rights, needs, choices, and social responsibilities.

Children are exposed to the themes of their culture from the time of their first exposure to stories. Zimet, Wiberg, and Blom (1971) did a multitheme content analysis of primers in thirteen nations and found numerous differences in these nations' first-grade textbooks. The primers differed in themes of traditionalism, work, play, conforming/compromising, caring/nurturing, and cleanliness/orderliness. Primers in the United States had frequent themes of caring and nurturing. They seldom had themes related to traditions, conforming/compromising, and cleanliness/orderliness. South Korean texts involved traditions, work, conforming/compromising, and cleanliness/orderliness. Texts from India also stressed traditions, work, conforming/compromising, and in addition, caring/nurturing. In general, the primers in European countries gave moderate attention to themes of play, work, and caring/nurturing and little attention to themes of tradition, conforming/compromising, and cleanliness/orderliness.

Cross-cultural psychologists have been interested in relationship of the theme of individual achievement motivation as reflected in folktales, personal narratives, stories elicited from stimulus pictures, and dream reports to economic development in cultures (LeVine, 1966; McClelland, 1958, 1971; Rosen, 1962). The appearance of achievement motivation themes in narratives does have a positive correlation with a society's economic growth and does predict individuals' persistence, willingness to take risks, and pursuit of difficult-to-attain goals. Achievement moti-

TABLE 7–2
Characteristics of texts

Text Pattern/Function	Examples	Key Words	Organization	Language Features
Narrative: text tells behavior/feelings/ thoughts of characters who may be real people, animals, or imaginary characters	Fictional stories, accounts of personal experiences, recounts of shared experiences	No typical key words other than *once, once upon a time, one time*	Setting Initiating event/complication Reaction Attempt Consequence Resolution Ending/coda	Major participants usually human or animals with human characteristics Mainly action verbs, but also verbs that refer to what characters felt, thought, or said Usually past tense Many linking verbs to do with time Written in first or third person Dialogue during which tense may change from past to present or future
Description: text tells what something is	House advertisement Botany Geography	*is called, can be defined as, is, can be interpreted as, is explained as, refers to, is a procedure for, is someone who, means*	Orientation Characteristics	Usually timeless present tense (*is, appears, grows*) Varied adjectives, adverbs, and prepositional phrases
Collection–enumeration: text gives a list of things that are related to a topic	Biology text (list characteristics of reptiles)	*an example is, for instance, another, next, finally, such as, to illustrate*	Topic introduced by general statement Classification locating what is being talked about	Factual, precise descriptive language Avoid first person and personal opinions

Text Pattern/Function	Examples	Key Words	Organization	Language Features
Sequence–procedure: text tells what happened or how to do something or make something	History texts, recipes, game rules, science experiments, craft instructions, appliance manuals	*first, next, then, second, third, following this step, finally, subsequently, from here . . . to, eventually, before, after*	Goal Materials list Methods	Detailed information of how, where, and when Linking words refer to time (*first, then, when*) Reader referred to in general way (*you*) or not mentioned (e.g., *glue parts A and B*) Mainly action verbs (*hold, paste, wash*)
Comparison–contrast: text shows how two things are the same or different	Science and social studies texts: e.g., comparing/contrasting insects and arachnids	*different, same, alike, similar, although, however, on the other hand, contrasted with, compared to, rather than, but, yet, still, instead of, nevertheless*	Topic Comparison Contrast Conclusion/summary	Parallel construction of sentences and paragraphs Factual, precise descriptive language (what they look like, what they have, why they do)
Cause–effect explanation: text gives reasons for why something happened	Science and history texts: e.g., mechanical explanation (how a pulley works), technological explanation (how a telephone works), system explanation (how a family functions), natural explanation (how thunderstorms occur)	*because, since, reasons, then, therefore, for this reason, results, effects, consequently, so, in order to, thus, depends on, influences, is a function of, produced, leads to, affects, hence*	Statement about phenomenon Sequenced explanation of how/why something occurs	Generalized nonhuman participants Mainly action verbs Some passive verbs Usually present tense

(continued)

TABLE 7–2, *continued*.

Text Pattern/Function	Examples	Key Words	Organization	Language Features
Problem–solution: text states a problem and offers solutions to problems	Ecological issues (cleaning up oil spills) Social issues (dealing with world hunger) Health issues (preventing AIDS)	*a problem is, a solution is*	Statement of problem Proposed solution Steps in solution Effectiveness of solution	Generalized participants (unnamed persons, objects, or elements of nature) Use of specific technical language
Argument–persuasion: text takes a position on an issue and justifies it	Sermons, newspaper editorials, political speeches	*therefore, so, because, the first reason*	Statement of position Background information Points with supporting evidence Summary/resolution	Generalized participants Often abstract ideas and opinions May use technical terms related to issue Often use emotive words and modals such as must, should Frequent use of passives

vation themes in stories are related to child-rearing practices and the status mobility that is available to people within a cultural group. Cultures that stress strong parent authority and cultures in which class status is determined by birth exhibit fewer achievement motivation themes in their stories.

Domino and Hannah (1987) explored the themes in stories produced by American and Chinese children ages 11 to 13 in response to story starters such as "Mother send Michael to the store to buy meat for supper. On the way home, Michael plays with friends and some meat is eaten by a dog. . . ." The stories from Chinese children evidenced greater social orientation and greater concern with authority and with morality. Compared to the stories by American children, the stories of the Chinese children included more people, both children and adult authorities, and transgressions were discovered and punished, often severely. In the stories of American children, there were significantly more themes of aggression, and children who committed negative acts were frequently never discovered. Actions and events in the stories of the Chinese children were more often determined by forces of nature or of a quasi-spirit world, whereas the events in the stories of American children were more often determined by the characters' intentions and plans. Domino and Hannah (1987) propose that these thematic differences in children's stories reflect cultural differences in child rearing, socialization, religious/ethical practices, and the role of the family.

Content Schemas

Culture affects not only story production but also story comprehension. With repeated experiences with the stories of one's culture, a person develops schemas for story content. Schemas are hierarchically organized conceptual units that describe general knowledge (Mandler, 1984). The content of many schemas is culture specific. Although in all cultures people eat, work, and have celebrations, the content of these events differs. Schemas are structures of expectation (Chafe, 1990); they guide the text comprehension process. Understanding a text requires more than understanding the words and sentences that compose the text. If the schemas a person uses to comprehend the text do not approximate the schemas used by the producer of the text, the person will likely misinterpret the text or not be able to determine the point of the text. Because the text appears "hard to follow" or appears to have no point, it is also likely that the person will not enjoy listening to or reading the text. Salisbury described the confusion an Alaskan Indian child might experience in reading a mainstream text:

> Many things confuse him. Dick and Jane are two gussick (Eskimo word for white person—derived from the Russian word cossack) children who play together. Yet he knows that boys and girls do not play together and do not share toys. They have a dog named Spot who comes indoors and does not work. They have a father who leaves for some mysterious place called "office" each day and never brings any food home with him. He drives a machine called an automobile on a hard covered road called a street which has a policeman on each corner. These policemen always smile, wear funny clothing and spend their time helping children to cross the street. Why do these children need this help? Dick and Jane's mother spends a lot of time in the kitchen cooking a strange food called "cookies" on a stove which has no flame in it.
>
> But the most bewildering part is yet to come. One day they drive out to the country which is a place where Dick and Jane's grandparents are kept. They do not live with the family and they are so glad to see Dick and Jane that one is certain that they have been ostracized from the rest of the family for some terrible reason. The old people live on something called a "farm," which is a place where many strange animals are kept—a peculiar beast called a "cow," some odd looking birds called "chickens" and a "horse" which looks like a deformed moose. (Salisbury, 1967, pp. 4–5)

Memory for text becomes distorted when texts contain unfamiliar schemas. Steffensen, Joag-Dev, and Anderson (1979) had Americans and Indians (from India) read reports of an American and an Indian wedding. American and Indian subjects took more time to read the unfamiliar schemas. They recalled more of the familiar schema passage, added more culturally appropriate information to the familiar passages, and produced more culturally based distortions when recalling the unfamiliar texts. The groups differed on what they considered to be important in the two passages, but they remembered best what they judged as important.

A similar study was conducted with African American and white teenagers (Reynolds, Taylor, Steffenson, Shirey, & Anderson, 1981). An episode was written on "sounding," an activity that takes place primarily in African American communities in which participants try to outdo each other in an exchange of insults (Labov, 1972). African American teenagers tended to see the episode as involving a friendly give-and-take, whereas white teenagers interpreted it as an ugly confrontation, sometimes involving physical violence. An African American student wrote, "Then everybody tried to get on the person side that joke were the best." A white student wrote, "Soon there was a riot. All the kids were fighting."

The strategies individuals use to comprehend texts with familiar and unfamiliar cultural schemas differ. Eleventh-grade American and Palauan students who were proficient readers were given two passages in the form of a letter from a woman to her sister describing the events surrounding a typical funeral in the two cultures (Pritchard, 1990). The students were asked to read the passages, and at the end of each sentence they were to talk out loud about what they were doing and thinking by (1) explaining what was happening in the letter, (2) explaining what they thought about as they read, (3) explaining what they did as they read, and (4) discussing anything else about the letter or how they read it. On the culturally familiar texts, students used more strategies involving *intersentential ties* (to relate the stimulus sentence to other portions of the passage by reading ahead, relating the immediate sentence to earlier sentences, or confirming/disconfirming an inference) and *background knowledge* (building understanding by visualizing, referring to the previous passage, relating the letter to personal experience, or speculating beyond information in the text). On the culturally unfamiliar texts, the students used more strategies related to *awareness* (to indicate how much progress they had made and any problems they were having with the task by referring to the experimental task or commenting on loss of concentration and failure to comprehend); *accepting ambiguity* (acknowledging problems by skipping words, asking questions, suspending judgment, or considering alternative inferences); and *establishing intrasentential ties* (trying to understand a particular sentence by rereading, paraphrasing, or using context cues to interpret a word).

In addition to the strategy differences used by all students on culturally familiar and unfamiliar texts, Pritchard (1990) observed differences in the strategies used by the American and Palauan students on the culturally unfamiliar letters. Although both groups used strategies related to awareness, accepting *ambiguity,* and intrasentential ties on the culturally unfamiliar texts, the American students made much greater use of strategies related to awareness and accepting ambiguity, and the Palauan students used primarily the intrasentential tie strategy of paraphrasing the stimulus sentence. Pritchard suggested that cultural background affected the strategies the students preferred. In general, Palauan culture discourages questioning and inferencing characteristic of the accepting ambiguity strategy, whereas American culture values flexibility and risk taking. The American strategies appeared to be more effective for achieving comprehension of culturally unfamiliar texts. American students gave summarizing or concluding statements for both the culturally familiar and unfamiliar letters, whereas Palauan students generally gave summarizing or concluding statements only for the culturally familiar text. Reluctance or inability to produce a concluding statement could represent a student's inability to integrate the information in the text.

Cultural differences in schema knowledge between students and teachers have the potential for affecting students' comprehension of school texts and teachers' evaluation and interpretation of students' text. Do the students lack specific schema knowledge, or are they just slow? What strategies do students use to comprehend text, and how successful are these strategies? Are ineffective strategies related to cultural styles or metacognitive deficits? Are the students' text productions really incoherent, or does the evaluator lack the necessary schema to recognize the coherence in the story?

Text Landscapes

Narrative texts have dual content. They have what Bruner (1986) called *landscape of action* and *landscape of consciousness.* Narratives may have only a landscape of action. Folktales, stories from oral cultures, and stories from young children often have only a landscape of action. Such stories consist of a sequence of action events with minimal information about the psychological states of the characters. In contrast, most modern Western stories and stories of children older than age nine devote considerable attention to the landscape of consciousness, that is, how the world is perceived and felt by the characters in the story. Ong (1982) suggested that writing permits reflection on language and self in a way not possible with oral language. In traditional oral narratives, characters are distinguished by external exploits. In written narratives, internal consciousness becomes increasingly important. In oral narratives, characters are flat; in written narratives, characters grow psychologically and become more rounded, like real persons.

Content analysis can surpass the thematic level to investigate peoples' motivations and explanations for events—to explore their landscapes of consciousness. The content analysis of verbatim explanations (CAVE) provides a means of assessing peoples' causal beliefs. Using the CAVE procedure, C. Peterson and Seligman (1984) looked at good and bad events reported in personal narratives and then looked for explanations for the given events. They rated each causal explanation on a seven-point scale in terms of internality, stability, and globality. Causes included other events, situational factors, behaviors of the narrator or others, and dispositions. The internal dimension refers to a cause within the person ("I'm not smart") or outside the person ("teachers are out to get me"). The stability dimension refers to how long lasting the cause is (a one-time instance or a life-long situation), and globality refers to how many aspects of one's life are affected. Oettingen (cited in C. Peterson & Seligman, 1984) used this system to analyze the newspaper articles in East and West Berlin of the 1984 Winter Olympics in Sarajevo, Yugoslavia. The explanations for performance in the events were compared. Although East Germany won significantly more medals than West Germany in those Olympics, their newspaper articles were far more pessimistic, conveying more a sense of hopelessness and power outside their control, while the West Berliners read more optimistic news with an emphasis on the personal skills and potential of their athletes.

How students explain activities in narratives can give insight into students' ways of coping in the classroom. Literature has suggested that students from lower socioeconomic backgrounds and some traditional cultures that have little or no literacy are more likely to be externally controlled (Wilcox, 1972). Conversely, literacy may facilitate the development of a landscape of consciousness and its associated metalinguistic and metacognitive behaviors. Ong (1982) maintained that literacy facilitates reflection. Olson and Astington (1986) reported evidence for a correlation between elaboration of speech act (state, claim, deny, concede) and mental state verbs (assume, infer, hypothesize) and the development of literacy. Many recent studies have reported on the metalinguistic and metacognitive deficits of learning disabled students (Baker & Brown, 1984; Englert, Raphael, Anderson, Gregg, & Anthony, 1989; Wong, 1985). The assumption of these studies appears to be that the metadeficits lead to the literacy deficits, but the literacy deficits may be contributing to the metadeficits (see also van Kleeck, chap. 3).

The CAVE analysis involves attributional analysis. Even when the superficial content of events in stories appears similar, the causal attribution that listeners/readers give to these events because of their belief and value systems can result in markedly different story interpretations. Albert (1986) had Hispanic and Anglo students and teachers read brief vignettes of student behavior and had them chose from four possible explanations for the behavior. The vignettes involve situations such as a student not wanting to talk in class, being caught by the principal coming into school late, or not wanting to take home a slip announcing an open house. In almost all cases, the Hispanic students and teachers attributed the behavior of the students in the vignettes to their being ashamed. Anglo students and teachers rarely attributed the behaviors to being ashamed. Anglos were more likely to give personality attributions (e.g., being shy) or to object to the event in the vignette (e.g., the principal shouldn't have stopped him because he wasn't doing anything wrong). Albert suggested that the higher attribution of "shame" to the behavior by Hispanics was related to the more collectivistic culture of Hispanics, which contrasts with the more individualistic Anglo culture.

Narrative Plots

Beliefs, values, and attributions affect the ways in which story plots are worked out, that is, the actual content of the plot and the ending of the story. A story plot must have a clear beginning, middle, and end, and it must be structured around a problem that the main character confronts and eventually resolves in some way (Aristotle, *Poetics*; Prince, 1973; Propp, 1968; Todorov, 1971).

Maranda and Maranda (1970) noted four types of narrative plot solutions:

1. Stories in which one power overwhelms another and there is no attempt at response. For example, a monster comes into town, smashes all the houses, and steals all the food, but the villagers do not respond.
2. Stories in which a character attempts a response but fails. Attempts are made to escape or to effect a rescue but are unsuccessful.

3. Stories in which a character nullifies the original threat or supplies what is lacking. The protagonist is successful in rendering the threat powerless in some way or in supplying what is lacking; however, the removal of the threat or deprivation may be temporary.
4. Stories in which not only is the threat nullified but the original circumstances are substantially transformed so that there is no possibility of the problem returning. The monster and all of its family are killed, jailed, or placed in a zoo, or characters discover a magic lamp that will fulfill all their needs.

These plots are developmental, with younger children producing levels 1 and 2 and older children producing levels 3 and 4. The plot types, however, are also affected by cultural beliefs. Those cultures that believe in fate and peoples' inability to effect change produce more stories of types 1 and 2 and far fewer, if any, stories of types 3 or 4. Ong's ideas (1982) on the impact of literacy suggest that narratives from oral cultures would not achieve a level-4 plot ending.

From the preschool years, gender differences affect story plots. Nicolopoulou and Scales (1990) observed that the stories of four- and five-year-old girls tended to have coherent plots with a stable set of characters and a continuous plot line. The girls structured their story content around stable sets of relationships—particularly family relationships. In contrast, the stories of four- and five-year-old boys had neither a clear plot nor a stable set of characters, nor did they develop their story themes in any systematic manner. Plots in the boys' stories centered on unrelated violent actions; their plots emphasized the landscape of action. Plots in girls' stories centered on the maintenance of social relationships; their plots emphasized the landscape of consciousness. Girls stories were judged to be of higher quality.

Other researchers have observed similar trends. Abrams (1977) noted that boys ages three to fourteen years told more stories of contests and villains and girls told more stories of domestic animals and deprivation. Botvin and Sutton-Smith (1977) observed that boys achieved Maranda level-3 and -4 plot endings by having their heros overcome their villains, while girls more often reached these levels through an alliance.

Gender differences in stories show no indication of decreasing with age. L. H. Peterson (1991) reported that in autobiographical essays written by college students, women more frequently chose topics focusing on crisis relationships with some other person (e.g., disagreement, breakup, concern for a sibling, or confrontation between cultures). Men chose topics that focused on themselves (e.g., physical challenge, crisis in vocation). Tannen (1990) reported similar observations. She also reported that men told stories in which they were the protagonists or antagonists, and for the most part, the stories they told made them look good. For example, they told stories of winning games or overcoming significant challenges. The women's stories tended to be about the norms of the community or joint actions of groups of people. When women did include themselves in the stories, they frequently told stories that made them look foolish. Johnstone (1989) observed that not only do men tell more stories in which they act alone, but when men and women tell about acting alone, the outcomes tend to differ. The majority of stories about acting alone told by men had happy outcomes. The majority of stories told by women in which they acted alone portrayed them suffering as a result of acting alone. Men's stories seldom included asking for help, whereas in nearly half of the women's stories, the protagonist asked for help. Table 7–3 summarizes gender differences in narratives.

Very few studies have considered the development of narrative skills in boys and girls separately. Yet the little literature that is available suggests that content and possibly structural complexity of narratives is affected by gender (Jett-Simpson & Masland, 1993; Kamler, 1993). Consequently, professionals may need to be cautious not only in applying narrative data to culturally diverse groups but also in applying it similarly to boys and girls from mainstream cultures.

The effects of culture on plots cannot be avoided by asking for retellings of stories. Although each person may watch the same film or listen to the same book, their focus will differ and they are likely to find a different purpose and plot for the story. Liebes (1988) had five culturally distinct groups watch an episode of *Dallas*. Groups were chosen from four widely different subcultures in Israel (Arabs, Moroccan Jews, new immigrants from Russia, and second-generation Israelis living in a kibbutz) and second-generation Israeli Americans in Los Angeles. A host couple invited two or more couples to meet in the living room of the host family and view an episode of

TABLE 7–3
Gender styles in narratives

Females	Males
Characters Both males and females Fewer characters, more detailed Often domestic animals; if wild animals are mentioned they are more likely friendly than ferocious Mention more household objects, products of nature (trees, flowers, fruit)	Characters Seldom females More characters, less detail More often wild or zoo animals More mention of transportation vehicles, occupational figures, insects
Themes Focus on relationships with others Deprivation, morality, disagreement, breakup, concern for sibling, confrontation between cultures, group membership, norms of the community Negotiate with villains; make friends of enemies	Themes Focus on self, self alone Villainy, aggression, hurt, misfortune, physical challenge, crisis in vocation, episode in self-confidence Defeat villains
Contemplative accounts	Action accounts—contests (intellectual, physical, nature [hunting, fishing])
Stories about themselves tend to make them look foolish	Stories about themselves put them in positive light
If act alone, suffer	If act alone, happy outcome
Protagonists ask for help	Protagonists rarely ask for help
Tell few jokes, especially to males or mixed groups	Tell more jokes

Dallas. They were then asked, "How would you retell the episode you just saw to somebody who has not seen it?" All groups were familiar with *Dallas.* Three types of retellings emerged: linear/sociological, segmented/psychological, thematic/ideological. Examples follow.

Linear/Sociological. These were retellings that sequentially related the activities in the episode and focused on the actions of the characters in terms of their roles in the story, that is, J.R.'s action in terms of his being the son of Elly and Jock Ewing, husband of Sue Ellen, and brother of Bobby.

The Arab and Morrocan groups retold their stories primarily in a linear manner and saw the plot as dealing with the social roles of the characters:

> William: JR is trying to get Sue Ellen and the child back home. So he goes off to try to get a monopoly of 25,000 barrels of oil, or maybe it is 50,000.
> Hyam: Yes, it was 25,000 barrels.
> George: To get his son back. He's trying to get a monopoly on the oil wells. So he takes all the oil in order to empty all of the refineries. (Liebes, 1988, p. 283)

Segmented/Psychological. Persons using segmented/psychological retellings retold selected portions of the story and focused on the characters, their motivations, and their interrelationships. Such retellings might focus on the causes and consequences of the personality of J.R., explaining what made him so competitive and how this attribute expresses itself in different situations.

The American and kibbutz groups offered segmented retellings, emphasizing not the sequence of events but the expression of personalities. In so doing, they frequently focused on one or two characters to the exclusion of the others in the episode.

> Sandy: Pam, you know, upset about a lot of things insider herself and that she wanted to kill herself and that her husband was trying to talk her into committing herself to the hospital to help her. This is the main thing got to me in this episode because, emotionally, that's was got to me, that she would want to kill herself. (Leibes, 1988, p. 283)

Thematic/Ideological. Persons engaging in thematic/ideological retellings searched for the theme or message in the story, rather than attending to the specific actions or psychological explanations for the actions.

The Russians generally ignored the specific story in favor of a thematic retelling concerned with the moral or message.

> Misha: The program reflects the reality in America.
>
> Sima: The financial problem plays an important role; JR wants to revenge himself through using his economic background. Through the oil wells. In this particular episode, the financial problem plays an important role.
>
> Rosa: The oil is the main theme. (Leibes, 1988, p. 283)

or another example:

> Misha: The program is propaganda for the American way of life. They show American characters. The program deals with the dilemma of life in America. It is actually advertising—or, more accurately, propaganda—for the American way of life. They show the average person, in an interesting way, the idea he should be striving towards. (Leibes, 1988, p. 285)

Even though the interviewer repeatedly attempted to get the discussants beyond the thematic level, they appeared to refuse to get into the details of the video.

Gee (1989) reported significant differences in how African American and white lower class students and white upper class adolescents interpreted the characters' activities in the following story.

> ***The Alligator River Story***
>
> Once upon a time there was a woman named Abigail who was in love with a man named Gregory. Gregory lived on the shore of a river. Abigail lived on the opposite shore of the river. The river which separated the two lovers was teeming with man-eating alligators. Abigail wanted to cross the river to be with Gregory. Unfortunately, the bridge had been washed out. So she went to ask Sinbad, a river boat captain, to take her across. He said he would be glad to if she would consent to go to bed with him preceding the voyage. She promptly refused and went to a friend named Ivan to explain her plight. Ivan did not want to be involved at all in the situation. Abigail felt her only alternative was to accept Sinbad's terms. Sinbad fulfilled his promise to Abigail and delivered her into the arms of Gregory. When she told Gregory about her amorous escapade in order to cross the river, Gregory cast her aside with disdain. Heartsick and dejected, Abigail turned to Slug with her tale of woe. Slug, feeling compassion for Abigail sought out Gregory and beat him brutally. Abigail was overjoyed at the sight of Gregory getting his due. As the sun sets on the horizon, we hear Abigail laughing at Gregory.

The plot of this story involved the motivations of the main character, Abigail, and several protagonists. The students were asked to discuss the story and come to consensus about how the characters should be ranked "from the most offensive to the least objectionable." The groups did not differ significantly in their rankings of the characters, but they did justify their decisions differently.

The African American students often began their discussion using pronouns, and not referring to the characters by name. They based their judgments of the characters' behaviors on their own knowledge of social norms—what their culture said was right or wrong and what one should and should not do—rather than on the specific information presented in the text. White students from the same socioeconomic group began their discussions by referring to the characters by name. They relied on the factual information provided in the text to make their judgments, reasoning about the psychological states of the characters. Their way of interpreting the text was consistent with the school's expectation of text comprehension.

Surprisingly, the upper class white students' approach to interpreting the text was as far removed from the lower class white students' approach as was the African American students' approach. The upper class white students used character names and avoided use of pronouns even after they had introduced the characters. Like the African American students, they did not base their evaluation of the characters on the information provided in the text alone. However, they also did not rely on societal norms. Instead they based their judgments on their own responses to the behavior and the degree to which their personal sensibilities were offended. For the African American students and the upper class white students, plot interpretation was not based on reading of the text alone. It was based on either broader life plots dictated by society or highly personalized plots of the individual.

How is text content (themes, schemas, landscapes, and plots) organized into a cohesive/coherent structure so that the text makes sense and makes a point for the listener/reader? The cohesion and coherence of a text is determined by the linguistic and paralinguistic style employed by the speakers and writers.

VARIATION IN TEXT STYLE

Barland (1975) defined style to include peoples' favorite forms of interaction, the depth of involvement sought, the extent to which they rely on the same channels for conveying information, and the extent to which they are tuned to the same level of meaning, such as factual versus emotional content. Communicative style both reflects and reinforces fundamental cultural beliefs about the way people are and the nature of interpersonal communication (Clancy, 1986). Variations in text style can result in difficulties in recognition of the text organization and misinterpretation of the text content.

Style in Topic Organization

Much of the work on communicative style has compared oral and literate texts, particularly narratives (Tannen, 1982a). Story styles have been labeled as oral and topic-associated or literate and topic-centered. Table 7–4 summarizes the characteristics of these two styles. An oral or topic-associated style frequently consists of a series of segments that are linked implicitly to an event or theme but with no explicit statements of an overall theme or point. A literate or topic-centered style is associated with books and school language. This style makes the temporal and cause–effect links between segments explicit. Topic-associated narratives are characteristic of some cultural groups in which the members share similar background knowledge and patterns of oral language performance (Cooley, 1979; Erickson, 1984; Gee, 1985; Michaels, 1985; Michaels & Collins, 1984; Tannen, 1984b). In a school context where the teacher may not share the child's background, such narratives appear incoherent.

Topic-centered and topic-associated narratives differ in their use of prosody, clause types, and conjunctions. In topic-centered narratives, the themes are developed through a linear progression of information. The child provides focused descriptions of a single event or object. Prosodically, topic-centered stories begin with a sustained rising tone. Changing tones (both rise-falls and fall-rises) are used to elaborate on the topic and low falling tones are used in closing.

In contrast, topic-centered narratives consist of a series of implicitly associated topics. Prosodically, rhythm and high hold pitches, rather than sharp rising and falling pitch contours, are used to organize information thematically. Many linguists have viewed topic-associated, oral narratives as having a poetic structure and have analyzed these oral narratives into verses and stanzas (Bright, 1982; Gee, 1985; Heath, 1983; Scollon & Scollon, 1981). Structurally, the topic-associating style is characterized by an absence of conjunctions other than *and,* which is used in relating anecdotes. This type of discourse is difficult to follow if one is expecting a narrative to focus on a single topic with clausal units marked off by sharp rising and falling pitches. The anecdotes in these narratives are not strung together randomly. Instead, the anecdotes are linked implicitly to a topical event or theme. The theme is not overtly stated but has to be inferred from the series of personal anecdotes. Thematic development is accomplished through anecdotal association rather than linear description. Erickson (1984) termed this pattern the "logic of the particular" and noted that it is commonly used by African Americans and Native Americans.

Style in Clausal Patterns

The cohesion strategies used in topic-centered and topic-associated styles vary not only in terms of the prosodic features used but also in terms of the intraclausal and interclausal complements used. Michaels and Collins (1984) studied the uses of complements within and across clause boundaries in narratives. They noted that in topic-associated narratives, the complements tended to be verbal complements; that is, they added information about a verbal process:

TABLE 7–4
Variations in text style

Literate Style	Oral Style
Linear progress of information on single event	Anecdotal, implicitly associated topics
Personal narratives begin by telling the listener what is coming	Personal narratives begin anywhere
Does not assume shared information with listener; talks about what is obvious to both speaker and listener	Assumes shared information; does not talk about what is obvious to both speaker and listener
Use of specific vocabulary	Frequent use of deictic and nonspecific words (e.g., *this, that, here, he, her,* etc.)
External, explicit evaluation (use words to explain characters' feelings and behavior and evaluate the quality of the story)	Internal, implicit evaluation (may be conveyed through intonation)
Cohesive characteristics:	Cohesive characteristics:
Begin with sustained rising tone; changing tones elaborate topic; falling tones close topic	Rhythm and high hold pitches organize information
Intraclausal nominal complements	Intraclausal verbal complements
Interclausal complements common; relative clauses to track characters	Interclausal complements rare; vowel elongation and high rise–fall contour on pronoun to track characters
Interclausal connectives varied and common; orient clauses with *but, because, so, therefore, conversely*, etc.	Interclausal connectives limited; orient clauses with *and, then,* and prosodic cues

> and then he dro:ve off *with 'em"*
> and he had a wreck on *his bike*
> and the peaches fell out *on the ground* (Michaels & Collins, 1984, p. 233)

These phrases add information about how he drove off, how he had a wreck, and where the peaches fell. In contrast, in topic-centered narratives, complements were frequently embedded against nominals referring to major characters in the story:

> he um . . . saw 'em *with the pears*
> this boy *on his bike* came along
> one of the kids there . . . was the one . . . *on the bike* (Michaels & Collins, 1984, p. 233)

Each of these prepositional phrases adds information about the nouns and pronouns. The identifying information is then used to maintain identity of references, to signal cohesive ties between characters and events in the narratives.

Interclausal components refer to syntactic structures such as infinitives, *that* complements and relative clauses. Interclausal complements enhance cohesion in discourse by explicitly mapping hierarchical relations onto clausal structure. By substituting superordinate and subordinate relations for simple conjunctions, interclausal complements serve two purposes: they order two clauses with respect to one another, and they provide additional information about a given noun phrase. In this second case, the information can then be used to establish co-identity in a later utterance. Children who use a topic-centered style used complex nominal syntax to describe characters in their stories (Michaels & Collins, 1984). Then, in referring back to these characters later in the story after other events or characters have been talked about, they again used complex syntax to reestablish the characters' identity:

> . . . there was a man/ . . . that was . . . picking some . . . pears// (Michaels & Collins, 1984, p. 235)

then later she says

> then/ . . . they . . . walked by the man/ who gave/ . . . wh-who was picking the pears// (p. 235)

In contrast, a child with a topic-associated style introduces his character

> it was about/ . . . this mān/ he was um/ . . . um . . . takes some um . . . pēach__/ . . . some . . . pēa:rs off the tŕee. (Michaels & Collins, 1984, p. 235)

The student with topic-associating style used two independent clauses where the student with topic-centered style used a single relative clause. This difference is important when it comes to reestablishing character identity. In the following passage, the child used vowel elongation and a high rise–fall contour on *man* to serve as a cue that he was talking about a previously mentioned character. To a listener unfamiliar with this use of intonation to track characters, the passage may be confusing or misleading because the listener may assume that "the man" is a new character.

> and when that . . . when he pa:ssed/ by that mâ:n/ . . . the man . . . the mâ:n came out the tŕee/ (Michaels & Collins, 1984, p. 235)

A third type of clausal organization is that of interclausal conjunctions. Clausal conjunctives such as *but, so, on the other hand, conversely* serve to orient a clause or series of clauses with respect to the preceding clauses. They serve either to replace an intonation or contextual cue or to duplicate its function. Compare the following two samples

> . . . he um . . . saw 'em with the peâ:rs
> so/
> . . . he thought/ . . . that . . . thēy stoled
> . . . his peaches// (Michaels & Collins, 1984, p. 236)

with

> the man came out the tŕee / saw the peârs was gô:ne / and then . . . he know who had gôt 'em/ (Michaels & Collins, 1984, p. 236)

The *then,* with a stressed high fall serves an implicit intonational signal, functionally equivalent to explicit conjunctions such as *so, therefore,* or *hence.* The chain of events and inferences is related, not with an explicit conjunction, but with a prosodic cue superimposed on what appears to be a temporal connective (Scott expands on various syntactic/literate styles in chap. 8).

Flexibility in Style

The oral narrative style has been associated with lower socioeconomic groups, but this is not necessarily the case. The oral style can occur whenever a group of people familiar with one another get together and begin to tell stories. Individuals or groups may use a highly oral style in some informal contexts and a highly literate style in formal contexts. Tannen (1984b) reported an instance of misunderstanding and misinterpretation that occurred when New Yorkers of Jewish background and natives of Los Angeles told stories during a Thanksgiving dinner. The New Yorkers' oral-style stories were marked by exaggerated paralinguistic and prosodic features. They used postural and gestural cues, marked shifts from high to low pitch, and varying rates of speech. The New Yorkers listening to the stories responded in like style during the story telling with comments such as "Oh:: Go::D" in a disbelieving tone. The point of the story was conveyed by the tone of the telling—through what Labov (1972) called *internal evaluation*. Without external, explicit evaluation, however, the Los Angeles natives who were listening asked "what does it mean?" The New Yorkers listening to the literate-style stories of the Los Angeles natives found their stories dull and uninteresting because they did not indicate their personal emotional response. The New Yorkers relied on a highly oral style in conversation but could switch to a literate style when required to do so for academic purposes.

Students may be aware that their communicative style differs from the mainstream, and they may attempt to modify their styles. In so doing, however, they may not make their communication more understandable to others. Gee (1989) analyzed narratives that an African American eleven-year-old girl told to a peer and an adult and that a white middle-class eleven-year-old girl told to an adult. He coded the narrative lines as informative (those that provide new information to the story) and expressive (those that carry emotive, performative, or expressive content but do not advance the narrative story line). He also noted the ways lines were linked together (temporal, logical, and expressive), the use of sound effects, and the use of gestures in the story telling. In her story to her peers, the African American student used more expressive lines and less informative lines, more expressive links and less temporal and logical links, and more sound effects and gestures than did the white student talking to an adult. The white student used informative lines and temporal and logical links almost exclusively in her story to an adult. When talking to an adult, the African American student did change styles, but the changes did not make her narrative more understandable to the adult. The African American student significantly reduced her use of expressive lines, expressive links, sound effects, and gestures. She did not, however, increase the number of informative lines and temporal and expressive links. Although she eliminated unique aspects of her communicative style, she did not replace what she eliminated with mainstream style elements. Apparently, the African American student was aware of some ways in which her style differed from the expectations of middle-class adults. She knew what to eliminate, but she did not know what to substitute in its place. Her narrative to her peers had a well-developed plot and was readily intelligible to individuals familiar with that communicative style. The narrative she produced for the adult would not have been interpretable by her peers or by mainstream adults.

This example illustrates that care must be taken when attempting to develop flexibility in communicate style. Adults should not imply that certain aspects of style are "bad" and should not be used. Rather, they should focus on the characteristics of the two styles and show how they each communicate their message. Indeed, if students reduce communicative aspects of one style, they will need to increase communicate aspects of the other style.

Expository Style

The majority of information on stylistic variations in texts has been done on narrative texts. Grabe (1987), however, was interested in determining if different text genres had different stylistic characteristics. He analyzed the syntactic and cohesion characteristics of texts varying in content (natural science, social science, and humanities) and audience (academic, introductory university, and popular). A complex factor analysis indicated that narrative texts were indeed significantly different in syntactic patterns and cohesive characteristics than all expository text. Among the expository texts were several subtypes, each also varying in their use of syntactic and cohesive characteristics. Grabe's work suggests that not only must students acquire a literate narrative style for school but they must also acquire several different types of expository style to succeed in higher grades (see Blachowicz, chap. 11; Ehren, chap. 15; Scott, chap. 8).

IMPLICATIONS

Effects of Text Variations

What is the significance of cultural variations in genre types and text structure, content, and style? These communication differences in multicultural societies may well result in multiple problems in the classroom (Erickson, 1984). There can be miscommunication at the implicit social level (the student is perceived as disrespectful and rude; the teacher is perceived as cold); misunderstanding at the explicit referential level (the student and teacher do not understand the meanings of each other's words); and misattribution and faulty assessment of the student's intentions and abilities (the student is perceived as unmotivated and/or learning disabled; the teacher is perceived as trying to make things difficult).

Distinguishing between students with true neurologically based language learning disabilities and students who have culturally based language differences is no simple task. In fact, it may be impossible in the majority of cases. Assessment procedures are themselves based on mainstream social and academic texts (i.e., ways of displaying knowledge and using language and the content of the knowledge), and nearly all the data on normal development have been collected from mainstream students (Westby, 1990). If students come from a highly literate background, have been exposed at home and school to a variety of literate text genres, and have had opportunities to participate in literate text activities, yet perform below other students of similar background on language activities in the classroom, the students may have a language learning disability. If, however, students come from a home where they have encountered minimal literacy and have not participated in extended monologue or literate style discourse, or if they come from any nondominant cultural group having values, beliefs, and communication patterns that differ from the mainstream, it is difficult to determine if the students are language disabled or are simply reflecting their past experiences with language. Many of the characteristics of texts of true language learning disabled students (associative organization, simple syntax, intonation to carry meaning, ambiguous reference) are also characteristics of the oral-style texts of students from other than mainstream cultures.

To succeed in school, students must be able to comprehend and produce a literate, topic-centered narrative. They must understand the structural organization and thematic content of texts that students are expected to read. *Teachers and speech-language pathologists should not be forced into determining if a student is "truly learning disabled" before providing assistance in learning the social and academic texts of school.* Although it may be impossible to determine which students are "truly learning disabled," it is not impossible to determine which students are not using the social and academic texts of the classroom. Children who do not exhibit the text characteristics documented for normally developing mainstream students are at risk for academic difficulties. All students lacking the social and academic texts of school should be assisted in acquiring them. This requires that all professionals who understand issues in language learning work together.

Changing Research Paradigms

Understanding and assessing discourse in culturally diverse populations and providing effective programs require methodological changes (see Lahey & Bloom, chap. 13). The usual quantitative language analyses (e.g., vocabulary size, syntactic complexity) are insufficient for gathering and interpreting data on discourse variations, and the traditional clinical interaction models are insufficient for developing communicative competence (Silliman & Wilkinson, 1991; chaps. 2, 6). To understand discourse variations and to implement appropriate programs, language specialists need a *thick description* (a term used by anthropologists to refer to detailed descriptions of all aspects of an environment) of the discourse and an understanding of how the discourse developed and is used.

Qualitative Methodology. Schools have not traditionally used thick description to understand student performance. Schools still tend to rely on quantitative, standardized testing approaches to qualify students for special services and to evaluate students' responses to these services. Gradually, schools are becoming aware of the incomplete and often inaccurate information of the quantitative paradigm (Eisner & Peshkin, 1990; Fetterman, 1988). A number of qualitative paradigms, which rely on thick descriptions, are finding their way into educational research. Qualitative approaches are not totally new; they have been used in anthropology and sociology for some time. Patton (1990) discussed a variety of qualitative approaches that are currently in use. Each qualitative approach asks different questions and uses different data. Each approach has something to offer professionals attempting to understand the discourse abilities of learning disabled and culturally different students in schools. Qualitative methodology provides multiple perspectives on text abilities.

For example, *ethnography,* a methodology developed in anthropology, assumes there is a culture for any behavior observed. *Culture* is defined as the collection of behavior patterns and beliefs that constitute "standards for deciding what is, standards for deciding what can be, standards for deciding how one feels about it, standards for deciding what to do about it, and standards for deciding how to go about doing it" (Goodenough, 1971, pp. 21–22). Schools represent a significant component of mainstream culture (Nelson, chap. 4). Ethnography asks "What is the culture of this group of people?" Observation and interviews are the source of data. Ethnography is useful in discovering the culture of the home, playground, therapy session, and the classroom and what social and academic texts students must understand and perform to function adequately within these environments. Cultural differences should always be understood when applying many of the observational suggestions presented by Silliman and Wilkinson in Chapter 6.

Another approach, *ethnomethodology,* which arose from the field of sociology, asks "How do people make sense of their everyday activities so as to behave in socially acceptable ways" (Wallace & Wolf, 1980)? Its goal is to determine what a complete stranger would have to learn to become a routinely functioning member of a group, a program, or a culture. Like ethnographers, ethnomethodologists conduct observations and interviews. They go a step farther, however, by conducting "experiments" in which they violate the scene by doing something that disrupts the normal flow of an activity and watching how people deal with this disruption. Learning disabled and culturally different students often experience problems in educational and social encounters because they unknowingly violate rules of behavior in the culture. Knowing what to do is not sufficient; one must also know what not to do. Ethnomethodological procedures can provide insight into the nature of the problems that learning disabled and culturally different students experience participating in the school environment. How do their language and behavior patterns violate the expectations of teachers and peers and result in their referral to special education or speech/language therapy?

Culture is based on a shared set of symbols. *Symbolic interactionism,* which arose from social psychology, asks "What common set of symbols and understandings have emerged to give meaning to people's interactions?" (Blumer, 1969; Mead, 1934). This approach places great emphasis on the importance of meaning and interpretation by the people involved and in so doing is a reaction to behavioristic and mechanistic stimulus–response psychology. Symbolic interactionism's premises include the following: (1) Humans act toward things on the basis of the meanings that the things have for them; (2) the meanings of things arise out of the social interactions one has with others; and (3) interactions with others depend on value and belief systems. Students' interpretations of a task and their own abilities will affect their performance (Athey & Holmes, 1969; Covington & Omelich, 1979; Myers & Paris, 1978). Professionals need to understand how students interpret the tasks they are given and the behavior of teachers and fellow students and how culture and learning disabilities affect a student's acquisition of the mainstream set of symbols.

Language assessment has generally looked only at the student—perhaps in a naturalistic context—but still only at the student. Students do not exist in isolation. They must communicate with peers in and out of the school environment; they must communicate with a variety of people within the school environment; they must communicate with a different set of people in their homes; and they must communicate with another set of people in their community. Understanding students requires an understanding of the nested set of systems in which they live and how these various systems have an impact on their behavior. *Systems theory* asks "How and why does a system function as a whole?" (Bronfenbrenner, 1979; Nelson, chap. 4). Systems theory is becoming increasingly important in dealing with and understanding real-world complexities, viewing things as whole entities embedded in a larger context. Holistic thinking is central to systems theory. A system is a whole that is greater than and different from its parts. The parts are so interconnected that one cannot deal with simple cause and effect (Lincoln & Guba, 1985). Changes in one part of the system lead to changes in all aspects of the system. The parts cannot be added in a linear way to achieve a whole. A system cannot be understood by an analysis of its parts. Systems theory is quickly being employed in the development of the Individual Family Service Plan (IFSP) required by Public Law 99–457 that provides funding to states to serve the birth-to-three population (Dunst, Trivette, Hamby, & Pollock, 1990; Trout & Foley, 1989). PL 99–457 requires that the plan developed for the handicapped child be developed with and for the child's family as well as for the child. To do so requires not only an understanding of the needs and resources of the child but also of the child's family and the community and region within which they live. Systems theory research needs to be applied to the school-age child. What types of communication are used in the parts of the system? How do the systems facilitate or inhibit students' performance? How do students function in different aspects of the system, and how can aspects of the students' home and community systems be used to facilitate success within the academic system?

Traditional assessment and intervention approaches have relied on linear cause–effect models. Deficits are identified as causes of the disability; these causes are treated, and supposedly changed, which should result in improvements in the student. People and the systems within which they live, however, often do not function in orderly, predictable ways. Dealing with a child, a family, or a school system may feel like dealing with chaos because there is little apparent organization to the systems. *Chaos theory,* or nonlinear dynamics, which has arisen out of physics and the natural sciences, asks "What is the underlying order, if any, of disorderly phenomena?" (Gleick, 1987). Chaos theory acknowledges that behavior cannot be explained on the basis of a linear string of cause–effect relationships. Chaos research is itself highly quantitative, but its assumptions can give us a new way of thinking about what we observe, how we observe, and what we know as a result of our observations. Chaos theory is beginning to expand beyond the natural sciences. It has the potential to give social scientists permission to feel comfortable describing nonlinear interventions and not to feel the need to impose a false order on observations. Chaos theory can allow us to find the predictability in the unpredictability of human behavior.

These holistic, interactive, qualitative approaches to research represent a paradigm shift away from the discrete point, quantitative, linear, and stimulus–response paradigms. Kuhn (1970) maintained that each paradigm shift produces a consequent shift in what are perceived as problems and as legitimate problem solutions. The transition from one paradigm to another is not achieved by a series of small cumulative changes. Rather, it is a reconstruction of the field from a new zeitgeist, a reconstruction that changes some of the field's most elementary theoretical principles as well as many of its goals and methods. New paradigms give professionals a different view of the world and the people in it. The traditional quantitative, ethnocentric approach to language learning disabilities will not serve teachers and clinicians well in understanding the language learning of culturally diverse students. If practitioners approach culturally diverse groups with predetermined concepts and explanations, they will overlook and even misinterpret data.

The Vygotsky Link. All of these qualitative methodologies involve a social–cultural perspective on understanding human behavior. Feldman (1989) stated, "we make the world not with boards, but with symbols, and the central cognitive task of childhood is the task of learning how to make worlds, chiefly with the language tools of culture" (p. 106). Social–cultural interactions direct children's cognitive and linguistic development.

Vygotsky's work (1962, 1978) provides a means of uniting the study of culturally organized experience with the study of cognitive/linguistic development. Several authors of this text also discussed his approach. Silliman and Wilkinson (chap. 2) and Palincsar and her colleagues (chap. 5) focused on Vygotsky's concept of collaboration between adults and children in the learning process. They used Vygotsky's work to show how one begins to understand a learner's potential. Van Kleeck (chap. 3) also discussed Vygotsky's work by commenting that "every function in a child's cultural development appears twice, first on a social level, later on an individual level."

Vygotsky denied the strict separation of individuals from their social environments. Instead, individuals and society are interactive components of a system, and cognitive and linguistic development are treated as the process of acquiring culture. Vygotsky referred to his approach as *sociocultural* or *sociohistorical.* Children's development cannot be understood by studying the children alone; one must also study the world within which the children live. Vygotsky adds that the "levels of generalization in a child correspond strictly to the levels in the development of social interaction. Any new level in the child's generalization abilities signifies a new level in the possibility for social interaction" (Vygotsky, 1956, p. 432, cited in Wertsch, 1983, p. 26). The greater children's exposure to social interaction, the greater their cognitive/linguistic development, and the greater their cognitive/linguistic development, the greater their potential for socialization.

Consequently, the study of culture, cognition, and language must incorporate the study of both the systems of social relations and internal cognitive activity. Leont'ev, founder with Vygotsky and Luria of the sociohistorical school, proposed " . . .if we removed human activity from the system of social relationships and social life, it would not exist . . . the human individual's activity is a system in the system of social relations" (Leont'ev, 1981, pp. 46–47, cited in Wertsch, 1985, p. 151). Human behavior does not exist outside of social relations.

As noted by the authors in Part 2 of this text, Vygotsky (1962) proposed that social contact facilitates children's development of cognitive processes in two ways: (1) Joint activities permit displaying, sharing, and practicing of cognitive processes so children can modify their current mode of performing. (2) In joint activities, adults or more advanced peers lighten the immediate task by assuming a metacognitive control and monitoring of the activity. In this way children learn not only the content of their culture, but they also learn how to learn, how to display their knowledge in culturally appropriate ways, and how to use metacognitive behaviors to control and monitor their performance on tasks. Children learn when they are assisted in performing activities within their zone of proximal development (ZPD). (See Palincsar et al., chap. 5, for a definition of "zone of proximal development" from Vygotsky, 1978. Also see Silliman & Wilkinson, chap. 6.)

Popular schema theory is compatible with the Russian ideas of development. Nelson (1981), discussing mechanisms of schema acquisition, maintained that schemata are built up from recurrent events occurring in social contexts; ". . . young children's scripts are initially acquired within contexts that are highly structured for them by adults" (p. 106). The work of researchers using the philosophical ideas of Vygotsky and the methods of ethnography, ethnomethodology, and symbolic interactionism has provided new understanding of the nature of discourse and the social–cultural variations in discourse.

Understanding and Assessing Text Diversity

Poor performance on standardized testing or on classroom academic tasks should not be viewed as a conclusive basis for placement in a special education program for communicatively handicapped/learning disabled students. Professionals can employ qualitative methodological approaches in prereferral strategies to avoid inappropriate referral and placement of culturally different students in special education (Garcia & Ortiz, 1988). By understanding how culture may affect students' language patterns, by examining the nature of the instruction that is provided, and by developing ecologically valid assessment processes, professionals can modify program strategies to accommodate students' strengths and needs.

Professionals involved in the education of culturally different students need to understand how cultural variations in texts affect school performance. They must be able to recognize cultural variations in text genres and text structure, content, and style, and they must be able to use this knowledge to attempt to determine if students' texts reflect cultural discourse styles or if they reflect language disorders. Successful evaluation and programming require understanding of the culture of the home and school. Professionals need to develop ecologically valid assessment procedures to elicit naturalistic language samples and to develop culturally sensitive intervention strategies. This will require using qualitative methodology—observing and interviewing teachers and students and their families—to develop thick descriptions of the communicative culture of home and school. The nature of the social texts that takes place in the classroom must be documented. For example, professionals must ask What is the structure of teacher-led lessons? What types of questions are asked? How do students get a turn? What is considered disruptive behavior? How do teachers deal with disruptive behavior? What types of responses are acceptable or unacceptable? Nelson (chap. 4) and Silliman and Wilkinson (chaps. 2, 6) provide additional information in these areas.

The academic text content must also be analyzed. What subject matter is presented? How familiar is the subject matter? How contextualized-decontextualized is the content? That is, is learning of the content supported by hands-on activities, field trips, and visuals, or must the content be learned from language alone? What text genres and text structures are used in classroom textbooks? What background knowledge is assumed by the textbooks?

It is also important to learn how students view the social and academic discourse of school. Are they uncomfortable participating in the social texts? Do they think participating may draw undue attention to them and alienate them from their peer group? How do they interpret the teacher's behavior? What do students think they must do to succeed in school? In developing intervention strategies, it is also helpful to know about the students' ecological systems. What support systems do students have? In what systems do they communicate—home, street corner, playground, church? What are their roles in these systems? How do different components of the system relate to each other? Is there a history of friction between the elements of the system?

Evaluation of text abilities of students may require eliciting a variety of texts having different functions and genres, using stimulus materials that reflect the experiences and values of the students' cultures, and for some individuals, collecting narratives in peer-group story-telling sessions. By understanding the distinction between language disorders and language differences, professionals can value the discourse abilities of culturally different students and foster the students' self-esteem; and by understanding how students' oral and written texts may differ from those of the school, professionals can facilitate students' acquisition of the literate text structures and styles required for academic success. For students from culturally diverse backgrounds, the determination of language learning problems cannot be made on the basis of a one-time evaluation. An evaluation of text abilities should be used only to document language abilities at a point in time, not to diagnose disability. Over time, text evaluations can be conducted to document students' development. Comparisons can be made among students of similar backgrounds who began at similar points. Those students who exhibit minimal or very slow change may have true language learning disabilities.

Facilitating Social and Academic School Texts

How can students with deficits or differences in text language be helped to acquire the social and academic texts of schools? One way is to use the methods by which normal mainstream students have acquired these skills. Such children have learned their discourse patterns through negotiated conversations with adults and more advanced peers. Vygotsky's concept of a ZPD, discussed also by Palincsar et al. (chap. 5) and others, provides a framework for facilitating children's language development. By using a variety of interactive teaching methods, in which students are supported in communicative interactions, students can learn the social and academic texts of schools. At least two major aspects of text development must be considered: (1) development of relevant content schema knowledge and (2) development of the structure and style of a variety of text genres.

Developing Content Schema Knowledge. Reading researchers have been particularly sensitive to the necessity of developing students' schema knowledge. Students cannot comprehend and produce texts if they do not possess the necessary schema knowledge. Before presenting textual information, adults need to determine what students know about the topic. The Pre-Reading Plan (PREP) (Langer, 1982) is useful in evaluating students' content knowledge. The PREP technique (which is also discussed by Blachowicz in chap. 11) consists of three steps:

1. Initial association with the concept: The adult asks the children to brainstorm about the concept by asking, "What do you think about when I say . . . ?"
2. Reflections on initial associations: After all the children are finished giving their responses, the teacher asks each of them, "What made you think of . . . ?"
3. Reformulation of knowledge: After all the children have responded in step 2, the adult asks, "Based on our discussion, do you have any new ideas about . . . ?"

In initiating and guiding the discussion, adults can ask specific questions and model possible responses as prompts for students who do not respond to the general questions. The nature of the students' responses gives insights into their level of knowledge about the topic. Students who give tangential associations or word sound-alike responses have little knowledge of the topic. Students who give appropriate examples or attributes of the idea have some knowledge. Students who give precise definitions, analogies, or link the concept to a superordinate concept have much knowledge about the topic. For students with little or some knowledge, adults should engage the students in activities or further discussion that will increase their schema knowledge before introducing the academic text. (See chap. 11 for specific examples.)

Developing Genres, Structures, and Style. The only way to acquire the social and academic texts of schools is to participate in the texts. Just as one would not expect a two-and-one-half-year-old to tell a story without assistance, one should also not expect a school-age student to be able to engage in the social and academic texts of school without supportive scaffolding (as per Silliman & Wilkinson, chap. 2). Intervention should not be a one-sided process—school personnel need to learn about the students' communication patterns in their homes and communities as much as students need to learn the schools' communication patterns.

Heath (1982a) described how knowledge of the communication patterns of the community and the communication requirements of the school were used to develop students' use of the social and academic texts of schools. Teachers in a community called Trackton began to use question types in their lessons that were characteristic of the types of questions children heard at home. Rather than asking for identification of specific objects or attributes of objects, which are typical of school lessons, the teachers asked questions about what was happening and what something was like or what it reminded students of. With these familiar questions, students began to participate in the social discourse of the classroom.

Yet students needed to be able to handle the usual school texts. Teachers taped some of the oral lessons. After class, teachers added to the tapes the specific types of questions that were required in school—labels, definitions, categorizations. Answers to these questions were provided by children adept at answering these types of questions. Class members then used the tapes in learning centers. Heath suggested that students were drawn to the learning centers because they could hear themselves giving responses similar to those in their community. In addition, they benefitted from hearing the kinds of questions and answers used in classroom discourse. Learning these strategies from tapes was less threatening than acquiring them in the classroom activities, where other students dominated the student–teacher interaction. Gradually, teachers asked specific Trackton students to help them prepare questions and answers to add to the tape. Trackton students then heard themselves responding to classroom discourse.

A speech-pathologist for a Pueblo Indian tribe in the Southwest provided a similar activity. She had elders of the tribe tape-record their story telling and draw pictures to go along with the stories on the tapes. She then worked with the elders to develop questions that could be asked about the stories. The children listened to the tapes and responded to the questions in the learning center.

Schools can enlist parents to assist their children in developing the school texts. A teacher and a speech-pathologist in a Southwestern city made visits to the homes of children in their program. They conducted informal ethnographic interviews to discover the families' values, beliefs, and activities and their goals for their children. Although many of the families had minimal experience with schools and had limited literacy skills, they all wanted their children to be able to read and write and be successful in school. The school staff enlisted their assistance in helping their children achieve the goal of reading. They explained to the families that reading stories to their children would help them become readers. The teacher and speech-pathologist developed a sequential series of "book report" forms to guide the parents in how to talk with their children about books. Children checked books out of the classroom library. Parents read the stories and then asked the one or two questions that were on the book report form. Questions on the book report forms followed the developmental sequence noted by Snow and Goldfield (1981) mentioned earlier in this paper. Each book report form addressed only one concept. Early forms required only labeling of pictures. Later forms required sequential retelling of some activities in the book, then discussion of cause–effect reactions (why certain things happened), how characters felt about events in the stories, problems in the stories, and how the problems were solved. In this manner parents were introduced to the mainstream episodic structure of narratives. A side effect of the project was that not only did the children become literate, but parents reported that their own reading skills improved, and several of them returned to school to obtain their graduation equivalency degrees.

Children can provide scaffolding for other children. Mounting data support collaborative learning and peer tutoring programs (Johnson, Johnson, Holubec, & Roy, 1984; Kagan, 1986; Sharan, 1990). Cooperative learning methods divide the class into small teams whose members are positively dependent on each other. Positive interdependence among teammates is created by task interest and reward structures, which make the achievement of any team member contribute to the rewards of all. Groups are limited to no more than six students—smaller for students new to cooperative learning. The groups are usually heterogeneous in terms of ability and ethnicity. The groups are arranged in circles to facilitate communication. Interdependence is promoted by requiring students to share instructional materials and develop a group product. Each student is assigned a role in the group, such as recorder, encourager, observer, or checker to ensure involvement. Adults model collaborative skills of communication and monitor students' behavior for any problems that arise with the task or the collaborative effort.

To be independent learners, students must eventually be able to comprehend and produce school texts without scaffolding support. The Kamehameha Program for Native Hawaiian students has used qualitative methodologies to develop an educational model that employs Vygotskian principles in curriculum strategies (Tharp & Gallimore, 1988). Staff have used qualitative approaches to gain understanding of children's cultural value systems and communicative interaction patterns. Teachers employ the children's values and interactional styles in lessons and provide a continuum of discourse teaching strategies that move children through stages of the ZPD from assisted, to self-directed, to unassisted automatized learning, and then to a higher level task, which again requires assistance. Initially, students are assisted in tasks by teachers or more capable students, who provide language scaffolds to guide task completion. Gradually, children develop the activity rules and language to use self-directed speech to complete the activity. With experience, the activity becomes automatized, and children no longer consciously think about how to perform it. The students are then ready to move to another higher cognitive task for which they will again require assistance to perform.

These steps are repeated through five components of the curriculum that involve increasingly decontextualized levels of text comprehension and production. The first component, called *concept/experience,* involves group discussion about concrete objects and events. In the *word play* component, pictures, posters, and charts are used for discussion. Word play is a transition stage that acquaints the children with meaningful contextualized print. In the third component, the *language-experience approach,* children dictate stories about a joint experience or activity, the teacher transcribes the stories on the chalkboard or chart paper, and the stories are used to introduce reading principles. The fourth component, the *experience text relationship,* involves developing comprehension of printed narrative texts by weaving of new school concepts with concepts of everyday life. The final component, the *concept-text application,* deals with the transition to complex expository text. Students must be able to summarize, synthesize, and speculate about the text and apply knowledge gained in follow-up projects such as a written report or a science project. The Kamehameha Program acknowledges the children's cultural language patterns and provides scaffolding support within students' ZPDs to provide a transition for them to independent functioning with the variety of texts required in school. Although the specific teacher–child interaction patterns vary across cultures, this basic framework could be applied to students from many cultures to assisting them in acquiring the genres, structures, and styles of school discourse.

SUMMARY

Changing times require changing paradigms. Professionals must acquire new data to understand the increasingly diverse populations of the United States. Teachers and clinicians must use new paradigms to development ecologically valid assessment procedures and culturally appropriate intervention strategies that will ensure all children the opportunity to reach their potential.

REFERENCES

Abrams, R. D. (1977). *Conflict resolution in children's storytelling: An application of Erikson's theory and the conflict enculturation model.* Unpublished doctoral dissertation. Columbia University, New York.

Abrams, D. M., & Sutton-Smith B. (1977). The development of the trickster in children's narrative. *Journal of American Folklore, 90,* 29–47.

Albert, R. (1986). Communication and attributional differences between Hispanics and Anglo-Americans. In Y. Y. Kim (Ed.), *Interethnic communication.* Newbury Park, CA: Sage.

American Council on Education. (1988). *One-third of a nation.* Washington, DC: American Council on Education.

Ames, L. (1966). Children's stories. *Genetic Psychology Monographs, 73,* 337–396.

Applebee, A. (1978). *The child's concept of story.* Chicago: University of Chicago Press.

Aristotle, (1952). Poetics. In *The works of Aristotle* (Vol. 2). Chicago: Encyclopedia Britannica. [Reprinted from W. D. Ross (Ed. and Trans.), *The works of Aristotle* (p. 129). New York: Oxford University Press]

Athey, I. J., & Holmes, J. A. (1969). *Reading success and personality characteristics in junior high school students.* Berkeley: University of California Press.

Baker, L., & Brown, A. (1984). Metacognitive skills and reading. In P. D. Pearson (Ed.), *Handbook of reading research.* New York: Longman.

Barlund, D. C. (1975). *Public and private self in Japan and the United States: Communicative styles of two cultures.* Tokyo, Simul.

Basso, E. (1987). *In favor of deceit.* Tucson: University of Arizona Press.

Bates, E. (1976). *Language and context: The development of pragmatics.* New York: Academic Press.

Bates, E. (1988). *From first words to grammar.* Cambridge, UK: Cambridge University Press.

Bauman, R. (1975). Verbal art as performance. *American Anthropologist, 77,* 290–311.

Bellugi, U., & Klima, E. (1966). Syntactic regularities in the speech of children. In J. Lyons & R. Wales (Eds.), *Psycholinguistic papers.* Edinburgh: Edinburgh University Press.

Berelson, B. (1971). *Content analysis in communication research.* New York: Hafner.

Black, J. B. (1985). An exposition on understanding expository text. In B. K. Britton & J. B. Black (Eds.), *Understanding expository text.* Hillsdale, NJ: Erlbaum.

Bloom, L. (1970). *Language development: Form and function in emerging grammars.* Cambridge, MA: MIT Press.

Blumer, H. (1969). *Symbolic interactionism.* Englewood Cliffs, NJ: Prentice-Hall.

Boggs, S. T. (1985). *Speaking relating and learning: A study of Hawaiian children at home and school.* Norwood, NJ: Ablex.

Bohannon, J. N., & Warren-Leubecker, A. (1993). Theoretical approaches to language acquisition. In J. B. Gleason (Ed.), *The development of language* (3rd ed.). New York: Merrill/Macmillan.

Botvin, G. J., & Sutton-Smith, B. (1977). The development of structural complexity in children's fantasy. *Developmental Psychology, 13,* 377–388.

Brady, M. K. (1984). *Some kind of power: Navajo children's skinwalker narratives.* Salt Lake City: University of Utah Press.

Brain, M. D. (1963). The ontogeny of English phrase structure: The first phase. *Languages, 39,* 1–13.

Bright, W. (1982). Poetic structure in oral narrative. In D. Tannen (Ed.), *Spoken and written language.* Norwood, NJ: Ablex.

Brinton, B., & Fujiki, M. (1989). *Conversational management with language-impaired children.* Rockville, MD: Aspen.

Britton, B. K., & Black, J. (1985). *Understanding expository text.* Hillsdale, NJ: Lawrence Erlbaum.

Bronfrenbrenner, U. (1979). *The ecology of human development: Experiments by nature and design.* Cambridge, MA: Harvard University Press.

Brown, G., & Yule, G. (1983). *Discourse analysis.* Cambridge, UK: Cambridge University Press.

Brown, R., & Fraser, C. (1963). The acquisition of syntax. In C. N. Cofer & B. Musgrave (Eds.), *Verbal behavior and learning: Problem and processes.* New York: McGraw-Hill.

Bruner, J. (1974). From communication to language: A psychological perspective. *Cognition, 3,* 255–287.

Bruner, J. (1985). Narrative and paradigmatic modes of thought. In E. Eisner (Ed.), *Learning and teaching: The ways of knowing.* Chicago: University of Chicago Press.

Bruner, J. (1986). *Actual minds, possible worlds.* Cambridge, MA: Harvard University Press.

Cazden, C. (1983). Adult assistance to language development: Scaffolds, models, and direct instruction. In R. Parker & F. Davis (Eds.), *Developing literacy.* Newark, DE: International Reading Association.

Cazden, C. (1988). *Classroom discourse: The language of teaching and learning.* Portsmouth, NH: Heinemann.

Chafe, W. (1990). Some things that narratives tell us about the mind. In B. K. Britton & A. D. Pellegrini (Eds.), *Narrative thought and narrative language.* Hillsdale, NJ: Erlbaum.

Chomsky, N. (1965). *Aspects of a theory of syntax.* Cambridge, MA: MIT Press.

Clancy, P. M. (1986). Acquiring communicative style in Japanese. In B. B. Schieffelin & E. Ochs (Eds.), *Language socialization across cultures.* Cambridge, UK: Cambridge University Press.

Clarke, J. H. (1990). *Patterns of thinking: Integrating learning skills in content teaching.* Boston: Allyn & Bacon.

Cole, M. (1985). The zone of proximal development: Where culture and cognition create each other. In J. V. Wertsch (Ed.), *Culture communication and cognition.* Cambridge, UK: Cambridge University Press.

Connor, U. (1987). Argumentative patterns in student essays: Cross-cultural differences. In U. Connor & R. Kaplan (Eds.), *Writing across cultures: Analysis of 12 texts.* Reading, MA: Addison-Wesley.

Connor, U., & Kaplan, R. (1987). *Writing across languages: Analysis of 12 texts.* Reading, MA: Addison-Wesley.

Connor, U., & McCogg, P. (1987). A contrastive study of English prose paraphrases. In U. Connor & R. Kaplan (Eds.), *Writing across cultures: Analysis of 12 texts.* Reading, MA: Addison-Wesley.

Cooley, R. (1979). Spokes in a wheel: A linguistic and rhetorical analysis of Native American public discourse. *Proceedings of the Fifth Annual Meeting of the Berkeley Linguistics Society* (pp. 552–557).Berkeley: University of California.

Covington, M. V., & Omelich, C. L. (1979). It's best to be able and virtuous too: Student and teacher evaluative responses to successful effort. *Journal of Educational Psychology, 71,* 688–700.

Davis, E. A. (1937). The development of linguistic skill in twins, singletons with siblings, and only children from five to ten years. *Child Welfare Monographs,* No. 14, Minneapolis: University of Minnesota Press.

DePaulo, B. M., & Jordan, A. (1982). Age changes in deceiving and detecting deceit. In R. S. Feldman (Ed.), *Development of nonverbal behavior in children.* New York: Springer-Verlag.

Domino, G., & Hannah, M. (1987). A comparative analysis of social values in Chinese and American children. *Journal of Cross-Cultural Psychology, 18,* 58–77.

Dundes, A. (1980). *Interpreting folklore.* Bloomington, IN: University of Indiana Press.

Dunst, C. J., Trivette, C. M., & Cross, A. H. (1988). *Enabling and empowering families.* Cambridge, MA: Brookline Books.

Dunst, C. J., Trivette, C. M., Hamby, D., & Pollock, B. (1990). Family systems correlates of the behavior of young children with handicaps. *Journal of Early Intervention, 14*(3), 204–218.

Eggington, W. G. (1987). Written academic discourse in Korean: Implications for effective communication. In U. Connor & R. Kaplan (Eds.), *Writing across cultures: Analysis of L2 texts.* Reading, MA: Addison-Wesley.

Eisner, E. W., & Peshkin, A. (1990). *Qualitative inquiry in education.* New York: Teachers College Press.

Englert, A. S., Raphael, T. E., Anderson, L. M., Gregg, S. L., & Anthony, H. M. (1989). *Learning Disabilities Quarterly, 5*(1), 5–24.

Erickson, F. (1984). Rhetoric, anecdote, and rhapsody: Coherence strategies in a conversation among black American adolescents. In D. Tannen (Ed.), *Coherence in spoken and written discourse.* Norwood, NJ: Ablex.

Feagans, L., & Short, E. (1984). Developmental differences in the comprehension and production of narratives by reading disabled and normally achieving children. *Child Development, 55,* 1727–1736.

Feldman, C. F. (1989). Monologue as problem-solving narrative. In K. Nelson (Ed.), *Narratives from the crib.* Cambridge, MA: Harvard University Press.

Fetterman, D. M. (1988). *Qualitative approaches to evaluation and education.* New York: Praeger.

Garcia, S. B., & Ortiz, A. A. (1988). Preventing inappropriate referrals of language minority students to special education. *New focus.* Weaton, MD: The National Clearing House for Bilingual Education.

Gee, J. (1985). The narrativization of experience in the oral style. *Journal of Education, 167,* 9–35.

Gee, J. (1989). Two styles of narrative construction and their linguistic and educational implications. *Discourse Processes, 12,* 287–307.

Gee, J., & Michaels, S. (1989). Discourse styles: Variations across speakers, situations, and tasks. *Discourse Processes, 12,* 263–265.

Gleick, J. (1987). *Chaos: Making a new science.* New York: Penguin.

Go, M. J. (1984). Quantitative content analysis. In W. Gudykunst & Y. Y. Kim (Eds.), *Methods for intercultural communication research.* Beverly Hills, CA: Sage.

Goodenough, W. (1971). *Culture, language, and society.* Reading, MA: Addison-Wesley.

Grabe, W. (1987). Contrastive rhetoric and text-type research. In U. Connor & R. Kaplan (Eds.), *Writing across cultures: Analysis of 12 texts.* Reading, MA: Addison-Wesley.

Green, J. L., Weade, R., & Graham, K. (1988). Lesson construction and student participation: A sociolinguistic analysis. In J. L. Green & J. O. Harker (Eds.), *Multiple perspective analysis of classroom discourse.* Norwood, NJ: Ablex.

Hardy, B. (1977). Narrative as a primary act of mind. In M. Meek, A. Warlow, & G. Barton (Eds.), *The cool web: The pattern of children's reading.* London: Bodley Head.

Heath, S. B. (1982a). Questioning at home and at school: A comparative study. In G. Spindler (Ed.), *Doing the ethnography of schooling.* New York: Holt, Rinehart & Winston.

Heath, S. B. (1982b). What no bedtime story means: Narrative skills at home and school. *Language in Society, 11*(2), 49–76.

Heath, S. B. (1983). *Ways with words.* Cambridge: Cambridge University Press.

Heath, S. B. (1986a). Sociocultural contexts of language development. In *Beyond language.* Los Angeles: Evaluation and Dissemination and Assessment Center.

Heath, S. B. (1986b). Talking a cross-cultural look at narratives. *Topics in Language Disorders, 7*(1), 84–94.

Heath, S. B. (1987). The literate essay: Using ethnography to explode myths. In J. A. Langer (Ed.), *Language, literacy, and culture: Issues of society and schooling.* Norwood, NJ: Ablex.

Highwater, J. (1981). *The primal mind: Vision and reality in Indian America.* Harper & Row: New York.

Indrasuta, C. (1988). Narrative styles in the writing of Thai and American students. In A. C. Purves (Ed.), *Writing across languages and cultures.* Newbury Park, CA: Sage.

Jacobs, M. (1959). *The content and style of an oral literature.* Chicago: University of Chicago Press.

Jett-Simpson, M., & Masland, S. (1993). Girls are no dodo birds! Exploring gender equity issues in the language arts classroom. *Language Arts, 70,* 104–108.

Johnson, J. (1982). Narratives: A new look at communication problems in language disorders. *Language Speech and Hearing Services in Schools, 13,* 144.

Johnson, D. W., Johnson, R. T., Holubec, E. J., & Roy, P. (1984). *Circles of learning.* Alexandria, VA: Association for Supervision and Curriculum Development.

Johnstone, B. (1989). *Community and context: How women and men construct their worlds in conversational narration.* Paper presented at Women in America: Legacies of race and ethnicity. Georgetown University: Washington, DC.

Kagan, S. (1986). Cooperative learning and sociocultural factors in schooling. In *Beyond language.* Los Angeles: Evaluation, Dissemination and Assessment Center.

Kamler, B. (1993). Constructing gender in the process writing classroom. *Language Arts, 70,* 93–103.

Kaplan, R. (1966). Cultural thought patterns in intercultural education. *Language Learning, 16,* 1–20.

Kaplan, R. (1987). Cultural thought patterns revisited. In U. Connor & R. Kaplan (Eds.), *Writing across languages: Analysis of 12 texts.* Reading, MA: Addison-Wesley.

Kintch, W., & Green, E. (1978). The role of culture-specific schemata in the comprehension and recall of stories. *Discourse Processes, 1,* 1–13.

Kluckhohn, F., & Strodtbeck, F. (1961). *Variations in value orientations.* New York: Row, Peterson.
Kuhn, T. (1970). *The structure of scientific revolutions.* Chicago: University of Chicago Press.
Labov, W. (1972). *Language in the inner city.* Philadelphia: University of Pennsylvania Press.
Langer, J. A. (1982). Facilitating text processing: The elaboration of prior knowledge. In J. A. Langer & M. Smith-Burke (Eds.), *Reader meets author: Bridging the gap.* Newark, DE: International Reading Association.
Leont'ev, A. N. (1981). The problem of activity in psychology. In J. V. Wertsch (Ed.), *The concept of activity in Soviet psychology.* Armonk, NY: Sharpe.
LeVine, R. (1966). *Dreams and deeds.* Chicago: University of Chicago Press.
Lincoln Y., & Guba, E. (1985). *Naturalistic inquiry.* Newbury Park, CA: Sage.
Liebes, T. (1988). Cultural differences in retelling of television fiction. *Critical Studies in Mass Communication, 5*(4), 277–292.
Lystad, M. (1974). *A child's world.* Rockville, MD: National Institute of Mental Health.
Mandler, J. M. (1984). *Stories, scripts and scenes: Aspects of schema theory.* Hillsdale, NJ: Erlbaum.
Maranda, K., & Maranda, P. (1970). *Structural models in folklore and transformational essays.* The Hague: Mouton.
Matsuyama, U. (1983). Can story grammar speak Japanese? *The Reading Teacher, 36,* 666–669.
McCarthy, D. (1954). Language development in children. In L. Carmichael (Ed.), *Manual of child psychology.* New York: Wiley.
McClelland, D. (1958). The use of measures of human motivation in the study of society. In J. Atkinson (Ed.), *Motives in fantasy, action, and society.* Princeton, NJ: Van Nostrand.
McClelland, D. (1971). *Motivational trends in society.* New York: General Learning Press.
McNeill, D. (1970). *The acquisition of language: The study of developmental psycholinguistics.* New York: Harper & Row.
Mead, G. (1934). *Mind, self and society.* Chicago: University of Chicago Press.
Mehan, H. (1979). *Learning lessons.* Cambridge: Harvard University Press.
Merritt, D., & Liles, B. (1987). Story grammar ability in children with and without language disorder: Story generation, story retelling, and story comprehension. *Journal of Speech and Hearing Research, 30,* 539–552.
Michaels, S. (1985). Hearing the connections in children's oral and written discourse. *Journal of Education, 167,* 36–56.
Michaels, S., & Collins, J. (1984). Oral discourse styles: Classroom interaction and the acquisition of literacy. In D. Tannen (Ed.), *Coherence in spoken and written discourse.* Norwood, NJ: Ablex.
Myers, M., & Paris, S. G. (1978). Children's metacognitive knowledge about reading. *Journal of Educational Psychology, 70,* 680–690.
Nelson, K. (1981). Social cognition in a script framework. In J. H. Flavell & L. Ross (Eds.), *Social cognitive development.* Cambridge, UK: Cambridge University Press.
Nelson, K. (Ed.). (1989). *Narratives from the crib.* Cambridge, MA: Harvard University Press.
Nicolopoulou, A., & Scales, B. (1990, March). *"Teenage Mutant Ninja Turtles" versus "The prince and the princess:" Gender differences in four-year-olds' stories.* Paper presented at the 11th annual ethnography in education research forum, Philadelphia.
Oller, J. (1979), *Language tests at school.* New York: Longman.
Olson, D., & Astington, J. (1986). Children's acquisition of metalinguistic and metacognitive verbs. In W. Demopoulos & A. Marras (Eds.), *Language learning and concept acquisition.* (pp. 184–199). Norwood, NJ: Ablex.
Ong, W. J. (1982). *Orality and literacy: The technologizing of the word.* New York: Metheun.
Patton, M. Q. (1990). *Qualitative evaluation and research methods.* Newbury Park, CA: Sage.
Peters, A. M. (1983). *The units of language acquisition.* Cambridge: Cambridge University Press.
Peterson, C., & McCabe, A. (1983). *Developmental psycholinguistics: Three ways of looking at a child's narrative.* New York: Plenum.
Peterson, C., & Seligman, M. (1984). *Content analysis of verbatim explanations: The CAVE technique for assessing explanatory style.* Unpublished paper. Department of Psychology, Virginia Institute and State University, Blacksburg, VA.
Peterson, L. H. (1991). Gender and the autobiographical essay: Research perspectives. *College Composition and Communication, 42*(2), 170–183.
Philips, S. (1983). *The invisible culture: Communication in classroom and community on the Warm Springs Indian Reservation.* New York: Longman.
Pitcher, E. G., & Prelinger, E. (1963). *Children tell stories.* New York: International Universities Press.
Polanyi, L. (1985). *Telling the American story.* Norwood, NJ: Ablex.
Prince, C. (1973). *The grammar of stories.* The Hague: Mouton.
Pritchard, R. (1990). The effects of cultural schemata on reading processing strategies. *Reading Research Quarterly, 25,* 273–295.
Propp, V. (1968). *Morphology of the folktale.* Austin, TX: University of Austin Press.
Purvis, A. C. (1988). *Writing across cultures: Issues in contrastive linguistics.* Newbury Park, CA: Sage.
Radin, P. (1956). *The trickster.* New York: Schocken Books.
Reynolds, R. E., Taylor, M. A., Steffensen, M. A., Shirey, L. L., & Anderson, R. C. (1981). *Cultural schemata and reading*

comprehension. Technical Report No. 201. Urbana: University of Illinois, Center for the Study of Reading.

Ripich, D. & Spinelli, F. (1985). *School discourse strategies*. San Diego, CA: College-Hill Press.

Rosen, B. (1962). Socialization and achievement motivation in Brazil. *American Sociological Review, 27,* 612–624.

Roth, F. P., & Spekman, N. J. (1986). Narrative discourse: Spontaneously generated stories of learning-disabled and normally achieving students. *Journal of Speech and Hearing Disorders, 51,* 8–23.

Salisbury, L. H. (1967). Teaching English to Alaskan natives. *Journal of American Indian Education, 6,* 4–5.

Schieffelin, B. B., & Ochs, E. (1986). *Language socialization across cultures*. Cambridge: New York.

Scollon, R., & Scollon, S. (1981). *Narrative, literacy and face in interethnic communication*. Norwood, NJ: Ablex.

Scollon, R., & Scollon, S. (1984). Cooking it up and boiling it down: Abstracts in Athabaskan children's story retellings. In D. Tannen (Ed.), *Coherence in spoken and written discourse*. Norwood, NJ: Ablex.

Sharan, S. (1990). *Cooperative learning*. New York: Praeger.

Silliman, E., & Wilkinson, L. C. (1991). *Communicating for learning: classroom observation and collaboration*. Rockville, MD: Aspen.

Skinner, B. F. (1957). *Verbal behavior*. New York: Appleton-Century-Crofts.

Snow, C., & Goldfield, B. (1981). Building stories: The emergence of information structures from conversation. In D. Tannen (Ed.), *Analyzing discourse: Text and talk*. Washington, DC: Georgetown University Press.

Soter, A. O. (1988). The second language learner and cultural transfer in narration. In A. C. Purves (Ed.), *Writing across languages and cultures*. Newbury Park, CA: Sage.

Staats, C., & Staats, A. (1957). Meaning established by classical conditioning. *Journal of Experimental Psychology, 54,* 74–80.

Starosta, W. (1984). Qualitative content analysis: A Burkeian perspective. In W. Gudykunst & Y. Y. Kim (Eds.), *Methods for intercultural communication research*. Beverly Hills: Sage.

Steffensen, M. S., Joag-Dev, C., & Anderson, R. C. (1979). A cross-cultural perspective on reading comprehension. *Reading Research Quarterly, 15,* 10–29.

Stein, N., & Glenn, C. (1979). An analysis of story comprehension in elementary school children. In R. O. Freedle (Ed.), *New directions in discourse processing*. Norwood, NJ: Ablex.

Stewart, E. C. (1972). *American cultural patterns*. Yarmouth, ME: Intercultural Press.

Stubbs, M. (1983). *Discourse analysis: The sociolinguistic analysis of natural language*. Chicago: University of Chicago Press.

Tannen, D. (1982a). The oral/literate continuum in discourse. In D. Tannen (Ed.), *Spoken and written language*. Norwood, NJ: Ablex.

Tannen, D. (Ed.) (1982b). *Spoken and written language: Exploring orality and literacy*. Norwood, NJ: Ablex.

Tannen, D. (Ed.) (1984a). *Coherence in spoken and written discourse*. Norwood, NJ: Ablex.

Tannen, D. (1984b). *Conversational style: Analyzing talk among friends*. Norwood, NJ: Ablex.

Tannen, D. (1990). *You just don't understand: Women and men in conversation*. New York: William Morrow.

Templin, M. C. (1957). Certain language skills in children: Their development and interrelationships. *Child Welfare Monographs,* No. 26, Minneapolis: University of Minnesota Press.

Tharp, R. G., & Gallimore, R. (1988). *Rousing minds to life*. Cambridge, UK: Cambridge University Press.

Todorov, T. (1971). The two principles of narrative. *Diacritics,* Fall.

Trout, M., & Foley, G. (1989). Working with families of handicapped infants and toddlers. *Topics in Language Disorders, 10*(1), 57–67.

Tseng, W., & Hsu, J. (1972). The Chinese attitude toward parental authority as expressed in Chinese children's stories. *Archives of General Psychiatry, 26,* 28–34.

Vygotsky, L. (1962). *Thought and language*. Cambridge, MA: MIT Press.

Vygotsky, L. (1978). In M. Cole, V. John-Steiner, S. Scribner, & E. Souberman (Eds. & Trans.). Cambridge: *Mind in society: The development of higher psychological processes*. Cambridge, MA: Harvard University Press.

Wallace, R. A., & Wolf, A. (1980). *Contemporary sociological thought*. Englewood Cliffs, NJ: Prentice-Hall.

Wertsch, J. V. (1983). The role of semiosis in L. S. Vygotsky's theory of human cognition. In B. Brain (Ed.), *The sociogenesis of language and human conduct*. New York: Plenum.

Westby, C. E. (1984). The development of narrative language abilities. In G. P. Wallach & K. G. Butler (Eds.), *Language learning disabilities in school-age children* (pp. 103–127). Baltimore, MD: Williams & Wilkins.

Westby, C. E. (1985). Learning to talk—Talking to learn: Oral–literate language differences. In C. Simon (Ed.), *Communication skills and classroom success: Therapy methodologies for language-learning disabled students*. San Diego: College-Hill.

Westby, C. E. (Ed.) (1986). Narrative discourse: Development and disorder. *Topics in Language Disorders, 7,* 1.

Westby, C. E. (1990). There's no such thing as culture-free testing. *Texas Journal of Audiology and Speech Pathology, 16,* 4–5.

Westby, C. E., Maggart, Z., & Van Dongen, R. (1984). *Oral narratives of students varying in reading ability*. Paper presented at the third international congress for the study of child language, Austin, TX.

Wilcox, K. (1972). Differential socialization in the classroom: Implications for equal opportunity. In G. Spindler (Ed.), *Doing the ethnography of schooling*. New York: Holt, Rinehart & Winston.

Wong, E. (1985). Metacognition and learning disabilities. In D. L. Forrest-Pressley, G. E. MacKinnon, & T. G. Waller (Eds.), *Metacognition, cognition, and human performance.* Orlando, FL: Academic Press.

Worth, S., & Adair, J. (1972). *Through Navajo eyes.* Bloomington: University of Indiana Press.

Wundt, W. (1916). *The elements of folk psychology.* London: Allen & Unwin.

Zimet, S., Wiberg, J., & Blom, G. (1971). Attitudes and values in primers from the U.S. and twelve other countries. *Journal of Social Psychology, 84,* 167–174.

8

A DISCOURSE CONTINUUM FOR SCHOOL-AGE STUDENTS

Impact of Modality and Genre

■ Cheryl M. Scott
Oklahoma State University

As expressed throughout this text, language clinicians and teachers subscribe to the notion that language assessment should be representative and intervention functional. Both goals require an understanding of language variation across a variety of individual, institutional, and family contexts (see Westby, chap. 7; Lahey & Bloom, chap. 13, and other authors in this volume). Sensitivity to language variation has been a guiding force for the past quarter century of child language research; researchers have gone to homes, classrooms, and playgrounds to record children in different settings with different interlocutors. Recent research in discourse analysis and written language has heightened interest even further. As language users of any age, speakers and writers search for the best fit between form and function. Depending on the task, the search involves more or less conscious awareness (see also van Kleeck, chap. 3).

Child language specialists are well versed in the nature of early form–function interactions. For the majority, mere mention of the utterance *mommy sock* conjures up visions of two-year-old Kathryn pointing out her mother's sock (the possession relation), and on another occasion, wanting help putting on her sock (the action relation) (Bloom, 1970). Kathryn did not yet have a sufficient stock of forms to fit with different meanings and functions. In a few short years, however, she was undoubtedly capable of several important contextual adjustments. She probably spoke with less complex grammatical forms when addressing children younger than herself (Shatz & Gelman, 1973). And, if Kathryn had begun telling stories, her narrative form was probably distinguishable from her conversational form, at both sentence and discourse levels.

Specialists may be less knowledgeable about language varieties characteristic of older children and adolescents. Transcripts of preschool language are familiar, but few researchers have studied verbatim accounts of language produced by teenagers, or for that matter, adult dialogue or monologue (e.g., Crystal & Davy, 1975). Developmental schedules and training paradigms for narrative discourse are familiar, but less is known about informational forms of language such as expository, opinion, or procedural text.[1] Language clinicians may be comfortable evaluating spoken language but less comfortable with written language (Wallach & Butler, chap. 1).

The purpose of this chapter is to present information about language varieties encountered and produced by school-age children and adolescents. The underlying premise is the belief that informed language assessment and intervention must be based on an intimate familiarity with the medium. What seems like a simple task, however, turns out to be quite complex, for several reasons. Although readers of this book undoubtedly function at very high levels of literacy, they are not unlike Chomsky's (1965) speaker–hearer who "knows" the language (tacit, implicit knowledge) but does not know the language (explicit knowledge). For instance, language specialists may not appreciate the fact that readers routinely read and comprehend sentences averaging

[1] In this chapter the terms *discourse* and *text* are used interchangeably. Modality (whether spoken or written) is not specified by the use of either term. Both terms refer to a unit of language, larger than a sentence, which shows a common theme as well as local and global cohesion patterns.

twenty-two words that contain several hierarchical levels of embedding. One task, then, is to develop conscious awareness of the forms and functions of higher level language, written and spoken. A second problem is that language facility, for form and function, continues to develop throughout elementary and secondary levels of schooling; however, the changes are slower and more subtle than in preschool children (see Scott, 1988c, for a detailed discussion). Both of these factors, one's lack of explicit knowledge about higher level discourse form and the subtle nature of developmental changes, make it easy to underestimate the significant impact of context on language.

The first section of this chapter outlines broadly the range of discourse types found in the ambient language and considers how discourse genre and modality affect text and sentence level structure. The second section focuses more specifically on functions and forms of language encountered by schoolchildren, and, in turn, the types of language they typically produce in that setting. A third section reviews literature that describes the developmental course of children's knowledge about different discourse genres and modes, as reflected in the linguistic analysis of texts they produce. The final section is concerned with applications of this information to language assessment and intervention. Taken together, the information presented should help language professionals find a better fit between testing and teaching paradigms and the everyday discourse requirements of school-age children and adolescents. The ultimate goals are to avoid teaching things these students already know about language and to find better ways of teaching the things they do not know.

LANGUAGE VARIATION AS A FUNCTION OF GENRE AND MODALITY

Whereas Chomsky (1965) characterized language as an infinite number of sentences, language might also be described as an almost limitless number of distinguishable types of discourse, or genres. In the field of rhetoric, discourse has traditionally been divided into narration, description, argument, and exposition types (Faigley, Cherry, Jolliffe, & Skinner, 1985). In any one of these types, there are many varieties. Within the broad category of narratives, for example, there are countless narrative varieties that differ according to function, setting, and knowledge base (Scott, 1988b; Westby, chap. 7). Thus, a fable told to a child to teach a moral is structured differently from a recount of an event told by a child at the request of an adult, although both could be characterized broadly as narratives. Likewise, expository or informational types of discourse, outlined in Westby, Chapter 7, might be of several broad structural types (e.g., descriptive, sequence, enumerative, cause–effect, compare–contrast, problem–solution) and could be further divided according to several parameters. For example, a page-long compare–contrast answer to an essay question would differ from a longer academic analysis. Even academic expository writing can be shown to vary along a number of continua, as illustrated recently by MacDonald (1989) in her comparison of humanities and social science discourse. Essentially then, the discourse taxonomic pie can be divided into pieces of any size depending on the purpose of the person doing the cutting. Language clinicians and teachers will need to look beyond the broad categories of discourse to discover the many unique characteristics of any one discourse sample.

Discourse occurs in either a spoken or written modality.[2] In recent treatments of discourse, genre and modality are frequently considered together along an oral–literate continuum (e.g., Horowitz & Samuels, 1987; Olson, 1977; Silliman & Wilkinson, chap. 2; Westby, chap. 7). At one end of the continuum is informal, spoken conversational discourse (called *chat* by Brown, Anderson, Shillcock, & Yule, 1984, or *unplanned* spoken language by Danielewicz, 1984). At the other extreme is formal, written academic/analytic discourse. The list of contrastive oral and written features in Table 8–1, adapted from Horowitz and Samuels (1987, p. 9), is typical of many recent descriptions of informal spoken chat, contrasted with formal expository/academic writing. The list highlights genre differences (narrative-like vs. expository-like); situation differences (interactive and contextualized vs. solitary and decontextualized); and form differences (e.g., linear vs. hierarchical). (See

[2]Beyond the obvious difference in medium, the terms *spoken* (oral) and *written language* have been inadequately defined (Horowitz & Samuels, 1987). Some use the terms in a more narrow sense to refer to the *products* of speaking and writing, which are available for analysis. Others use the terms more broadly to include *processes* of listening–speaking and reading–writing, which are more difficult to study. This chapter is concerned largely with spoken and written language *products*.

TABLE 8–1
Spoken and written language contrasts
From "Comprehending Oral and Written Language: Critical Contrasts for Literacy and Schooling" by R. Horowitz and S. J. Samuels, in *Comprehending Oral and Written Language* (p. 9) edited by R. Horowitz and S. J. Samuels, 1987, San Diego, CA: Academic Press. Copyright 1987 by Academic Press. Adapted by permission.

Spoken Language	Written Language
Narrative-like	Expository-like
Action oriented	Idea oriented
Event oriented	Argument oriented
Story oriented	Explanation oriented
Interactive (face-to-face)	Solitary (face-to-text)
Reciprocity between speaker and listener	Limited reciprocity between writer and reader
Shared context	Decontextualized
Implicit (elliptical)	Explicit
Interpersonal	Objective and distanced
Cohesion via paralinguistic cues	Cohesion through lexical cues
Simple linear structures	Complex hierarchical structures
Right branching with limited subordination	Left branching with multiple levels of subordination
Paratactic patterns	Hypotactic patterns
Repetition	Succinctness
Fleeting	Permanent

Silliman & Wilkinson, chap. 2; Palincsar, Brown, & Campione, chap. 5, for additional information on unplanned and planned discourse.)

Although such descriptions highlight important contrasts, there is increasing consensus that such spoken–written characterizations oversimplify, given the considerable overlap and intermingling along the oral–literate continuum. Typical examples are the planned, informational, and sometimes read speech (e.g., a presidential address delivered via TelePrompTer) compared with the chatty, personal letter, which might be written much as it would be spoken. The presidential address, although spoken, lies at the literate end of the continuum, while the written letter is closer to the oral end. Interestingly, the speech delivered by reading the teleprompter has been written but is processed by listening. A reverse example is a deaf college student who reads a spoken lecture in real time (e.g., a classroom closed-captioning system using a court reporter and computer, as described by Haydu & Patterson, 1990). Many additional examples defy the linearity implied, for either product or process, in the attempt to reduce discourse diversity to one continuum. Several examples in the school setting include dialogue journals, discussions about written material, and writing based on language experience approaches to reading. Computer applications, including electronic mail and speech synthesis for word processor writing, further complicate the picture.

Compelling as such examples may be, it is true that spoken and written language frequently serve quite different purposes. The permanency of writing leads to functions not found with spoken language including information storage and summary, labeling, literary form expansion, academic analysis, memory aids, and legal and financial procedures, as Wallach and Butler point out in their introductory chapter. The cases of writing and speaking exactly the same discourse under similar circumstances, for similar purposes, are rare. The relation between speech and writing is complementary; certain genres are *typically* spoken, and certain genres are *typically* written. Hence, it is best to consider genre and modality together, even though it can then be difficult to isolate the structural effects of either one.

Summarizing thus far, the attempt to provide an overview of discourse types and consequent influences on form is challenged on three fronts. First, the number of genres can be very large and new genres continue to be added (others perhaps dropping out) with technological changes. Second, genres do not "line up" in any neat way on an oral–literate continuum, making generalizations tenuous. Finally, the effects of genre and modality are difficult to separate, which is due to the fact that many types of discourse are typically found in only one mode. The remainder of this section outlines two recent lines of research on spoken and written language that bring some clarity to the discussion of form–function interactions.

Multidimensional Variation in Spoken and Written Text

For many years, writing was considered to be a derivative of spoken language, which was thought to be the primary modality (Bloomfield, 1933). Spoken and written language have only recently been treated as independent linguistic systems with important differences as well as similarities. There have been several approaches to the study of spoken and written language differences. Two treatments summarized next are the dimensional approach and the multidimensional approach.

In a dimensional approach, texts are compared along particular situational, functional, or processing parameters, for example, detached/involved, integrated/fragmented, formal/informal, or contextualized/decontextualized (Chafe, 1982; Chafe & Danielewicz, 1987). Having identified such functional distinctions, the linguistic features associated with each dimension are then identified. A case in point is the association of passive voice with detached texts where the mention of a specific agent is not important (e.g., in a science text, sentences such as *Lymph nodes are found in many places* would be common).

Biber's multidimensional approach (1986, 1988) is different in several respects. Previous researchers began with a functional interpretation and then searched for confirming features. Biber used multivariate statistical procedures to identify groups of co-occurring features, which were then interpreted in functional terms. Specifically, Biber's computational program searched for co-occurrences among sixty-seven structural features in a large corpus of spoken and written texts. The analysis revealed six dimensions, summarized in Table 8–2. In the table, each dimension is described generally, and examples of discourse types with high and low values on that dimension are listed. Finally, some of the structural features associated with high and low types are listed.

Biber defined a dimension as a "bundle of linguistic features that co-occur in texts because they work together to mark some common underlying function" (1988, p. 55). For each dimension, Table 8–2 gives examples of types of texts that have high and low values and their co-occurring linguistic structures. Any two genres can be compared by noting their place on the various dimension continua. For example, personal letters have a moderately high value on "involved versus informational," an intermediate value on "narrative versus nonnarrative," a moderately low value on "explicit versus situation-dependent reference," a moderately high value on "overt expression of persuasion," and so on. In a similar manner, values for professional letters could be noted and then compared with personal letters. Because no single dimension adequately describes any genre or comparisons between genres, Biber characterizes his system as multidimensional. Compared with previous unidimensional accounts, the multidimensional analysis is defended as more comprehensive and less a priori (Biber, 1988). As discussed in a later section of this chapter, Biber has recently applied his multidimensional discourse analysis model to the study of oral and literate characteristics of second-, fourth-, and sixth-grade reading materials (1991).

Absolute Differences in Spoken and Written Text

Considerable controversy surrounds the question of whether there are any absolute linguistic differences between spoken and written texts that are independent of genre (i.e., a result solely of speaking or writing the language). A related question is whether one mode is, in general, more complex than the other. Biber (1988) cited the results of his multidimensional analysis as evidence refuting the existence of an absolute dimension. If such a dimension existed, his methodology should have uncovered a set of co-occurring linguistic features that separated all spoken texts from all written texts. In all six dimensions, however, Biber found some overlap of spoken and written genres.

Close examination of Biber's data, however, reveals that three of the six dimensions (1, 3, and 5 in Table 8–2), did a good, albeit not perfect, job of distinguishing spoken and written texts. Spoken texts are typically involved (dimension 1), situation-dependent (dimension 3), and nonabstract (dimension 5). Written texts are typically informational, explicit, and abstract (the opposite end of dimen-

TABLE 8–2
Six dimensions of discourse identified by Biber (1988)

1. **Involved versus Informational**

General Description: Involved texts focus on interpersonal and affective content, using general terms. Produced under real-time constraints, these texts have low informational densities. Informational texts require careful word choice and have higher informational densities.

Very High (Involved) Genres: Face-to-face and telephone conversations.

Moderately High Genres: Personal letters, spontaneous speeches, interviews.

Features: Private verbs *(think, love)*, emphatics (*really*), *that*-deletions, present tense, WH questions, causative subordination (*because*), contractions, generalized and fragmented presentation of content indicated by hedges *(sort of),* discourse particles (*anyway, well*) clausal *and, be* as main verb, pro-verb *do,* pronoun *it,* second-person pronouns.

Very Low (Informational) Genres: Biographies, press reviews, academic prose, press reportage, official documents.

Moderately Low Genres: Science fiction, religion, humor, popular lore, editorials, hobbies.

Features: Nouns and prepositions in nominal groups, long words, higher type/token ratio (more varied vocabulary), attributive adjectives.

2. **Narrative versus Nonnarrative Concerns**

General Description: Narrative texts report past events, frequently with continuing results; hence, there are more verbs. Nonnarrative texts present expository and procedural information that emphasize nominal, descriptive, or argumentative information.

Very High (Narrative) Genres: Fiction (romantic, mystery, science, adventure).

Features: Past-tense and perfect-aspect verbs, third-person pronouns, public verbs *(tell, speak, say),* present participial clauses, synthetic negation.

Intermediate Genres: Prepared and spontaneous speeches, biographies, personal letters, humor, face-to-face conversation, press reportage.

Very Low (Nonnarrative) Genres: Broadcasts, professional letters, academic prose, hobbies, official documents.

Features: Present-tense verbs, attributive adjectives, fewer verbs (but infinitives and passives are emphasized).

3. **Explicit versus Situation-Dependent Reference**

General Description: Explicit texts have highly elaborated, text-internal reference, permitting extensive identification of nominals. Situation-dependent texts refer extensively to physical and temporal situations.

Very High (Explicit) Genres: Official documents, professional letters.

Moderately High Genres: Press reviews, academic prose, religion.

Features: WH relative clauses and other forms of nominal postmodification, phrasal coordination, nominalizations.

Very Low (Situation Dependent) Genres: Broadcasts.

Moderately Low Genres: Face-to-face, telephone conversations, fiction, personal letters.

Features: Place and time adverbials.

TABLE 8–2, *continued.*

4. **Overt Expression of Persuasion**

General Description: Texts with high values present the speaker or writer's own assessment of likelihood or advisability and attempt to persuade the addressee that certain events are desirable or probable.

Very High Genres: Professional letters, editorials.

Features: Prediction modals *(will, would),* necessity modals *(must),* and possibility modals *(may, can, could),* conditional clauses, persuasive verbs, infinitives, split auxiliaries.

Very Low Genres: Broadcasts, press reviews.

5. **Abstract versus Non-abstract Information**

General Description: Texts with a technical or conceptual focus; agents are relatively unimportant.

Very High Genres: Academic prose, official documents.

Features: Conjuncts, agentless and *by* passives, past participial clauses, relative pronoun and auxiliary deletions in relative clauses, adverbial subordination.

Intermediate Genres: Many genres are intermediate, indicating a mixture of the two types, e.g., hobbies, press reportage, press reviews, editorials.

Very Low Genres: Fiction, personal letters, face-to-face and telephone conversations.

6. **On-Line Informational Elaboration**

General Description: Texts that mark informational elaboration and express opinions, attitudes or personal statements of individuals, frequently under strict real-time conditions.

Very High Genres: Prepared and spontaneous speeches, interviews.

Moderately High Genres: Professional letters, editorials, religion.

Features: That complements to verbs and adjectives, *that* relatives in object positions, demonstratives, final prepositions, existential *there,* demonstrative pronouns, and WH relatives on object positions.

Very Low Genres: Fiction, personal letters, humor.

Features: Phrasal coordination.

sions 1, 3, and 5). Linguistic features that characterize the "written end" of these three dimensions, as shown in Table 8–2, include nouns and prepositions in nominal groups, long words, higher type/token ratios, attributive adjectives, WH relative clauses and other forms of noun postmodification, phrasal coordination, nominalization, and passives. For the practitioner, these findings have developmental and pedagogical significance. The act of writing, which by nature provides more processing time than speaking, draws on a subset of structures not tapped as frequently in spoken language. Judgments of maturity in writing, and indeed, overt efforts to teach a more "written" style, are informed by attempts to pinpoint structural differences attributable to modality alone. Although Biber would caution that these structures are not absolute concomitants of written language, they occur with enough frequency to warrant the attention of practitioners.

The same structures characterizing written texts in Biber's work (1988) figure prominently in Halliday's discussion of spoken versus written complexity. Halliday (1987) debated the widely held assumption that written language is structurally more complex than spoken, claiming that both are complex but in different ways. Writing is characterized by lexical density and embeddedness within nominal constructions (a hierarchical code). Speaking proceeds in clause complexes linked by coordinating and subordinating conjunctions (a linear code), as illustrated in the following comparison (from Halliday, 1987, p. 62, italics added):

More "Written"

Every previous visit had left me with *a sense of the risk to others in further attempts at action on my part.*

More "Spoken"

Whenever I'd visited there before I'd end up feeling that other people might get hurt if I tried to do anything more.

The preceding written version is a one-clause sentence that communicates basically the same information as the spoken four-clause sentence. The difference is that the spoken content unfolds in successive clauses (linked by connectives *whenever, that,* and *if,* while the written content is found in long and complex nominal groups (in italics). Both Biber (1988) and Halliday (1987) speculate that the real-time constraints of speaking, as opposed to writing, account in large part for such linguistic form differences.

Evidence for absolute differences might emerge more clearly in studies that compare spoken and written versions of the same material. Beaman (1984) reported findings that supported Halliday's thesis that complexity differences, rather than complexity per se, sets writing and speaking apart. Her adult subjects produced different kinds of subordination in their spoken and written renditions of *The Pear* story. Scott and Klutsenbaker (1989) compared spoken and written summaries of both narrative and expository material produced by eleven-, fourteen-, and twenty-one-year-old subjects. Their findings, discussed in the third section of this chapter, confirm Halliday's description of spoken versus written complexity. Applications of this information in language assessment and intervention will be addressed in the fourth and final section.

To conclude this overview of language variation as a function of genre and modality, one can find some order and consensus in the attempt to characterize form–function interactions. Although a potentially limitless number of spoken and written genres is to be accounted for, Biber's computational investigation identifies a limited number of dimensions based on co-occurrence patterns of linguistic features. The six dimensions provide a useful tool by which to characterize any single genre, or to compare several different language varieties. Whether or not there is an absolute spoken-written dimension, many investigators agree that forms favored in writing result in a hierarchical code, while speaking is a linear code. These structural differences are found when spoken and written versions of the same material are compared (e.g., a spoken and written version of the same story) but are accentuated when different genres are compared (e.g., conversation compared with academic prose).

LANGUAGE VARIETIES IN THE CLASSROOM

Schoolchildren and adolescents encounter many of the discourse types discussed in the previous section. Quite obviously, students are not yet writing editorials, reading official documents, writing professional letters, or delivering planned speeches (at least routinely). They do, however, read textbooks, write fiction, write informational reports, engage in small group discussion, and listen to lectures. To be sure, the attempt to survey classroom language contexts is challenged by a vast array of different practices across communities, schools, and classrooms (see Nelson, chap. 4). For example, students in Nancy Atwell's eighth-grade class in Boothbay Harbor, Maine, undoubtedly spend more of their school day writing than students in many other eighth-grade rooms; Atwell (1987b) has been at the forefront in developing writing-as-process curricula at the middle school level. Even within the same school, there may be discernible differences in language varieties depending on individually held philosophies and idiosyncratic methods. Heath (1987) reported many changes in classroom language among teachers who had gone from traditional to open classrooms. Given the variety of pedagogical beliefs and practices, it is perhaps fruitless to search for a "typical" classroom. Recognizing that schoolchildren will encounter variations across teachers (see Nelson, chap. 4), research nevertheless provides the following characterization of spoken and written discourse in schools. Familiarity with school discourse is motivated by an expanding literature documenting the effects of text variables on learning (e.g., Horowitz, 1990; Meyer & Freedle, 1979, 1984; Silliman & Wilkinson, chap. 2; Wallach & Butler, chap. 1). Biber (1991) notes that school discourse research falls into three main types of studies: comparisons of home and school spoken discourse (e.g., studies of teacher talk); analyses of school texts, particularly readability studies; and analyses of student writing. Each topic is addressed in this section.

Listening and Talking in the Classroom

Classroom ethnographers and several authors in the present volume concur that classroom discourse is fundamentally different from conversation outside the school. A moment's reflection reveals the major determinant—one adult in an authority relationship with twenty to thirty students. That adult is charged with maintaining an environment of order where learning can occur. As a result, "classroom language has overriding rules that reflect the teacher's authority to decide who speaks, on what topics, and for how long" (Heath, 1978, p. 6). Given this fundamental difference, what are the textual characteristics of classroom discourse encountered by students? What is the range of variation among different teachers? Does classroom discourse pose any unique processing problems for students? Do students listen mainly to teachers and tune out when other students are talking? Are there long stretches of informational monologue? Does subject matter affect classroom discourse? Is it possible that discourse differences among teachers bring about greater or lesser amounts of student learning? Although it is well-known that students spend most of their time listening, when they do speak, what are the discourse properties of their contributions? Following is a selective review of several studies that address these questions. Many comprehensive reviews of classroom discourse are available (e.g., Bloome & Knott, 1985; Edwards & Mercer, 1986; Nelson, 1984; Tattershall & Creaghead, 1985; Wallach & Miller, 1988). In addition, Nelson (chap. 4) and Silliman and Wilkinson (chap. 2) discuss various aspects of classroom discourse in this volume.

Many treatments of teacher input characterize the talk as either information based or management based (see Palincsar et al., chap. 5). That is, teachers are basically concerned with imparting information (and evaluating student's understanding of that information) or managing classroom behavior (Morine-Dershimer, 1988). Management-based input can be further categorized as general behavior and discourse management or more specific lesson management. Heath (1978) refers to the role of teachers engaged in the first type of management as "arbiters of good citizenship and order" (p. 11). Whether information or management based, teacher questions account for a high proportion of classroom discourse. This might seem odd, given the fact that

> Teachers know things and have to teach them; children know less and have to learn. Why then is it not the case that children ask all the questions and teachers do all the answering? (Edwards & Mercer, 1986, p. 197)

Advisability notwithstanding, teacher questions are the opening move of many tripartite exchanges comprising a question from the teacher, an answer from the student, and teacher evaluation of the answer (initiation–reply–feedback sequences, which are evaluated critically by Palincsar and her colleagues and Silliman and Wilkinson in chaps. 2 and 5, respectively).

These parameters can be illustrated in the context of real classrooms. Shuy (1988), interested in the question of variation across teachers, studied discourse patterns in six different fourth-grade language arts classes. Each class was videotaped six times, for a total corpus of thirty-six lessons. He found that teachers initiated 97% of all exchanges. Teachers varied in their ratios of information versus management talk. Across teachers, there was a fairly constant ratio of one question for every three utterances. For four teachers, the vast majority of these questions dealt with content, but two teachers used questions as indirect requests for behaviors with equal or greater frequency. The types of content questions within a knowledge-probing cycle differed across teachers. Some teachers asked the same question type repeatedly to different students, while others varied question types more in keeping with a natural conversation.

Lesson topic management techniques also varied in the six classrooms observed by Shuy (1988). One teacher consistently used a personal anecdote as an introduction into the lesson topic and proceeded through the lesson using discourse strategies judged by Shuy to be more conversational (e.g., tag questions). Another teacher managed by well-controlled bidding (hand raising by the children), short turns, and gave little indication whether the class was progressing toward the goal. Shuy called this style "management by withholding information" (p. 125). Reading through Shuy's rich examples of individual discourse management styles, one begins to get a sense of the pervasive influence of style on discourse topic. Shuy found that the teacher with the more naturalistic discourse management style elicited more topic branching and development from her students, whereas students of the more regulatory teacher tended to recycle "safe" topics.

Analyzing the same thirty-six language arts lessons as Shuy, Ramirez (1988) adapted the Sinclair and Coulthard (1975) functional analysis system to examine types of exchanges, moves, and acts. Ramirez was interested in the density of acts in exchanges, and as such his data provide a particularly revealing glimpse into the length features of any one participant's contribution. Although teachers were similar in the number of exchanges they initiated in a given lesson (ranging from thirty to forty), there were large differences between classrooms in student-initiated exchanges (which ranged from sixteen to less than one). When students initiated some type of exchange and the teacher replied, the students almost never followed up with another act (except, interestingly, in the classroom of the one teacher whose style was noted to be more naturalistic). Other differences among teachers included the following:

The density of acts in follow-up moves
The ratio of management acts and information acts
The ratio of indirect to direct management acts
The ratio of general management to lesson-related management
The ratio of metastatements to informatives
The ratio of metastatements to lesson-related management

No two teachers had the same *pattern* of discourse attributes; the result was six classrooms with unique discourse environments. The pattern of the teacher with the more naturalistic discourse style was of special note because this teacher was neither high nor low on any of the measures that differed significantly across the teachers. Rather, she seemed to travel a middle path.

One basic question about classroom discourse is the extent to which teachers typically "lecture," in the sense that their turns come to resemble a monologue. Presumably, the processing requirements for listening to a monologue would differ from those needed in discourse that resembles a dialogue with back-and-forth teacher and student turns. Although the opening moves of an exchange are most like a monologue (Ramirez, 1988), classroom dialogues can come to resemble a monologue when the content domain of successive exchanges is taken into account. For example, Edwards and Mercer (1986) showed how "recapping," a form of summarizing, takes place in a dialogue sequence: The teacher leaves open small slots for the students to fill, within an overall framework, which she herself provides. Both the lone "test" question and the longer recapping series of test questions serve the same underlying function—namely, the explicit checking of assumptions about shared information. But the series of questions serves the additional function of building a summary text over time. Thus, the potential for text building via collaborative dialogue should not be overlooked (as per Palincsar et al., chap. 5; Silliman & Wilkinson, chap. 2).

Subject matter is another variable that affects the top-level organizational characteristics of teacher talk and teacher–student discussion patterns. Heath (1978) reported that teachers in junior and senior high English and social studies classes restated questions more often, discussed the reasoning process more often, and used longer sentences. In short, these teachers organized classroom discourse in a way that allowed for verbal expansion via longer stretches of student discourse, as Nelson (chap. 4), also indicates. Science and math teachers, on the other hand, valued brief, concise answers as evidence that their students understood the material and fashioned classroom discourse accordingly. Once made aware of these patterns, science and math teachers agreed that expository/expanded discourse had a place in their classrooms as well as in humanities subjects and looked for ways to encourage such patterns.

Although students spend the majority of their time listening to teachers, they also listen to other students talking to teachers. In fact, there is evidence that the comments of other students are more salient than teacher talk. In a study by Morine-Dershimer and Tenenberg (1981), students watched videotapes of classroom sessions in which they had been a participant. Following this, they reported on "what they heard anybody saying." The students reported comments of other students—particularly high achieving students—more often than questions of teachers. Thus, students appear to believe that important content information can be found in other students' responses. Furthermore, the responses that got the most student attention were those that were pursued by the teacher in some manner, for example, by asking another question of the same student, or by directing the same question to another student.

Certainly, in most classrooms, the amount of time that students are listening far outweighs the time spent talking. When student talk is sanctioned, it is frequently found in student–student exchanges that accompany peer-group cooperative learning. Phillips (1985) studied peer-group conversations associated with school tasks in children ten to twelve years old. He found that at the start of a group session, children negotiate together to arrive at a general way of talking, termed "mode" by Phillips. Five modes were identified: operational, argumentational, hypothetical, experiential, and expositional. Linguistic markers associated with each mode appear in Figure 8–1.

FIGURE 8–1
Linguistic markers associated with types of peer-group school discourse identified by Phillips (1985)

Operational
- Deictics *this, that, these, those, it, them*
- Imperatives, not addressed to any named person
- Running commentary on things happening, apparent to group members
- Injunctions (*hang on a minute*)

Argumentational
- *Yes but* and *yes well* prefaces
- Assertive utterance—final tags *(will it, don't they)*
- *Because* subordinate clauses

Hypothetical
- *What about, how about, say* prefaces
- *If* subordinate clauses
- *Could* and *would* modal auxiliaries
- *Fairly, sort of,* and other imprecise modifiers, which leave precise details of proposition only vaguely defined (intentionally)

Experiential
- *I remember, once* prefaces indicating recall of a personal experience
- *You know Mr. X* followed by telling something about Mr. X
- Anecdotes containing direct quotes of one of the characters, precisely defined detail, and an ending

Expositional (occurs most frequently embedded in stretches of talk that are predominantly another mode)
- WH-questions

Contrary to what might be expected, the particular activity does not necessarily determine the mode that will be adopted by the group. Rather, the children themselves negotiate (indirectly) the mode to be used at the outset. Phillips provided the following example of a hypothetical discussion in the making:

> B: *what about* a bucket shaped roof . . . a bucket shaped roof . . . the rain falls in it and then it goes into your systems an' that
> E: you have sort of an automatic [interrupted]
> P: you have to clean the water
> R: yer don't
> P: you do
> A: yer do
> C: feel it
> E: *what about if* you have sort of an automatic thing what senses dirt, um if water i . . . s [drawn out] clean or dirty and you have two different um . . . (1985, p. 73)

Once chosen, however, Phillips believes that the mode does affect the cognitive activity. For example, in an activity of repairing an electrical circuit, the operational mode, if chosen, has the effect of encouraging action rather than thoughtful discussion and long-term planning. In the argumentational mode, children are more concerned with defending their own position than explaining why an alternative should be rejected. Unlike the operational mode, argumentational discourse in small groups supports thoughtful activity. Both hypothetical and experiential modes require that participants attend over long stretches of discourse because remarks are "on the floor" for extended periods of time. A hypothetical remark, for example, might bring up a possibility that is considered against others previously mentioned. Expositional discourse was defined as question–answer routines by Phillips. Unlike teacher–student exchanges, these episodes were rare in peer discussions. According to Phillips, such exchanges discourage reflective thought on the part of those not involved in the exchange. As noted previously, however, students do listen carefully to other students answering questions (Morine-Dershimer, 1988). So, this discrepancy remains to be resolved.

In summary, research on listening and speaking in classrooms underscores important connections between discourse and learning. Clearly, subject matter, individual teacher variation, and student peer conversational styles have an impact on learning. Because this line of inquiry is young, it remains for future discourse analysts to provide more detailed accounts of these connections. The practitioner who is aware of research to date, however, can maximize opportunities for classroom learning by advocating that teachers (1) use a variety of discourse moves; (2) provide more opportunities for extended student discourse; (3) provide opportunities for topic expansion in teacher–student exchanges; and (4) model argumentational, hypothetical, and experiential exchanges.

Reading in the Classroom

Textbooks serve as the main focus of both reading and writing activities in the classroom. In most school systems, teachers by the third or fourth grades are expected to use graded textbooks. The books may have been chosen by a district committee of teachers, frequently from a list of choices put together by another committee at the state level (i.e., the "de facto" curriculum described by Nelson in chap. 4). In recent years, methods of selection and textbooks themselves have increasingly come under fire from professional educators and laypersons alike. Many students have persistent difficulty comprehending material in assigned texts (D. Durkin, 1989). Frequently, as they progress through the system, students' commitment to reading and writing erodes (National Assessment of Educational Progress [NAEP], 1981, as reported by Langer, 1984b). Often-repeated criticisms include the following:

- Textbooks are written to conform to a bewildering array of requirements promulgated by state committees, leading to content that is test oriented and disconnected.
- Textbooks do not provide enough context to help readers make sense of facts. The books "mention" things and move on. They are summaries of summaries (i.e., they are too condensed). Hence, the material is quite dense, making comprehension difficult.
- The use of readability formulas contributes to stilted syntax and uninteresting vocabulary and can actually increase comprehension difficulties.
- Textbooks do not provide good models of top-level text structure.
- Writing assignments in textbooks call for rote repetition of text material and rarely call for text-level writing beyond the sentence level.

The following citation illustrates the point that the top-level organization of texts can be elusive. Figure 8–2 contains a portion of the table of contents from a

FIGURE 8–2
The subsection titles of two chapters in a third-grade language arts textbook

From *Language for Daily Use: Explorer Edition* by M. Dawson, M. Elwell, E. Johnson, and M. Zollinger, 1978, New York: Harcourt Brace Jovanovich.

Chapter 5 *Kinds of Sentences*
- Sentences that tell (declarative)
- Sentences that give orders or directions (commands)
- Sentences that show strong feeling
- Sentences that ask questions
- Word order in sentences
- Writing sentences
- How our language grows
- Writing interesting sentences (expanding noun and verb phrases)
- Using words correctly: brought
- Using words correctly: took
- Saying all the sounds in a word
- A book to read
- Checkup

Chapter 6 *Writing Good Paragraphs*
- Keeping to the topic
- Writing "hear" and "here"
- Writing good sentences in paragraphs
- Using different sentence beginnings
- Writing a paragraph in good order
- Making an outline
- How our language groups
- More contractions
- Writing to, too, and two
- A book to read
- Checkup

third-grade language arts text (Dawson, Elwell, Johnson, & Zollinger, 1978). Both chapters have a general title, followed by a listing of subsection titles. Notice the diversity of topics and text levels in the list of subsection titles. For example, in Chapter 6, it is difficult to see why a chapter on writing good paragraphs would contain a subsection entitled *Writing To, Too, and Two.* Equally puzzling is the logic of a subsection called *Saying All the Sounds in a Word* in Chapter 5, entitled *Kinds of Sentences.* A student taught the metacomprehension strategy of looking over section headings before reading would have been confused by these and other chapters in this particular text.

Writers of textbooks obviously need to consider the intended reader's cognitive, linguistic, and social development when they compose text. The use of readability formulas, however, as a way to tailor text remains controversial. Readability of text is generally determined by counts of sentence length (in words) and word length (in syllables). Texts with lower readability levels will be characterized by shorter (less complex) sentences and shorter (more frequent) words. In some cases, original texts (stories, articles) are rewritten for the purpose of lowering the readability level. As a fan of Marshall's *George and Martha* books (e.g., Marshall, 1974), I was particuarly interested in comparing the original story with an altered version I encountered in a second-grade basal textbook (*Inside and Out,* 1978). Study of the differences in the two versions revealed use of three methods of altering the original text to make it conform to a lower readability level (Green & Olsen, 1988): (1) substituting shorter, more frequent words, (2) deleting words and phrases, and (3) breaking up compound and complex sentences into simple sentences, with deletion of conjunctions. The result was a text in which the variety of cohesion markers found in natural texts, both lexical and grammatical, was narrowed. Substitution resulted in more frequent, but less specific words (e.g., instead of *pouring* soup into his *loafers,* George *puts* soup in his *shoes*). Sometimes, a change actually resulted in a meaning that was not intended by the original writer and did not fit the text (e.g., *had eaten* became *had to eat*). The net result was that logical relations in the altered text may indeed be more difficult for the reader to construct.

Another difference between the two texts was in the use of cognitive verbs. In the original version, the verb *said* was used six times, but *ask* and *sigh* were also found; the only cognitive verb in the adapted story was *said,* which was used nine times. Not only are characters rendered less interesting when they only *say* things, but the practice also seems ill-advised in light of the finding that children's use of cognitive verbs is one of the better predictors of reading ability (Torrance & Olson, 1984).

Green and Olsen (1988) investigated both preferences and comprehension for original and altered texts with fifty-eight second-grade children. For the group as a whole, the original texts (two narratives) held a slight advantage in terms of preference. Of particular interest was the fact that the least able readers had a much stronger preference for the *original* texts. Further, the readability-adapted texts were not significantly easier for children to understand. This finding suggests that practitioners examine the advisability of matching reading input and reading level via readability formulas, at least on an exclusive basis. Many textual features in addition to word and sentence length, the main ingredients of readability formulas, determine ease of comprehension (Biber, 1991). Like the parent–teacher who senses the preschooler's linguistic level and pitches his own child-directed-talk at a slightly higher level, the practitioner should provide some written text that encourages the school-age reader to work at understanding higher level text.

The *George and Martha* (Marshall, 1974) text mentioned previously and the texts used by Green and Olsen (1988) in their research were rewritten to conform to a particular readability level. Fry (1988) refers to this as *cheating,* which he contrasts with the notion of *writeability*—the initial writing of a text so that it will conform to a certain difficulty level. Fry (1988) recommends the latter practice and offers guidelines for writers to consider.

Whichever method is used to make texts fit particular difficulty levels, there are structural ramifications that extend beyond the sentence. Davison (1988) compared two children's science magazines, one that used readability formulas and another with a policy of not using the formulas. The readability-adapted magazine used a newspaper-like organization. Here, the most important facts were stated first, followed by second most important, and so on. In the second magazine, texts were sequentially organized in articles for younger children, and texts for older children followed a cause–effect logical structure. Davison claimed that connections between ideas are less transparent in the newspaper structure. The second magazine handled reader age differences by the overall length of the article and the topic, *not* by sentence length, which was similar in articles for younger and older children. In the readability-adapted magazine, however, articles for younger readers contained, predictably, shorter sentences.

Biber (1991) is critical of readability formulas as predictors of text difficulty because the formulas are too simplistic from a linguistic standpoint. Recently, Biber (1991) applied the multidimensional analysis, as described in the previous section, to second-, fourth-, and sixth-grade basal texts, science texts, and extracurricular texts (novels and comic books). Specifically, Biber compared the texts on three dimensions: integration/involvement, elaborated/situated, and abstract style (see structures typically associated with each dimension in Table 8–2). Basal readers were shown to be homogeneous (i.e., relatively unchanging) across grade levels in being situated (not elaborated) and nonabstract; there was some change between second and fourth grade as the basals became more informational and less involved. Science books, in comparison, showed more dimensional changes across grades, becoming more informational, elaborated, and involved. Compared to adult level texts, however, all school texts were found to be more "oral" (i.e., more involved, situated, and less abstract). The extracurricular texts examined by Biber varied considerably on these dimensions, some being quite "oral" and others more "literate." Biber's approach is promising as a more complete account of linguistic variation among school texts. Given his multidimensional data base for adult texts (Biber, 1988), the approach can also be used to compare school and adult-level texts with more precision than previously possible.

The last textbook issue addressed is the observation that textbooks are highly condensed treatments of topics, as Wallach and Butler also note in Chapter 1. Insight into this criticism comes from closely examining the structure of individual chapters. To this end, the author compared two chapters, one from a seventh-grade science text (Heimler, 1981) and the other from a ninth-grade science text (Lamb, Cuevas, & Lehrman, 1989), with the results shown in Table 8–3. Measures included the number of subsections per chapter, the average number of paragraphs per subsection, and the average number of sentences per paragraph. The subsection topic was explained in four or five short paragraphs, each paragraph containing only four or five sentences. Altogether, the topic was explained with sixteen to twenty-five sentences. Elaboration on any one topic was not characteristic of either the seventh- or ninth-grade science texts. In fact, the only difference between the seventh- and ninth-grade books was in sentence length, a finding not unexpected because the books undoubtedly meet grade-appropriate readability levels. However, differences in topic elaboration, although anticipated, were not found. Such differences might have taken the form of more paragraphs or longer paragraphs in the ninth-grade text.

A look at sentence structure in these same two textbooks illustrates points made in the first section of this chapter regarding structures typical of written language. In the following ninth-grade selection (also prevalent in the seventh-grade text), words in italics form complex nominal groups (a head noun with all pre- and postmodifying structures):

> *The law of universal gravitation* states that *the strength of an object's gravitational force* depends on *its mass. The more mass the object has, the more force it exerts on other objects. This force of attraction between most objects* is very small. However, *large objects such as the sun and the earth* have *large gravitational forces. These forces* are what keep *the earth* in *orbit around the sun* [emphasis added] (Lamb et al., 1989, p. 68)

Information embedded within nominal structures constitutes what Halliday (1987) calls "the hierarchical code of written language." Notice also that these postmodifying structures interrupt the subject noun and the verb (e.g., *strength* from *depends, force* from *is,* and *objects* from *have*), which increases processing difficulty (Perera, 1984). These postmodifying structures are less obviously a part of the teacher-talk texts shown in the literature (e.g., the sixth-grade excerpts in Nelson, 1984). When postmodifying structures are used in teacher-talk texts, they rarely interrupt subject nouns and verbs. Interestingly, sixth-grade teachers in Nelson's study (1984) spoke in sentences that are equally as long as the written sentences in the science texts.

Besides textbooks, workbooks are a second major source of written input in schools. Figure 8–3 contains two examples of written input found in elemen-

TABLE 8–3
A comparison of seventh- and ninth-grade science textbook chapters

	Seventh Grade (Life Sciences)	**Ninth Grade (Physical Sciences)**
Number of chapters in textbook	23	25
Chapter title	Animal Structures	Force and Acceleration
Number of subsections	7	9
Average number of paragraphs per subsection	4.3 (30/7)	4.8 (42/9)
Average number of sentences per paragraph	5.3 (158/30)	4.6 (191/42)
Average number of words per T-unit	10.8 (1,770/163)	14.8 (2,982/201)

FIGURE 8–3
Examples of workbook instructions that contain many metalinguistic words (i.e., words about language) and right-branching subordination

1. First-Grade Basal Workbook

Count the vowel letters in each word. Mark the letter that represents the vowel that you will hear in the word. Mark through the vowel letter that will be silent. Check your work as you hear the words.

Mark the letter that represents the vowel that you will hear in the word.

verb object

First level sub verb object

Second level obj sub verb adverbial

2. Fourth-Grade Basal Workbook

Read the sentences below. Then read the list of meanings given after the last sentence. Each of these meanings matches one of the boldface words in the sentences. Match each of the meanings with the correct boldface word. Then write the letter of the meaning in the space before the sentence in which the boldface word appears.

in the space before the sentence in which the boldface word appears.

adverbial

First level adverbial

Second level adverbial subject verb

tary workbooks. Several characteristics of workbook lexicon, sentence structure, and text pose challenges to children. Directions in workbooks are frequently difficult to understand, which is due to the high density of metalinguistic vocabulary combined with a multilayered, right-branching subordinate clause sentential syntax; in essence, strings of structures are used to qualify a head noun (e.g., prepositional phrases, relative clauses, and other nonfinite clauses). In example 1 in Figure 8–3, from a first-grade basal workbook, there are two levels of embedding postmodifying the second instance of *letter.* Example 2, from a fourth-grade workbook, also contains two levels of embedding postmodifying the word *space.*

Although school texts have been criticized on a number of fronts, Chall and Squire (1991), in their comprehensive review of textbooks and the publishing industry, find a number of encouraging signs. They note increased interest among text researchers and developers in maximizing factors such as cohesion, focusing, and top-level organization in content texts (mathematics, social studies, English, science) and an increase in nonnarrative (informational) selections in basal reading programs. They also find concern with the decline in textbook difficulty, which has continued over a fifty-year period. Uncritical acceptance of the notion that easier texts are better texts is being replaced by concern with effects on learning.

Writing in the Classroom

Children come to school with vastly different exposures to adult writing, as Heath (1983) demonstrated in her classic descriptions of literacy contexts in three communities of the Piedmont Carolinas. The children of townspeople (black and white mainstream families) observed adults using writing as memory aids (lists, recipes, etc.), messages, social and business letters, and financial transactions. The least frequent type of writing was expository or informational writing (e.g., tasks brought home from the job or church such as summaries of group meetings, annual reports, etc.). Although Tracton children (from a black working-class community) observed some of the same uses of writing (e.g., memory aids and messages), there were fewer occasions to observe adults reading or writing extended discourse (e.g., letters, reports). Roadville children (from a white working-class community) saw even less extended writing of any kind. The longest written pieces in Roadville homes were notes (in phrase form) prepared for church or club meetings and an occasional personal letter, both written largely by women.

Even though children bring a variety of literacy experiences to school, for many, the purposes and forms of school writing will constitute a new experience (see van Kleeck, chap. 3). And the nature of that experience with writing will vary considerably, depending on the curriculum model in force in the classroom the child enters (as in Nelson, chap. 4). Deford (1986) described effects of curriculum models (traditional, literature, and mastery learning) on writing process and products in three first-grade classrooms. The major finding was that the children's writing reflected classroom print experiences. For example, when vocabulary was controlled in the classroom, as in the basal readers used in the traditional classroom, then children's written vocabulary was similarly limited. Children in the literature-based room wrote on a greater variety of topics and in more genres. Texts produced by children in the traditional and mastery classrooms were produced on a single day in thirty to forty minutes, whereas texts written in the literature classroom were produced over a period of days with time devoted to revision. Effects of print input on writing products can even be found in traditional classrooms using different basal readers. Eckhoff (1983) found that second-grade children reading from a basal reader using simpler sentences wrote simpler sentences than children using a book with more complex sentence patterns. (See also Palincsar et al., chap. 5, for additional information on writing strategies in the classroom.)

Beginning in the mid-elementary years, contexts for writing become increasingly compartmentalized between instruction/evaluation and other purposes. Studying second- and third-grade writing contexts, Florio and Clark (1982) identified four major functions: (1) participatory/community (e.g., collaborative teacher–student writing of classroom rules); (2) knowledge of self and others (e.g., diaries); (3) privacy and recreation (e.g., letters and cards); and (4) demonstration of knowledge. Only the last type of writing was formally assessed and taught. Moreover, almost all instruction-related writing was "heavily crafted by the teacher herself and/or by the makers of educational materials" (Florio-Ruane, 1985, p. 52).

The major purpose of school writing, and consequently the major investment of school writing time, is in the evaluation of learning. This is increasingly the case as children progress through upper elementary and secondary grades, where most grading is based on written products of one form or another. To the contrary, very little grading is based on spoken language (Butrill, Niizawa, Biemer, Takahashi, & Hearn, 1989), with infrequent exceptions such as speech (or speech and drama) classes. Moffett (1988) states, more forcefully,

> It is impossible to understand the teaching of writing in America if one does not realize that, in one form or another, from the first grade through graduate school, it serves mostly to test reading—either reading comprehension or the comprehensiveness of one's reading. (p. 73)

In one of the most comprehensive investigations of secondary writing contexts, Applebee (1981, 1984) confirmed the major function of writing as a vehicle to test knowledge of specific content areas. Furthermore, this type of writing was rarely at the text level. Observations from sixty-eight ninth- and eleventh-grade classrooms, in a variety of subjects, revealed that although students spent 44% of their classroom time writing, only 3% was devoted to writing texts of paragraph length or longer. Real text composing, as distinguished from writing words, phrases, and single sentences, was extremely limited. Even when students were asked to compose, the task most often involved repeating what was already organized by the teacher or text, rather than extending or constructing new learning. The potential learning consequences of such practices were studied by Newell (1984), who found that material read by eleventh-grade students was better learned when they wrote essays over the content (as compared with note taking and answering study questions). Such results point out that teachers may have overlooked the value of text-level writing as a learning tool, even when the reason for writing is to demonstrate one's knowledge.

Applebee (1984) analyzed the longer texts that were available in his sample for overall quality, cohesion, and top-level text organization, applying the analysis system of rhetorical predicates developed by Meyer (1975, 1981). He found that the global and local text organization patterns used by students were distinguishable as a function of subject (science vs. social studies) and task (analytic vs. summary writing). He also compared the rhetorical organization patterns of students' writing with their textbooks in the same subjects. Textbook summary writing was organized primarily according to sequence (time ordering), for both social studies and science. Analytic social studies writing was predominantly causal, whereas analytic science texts were organized around comparisons (alternatives). Student writing was less consistent in the association between one major top-level structure with one type of writing (i.e., analytic or summary) but showed some developing similarities to textbook writing. Whatever the top-level organizational structure, other researchers have also been concerned about student report writing. Nordberg (1984) criticized reports as poorly written, reworded collections of facts taken from single sources.

In Applebee's (1984) data, writing for personal purposes, for example, self-discovery or exploring ideas with friends, has virtually disappeared *except among poorer writers,* who continued to receive some personal writing assignments. In the years since Applebee's classrooms were observed, however, some attempts have been made to broaden the functions of school writing beyond the confines of testing and textbook/teacher knowledge. Examples are Atwell's (1987a) transformation from teacher-chosen to student-chosen topics in her eighth-grade classes and Lumley's (1987) use of peer-group dialogue journals in high school classes. As Freedle and Fine (1983) argue, however, teachers who explore additional types of classroom writing should watch for potential violations of sociolinguistic constraints. As an example, they point out that in-class diary writing, characteristic of early elementary writing, tends to drop out as the year progresses. This is attributed to a mismatch between the appropriate use of diaries outside and inside the classroom (e.g., who may read it, what ideas can be expressed, etc.).

A final perspective for this section on linguistic contexts and requirements in schools concerns the students' level of involvement. Accumulating ethnographic and anecdotal evidence suggests that students are not passive participants in this melange of textbooks, teacher talk, and linguistic requirements. To the contrary, children as young as kindergarten search for patterns and purposes in their literacy schooling (Dyson, 1984). Early elementary children have been known to "scope out" the teacher's philosophy on writing pedagogy and then structure their compositions accordingly (Calkins, 1983). Anyone who has directly asked a student her opinion on these matters will not infrequently find thoughtful reflections on the purpose and value of the linguistic tasks students are asked to do. Indeed, from the first day of school, children have expectations and opinions. I recall the story told by one of my students whose son Noah was getting ready for his first day of kindergarten. Noah was excited but nervous about his first day, as was his mother. When picking him up after school then, she asked with some trepidation how his first day had gone. Noah replied, "Oh, it was okay, but I didn't even learn to read."

In the preceding paragraphs, school language has been examined for text level characteristics including genre, organization, length, and processing requirements. Current classroom discourse practices have many critics, including Langer (1984b), who provided the following critique:

- Students are taught to provide factual information but are not taught to critically examine information—their own or others.
- Students spend too much time doing seatwork and paperwork and too little time in thoughtful interaction, with teachers and other students.
- There is too little true instruction, and too much practice and testing.
- Teacher manuals accompanying basal readers exhort teaching comprehension but provide few suggestions on how this might be done.
- Writing assignments in student textbooks do not require text-level writing or critical thinking.
- Textbook passages are poor models of expository text structure and are therefore poor models for either reading or writing.
- Readability formulas can increase text difficulty by increasing the number of inferences required by readers.
- Students are disengaged from the subject matter and from reading and writing.

Examination of the way students spend their time in classrooms provides at least partial explanations for the discontent:

- Only 3% of secondary class time is spent in writing activities requiring text-level writing the length of a paragraph or longer (Applebee, 1981).
- Only 5% of secondary class time is spent in discussions organized purposely to promote speaking skills (Goodlad, 1984).
- A survey of seventeen-year-olds revealed that three quarters had not written anything in a two-week period (Graves, 1978).
- Half of class time (48%) at seventh, eighth, and ninth grade is spent in independent seatwork (Shumaker, Sheldon-Wildgen, & Sherman, 1980).
- Only 10% of all classroom work in upper elementary grades requires communication and co-operation between students (Galton, Simon, & Kroll, 1980).
- Half of class time (50%) is spent getting organized in the average elementary class (Gump, 1975).

These and other complaints find support in the results of the National Assessment of Educational Progress (1981), and are echoed in newspaper articles, news magazine reports (e.g., Leslie & Wingert, 1990), and televised panel discussions and interviews.

Ultimately at issue for language clinicians and teachers is whether students should be trained to conform to the school context, if indeed that context is flawed, or whether the context itself needs attention (Cazden & Haynes, 1987). By careful examination of and sensitivity to school discourse, educators should be in a better position to contribute to that debate and to problem solve, for both remedial and regular education applications. In the long run, one hopes to make better decisions about when to help the student fit the context (i.e., when the school language context is well suited for learning) and when to change the context itself (when it fails to facilitate learning).

LEARNING ABOUT LANGUAGE VARIATION

Most children enter school with a well-developed phrase structure grammar. They have also learned a great deal about the nature of conversational and narrative forms of discourse. Grammatical and lexical cohesion systems are in place. Because adults can easily chat with many five-year-olds about a variety of topics, it may seem that language learning, for all practical purposes, is nearly complete. Many language forms and functions, however, are learned in late childhood and in adolescence (K. Durkin, 1986; Nippold, 1988; Nippold, Schwarz, & Undlin, 1992; Romaine, 1984; Scott, 1984, 1988a, 1988c). Linguistic change may seem less obvious only because it is protracted and involves structures that occur less frequently in the language (Scott, 1988c).

As children become capable of producing longer stretches of discourse, they are faced with the necessity of tying together more and more sentences. As a result, sentence structure is increasingly influenced by discourse structure. Children learn a number of word order variations within the sentence as signals of theme and focus (e.g., adverbial fronting, cleft sentences). They learn that some cohesion structures are unique to certain genres—that it would be odd, for example, to end a narrative with the connective *in conclusion*. They learn to write for an invisible audience, requiring proficiency with forms used to make meaning more explicit (e.g., noun phrase postmodifiers, appositive structures, etc.). To comprehend and remember longer stretches of discourse such as classroom lectures, children must learn about top-level text structures typically associated with certain types of informational language. In sum, children and adolescents gradually learn the forms that define each genre as a unique type of discourse. The ways in which structures combine to produce these many discourse types was the subject of Biber's (1988) multidimensional analysis of language variation, as reported in the first section of this chapter.

Many linguistic systems and topics are relevant to the study of discourse development in school-age children and adolescents. This section offers a selective review of studies concerned with comparisons of children's text production across modalities and genres. Comparisons of this type bring into sharper focus the developmental course of language form and function interactions. The review concentrates on production of text rather than comprehension per se; in several studies, however, the production texts under analysis are recall/summary protocols. In other words, the texts are indirect representations of comprehended information.

Comparisons of Modality: Spoken and Written Language

Investigations comparing children's spoken and written language abilities have been designed with a focus on either form (e.g., sentence level syntax) or content (e.g., semantic propositions, story grammar elements, and types and amount of information). Researchers interested in form have analyzed a variety of structures within and across sentences. Several large-scale developmental investigations of speaking and writing track syntactic changes throughout the school years (Loban, 1976; O'Donnell, Griffin, & Norris, 1967). These and other studies comparing spoken and written form have been reviewed by Perera (1984, 1986) and Scott (1988c). When average sentence length (in words) is used as a metric of overall complexity, *writing eventually overtakes speaking in late elementary or early secondary years,* although studies differ in the exact point of crossover.

Kroll (1981) provided a developmental model of spoken and written form relationships that spans beginning to advanced writing levels. In this model, the first level of writing is called the *preparation phase.* When they begin to write, children are engrossed in the mechanics of writing—forming letters and spelling—to the extent that they have few energies left for composing. Consequently, grammatical form of self-generated written texts may lag behind when comparisons are made with spoken text. For instance, omissions may occur that would be uncommon in speech. By the age of seven, most children have entered a *consolidation phase* in which they are writing independently and drawing on their store of oral language competence. Grammatically, their writing is much like their speech, minus some of the pragmatic particles of conversation which they seem to realize are misplaced in writing (e.g., *I mean, you know, like*). In the next period, a *differentiation phase,* writing begins to contain forms that are more "written," for example, passive voice, nominalization, fronted adverbials, nonfinite verbs, and the like. (These and other structures favored in writing were discussed in the first section of the chapter.) Most children's writing shows initial signs of differentiation by the age of nine. Finally, in the later years of secondary school, most writers enter an *integration phase,* in which they can draw on both spoken and written competencies in their writing, depending on the demands of the task. At the extremes, they can even talk "writing" and write "talking" (Kroll, 1981, p. 53; see also Wallach and Butler, chap. 1).

Unlike the large-scale studies that tallied all structures used in spoken and written texts, then noted differences, Scott and Klutsenbaker (1989) used Halliday's (1987) model of hierarchical (written) versus linear (spoken) codes in a more selective comparison of spoken and written forms. Halliday characterized spoken form as strings of clause complexes connected by conjunctions. This contrasted with written language where the same information was coded hierarchically in complex nominal groups (via noun phrase pre- and postmodification structures). Scott and Klutsenbaker asked eleven-, fourteen-, and twenty-one-year-olds to summarize both orally and in writing two narrative and two expository video programs (N = 7, fifty-six texts). They then compared portions of the texts where the same information was coded. Analysis revealed steadily increasing amounts of structural distinctiveness along the lines described by Halliday (1987). Citations illustrating modality-specific structures that code the same information are shown in Figure 8–4. The first examples show instances of nominalization, where verbally coded information in speaking contrasts with nominally coded information in writing. In the second group of examples, verbally coded written information takes the form of attributive adjectives in speaking. Frequently, there is a clause savings in the written version; information that takes several clauses to code when speaking is coded in fewer clauses, but with more complex nominal groups, when writing.

As part of a study investigating age, modality, and genre effects on text, Pelligrini, Galda, and Rubin (1984) found that persuasive written texts had more causal conjunctions than persuasive spoken texts. They speculated that the slower pace of writing may have facilitated more integration of ideas. They also compared third- and fifth-grade texts and found that written grammatical cohesion (defined as reference, ellipsis, and substitution) was significantly higher than spoken cohesion in the third-grade texts. There was no further differentiation in the fifth-grade spoken–written comparisons.

Other studies of developing spoken and written language have been more concerned with content. Researchers with this interest have compared spoken and written versions of text for the presence of particular propositions and higher level text elements (e.g., story grammar elements, types of arguments). Generally, investigators have studied upper elementary and secondary students. One of the few cross-modality studies of younger children was reported recently by Horowitz (1990). She asked second-grade children (N = 32) to persuade parents to buy a Snoopy Sno Cone Machine. Although the spoken texts were longer, spoken and written texts contained the same number

FIGURE 8–4
Examples of differences in spoken and written versions of the same information

Examples from *Comparing Spoken and Written Summaries: Text Structure and Surface Form* by C. Scott and K. Klutsenbaker, 1989, November, paper presented at the Annual Convention of the American Speech-Language-Hearing Association, St. Louis.

NOMINALIZATION

Descriptive, expository (age fourteen)
Spoken: it starts *to flashflood*/
Written: *flashflooding* occurs/

Persuasive (age eleven)
Spoken: and on the car commercial they really *get excited* about the car when it goes/
Written: how it looks better when you add *excitement* or background/

Narrative (age eleven)
Spoken: and he went to the big city to see *if a fisherman would take him*/
Written: he went to the city to ask about *a fishing place*/

Narrative (age fourteen)
Spoken: finally his mom *talked* to his dad/ and they let him go down there/
Written: after *a discussion* they agree/

ATTRIBUTIVE ADJECTIVES

Narrative (age fourteen)
Spoken: one of the goats *went up a mountain off too far away from the herd*/
Written: Yanis followed one *wandering* goat up a mountain/

Descriptive, expository (age twenty-one)
Spoken: and it went into detail a little bit about how the *animals and plants adapted*/
Written: the program discussed some of the *adaptation techniques* that are observed in the desert/

of arguments. There were differences, however, in the types of arguments used. Whereas the spoken arguments were predominantly pleas (*please Mommy please*) and trades (*I'll stop bugging you if you get me the Sno Cone Machine*), the written arguments more narrowly focused on pleas. Perhaps more interesting than the group differences were the individual differences. Horowitz found considerable variation among the second graders in the overall level of performance and in the types of top-level organization used. Although some children used a list structure, others relied on cause–effect explanations. In the following example from Horowitz (1990, p. 125), a second grader wrote a persuasive piece that goes beyond pleas into trades, benefits, and anticipated counterarguments:

> please would you by that Snoopy snow Cone Machine it only cost 21.00 I'll try to ern it I'll take out the trash and make the beds and rake the yard and feed the dog and cat I'll clean the house my sisters room spesholy her room looks like a pig pen my room is not as bad as hers Then I think I'll 21.00 to by the snoopy snow cone Machine Iif I worked that hard I should get a Snoopy Snow cone Machine I'll buy a new thing for you

Hidi and Hildyard (1983) were interested in the extent to which discourse genre and modality (i.e., spoken or written production) interact. They hypothesized relative independence. Specifically, they expected to find structural differences between expository and narrative texts but few differences when comparing spoken and written versions of the same text. Children in grades 3 and 5 were asked to tell a story from a given setting and to produce an opinion about a given premise (*N* = 43, eighty-six texts). Scoring involved rating the texts for top-level structure and cohesion. Although the spoken productions were longer than the written productions, there were no differences in top-level well formedness. The written narratives of the children were likely to contain the same rating for text structure as the spoken stories (e.g., a well-developed plot brought to an adequate conclusion). Hidi and Hildyard concluded that a modality-independent organizational schemata guides both speaking and writing. A similar finding was reported in the Scott and Klutsenbaker (1989) study discussed earlier. Like the Hidi and Hildyard (1983) texts, written summaries were considerably shorter than spoken summaries. However, the length difference did not impair text well-formedness in terms of the presence of major text elements. Thus, if a spoken narrative contained all the major elements beginning with setting through to the conclusion, the written version almost always contained the same set of elements. This finding held for all subjects irrespective of age (eleven, fourteen, or twenty-one years) or language ability. It seems that discourse organizational schemata are powerful and general in their control over content. This is good news for practitioners, who should anticipate and encourage generalization of text organization from writing to speaking, or vice versa.

In a follow-up study, Hildyard and Hidi (1985) asked sixth-grade students to either speak or write narratives in response to a brief setting introduction (*N*=36, thirty-six texts). Unlike the results of their earlier work, the spoken and written texts in this study were of equal length. Whereas in the previous study, the authors rated top-level organization and quality, in this study, they counted the number of story elements present. They found an advantage for the written narratives, where students included an average of 6.8 elements per story, compared with 5.1 elements in the spoken samples. Hildyard and Hidi speculated that by the sixth grade, children have gained enough written fluency that they are able to take advantage of the fact that writing affords more time for generating and reviewing. Hence they can include more information when writing.

Hildyard and Hidi (1985) were also interested in the effect of modality on delayed recall of information. Four days after the narrative production task, they asked the sixth-grade children to either tell or write what they recalled about their story. Children who wrote the original story *and* also wrote the recall version remembered significantly more idea units than other subjects. This finding may be of particular interest to speech-language professionals and teachers and will be taken up again in the final section of the chapter.

Modality contributions to text production have been studied further by McCutchen (1987), who was motivated by the observation that writing is extremely difficult for many children, even those who use spoken language quite competently. She designed a study to test two potential sources of writing difficulty. McCutchen reasoned that if writing problems stem from modality factors only (i.e., the added burden of written transcription—physically producing letters and spelling), then written productions should be inferior to spoken in all genres. However, if writing problems stem from children's difficulties producing *extended* text, then modality would not affect the product although genre might have an impact. (Like Hidi & Hildyard, 1983, McCutchen was concerned with interactions between genre and modality.) Fourth-, sixth-, and eighth-grade boys spoke and wrote two narratives and two argument/persuasive texts (*N*=30, 240 texts). Texts were analyzed for length, structural elaboration, coherence, and cohesion.

In several respects, McCutchen's (1987) results resembled those of Hidi and Hildyard (1983; Hildyard & Hidi, 1985) but were interpreted differently. Although both narrative and argument written texts were shorter than spoken counterparts, they were not of poorer text quality in terms of coherence or in the arrangement and linking of information. Speaking seems to facilitate the *access* of information in the knowledge base, resulting in longer spoken texts. In narratives, for example, the greater length was achieved by relating more major events, but individual events were no more elaborated when spoken than when written. A coherence advantage, according to McCutchen, does not automatically accompany a length advantage. In fact, written argument texts were actually more coherent than their spoken counterparts, even though they were shorter in length. Specifically, they contained more explicit ties (e.g., connectives such as *another reason* or *so* and subordinate clauses, which link independent clauses). McCutchen interpreted her findings to support a model of discourse processing in which knowledge base, text organization (genre) competence, and modality interact. The speaking process, which fosters rapid access of information, might work at cross purposes with the careful logical–causal development required in argument texts. Rapid access has less of an impact on narrative text where temporal relations predominate.

Comparisons of Genre: Beyond Narratives

Since the early 1970s, an extensive literature has grown that discusses children's development of conversational discourse and spoken narrative discourse. Although less is known about children's narrative writing (as compared to narrative speaking), students of child language generally assume that children can both chat and tell/write stories with considerable aplomb long before they can produce opinion or informational types of discourse. During preschool and early elementary years, narratives predominate as discourse input. Kindergarten children are more proficient in processing narratives, as indicated by their ability to recall more narrative than expository information (Freedle & Hale, 1979). Studies reviewed next have looked into children's abilities to move beyond narratives to other forms of discourse with the accompanying appropriate shifts in form. Although both spoken and written modalities are sometimes studied, the major interest in these studies is genre. As was the case for research in modality comparisons, genre comparisons have been geared toward both form and content. Studies dealing primarily with form are reviewed first, followed by those emphasizing content.

McCutchen and Perfetti (1982) were interested in the development of local cohesion in essay and narrative writing of second-, fourth-, sixth-, and eighth-grade children. Children were given an initial and final sentence but could choose a topic. The sentences suggested either an expository or a narrative text. For example:

Expository

Initial: There are many things about ( ) that make it fun and exciting.

Final: So, while ( ) can be fun, there are those dangers that we must watch out for so that the fun is not spoiled. (p. 120)

Narrative

Initial: Bobby always enjoyed ( ). One day . . .

Final: Bobby still thought ( ) was fun, but Bobby knew he would have to be more careful from now on. (p. 124)

Their analyses revealed developmental change from unsuccessful connections (frequently, unclear pronominal reference) to remote connections, to local connections. McCutchen and Perfetti (1982) illustrated the difference between local and remote connections with the following example:

1. There are many things about football that make it fun and exciting.
2. The fun side of football is that you get to score winning touchdowns and be the hero of the game.
3. Another fun thing is playing against people who are equal to or better than you to see how good you really are. (p. 117)

Local connections exist between sentences 1, 2, and 3 (*fun* and *football* are repeated) and between 2 and 3 (*another* links the reason of 3 with that of 2). If sentence 3 had not used the word *another,* sentence 3 along with sentence 2 would both provide independent examples of the assertion that football is fun and as such were classified as remote connections.

The same developmental sequence occurred in essay and in narrative writing (i.e., progression from unsuccessful, to remote, to local connections) but began sooner and progressed more rapidly in narrative writing. For both discourse types, as local connections developed, sensitivity to topic constraints also increased. Sensitivity to topic constraints was considered to occur when the writer included information relevant to the closing stimulus sentence. Types of local connections were found to change both with age and discourse type. Although reference and lexical ties dominated at younger ages, other types of connections increased with age. Discourse type influenced the timing but not the sequence of connections. For example, second graders produced connections in narratives that did not appear in expository texts until the fourth grade.

The overall developmental trend from the McCutchen and Perfetti (1982) study is a shift from connections that result in a list-like text structure (where successive sentences are related to a topic sentence but not to each other) to connections in which sentences relate *both* to adjacent sentences and to the topic simultaneously. This more sophisticated pattern occurs earlier in narrative than expository writing. Examples of both types of texts follow:

Topic-connected only (list-like): Swimming is fun and exciting. Because we can play with our friends in the swimming pool. And we can have races. And we can play with a beach ball. And we can. . . . (p. 121)

> *Topic and adjacent sentence connected:* There are many things about football that make it exciting. The fun side of football is that you get to score winning touchdowns and be the hero of the game. Another fun thing is playing against people who are better than you to see how good you really are. You can also compete on a high school or college level if you. . . . (p. 120)

Extending the cross-genre research on cohesion to older subjects, Crowhurst (1987) examined types of cohesive ties (after Halliday & Hasan, 1976) used by students in grades 6, 10, and 12 in narrative and persuasive writing (315 texts). Students wrote in response to the same picture (a performing whale in midair), but instructions were designed to elicit either narrative or persuasive writing. Several differences emerged as a function of genre, age, and interactions. Some types of cohesion increased with grade level (e.g., lexical collocation and synonyms), while other types decreased (e.g., exophora, causal *so* conjunctions, and temporal *then* conjunctions). Genre differences included higher frequencies of pronominals, demonstratives, and indefinite *the,* and temporal conjunctions in narratives.

Detailed analysis by Crowhurst (1987) revealed that similar mean scores can be based on different uses of cohesion. Lexical repetition was a case in point. Sixth- and twelfth-grade students had similar scores but different *uses* of repetition in persuasive writing. Sixth graders achieved their score through an immature repetition of words, while twelfth-grade repetitions reflected greater elaboration and summary. A similar case occurred with conjunctions, where comparable overall scores obscured the greater variety of different conjunctive words used by older students.

Citing the consensus of several cross-genre comparisons of syntactic complexity, Rubin (1984) summarized the findings:

> First, discourse function exerts a profound effect on syntactic complexity. Within-age style shifts are of a magnitude equal to or exceeding between-age contrasts. Second there is a strong tendency for style-shifting in writing to increase with age. That is, more mature writers are sensitive to the differential stylistic demands of the various functions to a greater degree than younger writers. (p. 220)

According to Rubin (1984), persuasion brings about the highest degree of syntactic complexity, presumably because of its dependence on subordination to express logical relationships. In the studies cited by Rubin, syntactic complexity was measured by sentence length and/or subordination ratio.

Langer's (1985) results support Rubin's (1984) observations concerning cross-genre effects on form and extend the focus of study to content and text organization. In a cleverly designed procedure, Langer gathered spoken (retellings of read passages) and written samples, in both story and report genres, from third-, sixth-, and ninth-grade students ($N = 67$, 268 texts). She reported, in agreement with Rubin, that genre distinctions were greater than age distinctions in their effects on writing. Although stories were longer at grades 3 and 6, by the ninth grade, reports were longer than stories. At each grade, average sentence length was longer for reports.

Reports in Langer's study (1985) were distinguished from stories in terms of their top-level structure (i.e., types of rhetorical predicates, analyzed according to Meyer, 1975, 1981) and internal structure (extent of elaboration under top-level nodes). Whereas stories were organized according to temporal sequence nodes, reports were organized around information clusters with the title as a superordinate content node. There were no significant age effects for top-level structure. By the higher grades, however, genre significantly affected the amount of internal organization (i.e., the number of nodes at lower levels in the hierarchical content tree structure of the text). With age, reports became more internally structured than stories. Top-level structure also differentially affected the type of information included in the retelling of a read text. With stories, students recalled (retold) most of the information at high levels in the content organization and very little at lower levels; with reports, recall was more evenly distributed from higher to lower levels.

In summary, Langer (1985) found that third-grade students differentiate between stories and reports in their retelling and writing. They can even talk about some of the differences, citing the fiction versus fact distinction. Although growth occurred in both stories and reports, the changes in reports were more dramatic. Results suggested, further, that genre was more powerful than modality in its effects on the production of texts. These results support the need for genre-based intervention strategies that cut across modality, a point that is expanded later in this chapter.

To pursue the validity of these findings, Langer (1986) asked *how* children made meaning, as evidenced in their comments *about* reading/retelling and writing. In the previously described study (Langer, 1985), she had assigned children to either a think-aloud or retrospective condition. The think-aloud subjects reported their thoughts as they were reading/retelling and writing; the retrospective subjects reported their thoughts after the completion of the tasks. The resulting protocols were analyzed (Langer, 1986) via repeated scans for reasoning operations, monitoring behaviors, and other types of comments. A comment classified as a reasoning operation was one that questioned, hypothesized, assumed, validated, cited evidence, or otherwise reasoned about some aspect of the text content, for example, "maybe later on the boys will realize she's OK" (hypothesizing) or "let's see, what are some other things they have" (questioning) (see Langer, 1986, pp. 260–264). Results indicated that children employed different patterns of reasoning over the course of the reading/retelling versus writing activities. Reasoning that involved direct statements of text content (e.g., "this tells me the mole has weird ears") constituted 49% of the reading/retelling comments but only 36% of the writing comments. Reading/retelling comments were also more concerned with citing evidence for interpretations (e.g., "cause it says it was made by a small furry animal called a mole") and validating previous interpretations (e.g., "OK, that tells me the same thing"). Writing protocols, in contrast, were more concerned with hypothesizing and metacomment operations.

The second major analysis involved monitoring behaviors, including use and more conscious awareness comments. An example of a use comment was "I'll call it 'My First Day at Camp,'" while an awareness comment reflected more conscious reflection, for example, "it is a story, so I need to find an interesting title" (p. 236). While both reading and writing monitoring comments were largely concerned with meaning, writing contained a broader range of concerns with the text itself including goals and subgoals, genre, mechanics, and lexical choices. Another indication that children are more concerned with text structure during writing was the greater occurrence of comments focusing on global (as opposed to local) meaning in the writing protocols. In addition, although children were concerned largely with products rather than processes, they were more concerned with process during writing, where 37% of their comments reflected process concerns (e.g., "if I keep saying first day, first day, something will come to mind," p. 253). Age differences also were reflected in these comments. Third graders had less variety in the types of comments they made; they also made fewer reflective and evaluative comments both during and after finishing their reading and writing. In general, there were few genre differences. Finally, although the think-aloud (during) protocols were longer, there were few differences between think-aloud and retrospective (after) methods of eliciting comments.

Modality and Genre Development: A Summary

The cross-modality and cross-genre studies reviewed in the preceding sections contribute to an emerging account of how children come to control an increasing number of discourse types in both spoken and written mediums. By the age of ten for most children, one expects to see the beginning of divergence in spoken and written form. At least some form differences appear to be independent of genre, for example, the hierarchical coding of information in complex nominal groups with structures including nominalization and noun phrase postmodifying constructions (Scott & Klutsenbaker, 1989; e.g., see Figure 8–4). Gradually, written sentences become longer, and subordination within sentences increases when compared to spoken counterparts. There is evidence that by late elementary years, written text contains more explicit cohesion markers per unit measure than spoken text, at least for some cohesion systems (e.g., causal connectives). These findings, in part, appear to result from real-time processing differences in the two mediums. When content differences between children's written and spoken versions of a text are compared, there are few differences in top-level information, even though written versions are typically shorter. At lower levels of text organization, writing and speaking may, however, encourage coding of different types of information (McCutchen, 1987).

Comparisons across types of discourse have sometimes included both spoken and written modalities, but more often involve writing only. With very few exceptions (e.g., Langer's oral report retellings, 1985), children's development of spoken informational/expository discourse has not been addressed. Given these limitations, there is a consensus view that narrative competence precedes descriptive/informational writing, which in turn precedes persuasive/argument writing (Rubin, 1984). In the studies reviewed earlier, narrative superiority in younger children at early and mid-elementary levels was revealed in findings such as the earlier appearance of advanced cohesion systems and text length. There is also anecdotal evidence that children rely on narrative formats when other types of discourse are called for, in both speaking (Scott, 1988b) and writing (Crowhurst & Piche, 1979). To illustrate the former, when asked to give her opinion about seat belt laws, the child discussed by Scott (1988b) told about a dangerous episode when the emergency brake of the family car gave way (with the child inside). However, she never gave her own opinion about the law, nor could she discuss its merits or shortcomings. Narrative patterns of organization have also been reported to find their way into analytic writing of high school students. Applebee (1984) found that students beginning to write analytic texts sometimes start by embedding narrative stretches within a global analytic framework. Of the several types of expository text, Meyer, Brandt, and Bluth (1980) suggest that competence proceeds developmentally from description to antecedent/consequent, problem/solution, and finally comparison.

Opinions differ on the significance of the commonly reported developmental preeminence of narrative text. Langer (1985) cited the case study of Paul Bissex (Bissex, 1980), whose writing was predominantly informational in function between the ages of five and nine. Thus, when early self-generated texts of young children in the home setting are studied, capabilities that extend beyond narratives may be found. Other researchers attribute the difference to educational practice, stating that children lack experience with nonnarrative texts in the early elementary curriculum (e.g., see Christie, 1986, on informational writing; Crowhurst, 1987, on persuasive writing). Children as young as fourth grade can write persuasive texts, even though such texts will become better developed with age (Scardamalia, 1981). Because text develops within an institutional environment, it is difficult to separate the effects of pedagogical practices and inherent cognitive-linguistic factors on text acquisition.

Although information in this section has highlighted cross-genre and modality *comparisons,* it is important to remember that *within* each genre, development continues across the school years. Most types of analyses, if detailed enough, provide such evidence. When McCutchen and Perfetti (1982) studied cohesion in essay writing in second, fourth, sixth, and eighth graders, they found that the types of local connections changed with time. When Freedman (1987) studied written narratives of fifth, eighth, and twelfth graders, she uncovered considerable continuing change in text structure. When Applebee (1984) analyzed analytic writing of ninth and eleventh graders, he noted a change from unbalanced arguments (i.e., one point receives considerable discussion while others are abandoned quickly) to more balanced arguments in which several points are elaborated.

Furthermore, at any given developmental level, quality of writing will depend on the knowledge base in general and even more specifically on the particular *type* of knowledge (as also discussed by Milosky, chap. 10). In a study of expository writing by tenth graders, Langer (1984a) demonstrated that students with an extensive knowledge base did better on thesis/evidence assignments, while students with a better organized knowledge base did best on compare–contrast assignments. This finding reminds practitioners that students' higher level discourse products, sampled at any one point in time, will reflect a truly intricate complex of dependencies. While this may seem daunting on the assessment side, on the intervention side, one can envision many potential avenues for enhancing discourse skills. For example, if compare–contrast writing is the goal, this might be best accomplished with highly overlearned, well-organized topics.

Information presented to this point underscores the formidable developmental and educational challenges faced by all language learners. Discourse requirements for the last years of this millennium and beyond are many and varied. Each discourse genre has a unique discourse form that must be learned; genre affects form at lexical, phrase, sentence, and text levels. When children learn to write, the nature of the writing process (compared with the speaking process) will bring about additional alterations. Some children traverse such developmental challenges with a minimum of difficulty, learning to comprehend and produce these discourse varieties almost incidentally, or, according to some education critics, in spite of the educational system. For others, however, many varieties of discourse present special problems. In the final section of this chapter, findings from the developmental discourse literature are examined for their implications in language assessment and intervention.

IMPLICATIONS FOR ASSESSMENT AND INTERVENTION

Students with language learning disabilities—those students who, by definition, are not as "good at" language—face numerous discourse challenges, which accumulate in successive years in school. In any one assignment, difficulties might arise from several sources. This point became even clearer during a recent clinical session involving the author and a seventh-grade student with language learning problems. As part of an evaluation of reading comprehension, I devised three types of questions about a passage on Susan B. Anthony, taken from a seventh-grade social studies textbook. The questions included the following:

- Explicit/sentential (answer could be found directly within one sentence)
- Explicit/textual (answer could be found directly, but spanned several sentences)
- Implicit (answers involved inference and/or opinion and required text-level comprehension)

The question types followed a comprehension assessment format used in the study of readability by Green and Olsen (1988), as discussed earlier. Not surprisingly, this student handled the first type of question well but had difficulty with the second two types. Probing revealed many words she did not understand and a limited knowledge base for the topic. Moreover, she had difficulty with several types of subordination (as indicated by her inability to paraphrase and complete other sentences with the same structure). A short time later, I observed a ninth grader without language problems working on textbook questions about *Romeo and Juliet.* One question was particularly difficult. The answer could be found within one line of the play; however, it required inference, text-level comprehension, understanding of figurative language, and an appreciation of Shakespearean meter. The seventh grader having difficulty with a text on Susan B. Anthony would encounter Shakespeare in two short years. That she would find it very difficult seemed a forgone conclusion.

Language clinicians and teachers working with students with language learning disabilities have additional challenges that transcend the range and extent of the linguistic deficit. Debate over the construct of language disabilities has increased (see discussion of specific language impairment in Johnston, 1991; Lahey, 1990; Lahey & Bloom, chap. 13; Leonard, 1987, 1991; Wallach & Butler, chap. 1). Definition and identification issues in the field of learning disabilities have intensified (Cannon, 1991). Detailed knowledge regarding classroom discourse capabilities of language learning disabled (LLD) students is very limited (but see Silliman & Wilkinson, chap. 2). Assessment procedures, whether norm or criterion referenced, have seldom tapped discourse abilities of the types reviewed in this chapter. Investigators have concentrated on narrative discourse, almost to the exclusion of informational/expository discourse. And debate over how to best assess writing ability continues unabated in regular and special education circles. Still, several principles and practices are gleaned from the discourse literature that offer guidelines for clinical and educational practice with school-age LLD children.

Assessment Principles and Practices

Language clinicians have traditionally assessed language by administering batteries of standardized tests. Perhaps they also collect a conversational language sample, which is then analyzed for syntactic, semantic, and pragmatic information. Literature reviewed earlier and in other chapters of this text suggests several changes. Academically relevant discourse capabilities can be assessed only by studying those same behaviors directly. This means that practitioners will have to observe listening, speaking, reading, and writing within everyday school contexts, done for real school purposes.

Several authors who recommend examining a variety of discourse types comprehended and produced by any one student refer to this as *a portfolio approach* (e.g., Palincsar et al., chap. 5; Scott, 1988b, 1989; Scott & Erwin, 1992; Silliman & Wilkinson, chap. 6; Valencia, 1990; Wixson & Lipson, 1986). As they become available, written products, transcripts or tapes of spoken language, written observations, and notes by practitioners or students themselves are gathered and retained in a portfolio. Analysis of the portfolio record, over time, should reveal breadth, depth, and chronology in school discourse functioning.

A portfolio, then, is larger and more extensive than a test form or report card (although it could include these), but "smaller and more focused than a steamer trunk filled with accumulated artifacts" (Valencia, 1990, p. 339). Portfolios should be planned to meet specific purposes; contents should be selected to provide assessment information directly tied to goals of intervention/instruction. Parameters defining the types of information in the portfolio might include the following:

- Informational/expository as well as narrative discourse samples
- Samples spanning several different types of expository top-level structure (e.g., description and compare/contrast), depending on the developmental level of the student
- Several different types of narrative samples, relevant to the classroom, e.g., personal experience, autobiography, biography, historical summary
- Analytic as well as summary writing (Applebee, 1984)
- Student comments, written or spoken, regarding their own understanding, beliefs, practices, or opinions (whether positive or negative) about school/home literate language contexts or assignments
- Both spoken and written samples (spoken samples should include monologue and informational discourse, in addition to informal chat)
- Comparisons of spoken and written form on the same topic (permitting more direct comparisons of written language differentiation)
- Information about discourse-level requirements/routines in various classes taken by student (gained through student and/or teacher interview)
- Samples of student essay exam writing
- Texts produced on an impromptu basis versus texts produced over longer periods of time, with opportunities for planning and revision
- Documentation of various levels of comprehension for various types of texts, e.g., effects of top-level structure, length, background knowledge (see Langer, 1984b; D. Durkin, 1989, for a critique of norm-referenced reading comprehension tests)
- Observations about processes as well as products (i.e., what students *do* in the course of trying to generate literate products)

Portfolios in the author's clinical work in addition routinely include scraps of paper containing observations or direct quotes that reveal something interesting a student knows (or does not know) about language. For example, during snack time in a recent session, a ten-year-old spotted a bag of potato chips and another bag of pretzels. Told he would have to choose one, he said, while alternately pointing, "eeny, meeny, miny, mo—ancient ritual." Not only was the level of lexical development surprising, but his comment also revealed sophisticated figurative language and humor. Such information can counteract the tendency to *underestimate* what students with language learning disabilities know about language, simply because what they know has never been tapped in a wide variety of discourse contexts, or at least recorded. This information can also reveal the *pattern-seeking* strategies that older students frequently retain from their younger years. To illustrate, a seventh-grade LLD student offered her unsolicited definition of adjectives as "descripting" words.

The portfolio should always be open, with additions as relevant information becomes available in the course of intervention. The portfolio can be a repository for any and all information that bears on a student's linguistic knowledge, so long as that information is deemed to have instructional applications.

A second fundamental change in assessment practice is the evaluation of discourse processes in addition to products (actual texts produced by speakers and writers). *Process* refers to those strategies used in comprehending and generating discourse and the level of conscious awareness of those strategies. Compared to speaking, writing affords greater opportunity for conscious reflection on discourse generating strategies. Writing lends itself to an examination of actual processes involved in arriving at a final product (e.g., planning, generating, and revising strategies). Although some information about discourse processes can be found in portfolios containing anecdotal observations and successive drafts of texts, clinicians may wish to more specifically target the assessment of processes. According to Englert and Raphael (1988), poor writers spend less time planning, rereading, and revising. They use a partially different set of strategies for generating written text than better writers use. Hence, assessment efforts devoted to writing process may be time well spent. Scott and Erwin (1992) recently reviewed several approaches to the assessment of writing process and offer applicable developmental guidelines. Many techniques used ask writers to consciously state and analyze what they do when they write. Techniques reviewed by Faigley et al. (1985) include think-aloud protocols, reporting-in, stimulated recall, logs kept before, after, and during writing, and interviews (concurrent and post hoc). Research by Langer (1986) reviewed previously in this chapter could also be consulted for approaches to process assessment. Langer's work was designed for speaking as well as writing contexts. Other useful suggestions for capturing various process interactions with the literacy context can be found in Wixson and Lipson (1986).

Several excellent sources are available for language clinicians and teachers wishing to design either research or clinical assessment paradigms that target specific genre, modality, and production–comprehension interrelationships. Neville (1988) provides a detailed account of her five-year project with a large sample of Scottish schoolchildren (ages 8/9, 10/11, and 13/14). The project was designed to compare narrative and expository skills in both spoken and written form. Not only are her normative data useful, but her testing procedures could easily be adapted for individual testing with language disordered students. When compared to American schools, British schools appear to be more cognizant of the need for literacy training in the spoken mode (their term is "oracy" training), hence their interest in cross-mode and cross-genre assessment at the discourse level (in addition to Neville, see Brown et al., 1984).

A resource for those interested in writing tasks is Ruth and Murphy (1988). These authors provide an extensive review of the literature on tasks used to assess the writing skills of secondary and postsecondary students and how the task (i.e., topic, genre, instructions) affects the product.

For those clinicians who argue that these types of assessment approaches are too time-consuming and/or do not lead to intervention goals quickly enough, one need only look at the scores of adolescents in schools who have struggled year after year in special education programs (speech-language impaired, learning disabled, remedial reading). Perhaps as many students are not identified for special placements but become only marginally proficient at higher levels of academic discourse. A large number of students with language related learning difficulties either leave school as soon as they can, or graduate with serious deficiencies in their literate language competence. Crystal (1982) writes eloquently of the dilemma that amounts to the investment of time now or lost opportunities later.

Intervention Principles and Practices

LLD children and adolescents must function in the same discourse contexts common to other students. The most important single intervention principle suggested by the information reviewed in this chapter is that discourse contexts used in intervention should be expanded. *Students will not become competent with types of language that they do not experience.* This principle is highlighted further by a growing body of evidence that professionals, perhaps unwittingly, alter school discourse contexts for LLD students. These students hear different types of questions (Silliman & Leslie, 1980), have different kinds of experiences in reading groups (Duffy, 1982), and are asked to write different types of texts (Applebee, 1984).

Awareness Activities with A Variety of Texts. Intervention activities that teach conscious awareness of top-level organization patterns in academic discourse are recommended via direct work with school texts and other types of school discourse. Carefully crafted experiences with a variety of text structures should be expected to have broad impact. When a student realizes that a teacher's lecture is proceeding in an expository compare–contrast format, that student will be better able to comprehend and remember the content of that lecture. When the top-level text structure requirements of a written assignment are clear to a student, the product ought to reflect better organized content. And when a student is aware of textbook top-level structures characteristic of different courses, reading comprehension for material in those texts can also be expected to improve. Awareness of and facility with text structure should positively affect a variety of literate language requirements.

Awareness activities should include spoken as well as written language and discourse varieties that occur outside of school. The requirements of written school discourse should become clearer to students when comparisons are made with these additional discourse varieties. To encourage conscious awareness of spoken discourse, a variety of transcripts can be examined. The practice of showing students on paper what people say (whether taken from media materials or their own/peer speech) can be particularly helpful in building text awareness. Transcriptions of spoken discourse serve to demystify language, as the fleeting word is captured for conscious analysis. Because of the wide gaps between spoken and written language for many LLD students, verbatim transcriptions of their own spoken language can be used to motivate higher levels of written language (e.g., "look, that sentence was seventeen words long. Can you do some longer sentences when you write?").

To encourage conscious awareness of discourse outside the school context, many high interest texts are possible. Videotaped media material (interviews, analyses, reportage, personal narratives) provide good sources for text awareness (see Bourgault, 1985, for applications of media discourse). Variety of discourse exposure is the key. Interesting discourse can be found in unlikely places, as Biber (1991) demonstrated when he examined a *Spiderman* comic book. LLD students find texts outside typical school examples highly motivating. Texts such as newspaper articles, comic strips, product promotions, magazines, greeting cards, school newspapers and yearbooks, and copy about favorite stars and musicians are examples. When students gain experience with non-school texts, the characteristics of school texts, by comparison, become clearer to them.

Aside from variety, there is another important reason for expanding work on discourse to nonacademic texts. As shown earlier, textbook discourse can be highly stylized, both at sentence and text levels. Supplementary workbook material, particularly in language arts, also uses highly contrived, usually short, texts. For instance, a student might be asked to identify the top-level structure for a four-sentence paragraph in a workbook. Information outside the educational setting comes packaged differently. Thus, while shorter texts can be used for text-level awareness work in the beginning stages of intervention, students need doses of *real* text (i.e., text not composed for instructional purposes) alongside the contrived text. Such experiences also teach that real texts are seldom *exclusively* one type of top-level structure (e.g., a text might be a combination of description and compare–contrast).

Modeling of Process. This volume contains information about many formats for teaching text structure. Modeling-of-process approaches (e.g., reciprocal teaching) seem well suited as methods for teaching awareness of top-level text structure. Langer (1984b) draws parallels between such modeling approaches and the scaffolding accounts of earlier language learning (e.g., Bruner, 1978) and offers key characteristics of this type of instruction. Modeling approaches may require more intensive one-on-one service delivery, even though pull-out service delivery models are not currently in vogue.

Word and Sentence-Level Competence. Discourse-based approaches to intervention are compatible with intensive work on smaller types of language units. Words, phrases, and sentences "do the work" of discourse. If students cannot write the variety of complex sentence-level structures characteristic of written language (Halliday, 1987), their texts will not measure up, regardless of how well organized they are at higher levels. If students have not developed a knowledge base in the morphological structure of language, particularly later developing derivational morphology, their texts will be inadequate. Language clinicians might interpret the information in this chapter to indicate that work on phrase and sentence level grammar is unnecessary. They themselves might be bored by such work, and students, in the author's experience, may also be bored by the typical grammar curriculum in schools. Work on grammar should be continued, but such work should be specifically tied to a discourse base, using real texts. Students can be explicitly taught about specific form–function interactions and the propensity of particular types of discourse for particular forms. In addition to top-level structure, then, work at the sentence level with complex sentence patterns characteristic of informational and written text may also be required. Information presented in the first section of this chapter should be helpful in choosing target patterns.

Writing Has Many Functions. Knowledge base has been shown to have a powerful impact on the quality of writing and, as discussed earlier, interacts differently with different types of texts (Langer, 1984a). The "authorship potential" (Moffett, 1988) for topics we know about is higher than for those we know little about. Self-chosen topics are a mainstay of the process writing curricula advocated by many writing reformers (Atwell, 1987a, 1987b; Calkins, 1983; Graves, 1978, 1983). However, there is increasing awareness that process-based approaches to writing may not transfer to other educational contexts for writing where purpose is more restricted to the demonstration of knowledge (Applebee, 1984; Perelman, 1986). So, it seems wise to keep clearly in mind that there are several basic, underlying purposes for writing and that all are legitimate. Writing on self-chosen topics may be motivating, but it should not be the only avenue into writing. As indicated in the results of Hildyard and Hidi (1985), reported earlier, the use of writing as a *tool* for learning is also legitimate (i.e., a memory tool and a knowledge-expanding tool). Kroll (1981, p. 53) cited the novelist E. M. Forster's frequently quoted "How do I know what I think until I see what I say?" to underscore the importance of writing as a tool. Writing for purposes of evaluation will always be required in educational institutions; therefore, it is important for students to appreciate this purpose for writing and learn to do it better. Writing across the curriculum approaches are well-suited to learning contexts when students are trying to acquire knowledge at the same time that they write about it.

Genre as a Framework for Intervention. Literate language is more than reading and writing—a theme expressed throughout this text. Indeed, there are many ways in which spoken and written language support each other as literate language. The review of cross-modality and cross-genre research earlier in this chapter suggested that genre is more powerful than modality in its effect on the form of texts. This suggests that intervention should be genre-based with specific spoken and written assignments. For example, if compare–contrast expository texts are a goal, students could be asked to listen to a debate presenting pro and con positions on a controversial topic (spoken assignment). The students could then be asked to summarize what they heard (a written assignment). Finally, they can present the spoken equivalent of that summary to other class members (another spoken assignment). The general neglect of spoken language curriculum in American schools has been alluded to earlier. Phillips (1985) argues for well-crafted spoken language assignments in a classroom context, both speaking and listening. Students need to see the connection between types of oral discourse and forms of cognitive activity. He reminds us that "spoken language forms a text, too, and with current technology it is possible to capture these texts and study them" (p. 81).

Discourse Strengths as Avenues. Finally, it should again be stressed that if professionals look hard enough, they can often find some textual strengths in LLD students. Perhaps a student is genuinely much better at one type of text than another. Perhaps a knowledge-base strength or special interest would lead naturally to a particular type of text as an avenue into other types. Perhaps there are spoken language strengths that can be captured for written language competence, or vice versa. Perhaps a generally weak writer nevertheless uses a typically "written" form, or a low-frequency word that is effective in the text, or a clever phrasing. LLD students not infrequently do some things *right,* and finding those instances can be a powerful antidote for individuals who fail many times over every school day.

SUMMARY

Understanding form–function interactions in the varieties of academic discourse important to schoolchildren can help language professionals (1) find discourse strengths as well as weaknesses, (2) avoid teaching things students already know or do not need to learn, and (3) teach discourse skills with maximum generalization across the curriculum. Different types of discourse call for different grammatical forms. Students who control a wide variety of these forms and can "call them up" selectively as needed to comprehend and produce different discourse genres will be at an advantage in the classroom. Likewise, students who adopt a more hierarchical (nominally complex) code when writing will be judged more favorably. By the age of ten, children's writing begins to diverge in form from speaking. By the same age, children tell and write chronologically based narrative discourse with relative fluency and should be developing informational/expository writing. Detailed analyses reveal that development continues in all types of discourse throughout the school years.

REFERENCES

Applebee, A. (1981). *Writing in the secondary school.* Urbana, IL: National Council of Teachers of English, Research Report No. 21.

Applebee, A. (1984). *Contexts for learning to write.* Norwood, NJ: Ablex.

Atwell, N. (1987a). Everyone sits at a big desk: Discovering topics for writing. In D. Goswami & P. R. Stillman (Eds.), *Reclaiming the classroom: Teacher research as an agency for change* (pp. 178–187). Upper Montclair, NJ: Boynton/Cook.

Atwell, N. (1987b). *In the middle: Writing, reading, and learning with adolescents.* Portsmouth, NH: Heinemann.

Beaman, K. (1984). Coordination and subordination revisited: Syntactic complexity in spoken and written narrative discourse. In D. Tannen (Ed.), *Coherence in spoken and written discourse* (pp. 48–81). Norwood, NJ: Ablex.

Biber, D. (1986). Spoken and written textual dimensions in English: Resolving the contradictory findings. *Language, 62,* 384–414.
Biber, D. (1988). *Variation across speech and writing.* Cambridge, MA: Cambridge University Press.
Biber, D. (1991). Oral and literate characteristics of selected primary school reading materials. *Text, 11,* 73–96.
Bissex, G. (1980). *GYNS AT WRK: A child learns to write and read.* Cambridge, MA: Harvard University Press.
Bloom, L. (1970). *Language development: Form and function in emerging grammars.* Cambridge, MA: MIT Press.
Bloome, D., & Knott, G. (1985). Teacher–student discourse. In D. N. Ripich & F. M. Spinelli (Eds.), *School discourse problems* (pp. 53–78). San Diego, CA: College Hill Press.
Bloomfield, L. (1933). *Language.* New York: Holt, Rinehart & Winston.
Bourgault, R. (1985). Mass media and pragmatics: An approach for developing listening, speaking, and writing skills in secondary school students. In C. S. Simon (Ed.), *Communication skills and classroom success* (pp. 241–269). San Diego, CA: College Hill Press.
Brown, G., Anderson, A., Shillcock, R., & Yule, G. (1984). *Teaching talk: Strategies for production and assessment.* Cambridge, England: Cambridge University Press.
Bruner, J. (1978). On prelinguistic prerequisites of speech. In R. N. Campbell & P. T. Smith (Eds.), *Recent advances in the psychology of language* (Vol. 4a). New York: Plenum Press.
Butrill, J., Niizawa, J., Biemer, C., Takahashi, C., & Hearn, S. (1989). Serving the language learning disabled adolescent: A strategies-based model. *Language, Speech, and Hearing Services in Schools, 20,* 185–204.
Calkins, L. (1983). *Lessons from a child: On the teaching and learning of writing.* London: Heinemann.
Cannon, L. (1991). Construct of learning disabilities: Classification and definition. *LDA Newsbriefs, 26,* 1–16.
Cazden, C., & Haynes, C. (1987). A review of D. N. Ripich & F. M. Spinelli (Eds.), *School discourse problems.* San Diego, CA: College Hill Press. *Applied Psycholinguistics, 7,* 394–396.
Chafe, W. (1982). Integration and involvement in speaking, writing, and oral literature. In D. Tannen (Ed.), *Spoken and written language: Exploring orality and literacy* (pp. 35–53). Norwood, NJ: Ablex.
Chafe, W., & Danielewicz, J. (1987). Properties of spoken and written language. In R. Horowitz & S. J. Samuels (Eds.), *Comprehending oral and written language* (pp. 83–113). San Diego, CA: Academic Press.
Chall, J. S., & Squire, J. R. (1991). The publishing industry and textbooks. In R. Barr, M. Kamil, P. Mosenthal, & D. Pearson (Eds.), *Handbook of reading research* (pp. 120–146). White Plains, NY: Longman.
Chomsky, N. (1965). *Aspects of a theory of syntax.* Cambridge, MA: MIT Press.
Christie, F. (1986). Writing in the infants grades. In C. Painter & J. Martin (Eds.), *Writing to mean: Teaching genres across the curriculum* (pp. 118–135). Applied Linguistics Association of Australia, Occasional Papers, No. 9.
Crowhurst, M. (1987). Cohesion in argument and narration at three grade levels. *Research in the Teaching of English, 21,* 185–201.
Crowhurst, M., & Piche, G. (1979). Audience and mode of discourse effects on syntactic complexity in writing at two grade levels. *Research in the Teaching of English, 13,* 101–109.
Crystal, D. (1982). Terms, time, and teeth. *British Journal of Disorders of Communication, 17,* 3–19.
Crystal, D., & Davy, D. (1975). *Advanced conversational English.* London: Longman.
Danielewicz, J. M. (1984). The interaction between text and context: A study of how adults and children use spoken and written language in four contexts. In D. D. Pelligrini & T. D. Yawkey (Eds.), *The development of oral and written language in social contexts* (pp. 243–260). Norwood, NJ: Ablex.
Davison, A. (1988). Assigning grade levels without formulas: Some case studies. In B. L. Zakaluk & S. J. Samuels (Eds.), *Readability: Its past, present and future* (pp. 36–45). Newark, DE: International Reading Association.
Dawson, M., Elwell, M., Johnson, E., & Zollinger, M. (1978). *Language for daily use: Explorer edition.* New York: Harcourt Brace Jovanovich.
DeFord, D. (1986). Classroom contexts for literacy learning. In T. E. Raphael (Ed.), *The contexts of school-based literacy* (pp. 163–180). New York: Random House.
Duffy, G. G. (1982). Fighting off the alligators: What research in real classrooms has to say about reading instruction. *Journal of Reading Behavior, 14,* 351–373.
Durkin, D. (1989). *Teaching them to read* (5th ed.). Boston: Allyn & Bacon.
Durkin, K. (1986). *Language development in the school years.* London: Croom Helm.
Dyson, A. H. (1984). Learning to write/learning to do school: Emergent writers' interpretations of school literacy tasks. *Research in the Teaching of English, 18,* 233–264.
Eckhoff, B. (1983). How reading affects children's writing. *Language Arts, 60,* 607–616.
Edwards, D., & Mercer, N. (1986). Context and continuity: Classroom discourse and the development of shared knowledge. In K. Durkin (Ed.), *Language development in the school years* (pp. 172–202). London: Croom Helm.
Englert, C., & Raphael, T. (1988). Constructing well-formed prose: Process, structure, and metacognitive knowledge. *Exceptional Children, 54,* 513–520.
Faigley, L., Cherry, R., Jolliffe, D., & Skinner, A. (1985). *Assessing writer's knowledge and processes of composing.* Norwood, NJ: Ablex.
Florio, S., & Clark, C. M. (1982). The functions of writing in an elementary school classroom. *Research in the Teaching of English, 16,* 115–130.

Florio-Ruane, S. (1985). Learning about language in classrooms. *Volta Review, 87,* 47–55.

Freedle, R., & Fine, J. (1983). An interactional approach to the development of discourse. In J. Fine & R. Freedle (Eds.), *Developmental issues in discourse, Volume XI,* (pp. 143–168). Norwood, NJ: Ablex.

Freedle, R., & Hale, G. (1979). Acquisition of new comprehension schemata for expository prose by transfer of a narrative schema. In R. O. Freedle (Ed.), *New directions in discourse processing* (pp. 121–135). Norwood, NJ: Ablex.

Freedman, A. (1987). Development in story writing. *Applied Psycholinguistics, 8,* 153–170.

Fry, E. B. (1988). Writeability: Principles of writing for increased comprehension. In B. L. Zakaluk & S. J. Samuels (Eds.), *Readability: Its past, present and future* (pp. 77–97). Newark, DE: International Reading Association.

Galton, M., Simon, B., & Kroll, P. (1980). *Inside the primary classroom.* London: Routledge & Kegan Paul.

Goodlad, J. I. (1984). *A place called school: Prospects for the future.* New York: McGraw-Hill.

Graves, D. (1978). *Balance the basics: Let them write.* New York: Ford Foundation. (ERIC Document Reproduction Service No. ED 192 364)

Graves, D. (1983). *Writing: Teachers and children at work.* London: Heinemann.

Green, G. M., & Olsen, M. (1988). Preferences for and comprehension of original and readability adapted materials. In A. Davison & G. M. Green (Eds.), *Linguistic complexity and text comprehension* (pp. 115–140). Hillsdale, NJ: Lawrence Erlbaum.

Gump, P. (1975). Education as an environmental enterprise. In R. Weinberg & F. Wood (Eds.), *Observations of pupils and teachers in mainstream and special education.* Reston, VA: Council for Exceptional Children.

Halliday, M. A. K. (1987). Spoken and written modes of meaning. In R. Horowitz & S. J. Samuels (Eds.), *Comprehending oral and written language* (pp. 55–82). San Diego, CA: Academic Press.

Halliday, M. A. K., & Hasan, R. (1976). *Cohesion in English.* London: Longman.

Haydu, M. L., & Patterson, K. (1990, October). *The captioned classroom: Applications for the learning impaired adolescent.* Paper presented at the Fourth National Conference on the Habilitation and Rehabilitation of Hearing Impaired Adolescents, Omaha, NE.

Heath, S. B. (1978). Teacher talk: Language in the classroom. *Language in education: Theory and practice* (No. 9). Arlington, VA: Center for Applied Linguistics.

Heath, S. B. (1983). *Ways with words.* Cambridge, UK: Cambridge University Press.

Heath, S. B. (1987). A lot of talk about nothing. In D. Goswami & P. R. Stillman (Eds.), *Reclaiming the classroom: Teacher research as an agency for change* (pp. 39–48). Upper Montclair, NJ: Boynton/Cook.

Heimler, C. H. (1981). *Focus on life science.* New York: Merrill/Macmillan.

Hidi, S., & Hildyard, A. (1983). The comparison of oral and written productions in two discourse types. *Discourse Processes, 6,* 91–105.

Hildyard, A., & Hidi, S. (1985). Oral–written differences in the production and recall of narratives. In D. Olson, N. Torrance, & A. Hildyard (Eds.), *Literacy, language, and learning: The nature and consequences of reading and writing* (pp. 285–306). Cambridge, UK: Cambridge University Press.

Horowitz, R. (1990). Discourse organization in oral and written language: Critical contrasts for literacy and schooling. In J. H. A. L. de Jong & D. Stevenson (Eds.), *Individualizing the assessment of language abilities* (pp. 108–126). Clevdon, Avon, UK: Multilingual Matters.

Horowitz, R., & Samuels, S. J. (1987). Comprehending oral and written language: Critical contrasts for literacy and schooling. In R. Horowitz & S. J. Samuels (Eds.), *Comprehending oral and written language* (pp. 1–52). San Diego, CA: Academic Press.

Inside and Out. (1978). Newton, MA: Allyn & Bacon.

Johnston, J. (1991). The continuing relevance of cause: A reply to Leonard's "specific language impairment as a clinical category." *Language, Speech and Hearing Services in Schools, 22,* 75–79.

Kroll, B. (1981). Developmental relationships between speaking and writing. In B. Kroll & R. Vann (Eds.), *Exploring speaking–writing relationships: Connections and contrasts* (pp. 32–54). Champaign, IL: National Council of Teachers of English.

Lahey, M. (1990). Who shall be called language disordered? Some reflections and one perspective. *Journal of Speech and Hearing Disorders, 55,* 612–620.

Lamb, W. G., Cuevas, M. P., & Lehrman, R. L. (1989). *Physical Science.* Orlando, FL: Harcourt Brace Jovanovich.

Langer, J. (1984a). The effects of available information on responses to school writing tasks. *Research in the Teaching of English, 18,* 27–44.

Langer, J. (1984b). Literacy instruction in American schools: Problems and perspectives. *American Journal of Education, 93,* 107–132.

Langer, J. (1985). Children's sense of genre: A study of performance on parallel reading and writing tasks. *Written Communication, 2,* 157–187.

Langer, J. (1986). Reading, writing, and understanding: An analysis of the construction of meaning. *Written Communication, 3,* 219–267.

Leonard, L. (1987). Is specific language impairment a useful construct? In S. Rosenberg (Ed.), *Advances in applied psycholinguistics: Volume I. Disorders of first-language development* (pp. 1–39). New York: Cambridge University Press.

Leonard, L. (1991). Specific language impairment as a clinical category. *Language, Speech, and Hearing Services in Schools, 22,* 66–68.

Leslie, C., & Wingert, P. (1990, January). Not as easy as A, B, or C. *Newsweek Special Edition*, pp. 56–58.

Loban, W. (1976). *Language development: Kindergarten through grade twelve* (Report No. 18). Champaign, IL: National Council of Teachers of English.

Lumley, D. (1987). An analysis of peer group dialogue journals for classroom use. In D. Goswami & P. R. Stillman (Eds.), *Reclaiming the classroom: Teacher research as an agency for change* (pp. 167–177). Upper Montclair, NJ: Boynton/Cook.

MacDonald, S. (1989). Data-driven and conceptually driven academic discourse. *Written Communication, 6,* 411–435.

Marshall, J. (1974). *George and Martha.* Boston: Houghton Mifflin.

McCutchen, D. (1987). Children's discourse skill: Form and modality requirements of schooled writing. *Discourse Processes, 10,* 267–286.

McCutchen, D., & Perfetti, C. A. (1982). Coherence and connectedness in the development of discourse production. *Text, 2,* 113–139.

Meyer, B. (1975). *The organization of prose and its effects on memory.* New York: Elsevier.

Meyer, B. (1981). *Prose analysis procedures, purposes, and problems.* Tempe, AZ: University of Arizona, Department of Educational Psychology.

Meyer, B., Brandt, D., & Bluth G. (1980). Use of author's textual schema: Key for ninth-graders' comprehension. *Reading Research Quarterly, 16,* 72–103.

Meyer, B., & Freedle, R. O. (1979). Effects of different discourse types on recall (Report No. 6). Tempe, AZ: Arizona State University, Department of Educational Psychology.

Meyer, B., & Freedle, R. O. (1984). Effects of discourse types on recall. *American Educational Research Association Journal, 21,* 121–143.

Moffett, J. (1988). *Coming on center: Essays in English Education* (2nd ed.). Portsmouth, NH: Heinemann.

Morine-Dershimer, G. (1988). Comparing systems: How do we know? In J. L. Green & J. O. Harker (Eds.), *Multiple perspective analyses of classroom discourse* (pp. 195–214). Norwood, NJ: Ablex.

Morine-Dershimer, G., & Tenenberg, M. (1981). *Participant perspectives of classroom discourse. Executive summary of Final Report.* Syracuse, NY: Syracuse University Division for the Study of Teaching.

National Assessment of Educational Progress. (1981). *Reading, thinking, and writing: Results from the 1979–1980 national assessment of reading and literature* (Report No. 11–L–01). Denver, CO: Education Commission of the States.

Nelson, N. (1984). Beyond information processing: The language of teachers and textbooks. In G. P. Wallach & K. G. Butler (Eds.), *Language learning disabilities in school-age children* (p. 154–178). Baltimore: Williams & Wilkins.

Neville, M. (1988). *Assessing and teaching language: Literacy and oracy in schools.* London: Macmillan Education.

Newell, G. E. (1984). Learning from writing in two content areas: A case study/protocol analysis. *Research in the Teaching of English, 18,* 265–287.

Nippold, M. (1988). *Later language development: Ages nine through nineteen.* San Diego, CA: College Hill Press.

Nippold, M., Schwarz, I., & Undlin, R. (1992). Use and understanding of adverbial conjuncts: A developmental study of adolescents and young adults. *Journal of Speech and Hearing Research, 35,* 108–118.

Nordberg, B. (1984, April). *Let's not "write a report".* Paper presented at the annual meeting of the National Council of Teachers of English spring conference, Columbus, OH.

O'Donnell, R., Griffin, W., & Norris, R. (1967). *Syntax of kindergarten and elementary school children: A transformational analysis* (Report No. 8). Champaign, IL: National Council of Teachers of English.

Olson, D. (1977). From utterance to text: The bias of language in speech and writing. *The Harvard Educational Review, 47,* 257–281.

Pelligrini, A., Galda, L., & Rubin, D. (1984). Context in text: The development of oral and written language in two genres. *Child Development, 55,* 1549–1555.

Perelman, L. (1986). The context of classroom writing. *College English, 48,* 471–479.

Perera, K. (1984). *Children's writing and reading.* London: Basil Blackwell.

Perera, K. (1986). Language acquisition and writing. In P. Fletcher & M. Garman (Eds.), *Language acquisition* (2nd ed.) (pp. 494–533). Cambridge, UK: Cambridge University Press.

Phillips, T. (1985). Beyond lip-service: Discourse development after the age of nine. In G. Wells & J. Nicholls (Eds.), *Language and learning: An interactionist perspective* (pp. 59–82). London: Falmer Press.

Ramirez, A. (1988). Analyzing speech acts. In J. L. Green & J. O. Harker (Eds.), *Multiple perspective analyses of classroom discourse* (pp. 135–164). Norwood, NJ: Ablex.

Romaine, S. (1984). *The language of children and adolescents.* Oxford: Blackwell.

Rubin, D. L. (1984). The influence of communicative context on stylistic variations in writing. In D. D. Pellegrini & T. D. Yawkey (Eds.), *The development of oral and written language in social contexts* (pp. 213–232). Norwood, NJ: Ablex.

Ruth, L., & Murphy, S. (1988). *Designing writing tasks for the assessment of writing.* Norwood, NJ: Ablex.

Scardamalia, M. (1981). How children cope with the cognitive demands of writing. In C. Frederiksen & J. Dominic (Eds.), *Writing: The nature, development, and teaching of written communication. Vol 2. Writing: Process, development, communication* (pp. 81–103). Hillsdale, NJ: Lawrence Earlbaum.

Scott, C. (1984). Adverbial connectivity in conversations of children 6–12. *Journal of Child Language, 11,* 423–452.

Scott, C. (1988a). The development of complex sentences. *Topics in Language Disorders, 8,* 44–62.

Scott, C. (1988b). A perspective on the evaluation of school children's narratives. *Language, Speech, and Hearing Services in Schools, 19,* 67–82.

Scott, C. (1988c). Spoken and written syntax. In M. Nippold (Ed.), *Later language development: Ages 9 through 19* (pp. 49–95). San Diego, CA: College Hill Press.

Scott, C. (1989). Problem writers: Nature, assessment, and intervention. In A. Kamhi & H. Catts (Eds.), *Reading disabilities: A developmental language perspective* (pp. 303–344). Boston: College Hill Press.

Scott, C., & Erwin, D. (1992). Descriptive assessment of writing: Process and product. In J. Damico (Ed.), *Best practices in school speech-language pathology: Descriptive/nonstandardized language assessment* (pp. 87–98). San Antonio, TX: The Psychological Corporation.

Scott, C., & Klutsenbaker, K. (1989, November). *Comparing spoken and written summaries: Text structure and surface form.* Paper presented at the Annual Convention of the American Speech-Language-Hearing Association, St. Louis.

Shatz, M., & Gelman, R. (1973). The development of communication skills: Modifications in the speech of young children as a function of listener. *Monographs of the Society for Research in Child Development, 38* (Serial No. 152).

Shumaker, J., Sheldon-Wildgen, J., & Sherman, J. (1980). *An observational study of the academic and social behaviors of learning disabled adolescents in the regular classroom* (Report No. 22). Lawrence, KS: University of Kansas Institute for Research in Learning Disabilities.

Shuy, R. (1988). Identifying dimensions of classroom language. In J. L. Green & J. O. Harker (Eds.), *Multiple perspective analyses of classroom discourse* (pp. 113–134). Norwood, NJ: Ablex.

Silliman, E. R., & Leslie, S. (1980, November). *Instructional language: Comparisons of a regular and special educational classroom.* Paper presented at the Annual Convention of the American Speech-Language-Hearing Association, Detroit.

Sinclair, J. M., & Coulthard, R. M. (1975). *Toward an analysis of discourse: The English used by teachers and pupils.* London: Oxford University Press.

Tattershall, S., & Creaghead, N. (1985). A comparison of communication at home and school. In D. R. Ripich & F. M. Spinelli (Eds.), *School discourse problems* (pp. 29–52). San Diego, CA: College Hill Press.

Torrance, N., & Olson, D. R. (1984). Oral language competence and the acquisition of literacy. In D. D. Pellegrini & T. D. Yawkey (Eds.), *The development of oral and written language in social contexts* (pp. 167–182). Norwood, NJ: Ablex.

Valencia, S. (1990). A portfolio approach to classroom reading assessment: The whys, whats, and hows. *The Reading Teacher, 43,* 338–340.

Wallach, G., & Miller, L. (1988). *Language intervention and academic success.* Boston: College Hill Press.

Wixson, K. K., & Lipson, M. Y. (1986). Reading (dis)ability: An interactionist perspective. In T. Raphael & R. Reynolds (Eds.), *The contexts of school-based literacy* (pp. 131–148). New York: Random House.

9

EARLY LITERACY ACQUISITION

The Role of Phonological Awareness

■ Benita A. Blachman
Syracuse University

The role of phonological awareness in early literacy acquisition has been systematically investigated since the early 1970s, and the result has been called "a scientific success story" (Stanovich, 1987). As Stanovich (1991) explains: "One exciting outcome of research in reading . . . is that researchers have isolated a process that is a major determinant of the early acquisition of reading skill and one of the keys to the prevention of reading disability" (p. 22).

What is phonological awareness, and why has it generated such excitement in the research community? Simply stated, *phonological awareness* is an awareness of, and the ability to manipulate, the phonological segments represented in an alphabetic orthography. A child who can, for example, categorize words on the basis of common sounds (e.g., /hen/ and /hot/ go together because they both start with /h/); segment a word into its constituent phonemes; delete phonemes (e.g., "say /sun/ without the /s/"); or reverse phonemes is demonstrating an awareness of the segments of sound that an alphabet represents.

Research has shown that without this awareness, it is difficult for a young child to understand how alphabetic transcription works (e.g., why *sun* is written with three letters), and as a consequence, it is difficult to learn to decode. On the other hand, the research suggests that a child with phonological awareness and knowledge of how the sound segments are represented by letters of the alphabet will learn to recognize and spell words with much greater success than the child who lacks this understanding. This chapter will trace the empirically compelling research, conducted since the 1970s, that supports a causal reciprocal role for phonological awareness in reading acquisition and demonstrates that early intervention in phonological awareness can make a difference in a child's reading and spelling success.

THE RELATIONSHIP BETWEEN SPEECH AND THE ALPHABET

It has been said that "the mere fact that a child understands what is said to him tells us little about what speech segments he perceives" (Savin, 1972, p. 321). It might be more accurate to say that a child's comprehension of speech tells us little about how well he can *analyze* his speech into its constituent segments. Although of little consequence in becoming an adequate speaker–hearer of one's language, the realization that speech can be segmented and that these segmented units can be represented by printed forms is one of the fundamental tasks facing the beginning reader (I. Y. Liberman, 1971). When reading an alphabetic writing system such as English, in which the graphic symbols more or less represent the sounds of speech, the child must understand not only that the speech stream can be segmented into words and syllables but ultimately that even smaller sublexical units (phonemes) are accessible.

It is important to understand that the nature of the writing system interacts in very specific ways with the unit the readers must access from the speech stream. As discussed by I. Y. Liberman, Shankweiler, Fischer, and Carter (1974) and Gleitman and Rozin (1977), to develop a written representation of a language, one must decide what kind and size of unit will be represented. In the earliest writing systems, a meaningful unit—the word—was indicated with a single character or symbol. The Chinese logographic characters and the Japanese *kanji* characters (borrowed from the Chinese) are examples of this type of writing system. The young child learning to read Chinese need only make the link between the meaningful unit in the speech stream and the printed symbol, a task that is conceptually less difficult than abstracting smaller, meaningless units. Rozin, Poritsky, and Sotsky (1971) were able to demonstrate that American poor readers in second grade were able to learn selected English words more easily when they were represented by Chinese characters. Despite the ease with which poor readers might initially decipher a logographic system (much the way a preschooler initially identifies words on cereal boxes and soup cans by the holistic visual configuration), there are obvious disadvantages to dealing with an alphabetic system in this way. By memorizing an endless series of whole words, the child loses the economy of our alphabetic system, which allows an individual to read words never before encountered in print.

Historically, writing systems representing meaningless units, specifically syllables and phonemes, were developed after systems representing whole words (Gelb, 1963). The syllabary, in which the printed symbol stands for a unit of syllable size, is exemplified by the Japanese *kana*. Syllabaries typically represent a simple, open syllable (consonant-vowel [CV]) structure, unlike the more complex syllable structure in English. Some evidence from the high literacy rates reported among certain cultures using syllabic scripts (i.e., Cherokee, Japanese) suggests that creating a link between syllabic units in the speech stream and the printed notations representing these units is relatively easy for young children (Makita, 1968; Sakamoto & Makita, 1973; Walker, 1969; as reported by Gleitman & Rozin, 1973, and Rozin & Gleitman, 1977). Evidence also shows that children can segment speech into syllables before they can segment speech into phonemes (Liberman et al., 1974; Rosner & Simon, 1971).

The last (and relatively recent) developmental milestone in the history of writing systems was the abstraction of the phonemic segment from the speech stream and the development of a written notation to represent these small, abstract units. Some alphabetic languages, such as Finnish, are more nearly phonetic transcriptions than English. Nonetheless, like all the other alphabetic orthographies, English writing is, despite its greater abstractness, basically "a cipher on the phonemes of the language" (I. Y. Liberman & Shankweiler, 1979, p. 110). Once students unlock the alphabetic principle (understanding the relationship between speech and an alphabetic orthography), they are eventually able to read words seen in print for the first time by at least approximating their spoken form. However, there is nothing inherent in becoming an adequate speaker–hearer of English that illuminates for the child the specific linguistic units represented in our alphabetic script. Herein lies a significant problem for many beginning readers, as Wallach and Butler also pointed out in Chapter 1.

THE PROBLEM OF PHONOLOGICAL AWARENESS

Although it is obvious to literate adults that they have an alphabetic system in which graphic symbols more or less represent the sounds of speech, ample evidence indicates that this level of understanding of the structure of language develops over time and cannot be taken for granted in the kindergarten and first-grade child (Bruce, 1964; Liberman et al., 1974; Rosner & Simon, 1971). The work of A. M. Liberman, Cooper, Shankweiler, and Studdert-Kennedy (1967) and A. M. Liberman (1970) has helped professionals understand the complex relationship among the phonemes in the speech stream, which makes it difficult for the young child to access these phonemic segments (van Kleeck introduces the subject in chap. 3). When a speaker produces the word *bag*, for example, information about each segment is transmitted simultaneously. The vowel /æ/ exerts influence over the entire syllable, and the pronunciation of each phoneme depends on the context in which it occurs. Although the three segments of the written word *bag* can be easily identified, the individual phonemes that they represent are coarticulated during speech production (the consonants are folded into the vowels), creating a "merged" (A. M. Liberman et al., 1967; I. Y. Liberman, 1971) or "shingled" (Gleitman & Rozin, 1973) effect. The result is that one hears only a single acoustic unit—the syllable. (For a more detailed discussion, see Gleitman & Rozin, 1977; A. M. Liberman et al., 1967; I. Y. Liberman, 1971, 1973, 1982.)

Given the complex nature of the message the child must analyze to construct a link between the sounds of speech and the signs of print, it is not difficult to understand why a six-year-old beginning reader might have some difficulty. However, evidence now indicates that children who are proficient at this level of linguistic analysis (segmenting spoken language into phonemes) at an early age are more likely to become good readers (see also van Kleeck, chap. 3).

EARLY DEVELOPMENTAL STUDIES

The earliest investigations of phonological awareness explored the developmental nature of these skills and the relationship of these skills to reading. More recently, research has focused on the ability to train phonological awareness and on the effect of this training on reading and spelling acquisition.

During the early 1970s, several investigators found that the ability to analyze the spoken word into syllables or phonemes follows a developmental pattern (Bruce, 1964; Fox & Routh, 1975; Gleitman & Rozin, 1973; Liberman et al., 1974; Rosner & Simon, 1971; Savin, 1972; Zhurova, 1973). Various experimental measures were used in these studies, and several of these can be adapted for both assessment and remediation activities. For example, an elision task was used by Bruce (1964) to test the child's ability to analyze the spoken word. The examiner pronounced a word such as /fan/ and asked the child to produce the word that would result if one eliminated either the first, last, or middle sound. The subjects, who ranged in age from 5:7 to 7:6, were selected from three English Infant Schools. Children were grouped according to mental ages obtained on the Stanford Binet Intelligence Test. Results indicated that the children with a mental age below seven were unable to perform the task. Between the mental ages of seven and eight, the variability in scores reflected the different teaching techniques in the three different schools. Children obtaining the highest scores on the elision task had the most direct phonics teaching. By age nine, children from all three of the schools were able to perform the task with 80% accuracy.

This elision task was expanded to include words to be produced by the child after eliminating a syllable (e.g., "Say /cowboy/ without the /cow/"), as well as items that called for the oral manipulation of phonemes (e.g., "Say /belt/ without the /t/") (Rosner & Simon, 1971). This expanded task, the Auditory Analysis Test (AAT), was administered to children in kindergarten through sixth grade. Mean scores improved progressively from kindergarten upward, with the biggest change occurring between kindergarten and the end of grade 1. Rosner and Simon suggested that, while reading instruction was most likely a significant factor in children's ability to analyze language, language analysis skills might in turn affect their early reading ability.

A tapping task was developed by I. Y. Liberman et al. (1974) to measure children's ability to segment spoken words into syllables and phonemes. Children were required to indicate, by tapping a wooden dowel on the table, the number of segments (syllables for one group, phonemes for another) in words spoken by the examiner. The subjects included four-, five-, and six-year-olds in preschool, kindergarten, and first-grade classes. The results clearly indicated that it is easier for words to be segmented into syllables than into phonemes and that there is a developmental hierarchy in the performance of these language analysis tasks. At age four nearly half of the children could segment words into syllables, but none could segment into phonemes. Although there was not a marked increase in the ability to segment syllables at age five, 17% of the children could now segment by phonemes. By the end of the first grade, 90% could successfully perform the syllable segmentation task, while 70% were able to succeed in phoneme segmentation. Liberman et al., like Rosner and Simon (1971) and Bruce (1964), suggested that it was impossible from existing studies to sort out the effects of maturation and instruction when attempting to explain the steep rise during the first grade in the child's ability to analyze his spoken language—an issue also raised by van Kleeck in Chapter 3. Liberman postulated that regardless of instruction, results indicated a greater level of maturity was necessary to analyze words into phonemes than into syllables (I. Y. Liberman, 1973).

Others have confirmed the relative ease of syllable segmentation compared to phoneme segmentation using the Liberman Tapping Task (Blachman, 1983, 1984; Leong & Haines, 1978; Zifcak, 1981) and other experimental measures of phonological awareness (Fox & Routh, 1975; Goldstein, 1976; Treiman & Baron, 1981). More recent work by Treiman and her colleagues (Treiman, 1985; Treiman & Zukowski, 1991) suggests that helping children gain access to the two primary parts of the syllable—onsets and rimes (e.g., in the syllable *trip*, the onset is *tr* and the rime is *ip*)—might help children negotiate the transition from syllable awareness to awareness of phonemes (also see Adams, 1990; Goswami & Bryant, 1990, for more detailed discussions of this issue; see also van Kleeck, chap. 3). A reasonable question to ask would be why segmentation into syllables is easier than segmentation into phonemes. Liberman, Shankweiler, Blachman, Camp, and Werfelman (1980) offered the following explanation:

> As we noted earlier, the consonant segments of the phonemic message are typically folded, at the acoustic level, into the vowel. The result is that there is no acoustic criterion by which the phonemic segments are dependably marked. However, every syllable that is formed in this way contains a vocalic nucleus and, therefore, a peak of acoustic energy. These energy peaks provide audible cues that correspond to the syllable centers (Fletcher, 1929). Though such auditory cues could not in themselves help listeners to define exact syllable boundaries, they should make it easy for them to discover how many syllables there are and, in that sense, to do explicit segmentation (p. 196).

RELATIONSHIP OF PHONOLOGICAL AWARENESS TO READING

In addition to the developmental findings, researchers in the 1970s also began to explore the relationship between phonological awareness and the acquisition of beginning reading skills. Rosner and Simon (1971), for example, found significant partial correlations (with IQ held constant) between the AAT and the language arts subtests of the Stanford Achievement Test for grades 1 through 5. I. Y. Liberman and her colleagues (1974) were particularly interested in the 30% of the first graders in their study who could not segment words into phonemes at the end of first grade. They administered the word recognition subtest of the Wide Range Achievement Test (WRAT) to all children from the original study at the beginning of second grade. They found that half of the children in the lowest third of the class for reading had been unable to analyze words into phonemes on the tapping task administered the previous year. However, no children in the upper third of the class had failed the segmentation test in grade 1.

In several additional studies, significant relationships were also found between the child's phonological awareness and the acquisition of beginning reading skills. A significant correlation was found between phoneme segmentation and reading on the reading recognition subtest of the Peabody Individual Achievement Test (PIAT) (Fox & Routh, 1975). In a later study, Fox and Routh (1976) investigated the ability of bright four-year-olds to learn to decode pairs of letter-like forms, for example ▷| ±, having a one-to-one correspondence of simple English words (e.g., *me, see, way*). They found that the good segmenters were significantly better than the nonsegmenters at the decoding task. In fact, the nonsegmenters were not able to learn to decode the words in the trials allotted them. In another study of four-year-olds (Goldstein, 1976), scores on a word analysis/synthesis task accounted for a significant amount of the variance (independent of IQ) on two author-devised reading tests, administered after a thirteen-week reading training period.

With kindergarten children, ability to segment consonant-vowel-consonant (CVC) words into three distinct units was significantly related to scores one year later on the word recognition subtest of the WRAT (Helfgott, 1976). With first graders, there were significant correlations between phoneme segmentation ability (on the Liberman Tapping Task) and performance on the WRAT word recognition subtest, as well as the Gallistel-Ellis Test of Coding Skills (Blachman, 1983; Zifcak, 1981). In addition, Zifcak compared the ability of the Liberman Tapping Task, the Rosner AAT, and Read's (1971) invented spellings, along with IQ, socioeconomic status, sex, and age, to predict the reading scores of the first-grade sample. The single best predictor was the Liberman Tapping Task, accounting for more than 60% of the variance in reading achievement. The invented spellings also added significantly to the prediction, but none of the other variables made a significant contribution to the prediction of reading achievement. As part of a larger kindergarten and first-grade study investigating the relationship of several reading-related language measures to reading, Blachman (1984) found that phoneme segmentation combined with another phonological processing measure, rapid automatized naming of letters and colors (Denckla & Rudel, 1976), accounted for 68% of the variance in the WRAT reading scores of first-grade inner-city children. Syllable segmentation was not found to be a significant predictor of first-grade reading ability, perhaps because it is a much easier task for first-grade children in general and thus much less discriminating. I. Y. Liberman and Mann (1981), however, did find that syllable segmentation measured in kindergarten can significantly predict reading performance in first grade.

Using the Lindamood Auditory Conceptualization Test (LAC) (Lindamood & Lindamood, 1971), an instrument probably more familiar to speech-language pathologists than to others working with learning disabled children, Calfee, Lindamood, and Lindamood (1973) also investigated the relationship between reading and what those authors call "acoustic-phonetic" skills. By manipulating colored blocks, children indicate their awareness of the phonemic segments in speech. For example, if the examiner said "show me /ip/," a child might present two blocks of different colors. The examiner might then say "if that says /ip/, show me /pi/," and the student would be expected to reverse the order of the blocks. More complicated items include "if that says /vips/, show me /ips/" (p. 294). Students in kindergarten through twelfth grade were tested using the LAC and the reading and spelling subtests of the WRAT. Highly significant correlations were found across grade levels between LAC total score and a combined reading and spelling score. Of particular significance in this study was the stability of the relationship between these phoneme manipulation skills and reading and spelling scores from kindergarten through high school.

Overwhelming evidence from a host of longitudinal studies now indicates that performance on tasks measuring phonological awareness in kindergarten or first grade are powerful predictors of reading achievement (Blachman, 1984; Blachman & James, 1986; Bradley & Bryant, 1983, 1985; Juel, 1988; Juel, Griffith, & Gough, 1986; Lundberg, Olofsson, & Wall, 1980; Mann & Ditunno, 1990; Mann & Liberman, 1984; Share, Jorm, MacLean, & Matthews, 1984; Stanovich, Cunningham, & Cramer, 1984; Torneus, 1984; Vellutino & Scanlon, 1987). Several new studies have demonstrated that phonological awareness can be measured in even younger preschool children and that it remains a robust predictor of early reading success (Bryant, Bradley, MacLean, & Crossland, 1989; Bryant, MacLean, Bradley, & Crossland, 1990; MacLean, Bryant, & Bradley, 1987; Scarborough, 1990).

Correlation studies such as the ones discussed here, even when the findings are highly consistent, leave many questions unanswered. Of special interest is whether phonological awareness facilitates learning to read or is developed by learning to read. Van Kleeck (chap. 3) also raises this question. Researchers have presented data to support a variety of hypotheses regarding the nature of the relationship between phonological awareness and reading. For example, as shall be seen later in this chapter, phonological awareness training studies (e.g., Bradley & Bryant, 1983, 1985; Lundberg, Frost, & Peterson, 1988) and recent investigations of the relationship between the rhyming ability of three- and four-year-olds and early word recognition (Bryant et al., 1989; MacLean et al., 1987) offer convincing evidence that phonological awareness facilitates learning to read. On the other hand, Morais and his colleagues (Morais, 1991; Morais, Cary, Alegria, & Bertelson, 1979) have demonstrated that this awareness of the internal structure of language is developed as one learns to read an alphabetic orthography. In the Morais et al. (1979) study, for example, they compared literate adults (who only learned to read as adults) and illiterate adults from the same poor peasant background in Portugal on their ability to add or delete a phoneme at the beginning of a nonword. These researchers found that only the literate adults were successful. This suggested that the level of linguistic awareness required to segment language into phonemes does not develop as a matter of course but requires some training that is most often provided by formal reading instruction.

The data supporting these alternative hypotheses are not, however, in conflict. There is no reason for one interpretation regarding the direction of the relationship between phonological awareness and reading to preclude the other, when, in fact, a reciprocal relationship is more likely to be the case (Ehri, 1979; I. Y. Liberman, Liberman, Mattingly, & Shankweiler, 1980; Lundberg, 1991; Perfetti, Beck, Bell, & Hughes, 1987; Stuart & Coltheart, 1988). As Perfetti and his colleagues were able to demonstrate in their longitudinal study (Perfetti et al., 1987):

> The reciprocity hypothesis (i.e., that reflective phonemic knowledge and reading competence develop in mutual support) is not a denial of a causal role for phonemic awareness. It is instead a suggestion that the causal connection is only half the picture. The other half is that advancement in reading promotes increased reflective phonemic awareness, which in turn promotes further gains in reading. (p. 41)

For many youngsters, exposure to print (e.g., being read to) appears to trigger phonological awareness long before formal instruction begins, as discussed in great detail by van Kleeck (chap. 3). Yet other children fail to develop the most rudimentary connections between print and speech, even after exposure to formal reading instruction. This brings us to several additional questions: Can we train phonological awareness and, as a corollary, how do we do it? Does the training have a positive effect on reading?

TEACHING PHONOLOGICAL AWARENESS

To some extent, of course, all researchers do some training in phonological awareness by whatever modeling of the task they conduct before presenting the experimental test items. However, in many of the early studies, researchers wanted to know more specifically whether or not a child's phonological awareness could be improved by direct instructional activities (Elkonin, 1963, 1973; Fox & Routh, 1976; Helfgott, 1976; Kattke, 1978; Lewkowicz, 1980; Lewkowicz & Low, 1979; Marsh & Mineo, 1977; Olofsson & Lundberg, 1983; Rosner, 1974; Skjelfjord, 1976; Zhurova, 1973).

After using Rosner's (1973) AAT program from September to May, four-year-old preschoolers were successful with two-syllable tasks (e.g., "Say /cowboy/. Now say it again, but don't say /boy/"), and kindergartners were able to perform phoneme elision tasks with initial consonants (e.g., "Say /bat/. Now say it again, but don't say /b/") (Rosner, 1974, p. 381). Both groups made significant progress from pre- to posttesting. In another type of phonological awareness task, requiring four- and five-year-olds to identify which of two words begins or ends with a given sound, children improved significantly over four days of training and appeared to maintain this level of performance during four days of transfer tasks (Marsh & Mineo, 1977). In general, continuants (/s/, /m/, /f/, or /n/) were more easily matched than stops (/b/, /d/, /p/, /t/), although there was an interaction between position in the word and phoneme type. In the initial position, subjects were more successful with continuants, whereas the stops were more easily recognized in the final position.

The most detailed description of a successful model for training young children to segment words into phonemes was presented by Elkonin (1963, 1973). Showing children a simple line drawing of the word to be segmented and a row of squares depicting the exact number of phonemes in the pictured word, Elkonin and his colleagues taught the children to pronounce the word slowly and to push a counter into each square as each sound in the word was produced. The success rate of children using the counters, pictures, and diagrams was considerably higher than when the aids were not used in training segmentation skills. Five- and six-year-old children were able to master segmentation with this procedure.

An attempt has also been made to evaluate the effectiveness of each of the visual aids (counters, squares, and pictures) used in the Elkonin procedure (Lewkowicz & Low, 1979). Testing kindergarten children at the beginning of the year, the authors found that squares and counters were the most important in helping children segment successfully. However, once children had learned to segment two-phoneme words correctly using the aids, the use of the aids did not improve the three-phoneme segmentation. Based on their subjects' mastery of two- and three-phoneme word segmentation, the authors suggested that this skill is not too difficult to teach to kindergarten children. This finding was confirmed by other researchers (Helfgott, 1976; Kattke, 1978) using the diagram and other elements of the Elkonin procedure in their training. All of these researchers emphasized initial training with kindergarten children on two-phoneme words (consonant-vowel and vowel-consonant), having found them easier than three-phoneme words to segment.

EFFECTS OF PHONOLOGICAL AWARENESS INSTRUCTION ON LITERACY ACQUISITION

Despite numerous correlational studies documenting the contribution of phonological awareness to beginning reading success, and despite evidence that we can develop phoneme awareness in young children, it was only in the last decade that researchers were able to demonstrate clearly the effect of training on reading. Although some training studies were completed in the 1970s, insufficient data, small sample size, and attempts to evaluate too many program components at the same time made it difficult to isolate the effect of training in phoneme awareness on reading and spelling.

In 1973, for example, Elkonin reported that the kindergarten children in his studies were able to master "sound analysis of words," and this was followed by "improvement in various aspects of literacy" (p. 569); however, no data were reported to document the success of the trained children. About the same time, Rosner (1971) provided some very preliminary support for the effect of phonological awareness training on the development of reading. He trained a small (n = 8) experimental group of nonreading first graders in segmentation skills, using the auditory component of an earlier version of his 1973 Perceptual Skills Curriculum (e.g., "Say /fat/. Now say it again without the /f/"). A control group matched for IQ and auditory analysis scores before training did not receive this special instruction, although both groups were being taught to read during this period. At the end of about three and one-half months of training, the experimental group had significantly higher scores on the AAT. In addition, the children were also tested on their ability to read words from the instructional material and "transfer" words not included in the training program. The experimental group was able to read significantly more words from both reading lists than the control group.

Another first-grade study demonstrated the effectiveness of a tutorial reading program that included training in analysis and synthesis (Wallach & Wallach, 1976). Low-readiness first graders in an inner-city school were tutored by minority mothers. In addition, the children received regular classroom reading instruction. Part I of the program emphasized recognition of sounds at the beginning of words and sound–symbol relationships; Part II emphasized recognition and manipulation of sounds in all positions of the word and direct instruction in blending phonetically regular CVC words; and Part III moved into the regular classroom reading materials. At the end of the year, the experimental children performed significantly better than the control children on experimenter-devised and standardized reading measures.

In one of the few studies with older children, Williams (1980) evaluated the effectiveness of her program ("The ABD's of Reading"), designed to teach phonemic analysis, blending, and decoding to learning disabled children between the ages of seven and twelve. Specific materials were prepared for the teacher to instruct children in analysis of words into syllables; analysis of words into phonemes (first working with syllables of two and then three phonemes); and blending of two-phoneme and then three-phoneme CVC units. A modification of the Elkonin (1973) visual aids was used, with wooden squares representing first the syllables and then the phonemes. After the emphasis on segmental analysis, letter–sound correspondences were taught, and letter symbols were placed on the wooden squares. The students were then taught to read (decode) and construct (encode) CVC combinations and later CCVC, CVCC, and CCVCC combinations, followed by two-syllable words with these same patterns.

Classrooms were randomly assigned to either an instructional treatment or nontreatment control group. The program was used for twenty minutes a day, three to four times a week, for about six months to supplement whatever reading program was used in the classroom. There were no differences between groups on a pretest measuring sound–symbol associations, phoneme analysis and blending, and decoding of CVC words. However, on posttests based on data from twenty experimental groups (n = 60) and fourteen control groups (n = 42), the experimental groups performed significantly better than the control groups on eight of nine subtests. To measure the child's success at decoding novel CVC nonsense and real word combinations (half of the items had been included in the instructional program, and the other half were new combinations), two transfer tasks were administered at two different points in the training program. Again, results (based on twenty-eight experimental subjects and twenty-eight control subjects who completed both tests) indicated that correct responses were significantly higher for the experimental than the control subjects. Williams's work demonstrated the effectiveness of teaching these skills to older (age seven to twelve) learning disabled students. Williams agreed with others (Elkonin, 1963, 1973; I. Y. Liberman, 1971; I. Y. Liberman et al., 1980; I. Y. Liberman & Shankweiler, 1979) that these skills should be emphasized in beginning reading instruction.

The Wallach and Wallach (1976) and the Williams studies evaluated many program components; consequently, the specific effect on reading of training in phoneme analysis skills could not be isolated. One might also suggest that the effectiveness of the training may have been due to the increased reading time given to experimental subjects rather than the specific activities used. Since the early 1980s, however, numerous training studies here and abroad have confirmed the value of providing instruction in phonological awareness to beginning readers (Ball & Blachman, 1988, 1991; Blachman, Ball, Black, & Tangel, 1991; Bradley & Bryant, 1983, 1985; Byrne & Fielding-Barnsley, 1991a; Cunningham, 1990; Fox & Routh, 1984; Lundberg et al., 1988; Treiman & Baron,

1983). The results of these studies have been so consistent in demonstrating a positive effect on reading and/or spelling ability, that Adams (1990) concluded after a recent review of the phonological awareness literature that "The evidence is compelling: Toward the goal of efficient and effective reading instruction, explicit training of phonemic awareness is invaluable" (p. 331).

Manipulating Instructional Components

The intervention activities created for many of these training studies are applicable to a variety of classroom and clinical settings (for a more complete description of these activities see Blachman, 1991). Researchers have worked with children in large and small groups, as well as individually. Another important component that has been manipulated is whether the phonological awareness instruction is combined with instruction that links the phonological segments to the letters of the alphabet. For example, by electing to focus specifically on enhancing phonological awareness *without* providing instruction in the connections between the sound segments and letters, Lundberg et al. (1988) demonstrated that phonological awareness can be heightened outside the context of literacy instruction. They also challenged the idea that phonological awareness is only a consequence of reading instruction. In the Lundberg et al. study of 235 nonreading Danish kindergarten children, classroom teachers provided eight months of training to the entire group of fifteen to twenty students in each classroom. During the first two months, the children participated in a variety of listening games and rhyming activities and learned first to segment sentences into words and then multisyllabic words into syllables. During the third month, children were taught to identify the initial phoneme in words that begin with continuous sound letters. By the fifth month, children were learning to segment two-phoneme items.

After the intervention, the children who had participated in the phonological awareness intervention demonstrated superior skill on tasks requiring word, syllable, and phoneme segmentation and synthesis, although the groups did not differ on tests of beginning reading at the end of kindergarten. When the children were tested at the end of first grade, the treatment children significantly outperformed the control children on measures of both reading and spelling. Thus, once the children were exposed to formal reading and spelling instruction in grades 1 and 2, children who had participated in the phonological awareness intervention in kindergarten appeared to be better prepared to take advantage of that instruction than the control children. It is important to note that although the kindergarten program emphasized games, the authors had learned from earlier research (Olofsson & Lundberg, 1983) that structure was a critical variable in the success of the program. In their 1983 study, these researchers had varied structure across treatment conditions. Children in the most structured condition participated in three to four lessons per week for fifteen to thirty minutes; children in the least structured condition participated in phoneme awareness activities that their teachers introduced spontaneously during normal play activities, as per van Kleeck (chap. 3). Only the most structured group showed improvement on the posttest.

In a more recent study in the United States, Cunningham (1990) provided ten weeks (twenty lessons, fifteen to twenty minutes each) of phoneme awareness instruction to small groups of kindergarten children. As in the Lundberg study, Cunningham did not provide explicit training in sound–symbol correspondences. Her intervention was adapted from "The ABD's of Reading" (Williams, 1979) described earlier in this chapter. Wooden markers were used to represent the sounds in words, and worksheets depicted a series of boxes that corresponded to the number of phonemes in the word to be analyzed (e.g., three boxes for *cot*). Children learned to put an "x" in the appropriate box to represent the first, middle, or final sound in a spoken word. After the intervention, the treatment children in both kindergarten and first grade outperformed the control children on measures of phoneme awareness and on a general measure of reading ability.

These studies demonstrate the facilitating effect on reading of training in phoneme awareness. In the Lundberg et al. (1988) study, in particular, the researchers were able to isolate the effect of phonological awareness by heightening phonological awareness outside the context of literacy instruction. That is, these Danish kindergarten children did not have instruction in sound–symbol correspondences during the intervention, nor was such instruction part of the typical kindergarten curriculum. However, once these children were exposed to formal instruction in reading and writing in first grade, the treatment children in the Lundberg study demonstrated that they had an edge over those who had not participated in activities to enhance phonological awareness. In this way, Lundberg and his colleagues answered an important theoretical question regarding the value of training in phonological awareness uncontaminated by instruction in reading. This does not mean, however, that providing phonological awareness instruction without also enabling children to understand how the sound segments connect to letters is the most pedagogically sound practice. As the next group of studies illustrates, considerable evidence indicates that the benefits of training in phonological awareness can be enhanced when the connections between the sound segments in words and letters are made explicit during training.

Connecting Sound Segments to Letters

In a landmark longitudinal and experimental training study in England, Bradley and Bryant (1983, 1985) established a causal relationship between phonological awareness and reading achievement. The study also demonstrates the incremental benefit of combining phonological awareness instruction with letter-sound instruction. In their longitudinal work, Bradley and Bryant found a significant relationship between the phoneme awareness of 368 four- and five-year-olds and the reading and spelling achievement of these same children three years later. During the second year of study, sixty-five of the children with the lowest pretest scores on phonological awareness (as measured by a test of sound categorization) were assigned to one of four groups matched on IQ, age, sex, and sound categorization ability. Children in the first group learned to categorize pictures on the basis of shared sounds. For example, children learned that *hen* could be grouped with *men* and *pen* because they rhymed. They also learned that *hen* could be grouped with *hat* and *hill* because they shared the same initial sound; that *hen* could be grouped with *pin* and *sun* because they shared an end sound; and that *hen* could be grouped with *leg* and *net* because the middle sound was shared. The children in the second group learned to categorize the same pictures on the basis of shared sounds, but in addition they learned to represent the common sounds with plastic letters. The children in the third group learned to categorize the same pictures on the basis of semantic categories (e.g., they were taught that *hen* and *dog* could be grouped together because they are both animals). A fourth group received no intervention.

The intervention for the first groups and the semantic categorization control group consisted of forty individual lessons over a period of two years. After the training, the children who had received the sound categorization instruction scored somewhat higher on posttests of reading and spelling than the untrained children. The most successful children, however, were the ones who were instructed in sound categorization and who were also taught to make the connections between the sound segments and letters. These children significantly outperformed both control groups in reading and spelling and had significantly higher spelling scores than the children who had received only the sound categorization training. Despite the relatively limited nature of the intervention (forty lessons spread over a two-year period), a follow-up study four years after the conclusion of the original study revealed that the children who were taught to make the connections between sound segments and letters, in combination with instruction in sound categorization, were still the most successful in reading and spelling (Bradley, 1988). Thus, the Bradley and Bryant study (1983) demonstrates that the value of phoneme awareness instruction is increased by connecting the sound segments in words to their corresponding printed symbols (see also Hohn & Ehri, 1983).

In a recent study in Australia, Byrne and Fielding-Barnsley (1991a) have shown that the phonological awareness task of sound categorization (modified and referred to here as *phoneme identity*) can be taught to four-year-old preschool children. Using a subset of the sounds illustrated in a new program entitled Sound Foundations (Byrne & Fielding-Barnsley, 1991b), children were introduced to specific sounds (e.g., /s/, /m/, /t/, /l/, /p/) in either the initial or final position through jingles or poems presented by the experimenter. Next, the experimenter introduced a large color poster that depicted objects that begin (or end) with the target sound. (There are two posters for each sound. One poster depicts items that *begin* with a given sound, and the second presents pictures of objects that *end* with a given sound. For the vowel sound /æ/, the pictures represent objects with the sound in the initial position only. About 60% of the pictures on each poster begin or end with a given sound.) Each child in the group was asked to find pictures that begin with the target sound (hence, the name "phoneme identity"). In the next lesson, each child was asked to identify pictures that ended with the same target sound. Worksheets were also used to give children an opportunity to identify and to color drawings that represented a given sound. Eventually, games were introduced that reinforced the learned sounds in both the initial and final position. The children were also taught to recognize the letter that represented each target phoneme (i.e., /s/, /m/, /l/, /t/, /p/, /æ/). Over a twelve-week period, there were twelve training sessions, each lasting for twenty to thirty minutes. The control children received the same number of training sessions and used the same materials. The object of their lessons, however, was to identify and categorize pictures on the basis of semantic categories (e.g., animals). After the training, the treatment children showed greater gains in phoneme identity (the measure of phoneme awareness used in this study) than the controls. This was true of performance on measures of untrained phonemes as well as measures of trained phonemes. The treatment children were also significantly more successful on a forced choice word recognition test (e.g., "Does this [*sat*, e.g.] say 'sat' or 'mat?'?" p. 452]). The authors concluded, as have others (e.g., Gough & Walsh, 1991), that children need both phonological awareness and knowledge of how the sound segments are represented by letters to understand the alphabetic principle.

The phonological awareness training studies reviewed thus far have demonstrated the following: (1) phonological awareness can be heightened even in preliterate children, (2) heightening phonological awareness facilitates later reading and spelling performance, and (3) the value of phoneme awareness instruction is increased when connections are made between the sound segments and their corresponding printed symbols. What is not known from these studies is whether an increase in letter–sound knowledge alone can make a difference in early literacy acquisition. For example, it would be reasonable to ask if the letter–sound component of the study by Bradley and Bryant (1983) was responsible for the superior reading and spelling of the children who were instructed in phoneme awareness and who were also taught to make the connections between the sound segments in words and the letters of the alphabet. Because Bradley and Bryant did not have a letter–sound training-only condition, it was not possible to answer this question.

To investigate this question, Ball and Blachman (1988, 1991) randomly assigned ninety nonreading kindergarten children to one of three groups. The children in the first group received instruction in phonological awareness that also included a sound–symbol component. The children in the second group participated in a variety of language activities (e.g., listening to stories, vocabulary development) but used the identical materials to learn sound–symbol associations that were used by the children in the phoneme awareness group. Children in both of these conditions met in groups of four or five, four times per week, for fifteen to twenty minutes, for seven weeks. A third group received no special instruction.

The children in the phoneme awareness condition participated in carefully structured three-part lessons. Each day the lesson began with a *say-it-and-move-it* activity. Children learned to move a disk (and other manipulatives, e.g., blocks and tiles) from the top half of an eight and one-half- by eleven-inch laminated sheet to the bottom half of the sheet to represent the sounds in one-, two-, or three-phoneme spoken items. Initially, the children learned to represent one sound (e.g., /i/) with one disk, followed by one sound repeated twice (e.g., /i/ /i/). The children then progressed to the segmentation of two-phoneme words (e.g., *it*), and eventually three-phoneme words (e.g., *sit*) were introduced. With two- and three-phoneme words, the examiner said the word slowly and, at the same time, modeled for the children how to move one disk for each sound. Next, the children were instructed to "say-it-and-move-it." To facilitate saying the words slowly with a minimum of distortion, words were initially selected that begin with continuous sound letters (e.g., *s*un, *l*ip, *f*an). During the last few weeks of the intervention, children who had mastered specified letter sounds were given letter tiles (in addition to their blank tiles) to use during the say-it-and-move-it-activity. However, the words to be segmented never included more than one of the letters on the letter tiles. For example, the children who had mastered the sounds of /a/ and /i/ were given an /a/ tile and an /i/ tile, as well as blank tiles. Among the words in the say-it-and-move-it lesson for that day might have been *lip* and *fan*.

The second activity in each three-part lesson for the phoneme awareness condition was a *segmentation-related* activity. These included, for example, a sound categorization activity adapted from Bradley and Bryant (1983) in which children were taught to group words on the basis of shared sounds. In this activity three or four pictures were placed in front of the children. The children had to decide which picture did not begin (or end) like the others. On another day, Elkonin-style segmentation cards were used to practice phoneme segmentation (a picture of the object to be segmented is in the top half of the page, and boxes representing the number of sounds in the pictured item are in the bottom half of the page). On yet another day, the segmentation-related activity might involve sound blending. Often, a puppet was used to tell stories, and the children had to correct (by blending the sounds together) any words that were mispronounced (segmented into their constituent phonemes) by the puppet.

The third part of each phoneme awareness lesson emphasized the teaching of letter names and sounds. Illustrated alphabet cards were used to introduce the names and sounds of nine letters *(a, m, t, i, s, r, u, b, f)*. For example, the letter *r* was introduced by a picture of a *r*ed *r*ooster in *r*ed *r*unning shoes. Children also played a variety of games (e.g., a version of Bingo) to reinforce the letter names and sounds that were learned during this part of each lesson.

Before the intervention, the children in the three groups did not differ on age, sex, race, socioeconomic status (SES) level, Peabody Picture Vocabulary Test—Revised (PPVT-R), letter name knowledge, letter sound knowledge, or reading ability. After the intervention, the children who were trained in phoneme awareness plus letter sounds significantly outperformed both the language activities control group and the no intervention control group on measures of phoneme awareness, reading, and developmental spelling. Of particular importance in this study was the performance of the language activities group, who had letter sound training, which was identical to that of the phoneme awareness group. After the intervention, the language activities group did not differ from the phoneme awareness group on letter sound knowledge. However, despite having letter sound knowledge that was equivalent to that of the phoneme awareness group, the language activities group did not differ from the no treatment control group on phoneme awareness, reading, or developmental spelling. Thus, it is clear from these results that *it is not letter sound knowledge alone* that is responsible for improvement in beginning reading and spelling skill. Rather, it is the *combination* of phoneme awareness instruction and letter sound knowledge that benefits early literacy acquisition (see also Ehri & Wilce, 1987).

A Classroom Model for Heightening Phonological Awareness

The training studies reviewed thus far offer strikingly consistent support for the value of providing instruction in phoneme awareness to preschool, kindergarten, and first-grade children. It is this evidence that has prompted researchers to recommend that teachers provide this instruction early—before children have had a chance to fail in reading and spelling (Adams, 1990; Blachman, 1989, 1991; Juel, 1988). Unfortunately, despite the research, activities to build skills in phonological awareness are not typically incorporated into the kindergarten curriculum. Although more teachers and clinicians are now aware of the value of phonological awareness, knowing exactly what to do to teach it is a different matter. Recently, however, articles have begun to appear that are directed to the practitioner and that focus on clinical applications of the research in phonological awareness (see, e.g., Blachman, 1991; Catts, 1991). A new program, published in Australia, is available to facilitate instruction in this skill (Sound Foundations, Byrne & Fielding-Barnsley, 1991b).

Perhaps of greatest concern is the fact that in almost all of the previous phonological awareness training studies, the intervention was conducted *outside* the regular classroom using specially trained teachers and clinicians who were brought to the schools by the researchers (see, e.g., Ball & Blachman, 1988, 1991; Bradley & Bryant, 1983, 1985; Byrne & Fielding-Barnsley, 1991a; Cunningham, 1990). (Although Lundberg et al., 1988, did conduct their Danish training study in kindergarten classrooms, the kindergarten children were a year older than those in kindergartens in the United States.) "Outside classroom" training has made it difficult to know whether the instructional strategies evaluated in these studies would be as effective when incorporated into the regular school day by classroom teachers. To answer this question, a new study was undertaken to investigate the effectiveness of instruction in phonological awareness provided in regular kindergarten classrooms by kindergarten teachers and their teaching assistants (Blachman et al., 1991).

This kindergarten training study was conducted in four, demographically comparable, low-income, inner-city schools in upstate New York. The eighty-four treatment children were drawn from all ten of the kindergarten classrooms in two of the schools; the seventy-five control children were drawn from all eight of the kindergarten classrooms in the other two schools. Before the intervention, there were no differences in the two groups of children on age, sex, race, SES level (i.e., 86% of the treatment group and 83% of the control group received free or supported lunch), PPVT-R scores, phoneme awareness, letter name and letter sound knowledge, or reading. The scores of both groups tended to cluster in the lower end of the average range on the PPVT-R (M = 91). Both groups of children had equally limited knowledge of the alphabet before the intervention (i.e., each group knew, on average, only two letter sounds when pretested in January of the kindergarten year). These four schools typically reported a high incidence of reading failure and had limited resources to cope with this failure. Thus, an attempt was made not only to evaluate the effectiveness of a classroom-based and teacher-conducted phoneme awareness intervention but also to evaluate its effectiveness in schools in which reading achievement was a major concern.

The teachers and their classroom teaching assistants participated in seven, two-hour in-service workshops to learn how to implement the phoneme awareness intervention. The intervention (modeled after Ball & Blachman, 1988, 1991) was expanded from twenty-eight to forty-one lessons conducted over eleven weeks. The classroom teachers or teaching assistants met with the treatment children in groups of four or five, four times per week, for fifteen- to twenty-minute lessons. Each lesson consisted of the same three parts described earlier: say-it-and-move-it, segmentation-related activities, and letter name and letter-sound instruction. However, because the intervention lasted longer than the intervention in our earlier study (eleven weeks instead of seven), some of the children in this study progressed to using letter tiles to represent each sound in a three-phoneme real word (e.g., *sat*). Children in each group who had not mastered letter sounds continued to use all blank tiles to segment words during the say-it-and-move-it activity. The control children in this study participated in a traditional kindergarten curriculum that included whole class instruction in letter names and sounds.

At the end of eleven weeks, children in both groups were assessed in phonological awareness, letter name and letter sound knowledge, reading, and invented spelling. The children who had participated in the phonological awareness intervention significantly outperformed the control children on measures of phoneme awareness, letter name and letter sound knowledge, reading phonetically regular words and nonwords, and invented spelling. Thus, although the treatment and control children both had limited knowledge of the alphabet before the intervention, after the intervention, the treatment children demonstrated a more sophisticated awareness of the internal structure of words. Evidence for this comes from their ability to segment words into the segments of sound that are represented in an alphabetic orthography, from their ability to connect these sound segments to the letters that represent these sounds, and from their ability to use this information to begin to read words and nonwords that conform to phonetically regular patterns.

Perhaps the most convincing evidence of the treatment children's superior knowledge of the internal structure of words was seen in their performance on a measure of invented spelling (Tangel & Blachman, 1992). These early spellings give us some insight into how children perceive the sound system of their language (see Read, 1986, for detailed discussion). Although the children did not write any words during the intervention, they were asked to write five words as a posttest. The words, originally selected by Ball and Blachman (1991), were *lap, sick, pretty, train,* and *elephant*. A developmental scoring procedure was developed to measure the extent to which the spelling of each dictated word captured the phonetic structure of the word (see Tangel & Blachman, 1992, for the unabbreviated scoring procedure). The scale (adapted from I. Y. Liberman, Rubin, Duques, & Carlisle, 1985) takes into account the number of phonemes represented and the level of orthographic representation (the use of phonetically related or conventional letters). For example, for the word *train* points were awarded as shown in Table 9–1.

Using similar criteria to evaluate the spelling of each word produced by the children, Tangel and Blachman (1992) found that the treatment children produced more sophisticated invented spellings for each word sampled. For example, for the word *sick*, 31% of the treatment children represented all of the phonemes of the word with conventional letters (e.g., *sik, sic*). None of the control children demonstrated this level of sophistication. The spellings of the treatment children, in general, were more sophisticated in terms of the number of phonemes represented, the sequencing of phonemes, and orthographic features. We were also interested in determining the representation of treatment and control children among our top, middle, and bottom invented spellers. When treatment and control groups were merged and the children rank ordered,

TABLE 9–1
Developmental scoring for invented spellings of *train*

Response	Criteria	Points
FMTXBR	Random string	0
J	Phonetically related letter	1
T	Correct first letter	2
JRA, TAN	More than one phoneme, but not all, with phonetically related or conventional letters	3
HRAN, TREN	All phonemes with mix of phonetically related and conventional letters	4
TRANE	All phonemes with conventional letters; attempt to mark long vowel	5
TRAIN	Correct spelling	6

51% of the treatment children ranked among the top third of invented spellers, while only 17% of the control children were in this group. Thus, the results clearly indicate that the invented spellings produced by the treatment children were developmentally superior to those produced by children who did not have instruction in phoneme awareness. Previous research has indicated that the level of sophistication of a child's invented spelling is related to first-grade reading success (Ferroli & Shanahan, 1987; Mann, Tobin, & Wilson, 1987; Morris & Perney, 1984). Now there is also evidence that training in phonological awareness that includes instruction in sound–symbol associations can enhance a child's invented spelling.

One of the central questions of this study (Blachman et al., 1991) was whether phoneme awareness instruction provided in the regular classroom was as effective as it had proven to be in previous studies that were conducted under more controlled conditions (provided outside the classroom by specially trained experimenters). The results clearly indicate that regular classroom teachers can incorporate these activities into the regular school day and that the training has a positive effect on important beginning reading and spelling skills. In addition, long-term follow-up studies provide evidence that this early emphasis on phonological awareness can have benefits for years to come (see, e.g., Bradley, 1988; Lundberg et al., 1988).

It is important for teachers and clinicians working with young children to recognize that, although the evidence to support the inclusion of phonological awareness activities in the curriculum appears incontrovertible, popular practices frequently fail to reflect the current research base. For example, although learning about the segmental nature of speech and its relationship to print has proven to be critical to reading success, some influential members of the reading community argue just the opposite. Goodman and Goodman (1979), vocal proponents of whole language instruction, argue that the use of written language does not require a "high level of conscious awareness of the units . . . " (p. 139). They suggest, in fact, that activities that require "breaking whole (natural) language into bite-size, abstract little pieces . . . words, syllables, and isolated sounds" (Goodman, 1986, p. 7) makes learning to read more difficult. Unfortunately, teachers who adhere rigidly to this tenet of whole language avoid doing many of the activities that research has shown promotes beginning literacy.

Ideally, one would want phonological awareness activities to be integrated into a classroom rich in oral and written language activities. The value of reading to children and of giving children opportunities to talk and write about their experiences and opportunities to learn basic concepts about print has been well documented (Anderson, Hiebert, Scott, & Wilkinson, 1985; Silliman & Wilkinson, chap. 2; van Kleeck, chap. 3). Through these and other activities (e.g., playing oral language games, e.g., rhyming; see Bryant et al., 1989; MacLean et al., 1987; van Kleeck, chap. 3), some children will discover the internal structure of words on their own. Other children need the structured opportunities that focused phonological awareness activities provide in order to learn about the internal structure of words. Those of us interested in promoting literacy acquisition need to make sure that our classrooms provide opportunities for children to develop phonological awareness.

Getting from Phonological Awareness to Word Recognition

When the children in our kindergarten study (Blachman et al., 1991) entered first grade, the nature of the instruction changed. Once the children could demonstrate an understanding of the segmental nature of speech by segmenting one-, two-, and three-phoneme items, and once they knew about half of the letter sounds, we felt the children were ready to move into more formal reading instruction. To build on the phonological awareness developed in kindergarten, our first-grade program emphasized the alphabetic code. The treatment children followed a five-part lesson that had been used with success in other inner-city schools (Blachman, 1987). The control children followed a traditional basal reading program. The experimental treatment consisted of (1) a brief review of sound–symbol associations; (2) instruction in phoneme analysis and blending by manipulating individual letters on a small pocket-chart (e.g., changing *sat* to *sam* to *ham*, *ham* to *him*); 3) a brief review of phonetically regular words and high frequency sight words; (4) reading stories from phonetically controlled readers, basal readers (basal workbooks were not used) and trade books; (5) written dictation of phonetically regular words and sentences.

At the end of first grade, the treatment children significantly outperformed the control children on measures of phoneme awareness, letter names and sounds, three measures of word recognition, a developmental spelling test, and a standardized spelling measure. In addition, fewer treatment children were recommended for retention in grade 1, and fewer treatment children were referred for remedial reading instruction from Chapter 1 reading teachers. A preliminary follow-up study from the end of second grade suggests that the children who participated in this phoneme awareness intervention in kindergarten, followed by a program that emphasized the alphabetic code in grade 1, maintained their superiority in reading at the end of second grade.

Although other methods of reading instruction might be selected to follow an early emphasis on phonological awareness, the code-emphasis model outlined earlier provides a logical extension of the earlier phonological awareness activities. This first-grade program provides an opportunity for children to develop accurate and fluent word recognition early in the reading process. The evidence continues to mount that accurate and fluent word identification is both critical in reading success (Adams, 1990; Ehri, 1991; Stanovich, 1991; Vellutino, 1991) *and* the source of the difficulty in most cases of reading disability (Chall, 1983; Gough & Tunmer, 1986; Vellutino, 1979). Thus, if the ultimate goal is the prevention of reading failure, developing phonological awareness and accurate and fluent word identification early in the child's process of literacy acquisition seems to be essential (Adams, 1990; Stanovich, 1986). Additional support for this proposal comes from Juel's (1988) longitudinal study of the reading development of fifty-four children from first to fourth grade:

> Children who became poor readers entered first grade with little phonemic awareness. Although their phonemic awareness steadily increased in first grade, they left this grade with a little less phonemic awareness than that which the children who became average or good readers possessed upon entering first grade. . . . [P]oor entering phonemic awareness appeared to contribute to a very slow start in learning spelling–sound correspondences. . . . By the end of fourth grade the poor decoders had still not achieved the level of decoding that the average to good readers had achieved by the beginning of second grade. (p. 444)

Among the fifty-four children Juel followed, it was the poor decoders who disliked reading and did less of it. This led to fewer opportunities for vocabulary growth and for exposure to new ideas and concepts. This vicious cycle has disastrous consequences for later reading comprehension. As explained by Stanovich (1986), early problems in phonological awareness and spelling-to-sound-mapping result in difficulty breaking the code. This is followed by fewer opportunities to read at school and unrewarding reading experiences. With less practice, the poorer readers are delayed in the development of automatic word recognition strategies. When automatic word recognition strategies are not in place, the poorer reader must use valuable cognitive resources (see Lahey & Bloom's discussion, chap. 13) for word recognition, reducing the resources available for comprehension (see also Perfetti, 1985; Vellutino, 1991). Because reading itself fosters many of the skills important in reading comprehension, such as vocabulary development and increased general knowledge, a marked reduction in reading experiences exacerbates the differences between good and poor readers. Juel (1988) suggests that in her study it was this cycle of failure, beginning with poor phonemic awareness, that was responsible for the increasing gap between the good and poor readers in both reading comprehension and written stories. One of the most discouraging findings in the Juel study was the fact that there was a probability of .88 that a child who was a poor reader at the end of first grade was still a poor reader at the end of fourth grade. Gough and Juel (1991) conclude from this study that "what seems essential is to insure that children learn to decode in first grade. If decoding skill does not arrive then, it may be very hard to change the direction that reading achievement takes" (p. 55).

As discussed earlier, and in several places in this text, popular practices do not always reflect the current research base. Many whole language theorists, for example, reject direct instruction methods in word recognition because these methods violate the basic philosophy of "whole language." Whole language advocates believe that children acquire written language in the same way that they acquire oral language. That is, if oral language is acquired naturally by immersion in a rich oral language environment, then written language can be acquired by immersion in an environment rich in printed language (Vellutino, 1991). Thus, whole language advocates believe that "the language a child encounters in print should be as 'whole' as the language he or she encounters in the natural environment, rather than fractioned into words, syllables, or individual sounds" (Vellutino, 1991, p. 439). Although some children may be quite successful in inducing the alphabetic principle and becoming fluent in word recognition through immersion in a print-rich environment and opportunities to play with oral and written language, many others will not be so fortunate. For children who do not develop fluent word recognition skills, their future as readers is bleak. The effectiveness of early and direct instruction in code-based strategies (beginning with activities to facilitate phonological awareness, letter–sound knowledge, and decoding or word recognition) has been extensively documented (Adams, 1990; Chall, 1967, 1989; Williams, 1986). *It is critical that professionals continue to support the inclusion of code-based strategies in beginning literacy programs if they hope to reduce the incidence of reading failure.* It is also important to recognize that no one has suggested that the code-based strategies preclude the use of meaning based strategies. In fact, the importance of meaning in all literacy instruction is emphasized by those who stress an early emphasis on the code (Adams, 1990; I. Y. Liberman & Liberman, 1990; Vellutino, 1991). Vellutino's (1991) recent summary of the research regarding the code-oriented versus whole language oriented controversy says it best:

> The implications of the research for teaching children to read should be apparent. The most basic dictate seems to be that instruction that promotes facility in word identification is vitally important to success in reading. Accordingly, instruction that facilitates both phoneme awareness and alphabetic coding is vitally important to success in reading. However, nothing in the research precludes the use of whole language type activities in teaching reading, such as the use of context for monitoring and predictive purposes, vocabulary enrichment to imbue printed words with meaning, discussion that would encourage reading for comprehension, integration of reading, writing, and spelling to concretize the relationships between and among these representational systems, and so forth. Conversely, the research runs counter to exclusive versions of either whole language or code-oriented approaches to reading instruction. In other words, the research supports a balanced approach. (p. 442)

ASSESSMENT ISSUES

As discussed earlier, many of the intervention activities used in the phoneme awareness training studies can be adapted for classroom use. It is also the case that the measures used in these studies to *assess* phoneme awareness can be adapted by the clinician wishing to assess phonological awareness in the young child. However, there is no "cookbook" providing clear guidelines about which phoneme awareness task to administer to which child.

What is known from the literature is that regardless of how phonological awareness has been measured (e.g., sound counting, sound deletion, sound manipulation [reversing phonemes], sound categorization), it has been shown to be significantly related to reading achievement. Two studies of task comparability (Stanovich, Cunningham, & Cramer, 1984; Yopp, 1988) found that, despite the variety in task demand, the phonological awareness tasks shared a large amount of variance, thus supporting the construct validity of the concept of phonological awareness (see also Vellutino & Scanlon, 1987). In addition, these studies provided information regarding a hierarchy of task difficulty. Specifically, among the phoneme awareness tasks evaluated, rhyming proved to be the easiest and phoneme deletion the most difficult. Phoneme segmentation and phoneme counting fall in between. But which of these tasks is appropriate for a kindergarten child, a first-grade child, or an older remedial student?

For the kindergarten child, rhyme detection and production have been found to be the easiest phoneme awareness tasks. Consequently, when rhyming has been measured at the end of kindergarten, it has been found to be less predictive of reading achievement than other measures of phonological awareness (Blachman, 1984; Stanovich et al, 1984; Yopp, 1988). On the other hand, knowledge of nursery rhymes and rhyme detection in three- and four-year-olds is strongly related to beginning word recognition ability (Bryant et al. 1989; MacLean et al., 1987; van Kleeck, chap. 3). In a more recent study by Bryant and his colleagues (1990), new evidence is presented to indicate that "there is a developmental path from early sensitivity to rhyme to awareness of phonemes a year or more later, and this awareness of phonemes is strongly related to reading" (p. 435). The data also provide evidence that sensitivity to rhyme makes a direct contribution to reading that is separate from the relationship between phoneme awareness and reading. Thus, ability to detect and produce rhyme may be a particularly useful assessment measure with preschool children, and kindergarten children who do not demonstrate facility with rhyme should be given ample opportunities to develop this skill.

When more conceptually demanding tasks (e.g., asking the child to segment words into phonemes) are administered to kindergarten children, educators and clinicians appear to be somewhat confused regarding interpretation of performance. The developmental literature indicates that the majority of kindergarten children will not be able to segment words into phonemes, despite their ability to rhyme and to segment words into the more readily identifiable syllabic unit (Blachman 1984; I. Y. Liberman et al., 1974; Stanovich et al., 1984; Yopp, 1988). Yet, in some cases "failure" on a test of phoneme segmentation in kindergarten has been used to indicate that the child cannot profit from an approach to reading that emphasizes the alphabetic code and, instead, would benefit from an approach that emphasizes whole words. On the contrary, research has indicated that instruction in phonological awareness and alphabetic coding in kindergarten and first grade may have the greatest benefit for those with low phonological awareness pretest scores (Bradley & Bryant, 1983, 1985; Stanovich, 1986; Torneus, 1984). Thus, to exclude a child from activities that could enhance phonological awareness in kindergarten, because of "failure" on a kindergarten test of phonological awareness, is likely to be detrimental to that child's literacy acquisition.

For the first-grade child, the literature suggests that by the end of the year most children will be able to count phonemes, segment phonemes, or delete initial phonemes in one-, two-, or three-phoneme items. For example, in a now classic study by Liberman et al. (1974), the developmental data indicated that at the end of the first-grade year, 70% of the children were successful at segmenting words in one-, two, and three-phoneme items, as mentioned previously in this chapter. Thus, these tasks appear to be appropriate assessment measures to identify children in first grade who need direct instruction in phonological awareness. A more conceptually demanding task, such as phoneme deletion or phoneme manipulation, might be more appropriate for assessment of an older child (see, e.g., Pratt & Brady, 1988, for data on tasks used with third-grade children).

Despite the extensive literature on the relationship of phonological awareness to reading success, tasks to specifically assess phonological awareness are still not routinely included in kindergarten and first-grade assessments. There is also an extensive literature relating other phonological processing skills to reading (i.e., the phonological processes involved in lexical access and in the efficient storage of verbal information in working memory). Yet measures assessing these critical phonological skills are often missing when we assess young children. Evidence indicates that when measures sensitive to these three phonological processing skills (e.g., phonological awareness, lexical access, and verbal memory) are used to predict end of first-grade reading ability, it is possible to account for more than 74% of the variance in first-grade reading achievement (Blachman, 1983). This is a considerable improvement over the 50% usually explained by the better predictive instruments (Lindsay & Wedell, 1982; Pikulski, 1974). It is important to remember that if an assessment battery fails to reflect the phonological processing variables important in early reading, then obviously the assessment results will fail to demonstrate the relationship that exists between these language skills and reading success. When assessing young children, teachers and clinicians need to make sure that their screening and assessment instruments include those language measures that are directly related to early reading acquisition.

UNSOLVED PROBLEMS

The focus in this chapter has been on the necessity of acquiring phonological awareness and letter sound knowledge for beginning literacy acquisition. However, this is not the same as saying that phonological awareness and letter knowledge are sufficient for reading success. In Byrne and Fielding-Barnsley's (1991a) study, for example, the researchers not only examined the children who had attained a certain level of success on measures of phoneme identity, letter knowledge, and word recognition but also examined the children who, despite success on measures of phoneme identity and letter knowledge, were not successful on the word recognition task. The researchers ask an important question: "What is needed in addition to phonemic awareness and letter knowledge?" (p. 455). They suggest, as a partial response to their question, that one thing that is needed is increased emphasis on the application of phonological awareness to the reading task, through a more "meta-level" of instruction as opposed to a more "skill and drill" approach. As noted by Byrne and Fielding-Barnsley, when Cunningham (1990) compared these two approaches to phoneme awareness instruction with kindergarten and first-grade children, she found that all groups improved in reading achievement, but the greatest improvement was seen in the first-grade children who had the "meta-level" of instruction (see van Kleeck, chap. 3, for more details).

In future research, professionals need to look at both the children who are successful in our training programs as well as those who are not successful. The Byrne and Fielding-Barnsley study provides a good example by identifying a small subgroup of children who, despite success in phoneme identity and letter knowledge, were not successful on their word recognition task. However, because the children in this study were so young (between the ages of four and five), it is unclear what will happen when children in this "phonologically aware" subgroup are given repeated opportunities to apply their knowledge of the alphabetic principle in real reading contexts (the importance of this applied practice has been well documented; see, e.g., Adams, 1990; Anderson et al., 1985). It is important to ask these questions.

Another question to explore is the relationship among the various phonological processing skills known to contribute to reading deficits (I. Y. Liberman & Shankweiler, 1985; Wagner & Torgesen, 1987). In addition to problems in phonological awareness, there is extensive documentation of problems in the retrieval of phonological information (demonstrated by slowness on rapid naming tasks) (see German, chap. 12; Lahey & Bloom, chap. 13; see also Wolf, 1991, for a review of the naming speed literature) and in the phonological processes needed for efficient storage of verbal information in working memory (see Brady, 1991, for a review of the role of working memory in reading). Although practitioners' understanding of phonological awareness, and their ability to facilitate its development, increased dramatically in the 1980s and 1990s, Torgesen (1991) suggested that it is unlikely that problems in phonological awareness, by themselves, account for the most intractable long-term reading disabilities. Torgesen also points out that, despite the ability to train phonological awareness and to demonstrate the benefit of this training on reading, similarly convincing demonstrations of training effects in the other areas of phonological processing are lacking. In Wolf's (1991) discussion of naming-rate deficits in poor readers and Torgesen's (1991) discussion of severe memory span deficits, both researchers provide data to document the enduring nature of these phonological processing problems in severely disabled readers. Developing effective remediation strategies to cope with the variety of phonological processing problems experienced by severely disabled readers continues to present a formidable challenge for both researchers and practitioners.

SUMMARY

As seen in this chapter, an abundance of research now supports a causal role for phonological awareness in early literacy acquisition. The evidence clearly indicates that an awareness of internal structure of words facilitates success in learning how to read and spell. In addition, professionals know how to heighten phonological awareness in young children. Furthermore, evidence indicates that children who have had instruction in phonological awareness demonstrate reading and spelling skills that are superior to those of children who have not had this instruction.

Given the critical role of phonological awareness in learning how to read, it is important for teachers and clinicians to provide ample opportunities for children to learn about the phonological segments that are represented in an alphabetic orthography. Although many children will acquire this knowledge on their own, other children will not be so fortunate and will need the kind of systematic instruction described in this chapter. As language specialists create the rich oral and written language environments that all children should experience, they should not lose sight of the fact that they must also provide for the individual differences in phonological abilities that children bring to early literacy activities (I. Y. Liberman & Shankweiler, 1991). Phonological awareness, combined with knowledge of how the sound segments connect to letters, leads to more accurate word recognition; and word recognition, by every account, is vitally important to reading success (Adams, 1990; Vellutino, 1991). If professionals wish to reduce the incidence of reading failure, their instructional practices must reflect these facts.

REFERENCES

Adams, M. J. (1990). *Beginning to read: Thinking and learning about print*. Cambridge, MA: MIT Press.

Anderson, R., Hiebert, E., Scott, J., & Wilkinson, I. (Eds.). (1985). *Becoming a nation of readers: The report of the Commission on Reading*. Washington, DC: National Institute of Education.

Ball, E. W., & Blachman, B. A. (1988). Phoneme segmentation training: Effect on reading readiness. *Annals of Dyslexia, 38,* 208–225.

Ball, E. W., & Blachman, B. A. (1991). Does phoneme awareness training in kindergarten make a difference in early word recognition and developmental spelling? *Reading Research Quarterly, 26*(1), 49–66.

Blachman, B. (1983). Are we assessing the linguistic factors critical in early reading? *Annals of Dyslexia, 33,* 91–109.

Blachman, B. (1984). Relationship of rapid naming ability and language analysis skill to kindergarten and first-grade reading achievement. *Journal of Educational Psychology, 76,* 610–622.

Blachman, B. A. (1987). An alternative classroom reading program for learning disabled and other low-achieving children. In R. Bowler (Ed.), *Intimacy with language: A forgotten basic in teacher education*. Baltimore: Orton Dyslexia Society.

Blachman, B. (1989). Phonological awareness and word recognition: Assessment and intervention. In A. G. Kamhi & H. W. Catts (Eds.), *Reading disabilities: A developmental language perspective* (pp. 133–158). Boston: College-Hill Press.

Blachman, B. A. (1991). Early intervention for children's reading problems: Clinical applications of the research in phonological awareness. *Topics in Language Disorders, 12*(1), 51–65.

Blachman, B. A., Ball, E., Black, S., & Tangel, D. (1991). *Promising practices for beginning reading instruction: Teaching phoneme awareness in the kindergarten classroom.* Manuscript submitted for publication.

Blachman, B., & James, S. (October, 1986). *A longitudinal study of metalinguistic abilities and reading achievement in primary grade children*. Paper presented at the meeting of the International Academy for Research in Learning Disabilities, Northwestern University, Evanston, IL.

Bradley, L. (1988). Making connections in learning to read and spell. *Applied Cognitive Psychology, 2,* 3–18.

Bradley, L., & Bryant, P. (1983). Categorizing sounds and learning to read: A causal connection. *Nature, 30,* 419–421.

Bradley, L., & Bryant, P. (1985). *Rhyme and reason in reading and spelling*. Ann Arbor: University of Michigan Press.

Brady, S. A. (1991). The role of working memory in reading disability. In S. A. Brady & D. P. Shankweiler (Eds.), *Phonological processes in literacy; A tribute to Isabelle Y. Liberman* (pp. 129–151). Hillsdale, NJ: Lawrence Erlbaum.

Bruce, L. J. (1964). The analysis of word sounds by young children. *British Journal of Educational Psychology, 34,* 158–170.

Bryant, P. E., Bradley, L., MacLean, M., & Crossland, J. (1989). Nursery rhymes, phonological skills and reading. *Journal of Child Language, 16,* 407–428.

Bryant, P. E., MacLean, M., Bradley, L. L., & Crossland, J. (1990). Rhyme and alliteration, phoneme detection, and learning to read. *Developmental Psychology, 26,* 429–438.

Byrne, B., & Fielding-Barnsley, R. (1991a). Evaluation of a program to teach phonemic awareness to young children. *Journal of Educational Psychology, 83,* 451–455.

Byrne, B., & Fielding-Barnsley, R. (1991b). *Sound foundations.* Artarmon, New South Wales, Australia: Leyden Educational Publishers.

Calfee, R. C., Lindamood, P., & Lindamood, C. (1973). Acoustic-phonetic skills and reading—kindergarten through 12th grade. *Journal of Educational Psychology, 64,* 293–298.

Catts, H. W. (1991). Facilitating phonological awareness: Role of speech-language pathologists. *Language, Speech, and Hearing Services in the Schools, 22,* 196–203.

Chall, J. S. (1967). *Learning to read: The great debate*. New York: McGraw-Hill.

Chall, J. S. (1983). *Stages of reading development*. New York: McGraw-Hill.

Chall, J. S. (1989). *Learning to read: The great debate* 20 years later: A response to "Debunking the great phonics myth." *Phi Delta Kappan, 70,* 521–538.

Cunningham, A. E. (1990). Explicit v. implicit instruction in phonemic awareness. *Journal of Experimental Child Psychology, 50*(3), 429–444.

Denckla, M. B., & Rudel, R. G. (1976). Rapid "automatized" naming (R. A. N.): Dyslexia differentiated from other learning disabilities. *Neuropsychologia, 14,* 471–479.

Ehri, L. C. (1979). Linguistic insight: Threshold of reading acquisition. In T. G. Waller & G. E. MacKinnon (Eds.), *Reading research: Advances in theory and practice* (Vol. 1). New York: Academic Press.

Ehri, L. (1991). Learning to read and spell words. In L. Rieben & C. A. Perfetti (Eds.), *Learning to read: Basic research and its implications* (pp. 57–73). Hillsdale, NJ: Lawrence Erlbaum Associates.

Ehri, L., & Wilce, L. (1987). Does learning to spell help beginners learn to read words? *Reading Research Quarterly, 12,* 47–65.

Elkonin, D. B. (1963). The psychology of mastering the elements of reading. In B. Simon & J. Simon (Eds.), *Educational psychology in the U. S. S. R.* London: Routledge & Kegan Paul.

Elkonin, D. B. (1973). U. S. S. R. In J. Downing (Ed.), *Comparative reading*. New York: Macmillan.

Ferroli, L., & Shanahan, T. (1987). Kindergarten spelling: Explaining its relationship to first-grade reading. In J. E. Readence & R. S. Baldwin (Eds.), *Research in literacy: Merging perspectives. Thirty-sixth Yearbook of the National Reading Conference* (pp. 93–99). Rochester, NY: National Reading Conference.

Fletcher, H. (1929). *Speech and hearing*. New York: Van Nostrand.

Fox, B., & Routh, D. K. (1975). Analysing spoken language into words, syllables, and phonemes: A developmental study. *Journal of Psycholinguistic Research, 4,* 331–342.

Fox, B., & Routh, D. K. (1976). Phonemic analysis and synthesis as word-attack skills. *Journal of Educational Psychology, 68,* 70–74.

Fox, B., & Routh, D. K. (1984). Phonemic analysis and synthesis as word attack skills: Revisited. *Journal of Educational Psychology, 76,* 1059–1061.

Gelb, I. J. (1963). *A study of writing*. Chicago: University of Chicago Press.

Gleitman, L. R., & Rozin, P. (1973). Teaching reading by use of a syllabary. *Reading Research Quarterly, 8,* 447–483.

Gleitman, L. R., & Rozin, P. (1977). The structure and acquisition of reading I: Relations between orthographies and the structure of language. In A. S. Reber & D. L. Scarborough (Eds.), *Toward a psychology of reading: The proceedings of the CUNY Conference* (pp. 1–53), Hillsdale, NJ: Lawrence Erlbaum.

Goldstein, D. M. (1976). Cognitive-linguistic functioning and learning to read in preschoolers. *Journal of Educational Psychology, 68,* 680–688.

Goodman, K. S. (1986). *What's whole in whole language: A parent-teacher guide*. Portsmouth, NH: Heinemann.

Goodman, K. S., & Goodman, Y. M. (1979). Learning to read is natural. In L. B. Resnick & P. A. Weaver (Eds.), *Theory and practice of early reading* (Vol. 1, pp. 137–154). Hillsdale, NJ: Lawrence Erlbaum.

Goswami, U., & Bryant, P. (1990). *Phonological skills and learning to read*. East Sussex, UK: Lawrence Erlbaum.

Gough, P. B., & Juel, C. (1991). The first stages of word recognition. In L. Rieben & C. A. Perfetti (Eds.). *Learning to read: Basic research and its implications* (pp. 47–56). Hillsdale, NJ: Lawrence Erlbaum.

Gough, P. B., & Tunmer, W. E. (1986). Decoding, reading, and reading disability. *Remedial and Special Education, 7,* 6–10.

Gough, P. B., & Walsh, M. (1991). Chinese, Phoenicians, and the orthographic cipher of English. In S. A. Brady & D. P. Shankweiler (Eds.), *Phonological processes in literacy: A tribute to Isabelle Y. Liberman* (pp. 199–209). Hillsdale, NJ: Lawrence Erlbaum

Helfgott, J. (1976). Phonemic segmentation and blending skills of kindergarten children: Implications for beginning reading acquisition. *Contemporary Educational Psychology, 1,* 157–169.

Hohn, W., & Ehri, L. (1983). Do alphabet letters help prereaders acquire phonemic segmentation skills? *Journal of Educational Psychology, 75,* 752–762.

Juel, C. (1988). Learning to read and write: A longitudinal study of 54 children from first through fourth grades. *Journal of Educational Psychology, 80,* 437–447.

Juel, C., Griffith, P., & Gough, P. (1986). Acquisition of literacy: A longitudinal study of children in first and second grade. *Journal of Educational Psychology, 78,* 243–255.

Kattke, M. L. (1978). The ability of kindergarten children to analyze 2-phoneme words (Doctoral dissertation, Columbia University Teachers College). *Dissertation Abstracts International, 39,* 3472A. (University Microfilms No. 78-22, 058).

Leong, C. K., & Haines, C. F. (1978). Beginning readers' analysis of words and sentences. *Journal of Reading Behavior, 10,* 393–407.

Lewkowicz, N. K. (1980). Phonemic awareness training: What to teach and how to teach it. *Journal of Educational Psychology, 72,* 686–700.

Lewkowicz, N. K., & Low, L. Y. (1979). Effects of visual aids and word structure on phonemic segmentation. *Contemporary Educational Psychology, 4,* 238–252.

Liberman, A. M. (1970). The grammars of speech and language. *Cognitive Psychology, 1,* 301–323.

Liberman, A. M., Cooper, F. S., Shankweiler, D., & Studdert-Kennedy, M. (1967). Perception of the speech code. *Psychological Review, 74,* 431–461.

Liberman, I. Y. (1971). Basic research in speech and lateralization of language: Some implications for reading disability. *Bulletin of the Orton Society, 21,* 71–87.

Liberman, I. Y. (1973). Segmentation of the spoken word and reading acquisition. *Bulletin of the Orton Society, 23,* 65–77.

Liberman, I. Y. (1982). A language-oriented view of reading and its disabilities. In H. Myklebust (Ed.), *Progress in learning disabilities* (Vol. 5, pp. 81–101). New York: Grune & Stratton.

Liberman, I. Y., & Liberman, A. M. (1990). Whole language vs. code emphasis: Underlying assumptions and their implications for reading instruction. *Annals of Dyslexia, 40,* 51–76.

Liberman, I. Y., Liberman, A. M., Mattingly, I. G., & Shankweiler, D. (1980). Orthography and the beginning reader. In J. Kavanagh & R. Venezky (Eds.), *Orthography, reading and dyslexia* (pp. 137–153). Baltimore: University Park Press.

Liberman, I. Y., & Mann, V. (1981). Should reading instruction and remediation vary with the sex of the child? In A. Ansara, N. Geschwind, A. Galaburda, M. Albert, & N. Gartrell (Eds.), *Sex differences in dyslexia.* Towson, MD: The Orton Dyslexia Society.

Liberman, I. Y., Rubin, H., Duques, S., & Carlisle, J. (1985). Linguistic abilities and spelling proficiency in kindergartners and adult poor spellers. In D. Gray & J. Kavanagh (Eds.), *Biobehavioral measures of dyslexia* (pp. 163–176). Parkton, MD: York Press.

Liberman, I. Y., & Shankweiler, D. (1979). Speech, the alphabet, and teaching children to read. In L. Resnick & P. Weaver (Eds.), *Theory and practice of early reading* (Vol. 2, pp. 109–132). Hillsdale, NJ: Lawrence Erlbaum.

Liberman, I. Y., & Shankweiler, D. (1985). Phonology and the problems of learning to read and write. *Remedial and Special Education, 6,* 8–17.

Liberman, I. Y., & Shankweiler, D. (1991). Phonology and beginning reading: A tutorial. In L. Rieben & C. A. Perfetti (Eds.), *Learning to read: Basic research and its implications* (pp. 3–17). Hillsdale, NJ: Lawrence Erlbaum.

Liberman, I. Y., Shankweiler, D., Blachman, B. A., Camp, L., & Werfelman, M. (1980). Steps toward literacy: A linguistic approach. In P. Levinson & C. Sloan (Eds.), *Auditory processing and language: Clinical and research perspectives* (pp. 189–215). New York: Grune & Stratton.

Liberman, I. Y., Shankweiler, D., Fischer, F. W., & Carter, B. (1974). Explicit syllable and phoneme segmentation in the young child. *Journal of Experimental Child Psychology, 18,* 201–212.

Lindamood, C. H., & Lindamood, P. C. (1971). *L. A. C. test: Lindamood auditory conceptualization test.* Boston: Teaching Resources.

Lindsay, G. A., & Wedell, K. (1982). The early identification of "at risk" children revisited. *Journal of Learning Disabilities, 15,* 212–217.

Lundberg, I. (1991). Phonemic awareness can be developed without reading instruction. In S. A. Brady & D. P. Shankweiler (Eds.), *Phonological processes in literacy: A tribute to Isabelle Y. Liberman* (pp. 47–53). Hillsdale, NJ: Lawrence Erlbaum.

Lundberg, I., Frost, J., & Peterson, O. (1988). Effects of an extensive program for stimulating phonological awareness in preschool children. *Reading Research Quarterly, 23,* 263–284.

Lundberg, I., Olofsson, A., & Wall, S. (1980). Reading and spelling skill in the first school years predicted from phonemic awareness skills in kindergarten. *Scandinavian Journal of Psychology, 21,* 159–173.

MacLean, M., Bryant, P., & Bradley, L. (1987). Rhymes, nursery rhymes, and reading in early childhood. *Merrill-Palmer Quarterly, 33,* 255–281.

Makita, K. (1968). The rarity of reading disability in Japanese children. *American Journal of Orthopsychiatry, 38,* 599–614.

Mann, V. A., & Ditunno, P. (1990). Phonological deficiencies: Effective predictors of future reading problems. In G. Pavlides (Ed.), *Dyslexia: A neuropsychological and learning perspective* (pp. 105–131). Sussex: Wiley.

Mann, V. A., & Liberman, I. Y. (1984). Phonological awareness and verbal short-term memory: Can they presage early reading problems? *Journal of Learning Disabilities, 17,* 592–599.

Mann, V., Tobin, P., & Wilson, R. (1987). Measuring phonological awareness through the invented spellings of kindergarten children. *Merrill-Palmer Quarterly, 33,* 365–391.

Marsh, G., & Mineo, R. J. (1977). Training preschool children to recognize phonemes in words. *Journal of Educational Psychology, 69,* 748–753.

Morais, J. (1991). Constraints on the development of phonemic awareness. In S. A. Brady & D. P. Shankweiler (Eds.), *Phonological processes in literacy: A tribute to Isabelle Y. Liberman* (pp. 5–27). Hillsdale, NJ: Lawrence Erlbaum Associates.

Morais, J., Cary, L., Alegria, J., & Bertelson, P. (1979). Does awareness of speech as a sequence of phones arise spontaneously? *Cognition, 7,* 323–331.

Morris, D., & Perney, J. (1984). Developmental spelling as a predictor of first-grade reading achievement. *Elementary School Journal, 84,* 441–457.

Olofsson, A., & Lundberg, I. (1983). Can phonemic awareness be trained in kindergarten? *Scandinavian Journal of Psychology, 24,* 35–44.

Perfetti, C. A. (1985). *Reading ability*. New York: Oxford University Press.

Perfetti, C. A. (1991). Representations and awareness in the acquisition of reading competence. In L. Rieben & C. A. Perfetti (Eds.), *Learning to read: Basic research and its implications* (pp. 33–44). Hillsdale, NJ: Lawrence Erlbaum.

Perfetti, C. A., Beck, I., Bell, L., & Hughes, C. (1987). Phonemic knowledge and learning to read are reciprocal: A longitudinal study of first grade children. In K. Stanovich (Ed.), Children's reading and the development of phonological awareness [Special issue]. *Merrill-Palmer Quarterly, 33*(3), 283–320.
Pikulski, J. J. (1974). Assessment of prereading skills: A review of frequently employed measures. *Reading World, 13,* 171–197.
Pratt, A. C., & Brady, S. (1988). Relation of phonological awareness to reading disability in children and adults. *Journal of Educational Psychology, 80,* 319–323.
Read, C. (1971). Preschool children's knowledge of English phonology. *Harvard Educational Review, 41,* 1–34.
Read, C. (1986). *Children's creative spellings*. London: Routledge & Kegan Paul.
Rosner, J. (1971). *Phonic analysis training and beginning reading skills*. Pittsburgh: University of Pittsburgh Learning Research and Development Center. (ERIC Document Reproduction Service No. ED 059-029)
Rosner, J. (1973). *The perceptual skills curriculum*. New York: Walker Educational Book Company.
Rosner, J. (1974). Auditory analysis training with prereaders. *The Reading Teacher, 27,* 379–384.
Rosner, J., & Simon, D. (1971). The auditory analysis test: An initial report. *Journal of Learning Disabilities, 4,* 40–48.
Rozin, P., & Gleitman, L. (1977). The structure and acquisition of reading II: The reading process and the acquisition of the alphabetic principle. In A. S. Reber & D. L. Scarborough (Eds.), *Toward a psychology of reading: The proceedings of the CUNY conference* (pp. 55–141). Hillsdale, NJ: Lawrence Erlbaum.
Rozin, P., Poritsky, S., & Sotsky, R. (1971). American children with reading problems can easily learn to read English represented by Chinese characters. *Science, 171,* 1264–1267.
Sakamoto, T., & Makita, K. (1973). Japan. In J. Downing (Ed.), *Comparative reading: Cross-national studies of behavior and processes in reading and writing*. New York: Macmillan.
Savin, H. B. (1972). What the child knows about speech when he starts to learn to read. In J. F. Kavanagh & I. G. Mattingly (Eds.), *Language by ear and by eye: The relationships between speech and reading* (pp. 319–326). Cambridge, MA: MIT Press.
Scarborough, H. S. (1990). Very early language deficits in dyslexic children. *Child Development, 61,* 1728–1743.
Share, D. J., Jorm, A. F., MacLean, R., & Matthews, R. (1984). Sources of individual differences in reading achievement. *Journal of Educational Psychology, 76,* 466–477.
Skjelfjord, V. J. (1976). Teaching children to segment spoken words as an aid in learning to read. *Journal of Learning Disabilities, 9,* 297–306.
Stanovich, K. E. (1986). Matthew effects in reading: Some consequences of individual differences in the acquisition of literacy. *Reading Research Quarterly, 21,* 360–407.
Stanovich, K. E. (Ed.). (1987). Introduction. Children's reading and the development of phonological awareness [Special issue]. *Merrill-Palmer Quarterly, 33*(3).
Stanovich, K. E. (1991). Changing models of reading and reading acquisition. In L. Rieben & C. A. Perfetti (Eds.), *Learning to read: Basic research and its implications* (pp. 19–31). Hillsdale, NJ: Lawrence Erlbaum.
Stanovich, K. E., Cunningham, A. E., & Cramer, B. B. (1984). Assessing phonological awareness in kindergarten children: Issues of task comparability. *Journal of Experimental Child Psychology, 38,* 175–190.
Stuart, M., & Coltheart, M. (1988). Does reading develop in a sequence of stages? *Cognition, 30,* 139–181.
Tangel, D., & Blachman, B. A. (1992). Effect of phoneme awareness instruction on kindergarten children's invented spelling. *Journal of Reading Behavior, 24*(2), 233–261.
Torgesen, J. K. (1991). Cross-age consistency in phonological processing. In S. A. Brady & D. P. Shankweiler (Eds.), *Phonological processes in literacy: A tribute to Isabelle Y. Liberman* (pp. 187–193). Hillsdale, NJ: Lawrence Erlbaum.
Torneus, M. (1984). Phonological awareness and reading: A chicken and egg problem? *Journal of Educational Psychology, 76,* 1346–1358.
Treiman, R. (1985). Onsets and rimes as units of spoken syllables: Evidence from children. *Journal of Experimental Child Psychology, 39,* 161–181.
Treiman, R., & Baron, J. (1981). Segmental analysis ability: Development and relation to reading ability. In G. E. MacKinnon & T. G. Waller (Eds.), *Reading research: Advances in theory and practice* (Vol. 3, pp. 159–198). New York: Academic Press.
Treiman, R., & Baron, J. (1983). Phonemic-analysis training helps children benefit from spelling-sound rules. *Memory & Cognition, 11,* 382–389.
Treiman, R., & Zukowski, A. (1991). Levels of phonological awareness. In S. A. Brady & D. P. Shankweiler (Eds.), *Phonological processes in literacy: A tribute to Isabelle Y. Liberman* (pp. 67–83). Hillsdale, NJ: Lawrence Erlbaum.
Vellutino, F. R. (1979). *Dyslexia: Theory and research.* Cambridge, MA: MIT Press.
Vellutino, F. R. (1991). Introduction to three studies on reading acquisition: Convergent findings on theoretical foundations of code-oriented versus whole-language approaches to reading instruction. *Journal of Educational Psychology, 83,* 437–443.
Vellutino, F. R., & Scanlon, D. M. (1987). Phonological coding, phonological awareness, and reading ability: Evidence from a longitudinal and experimental study. *Merrill-Palmer Quarterly, 33,* 321–363.

Wagner, R., & Torgesen, J. (1987). The nature of phonological processing and its causal role in the acquisition of reading skills. *Psychological Review, 101,* 192–212.

Walker, W. (1969). Notes on native writing systems and the design of native literacy programs. *Anthropological Linguistics, 11,* 148–166.

Wallach, M. A., & Wallach, L. (1976). *Teaching all children to read*. Chicago: University of Chicago Press.

Williams, J. (1979). The ABD's of reading: A program for the learning disabled. In L. B. Resnick & P. A. Weaver (Eds.), *Theory and practice of early reading* (Vol. 3, pp. 179–195). Hillsdale, NJ: Lawrence Erlbaum.

Williams, J. (1980). Teaching decoding with an emphasis on phoneme analysis and phoneme blending. *Journal of Educational Psychology, 72,* 1–15.

Williams, J. (1986). The role of phonemic analysis in reading. In J. Torgesen & B. Wong (Eds.), *Psychological and educational perspectives on learning disabilities* (pp. 399–416). Orlando, FL: Academic Press.

Wolf, M. (1991). Naming speed and reading: The contribution of the cognitive neurosciences. *Reading Research Quarterly, 26,* 123–141.

Yopp, H. K. (1988). The validity and reliability of phonemic awareness tests. *Reading Research Quarterly, 23,* 159–177.

Zhurova, L. Y. (1973). The development of analysis of words into their sounds by preschool children. In C. A. Ferguson & D. I. Slobin (Eds.), *Studies of child language development.* New York: Holt, Rinehart & Winston.

Zifcak, M. (1981). Phonological awareness and reading acquisition. *Contemporary Educational Psychology, 6,* 117–126.

10

NONLITERAL LANGUAGE ABILITIES

Seeing the Forest for the Trees

■ Linda M. Milosky
Syracuse University

In the opening act of *Cyrano de Bergerac,* a lord attempting to insult Cyrano says "Your . . . your nose is . . . errr . . . Your nose . . . is very large." Cyrano responds:

> Ah, no, young man, that is not enough! You might have said, dear me there are a thousand things . . . varying the tone . . . For instance . . . here you are: Aggressive: "I, monsieur, if I had such a nose, nothing would serve but I must cut it off!" . . . Descriptive: "It is a crag . . . a peak . . . a promontory! . . . A promontory, did I say? It is a peninsula." Mincing: "Do you so dote on birds, you have, fond as a father, been at pains to fit the little darlings with a roost?" Tender: "Have a little sunshade made for it. It might get freckled!" Dramatic: "It is the Red Sea when it bleeds." Admiring: "What a sign for a perfumer's shop!" Simple: "A monument! When is admission free?" Deferent: "Suffer, monsieur, that I should pay you my respects: that is what I call possessing a house of your own!" Rustic: "Hi, boys! Call that a nose? Ye don't gull me! It's either a prize carrot or else a stunted gourd." (Rostand, 1898)

Cyrano ends the speech by stating to the lord

> That, my dear sir, or something not unlike, is what you would have said to me, had you the smallest leaven of letters or of wit; but of wit, O most pitiable of objects made by God, you never had a rudiment, and of letters, you have just those that are needed to spell 'fool'!

In this well-known speech, Cyrano clearly conveys that linguistic creativity and verbal agility are highly valued. He uses a variety of the literary devices such as metaphor, simile, irony, and hyperbole to demonstrate the many ways the lord might have cleverly worded an insult. Although this commentary is contained within a piece of nineteenth-century literature, the ability to communicate effectively, creatively, and nonliterally is still highly valued and necessary in many present-day cultures. Figurative or nonliteral language has sometimes mistakenly been considered strictly within the purview of the language arts class. However, even superficial examination of social conversation, the various mass media, classroom exchanges, language within the workplace, and religious and cultural institutions reveals its pervasiveness.

- On one episode of "The Cosby Show," nonliteral uses occurred over 10 times per minute of dialogue.
- A page from a recent issue of *Teen* magazine revealed thirty-eight figurative uses on one page.
- Children's popular literature, beginning with preschool stories that parents read to children, is rife with instances of nonliteral language. *Miss Nelson Has a Field Day,* a very popular book for beginning readers, contained between one and two figurative uses per page. This book only has three or four sentences per page. The Berenstain Bear series, popular with preschoolers and early elementary school children, contains many instances of idioms, hyperbole, and irony. The humor in the Amelia Bedelia series, popular with later elementary school children, is based largely on the main character's literal interpretation of utterances intended figuratively.
- An average of 36% of teachers' utterances to students in grades kindergarten through eight contained nonliteral uses of language in a study conducted by Lazar, Warr-Leeper, Nicholson, and Johnson (1989). This figure may underestimate how often they occur, because more than one nonliteral use per utterance can and often does occur.

In everyday conversation, speakers often prefer indirectness in the form of nonliteral language over direct, literal statements. Pollio, Barlow, Fine, and Pollio (1977) estimated that nonliteral uses occur at a rate of four per minute in "free discourse." Although Grice (1975) proposes that the cooperative speaker is brief, informative, relevant, clear, and truthful, in fact, very often, speakers use nonliteral language in an indirect fashion to achieve a variety of social goals. These goals might include the desire to be more polite, clever, or more descriptive, to criticize, to tease, to achieve solidarity, or to be humorous. In turn, listeners may be judged as unintelligent or "dense" if they do not understand a speaker's nonliteral intent.

Cultural variables may affect the nature and number of metaphors that are used by speakers and comprehended by listeners. For example, African American culture has a rich heritage of figurative language use. Some of this figurative language use may have arisen as a result of the oppression of slavery and subsequent discrimination. Slaves used numerous metaphors in speech and in song to conceal their messages of hope and escape plans from slave owners and foremen. Examples of linguistic creativity in current-day African American culture are evidenced in verbal rituals such as sounding, marking, signifying, the lyrics of rap music, and the style of rhetoric often used in preaching in African American churches (Smitherman, 1986).

Nonliteral language comprehension and production not only are important in social situations but also become increasingly necessary for academic success as children progress in school. Pollio, Smith, and Pollio (1990) cite data from written text that suggest that "the average third grader will have to deal with one figure of speech every two pages. The average eleventh grader will have to deal with approximately 5 per page" (p. 143). The literature that students read contains instances of metaphor, simile, irony, hyperbole, and many other nonliteral forms.

The terminology used in teaching also often reflects use of metaphors or analogies. Teachers speak of the earth having a core, of mapping the brain, of nerve impulses traveling, of election day landslides, and of presidential contests. Thus, much important academic information is conveyed through the use of metaphors. Children are exposed to nonliteral language very early in the preschool years, so that relegating assessment and intervention of figurative language to adolescence and adulthood is inappropriate. For example, the following passage is from the Berenstain Bear series, books that are read to preschool-age children by their parents or teachers. In this story, the bears have just asked their father for some money.

> "A video game! At the mall!" Papa shouted. "You must think I'm made of money!" The cubs thought no such thing, and when they pictured it, it seemed very strange. Mama could see that they were puzzled and she explained: "Made of money is just a figure of speech, my dears." That's when the cubs realized that the situation was serious. Because Papa Bear only used figures of speech when he was upset. (Berenstain & Berenstain, 1983, pp. 11–12)

The preceding example illustrates that not only does figurative language occur in children's literature but its use and metalinguistic discussion of its use are integral points of this story.

Individuals who cannot comprehend or adequately use nonliteral language may have difficulty grasping academic concepts that are presented with such metaphoric vehicles. They also may be devalued by society and may be considered to be unintelligent. To say that someone is very "literal" implies both a failure to recognize more abstract or figurative senses of words and a lack of imagination; in its colloquial use, it also may mean that someone is "slow" or "dense."

Children with language and learning disabilities[1] exhibit difficulty with nonliteral language comprehension relative to their age-matched peers (Jones & Stone, 1989; Nippold & Fey, 1983; Seidenberg & Bernstein, 1986). Blalock (1982) found that sixty-three of eighty young adults who had been labeled language learning disabled (LLD) as children reported continued difficulty with language comprehension; these young adults cited particular problems with rapid, humorous conversational exchanges, where nonliteral uses might be common. Many of the

---

Throughout this chapter, the abbreviation LLD will be used to stand for the term *language learning disabled.* When reporting research, the terms *language disordered* or *language impaired* may be used on occasion because those terms were used by the investigators to describe their subjects. All three terms refer to children with specific and significant delays in expressive and/or receptive language, without sensory, cognitive, or emotional impairment. The terms *language impaired* or *language disordered* are particularly likely to be used in studies of preschool children (for whom the term LLD may not be appropriate).

young adults stated that they felt at a real social disadvantage in such conversational exchanges. They reported that their major strategy was to not say much, to nod, and to smile when others laughed.

Consider how impoverished messages would be without such uses. The messages of the communication board user who has a board with a limited number of fixed symbols or words are likely to sound telegraphic and concrete. Naive conversational partners may falsely assume diminished intelligence on the part of the speaker. Such concrete language also may be interpreted as rude when it is used to convey requests. The methods speakers use to convey politeness rely on being indirect. Indeed, some authors consider indirect requests as a form of figurative language. As these examples illustrate, speakers rely heavily on being able to express their thoughts in many different ways to communicate subtle nuances and to achieve multiple communication goals. Thus, figurative language comprehension and use are central to the language learning process and may present particular challenges to individuals with language disorders.

DOES NONLITERAL LANGUAGE EXIST AS A DISTINCT ENTITY?

Having delineated the frequency and importance of nonliteral language, it may seem contradictory to pose the question "Is there such a thing as nonliteral language?" By using the term *nonliteral,* a dichotomous classification of language is implied: literal language and nonliteral language. However, when coding a stretch of discourse for occurrences of nonliteral language, one is struck by the fact that many very commonly used terms are used in a nonliteral sense. Indeed, many scholars (e.g., Lakoff & Johnson, 1980) maintain that all words are metaphoric in origin. For example, as Hardison (1966) states, the phrase "running water" is rarely thought of as figurative. However, if one were asked to define *run,* presumably the definition would mention some action by the legs. In fact, *The American College Dictionary* (1968) lists 104 definitions for the word *run,* most of which do not include the notion of action by the legs, providing evidence of the many senses in which a word can be used. *A Dictionary of American Idioms* (Makkai, 1987) includes the following entries (all of which are likely to occur in a school context): "out of place," "keep time," "have to do with," "out of turn," "hand over," "keep in mind." Although these are listed in the idiom dictionary, they are so familiar that many would not consider them to be idiomatic. It becomes apparent that the literal/nonliteral distinction is a matter of degree; therefore, it may be best to use the notion of continuum when talking about literal or nonliteral senses of words, phrases, or sentences.

THE VARIETY OF NONLITERAL FORMS

Individuals use language to express something other than the literal meaning of the words in many ways. Corbett (1971) cites seventeen ways in which figures of speech are used to achieve distinct communicative goals. This chapter focuses on three common types of nonliteral language: metaphors, idioms, and irony. The discussion of each type of nonliteral language focuses not only on the form that each takes but also on the communicative goals that may be achieved.

Developmental research on nonliteral language forms is provided, with a general caveat. Children's comprehension and production of nonliteral forms is very task- and stimulus-dependent. That is, the age at which children are able to interpret or use a particular metaphor, for example, differs depending on the difficulty of the task used and on the particular metaphor chosen. Pollio and Pollio (1979) distinguish three kinds of mastery—use of a form, comprehension of it, and metalinguistic knowledge of it (or the ability to explain it). Practitioners and researchers must keep these distinctions in mind when examining and drawing conclusions about children's nonliteral language skills.

The final sections of the chapter describe in detail the information available to date about LLD children's figurative language skills. Revision of current assessment and intervention techniques for nonliteral language is suggested.

METAPHORS AND SIMILES

Metaphors are symbolic devices that are used to highlight the similarity between entities. To be nonliteral, these entities must come from distinctly different categories. For example, calling a devious person "a little snake" is metaphorical, while calling a worm a little snake is not. The sentence "Ghandi was a magician," contains a topic or entity being described (Ghandi) and a vehicle or the entity being used as the descriptor (a magician.) A ground or the features common to both (people who can make unusual or seemingly impossible things happen) is implied by the use of the device; the ground must be inferred by the listener. To be metaphoric, the statement cannot be literally true (e.g., Ghandi was not, by trade, an individual who performed tricks for amusement).

Metaphoric Forms

Metaphors may be expressed in a variety of forms, and these are exemplified in Table 10–1. Verbal metaphors may be expressed in a single word, in a sentence, and across several sentences. Both the topic and the vehicle may be mentioned, as in the Ghandi example, or only the vehicle may be mentioned with the topic evident from nonlinguistic context. For example, while watching a particularly ferocious player in a football game, one viewer might say to another "What a tiger!" The speaker expresses a metaphor in a single word, using the vehicle of tiger to comment on the topic of the football player seen on the television.

TABLE 10–1
Metaphors, similes, and allegory

Metaphoric Forms	
Metaphor	A statement of comparison between two entities that come from distinctly different categories. Two types of metaphor are predicative and proportional metaphors.
Predicative Metaphor	Metaphor that makes a single similarity statement.
Example	"Ghandi was a magician."
Proportional Metaphor	Expresses an analogy of the form A:B::C:D.
Examples	"[Mr. Allen's attorney] is to slow what a dog whistle is to the normal range of human hearing." (Grimes, 1993)
	"Johnny's knee was a tomato that squirted juice." (Leonard, Kail, 1984).
Simile	A metaphoric comparison overtly marked by using the terms *like* or *as.*
Example	"Rosa Parks was as courageous as Daniel."
	"Ghandi was like a magician."
Allegory	A metaphor extended across a whole piece of discourse, in which the topic of the metaphor (in this case, an attorney preparing a defense) is never mentioned.
Example	"There was a great turtle who was preparing to have a family. She searched endlessly for the proper beach, because she wanted just the right conditions. When she found a beach, she painstakingly began to build a mound, bit by bit, over the turtle eggs that she had laid. She wanted to disguise the eggs well enough so that the mongoose and rats wouldn't eat them. Other turtles laughed at how particular she was, but she knew how to hatch those babies. And that's all she really wanted: to hatch those babies so that they would develop properly."

Metaphors expressed in a single sentence may take the form of predicative metaphors and proportional metaphors. A predicative metaphor makes a single similarity statement. The metaphor about Ghandi given previously is a predicative metaphor. A proportional metaphor expresses an analogy of the form A:B::C:D. In the proportional metaphor taken from Nippold, Leonard, and Kail (1984), "Johnny's knee was a tomato that squirted juice," the analogy is "knee:X::tomato:juice." When a metaphor is extended across a whole piece of discourse (e.g., a story), the device is called *allegory*. For example, *The Butter Battle Book* by Dr. Seuss (1984) provides an allegory demonstrating the senselessness of nuclear war.

As is evident from the previous examples, metaphors do not contain overt linguistic marking signaling a comparison between two entities. When comparisons are overtly marked by using terms such as *like* or *as*, the comparisons are called *similes* (e.g., "Gandhi was like a magician"; "Rosa Parks was as courageous as Daniel"). The "as . . . as" form of simile not only marks the comparison, but it also explicitly states the ground for the comparison (in this case, courage).

Although commonly defined as literary devices or "figures of speech," metaphors need not be linguistic (Verbrugge, 1984). For example, during a birthday ceremony for children at a local preschool, the birthday child walked around a hoop while the other children counted aloud. The number of times the child circled the hoop was determined by her age, a relation made explicit by the teacher's instructions. Thus, one trip around the hoop was a metaphor for one year of the child's life.

The Communicative Value of Metaphors

Why do speakers use metaphors when they could express themselves more directly, using more literal language to describe or refer to an entity, quality, or action? According to Winner (1988), a metaphor is not simply a substitute for a term or a similarity statement about an entity. Rather, a metaphor transforms a topic (Richards, 1936). That is, language users "look at the topic (the principal subject) from the perspective of the vehicle (the subsidiary subject) so that [their] perception of the topic (but not the vehicle) is altered" (Winner, 1988, p. 22). Indeed, the similarity relation in metaphor is asymmetrical (Ortony, 1986). Calling a person a snake does not convey the same relation as calling a snake a person. In fact, the latter seems nonsensical.

Thus, metaphors are used "to clarify, illuminate, or explain" (Winner, 1988, p. 22). They may help people see the unfamiliar in terms of the familiar; that is, they may help listeners use prior knowledge to understand new information. While one may think of metaphors as more abstract, in fact, they may make something that is abstract more concrete. Moore (1988) provides an example of a preschool child coming to understand her father's death in terms of loss of a helium balloon that floated away from her grasp. As mentioned previously, use of metaphors is rife in teaching. Teachers often rely on familiar concepts or relationships to explain new ones, and in the process, metaphors may be used. Pearson, Raphael, TePaske, and Hyser (1981) demonstrate that when eight- and eleven-year-old children are presented with paragraphs about unfamiliar topics, they remember sentences containing a metaphor with a familiar vehicle better than literal paraphrases of the same sentence. Thus, retention of unfamiliar material may be enhanced by metaphorically conveying it in terms of the familiar.

Metaphors also help highlight one aspect of something in a particularly graphic way (e.g., Cyrano's use of "crag," "peak," and "promontory," all prominent landforms, to describe his nose). Metaphors may give rise to very vivid images, allowing one-word descriptions when use of literal language would require several words or phrases.

The communicative functions that metaphors serve exceed the functions of description or illumination. Metaphors allow speakers to avoid stating the obvious. As indicated in Cyrano's speech at the beginning of this chapter, stating the obvious may be considered dull or unintelligent. Speakers generally observe certain principles to make conversation a successful, cooperative endeavor (Grice, 1975). One of the principles that Grice (1975) proposes is the maxim of quantity. This principle states that speakers say what is necessary, no more or no less. Thus, speakers often avoid stating the obvious; metaphors may allow them to do so. For example, on seeing a sleeping child, it might seem foolish to say "He's sleeping." However, a speaker might comment "I see that we've lost someone." The comment no longer seems redundant with the nonlinguistic information in context.

A speaker's choice of metaphors also may express an attitude. For example, the statement "Life is a gift" conveys a very different attitude from "Life is a curse." The goal of these statements is not to better explain what life is, but rather to express the speaker's viewpoint. Thus, metaphoric comprehension and use not only involve the "cold" cognitive skills of analogical reasoning but also may require social and emotional cognition. Indeed, Pollio and Smith (1980) maintain that the success of a given metaphor may depend largely on the speaker's and listener's shared knowledge and their knowledge of each other.

Development of Metaphoric Skills

The developmental literature regarding children's use and comprehension of metaphors is reviewed next. As mentioned previously, the nature of the tasks used to examine children's skills will determine, in part, performance at any given age. However, examining the relative difficulty of various tasks or various kinds of metaphors provides very useful clinical information.

Development of Metaphor Production. The age or language level at which children begin producing metaphors is a subject of debate. Review of the research on metaphor production reveals several studies during the 1970s and early 1980s that claimed that children produce metaphorical utterances when their language production abilities still consist of only one- or two-word utterances. For example, Billow (1981) examined spontaneous metaphor in children ages two to six years of age. He reported that metaphors occurred across this age range, with the highest number of occurrences in children aged 3.1 to 3.6 years. Vosniadou (1987) cites as an example an eighteen-month-old's calling a toy car a "snake" as the child twisted and turned it up his mother's arm (from Winner, McCarthy, Kleinman, & Gardner, 1984). Metaphors, however, must be distinguished from pretend play utterances. Vosniadou (1987) provides a set of criteria that distinguishes children's overextensions and pretend play utterances from true metaphors. She suggests the following: (1) The reason for using metaphor is to compare two concepts, but the reason for renaming an object in play is to have that object stand for the other, named object. (2) The goal in using a metaphor is to communicate something about the topic of the metaphor, while in pretend play, the goal is to rename an object so that it fits into the play theme; no comment is made about the object itself. (3) Metaphors convey similarities, while similarity is not necessary between objects and their pretend renamings. In addition, the similarities being highlighted must be from conventionally different categories (e.g., "The pen is a mighty sword" is metaphorical; "A pen is an inky pencil" is not metaphorical). Therefore, Vosniadou suggests that children must base the metaphor on some comprehensible similarity between two entities, and they must be aware that the entities belong to different categories.

To return to the example cited earlier of the child calling a car a snake while twisting and turning it up his mother's arm (Winner et al., 1984), Vosniadou (1987) argues that the child is not attempting to say something about toy cars. Therefore, the utterance is not metaphorical. Vosniadou's criteria would also cast doubt on the metaphoricity of some of Billow's (1981) data. For example, Billow provides the following example of the protocol he used to determine that an utterance was metaphorical:

> Child (age 3.5): "It's going for a walk in the forest (taking little rubber animal and gliding it around observer's back) and it's going to eat some grass (animal reaches observer's hair)."
> Observer: (after 7 min.) "Where's the grass?"
> Child: (Points to green rug.)
> Observer: "What's this?" (observer's hair)
> Child: "Grass."
> Observer: "What's this?" (pointing to observer's hair again)
> Child: "Hair." (Billow, 1981, p. 435)

The child was clearly renaming hair as grass when engaged in pretend play with the toy animal. The observer's prompts led the child to label the hair as grass again, but there is no evidence that the child is attempting to compare hair to grass. Given the timetable for the emergence and blossoming of symbolic play, it is not surprising that Billow found the greatest number of what he termed "metaphors" at age 3.1 to 3.6 years.

Intentional violation of a category is not sufficient to label an utterance metaphorical; there must also be an intent to compare. Vosniadou (1987) notes that recent research on children's categorization abilities shows that young children may have much more clearly defined categories than previously thought. Thus, children may be capable of intentionally violating those categories at an earlier age. However, intentional violation of the category is insufficient. In pretend play, a child may intentionally violate a category or naming convention because an object necessary to the play theme is absent. The child must also have an intent to compare the two entities or to see one from the perspective of the other. Thus, one of the criteria for determining metaphorical use is the speaker's intention—was there an intent to compare? Naturally, this may be difficult to determine in young children. However, evidence that children know the "real" name of an object cannot prove metaphoric intent.

Using Vosniadou's (1987) criteria, it seems likely that findings reported during the late 1970s and early 1980s failed to differentiate between pretend play renamings and metaphor production. Vosniadou and Ortony (1983) did demonstrate that four-year-old children could differentiate between literal and nonliteral similarity, suggesting that their renamings could indeed be intentionally metaphorical. Gentner (1988) reports a two-year-old saying that a crescent moon was "bent, like a banana." She argues that young children do produce metaphors much more readily than their comprehension suggests they should. Gentner adds that these early metaphors may be restricted to highlighting similarities in appearance but not in function or other relational aspects.

Metaphoric Preferences. Results of sentence completion tasks suggest that four-year-old children can produce conventional comparisons in simile form. Gardner, Kircher, Winner, and Perkins (1975) required subjects from four to nineteen years to complete similes such as "He looks as gigantic as . . ."). They found that all groups used conventional metaphoric endings most of the time. That is, the groups completed the simile nonliterally but used familiar comparisons ("as gigantic as a skyscraper").

The nature of children's metaphors seems to progress from perceptual bases to more conceptual relations. Both naturalistic observation and performance on experimental tasks reveal similar metaphoric preferences in production. Children's early metaphors are likely to be based on perceptual or appearance-based similarities. Thus, a cloud might be described as "whipped cream." Metaphors with a functional basis (e.g., "The Tigers annihilated the Blue Jays") or "psychologically minded" metaphors (e.g., "He's a rock") are more likely to occur later. However, in the sentence-completion task used by Gardner et al. (1975), preschoolers occasionally provided novel, appropriate psychologically based metaphors (e.g., "sad as a pimple," "stony as a stupid person"). Such developmental preferences may be seen in multiple-choice completion tasks described later.

Billow (1981) and Gardner and Winner (1982) noted a reduction with age in metaphor use in preschool and elementary schoolchildren's spontaneous speech. Silberstein, Gardner, Phelps, and Winner (1982) explain their failure to find increases in literal preferences in elementary school by suggesting that the task they used may have predisposed children to make metaphorical choices. Another possible explanation is based on the criteria explicated previously regarding a truly metaphorical utterance. Vosniadou (1987) argues that this putative reduction may be a false one. Rather, it may be a function of having classified some of younger children's utterances as metaphorical when the children were not intentionally making a metaphorical comparison.

Comprehension of Metaphors. The ability to comprehend metaphors involves several comparison skills. To comprehend a predicative metaphor, listeners must recognize that the topic is not a member of the vehicle's category (i.e., Ghandi did not make a hobby of doing party tricks and pulling rabbits out of hats). That recognition then may drive listeners to infer that a comparison is being made. Once listeners realize that a comparison of similarity is being made, they must discover the relevant similar dimension(s) (e.g., what do Ghandi and a magician have in common?). At the same time, listeners must *ignore the irrelevant similarities* (e.g., they both wear clothes; they both are involved with the public). Furthermore, it is important to not extend the metaphor on dimensions that, in fact, are dissimilar. For example, while a magician's effects are as a result of sleight of hand, Ghandi's effects were not. It would be erroneous in interpreting the Ghandi metaphor to assume that all of the effects Ghandi achieved did not actually happen but only appeared to happen.

In a proportional metaphor, the similarity being addressed requires listeners to understand a relationship between two entities (one a topic and the other a vehicle). Then listeners transfer the nature of that relationship to another entity (a second vehicle), with the fourth element (a topic) and the relationship being inferred. For the proportional metaphor "Johnny's knee was a tomato that squirted juice" (Nippold et al., 1984), listeners must understand the relationship between *tomato* and *juice*. Then they transfer that relationship to *knee* to infer that the unmentioned topic is blood.

Overt marking of the comparison may make comprehension easier. As mentioned previously, the statements "Ghandi was like a magician" and "Rosa Parks was as courageous as Daniel," are similes. They function in the same way as metaphors. However, they may be easier to process because they explicitly indicate a comparison between the topic and the vehicle. In addition, similes employing the "as (attribute) as" form explicitly state the ground of the comparison. Research comparing comprehension of similes and metaphors does indeed suggest that similes may be easier to understand (Seidenberg & Bernstein, 1986; Vosniadou & Ortony, 1986).

Some researchers believe that development of metaphor comprehension depends largely on changes in general cognitive capacity or general linguistic ability. Others argue that specific linguistic knowledge, experiences with metaphors, and real-world experiences are the major determinants of level of metaphor comprehension. Naturally, all these factors play a role; disputes center on the degree of importance of any one factor.

Johnson (1991) takes the neo-Piagetian position that changes in metaphor comprehension depend on changes in general cognitive (mental-attentional) capacity. She recently examined the effect of two subject variables, general language proficiency and socioeconomic status, on metaphor comprehension while controlling for nonverbal cognitive ability. Johnson reports that linguistic ability, knowledge base, and mental capacity all play a role in the development of metaphoric skill, but she argues that the largest role is played by general mental capacity. Her study, however, did not examine the role of specific linguistic knowledge and specific background knowledge on metaphor comprehension.

Keil (1986) argues that the ability to interpret an utterance metaphorically depends heavily on the degree of elaboration of the listener's knowledge of the topic, vehicle, and ground. Thus, he says that a child's ability to identify a word, for example, on a picture vocabulary task, is not a sufficient measure of what the child knows about the word. A child may be able to identify one word based on knowing only a minimal amount of information about it. The child may be able to identify another word based on very elaborated knowledge about it. Performance on a recognition task will appear identical for the two words. In contrast, when those words are used in a metaphorical task, for example, the child may be able to interpret a metaphor only when using a word for which she has elaborated knowledge. Thus, a child's world knowledge of the topic and vehicle of the metaphor affects the degree of understanding. If a speaker uses a dance metaphor (e.g., "I'm tired of do-si-do-ing with you"), the meaning may be lost to a listener who has never square danced.

Not surprisingly, presentation of metaphors in a meaningful linguistic context improves comprehension. A facilitating context helps the listener call up world knowledge related to the metaphoric topic and vehicle. Most investigations examining contextual effects have provided short stories with the metaphor appearing in a final sentence. Vosniadou and her colleagues, in a series of studies (Vosniadou, 1987; Vosniadou & Ortony, 1986; Vosniadou, Ortony, Reynolds, & Wilson, 1984), provided richer contexts both for the occurrence of the metaphor and for the child's demonstration of the meaning of it. In their studies, children heard short paragraphs and then acted out with toys the meaning of the final sentence, which contained a metaphor. The use of this "toy-world" environment substantially increased children's performance. The results led Vosniadou to consider the nature of metaphor comprehension and the tasks used to assess it.

Vosniadou (1987) identified three potential sources of difficulty in a listener's ability to demonstrate comprehension of a metaphor. (1) The listener may not realize that the statement "X is Y" is actually a comparison and so may interpret the statement literally. (2) The listener may realize that a comparison is being made but may not see the similarity between X and Y. (3) The listener may understand the comparison and may comprehend the metaphor but may be unable to express or explain that understanding. Obviously, then, children's performance depends on the nature of the task used to assess comprehension, on their knowledge of the entities being compared, and their ability to compare the entities. Results of studies that examine these aspects will be addressed next.

To date, four major types of comprehension tasks generally have been used to assess metaphor comprehension: enactment tasks, paraphrase or explanation tasks, multiple-choice or forced choice tasks, and sentence completion tasks. Enactment tasks appear to be easiest for children to perform. Vosniadou et al. (1984) examined children's ability to comprehend metaphors in story contexts, using entities with which children are familiar. They measured children's comprehension through the use of an enactment task, which did not require paraphrase. They found that four-year-olds were able to act out interpretations of metaphors in a toy-world environment. Obviously, in this study, the familiar story contexts as well as the enactment task aided children's performance. Vosniadou and Ortony (1986), however, directly compared the paraphrase and enactment tasks with six-year-old children and found a greater number of literal responses in the paraphrase task. They cite three possible reasons for the performance difference between paraphrase and enactment tasks. The first is that enactment does not require as much metacognitive or metalinguistic ability as the paraphrase task; that is, children need not talk about how they linked the topic and the vehicle (see van Kleeck, chap. 3).

Enactment may also increase the likelihood that children will process the information in the stories. Further support for the processing explanation comes from a study by Pellegrini and Galda (1982). They examined children's processing of narratives in a training study. Subjects engaged in one of three activities after hearing a narrative: dramatically enact the story, discuss the story, or draw a picture about the story. Children's comprehension/memory for the story in the dramatic enactment condition was superior to discussion of the story and to drawing a picture about it. Thus, enactment may facilitate metaphor comprehension because the contextual cues have been processed and retained more thoroughly.

Finally, Vosniadou and Ortony (1986) suggest that the context of the toy-world is likely to restrict the possible meanings of the metaphor, although permitting both literal and figurative interpretations. This restriction of meanings also would be likely to occur in real-life communicative contexts.

Sentence completion tasks that offer choices also reveal information about children's comprehension and production preferences for metaphors. As mentioned in the prior discussion of metaphor production, Gardner et al. (1975) had subjects complete similes (e.g., "He was as gigantic as..."). Immediately after each sentence completion, the investigator asked subjects to choose among one of four endings that the investigator presented. The choices included a *literal comparison* (e.g., "He was as gigantic as the most gigantic person in the whole world"); a *conventional comparison* ("He was as gigantic as a skyscraper in the center of town"); *a novel, but appropriate simile* ("He was as gigantic as a double-decker cone in a baby's hand"); and *an inappropriate ending* ("He was as gigantic as a clock from a department store"). The subjects included preschoolers (aged 3 and 4), 7-, 11-, 14-, and 19-year-olds. Subjects were asked to justify or explain each choice. Four-year-olds showed no difference in choosing among the four types, suggesting that they may have chosen randomly. They also were unable to justify their choices. Seven-year-olds preferred literal responses, 11-year-olds preferred conventional responses, and 14- and 19-year-olds chose either appropriate or conventional responses. These preferences contrast somewhat with the production findings, where seven-year-olds' completions were conventionally metaphoric more than 80% of the time. The authors speculate that whereas conventional comparisons may have arisen spontaneously on the completion, these subjects were reluctant to choose a metaphorical ending because of their inability to justify their choice. When seven-year-old subjects did choose metaphoric endings, their explanations often lacked appreciation of the metaphor. This finding suggests once again that metalinguistic explanations reflect a different level of comprehension than does a multiple choice task (van Kleeck, chap. 3). Several other investigators also have contrasted performance on paraphrase and multiple-choice tasks. Not surprisingly, performance on multiple-choice tasks consistently has been better than on paraphrase tasks (Winner, Engel, & Gardner, 1980; Winner, Rosenstiel, & Gardner, 1976). These findings also suggest that, depending on the criteria one proposes for "comprehension" of a metaphor, metaphoric production may precede comprehension.

Ease of metaphor comprehension also may vary with the type of similarities that are being highlighted. Some research shows that metaphors based on sensory properties may be easier for children to understand. Metaphors that draw similarities between physical entities and psychological states may be more difficult (Silberstein et al., 1982; Winner et al., 1976). Attributional or appearance-based metaphors ("jelly beans are like balloons") are understood earlier than relational metaphors ("a camera is like a tape recorder"), in which the similarity highlighted is based on nonperceptual relations (e.g., function, action performed) (Gentner, 1988).

Silberstein et al. (1982) administered a multiple-choice sentence completion task to subjects aged six through twenty years, to determine subjects' preferences for different types of grounds for metaphors. Subjects were given five choices for each sentence to be completed. Seven different types of endings were rotated through the five choices. Of the seven types, five were based on one ground (e.g., color, shape, sound, movement, conceptual); one was based on a combination of grounds (e.g., color and shape); and one was literal. Examples of the different types of grounds are contained in Table 10–2. Subjects' preferences changed with age; youngest subjects preferred shape and color grounds, which are static and perceptually based. Subjects of intermediate age preferred movement and sound grounds, which are dynamic and perceptually based. Oldest subjects preferred conceptually based grounds. All subjects except first-grade children preferred combination grounds such as color and movement or color and conceptual. The authors also noted considerable variability of preferences within grades. They found that children's ability to explain their choices appropriately rose with grade level and depended on the type of ground chosen. First-grade subjects had little difficulty explaining their choices when the ground was perceptually based. Fifth graders explained conceptually based grounds appropriately approximately two thirds of the time. The authors also found that preference for literal endings generally decreased, except during eighth and tenth grades, when approximately one quarter of the subjects preferred literal endings. Unlike younger children, however, these subjects were aware of the metaphorical choices and often offered explicit rejection of them, stating that they preferred directness.

In contrast with the preceding findings that perceptual metaphors are easier than psychological ones, Nippold et al. (1984) contrasted comprehension of psychological metaphors with perceptual metaphors in seven- and nine-year-old children. They found no difference between the two. However, as Waggoner and Palermo (1989) point out, the forced choice task that Nippold et al. used involved a choice between a psychological state and a physical state on about half the trials. For example, for the stimulus sentence "Kathy was a camera watching the children in the show," the choices were that Kathy "saw and remembered everything" or "sat next to a friend." These psychological versus physical choices may have made the task easier for children.

Naturally, experience with a specific metaphor affects understanding as well. So-called frozen metaphors (e.g., "She is a rock in time of trouble") are metaphors that are very commonly used. Indeed, they may be used so frequently that they are considered idioms. Pollio and Pollio (1979) found frozen metaphors easier to comprehend than novel metaphors for fourth- through eighth-grade children. They also found a positive correlation between children's comprehension of novel and frozen metaphors. Comprehension for both types steadily increased between grades 4 and 8. In Pollio and Pollio's data, one sees evidence that metaphor compre-

TABLE 10–2
Types of grounds used by Silberstein et al. (1982) in a metaphoric preference task
Examples from "Autumn Leaves and Old Photographs: The Development of Metaphor Preferences" L. Silberstein, H. Gardner, E. Phelps, and E. Winner, 1982, *Journal of Experimental Child Psychology, 34*, p. 140.

Type	Example
Static perceptual grounds	
Color	The volcano is a bright fire truck.
Shape	A wave in the ocean is a curl of hair.
Dynamic perceptual grounds	
Sound	The rattlesnake was a hissing kettle.
Movement	A volcano is a whale spouting water.
Conceptual grounds	
Obstruction	A traffic jam is getting your zipper stuck halfway.
Impending danger	The rattlesnake was a storm cloud.
Combination grounds	
Color and movement	The snowflake is a falling paper airplane.
Color and shape	The popped red balloon is an apple peel.

hension continues to develop well into adolescence. At grade 8, their subjects still were only achieving approximately 63% correct for novel forms and 80% correct for frozen forms.

In addition to experience with specific metaphors, the degree to which one's family or culture engages in figurative language may affect understanding of metaphors. Ortony, Turner, and Larson-Shapiro (1985) examined the figurative language abilities of inner-city African American children who engaged in sounding. *Sounding* is a ritualized trading of insults, and these insults are accomplished through the use of hyperbole (exaggeration), irony, or metaphor. Ortony et al. (1985) provide the following example:

> Larry: Man, you so poor your roaches and rats eat lunch out.
> Reggie: Well, you so poor the rats and roaches take you out to lunch. (p. 26)

Findings of the study suggest children who engage in more sounding may perform better on conventional metaphor comprehension tasks.

The ability to deal with conversational metaphors clearly depends on many factors, several of which also are relevant to the discussion of idioms. As noted previously, many idioms are actually frozen metaphors. Thus, their comprehension and use may follow the patterns noted for metaphors.

IDIOMS

Idioms are commonly used expressions whose meanings may not be derivable by determining the meanings of each of the individual words. The degree to which one can determine an idiom's figurative meaning from the literal meaning of the words has been termed the degree of *metaphoric transparency/opacity.* For example, the idiom "skating on thin ice" is considered relatively transparent. The meaning of danger or trouble is easily conveyed by imagining the consequences of skating on ice that is not sufficiently solid. In contrast, the figurative meanings of some idioms may seem totally unrelated to any literal sense of the words (e.g., "spill the beans"). Such idioms are considered to be opaque. Linguists have, however, traced the origins of many of these seemingly opaque idioms. For example, the phrase "kick the bucket" is often cited as being opaque or nondecomposable, but Hendrickson (1987) states that its meaning may be related to the process by which hogs were slaughtered years ago. The animals' heels were tied to a wooden block, and the rope was thrown over a pulley to hoist the animals up. The block was raised in a manner similar to drawing a bucket up from a well. Thus, the block became known as the "bucket," and the kicking of the animals' heels against the bucket led to the idiom for death. In reading dictionaries of word and phrase origins, it becomes clear that many seemingly opaque idioms may at one time have been transparent.

Many commonly used constructions are idiomatic and were once novel metaphors. Through overuse and language change, they "die" and lose their metaphoricity and come to be processed as literal. For example, it is unlikely that most listeners would consider the "table legs" or "hands of the clock" to be metaphoric or idiomatic. Yet the comparison to body parts is evident when one inspects such phrases. Similarly, inspection of idiom dictionaries (Clark, 1988; Makkai, 1987) reveals entries such as "hold on," "shut up," and "bring up." Most speakers and listeners would not consider these verb plus particle constructions to be figurative. However, because those who speak English as a second language (ESL speakers) are likely to have considerable difficulty with some of these forms, they are listed in idiom dictionaries. An ESL teacher reported that a six-year-old student in her class came running up to her, crying, and saying that another pupil was accusing him of stealing something. When she investigated further, the other child, rather bemused, said that all he had done was to tell the boy to "take his turn" in the game they were playing.

The prevalence and meaning of an idiom may be specific to an ethnic group, a local dialect, or sociocultural group. The idiom "You sure put your foot in that" when said in an African American community is a compliment meaning "You really gave it your all" or "You put your own personal mark on that"; however, many European Americans may associate it with another idiom, putting one's foot in one's mouth, and thus may infer a negative meaning. Specific idioms also may be more characteristic of one generation than another (e.g., my mother spoke of a very attractive dress as "the cat's pajamas," meaning "the best," while today teens might talk of an item of fashionable clothing as being "rad"). Idioms also vary from language to language. For example, Levorato and Cacciari (1992) used the Italian idiom "perdersi in un bicchier d'acqua," which, roughly translated, means to become very upset over nothing. If one translates an idiom literally word by word from a foreign language, the meaning of the idiom often is lost, and the resulting phrase often may be nonsensical (Clark, 1988). Again using the above example, the literal translation of the Italian idiom is "to get lost in a glass of water." The idiom in English that might convey this meaning is "to lose one's head over nothing" (Levorato & Cacciari, 1992).

Communicative Functions of Idioms

Idioms may serve a variety of communicative purposes, including expression of an attitude, establishment of "in-group" solidarity, or being indirect. A speaker may express an attitude by the choice of idiom; when someone dies, a speaker may say that the individual "kicked the bucket," "passed away," or "went to meet his Maker." Each of these choices reflects a different attitude toward the event. The goal of using nonliteral euphemisms (more mild versions of a harsh descriptor) may be to achieve politeness or distance by being indirect. Hence, so many idioms for talking about death may exist because it is a subject that is uncomfortable and emotional, leading to a proliferation of terms for avoiding direct expression of the event. Idioms also may be used to establish or acknowledge familiarity or common ground, as in being part of an "in-group." Certainly, comprehension of idioms is necessary to understand informal social conversation, and much humor is conveyed through the use of idioms and metaphors.

Theories about Idiom Acquisition

At least two explanations have been offered regarding how children acquire idioms. The idiom-as-giant-word hypothesis argues that children treat idioms as a single, large word. Therefore, children are thought to acquire idioms as they do other words, with idioms having entries in the mental lexicon separate from any of the entries for the individual words. In contrast, others have argued that many idioms are comprehended by examining the relation between the literal meanings of the words and the situation in which an idiom occurs and then recognizing the metaphorical nature of the idiom (e.g., "You're skating on thin ice" said to a child who is precariously tipping his chair on two legs). Naturally, this explanation can be applied only to idioms that are relatively metaphorically transparent.

As with metaphor comprehension, the developmental data reveal that performance depends on both the specific idiom and the task in which idiom comprehension is assessed. Brinton, Fujiki, and Mackey (1985) demonstrated this idiom-dependent variability in performance. They examined the ability of kindergarten, second-, fourth-, and sixth-grade students to understand six idioms. Table 10–3 presents the results of their study. If one examines only the overall means per age group, a general pattern of increase in idiom comprehension is seen. However, examining performance on individual idioms reveals that the pattern of increase is inconsistent across idioms. For example, performance on "let the cat out of the bag" and on "lend me a hand" changed very little across age groups. "Let the cat out of the bag" was understood by very few children, whereas "lend me a hand" was understood by eleven to fifteen children in each age group of twenty children. In contrast, comprehension of "all tied up" changed consid-

TABLE 10–3
Differences in idiom comprehension by idiom
Data from "Elementary School Age Children's Comprehension of Specific Idiomatic Expressions" by B. Brinton, M. Fujiki, and T. Mackey, 1985, *Journal of Communication Disorders, 18,* 250, 251.

	Percent Correct			
Idiom	**Kindergarten**	**Second Grade**	**Fourth Grade**	**Sixth Grade**
hit the ceiling	0	10	20	35
let the cat out of the bag	0	0	5	20
got carried away	35	95	100	90
now you're cooking	25	75	85	85
all tied up	5	30	55	75
lend me a hand	65	55	70	75
Total	22	44	56	62

erably with age. How might one account for these differences in comprehension among idioms?

Factors Affecting Idiom Comprehension

A number of interrelated factors affect ease of comprehension of a given idiom. For example, how often a child hears an idiom is likely to be a key factor in comprehension, but frequency of use of various idioms has only recently begun to be considered as a factor in investigations of idiom comprehension. Nippold and Rudzinski (1993) examined the effect of familiarity on subjects' performance by having a separate group of adolescents rate each of their idiom stimuli on a familiarity scale. They found that high familiarity idioms were easier to understand than low and mid familiarity idioms. The majority of other studies cited failed to mention any attempts to control for frequency in their selection of idioms for stimuli.

The context in which an idiom occurs clearly affects the accuracy with which the idiom's meaning is comprehended. Several studies (Ackerman, 1982; Cacciari & Levorato, 1989; Gibbs, 1987; Levorato & Cacciari, 1992; Prinz, 1983) have presented idioms in contexts that facilitated either the literal or figurative interpretation of the idiom. In all studies, context facilitated children's recognition of nonliteral intent. That is, children were more likely to choose nonliteral alternatives in multiple-choice tasks, and they were more likely to offer nonliteral explanations of idiom meaning.

As stated previously, idioms vary in the degree to which their figurative meanings can be discerned from analysis of their literal meanings. In general, more transparent idioms are developmentally easier for children to comprehend. Gibbs (1987) examined idiom comprehension in kindergarten, first-, third-, and fourth-grade children and found that transparent idioms were acquired earlier than opaque idioms. Nippold and Rudzinski (1993) also found that high familiarity idioms, which were easier for subjects to understand, also tended to be transparent.

Gibbs (1987) also investigated the effect of syntactic flexibility on idiom comprehension. *Syntactic flexibility* refers to the degree to which idioms can be transformed syntactically. For example, a speaker can say "Sue cut Joe down to size" or "Joe was cut down to size by Sue," but one would not say "Sue's throat was jumped down by Joe," in place of "Joe jumped down Sue's throat." Idioms like "jump down one's throat" that are not syntactically flexible are referred to as *frozen.* Gibbs and Gonzalez (1985) found that adults processed syntactically frozen idioms more rapidly than idioms that could undergo various syntactic transformations when both types were embedded within a story context. They also found that flexible idioms were remembered better than frozen ones on a cued recall task. Gibbs and Gonzales (1985) concluded that the flexible idioms required more processing to access their meaning than the frozen idioms. Thus, one might expect syntactically frozen idioms to be acquired earlier because their form is more invariant and thus is a more reliable cue to nonliteral intent. Gibbs (1987) did find that kindergarten and first-grade children understood syntactically frozen idioms better than syntactically flexible ones. Third- and fourth-grade children, however, understood the two types of idioms equally well.

Lexical flexibility, or the degree to which words in the idiom can be replaced, also varies among idioms (Gibbs & Nayak, 1989), and syntactic flexibility seems to be highly related to lexical flexibility. One can say "button your lips" or "fasten your lips"; and the agricultural variation of "raining cats and dogs" is "raining pitchforks, hammer handles, darning needles, and chicken coops." The idiom "chew the fat," however, remains invariant. Gibbs, Nayak, Bolton, and Keppel (1989) found that lexically flexible idioms also were more likely to be considered decomposable. Again, one might expect children to learn lexically invariant idioms more readily than those that were flexible, but this factor has not been investigated in children. Some anecdotal evidence suggests that children's compositional analysis of idioms and recognition of the individual words in the idiom may lag behind their comprehension of the idiom's general meaning and their acquisition of the general phonetic form of the idiom. For example, the six-year-old daughter of a friend of the author, when cautioned not to divulge a secret surprise for her brother, pressed her lips together and announced, "My lips are soiled."

The number of figurative meanings that an idiom has also seems to affect ease of processing. For example, as Mueller and Gibbs (1987) note, the idiom "on the rocks" can mean "in trouble" or "over ice," whereas "in a flash" is only used to mean "rapidly." Mueller and Gibbs (1987) found that adults recognized idioms with more than one figurative meaning faster and more accurately than they recognized idioms with only one figurative meaning. They propose that the faster access of multiple-meaning idioms is because such idioms have multiple entries in the mental lexicon. If searching occurs randomly, the probability of recognizing an idiom with multiple entries is greater. While searching of the mental lexicon may occur randomly when idioms are presented in isolation, it is unclear whether idioms used in context would demonstrate the same effect.

The prosodic elements of speech may also play a role in the likelihood of an idiom being recognized as such and therefore comprehended figuratively rather than literally. Van Lancker and Canter (1981) presented speakers with sentence pairs containing idioms and their literal counterparts and asked the speakers to try to maximally convey the meanings. Listeners easily identified which meaning was intended by the speakers. Van Lancker, Canter, and Terbeek (1981) performed acoustic analyses on the sentence pairs. They found that idioms were said more rapidly, had different pitch contours, and were said with less articulatory precision than their literal counterparts. Their findings also suggest that when idioms are uttered within a meaningful linguistic context, speakers may rely less on prosodic cues to mark the intended meaning. Rather, listeners may rely on linguistic contextual cues. Further research is warranted on the role of intonational cues in idiom recognition and comprehension when idioms are presented in context.

A child's ability to comprehend an idiom is likely to depend on the task used to assess comprehension. As indicated in the section on metaphor, paraphrase tasks are more difficult than multiple-choice tasks or forced choice tasks. In addition, the nature of the choices offered on multiple- or forced choice tasks may influence subject's responses. Brinton et al. (1985) used pictorial representations of literal and figurative interpretations and two foil pictures. As they note in their discussion, the literal interpretation and the depiction of "lend me a hand" are much less plausible than literal interpretations of other idioms. Similarly, one of Gibbs's (1987, 1991) stimuli was "jump down your throat," with the forced choice question asking "Did Tommy's mother crawl into his mouth?"

As indicated previously, idioms are pervasive, and new idioms are continually emerging in the language. The skills that an individual uses to understand idioms may vary with the idiom (Levorato & Cacciari, 1992; Nippold & Rudzinski, 1993). Opaque idioms may be learned as single units, or giant words. Transparent idioms may be more amenable to analysis, and thus their meaning may be learned by considering their literal meaning. In contrast, in ironic utterances, there is a specific constant relation between the literal and figurative meaning of the utterance (i.e., that of opposition or irrelevance). In addition, the unit of processing in dealing with idioms is a word or phrase, whereas irony involves whole utterances.

IRONY

Irony is a form of figurative language that often extends over whole utterances. The classic rhetorical definition of irony is one in which a speaker says the opposite of what he believes, violating Grice's (1975) maxim of truthfulness. Deception (i.e., lies), however, also requires that the speaker say the opposite of what he believes. The difference between irony and deception is that in the case of irony, the speaker does not want the listener to believe the statement. That is, the speaker makes a false statement, but the listener must recognize that the statement is false. Thus, if a child spills her milk and her brother says "Nice going," the brother is making a negative statement using positive words. He intends for his sister to recognize the discrepancy and his critical intent. In contrast, if the child drew a picture, and her brother said "Nice going," he might be attempting to deceive her to encourage her. Therefore, even though he thought the picture was bad, he wanted his sister to believe that he thought the picture was nice. In deception, the speaker wishes to be considered sincere, whereas in irony, the speaker wishes to convey lack of sincerity.

Irony need not always involve saying the opposite of what one means. Violating Grice's (1975) maxim of relevance also can result in irony. Winner (1988) cites the example of two women discussing a blind date. When asked by her friend, "How was your blind date last night?" the woman answers, "Oh, he had nice shoes." Clark argues that because the woman obviously had little interest in the quality of her dates' shoes, by being irrelevant, the friend is being ironic.

Why should practitioners be interested in irony? After all, do language specialists really want to teach students to be sarcastic, one might ask? Irony occurs frequently in literature and the media. Comprehension of irony also is important for social interaction, as it is a common vehicle for humor and criticism. A colleague of the author's recently reported a revealing classroom interaction with a preschool LI child. The children had just completed an activity in which they had been barefoot, and they were now engaged in putting shoes and socks back on. The LI child came up to the clinician and thrust a dirty, odoriferous sock under her nose. Without thinking, she said "Oh, thanks a lot, David." The child immediately smiled proudly and stuck the sock back under her nose. A teacher's aide, delightedly watching the interaction, reminded the speech-language pathologist of her own frequently repeated warnings to be careful about the use of irony with these young children. The child obviously had taken the remark as being sincere. However, the clinician noted her initial irritated response to the child when he did it the second time; she had briefly perceived the child as ignoring her response and thus as misbehaving. Irony comprehension involves reading multiple cues of facial expression, intonation, knowledge about the speaker, and knowledge about events. As such, it may present particular problems for LLD children.

The purpose of using irony is to convey an attitude, often critical in nature (Winner, 1988). However, irony may also be used to tease, to be humorous, or to console. For example, while at the ballet, an exchange was overheard between a couple settling into their seventh row center seats. The man, who seemed to be attempting a joke as well as hoping for praise, said, "I really have to apologize for these seats." His date, however, did not recognize the ironic intent and replied "Oh these seats seem just fine to me."

Winner (1988) suggests that irony is difficult for young children to understand because, to correctly process the utterance, the listener has to discern the speaker's attitude and relate it to the utterance. Winner hypothesizes two components to correctly comprehending irony: the listener needs to develop correct first- and second-order beliefs. First-order beliefs are the listener's beliefs about whether or not the speaker is being truthful. So, if the boy tells his sister, "Nice going" when she spills the milk, she must decide whether or not he really thinks it was nice. Second-order beliefs are the listener's beliefs about the speaker's sincerity. The sister also must ask herself whether or not her brother wants her to believe he thinks it is nice.

Children's and adults' comprehension of irony generally has been studied by presenting subjects with brief stories or scenarios in which a final remark by a character is potentially ironic. Subjects are then questioned about their interpretation of the final remark. Research on the development of irony comprehension (Ackerman, 1983; Demorest, Meyer, Phelps, Gardner, & Winner, 1984; Winner, 1988) suggests that children first may take an ironic utterance literally (e.g., they will consider "Nice going" to be a compliment). When a speaker makes such a comment after some negative event (e.g., a child losing a race), six-year-old children may consider the speaker to be mistaken (i.e., the speaker thought the child did well in the race, but he did not). Another early strategy reported by Demorest et al. is for children to change the nature of the preceding event to a positive one when recalling it, so that the event is consistent with a literal interpretation of the remark. For example, in the preceding example, a child loses a race, and a speaker says "You're a great runner." When children are asked whether the child won or lost the race, they may report that the child won the race.

A further development in nonliteral comprehension occurs, according to Winner (1988), when children develop first-order beliefs (recognition that a speaker may not mean what she says). Winner (1988) and Demorest et al. (1984) report that many of the nine-year-old children whom they studied reconciled a negative story event with a seemingly positive utterance by assuming that the speaker was telling a lie. They speculated that perhaps the speaker wanted to make the listener feel better about the negative event. However, Capelli, Nakagawa, and Madden (1990) and Hardy and Milosky (1991) found that deception was rarely offered as an explanation for a seemingly positive remark being made after a negative event. This difference may arise from methodological differences. Some of the studies used only forced choice questions to determine children's perception of the speaker's intent (e.g., "Did X want Y to feel bad or good?" Or "Was X being nice or mean?"). Younger children may be reluctant to ascribe malicious intent to a speaker. Hence, they choose the more socially acceptable alternative.

Several of the previously cited studies have found that nine-year-old children sometimes infer that a speaker's intent was consistent with irony. Demorest et al. (1984), however, reported that even at thirteen years of age, ironic intent was sometimes difficult for subjects to discern. Furthermore, in Ackerman's (1983) study, adults occasionally interpreted utterances with ironic intent as sincere. Consider how often you hear someone say "I was only joking" or "I was being sarcastic." In natural conversations, ironic intent may fail to be conveyed with some regularity.

Returning to the methodological issues that are of interest to both clinicians and researchers, use of closed-ended questions (e.g., "Was the speaker being nice or mean?") does not allow other possible interpretations of the intent of such remarks. Ford and Milosky (1991) and Hardy and Milosky (1991) found that children may infer that a speaker's intent when making a potentially ironic remark was to make a friendly joke or to express jealousy. Use of open-ended questions poses problems when children can comprehend ironic intent but lack the resources to be able to express that clearly. Thus, in attempting to discern children's interpretation of a potentially ironic remark, it may be beneficial to ask open-ended questions and then follow them with closed-ended versions when necessary.

What factors might lead a listener to assume that an utterance was intended ironically? Casual observation of conversations suggests that several cues may play a role. The nature of the event or entity that precipitated the remark is often critical information; it is the incongruence of a negative event followed by a "positive" remark that leads a listener to infer irony (e.g., the fact that a child spilled milk or lost a race and the speaker said "Nice going"). A speaker's intonation pattern (e.g., sarcastic tone of voice); facial expression (e.g., rolling of eyes); gestures (e.g., slapping forehead); and choice of words (e.g., "likely story") may provide the listener with cues. Another factor that clearly is important is the degree of shared knowledge between the speaker and listener (what is the speaker's attitude toward the topic); the speaker's general attitude or feelings about the listener (are they friendly or is there animosity between them?); and the prior conversational history of the participants (e.g., is the speaker often ironic?). Hardy and Milosky (1991) found that when two story characters were reported to have had a history of negative interactions, then both six- and nine-year-old children were more likely to interpret one character's remark as ironic and critical than when the interaction history was positive.

Review of the literature and anecdotal evidence suggest that successful use of irony is difficult, and many of the necessary skills lie in the domain of social cognition (Winner, 1988). Because social cognitive skills develop as a result of interaction with others, and the use of language often is required to negotiate higher level social interactions, further research may reveal that LLD children may have particular difficulty with such forms.

LLD CHILDREN'S FIGURATIVE LANGUAGE ABILITIES

This section reviews the studies that have examined LLD children's comprehension and production of figurative language. Because relatively few such studies have been conducted, the section also includes LLD children's performance on tasks that may be component skills in figurative language processing.

One focus of the studies of LLD children has been their ability to use linguistic context to interpret a variety of figurative language forms. In a comparison of third- through sixth-grade learning disabled and non-learning disabled students, Seidenberg and Bernstein (1986) found that students' ability to understand metaphors and similes in a story context increased with grade level. Although non-learning disabled students performed better than learning disabled students on both metaphor and simile comprehension tasks, the difference between the groups was rather small for simile comprehension, whereas for metaphor comprehension there was a much larger gap. Therefore, the findings suggest that learning disabled students may profit from the explicit linguistic markings of comparison that are contained in a simile. The authors suggest that a metacognitive deficit may account for learning disabled students' failure to realize that a metaphoric interpretation of an utterance is necessary. Jones and Stone (1989) compared LLD and same-age normally achieving sixteen- to eighteen-year-olds on comprehension of metaphors embedded in three-sentence stories. They speculated that the poorer performance of LLD subjects may have been due to poor inferencing skills or impoverished semantic networks. It is unclear from the single example given to what degree context supported a metaphoric interpretation.

The previously cited studies compared LLD subjects to their same-age or same-grade peers; it is also of interest to know whether LLD individuals' nonliteral language performance is similar to younger children matched for language abilities. Few studies have matched subjects for language abilities. One study, by Shatz, Shulman, and Bernstein (1980), compared LD and younger normal children's ability to make use of prior utterances in interpreting indirect requests for information and action. Although subjects in this study were not matched directly, the younger normal children displayed language abilities similar to those of the language disordered children. Indirect requests have often been considered nonliteral because an indirect request for action (e.g., "Would you please pass the salt?") requires more than a "yes" response to the literal interpretation of the request. It requires performing the action mentioned. Shatz et al. (1980) provided children with several requests of one type to create a "response set," or expectation regarding the desired response (i.e., action or information). Shatz et al. found that language disordered children were less likely than younger normal children to use the response set created by a series of prior requests to respond appropriately to requests for information versus requests for action.

A second study, by Nippold and Fey (1983), compared the metaphor comprehension and nonverbal combinatorial reasoning skills of a group of nine- to eleven-year-old children who had been diagnosed as language disordered during their preschool years with a group of normally developing nine- to eleven-year-olds. Nippold and Fey chose to investigate these two sets of skills based on previous evidence that they were related in normally developing children (Billow, 1975). The two subject groups that Nippold and Fey studied demonstrated no differences in their performance on several literal language tasks and overall nonverbal cognition. Subjects were asked to explain metaphors. They were also asked to perform a nonverbal task that assessed combinatorial reasoning, that is, the ability to group objects in all possible combinations. Nippold and Fey found that the children with a history of language impairment performed significantly more poorly than the control group on both tasks. Thus, nonliteral language performance may be a sensitive indicator of continued language difficulty in preadolescents.

Although several sources posit that LLD children may have difficulty with idiom comprehension, little empirical evidence available supports or refutes this contention. Strand's (1982) study is one exception. She examined idiom comprehension of eighteen language disordered children between the ages of seven and thirteen years. She compared the performance of language disordered subjects with forty normally developing children between the age of five and eleven years. The task involved picture identification of the idiomatic meaning and explanation of the idiomatic meaning after picture selection. She found that language disordered students performed consistently more poorly than their chronological-age (CA) peers but that each group's performance improved at about the same rate over the age span studied. Although this study suggests that language disordered students may perform like younger normals (i.e., perhaps like language-age matches), further investigation is needed to determine the nature of language disordered children's difficulties.

The ability of LLD children to comprehend idioms is of interest not only for practical reasons but also because of what it may tell clinicians and educators about the nature of language disorders (see Wallach & Butler, chap. 1). Idioms are of interest because LLD children may have enough experience with familiar idioms to know their meaning (and hence may perform more like their same-age peers); in contrast, their ability to deduce the meaning of unfamiliar idioms may depend more on linguistic and nonlinguistic inferencing skills. Hence, they may perform more like younger children whose language abilities are similar to theirs.

For certain figurative forms, one might expect LLD children to perform better than their language-age matches. For example, idiom comprehension might be better because the older LLD children may have heard idioms more often than their younger language-age matches. Ezell and Goldstein (1991) reported that mentally retarded children comprehended more idioms in a meaningful context than language-matched younger normal children. This suggests that linguistic and real-world experience may influence idiom comprehension.

Other data that suggest that language disordered children might experience greater difficulty with processing or use of idiomatic expressions come from Watkins and Rice's (1991) study of their use of verb plus particle constructions. This study is relevant because many idioms take the form of verb plus particle constructions (e.g., "*kick off* the evening," "*run up* a tab," "*ride out* the storm"). These investigators contrasted the abilities of LI children with language-matched and age-matched preschoolers on a task requiring use of verb plus preposition constructions (e.g., "jump off the chair") and verb plus particle constructions (e.g., "kick off the shoe"). They found that

LI subjects performed more poorly than their language-age and CA matches on the verb plus particle constructions.

Nonliteral language comprehension may involve recognizing the discrepancy between the literal meaning of an utterance and the context in which the utterance is said. Some investigators have suggested that it is this discrepancy that drives the listener to infer nonliteral intent. If this is so, comprehension monitoring skills, in which a child recognizes discrepancies, and inferencing skills would seem to play a major role in the acquisition of figurative language abilities.

Comprehension monitoring is the term that has been used to describe the process by which a listener or reader recognizes contradictions or incongruities in discourse. Skarakis-Doyle and Mullin (1990) compared the comprehension monitoring abilities of language disordered students and language-age matched controls. The findings suggested that language disordered children perform like their language-age matched controls in recognizing ambiguity. The authors attribute the language disordered children's performance to deficits not only in comprehension but also in social communicative knowledge. Thus, one might predict that language disordered children may have difficulty in using a seeming contradiction between utterances to drive them to make an ironic, nonliteral interpretation, for example.

As stated previously, inferencing skills also may be required in some figurative language comprehension. Crais and Chapman (1987) found that LLD children's inferencing abilities in a story comprehension task was like that of their language-matched peers. Weismer (1985), in contrast, found inferencing impaired in her language disordered children relative to their controls.

Another skill that may be required for comprehension of some metaphors is analogical reasoning. Nippold, Erskine, and Freed (1988) examined three different forms of analogical reasoning in LI and normally developing children. They found no differences between the groups when nonverbal intelligence was statistically controlled. One of the tasks was a verbal analogical reasoning task (e.g., "*Ear* goes with *radio* and *eye* goes with. . . . Is it *newspaper, glasses,* or *eyebrow?*"). Thus, the task is somewhat similar to the kind of reasoning that occurs in certain metaphors and metaphorically transparent idioms. All the stimuli in the verbal task were presented simultaneously in picture form as well, suggesting that when LI children have nonverbal support for comparisons, they perform like their normal peers.

Successful comprehension of irony and some idioms may be facilitated by information from prosodic elements of talk. Paralinguistic cues have been considered to be a developmentally earlier, more accessible route to language comprehension. Perhaps this is because young infants differentially respond to intonation before comprehending the linguistic elements of a message. Yet Cruttenden (1974, 1985) has shown that acquisition of various intonational contrasts continues after ten years of age. Few investigations have been conducted on LLD children's use of intonation in language comprehension and none on its use in figurative language comprehension. Berk, Doehring, and Bryans (1983) compared language disordered and language-normal children aged five to eleven years on judgments of angry, happy, or sad tone of voice. Many of the normally developing children had near-perfect performance. Performance of language disordered children improved with age, although they continued to evidence deficits in interpreting tone of voice.

As the previous review makes evident, research on the figurative language abilities of LLD students is very limited. However, it is clear, based on the frequency of use of such forms, and the importance of these forms in academic learning and social interaction, that investigation, assessment, and remediation of the figurative language skills of LLD children must be conducted.

CLINICAL IMPLICATIONS

The developmental literature reviewed previously provides professionals with many guidelines for the construction and implementation of assessment and intervention protocols. The world of children provides language specialists with an abundance of natural opportunities on which to capitalize when working with students. On the other hand, the long-term effectiveness of training students on lists of idioms or metaphors in workbooks is suspect (see also Ehren, chap. 15). Instead, taking advantage of students' classroom activities and material, their social activities, and their culture and teaching in the social milieu is likely to result in enhanced processing of figurative language (see also Nelson, chap. 4; Westby, chap. 7).

The purpose of using "real-life" examples rather than pages from workbooks is not to simply develop an alternative list of common figures of speech. Rather, these instances of figurative language in context will be motivated by real communicative goals. That is, the sportscaster's announcements that "the Jazz downed the Knicks" and "the Mets squeaked by the Sox" have a purpose—to inform fans of outcomes in an exciting manner. A teacher's or textbook's use of a galaxy to explain atomic structure will illuminate the new in terms of the old. A friend's bantering comment, "Oh it's rough having so much talent," provides a compliment in a humorous way. If professionals consider that one function of a metaphor is to illuminate or to explain, they might then be guided by the question When are speakers likely to need vivid descriptors? Two common communicative situations arise immediately. The first is when one party cannot or has not experienced firsthand the topic of the metaphor; this is a common occurrence when individuals talk about entities removed in time and/or space. For example, if a speaker wants to convey how beautiful the snow and ice are on a sunny morning to a friend in Florida, she would not convey excitement by saying that it was "all white and sparkly." She might instead talk of "crystalline blankets"; in describing the driving conditions, she might talk of a sleigh ride. The other situation is when the topic of the metaphor is unfamiliar to the listener—as when one talks about some new entity using descriptive terms related to an entity with which the listener is familiar. When parents explain death to young children, they typically use a variety of metaphors—sleep or a long trip away, for example.

Certainly, being persuasive in an argument requires highlighting the right features of an entity. For example, students often sell items to raise money for class trips or nonprofit organizations. Sales talk, particularly when presented in the media, often uses vivid description, with metaphors and idioms common. Clinicians might have students make a commercial about a product they are trying to sell. Videotaping the commercial may enhance students' interest.

Metaphors also may be appropriate to express a particular attitude or strong feeling about an entity or event. A literal description may not convey the same force as a metaphoric usage (e.g., "I felt sad when I heard the news" vs. "I was devastated when I heard the news"). Thus, in addition to teaching students component skills in interpreting such language, one should teach them the purpose for which it is being used.

In creating assessment and intervention tasks, the literature on normal development of figurative language may be used to some extent to guide professionals' decisions about task difficulty and suitability. In addition, the literature examining LLD children's performance, although limited, can inform clinician decisions. In the following sections, guidelines for assessing and promoting the various kinds of figurative language abilities are considered. These procedures are written in a form that should allow them to be carried out by either teachers or speech-language clinicians. For the sake of brevity, the terms *clinician* or *language specialist* will be used.

The previously reviewed literature makes clear three general aspects of figurative language comprehension and use that clinicians will want to consider in creating assessment and intervention materials: the first is the context in which the figurative language occurs, the second is the composition of the utterance containing figurative language, and the third is the type of task used.

Creating and Using Appropriate Contexts

One clear finding of the research literature is that both children and adults are more easily able to process nonliteral language when that language is presented in a meaningful context. Contexts may facilitate comprehension by providing information that is redundant with the meaning of the figurative language. They also may provide information that militates against or makes unlikely a literal meaning. Context may be linguistic, as when a short story or other conversation precedes a metaphor, or largely nonlinguistic (e.g., a series of events that occur, a role play of such events, or a video of such events).

Given the difficulty LLD children may have in integrating information across a series of utterances and making inferences, language specialists may wish to evaluate the relative efficacy of verbal versus nonverbal contexts. It may be easier for the LLD child to first process the linguistic metaphor in relation to nonverbally presented events. Later, the child might receive information relevant to the figurative use in the form of prior linguistic utterances. For example, a clinician might play a small portion of a television show or movie, using no sound, that portrays some distinctive action or entity and is followed by a figurative use. Alternatively, some students in a group might be asked to act out a largely nonverbal scenario followed by a nonliteral remark. The clinician may then teach students how to analyze the context to gain information regarding meaning or intent.

Contextual information that is presented either linguistically or nonlinguistically may consist of information about the speakers, the relationship between the speakers, the event in which the talk is occurring, the motivation behind the conversation, or the place in which the talk is occurring. In both assessment and intervention, clinicians may wish to consider how variation of contextual elements affects a student's interpretation of a nonliteral remark. For example, Hardy and Milosky (1991) found that children's interpretations of ironic remarks varied depending on who said the remark. When children were given a story about a bully saying something to another child, they were more likely to interpret a remark such as "You sure did great!" as ironic. That is, they thought that the speaker was being mean or teasing when the speaker was a bully. If the same utterance ("You sure did great!") was said by a friend of the other character, it was likely to be interpreted as sincere and complimentary. Thus, if clinicians wish to create contexts for teaching irony, they might consider using characters who are likely to be ironic. For example, Lucy, Oscar the Grouch, or Bart Simpson would be much more likely to make ironic remarks than Charlie Brown or Big Bird.

Naturally, the degree of facilitating context may be systematically varied along a continuum from context that is essentially redundant with a metaphor, idiom, or ironic utterance to context that is only minimally revealing. For example, an idiom may be placed fairly early in a conversation or story, or it may be placed later, with several redundant cues having preceded its occurrence. Figure 10–1 provides examples of varying degrees of context that may precede a figurative use.

FIGURE 10–1
Examples of different degrees of supporting linguistic context to aid in idiom or metaphor interpretation

The following contexts provide examples of increasing degrees of linguistic context from which a listener may infer meaning of the idiom. Each context uses the cues presented in the prior context, in addition to introducing the new, underlined cues. There are, of course, many other kinds of cues one might incorporate into such tasks.

Metalinguistic task	What does "spill the beans" mean?
Animate agent	The <u>man</u> spilled the beans.
State of mind of agent	The <u>nervous</u> man spilled the beans.
Event	The nervous man spilled the beans <u>about the birthday party.</u>
Mention of contrasting state	The woman's friends wanted to throw a surprise birthday party for her. They worked hard to <u>keep it a secret.</u> A nervous man spilled the beans about the <u>surprise</u> birthday party.
Linguistic marking of contrast	The woman's friends wanted to throw a surprise birthday party for her. They worked hard to keep it a secret, <u>but</u> a nervous man accidentally spilled the beans about the surprise birthday party.

The last example provides a context that is essentially redundant with the meaning of the idiom. In assessing comprehension, clinicians need to consider if the context is essentially redundant with idiom meaning; in such a case, a child would not need to understand the idiom to respond correctly. However, such redundancy may be valuable when first introducing idioms and when teaching students to use contextual information to guess idiom meaning.

If the prior context is conveyed linguistically, through prior conversation or in a short passage, enactment of linguistic stimuli may result in more thorough processing of material, a technique that may be particularly appropriate for younger children. Depending on the type of figure being taught, clinicians might engage the students in analysis of perceptual or conceptual aspects of the depicted situation and the character's emotion or responses to the situation. Students could be encouraged to note intonation, facial expressions, and gestures, the character's goals in making a statement, and how all of these are conveyed by the character's choice of nonliteral language.

Teaching students how to analyze context may address two different sources of difficulty. One type of erroneous response to figurative language is for the child to simply take the remark literally; another is for the child to recognize that the remark does not make sense literally but not know how to figure out the nonliteral meaning. In assessing a child's abilities with specific nonliteral language forms, the clinician should differentiate instances in which the child seems to take an utterance literally from instances in which the child provides some indication that he does not understand the meaning or that the utterance does not make sense. When the utterance does not make sense, the child is recognizing a communication problem and may actively seek an explanation or clues to

FIGURE 10–1, *continued.*

Idiom meaning stated	The woman's friends wanted to throw a surprise birthday party for her. They worked hard to keep it a secret. One man saw her at work every day and was nervous that <u>he would give away the secret. One day his fears came true.</u> The nervous man accidentally spilled the beans about the surprise birthday party.
Meaning stated and exemplified	The woman's friends wanted to throw a surprise birthday party for her. They worked hard to keep it a secret. One man saw her at work every day and was nervous that he would give away the secret. One day his fears came true. He was talking to her and said "<u>I'll see you on Sunday at the par . . . Ooops!</u>" The nervous man accidentally spilled the beans about the surprise birthday party.

meaning. For example, a graduate clinician recently used the term "heart of gold" with one of her students; the student subsequently asked her to draw a picture of it. When the clinician questioned her further, the student queried "Is it really made of gold?" This sequence provides evidence that the student knew there was something unusual in what had been said.

Clinicians need to make the previously illustrated distinction, because different skills may need to be taught. When a child takes a nonliteral remark literally, without questioning the meaning or sense, intervention might focus on recognition of inconsistencies or anomalies in a story or communicative interaction. The literature on training comprehension monitoring skills provides several examples of this type of training (Dollaghan & Kaston, 1986; Palincsar & Brown, 1984).

When a student recognizes that the remark is not to be taken literally but does not seem to be able to use context to determine cues to meaning, two techniques may facilitate students' use of context: one that teaches recognition and interpretation of the different types of cues (Sternberg, 1987) and the other that teaches students to make implicit inferences explicit through use of a question generating technique (Franks et al., 1982).

Sternberg (1987) researched the processes and cues that individuals may use to determine the meaning of an unfamiliar word in a passage. Briefly, he taught both students and adults to separate relevant from irrelevant information in beginning to form a definition, to combine the relevant cues in a way that yields a workable definition, and to relate prior knowledge about the relevant cues to new information about the word. The cues that Sternberg teaches are exemplified in Table 10–4. Sternberg found that both adult readers and students demonstrate enhanced performance when given practice using this approach.

Students' comprehension may also be facilitated by explicitly stating the implicit inferences that may be signaled in text (see also Wallach & Butler, chap. 1). Franks et al. (1982) taught students who were poor readers to make explicit relationships in the text that were implied and required inferences. Students evaluated sentences to determine if the relation

TABLE 10–4
Cues for learning vocabulary from linguistic context
From "Most Vocabulary Is Learned from Context" by R. Sternberg, in *The Nature of Vocabulary Acquisition* (p. 92) edited by M. McKeown and M. Curtis, 1987, Hillsdale, NJ: Lawrence Erlbaum. Copyright 1987 by Lawrence Erlbaum. Adapted by permission.

Cue Type	Example
Temporal cues	Duration, frequency, or when something can occur
Example	"In the morning"
Spatial cues	Location of *X*, possible locations
Example	"In the kitchen"
Value cues	Worth, desirability, or affect that it arouses
Example	"I just love it"
Stative descriptive cues	Properties of *X*—shape, color, feel, odor
Example	"It was strong"
Functional descriptive cues	Purpose of *X*, actions it can perform, potential uses
Example	"She needed it to get going"
Class membership	Classes to which it belongs
Example	"What a beverage!"
Equivalence cues	Cues regarding meaning or contrasts (antonyms)
Example	"The song about it is called 'Java Jive.'"
Causal/enablement cues	Causes or enabling conditions for *X*
Example	"You have to have hot water in order to make it."

between the character and an action seemed arbitrary. "For example, given the statement, 'The kind man bought the milk,' the students were asked, 'Is there any more reason to mention that a kind man bought the milk than a tall man or a mean man?" (p. 419). The students then learned to activate knowledge that made relationships between character and action less arbitrary. Students generated a reason or context to help understand why the person was performing action. In the preceding example, they were asked what they knew about kind people and their actions and then were asked to connect that knowledge with the milk purchase. Eventually, students used these elaboration strategies while reading passages. Consequently, their scores improved to the level achieved by good readers. Professionals might consider how this type of training might be used with passages or interactions containing figurative language to help students infer nonliteral intent and the specific meaning of that intent.

One note of caution is in order when students are presented with written passages: Their reading ability may circumscribe their use of contextual cues. Leu, Simons, and DeGroff (1986) have shown that poor readers may be forced to use the predictability contained in contextual information to simply decode words. When a reader uses context for such simple processes as decoding, then she may not be able to use context for the higher level comprehension processes of inferencing, cue analysis, and getting the gist out of a section of discourse, as Wallach and Butler also point out in Chapter 1.

When clinicians teach students to use the contextual analysis skills described earlier, they are teaching metalinguistic strategies. Research on teaching metalinguistic or metacognitive strategies (Pressley, Borkowski, & O'Sullivan, 1984) shows that when children are just taught a strategy, there is little improvement in the skill for which that strategy is designed. Indeed, it is necessary to teach the strategy, to teach how the strategy is helpful, and to show how it works (Pressley et al., 1984). This second step involves pointing out to children that when they use the strategy, some communicative goal is achieved (or their score improves on an academic task), because children do not necessarily connect the two events. Finally, good metalinguistic or metacognitive instruction also includes knowing how to monitor the effectiveness of the strategy and how to know which strategy to choose in a given situation (see Ehren's discussion of strategies in chap. 15).

Target Utterances Containing Figurative Language

Research suggests that conventional figurative uses will be easiest for children to comprehend and produce, with appreciation of novel uses developing later. Thus, when teaching metaphors or similes, one might start with comparisons such as "Her hands were as cold as ice," "The athlete was a star," or "My father was a bear this morning." Utterances that are frequently used ironically, such as "Thanks a lot," "That's a likely story," or "Nice going," may be easier for children to interpret than if one begins with less common, more situation-specific utterances said with ironic intent (e.g., "That's a great dress"). Consulting popular television shows and listening to students' conversations are likely to yield a variety of the more commonly occurring idioms. In addition, Nippold and Rudzinski (1993) provide familiarity ratings by adolescents for twenty-four idioms.

In distinguishing literal versus figurative meanings, it also may be valuable to illustrate the concept initially with those idioms whose literal senses are implausible or meaningless (e.g., "She jumped down his throat," "it's raining cats and dogs," "the test was a piece of cake," "He has a frog in his throat," "the cat's got her tongue"). Both the Amelia Bedelia series by Peggy Parish and Fred Gwynne's books use as their central focus children's literal misinterpretations of idioms.

The developmental literature in both comprehension and production of metaphors suggests that perceptual metaphors, based on static physical characteristics such as color and shape (e.g., "the rattlesnake was a long rope"; "the volcano is a bright red fire truck") may be easiest for children. Dynamic physical characteristics such as sound and movement (e.g., "the rattlesnake was soap sliding along the bathtub") follow. Functional characteristics or what an entity is used for ("the pen is a mighty sword") come next. Metaphors making comparisons based on psychological characteristics ("the rattlesnake was a storm cloud") generally are the latest acquisition. Clinicians also may use these guidelines when evaluating the difficulty of transparent idioms.

After identifying those prominent characteristics, students might be asked what entity or action really calls forth that characteristic. By asking for prominent characteristics, the clinician may avoid the pitfall of presenting metaphors as if they were simply comparison statements; rather, students may be more likely to see the transformative nature of metaphors—thinking about one thing in terms of another.

The opportunity to teach the transformative nature of metaphors is present throughout the school day. Teachers constantly provide images for students to use in learning. It will enhance learning of subject matter and learning of figurative language skills if students are provided opportunities to transform a concept into something with which they are familiar.

For example, a recent article in *The New York Times Magazine* (Jetter, 1993) cited the pioneering work of Bob Moses in teaching the language of mathematics, in general, and algebra, in particular, to students attending poor inner-city or rural schools—schools that traditionally have failed to teach this material successfully. Moses, Kamii, Swap, and Howard (1989) described how they used concepts that are meaningful to students to introduce the more abstract aspects of the language of algebra. One example cited was how Moses used a trip on the Boston subway to help students understand negative numbers. He took the students on a subway trip that started at a stop near their school. They rode into the city, got off and caught the train in the other direction, rode back *past* their correct stop to the end of the line, and then returned to their stop. Back at school, the class spent time diagraming, in increasingly abstract ways, the journey they had taken. These abstractions appeared more and more similar to the number line, and allowed the students to see the number line, including negative numbers, in relation to a common experience—that of riding the subway.

Figurative language also presents an excellent opportunity to explore cultural diversity and to recognize how that diversity may affect performance on tasks involving figurative language. For example, idioms are such commonly occurring figures of speech that interaction would be severely compromised without the ability to understand them. Given that idioms change with time, and differ across ethnic or social groups, examining idioms in different ethnic, social, and age groups provides an opportunity to explore cultural and linguistic diversity as it occurs in natural communicative interaction.

Rap music is a particularly rich source of current figurative language, but the origins of particular terms may be less recent. The rap group Kris Kross uses the term *mack* in the lyrics of one of its songs. According to Fab 5 Freddy, the author of a dictionary of hip-hop terms entitled *Fresh Fly Flavor* (1992), the term means "1. A flamboyant life style supported by women; 2. Being in control of a situation with your wit as the chief tool." Freddy traces the term's origin back to the eighteenth-century British movement called *Dandyism.* British dandies, known for their wit and dress, were called *macaronis;* hence, the appearance of the term in the song "Yankee Doodle." Freddy reports that the term was picked up by pimps in the late 1950s but that the current meaning has been broadened and softened. As Freddy states, "once again, a word or phrase has been snatched up by ultra-urban contemporary black youth, reformed, and spit back out into mainstream culture." Interesting, relevant materials for students may also be garnered from television shows, newspapers, radio, literature, religious sermons, and tape recordings of conversations.

Idioms present a particular challenge to children and adults who are learning English as a second language. Simply observing the interactions of these children may provide ample material for remediation. As indicated earlier, basic classroom directions such as "line up," "take turns," and "keep in mind," may not seem idiomatic, but they are, especially to the ear of a nonnative speaker. Recording a day's classroom conversation should provide many examples that, when taught, may help these children verbally negotiate classroom procedures, rather than being forced to rely on observation of others. In addition, in the course of metalinguistic teaching of second language learners, the true complexity of learning language is likely to become evident, as a colleague recently discovered. She was teaching an ESL adolescent about degrees of formality in addressing different listeners. She used the example, "You don't say 'What's up?' when talking to the principal." The student looked puzzled and responded, "But you weren't surprised!" The teacher, in turn, was mystified and after a few iterations of this dialogue, she realized the student was referring to the fact that, in a lesson on idioms, he had previously learned that "You don't say!" was an expression of surprise. This incident underscores the previously discussed importance of rich context in teaching language meaning.

A child's prior knowledge is likely to affect the ability to interpret any single figurative use and the context in which that figure occurs. Vosniadou (1987) has shown that when children are familiar with a domain, and can use their world knowledge, they are more likely to successfully interpret a metaphorical statement. In such situations, strong background knowledge makes a literal interpretation highly unlikely; children are driven to a metaphorical or an ironic interpretation. Thus, care must be taken both in choosing the figures of speech one uses and also in constructing the contextual information that clinicians hope will facilitate comprehension or use. For example, consider one of the metaphoric idioms from the Test of Language Competence (Wiig & Secord, 1988): The situation involves two girls talking about a friend running for class president and with one saying "She's holding all the aces." Correct interpretation of this idiom may require some knowledge of card playing, an assumption that may be erroneous, for example, among some members of Southern communities because the Southern Baptist tradition does not allow card playing. Other expressions that would not be appropriate are "the deck is stacked in her favor" or "I'd put my money on her." In these same communities, however, spectator sports are a very popular pastime that pervades many aspects of life, so saying "The score is in her favor" might better allow students to use their background knowledge to interpret the nonliteral intent.

Another important dimension that affects ease of comprehension is the form that is used to express the metaphor. Seidenberg and Bernstein (1986) demonstrated that language disordered children had greater success in interpretation when overt linguistic marking of the comparison (i.e., a simile) was used than when there was no linguistic indication of comparison (i.e., a traditional metaphor). Reynolds and Ortony (1980) reported similar findings for normally developing children. Both of these studies used the "like" form of simile. In working with children who are having difficulty comprehending such forms, it may be useful to begin with the "as . . . as" form (e.g., "as poor as a church mouse"; "as fresh as a daisy"; "as quiet as a tomb"), which states the ground of the comparison and then progress to the "like" form.

Task Variables

As indicated in the earlier sections of this chapter, the tasks that one uses to assess children's comprehension and use of figurative language are very likely to affect the degree of success that children demonstrate. Figure 10–2 provides examples of these tasks.

FIGURE 10–2
Examples of tasks used to assess idiom and metaphor comprehension
continued

Matching Words with Sensory Properties of Physical Stimuli
Children asked to match pairs of stimuli *(e.g., red and blue chips; two musical pieces)* to antonym pairs *(e.g., happy–sad, hard–soft)*
(Gardner, 1974)

Enactment
Children asked to act out stories in which a metaphor was embedded. Children given a board on which a setting (park, buildings) was laid out and given miniature toys relevant to each story. None of the toys was the literal referent used in the metaphor (e.g., there were no toy birds or nests for the story containing the metaphor *Sally was a bird flying to her nest*).
(Vosniadou & Ortony, 1986)

Forced Choice
The bird was a rainbow flying in the sky.
That means the bird:
1. was very colorful
2. was making a nest
(Nippold, Leonard, & Kail, 1984)

Sentence-Completion Task
Things don't have to be huge in size to look that way. Look at that boy standing over there. He looks as gigantic as ____.
The football player was a ____.
(Gardner, Kircher, Winner, & Perkins, 1975)

FIGURE 10–2, *continued.*

Multiple-Choice Meaning Task:
Things don't have to be huge in size to look that way. Look at that boy standing over there. He looks as gigantic as:

Literal choice:	*as gigantic as the most gigantic person in the whole world*
Conventional metaphor:	*as gigantic as a skyscraper in the center of town*
Appropriate metaphor:	*as gigantic as a double-decker cone in a baby's hand*
Inappropriate choice:	*as gigantic as a clock from a department store*

(Gardner, et al., 1975)

Multiple-Choice Metaphoric Preferences Task (All answers correct; purpose is to determine the grounds children prefer):
The popped red balloon is:
___ *a limp washcloth* (shape)
___ *a bottle of ketchup* (color)
___ *a washed away sandcastle* (conceptual: impermanence)
___ *an empty auditorium after a concert* (sound)
___ *an apple peel* (combination: color and shape)
(Silberstein, Gardner, Phelps, & Winner, 1982)

Paraphrase/Explanation Task
"The smell of her perfume was bright sunshine." Explain what that means.
(Winner, Rosenstiel, & Gardner, 1976)

Task formats may include enactment of meanings with toys or in dramatic role play, multiple-choice paradigms, sentence completion tasks, response to yes–no questions regarding meanings and intents, and paraphrase tasks. Of these, paraphrase has been shown consistently to be the most difficult or latest developing. However, it may be the only technique that allows clinicians to determine the nuances of a student's understanding.

SUMMARY

Figurative language is pervasive, necessary, and has its roots in language development occurring in the preschool years. It is used to achieve a wide variety of communicative goals, and these goals are intrinsic to the nature of figurative language. Its development spans the school years, and LLD students may have a particularly difficult time with learning to use it adroitly.

One way in which figurative language typically has been taught is to present a worksheet with a list of idioms or metaphors to be learned. This primarily may enhance students' abilities to read fortune cookies, because that is one of the few instances in real life where people are presented with metaphors, idioms, or proverbs completely unrelated to the ongoing discourse. In contrast, this chapter advocates that when teaching figurative language use, the clinician should present communicatively natural instances of nonliteral language, provide a rationale for using such language, and then illustrate that motivation in the stimuli. In this way, students may have practice incorporating all the sources of knowledge that they typically would have when interpreting figurative language. What will ultimately motivate students to learn and use such language is seeing how figurative language can aid them in pursuit of their goals—to run for class office, to write a clever Valentine, to be humorous, or to reflect on the lyrics in rap music.

In summary, language specialists who deal with LLD children on a daily basis may feel that figurative language is not central to intervention. On the contrary, as this chapter demonstrates, many of children's ongoing communicative needs will be met by intervention in this important area of communication.

REFERENCES

Ackerman, B. (1982). On comprehending idioms: Do children get the picture? *Journal of Experimental Child Psychology, 33,* 439–454.

Ackerman, B. (1983). Form and function in children's understanding of ironic utterances. *Journal of Experimental Child Psychology: General, 35,* 487–508.

American College Dictionary. (1968). New York: Random House.

Berenstain, S., & Berenstain, J. (1983). *The Berenstain bears' trouble with money.* New York: Random House.

Berk, S., Doehring, D., & Bryans, B. (1983). Judgments of vocal affect by language-delayed children. *Journal of Communication Disorders, 16,* 49–56.

Billow, R. (1975). A cognitive developmental study of metaphor comprehension. *Developmental Psychology, 11,* 415–423.

Billow, R. (1981). Observing spontaneous metaphor in children. *Journal of Experimental Child Psychology, 31,* 415–423.

Blalock, J. (1982). Persistent auditory language deficits in adults with learning disabilities. *Journal of Learning Disabilities, 15,* 604–609.

Brinton, B., Fujiki, M., & Mackey, T. (1985). Elementary school age children's comprehension of specific idiomatic expressions. *Journal of Communication Disorders, 18,* 245–257.

Cacciari, C., & Levorato, M. (1989). How children understand idioms in discourse. *Journal of Child Language, 16,* 387–405.

Capelli, C., Nakagawa, N., & Madden, C. (1990). How children understand sarcasm. The role of context and intonation. *Child Development, 61,* 1824–1841.

Clark, J. (1988). *Word wise: A dictionary of English idioms.* New York: Henry Holt.

Corbett, E. (1971). *Classical rhetoric for the modern student.* New York: Oxford University Press.

Crais, E., & Chapman, R. (1987). Story recall and inferencing skills in language/learning-disabled and nondisabled children. *Journal of Speech and Hearing Disorders, 52,* 50–55.

Cruttenden, A. (1974). An experiment involving comprehension of intonation in children from 7 to 10. *Journal of Child Language, 1,* 221–231.

Cruttenden, A. (1985). Intonation comprehension in ten-year-olds. *Journal of Child Language, 12,* 643–661.

Demorest, A., Meyer, C., Phelps, E., Gardner, H., & Winner, E. (1984). Words speak louder than actions: Understanding deliberately false remarks. *Child Development, 55,* 1527–1534.

Dollaghan, C., & Kaston, N. (1986). A comprehension monitoring program for language-impaired children. *Journal of Speech and Hearing Disorders, 51,* 264–271.

Ezell, H., & Goldstein, H. (1991). Comparison of idiom comprehension of normal children and children with mental retardation. *Journal of Speech and Hearing Research, 34,* 812–819.

Fab 5 Freddy. (1992). *Fresh fly flavor.* Stamford: Longmeadow Press.

Ford, J., & Milosky, L. (1991). *The effect of age and intonation on children's understanding of ironic utterances.* Paper presented at the American Speech-Language-Hearing Association, Atlanta, GA.

Franks, J., Vye, N., Auble, P., Mezynski, K., Perfetto, G., Bransford, J., Stein, B., & Littlefield, J. (1982). Learning from explicit versus implicit texts. *Journal of Experimental Psychology: General, 111,* 414–422.

Gardner, H. (1974). Metaphors and modalities: How children project polar adjectives onto diverse domains. *Child Development, 45,* 84–91.

Gardner, H., Kircher, M., Winner, E., & Perkins, D. (1975). Children's metaphoric productions and preferences. *Journal of Child Language, 2,* 125–141.

Gardner, H., & Winner, E. (1982). First intimations of artistry. In S. Strauss (Ed.), *U-shaped behavioral growth.* New York: Academic Press.

Gentner, D. (1988). Metaphor as structure mapping: The relational shift. *Child Development, 59,* 47–59.

Gibbs, R. (1987). Linguistic factors in children's understanding of idioms. *Journal of Child Language, 14,* 569–586.

Gibbs, R. (1991). Semantic analyzability in children's understanding of idioms. *Journal of Speech and Hearing Research, 34,* 613–620.

Gibbs, R., & Gonzales, G. (1985). Syntactic frozenness in processing and remembering idioms. *Cognition, 20,* 243–259.

Gibbs, R., & Nayak, N. (1989). Psycholinguistic studies on the syntactic behavior of idioms. *Cognitive Psychology, 21,* 100–138.

Gibbs, R., Nayak, N., Bolton, J., & Keppel, M. (1989). Speakers' assumptions about the lexical flexibility of idioms. *Memory and Cognition, 17,* 58–68.

Grice, H. (1975). Logic and conversation. In P. Cole & J. Morgan (Eds.), *Syntax and semantics: Speech acts* (pp. 41–58). New York: Academic Press.

Grimes, W. (1993, March 26). Farrow tries to avoid role of a woman scorned. *New York Times,* p. B4.

Hardison, O. (1966). *Practical rhetoric.* Norwalk, CT: Appleton-Century-Crofts.

Hardy, D., & Milosky, L. (1991). *The effects of age and social background information on interpretation of remarks in story contexts.* Paper presented at the American Speech-Language-Hearing Association, Atlanta, GA.

Hendrickson, R. (1987). *The Henry Holt encyclopedia of word and phrase origins.* New York: Henry Holt.

Jetter, A. (1993, February 20). Mississippi learning. *The New York Times Magazine,* pp. 28–35, 50, 51, 64, 72.

Johnson, J. (1991). Developmental versus language-based factors in metaphor interpretation. *Journal of Educational Psychology, 83,* 470–483.

Jones, J., & Stone, A. (1989). Metaphor comprehension by a language learning disabled and normally achieving adolescent boys. *Learning Disability Quarterly, 12,* 251–260.

Keil, F. (1986). Conceptual domains and the acquisition of metaphor. *Cognitive Development, 1,* 73–96.

Lakoff, G., & Johnson, M. (1980). *Metaphors we live by.* Chicago: University of Chicago Press.

Lazar, R., Warr-Leeper, G., Nicholson, C., & Johnson, S. (1989). Elementary school teachers' use of multiple meaning expressions. *Language, Speech, and Hearing Services in the Schools, 20,* 420–429.

Leu D., Jr., Simons, H., & DeGroff, L. (1986). Predictable texts and interactive-compensatory hypotheses: Evaluating individual differences in reading ability, context use, and comprehension. *Journal of Educational Psychology, 78,* 347–352.

Levorato, M., & Cacciari, C. (1992). Children's comprehension and production of idioms: The role of context and familiarity. *Journal of Child Language, 19,* 415–433.

Makkai, A. (1987). *A dictionary of American idioms.* New York: Barron's.

Moore, B. (1988). A young child's use of a physical-psychological metaphor. *Metaphor and Symbolic Activity, 3,* 223–232.

Moses, R., Kamii, M., Swap, S., & Howard, J. (1989). The Algebra Project: Organizing in the spirit of Ella. *Harvard Educational Review, 59,* 27–47.

Mueller, R., & Gibbs, R. (1987). Processing idioms with multiple meanings. *Journal of Psycholinguistic Research, 16,* 63–81.

Nippold, M., Erskine, B., & Freed, D. (1988). Proportional and functional analogical reasoning in normal and language-impaired children. *Journal of Speech and Hearing Disorders, 53,* 440–448.

Nippold, M., & Fey, S. (1983). Metaphoric understanding in preadolescents having a history of language acquisition difficulties. *Language, Speech, and Hearing Services in Schools, 14,* 171–180.

Nippold, M., Leonard, L., & Kail, R. (1984). Syntactic and conceptual factors in children's understanding of metaphors. *Journal of Speech and Hearing Research, 27,* 197–205.

Nippold, M., & Rudzinski, M. (1993). Familiarity and transparency in idiom explanation: A developmental study of children and adolescents. *Journal of Speech and Hearing Research, 36,* 728–737.

Ortony, A. (1986). Some problems for models of metaphor comprehension and their developmental implications. *Communication and Cognition, 19,* 347–366.

Ortony, A., Turner, T., & Larson-Shapiro, N. (1985). Cultural and instructional influences on figurative language comprehension by inner city children. *Research in the Teaching of English, 19,* 25–36.

Palincsar, A., & Brown, A. (1984). Reciprocal teaching of comprehension-fostering and comprehension-monitoring activities. *Cognition and Instruction, 1,* 117–175.

Pearson, P., Raphael, R., TePaske, R., & Hyser, H. (1981). The function of metaphor in children's recall of expository passages. *Journal of Reading Behavior, 13,* 249–261.

Pellegrini, A., & Galda, L. (1982). The effect of thematic-fantasy play training on the development of children's story comprehension. *American Educational Research Journal, 19,* 443–452.

Pollio, H., Barlow, J., Fine, H., & Pollio, M. (1977). *Psychology and the poetics of growth.* Hillsdale, NJ: Lawrence Erlbaum.

Pollio, H., & Smith, M. (1980). Metaphoric competence and complex human problem solving. In R. Honeck & R. Hoffman (Eds.), *Cognition and figurative language.* Hillsdale, NJ: Lawrence Erlbaum.

Pollio, H., Smith, M., & Pollio, M. (1990). Figurative language and cognitive psychology. *Language and Cognitive Processes, 5,* 141–167.

Pollio, M., & Pollio, H. (1979). A test of metaphoric comprehension and some preliminary data. *Journal of Child Language, 6,* 111–120.

Pressley, M., Borkowski, J., & O'Sullivan, J. (1984). Memory strategy instruction is made of this: Metamemory and durable strategy use. *Educational Psychologist, 19,* 94–107.

Prinz, P. (1983). The development of idiomatic meaning in children. *Language and Speech, 26,* 263–272.

Reynolds, R., & Ortony, A. (1980). Some issues in the measurement of children's comprehension of metaphorical language. *Child Development, 51,* 1110–1119.

Richards, I. (1936). *The philosophy of rhetoric.* London: Oxford University Press.

Rostand, E. (1898). *Cyrano de Bergerac.* New York: Doubleday & McClure.

Seidenberg, P., & Bernstein, D. (1986). The comprehension of similes and metaphors by learning-disabled and nonlearning-disabled children. *Language, Speech, and Hearing Services in the Schools, 17,* 219–229.

Seuss, Dr. (1984). *The butter battle book.* New York: Random House.

Shatz, M., Shulman, M., & Bernstein, D. (1980). The responses of language disordered children to indirect directives in varying contexts. *Applied Psycholinguistics, 1,* 295–306.

Silberstein, L., Gardner, H., Phelps, E., & Winner, E. (1982). Autumn leaves and old photographs: The development of metaphor preferences. *Journal of Experimental Child Psychology, 34,* 135–150.

Skarakis-Doyle, E., & Mullin, K. (1990). Comprehension monitoring in language-disordered children: A preliminary investigation of cognitive and linguistic factors. *Journal of Speech and Hearing Disorders, 55,* 700–705.

Smitherman, G. (1986). *Talkin and testifyin: The language of Black America.* Detroit: Wayne State University Press.

Sternberg, R. (1987). Most vocabulary is learned from context. In M. McKeown & M. Curtis (Eds.), *The nature of vocabulary acquisition.* Hillsdale, NJ: Lawrence Erlbaum.

Strand, K. (1982). The development of idiom comprehension in language-disordered children. In *Proceedings from the third Wisconsin symposium on research in child language disorders* (pp. 171–182). Madison: Department of Communication Disorders and University of Wisconsin-Extension, University of Wisconsin-Madison.

Van Lancker, D., & Canter, G. (1981). Idiomatic versus literal interpretations of ditropically ambiguous sentences. *Journal of Speech and Hearing Research, 46,* 64–69.

Van Lancker, D., Canter, G., & Terbeek, D. (1981). Disambiguation of ditropic sentences: acoustic and phonetic cues. *Journal of Speech and Hearing Research, 24,* 330–335.

Verbrugge, R. (1984). The role of metaphor in our perception of language. *Annals of the New York Academy of Sciences, 433,* 167–183.

Vosniadou, S. (1987). Children and metaphors. *Child Development, 58,* 870–885.

Vosniadou, S., & Ortony, A. (1983). The emergence of the literal-metaphorical-anomalous distinction in young children. *Child Development, 54,* 154–161.

Vosniadou, S., & Ortony, A. (1986). Testing the metaphoric competence of the young child: Paraphrase vs. enactment. *Human Development, 29,* 226–230.

Vosniadou, S., Ortony, A., Reynolds, R., & Wilson, P. (1984). Sources of difficulty in children's understanding of metaphorical language. *Child Development, 55,* 1588–1606.

Waggoner, J., & Palermo, D. (1989). Betty is a bouncing bubble: Children's comprehension of emotion-descriptive metaphors. *Developmental Psychology, 25,* 152–163.

Watkins, R., & Rice, M. (1991). Verb particle and preposition acquisition in language-impaired preschoolers. *Journal of Speech and Hearing Research, 34,* 1136–1141.

Weismer, S. (1985). Constructive comprehension abilities exhibited by language-disordered children. *Journal of Speech and Hearing Research, 28,* 175–184.

Wiig, E., & Secord, W. (1988). *Test of language competence—Expanded edition.* San Antonio: Psychological Corporation.

Winner, E. (1988). *The point of words.* Cambridge: Harvard University Press.

Winner, E., Engel, M., & Gardner, H. (1980). Misunderstanding metaphor: What's the problem? *Journal of Experimental Child Psychology, 30,* 22–32.

Winner, E., McCarthy, M., Kleinman, S., & Gardner, H. (1984). First metaphors. *New Directions for Child Development, 3,* 29–42.

Winner, E., Rosenstiel, A., & Gardner, H. (1976). The development of metaphoric understanding. *Developmental Psychology, 12,* 289–297.

11

PROBLEM-SOLVING STRATEGIES FOR ACADEMIC SUCCESS

■ Camille L. Z. Blachowicz
National-Louis University

COMPREHENSION AS PROBLEM SOLVING

Imagine being in a foreign country watching a televised sport that is unfamiliar to you. How do you make sense of what is going on? Thinking of the games you know, you look for the opposing teams, using the colors of jerseys to help you determine the opponents. Next, you watch for some sort of score, to determine the purpose of the game and to understand how points are accumulated. Later, you note who the nonplayers are, hypothesize that they are officials, and watch for interruptions in the game to help learn about approved and disapproved procedures. You begin to solve the puzzle of the game by using what you already know to make hypotheses about what is going on. As you become more sophisticated in your observation, these hypotheses are confirmed or changed until you understand the game.

From the infant learning to take her first steps, to the student involved in the more abstract problems of geometry and physics, learners start with what they know, hypothesize what could be, and strive to collect, integrate, and evaluate information that will help them reconcile something "new" with something "known." In the most basic sense, all learning, all "meaning making" involves problem solving (Lahey & Bloom, chap. 13; Miller, Galanter, & Pribram, 1960; Milosky, chap. 10; Newell & Simon, 1972).

These processes of connecting new knowledge with already existing knowledge structures, or the changing of knowledge structures in light of new knowledge, are reflected in Piaget's notions of assimilation and accommodation (1959) and in more recent constructive views of learning (D. E. Rumelhart, 1980). Both historical and contemporary views of reading comprehension stress a similarly dynamic view of comprehension, characterizing it as "reasoning" (Thorndike, 1917), as "thought getting and thought manipulating" (Huey, 1908/1968), in which the reader interacts, or "transacts" (Rosenblatt, 1978) with the text being read.

Like problem solving in general, reading comprehension requires that the reader be active, bring knowledge to the act of comprehending, make hypotheses and set purposes for reading, and gather information and make inferences before coming to a resolution. This theoretical perspective is supported by evidence that suggests that good readers *do* engage in these types of behaviors. They use their prior knowledge to self-question and hypothesize (Mandler & Johnson, 1977; D. R. Rumelhart, 1975). Further, good readers integrate information across the text and with their prior knowledge (Collins, Brown, & Larkin, 1980) and monitor these processes and their own learning (Brown, Bransford, Ferrarra, & Campione, 1983; Palincsar, Brown, & Campione, chap. 5; Silliman & Wilkinson, chap. 2).

What allows readers to engage in these processes is their prior knowledge of the world and how it works. If a reader sees a sentence such as

> The young girl wore her best dress and carried a brightly wrapped box.

the reader's knowledge of the world might lead to the hypothesis that the child was ready for a party, some sort of party where gift giving was appropriate. These are inferences the reader must make from past knowledge and are cued by, but not directly stated by, the author in this simple example.

It is critical to note that vocabulary is the surface manifestation of underlying prior conceptual knowledge. A reader who responds to the question "Where is the girl [in the preceding example] going?" with the answer "To a *birthday party* because she is carrying a *present*" reveals the nature of his prior experiences by the words chosen to express it. Someone from Pakistan might describe her dress as a *sari* and the present as one for *divali,* because the inferences drawn from author's clues reflect not only general cross-cultural schemata, such as the one for *party* but also the cultural bases of knowledge of each reader (Steffensen, Joag-dev, & Anderson, 1979; see also Westby, chap. 7).

Research also amply documents that the relationship between vocabulary knowledge and reading comprehension is a strong and significant one (Davis, 1944, 1968; Spearitt, 1972). As with the growth of conceptual knowledge, with which it is intimately connected, word learning occurs when learners are exposed to novel information about new words or about terms they have already encountered. This information can be gathered either incidentally, through repeated encounters with a word in contextual, communicative situations, or intentionally, through self-directed or other-directed instruction (Beck & McKeown, 1991; Nagy, 1988). In both cases, the process is analogous to the problem solving described earlier. Consider the dialogue of one fifth-grade student with his teacher when the teacher tried to encourage the student to verbalize his thinking process:

> Student: Well, what is an antidote anyhow?
> Teacher: What do you think it could be?
> Student: The guy took it after the poison.
> Teacher: So . . . ?
> Student: So, is it like medicine? [Student hypothesizes a connection to a known term.]
> Teacher: What do you think?
> Student: Well, he gets better and doesn't die. [Refers to subsequent context.]
> Teacher: So . . . ?
> Student: So, it's medicine or like a cure.

Here, the student uses past knowledge, hypothesizes a connection, and uses the rest of the text to test, and in this case, verify the new word meaning.

PROBLEM SOLVING AND ACADEMIC SUCCESS

For students experiencing academic difficulty, both the conceptual and the metacognitive components of the problem-solving process can be areas of difficulty. The ability to integrate new and old information presupposes a well-developed knowledge base as a foundation for comprehension (see Lahey & Bloom, chap. 13). Variations in the breadth and depth of world and school related prior knowledge have a significant effect on the ability to comprehend (Spiro & Meyers, 1984). Using our earlier example, a student without past (firsthand or vicarious) experience of attending a birthday party would not be able to use the cues given by the author to answer the inferential question, "Where is the girl going?" Further, the ability to appropriately implement and control comprehension problem solving processes has differentiated able from less able readers in a number of studies (August, Flavell, & Clift, 1984; Ryan, 1981). Less able readers do not adjust their reading for different purposes and they are not as easily able to shift hypotheses or change approaches when breakdowns of comprehension occur—similar to Scott's discussion of writing in Chapter 8. For example, with the earlier example, consider an added sentence:

> The young girl wore her best dress and carried a brightly wrapped box. The decorated tree and green and red tablecloths made the room look festive.

A capable reader will shift from "birthday party" to "Christmas" on encountering the second sentence. However, some readers who experience problems with shifting or modifying their initial hypotheses would not use later clues to modify their first impressions, even though they had the appropriate experiential background (Forrest-Pressley & Waller, 1984; Kimmell & MacGinitie, 1985).

Moreover, students experiencing academic problems often have well-documented deficits in word knowledge (German, chap. 12; Simmons & Kameenui, 1986) as well as in the contextual use of strategies necessary for independent word learning (Golinkoff, 1975–1976; Olshavsky, 1978). If the example had been

> The young girl wore her best dress and carried a brightly wrapped box. The *holly, wassail bowl,* and *yule log* made the room look festive.

even a student with a firmly established concept of "Christmas" would need a highly sophisticated vocabulary to use the clues in the second sentence to determine what holiday was taking place.

In sum, theoretical perspectives on comprehension, studies of good readers, and research on learners who have academic difficulty all suggest that a problem-solving model of comprehension and vocabulary is appropriate as a model on which to base instructional design for academic success. How to design and implement such instruction will be the focus of this chapter.

INSTRUCTION FOR ACADEMIC SUCCESS

Since its inception, the National Assessment of Academic Progress (NAEP) has targeted comprehension instruction as an area in need of renewed effort. In the last two decades, observational studies of both primary and middle school classrooms suggested that effective teaching of comprehension was not a major component of school reading programs, whereas assessment and "mentioning" of comprehension took a major part of the time (Durkin, 1978–1979; see also Silliman & Wilkinson, chap. 2). Moreover, older materials most used by teachers did not present coherent teaching programs for comprehension (Beck, McKeown, McCaslin, & Burkes, 1979). Further, even teachers who tried to target the comprehension area often focused on a low level of literal comprehension (Durkin, 1978–1979; Guszak, 1967) rather than higher level process-oriented instruction.

This general instructional concern has generated current theoretical perspectives on comprehension and vocabulary instruction, which have dovetailed nicely with research on students experiencing academic difficulty to suggest that an active, problem solving emphasis is appropriate for greater academic success. Indeed, intervention programs sharing this perspective have begun to provide results from which principles of instruction are emerging (Palincsar et al., chap. 5). At a minimum, instruction for academic success should (1) focus on strategic processes rather than on drill of isolated skills (Ehren, chap. 15; Paris, Wasik, & Turner, 1991); (2) require active participation on the part of the learner with discussion and writing taking major roles along with reading (Pearson & Fielding, 1991); and (3) include modeling by adult experts to scaffold for young readers (Roehler & Duffy, 1991; see also Silliman & Wilkinson, chap. 2).

Scaffolding, as discussed by Silliman and Wilkinson, provides information for the learner about the knowledge of content required for comprehension, the knowledge about text structures used for organizing the content, and knowledge about the processes for gaining and evaluating these contents and structures. The teacher's or clinician's role is to share this knowledge, model the strategies in instruction, and support the student in independent practice (Roehler & Duffy, 1991; Nelson, chap. 4; Silliman & Wilkinson, chap. 2).

It is also helpful to define the learner's role in the problem solving process. From the learner's perspective, the basic steps in a problem solving process that can be applied to comprehending new text and vocabulary follow:

1. Assess what you already know and think (i.e., what knowledge structures already exist).
2. Set a purpose (i.e., goal, prediction, something to be verified, question to be answered).
3. Monitor as you read (by asking yourself if you understand and using "fix-up" strategies when you do not).
4. Make a final evaluation and use what you read (i.e., evaluate and pull together your thoughts and respond in some way, even if only to say you have understood well enough to stop reading).

These processes are all recursive and take place until the reader is satisfied that the purposes for reading have been met, the questions answered, the initial hypotheses verified or reformulated. In instructional situations, when a teacher, clinician, or peers are present, verbal interaction and group problem solving provide models for later independent processes. With this instructional framework in mind, the remainder of this chapter will present examples and alternatives that stress the instructional and learner problem solving attributes detailed previously. These examples and alternatives are organized to reflect some areas common to students experiencing academic difficulty:

- Problems with narrative comprehension
- Problems with expository comprehension
- Problems in making connections across a text
- Problems with vocabulary

PROBLEMS WITH NARRATIVE COMPREHENSION

Students who have difficulty with narrative comprehension frequently have problems retelling stories in a coherent manner. Some "see the trees and not the forest," recounting isolated details from their reading without any coherent framework. Often, their retellings are not well organized or not systematically presented. Such readers have difficulty in connecting information across the text and often get "lost" in what they read without any recognition that they do not understand (Daneman, 1991; K. S. Goodman, 1969; Scott, chap. 8; Silliman & Wilkinson, chap. 2; Spiro & Myers, 1984).

Other students glean a general vague topic from a narrative selection but cannot flesh out this topic with details about the event structure of the selection, the motivation of the characters, or a wider theme. Sometimes, these more "global" readers decide on an interpretation of a text early in reading and do not refine or change that idea even after completing the whole text. They tend to stick with an early, vague idea and not change it, even when a good many ideas do not support their initial impression. Though these two profiles of behavior are not meant as rigid categorizations, the tendency to rely on details in the text without regard to overall structure, as well as the converse overreliance on gist without reference to details, are two tendencies of strategy "overreliance" that can be addressed by remedial instruction (Y. M. Goodman, Watson, & Burke, 1987).

The Directed Reading–Thinking Activity: An Instructional Prototype

A basic prototypical instructional routine for helping students with narrative comprehension is the Directed Reading–Thinking Activity (DR-TA) (Davidson & Wilkerson, 1988; Stauffer, 1969). This process is consistent with a problem solving model because it attempts to develop the following abilities in readers:

1. Set their own purpose for reading.
2. Modify their reading in accordance with the purpose they set.
3. Make and change decisions about content depending on the state of their knowledge at different points in reading a selection.
4. Suspend judgment while looking for information.
5. Synthesize information across the text.

Stauffer based his model on the belief that reading is a reasoning process that involves the reader in the reconstruction of the author's message. This building of the message begins with the reader's generation of a hypothesis about a selection and involves the maintenance or modification of these "theories about the story" as the reading proceeds. For the teacher, guiding the way through a selection using the DR-TA involves the readers in three processes: *predict*—eliciting predictions about what is to be read; *read*—having the students read to gather clues related to their prediction; and *test*—having the students use these clues, their own knowledge, and inferencing and reasoning ability to verify or change their predictions. The process is a recursive one that continues across chunks of the text until a satisfactory interpretation is reached.

The teacher usually begins with the title or some small chunk of the story to get the group to make some initial predictions. For example, using the story "How Jesse Makes Friends" (Figure 11–1), the teacher might start with the title and the cover picture of a young girl sitting, alone, on her porch, and say: "Look at the title and picture of this selection. Who do you think Jesse is and what kind of problem does she have?" These should elicit the obvious, the facts that the problem is about a girl named Jesse who needs to make friends. Then one can move on to a reading-generating prediction. "Why do you think Jesse needs to make friends? Why doesn't she have friends already?"

One can then use the hypotheses generated by this discussion ("She's mean, so kids don't like her" or "She lives far out of town and can't go to play at anyone's house") as predictions about the forthcoming content. The teacher then has the students read the first part of the selection to a designated point to find out why Jesse needs to make friends. Readers learn that she has just moved into a new neighborhood in the summer when school is out.

Further prediction ("What would you do if you were in this situation?" "How might Jesse go about it?" "Will these ideas work?") can drive the rest of the reading and discussion, which proceeds by chunks, predictions, reading, and discussion, repeating the process until the selection is finished. (See Silliman & Wilkinson, chaps. 2, 6, for additional information.)

Modifying the Directed Reading–Thinking Activity Process

This general predictive process can be modified in many ways for variety and for use with students with differing needs. One way is to incorporate more writing into the process (as Scott also suggests in chap. 8). As students finish a particular section, they can write their evaluations of their earlier predictions and extrapolate to the next section. A written DR-TA format can also be constructed to provide a "reading guide" for students as they read a narrative.

FIGURE 11–1
Reading guide for "How Jesse Makes Friends"

READING GUIDE —"How Jesse Makes Friends"

Use separate sheets of paper to respond to these questions as you read. Follow the directions that tell you when, and how far, to read.

LOOK at the title and picture on the first page.

1. Who do you think Jesse is, and what kind of problem does she have?

READ to the bottom of page 2 to see what the author tells you.

2. Were you on target? Who is Jesse, and what is her problem? What would *you* do if *you* were Jesse?

READ to the bottom of page 3 to see what Jesse does first.

3. Did Jesse do what you would have done? Explain. Do you think her plan is a good one? Why or why not?

READ to the end of the selection to see if her idea works.

4. Did it work? Do you think your plan would have been better? Explain.
5. What is your response to this selection? Do you think the author did a good job? What would you have done differently and why?

Other variations might include the following:

1. Make a chart with the headings *prediction, proved/disproved, no information, page,* and let students fill in their predictions as they make them. Then, as they read, they can find information to prove or disprove their initial ideas. This is especially useful for the students who tend to retain early, unproductive ideas about what they are reading. Making the "disprove" procedure as productive as the "prove" procedure focuses on the fact that verification procedures are more important than being initially correct in predicting what the author will tell you.

2. Make your own mystery. Clinicians can capitalize on the popularity of "Choose Your Own Mystery and Adventure" books by making their own. Find a "cliff-hanger" story, and photocopy it, cut and paste it so that each part to be read is on a separate page. At the bottom of each page, put the "cliff-hanger" question, for example, "Will Ludwig see Bertha and her new boyfriend in time to warn them of the tidal wave?" Have students complete each section with their prediction and compare it with the author's solution of the problem. Students also like to prepare these for other students. To do so, they have to "think like the teacher," which is a test of transfer of the modeled processes.

3. For students who are very reluctant to make predictions, prepare two or three alternative predictions for each stopping point in the selection. Let them choose and verify or disprove after reading. This takes the pressure off the "afraid to risk" students but lets them be involved in the thinking process.

4. Pick a story that is easily visualized. Have your students be movie directors, and at each point, describe or draw what the next scene will be like. This can also be combined with an art or video activity.

Other Predictive Guided Reading Approaches

Other guided processes reflect the same philosophy as the DR-TA. One of these is the ReQuest Procedure (Manzo, 1969), which is especially useful for the student who needs support early in the reading of a new selection, for those who get "lost" early. In this process the student and teacher silently read sections of a selection and then take turns asking and answering questions about it. The teacher's job is to model good questioning behavior, to give feedback, and to determine when the student has established enough of a purpose and sense of the selection to continue reading independently. The student, in a sense, becomes an "apprentice" in the reading process (see Wallach & Butler, chap. 1).

Another related method is the Creative Problem Solving method (Lundsteen, 1974), which uses multiple readings of the selection to deal with certain specific problems. In this process students first read the story quickly to learn who the characters are and what they are like, details that are charted on the board or on a personal record sheet. As soon as students are able, they discuss this with the group and teacher. Then they go back and focus on the problems of the characters, trying to isolate the main problem, problems, or goal. The teacher or clinician asks students to use the text to verify their hypotheses when there are conflicting views. In the last phase, the students discuss the solution to the problem(s). Each reading time is focused, and time may vary depending on the complexity of the task. The tasks focus on the basic elements of story structure to model a comprehension strategy for understanding a narrative (Graesser, Golding, & Long, 1991; Stein & Glenn, 1979; see also Scott, chap. 8).

Building Knowledge of Narrative Structure

Besides guiding students in a general problem solving process for reading, the teacher can help students experiencing difficulty with narrative comprehension by increasing their knowledge base about the varieties of narrative structure and literary convention. By having a better understanding of how stories work, students increase their ability to predict how the author will develop a story. Recognition of structure also provides a cognitive peg on which to hang a more generalized comprehension strategy, assisting the development of the students' ability to make predictions by building their knowledge base of how stories work.

Many educators and researchers have investigated the teaching of story structure to children as an instructional tool for comprehension development (Pearson & Fielding, 1991). Story grammars provide the teacher with a framework for analyzing retellings and a structure by which the student may organize recall. Teachers can ask students to fill a story frame as they read and use the frame as a retelling structure, a note-taking structure or as a framework for planning a written story (Figure 11–2).

Further, just as stories share a generalizable structure, authors also adopt conventions. Any child who

FIGURE 11–2
Story Grammar frame filled in for "How Jesse Makes Friends"

STORY FRAME	
Setting (Where and when does the story takes place?): - a small town - Jesse's new home	
Characters (Who is in the story?): Jesse Mom Dad neighborhood kids	
Problem/Goal (What do the main characters want to do? What problem do they want to solve?): Jesse wants to make friends in new town	
Actions (What happens to move them toward the goal/solution?): - Mom buys Jesse a magic set - Jesse puts on a magic show	Complications (new problems/obstacles): - Jesse needs to learn magic
Resolution (What is the outcome?): - Jesse meets local kids who may become friends	
Issue (author's purpose): - you need to take action to meet people	

begins a selection "Once upon a time . . ." and finishes ". . . and they lived happily ever after" has begun to recognize conventions of stories. Teachers can amplify this base by teaching students about genre. This can be done by having students read several pieces of one type and generalizing structural and conventional similarities. One way to do this is to use Venn diagrams to compare and contrast selections (Figure 11–3). When several narratives of one genre are compared, conventions can be determined and used to predict what will be forthcoming in later read selections. In sum, exposure to a variety of narrative structures, making structures explicit through diagrammatic means and involving the students in predictive reading instruction are all research- and classroom-documented means for improving narrative comprehension (Pearson & Fielding, 1991; Wallach & Butler, chap. 1).

PROBLEMS WITH EXPOSITORY COMPREHENSION

Expository text, as discussed by Scott in Chapter 8, and Westby in Chapter 7, presents a double difficulty for readers: unfamiliar content and a wide variety of organizational patterns. Unlike narrative structure, which is basic not only to oral stories but also to TV and movie formats, expository structures are ones with which most readers have less experience outside the school setting (Scott, chap. 8).

Some students who have difficulty with exposition are "fact accumulators" who try to remember every fact and detail without using structure to help them organize and find coherence. Even students who can use the structure of narrative to assist them frequently have difficulty with understanding the organizational and argument structure of a textbook chapter or of a free-standing piece of expository writing. They also have difficulty with vocabulary, which will be addressed later in this chapter. More than in a narrative, the *structures* of arguments and organization must be stressed to help students understand (see Scott, chap. 6, for additional information).

Predictive Models for Exposition

The K-W-L Plus (Carr & Ogle, 1987) is a predictive model for reading exposition that helps students

FIGURE 11–3
Compare and contrast frame

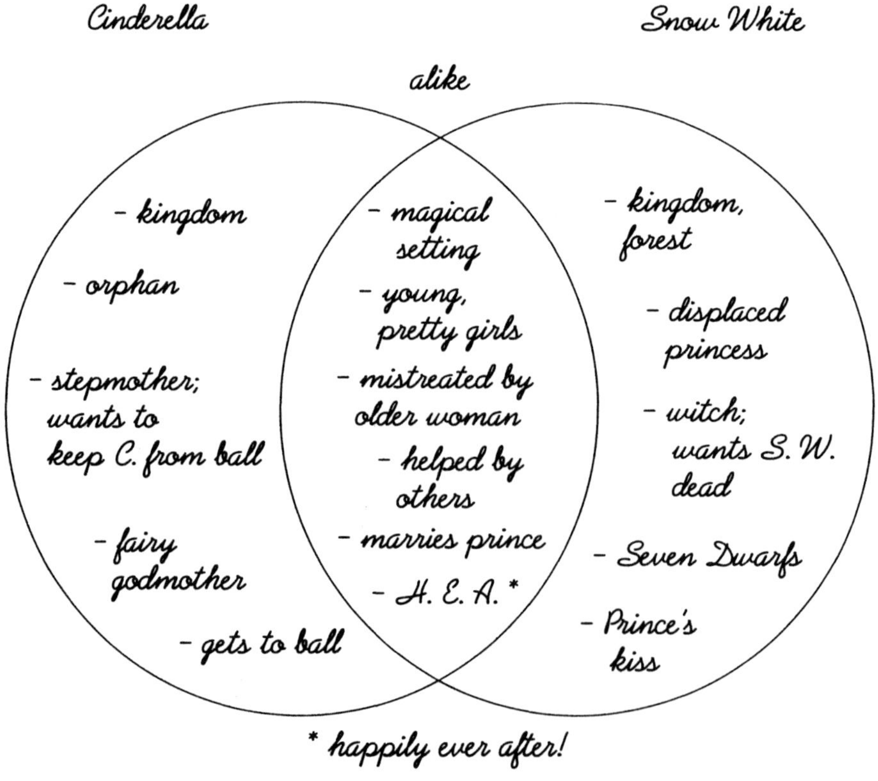

FIGURE 11–4
K-W-L chart on giraffes

GIRAFFES

What I know	What I want to know	What I learned
- spots - tall - in Africa - run fast	How big are they? What do they eat? How do they defend themselves	(See Fig. 11-5)

become more active readers of informational materials. It asks students to do the following:

1. Brainstorm before reading (Ask, What Do I *K*now?)
2. Set purposes before reading (What Do I *W*ant to Find Out?)
3. Consolidate after reading (What Did I *L*earn?)
4. Organize information into a framework for retention (Plus, which means making an original graphic or outline organizer)

The teacher leads the students through brainstorming about a topic before reading. This brainstorm raises some questions about the topic, and the teacher or clinician leads the students into asking more questions about what they want to get out of reading. For example, before reading the selection "Jake the Giraffe," the teacher asks the students to generate the information that they already know about giraffes. Following this, the teacher asks students to formulate questions as to what they would like to know about giraffes. These questions set a personal purpose for reading.

After silent reading, the students regroup and reflect on their original questions, answer them, and add to what they know about the topic. Throughout the process, the teacher supports the students in recording the data, ideas, and questions on a record chart (Figure 11–4).

The last stage, the "plus," involves organizing what is known in a graphic form such as the ones that will be described later. The use of graphic organizers, maps, webs, and the like helps students begin to visualize and use the organizational patterns of expository material, itself a valuable tool for developing expository comprehension.

Building Knowledge of Expository Structure

Unlike a story, exposition does not have a single recognizable structure but commonly has multiple patterns within the same piece, especially in textbook design. Some of the common ways authors organize their content (see Scott, chap. 8; Westby, chap. 7) follow:

1. Simple description or list of attributes
2. Time or procedural sequence
3. Problem–solution
4. Argument/ideas-details
5. Cause–effect
6. Compare–contrast

Graphic representations, webs, maps, or other schematic outlines can help students to visualize and organize content into a structured form. The free map or web asks students to organize information about what is read in some "chunked" format meaningful to them. For example, the descriptive selection on giraffes used for the K-W-L may be organized by the basic categories of information the author provides on giraffes (Figure 11–5). The mapping can be done after brainstorming has elicited all the information that has been learned after reading. The teacher or clinician then helps the students organize the information in some structured fashion, often in the same way that the author has structured the selection. This may be done deductively, with the teacher providing the frame, or inductively, with the students generating the categories. The latter should be the goal, if not the starting point, of systematic mapping instruction.

Teachers can also structure particular frames for different expository types. The compare–contrast frame used earlier also lends itself to expository comparisons. For problem-solution organization, the problem frame might look like Figure 11–6.

For a cause–effect organization, Figure 11–7 might be used.

In most instances, work with expository text structure is considered more difficult than work with more familiar narrative forms. Although simplified forms of

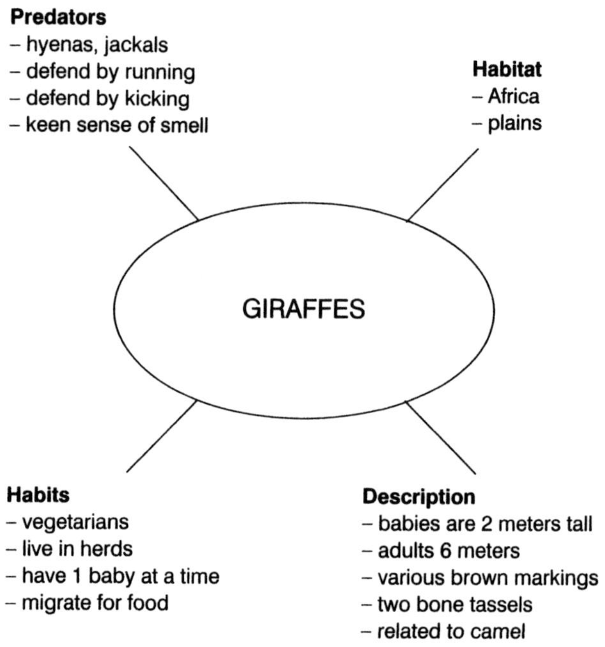

FIGURE 11–5
Content map—"Jake the Giraffe"

FIGURE 11–6
Problem–solution frame

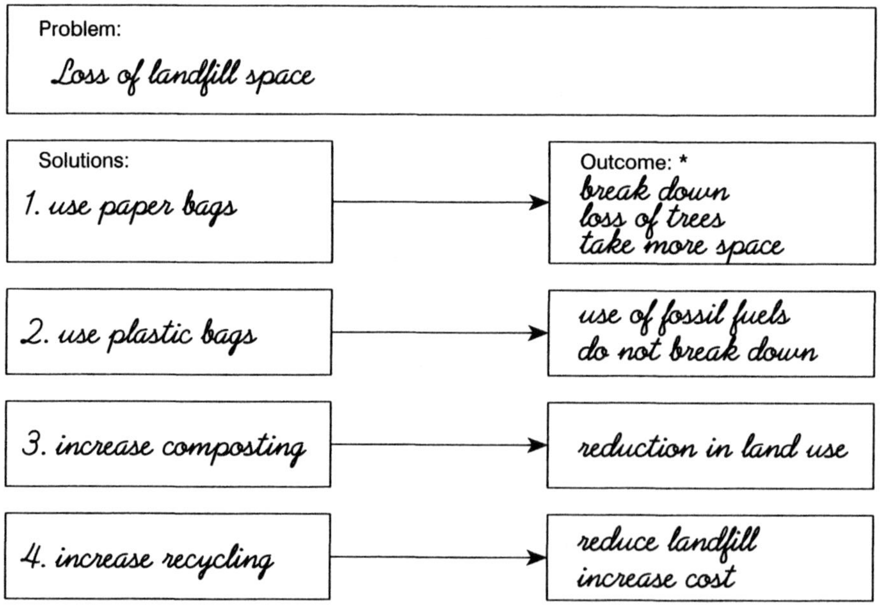

*Use this category in a selection that describes attempts to solve a problem that had different results.

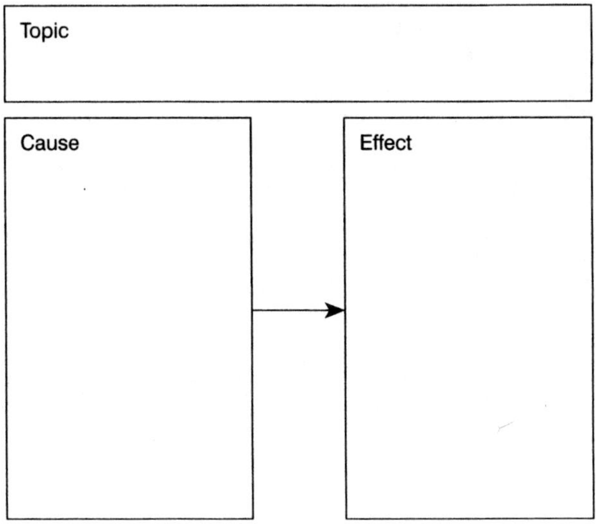

FIGURE 11–7
Cause–effect frame

the maps and other techniques can be used with appropriate support, teachers and clinicians need to consider the students' age and the cognitive, linguistic, and task difficulties of these techniques before trying to implement them. Further, age appropriateness may rule out more complex cognitive and response alternatives for young readers, as van Kleeck (chap. 3) and others suggest.

Other Expository Techniques

Reciprocal teaching, the topic of Chapter 5, is another methodology for helping students read predictively and monitor their comprehension of exposition. It involves a prediction and verification mode similar to the K-W-L and DR-TA but also includes, as Palincsar and her colleagues point out in Chapter 5, self-questioning and summarizing as a powerful component for prose learning.

Summarization remains a powerful tool for enhancing comprehension and recall of text. Day (1980) has formulated five rules to help students construct appropriate summaries:

1. Delete trivial information.
2. Delete redundant information.
3. Provide a superordinate term for any elements of information.
4. Find a main idea, if possible.
5. Construct a main idea if one is not given.

What is essential in implementing the development of these strategies is that the teacher or clinician provides modeling for the students and constant feedback on their own attempts, as Silliman and Wilkinson (chap. 2) and Nelson (chap. 4) suggest. In one summarization application study (Cunningham, 1982), students showed significant improvement by being given short passages to summarize and immediate feedback in the form of comparing their summary with a teacher model.

The "cross-out method" is another way in which the processes for summarization are practiced. Students are presented with short paragraphs and asked to cross out all irrelevant and redundant information. The comparison of student with student and with teacher provides the feedback needed before steps 3 to 5 of the preceding summarization process.

Rereading is one text-learning technique that is often overlooked because of its simplicity. Many times students, especially those who are less able, view rereading as somehow "cheating," not realizing that most adult readers read important informational materials more than one time.

One method that employs structured rereadings in the ConStruct (conceptual restructuring) method (Vaughan, 1984). The students read the materials through once and begin a graphic overview of the text, much like the map shown earlier. Then they read a second time to add more information or revise their earlier categories. Then they read a third time for more elaboration. In all tests of the ConStruct model, students who participated in the rereading and charting outperformed students who had read and answered questions on the same material.

A closely related method based on inductive questioning was proposed by Taba (1962) and continues to be used with success for content instruction (Barr & Johnson, 1991). In this model, rereading is tied to teacher questioning. The teacher first asks a series of literal questions about a text. Students reread until they are able to answer questions at this level. The teacher then asks inferential questions about the material. Students use the earlier gained literal information along with further rereading to answer these questions. Last, the teacher focuses on critical and evaluative questions. Normally, little rereading is required by this point, but, if it is, further rereading takes place.

Both of these models attempt to help students build the habit of coupling rereading with self-monitoring and recording to gain control of expository materials. Clinicians and teachers using these methods are reminded of both the cognitive and linguistic complexity of the task when applying such methods to students with language and learning disabilities (see Wallach & Butler, chap. 1).

PROBLEMS IN MAKING CONNECTIONS ACROSS A TEXT

Connecting information found in different locations in a text is a difficult problem in both narrative and expository reading. Many students focus on only single items of literal level information rather than collecting data as they read. This is painfully obvious with students in a question answering task. Students who use this strategy tend to look for some key words in a question, search for those same words in the text, and frame an answer based on the single sentence in which they locate a match.

Other students fixate on a particular topic early in their reading and do not use author clues across the text to modify their initial impression. These students tend to answer all questions from their own knowledge base, rather than using text information. An example of this type of behavior was exhibited by a student reading a selection about a "roomer." Early in the text he seized on the homophone "rumor" and answered all questions from a base relating to intrigue among friends rather than revising his earlier opinion to reflect a story about a rooming house.

Developing diversified strategies for answering questions is one way to emphasize the need to collect information across a text. Raphael (1982) suggests explicit strategy instruction in developing the ability to recognize that specific information search-and-integrate strategies are required for different types of questions. For example, some questions merely ask students to locate the information the author has explicitly given in one place in the text; these are "right here" questions that ask you to look for literal level information usually located in a single location. Other questions can best be answered by looking for explicit and implicit cues scattered across a text, for these you must "think and search." A third type of question requires students to add significant amounts of extra textual information to what the author tells students in order to answer the questions; these are "author and you" questions. Last, there are divergent questions answered primarily from students' own knowledge base; these are "on your own questions."

In their Question–Answer–Relationship (QAR) training studies, Raphael and Pearson (1985) found that direct instruction, modeling, and feedback on these strategies produced great benefits for poor readers, as did related studies with younger readers (Hansen & Pearson, 1983). Students are presented with a text and questions and must judge what type of search method is appropriate for each question. They might hypothesize that a question can be answered by looking for one specific item of information. Then, they attempt to answer the question and discuss as a group what the most successful search strategy was. The teacher or clinician models the process by taking a turn in the hypothesizing and search process with the ultimate goal of developing a repertoire of question answering and text search strategies for students.

One enjoyable application of these processes in a group situation is the "Comprehension Court" technique (Sentell & Blachowicz, 1989). This is a discussion process that draws on the students' gathering of "evidence" to support their "case." Students first read a selection with a general purpose. After first reading, two groups are formed and are presented with a set of questions. For example, for the story "The Changeling,"[1] which tells of a seal turned child, rescued by a childless couple, the students might be asked to gather evidence to support their opinions on the three statements shown in Figure 11–8.

The first statement shown in Figure 11–8, "Fishing was a major activity of this town," requires a fairly low level of information gathering and inference. There are many allusions to fishing equipment, fisherman, and the like in the selection, which is also set in a small town by the sea. Students need to look across the selection for clues, which are amply provided by the author.

For the second statement, "The changeling's parents were selfish," two different opinions can be supported by the evidence, and students also need to use their own knowledge of animals, family life, and the term *selfish*.

For the last statement, "The author's style was a good one for this story," students need to work on an evaluative level and use their outside criteria for the "good for this story" idea.

---

[1]Nonexistent text based on oral tradition stories.

FIGURE 11–8
Comprehension court evidence sheet

Title: "The Changeling"

Statements:

1. Fishing was a major activity in this town.
2. The changeling's parents were selfish.
3. The author's style was a good one for this story.

Statement	Evidence (key words and page)	Agree	Disagree
1.	- fishing boats - p. 3 - fisherman - p. 5 - no other sources of labor discussed (inference)	✔	
2.	- child longed for sea but father wouldn't let go - p. 7 - mother held child tight - p. 11 - parents grieved when child returned to sea - p. 14	✔	
3.	- various choices of language - too plain - no description of changeling - nothing about feelings		✔

After the groups amass their evidence and decide their position, the teacher calls the "court" into session. Each statement is discussed and the evidence weighed. Students become models for others as they explain their reasoning and go back to the text to read sections that support their views. Difficult statements often are cause for "continuance" as students seek more information, and some result in a "hung jury" because both points of view are well supported. This is an enjoyable way to get students to become active in inferencing across a text (Milosky, chap. 10).

Cloze Process

Use of the cloze process also gives students practice in making inferences, in this case, "on line," as they read the selection. By presenting readers with passages with some of the words deleted, the teacher or clinician can lead the reader to make predictions about word appropriateness and meaning, much as the DR-TA guided the reader to make predictions about larger chunks of text. Depending on the ways the deleted words are chosen, the teacher can focus the readers on using prior text, subsequent text, or particular types of words. For students who experience academic difficulty, modifications of the cloze process can provide supportive structures for developing on-line processing without exceeding their linguistic or task performance capability.

A standard cloze passage is constructed by deleting every fifth word of a passage or by using some preselected pattern that does not delete more than 20% of the words. A significant chunk of text must be used to give students more than a "fill-in-the blanks" experience. Cloze passages may be easily prepared by placing a sheet protector over a page or pages of a selection and using a marker to block out certain words.

The student is first asked to skim the passage, for gist, and then goes back to supply appropriate terms to complete the passage. This first skimming is essential because focusing on meaning and inferencing requires a "sense of the passage." Indeed, the teacher or clinician might wish to discuss the gist before proceeding with any cloze activities. The basic objective is to model for the student the process of generating predictions about what might be appropriate and using the total context to test these hypotheses. Unlike cloze used for assessment, synonymous matches are appropriate in cloze used for instruction. The cloze process can be modified in many ways (Blachowicz, 1977). One problem readers may have is a total loss of context some place in the passage. Some students have so little reading stamina that they get far off the track and are unable to continue the passage in a meaningful way. The "zip" procedure can be used to supply constant, immediate feedback so that the correct context is cumulative. The most effective technique for "zip" is putting the story or passage on an overhead transparency using masking tape to block out the designated words. The students skim for gist and then supply the masked words one at a time. As each possibility is predicted and discussed, the tape is pulled (or "zipped," hence the name), so that the readers have immediate feedback from the text as well as receive additional context from which to make further predictions. Students enjoy preparing zip passages for others and can use the sheet protector method for individual passages.

The maze procedure (Guthrie, Seifert, Burnham, & Kaplan, 1974) can be useful for students who have problems with word retrieval (German, chap. 12). In the chosen passage, words are not deleted. Rather, two distractors are supplied for each chosen item, providing a limited and manageable choice format. Distinctions can focus on semantic, syntactic, or graphophonic distinctions, depending on the need of the students (Figure 11–9).

When the goal is to present new words, the synonym cloze process can be quite useful. The words to be learned are circled for special attention but left visible. The students, as always, survey for gist, and then go through the text supplying words they know that would make sense as alternatives for the new words. This synonym generation helps students to make associations between words they know and the new word (Figure 11–10).

In essence, the students provide their own synonyms, definitions, or descriptions for the new words by using clues from the context. In synonym

quickly
slowly
happily
The Grand Vizier__________ crept across the room to

the sleeping Hodja. He reached under the bed searching for

gun
scissors
knife
the sharp blade of the__________ that Hodja kept for

careful
careless
clumsy
protection. As he searched, he was__________ not to

make a sound . . .

FIGURE 11–9
Maze cloze for "Hodja Saves the Day"
(Nonexistent text based on oral tradition stories.)

The leader is usually responsible for the procedural

matters that occur during discussion. Generally, the leader

will state the *main idea* (topic) to be discussed. She may call

on individuals, request *certain* (specific) information, or

raise pertinent *questions* (inquiries) to start a discussion.

At the end, the leader *pulls together* (summarizes) what has been

said and helps the group prepare a/an *plans* (agenda) for the

things to be discussed at the next meeting.

FIGURE 11–10
Synonym cloze for "analyzing group processes"

cloze, as in many cloze modifications, the student may supply more than one word for each omitted word. Synonym cloze is most useful for content area classes with technical vocabulary. If students can generate *eye dropper* for *pipette,* or *earth studier* for *geologist,* they are well on their way to a better understanding of their science texts.

PROBLEMS WITH VOCABULARY

Students experiencing academic difficulty frequently have a less extensive lexicon than more successful students (Becker, 1977). Also, they have fewer semantic associations for the words with which they are acquainted (Graves & Slater, 1987) and less efficient strategies for gaining word meanings from context (McKeown, 1985). In short, they know less about fewer words than do more successful students.

Current views on the development of vocabulary knowledge are consistent with the general trend toward incorporating cognitive learning principles in literacy education. New guidelines for approaching vocabulary instruction have emerged (Beck & McKeown, 1991). This focus considers the development of vocabulary as taking place within the more generalized development of comprehension (Blachowicz, 1985; Johnson & Pearson, 1984; Mezynski, 1983).

Such a model suggests that students look on the problem of unknown words in the same way they might consider a problem in science or mathematics. The unknown word can generate questions and predictions that must be resolved by close inspection of the clues the author provides and through application of already gained knowledge and reasoning principles. Although this model is process oriented, the need for substantial content suggests that literacy instruction be extended beyond a focus on a narrative literature base to a balanced approach where learning in the content areas is again receiving a major focus (Berger & Robinson, 1982).

Guidelines for Vocabulary Instruction in Content Classes

1. Establish what learners already know: The importance of activating learners' prior knowledge is well established in both the psychological and pedagogical research of the last fifteen years (Anderson, 1977; Milosky, chap. 10). The knowledge itself forms a basis for new learning, allows the teacher to assess what the student knows and, in a group setting, provides input for other students. Further, the generation processes—brainstorming, for example—engage the learner in an active way in the learning process.

2. Highlight the new: Rather than preteach the exact meaning of new words, which often leads to the teacher "feeding" the students, highlighting involves having the teacher lead the students to generate hypotheses about certain preselected terms. As well as defining the "problem" to be solved, highlighting cues the students to take better advantage of incidental cues that occur in contextual learning (Elley, 1989).

3. Generate possible connections between the "known" and the "new": In this stage students set up the problem they wish to resolve. They generate possible connections, which they will try to verify, clarify, or refute as they examine the text the author provides. At critical issue here is the need to include *known* words and concepts in every introduction of *new* words and concepts. If this is not done and students are confronted by lists of unknown words, without any topical or relational cues, they cannot begin to make these linkages.

4. Gather information to apply to the problem: Actual contextual reading is a critical way to gather information about the hypothesized connections between the new terms and concepts that students already know. Along with reading, experimentation, interview, observation, or any other skills and strategies developed in content learning can be applied to contextualize the word knowledge within a larger framework.

5. Self-monitoring and consolidation: In the self-monitoring stage, students attempt to draw some conclusions about the hypothesized relationships from the information they have gathered. They may find that they had a correct conceptualization of a new word, that they must modify their prediction, or that they don't yet have enough information and must go back and reexamine the text for more information. This responding to the question "Do I understand this?" is the process of self-monitoring so important to metacognitive development (Garner, 1987). Many times monitoring suggests that students must loop back into the process to gather more information. This involves reinspection of the text, discussion among students or with the teacher, purposeful use of references, and so on.

Consolidation of the word's meaning—its assimilation into students' existing knowledge structures or the accommodation of these new structures—takes place during this process as well as later when the student uses the word in meaningful reading, writing, speaking, listening, construction, or other demonstrations of contextualized learning (Anderson & Nagy, 1991). Encountering the word in contextual reading, using it in discussion, and writing it in meaningful discourse are the primary ways that students develop ownership of the term. If planned practice of other types takes place, it should involve the learner in using the new knowledge base to make semantic decisions about the word rather than passive definitional responses (Beck, Perfetti, & McKeown, 1982).

The three examples presented next each use prereading vocabulary to initiate a lesson. Using vocabulary as an entry point in the selection allows the teacher or clinician to highlight important words along with preparing concepts of the selection. It also raises issues about the selection that can stimulate questions that provide a purpose for reading.

Vocab-O-Gram. The Vocab-O-Gram (Blachowicz, 1986) is one device for focusing prereading predictions using vocabulary. It is a charting process appropriate for narrative selections that asks students to organize vocabulary in relationship to the structure of the selection, the story grammar (as discussed earlier in this chapter). Consider the vocabulary from the selection, "Hodja Saves the Day" shown in Figure 11–11.

The teacher and student(s) read through the list of vocabulary. Then the teacher asks questions that focus on the elements of story grammar and help students make predictions by entering the words

FIGURE 11–11
Vocab-O-Gram for "Hodja Saves the Day"

Vocabulary:

splendid, palace, outraged, trick, Hodja, Grand Vizier, turban, dungeon, Mt. Ararat, Allah, timberline, executioner, judge, wisdom

Do you have ideas about the ...

Setting: (Where does the story take place?) - in a kengdom (palace, dungeon) - far away, maybe in mountains (Mt. Ararat, timberline, Hodja = foreign)	Characters: (Who is in the story?) Hodja (he saves the day) Grand Vizier executioner judge maybe a king and criminal
Problem: (. . .of the story?) - somebody commits a crime (dungeon, executioner)	Action: (What kinds of things happen?) - there is a crime - there is a trial (judge) - somebody may be put to death (executioner)
Resolution: (How does this end?) Hodja saves day - maybe with a trick or wisdom	Other: Allah is god, I think. Maybe god is annoyed.

(Put clue words in the boxes.)

into a plausible location on the Vocab-O-Gram chart. Possible teacher questions and probing follow:

1. Look at the word list for this story. Do we have any clues to where this story might take place? (In a kingdom, cue words—*palace, dungeon.*) Students can use unfamiliar words to help localize—e.g., Mt. Ararat—mountainous place, sound foreign as do some other words—*Hodja, Grand Vizier.*)
2. Do we have any clues who the characters might be? (Palace people: *king, executioner, Allah, Grand Vizier* might be a person, *Hodja* might be a person.)
3. Do we have any clues to the problem? (If there is a dungeon and executioner, someone committed a crime.)
4. Do we have any clues to how characters will solve problem? (*Wisdom, trick.*)
5. We've made some predictions about this story, that it takes place in a mountain kingdom, that someone commits a crime, and that wisdom enters into the solution. Any other predictions or comments you'd like to make? (Teacher takes comments and predictions.) Let's read the selection to see how close our predictions come to what the author decided to write.

After the students have read the selection, they come together to discuss the match between their predictions and the selection. As the discussion progresses, words are moved in the Vocab-O-Gram chart, and other key words from the selection may be added. The vocabulary of many narratives allows some prediction about the selection in one or more categories of the Vocab-O-Gram. The teacher or clinician can use the chart to help the students structure a summarization of the selection after reading. The students can use the categorized words as cues for summarization and also use them in their written summary.

Story Impressions. The story impressions technique (McGinley & Denner, 1987) uses the same principles as Vocab-O-Gram to structure a prereading writing activity stimulated by vocabulary. The teacher presents a list of words for the students and asks them to write a summary of a story they might write using as many of the designated vocabulary words as seem to fit. They may make guesses about partly known or unknown words or choose to omit them. As with all predictive work with words, it is necessary that students know at least some of the words so they can begin to conceive of a story framework that might incorporate them.

After writing their short-story summaries, the students read and share them, noting where their ideas overlap. The students then read the selection, comparing their story using the words with the one the author has chosen to write. Comparisons can be made between author's use of the words and use by the students by rereading both the selection and student writing.

Knowledge Rating. Knowledge ratings (Blachowicz, 1986) emphasize that knowing a word is not an "all or nothing proposition." Word knowledge develops along a continuum, from the unknown, to the acquainted to the richly known. Most of us know some words well, know some words in a more general, impressionistic or multiple way, and are totally unfamiliar with other words. Because we learn a great many of our words through contextual exposure, word knowledge accrues over time. Terms that are unknown come to our attention, take on some associations and early defining characteristics, and are later known in a more refined and abstract way (Anderson & Nagy, 1991.)

For knowledge rating, students are presented with a list of words and first asked to rate their knowledge of each (Figure 11–12).

Rate your knowledge of these words.			
Word	Know well	Seen/heard it	Don't know
apartment	✔		
villa		✔	
geodesic dome		✔	
teepee	✔		
trullo			✔
yurt			✔
high rise	✔		
lean-to		✔	

FIGURE 11–12
Knowledge rating

They are encouraged to work in pairs or groups to share their ideas about the words before the teacher leads a general discussion. The focus of the discussion is to use the word to make predictions about the selection, much as in the earlier noted techniques. When words from a narrative are rated, the predictions relate to the story structure. In this case, for an expository social studies chapter, the teacher might ask the following questions:

1. Do you have any idea what the topic of this chapter might be? (Call students' attention to the topic of "dwellings.") Why?
2. Are these all contemporary, U.S. dwellings? (Explain.)
3. Can you predict what the author will tell you about each of these dwellings? (Where they are located; what they look like; who lives in them.) Let's read to find out this information about each of these words.

Postreading discussion focuses on the questions raised before reading and the location, description, and people associated with each term. This technique can also be coupled with writing, as in story impressions, though the lack of prior content knowledge in most expository situations may limit the amount of writing that can be done before reading.

SUMMARY

This chapter has presented a model for comprehension and vocabulary development that is consistent with a cognitive model of problem solving. The instructional techniques described are examples of current "best practice" in literacy instruction. They view the reader as an active hypothesizer, data collector, and reflector and view the teacher as a model, guide, and scaffolder (Silliman & Wilkinson, chap. 2). With the modifications necessary for use with particular students, such as changes for pacing, presentation, and appropriate ways of responding, these instructional approaches provide a starting point for developing the comprehension strategies and vocabulary knowledge necessary for academic success.

REFERENCES

Anderson, R. C. (1977). The notion of schemata and the educational enterprise. In R. C. Anderson, R. J. Spiro, & W. E. Montague, *Schooling and the acquisition of knowledge.* Hillsdale, NJ: Lawrence Erlbaum.

Anderson, R. C., & Nagy, W. E. (1991). Word meanings. In R. Barr, M. Kamil, P. Mosenthal, & P. D. Pearson (Eds.), *Handbook of reading research* (Vol. 2, pp. 789–814). White Plains, NY: Longman.

August, D. L., Flavell, J. H., & Clift, R. (1984). Comparison of comprehension monitoring of skilled and less-skilled readers. *Reading Research Quarterly, 20,* 39–53.

Barr, R., & Johnson, B. (1991). *Teaching reading in elementary classrooms: Developing independent readers.* White Plains, NY: Longman.

Beck, I., & McKeown, M. (1991). Conditions of vocabulary acquisition. In R. Barr, M. Kamil, P. Mosenthal, & P. D. Pearson (Eds.), *Handbook of reading research* (Vol. 2). White Plains, NY: Longman.

Beck, I., McKeown, M. C., McCaslin, E. C., & Burkes, A. M. (1979). *Instructional dimensions that may affect reading comprehension: Examples from two commercial reading programs.* Pittsburgh: University of Pittsburgh, Learning Research and Development Center.

Beck, I., Perfetti, C., & McKeown, M. (1982). Effects of long-term vocabulary instruction on lexical access and reading comprehension. *Journal of Educational Psychology, 74,* 506–521.

Becker, W. C. (1977). Teaching reading and language to the disadvantaged—what we have learned from field research. *Harvard Educational Review, 47,* 518–543.

Berger, A., & Robinson, H. A. (Eds.). (1982). *Secondary school reading: What research reveals from classroom practice.* Urbana, IL: ERIC Clearinghouse on Reading and Communication Skills and the National Conference on Research in English.

Blachowicz, C. L. Z. (1977). Cloze activities for primary readers. *Reading Teacher, 31,* 300–302.

Blachowicz, C. L. Z. (1985). Vocabulary development and reading: From research to instruction. *The Reading Teacher, 38,* 876–881.

Blachowicz, C. L. Z. (1986). Making connection: Alternatives to the vocabulary notebook. *Journal of Reading, 29,* 643–649.

Brown, A. L., Bransford, J. D., Ferrarra, R. A., & Campione, J. C. (1983). Learning, remembering and understanding. In J. H. Flavell & E. M. Markman (Eds.) *Handbook of child psychology* (Vol. 3, 4th ed., pp. 243–291). New York: Wiley.

Carr, E. M., & Ogle, D. M. (1987). A strategy for comprehension and summarization. *Journal of Reading, 30,* 626–631.

Collins, A., Brown, J. S., & Larkin, K. M. (1980). Inference in text understanding. In R. J. Spiro, B. C. Bruce, & W. F. Brewer (Eds.), *Theoretical issues in reading comprehension.* Hillsdale, NJ: Lawrence Erlbaum.

Cunningham, J. W. (1982). Generating interactions between schemata and text. In J. A. Niles & L. A. Harris (Eds.), *New inquiries into reading research* (31st Yearbook of the National Reading Conference) (pp. 42–47). Albany, NY: National Reading Conference.

Daneman, M. (1991). Individual differences in reading skill. In R. Barr, M. Kamil, P. Mosenthal, & P. D. Pearson (Eds.), *Handbook of reading research* (Vol. 2, pp. 512–538). White Plains, NY: Longman.

Davidson, J. L., & Wilkerson, B. C. (1988). *Directed reading–thinking activities.* Monroe, NY: Trillium Press.

Davis, F. B. (1944). Fundamental factors of comprehension in reading. *Psychometrika, 9,* 185–197.

Davis, F. B. (1968). Research in comprehension in reading. *Reading Research Quarterly, 3,* 499–544.

Day, J. D. (1980). *Teaching summarization skills: A comparison of training methods.* Unpublished doctoral dissertation, University of Illinois.

Durkin, D. (1978–1979). What classroom observations reveal about reading comprehension instruction. *Reading Research Quarterly, 14,* 481–533.

Elley, W. B. (1989). Vocabulary acquisition from listening to stories. *Reading Research Quarterly, 24,* 174–187.

Forrest-Pressley, D. L., & Waller, T. G. (1984). *Metacognition, cognition and reading.* New York: Springer-Verlag.

Garner, R. (1987). *Metacognition and reading comprehension.* Norwood, NJ: Ablex.

Graves, M. F., & Slater, W. H. (April 1987). *The development of reading vocabularies of rural disadvantaged students, inner-city disadvantaged students, and middle-class suburban students.* Paper presented at the meeting of the American Educational Research Association, Washington, DC.

Golinkoff, R. M. (1975–1976). A comparison of reading comprehension processes in good and poor comprehenders. *Reading Research Quarterly, 11,* 423–659.

Goodman, K. S. (1969). Analysis of reading miscues: Applied psycholinguistics. *Reading Research Quarterly, 5,* 9–30.

Goodman, Y. M., Watson, D., & Burke, C. L. (1987). *Reading miscue analysis.* New York: Richard C. Owen.

Graesser, A., Golding, J. M., & Long, D. L. (1991). Narrative representation and comprehension. In R. Barr, M. Kamil, P. Mosenthal, & P. D. Pearson (Eds.) *Handbook of reading research* (Vol. 2). White Plains, NY: Longman.

Guszak, F. J. (1967). Teacher questioning and reading. *The Reading Teacher, 21,* 227–234.

Guthrie, J. T., Seifert, M., Burnham, N. A., & Kaplan, R. (1974). The maze technique to assess and monitor reading comprehension. *The Reading Teacher, 28,* 161–168.

Hansen, J., & Pearson, P. D. (1983). An instructional study: Improving the inferential comprehension of good and poor fourth grade readers. *Journal of Educational Psychology, 75,* 821–829.

Huey, E. B. (1968). *The psychology and pedagogy of reading.* Cambridge, MA: MIT Press. (Original work published 1908)

Johnson, D., & Pearson, P. D. (1984). *Teaching reading vocabulary* (2nd ed.). New York: Holt, Rinehart & Winston.

Kimmell, S., & MacGinitie, W. H. (1985). Helping students revise hypotheses while reading. *The Reading Teacher, 37,* 768–771.

Lundsteen, S. (1974). Questioning to develop creative problem solving. *Elementary English, 51*(5), 645–650.

Mandler, J., & Johnson, N. S. (1977). Remembrance of things parsed: Story structure and recall. *Cognitive Psychology, 9,* 111–151.

Manzo, A. V. (1969). The ReQuest procedure. *Journal of Reading, 11,* 123–126.

McGinley, W. J., & Denner, P. R. (1987). Story impressions: A prereading/writing activity. *Journal of Reading, 30,* 248–253.

McKeown, M. (1985). The acquisition of word meaning from context by children of high and low ability. *Reading Research Quarterly, 20,* 482–496.

Mezynski, K. (1983). Issues concerning the acquisition of knowledge: Effects of vocabulary training on reading comprehension. *Review of Educational Research, 53,* 253–279.

Miller, G. A., Galanter, E., & Pribram, K. H. (1960). *Plans and the structure of behavior.* New York: Holt, Rinehart & Winston.

Nagy, W. E. (1988). *Teaching vocabulary to improve reading comprehension.* Newark, DE: International Reading Association.

Newell, A., & Simon, H. A. (1972). *Human problem solving.* Englewood Cliffs, NJ: Prentice-Hall.

Olshavsky, J. E. (1978). Comprehension profiles of good and poor readers across materials of increasing difficulty. In P. D. Pearson & J. Hansen (Eds.), *Reading: Disciplined inquiry into process and practice* (27th Yearbook of the National Reading Conference) (pp. 73–76). Clemson, SC: The National Reading Conference.

Paris, S. G., Wasik, B. A., & Turner, J. C. (1991). The development of strategic readers. In R. Barr, M. Kamil, P. Mosenthal, & P. D. Pearson (Eds.), *Handbook of reading research* (Vol. 2, pp. 267–278). White Plains, NY: Longman.

Pearson, P. D., & Fielding, L. (1991). Comprehension instruction. In R. Barr, M. Kamil, P. Mosenthal, & P. D. Pearson (Eds.), *Handbook of reading research* (Vol. 2). White Plains, NY: Longman.

Piaget, J. (1959). *The language and thought of the child.* London: Routledge & Kegan Paul.

Raphael, T. E. (1982). Question answering strategies for children. *Reading Teacher, 36,* 186–190.

Raphael, T. E., & Pearson, P. D. (1985). Increasing students' awareness of sources of information for answering questions. *American Educational Research Journal, 2,* 217–236.

Roehler, L. R., & Duffy, G. D. (1991). Teachers instructional actions. In R. Barr, M. Kamil, P. Mosenthal, & P. D. Pearson (Eds.), *Handbook of reading research* (Vol. 2). White Plains, NY: Longman.

Rosenblatt, L. M. (1978). *The reader, the text, the poem.* Carbondale, IL: Southern Illinois Press.

Rumelhart, D. E. (1980). Schemata: The building blocks of cognition. In R. J. Spiro, B. C. Bruce, & W. F. Brewer (Eds.), *Theoretical issues in reading comprehension.* Hillsdale, NJ: Lawrence Erlbaum.

Rumelhart, D. R. (1975). Notes of a schema for stories. In D. G. Bobrow & A. M. Collins (Eds.), *Representation and understanding* (pp. 211–236). New York: Academic Press.

Ryan, E. B. (1981). Identifying and remediating failures in reading comprehension: Toward an instructional approach for poor comprehenders. In T. G. Waller & G. E. MacKinnon (Eds.), *Advances in reading research* (Vol. 2). New York: Academic Press.

Sentell, C., & Blachowicz, C. L. Z. (1989). Comprehension court: A process approach to inference instruction. *The Reading Teacher, 43,* 347–348.

Simmons, D. C., & Kameenui, E. J. (1986). Articulating learning disabilities for the public: A case of professional riddles. *Learning Disabilities Quarterly, 9,* 304–314.

Spearitt, D. (1972). Identification of subskills in reading by maximum likelihood factor analysis. *Reading Research Quarterly, 8,* 92–111.

Spiro, R. J., & Meyers, A. (1984). Individual differences and underlying cognitive processes. In P. D. Pearson, M. Kamil, R. Barr, & P. Mosenthal (Eds.), *Handbook of reading research* (Vol. 1). White Plains, NY: Longman.

Stauffer, R. S. (1969). *Directing reading maturity as a cognitive process.* New York: Harper & Row.

Steffensen, M. S., Joag-dev, C., & Anderson, R. C. (1979). A cross cultural perspective on reading comprehension. *Reading Research Quarterly, 15,* 10–29.

Stein, N. L., & Glenn, C. G. (1979). An analysis of story comprehension in elementary school children. In Freedle, R. O. (Ed.), *Advances in discourse processing: Vol. 2. New directions in discourse processing.* Norwood, NJ: Ablex.

Taba, H. (1962). *Curriculum development: Theory and practice.* New York: Harcourt Brace & World.

Thorndike, E. L. (1917). Reading as reasoning: A study of mistakes in paragraph reading. *Journal of Educational Psychology, 6,* 323–332.

Vaughan, J. L. (1984). Concept structuring: The technique and empirical evidence. In S. D. Holley & D. F. Dansereau (Eds.), *Spatial learning strategies: Techniques, applications and related issues* (pp. 127–147). New York: Academic Press.

12

WORD FINDING DIFFICULTIES IN CHILDREN AND ADOLESCENTS

■ Diane J. German
National-Louis University

This chapter presents an overview of a significant oral language difficulty observed in children and adolescents: word finding or word retrieval difficulties. Word finding problems are of interest to professionals who are working with language learning disabled (LLD) students because of the pervasive nature of word finding problems in these students and the impact of word finding difficulties on their communicative and academic success. Topics to be discussed include (1) definition and characteristics of word finding difficulties; (2) patterns of development in word finding; (3) life span of word finding skills; (4) word finding and reading; and (5) assessment and programming for students with word finding difficulties.

DEFINITION AND CHARACTERISTICS

Nature and Definitions of Word Finding Difficulties

Definitions of word finding difficulties have included both their source and characteristics. Those definitions that focus on identifying the source of this language difficulty have defined word finding problems as either a difficulty of information storage or a difficulty of information retrieval. In part, the perspectives are based on research in memory processes that suggests that all items in memory have both a "storage strength" and a "retrieval strength" (Bjork & Bjork, 1992). Nippold (1992) explains that "*storage strength* is a measure of how well the item has been learned and *retrieval strength* is the ease with which that item can be accessed from memory on a given occasion" (p. 2). In relationship to vocabulary, the storage strength of a particular word refers to the extent and depth of knowledge available for that word; the retrieval strength for the same word refers to the ease with which it can be assessed in spontaneous usage. The perspective that suggests that vocabulary deficits or lack of word knowledge underlie word finding difficulties views them as a deficit in the learning and storing of vocabulary meanings. Here, the word finding difficulty is seen as the result of reduced storage strength. An alternative perspective suggests that an inability to retrieve target words underlies word finding difficulties. Here, word finding difficulties are defined as a difficulty in the processes involved in the retrieval of vocabulary. Thus, the word finding difficulty is viewed as reduced retrieval strength (see also Blachowicz, chap. 11; Blachman, chap. 9).

Applying these perspectives to children, Kail, Hale, Leonard, and Nippold (1984) formulated two hypotheses for describing the source of word finding difficulties in children: (1) the storage hypothesis and (2) the retrieval hypothesis. The storage hypothesis implies that children with language difficulties manifest problems in word finding because their vocabulary repertoires are limited or poorly established; that is, their vocabulary knowledge is shallow and underdeveloped. By contrast, the retrieval hypothesis proposes that the word finding problems are due to impaired accessing of the labels children have stored in memory. To investigate these hypotheses, Kail et al. (1984) created a series of tasks examining children's abilities to generate words on free recall, cued recall, and repeated recall tests. They studied students with both comprehension and production difficulties. Results showed that word finding difficulties occurred "in part because . . . representations of the words in memory [were] not as extensive or as well established which [made] it difficult for a retrieval algorithm to recover them" (p 46). Further, those authors suggest that the semantic memory of children with word finding difficulties may contain either fewer word entries or meager associations and weaker links between word entries. That is, these children may have had limited exposure to certain word meanings they are asked to retrieve. For example, the word *seal* has multiple meanings. Indeed, a child may know only one meaning for a word, knowing *seal* as an animal but not as a tool for stamping designs or as a verb in "sealing one's fate." Children can also have peripheral knowledge, being unaware of the subtle meanings that differentiate a target word from associated words (e.g., differentiating *seal* from *emblem*).

Discussions of word finding difficulties in the literature suggest that causes of word finding difficulties exceed students' lack of knowledge of target words. In fact, a recurring theme across disciplines regarding the nature of word finding difficulties is the noted discrepancy between children's *comprehension* and *retrieval* of target vocabulary. That is, students appear to be familiar with and to understand the words that they have difficulty retrieving. Definitions of word finding difficulties from the speech and language literature have described word finding as a breakdown in "form," "performance," or "semantics." For example, Lahey (1988) described problems in word finding as a disruption in the interaction between content and form. Lahey describes this content–form disruption by saying that children with word finding difficulties "circumlocute, or talk around the idea they are trying to communicate, having difficulty in recalling the form that represents the content they wish to express" (1988, p. 27). Other authors, such as Carrow-Woolfolk and Lynch (1982), say that word finding difficulties are a breakdown in language performance, a problem with formulation and language production. They report that in "language formulation problems, a child cannot match his output to what he wants to say, resulting in problems of word finding . . . and that a child . . . knows the words, but words are not easily available to him/her to generate language with fluency and in sequence" (p. 222).

One of the classic definitions of word finding difficulties in children emerges from the learning disabilities literature. D. Johnson and Myklebust (1967) defined word finding difficulties as an "auditory expressive language" difficulty resulting from problem in reauditorization (remembering what words sound like) and word selection. They indicated that children with learning disabilities often have word finding difficulties in the presence of age-appropriate understanding of the target word referent. More recently, the language and learning disabilities literature also defines word finding difficulties as going beyond word meanings. Wiig and Semel (1984) indicate that the word finding difficulties observed in children with learning disabilities cannot be "attributed to limited vocabulary development," because these "problems occur even when the words children are trying to recall and retrieve are familiar to them and easily recognized on picture vocabulary tasks" (p. 113). They attribute many word finding problems to a lack of "efficiency in locating and retrieving" stored words from long-term memory. Similarly, Wiig and Becker-Caplan (1984) define word-finding difficulties as an inability to "call up an intended word from the stored lexicon" (p. 1). Finally, Lerner (1988) describes this language difficulty as an expressive language difficulty; children substitute words or talk around words they cannot retrieve.

The reading literature has examined children's naming errors to better understand the processes underlying word finding skills. Katz (1986) explored the source of naming errors in poor readers. He reported that students' word finding errors often resembled the phonological structure of the target word (e.g., *bulb* for *globe*). He hypothesized that the phonological closeness was due to either an incomplete specification of the phonological aspects of the word in the lexicon or deficient retrieval of the stored phonological information. Similarly, Rubin and Liberman (1983) suggested that phonetic errors, which retain the generic phonemic elements of the target words, suggest a breakdown in either the storage of the phonological representation of the target word or in the efficiency of the short-term memory processes. They indicated, however, that semantic errors, where the retention of generic phonemic attributes is rare, suggest something different. They conclude that "the substitution that is similar in meaning only is not indicative of higher cognitive functioning, as might be assumed, but rather serves as a disguise for a phonological deficit affecting both oral and written language performance" (Rubin & Liberman, 1983, p. 117).

Although a weak phonological representation may be the source of some phonological and semantic naming errors, difficulty in retrieving the phonological or semantic schema could be the source of others. For example, German (1982, 1984) found that children with learning disabilities (LD) produced semantic, phonemic, and other unique target word substitutions (semantic, *hat* for *crown;* phonemic, *shoehorn* for *horseshoe;* and circumlocutory, *king hat* for *crown*) that suggest tacit knowledge of the target word. Further, these students produced these substitutions on words that they were able to retrieve in other naming contexts. These word finding inconsistencies indicate correct retrieval at an earlier point in time, suggesting word comprehension. Thus, these naming errors may be more typical of weak retrieval processes specific to semantic and phonological lexicons, rather than poor storage of the target word's name.

In summary, evidence supports both explanations for the presence of word finding difficulties; that is, both storage and retrieval hypotheses may be valid. Some language and learning disabled children may produce naming errors that are due to incomplete representations of the semantic or phonological schema of target words; other students display similar naming errors but have underlying difficulties in the retrieval processes of the stored semantic and phonological specifications. However, these distinctions are complex and difficult to differentiate in practice.

Inconsistencies reported across populations and age levels should be expected in view of the heterogeneity that exists in language, learning, and reading disabled populations (see Wallach & Butler, chap. 1; Lahey & Bloom, chap. 13). German (1992) therefore has proposed three subgroups of students who demonstrate word finding difficulties.

Subgroup 1: Retrieval Difficulties. Students in subgroup 1 are those who have word finding difficulties in the presence of apparently intact understanding of oral language, which is the classic definition of word finding difficulties in children and adults. These students have difficulty retrieving words whose referents they understand (i.e., vocabulary words whose meanings students comprehend and words they have retrieved without difficulty in other contexts). Word finding difficulties in subgroup 1 are a problem in *production* (Carrow-Woolfolk & Lynch, 1982; D. Johnson & Myklebust, 1967; Lahey, 1988; Lerner, 1988; Wiig & Semel, 1984). Moreover, research shows that students in subgroup 1 demonstrate understanding of vocabulary that is as good as control groups consisting of good readers (Rubin & Liberman, 1983; Wolf & Goodglass, 1986) and non-learning disabled students (German, 1979, 1984, 1985).

Subgroup 2: Comprehension Difficulties. In contrast, students in subgroup 2 have problems understanding language; they have difficulty using words that are unfamiliar or unknown or whose meanings are unstable. These students have little difficulty with words whose target word referents are more fully represented in their lexicons. Smith (1991) indicates that word finding problems can stem from "semantic problems that limit the richness of the knowledge one has stored about the word or access to this knowledge" (p. 200). Along with other semantic difficulties, such students can have problems using words that stem from shallow word meanings, problems in reference shifting, and weak analytic and synthesis skills.

Subgroup 3: Comprehension and Retrieval Difficulties. Last, students in subgroup 3 exhibit both comprehension and retrieval difficulties. That is, they have underlying problems learning meanings and problems retrieving words they comprehend. As reported earlier, Kail et al. (1984) studied language impaired students with a composite receptive–expressive language score of 3 years 2 months below chronological age. These students, characteristic of subgroup 3, manifested difficulty on both receptive language measures and word finding measures of known color and shape names (the confrontation subtest of the Clinical Evaluation of Language Function, Semel & Wiig, 1980) and on experimental recall tasks. These students were judged to have word finding difficulties on known words and difficulty finding words because representations of words in memory were not well established.

In conclusion, understanding the characteristics of subgroups of students is one of the major challenges facing professionals working with students with language difficulties today. However, practitioners must make the effort to carefully describe word finding patterns across contexts and curriculum content, as also discussed by Nelson (chap. 4) and other authors of this text.

Students' Characteristics

Students with word finding difficulties may exhibit problems retrieving specific words, phrases, or discourse. Difficulties in retrieval of specific words may be apparent in both single word retrieval contexts and discourse.

In the classroom, these students have difficulty relating character names, locations, dates, and specific facts from a story (see Blachowicz, chap. 11). When they also have difficulty retrieving phrase units, they usually have problems relating experiences or events to peers and teachers in conversational situations. Some students may also have difficulty retrieving the narrative schema of the discourse, using placeholders such as *who, when, where,* and *how.* Low language productivity during discourse in discussions and in social situations results.

Single Word Retrieval Contexts. The language patterns of students with retrieval difficulties in single word retrieval contexts are frequently described with respect to their accuracy (German 1986, 1989; Wiig & Semel, 1984) and speed in retrieval (Denckla & Rudel, 1974, 1976b; German 1986, 1989; Wiig & Semel, 1984). (See also the section on assessment later in this chapter.) These students may perform as either inaccurate respondents, slow respondents, or both. For example, a child in math class who quickly (within 4 seconds) says "numerator" when asked the name of the "denominator" would be considered a fast but inaccurate retriever. In contrast, a child who looks at the same math problem, then after a delay (4 seconds or greater), says "numerator" would be considered a slow and inaccurate retriever. Other students may be slow but accurate retrievers, saying "denominator" after looking at the problem for 4 seconds or more (German, 1986, 1989).

Students with word finding difficulties in single word retrieval contexts also manifest unique substitution responses when they cannot retrieve a target word (Fried-Oken, 1984). Examples of these substitution responses include semantic (*fireman* for *policemen* in a social studies unit); phonemic (*eliminate* for *estimate* in a math class); nonspecific words (*things* for *toys* in a free-play situation); or multiword substitutions (e.g., "the man who makes you follow the rules" for *referee* in a discourse about football) (German 1986, 1989). Substitutions of this nature suggest that the students have knowledge of the target word, as noted earlier. Some students use gestures (miming of the unretrieved target word) and/or extra verbalizations, that is, metalinguistic comments ("it starts with a *b*") or metacognitive comments ("I know it, but can't think of it") when called on in class (Fried-Oken, 1984; German, 1985, 1986, 1989; D. Johnson & Myklebust, 1967; Wiig & Semel, 1984).

Discourse. A somewhat newer area of study is the investigation of children's word-finding skills in discourse. However, only three child studies have specifically analyzed narratives for the presence of specific word-finding characteristics. German (1987) studied children with and without word finding difficulties. This research revealed two spontaneous language profiles as being unique to children with word-finding problems: profile 1: low language productivity, with few word-finding behaviors, or profile 2: adequate language productivity with more of the characteristics typical of children with word-finding problems, that is, repetitions, reformulations, and substitutions. In a second investigation, German and Simon (1991) reported that children with word finding difficulties manifested significantly more T-units (*T-units,* also described by Scott in chap. 8, refers to the main clause of an utterance and all its subordinate clauses) with word finding characteristics in their narratives than did children without word finding behaviors. Specifically, they produced a greater percentage of T-units with repetitions, reformulations, substitutions, empty words, delays, and insertions than their normal counterparts. The highest percentage of T-units contained repetitions, reformulations, and substitutions. These findings are consistent with earlier investigations of children's word finding skills (German, 1987; Wiig & Semel, 1975). Similar findings were reported in an investigation of the frequency and type of communication breakdowns present in both the narratives and conversational discourse of children with language difficulties. MacLachlan and Chapman (1988) evaluated subjects' narratives and conversations for the presence of stalls, repairs, and abandoned utterances. They reported that children with language difficulties manifested the following: (1) a significantly greater number of communication breakdowns per communication unit in narration as compared to conversation; (2) longer communication units contained more communication breakdowns; and (3) groups did not differ in the type of communication breakdowns manifested. MacLachlan and Chapman (1988) concluded that the type of discourse task (narration) and the length of the communication unit accounted for the increased communication breakdowns in the language disabled group (see also Scott, chap. 8).

Based on the findings from these investigations, German and Simon (1991) concluded that the language profiles of children with word finding difficulties in discourse can be described with respect to their language productivity and the incidence of specific word finding behaviors in their discourse. Students with difficulties retrieving specific words or phrases in discourse may, however, provide story descriptions of adequate length. Nevertheless, their discourse is characterized by word-finding difficulties, that is, a significant number of repetitions, reformulations, target-word substitutions, insertions, empty words, time fillers, and delays (Table 12–1). By contrast, students with difficulties retrieving discourse components provided stories of limited length with or without the word finding characteristics indicated earlier.

Discourse is a multilevel process, as discussed throughout this text. Therefore, it might be argued that the problems with discourse described in the previous section have an underlying basis that surpasses breakdowns in retrieval. For example, a high incidence of repetitions and time fillers may be indicative of fluency problems; a high incidence of time fillers or empty words may be the result of stylistic variations. However, researchers reiterate that students with bona fide word finding difficulties have some of the symptoms that occur in the discourse patterns such as those mentioned earlier: (1) prolonged pauses and circumlocutions; (2) use of empty place holders and stereotyped meaningless phrases; (3) excessive use of starters, indefinites, and words lacking specificity; and (4) redundant and perseverative repetitions and substitutions of prefixes and suffixes (Wiig & Semel, 1984).

Investigations focusing on communication breakdowns in children's narratives indirectly support the presence of word finding difficulties in discourse. A. R. Johnson, Johnston, and Weinrich (1984) classified some children's utterances as representative of pragmatic errors when they may be indicative of concurrent word finding difficulties in discourse, which contribute to pragmatic difficulties.

For example, overlap between word finding and pragmatic difficulties can be observed in verbal sequences labeled as *reformulations* that could be contributing to behaviors categorized as "difficulty in establishing a topic." Similarly, verbal sequences labeled as *repetitions* could be contributing to behaviors labeled as "use of redundant information." Last, sequences labeled as *insertions* and *empty words*

TABLE 12–1
Characteristics of word finding difficulties in discourse

Word-Finding Behaviors	Definition	Example
Word repetitions	Unnecessary repetitions of words or phrases.	I *ran, ran* to first base. *I ran to first, I ran to first* base.
Word reformulations	Changes in word choice or grammatical reformulations within one entry.	*They were*, to *He was* going.
Substitutions	Target word substitutions that occur in each entry. Major substitution types include semantic, perceptual, nonspecific words, and other categories.	Mary bought *money.* *(tickets)*
Insertions	Insertion of words that comment on the language process itself.	They are at are a a . . . . *I forgot what that is called*.
Empty words	Use of words or phrases that lack specificity, including stereotyped phrases.	*Oh*, it is that *thing-a-ma-jig* you put on the *what-cha-ma-call-it.*
Time fillers	Vowel sounds or syllables that are time fillers verbalized to fill in while the child tries to retrieve the target word (3 or more per entry).	*um, er, ah* He is looking through the *um, er, ah* binoculars.
Delays	Prolonged pauses of 6 seconds or more without verbalizations within an entry.	He is *[8 seconds]* playing *[6 seconds]* tennis.

may be the same as those described as "making a comment." Correspondingly, McCord and Haynes (1988) assessed conversational abilities of LD children. They identified nine categories of language behavior observed in conversations, some of which may be representative of word finding difficulties in discourse. These included use of "nonspecific vocabulary," and "linguistic nonfluency such as repetition or unusual pauses," "revision behavior," and "delays before responding." These same patterns have been discussed in the word-finding literature as target word substitutions, repetitions, reformulations, and delays, respectively (German, 1987). Liles and Purcell (1987) classified potential word-finding behaviors such as miscues, repairs, reformulations, self-corrections, false starts, and filled pauses as verbal departures and repairs present during discourse. Similarly, Knight-Arest (1984) classified word-finding characteristics as word repetitions, incomplete sentences, and the use of *uh* and *um* (time fillers) as "garbles." She reported that together with indefinite references, "garbles" rendered LD students' communications confusing and vague. Although these patterns emerged from investigations exploring more general aspects of children's discourse, the findings suggest the presence of word finding problems.

The discourse problems of children with language, learning, and reading difficulties are well documented (Roth, 1986). Studies have provided information about LD children's conversations and narratives (Bryan, Donahue, & Pearl, 1981; Donahue, 1984; Feagans & McKinney, 1982; Feagans & Short, 1984; Noel, 1980; Ripich & Griffith, 1988; Roth & Speckman, 1985, 1986; Speckman, 1981; Tuch, 1977; Westby, 1984). Studies have also indicated that children demonstrate production deficits in discourse in the presence of good story comprehension (Feagans & McKinney, 1982; Feagans & Short, 1984; Fry, Johnson, & Muehl, 1970; Loban, 1963; Smiley, Oakley, Worthen, Campione, & Brown, 1977; Weaver & Dickinson, 1979). Feagans and Short (1984) reported that children with reading difficulties comprehended spoken narratives in a comparable fashion to their normal peers. However, they performed more poorly on a variety of production measures: that is, they produced fewer action units, words, and complex sentences and manifested more nonreferential pronouns in their narrative than their normal-learning counterparts. Garnett (1986) also reported that some LD students (1) have adequate knowledge of story structure for comprehension but insufficient for story retelling; (2) produce stories and retellings that are impoverished with respect to the amount of information provided; and (3) produce narratives that are less explicit and that lack adequate orienting information and story-binding components. She suggests that poor narrative performance may be due to poor story grammar knowledge, specific linguistic deficits involving the use of cohesive ties, and general deficits in retrieval strategies. She recommends consideration of all three of these factors in intervention. Garnett also points out that retrieval strategies might be considered in the intervention programs of children with discourse difficulties. Therefore, although the underlying cause for narrative production difficulties is not yet clear, certainly, retrieval difficulty may be a possible contributing factor.

PATTERNS OF DEVELOPMENT IN WORD FINDING

Clinicians and teachers must have knowledge of developmental patterns for word finding skills so that they may identify word finding deficits in children with language learning disabilities. Of particular interest is the impact of maturation on children's naming accuracy, naming speed, and naming substitutions. Some studies on small populations report that fluent naming is a skill that develops gradually during childhood (Denckla & Rudel, 1974). Developmental trends are indicated across age groups in naming accuracy and speed (Rudel, Denckla, Broman, & Hirsch, 1980; Wiegel-Crump & Dennis, 1986).

Fried-Oken (1982), investigating normal-developing four- to nine-year-olds, reported that accuracy in naming improved with age and vocabulary growth. German (1986, 1989, 1990) also reported significant correlations and group differences between naming accuracy, naming speed, and age. In the first of a set of investigations, German (1986, 1989) used the Test of Word Finding (TWF) (primary and intermediate forms) to assess naming accuracy and naming speed in 1,200 first- through sixth-grade students (200 subjects at each grade level) (Figures 12–1 and 12–2). The study results demonstrated that both accuracy and speed increased with maturation from first through fifth grade, with a plateau between fifth and sixth grade (See Figures 12–1 and 12–2).

In a second set of investigations, German (1990) used the Test of Adolescent/Adult Word Finding (TAWF) to evaluate naming accuracy and speed of

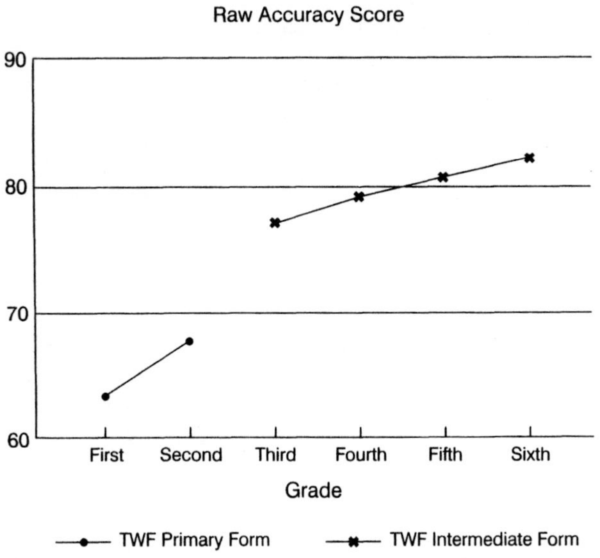

FIGURE 12–1
Mean raw accuracy scores for normal learning elementary-age students, first through sixth grade, on the Test of Word Finding (TWF)
Adapted from *National College of Education Test of Word Finding* by D. J. N. German, 1986, Chicago: Riverside. Copyright 1986 by the Riverside Publishing Company.

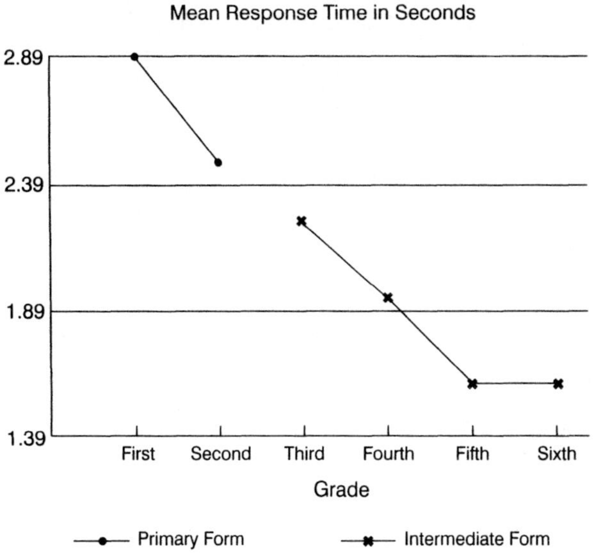

FIGURE 12–2
Mean response time for normal learning and normal word finding elementary-age students, first through sixth grade, on the Test of Word Finding
Adapted from *National College of Education Test of Word Finding* by D. J. N. German, 1986, Chicago: Riverside. Copyright 1986 by the Riverside Publishing Company.

1,200 seventh- through twelfth-grade students (200 subjects at each grade level). Again, accuracy and speed continued to increase with maturation with a differentiation of scores across middle and secondary school grades (Figures 12–3 and 12–4). Specifically, seventh- and eighth-grade students had similar accuracy scores; ninth- through eleventh-grade students manifested higher accuracy scores than lower grades; and twelfth-grade students manifested the highest accuracy scores (see Figure 12–3). Response time decreased significantly from grade 7 to 9 with minor differences from grade 9 to 12 (see Figure 12–4).

Finally, a third set of analyses of adults also revealed consistent change in both speed and accuracy with advancing age (German, 1990) (see Figures 12–3 and 12–4). However, the observed relationship for adults differed from that observed for the elementary and adolescent students. The comparison of accuracy scores and response time at each of the adult age levels reflected reverse trends with accuracy scores decreasing and response time increasing with age. Specifically, the adults in the 20:0 to 39:11 age group showed improvement in both word finding accuracy and speed compared with the twelfth-grade students. However, these skills declined in the 40:0 to 59:11 age group, with the sixty- to eighty-year-olds manifesting the lowest accuracy scores and the slowest response times in the adult sample (see Figures 12–3 and 12–4). These findings suggest that naming speed follows a developmental pattern similar to that observed in naming accuracy. That is, both improve from first through twelfth grade and up to middle adulthood and then decline as an adult ages, findings consistent with other studies of word finding skills in aging adults (Albert, Heller, & Milberg, 1988).

Investigations studying stages of retrieval on automatized and nonautomatized tasks also reported developmental trends. Wolf, Bally, and Morris (1986) investigated 115 average readers from kindergarten to grade 4. They identified three developmental stages of symbol-retrieval fluency on letters and numbers (automatized) and colors and objects (nonautomatized):

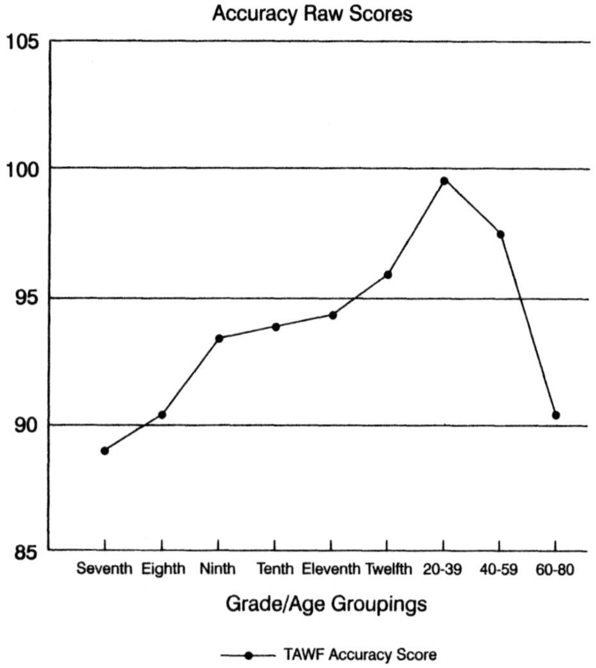

FIGURE 12–3
Mean raw accuracy scores for secondary students, seventh through twelfth grade, and adults, aged twenty to eighty years, on the Test of Adolescent/Adult Word Finding (TAWF)

Adapted from *National College of Education Test of Word Finding Skills (TAWF)* by D. J. German, 1990, Chicago: Riverside. Copyright 1990 by the Riverside Publishing Company.

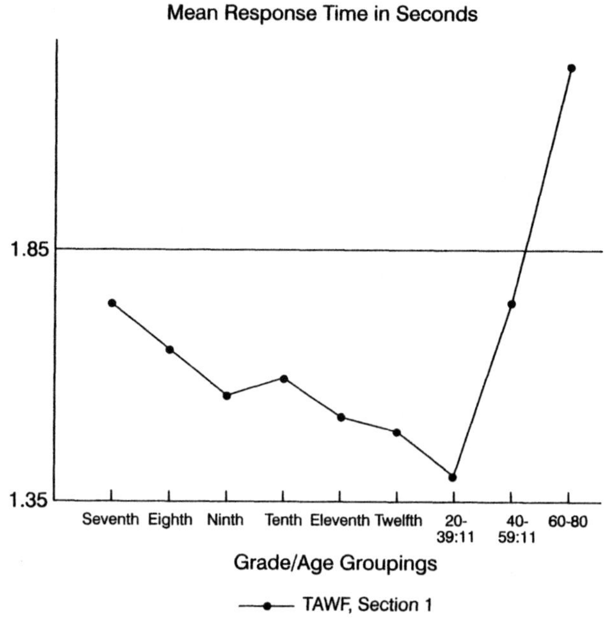

FIGURE 12–4
Mean response times of secondary students, seventh through twelfth grade, and adults, aged twenty to eighty years, on the Test of Adolescent/Adult Word Finding (TAWF)

Adapted from *National College of Education Test of Word Finding Skills (TAWF)* by D. J. German, 1990, Chicago: Riverside. Copyright 1990 by the Riverside Publishing Company.

- Stage 1, five to six years: This is a predifferentiation period when naming in automatized versus nonautomatized contexts is not differentiated (i.e., naming speed was similar across tasks of naming numbers, colors, letters, and objects).
- Stage 2, six to seven years: This is a symbol automatization period when there is a clear distinction between naming in automatized versus nonautomatized contexts (i.e., letter and number naming was faster than color and object naming).
- Stage 3, seven to eight years: This is a fluency period, during which speed of retrieval for all symbol sets approaches adult naming rates and naming errors (on letters, numbers, objects, and colors) are few.

Developmental trends also exist for the use of target word substitutions. Rudel et al. (1980) found that younger children tended to produce more "don't know" responses or unclassifiable or perceptual errors. Older children tended to produce more substitutions that were similar to error responses made by aphasics (circumlocution and paraphasic substitutions). Part-whole and half-right paraphasic (horseshoe for shoehorn) errors and phonemic errors were used to a lesser degree and reflected smaller increases with age. Wiegel-Crump and Dennis (1986), studying fifty normal children's (six to fourteen years) ability to produce names in response to descriptions, rhyming words, and pictures, also reported differences between younger and older children's naming responses. Younger children produced more syntagmatic substitutions (related to the target word, but of a different grammatical class, e.g., *food* or *meat* for *eat*) and paradigmatic associative responses (*glasses* for *mirror, toaster* for *butter*) to the target word. Although responses for all ages (six to fourteen years) tended to be semantically related (in the same semantic category) to the target word, the number of elements shared between the target word and the substitution increased with age. Responses that were only phonetically similar to the target word were not present at any age.

Studies examining developmental trends of word finding skills in discourse are also available. Litowitz and German (1990) examined the presence of word finding characteristics in the spontaneous narratives of 856 normal-developing children in grades 1 to 6 (normative sample for the TWF in Discourse [TWFD], German, 1991). The study considered the average number of words per T-unit representative of a particular word finding behavior (repetitions, reformulations, substitutions, insertions, empty words) and, where appropriate, the occurrence of specific word finding behaviors per T-unit in students' narratives (time fillers and delays).

The findings (Litowitz & German, 1990) indicated that only 2% of all T-units produced in the narratives included one or more of these word finding behaviors, with the most common types being repetitions, reformulations and substitutions, in descending rank order, followed by empty words, insertions, and time fillers, and least frequent, delays. The overall percentages of these characteristics remained relatively stable across grades. A shift was observed, however, in the pattern of word finding behaviors that accounted for the most frequent word finding characteristic at different grades.

Specifically, only substitutions and delays declined significantly across grades (Figures 12–5 and 12–6). Word substitutions rose significantly at second grade and dropped off sharply at sixth grade. Delays showed a steady decline across grades; they were especially steep from fourth grade on (see Figure 12–6). Categories for parenthetical remarks—empty words and insertions—showed a significant increase with maturation, with both rising from third grade on (Figure 12–7). Repetitions and word reformulations showed a pattern similar to each other: They were fairly consistent, with a small rise at fifth grade and falling to the lowest incidence in the sixth grade (Figure 12–8). Time fillers varied minimally from grade to

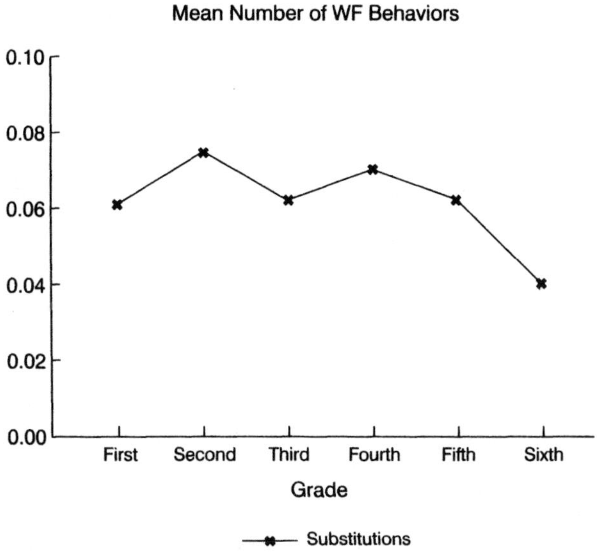

FIGURE 12–5
Mean number of substitutions on the Test of Word Finding in Discourse (TWFD): A significant linear and quadratic trend is shown for the sixth-grade levels
Adapted from *Test of Word Finding in Discourse (TWFD)* by D. J. German, 1991, Chicago: Riverside. Copyright 1991 by the Riverside Publishing Company.

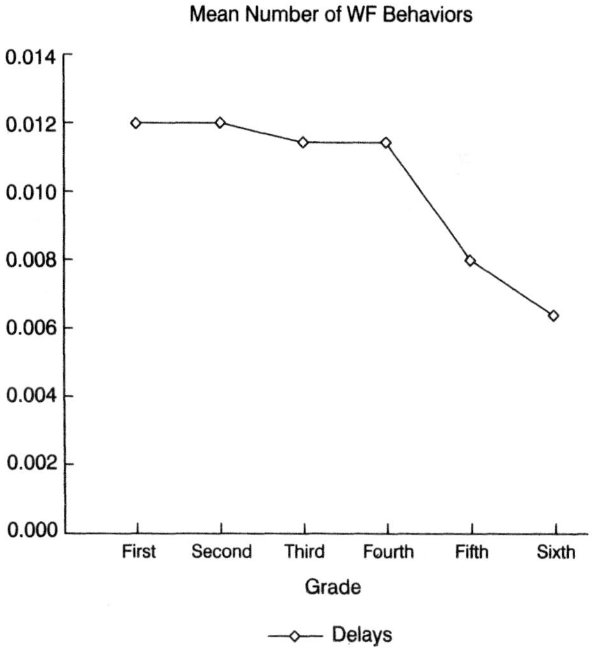

FIGURE 12–6
Mean number of delays on the Test of Word Finding in Discourse (TWFD): A significant linear trend is shown for the sixth-grade levels
Adapted from *Test of Word Finding in Discourse (TWFD)* by D. J. German, 1991, Chicago: Riverside. Copyright 1991 by the Riverside Publishing Company.

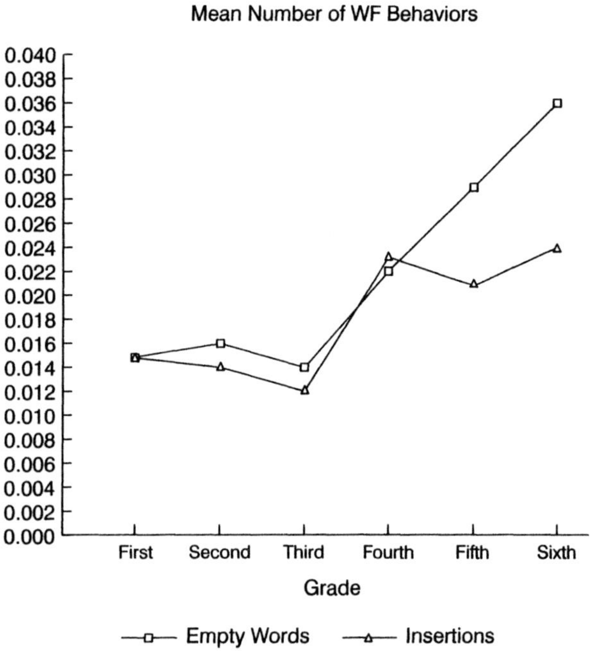

FIGURE 12–7
Mean number of empty words and insertions on the Test of Word Finding in Discourse (TWFD): A significant linear trend is shown for the sixth-grade levels

Adapted from *Test of Word Finding in Discourse (TWFD)* by D. J. German, 1991, Chicago: Riverside. Copyright 1991 by the Riverside Publishing Company.

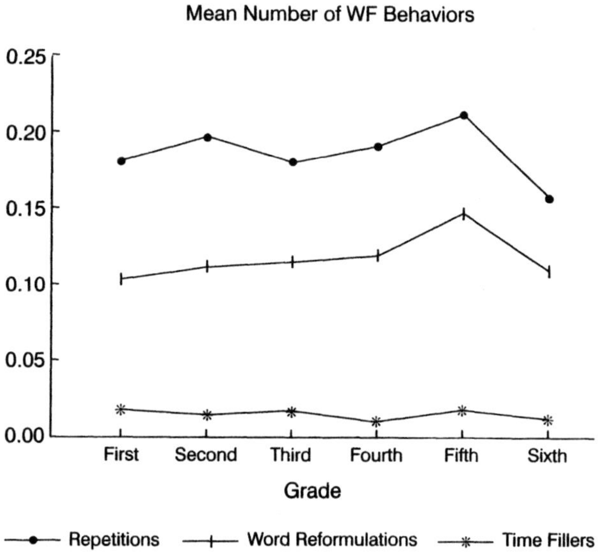

FIGURE 12–8
Mean number of repetitions, word reformulations, and time fillers on the Test of Word Finding in Discourse (TWFD): No significant linear or quadratic trend is seen for the sixth-grade levels

Adapted from *Test of Word Finding in Discourse (TWFD)* by D. J. German, 1991, Chicago: Riverside. Copyright 1991 by the Riverside Publishing Company.

grade, with the largest fluctuations at fourth, fifth, and sixth grade (see Figure 12–8). In summary, the most noteworthy indicators of developmental change in word finding were substitutions, empty words, and insertions. There are noticeable (if not significant) changes throughout the elementary school years. However, the most significant times developmentally for change seem to occur during second, fifth, and sixth grades. These findings have both theoretical and practical implications for teachers and clinicians.

First, in their own right, the findings (Litowitz & German, 1990) relative to single word naming skills, provide experimental support for what has clinically been observed: Differences exist between immature and mature word finding systems, and the efficiency of the system, at least with respect to naming accuracy and speed, changes over time. In addition, word finding interruptions in normal children's discourse is discontinuous and occurs in clusters (Litowitz & German (1990). Of interest is whether the development in word finding and naming confirm and reflect similar shifts in underlying cognitive and language competencies. Litowitz and German (1990) suggest that the first transition period, second grade, may reflect changes in semantic processing in children's word finding in discourse. It may be that as the vocabularies of second graders increase, their attention must be deployed to lexical choices, as evidenced by increased substitutions (see Lahey & Bloom, chap. 13). It is also possible that second graders are simply beginning to be more aware of their listeners' needs for shared lexical reference; they may be at a critical point in their integration of perceptual information with lexical–semantic knowledge. The later transition period suggests that a somewhat different process is occurring. Particularly at sixth grade, this second transition may indicate increased metalinguistic awareness (see van Kleeck, chap. 3). As Kowal, O'Connell, and Sabin (1975) note

> The PR's [parenthetical remarks] present in the older students seem to be inserted into on going [sic] speech to avoid (silent) interruptions and allow continuous speech at points where the speaker does not know how to start or to continue an utterance. The use of such a rhetoric device is part of the acquisition of verbal skills. (p. 203)

In all, available research suggests that a developmental dimension operates with regard to naming accuracy, naming speed, target word substitutions, and word finding characteristics. These developmental findings provide a reference point for students with language difficulties. Because practitioners are often unsure of what is considered typical versus atypical with respect to these indices, an awareness of these trends can help them in their work with students with and without word finding difficulties. For example, a high incidence of parenthetical remarks only (empty words, insertions, time fillers) present in an intermediate grade student's discourse should not be interpreted as an indication of a word finding difficulty, because it is now known that intermediate grade children typically display this behavior. By comparison, a high incidence in the use of repetitions, reformulations, and substitutions in older students may be diagnostic.

WORD FINDING AND READING DIFFICULTIES

Word Finding and Reading Relationship

Numerous investigators have reported a significant relationship between word finding ability and reading (Denckla & Rudel, 1974, 1976a; Katz, 1986; Murphy, Pollatsek, & Well, 1988; Wolf, 1991; Wolf & Goodglass, 1986). Wolf and Goodglass (1986) report that subtle dysnomia, or naming difficulty, is the most frequent characteristic of dyslexic children. Mattis, French, and Rapin (1975) identified a syndrome of dyslexia in which word-finding difficulties constituted a critical factor. Wolf (1980) reported patterns of naming behavior of poor readers that distinguished them from good readers: (1) greater discrepancies between receptive and expressive measures; (2) greater deficiencies in phonological fluency and letter naming; (3) erratic naming unaffected by target word frequency; and (4) substantial response differences. Murphy et al. (1988) found that poor readers displayed subtle oral language problems, of which word finding difficulty was one symptom. Liberman and Shankweiler (1985) have also indicated that poor readers have word finding problems. Students' naming difficulties often interfere with their ability to use language to store content. Continuity is disrupted, and the result is poor comprehension of text (Spear & Sternberg 1987; see also Blachowicz, chap. 11; Scott, chap. 8).

Results of correlational studies have also shown a strong relationship between reading and word-finding skills (Murphy et al., 1988; Semel & Wiig, 1980). In particular, Wolf (1980) reported substantial correlations (.74) between the naming and reading tests scores of poor and good readers between the ages of six and eleven. She concluded that the relationship between reading and word-retrieval processes is so strong that a dysfunction in one may predict a dysfunction in the other process.

Word Finding and Word Recognition

Investigations focused on word recognition skills of children with reading difficulties and word finding difficulties have provided insights into the impact of word finding skills on reading. Word recognition involves a process whereby a reader decodes words by matching letters with sounds (Lerner, 1988). For word recognition to facilitate reading comprehension, word identification needs to be automatic. If not, the reader is forced to expend significant processing energy on decoding rather than on the process of obtaining meaning from the text (see also Lahey & Bloom, chap. 13). Students who are poorer readers appear to have difficulty establishing automaticity in word identification and in word retrieval. For example, Rubin and Liberman (1983) indicate that because word-decoding requires assessing the phonological representation of the printed word, poor readers' decoding difficulties may be a function of their inability to assess the phonological representation of words they know (see also Blachman, chap. 9; van Kleeck, chap. 3). Katz (1986) concurs with Rubin and Liberman, suggesting that poor readers have difficulty retrieving the phonological properties of words rather than word meanings.

Similarly, Smith (1991) has noted that children with word finding difficulties manifest problems in establishing automaticity in word recognition. She states that students with word finding difficulties have difficulty retrieving which sounds go with what letters, even though they can identify the letter sounds in isolation. Sounding out words becomes more difficult because these students forget the first letter while struggling to retrieve the second. According to Smith (1991), the lack of automaticity in word recognition interferes with students' comprehension of text. As they "belabor the decoding of each word, their capacity to remember and integrate information from previous sentences is reduced and comprehension becomes impaired" (p. 162).

Word Finding Automaticity and Reading

Findings from other investigations have specifically supported a relationship between reading and automaticity in word finding. Poorer readers manifest slower naming times than average readers on continuous naming tasks (colors, letters, numbers, and objects) (Wolf, 1991). Because slower naming times on these tasks are said to be associated with the level of automaticity that children can establish in subprocesses of reading (Wolf, 1991), authors suggest that poorer readers also have difficulty establishing automaticity in word identification and in word retrieval. Bowers, Steffy, and Tate (1988), in a study of eight- to eleven-year-old students with dyslexia, reported that dyslexics "may have a specific deficit in naming automaticity" (p. 304). Recall that Blachman (1984; chap. 9) reported that students who were most likely to be among the better readers at the end of first grade were those who not only had greater facility in phoneme segmentation but also had better word retrieval skills on Rapid Automatized Naming (RAN) tasks (Denckla & Rudel, 1974, 1976b). Blachman (1984) further reported that students with poor word retrieval skills on RAN tasks do not necessarily demonstrate difficulties with phonological segmentation tasks. This suggests that tasks to assess word finding skills and tasks that assess phonological segmentation may be assessing different aspects of the linguistic/reading process.

Confrontation Naming and Reading

In contrast to continuous naming tasks (rapid naming of serially presented visual stimuli), performance on discrete naming formats (confrontation naming tasks where stimuli is presented one at a time) have also differentiated poor from average readers (Swanson, 1989, cited in Wolf, 1991). Katz (1986) reported that poor readers exhibit naming difficulties in naming pictured objects with low-frequency polysyllabic names. Wolf and Goodglass (1986), using similar naming tasks, reported that picture naming of objects by kindergarten children predicted both oral and silent reading in second grade and correlated with reading comprehension in the middle grades. In summary, the naming difficulties manifested by children with reading difficulties on both discrete and continuous naming formats have led researchers to suggest that children with reading disabilities may be "impeded in naming-retrieval rate at the most basic level of cognitive requirements as well as at the level required for continuous naming" (Wolf, 1991, p. 128).

Word Finding and Specific Reading Processes

Some authors have indicated that the impact of word finding abilities on students' reading manifests itself differently depending on the reading process involved, that is, word recognition, oral reading, and/or reading comprehension. Wolf, Bally, and Morris (1984) examined the relationship between different reading skills (i.e., word recognition, comprehension) and word-retrieval abilities (i.e., continuous naming in automatized and nonautomatized naming contexts). They studied average and impaired readers, kindergarten through second grade. Although average readers were found to undergo various stages in naming skills, impaired readers showed less change in naming skills over time. Retrieval rates for all naming categories were also significantly slower than that of first-grade average readers. In addition, the retrieval–reading relationship of average readers over time differed from that observed in children with reading difficulties. Both groups evidenced weaker relationships between reading comprehension and retrieval with no significant relationship between nonautomatized symbol speed and reading by grade 2. Groups differed, however, with respect to automatized stimuli retrieval, oral reading, and word recognition. For average readers, correlations between automatized stimuli retrieval, oral reading, and word recognition decreased with advancing grade; similar comparisons revealed increased correlations with grade for poorer readers. These findings indicate that for impaired readers development of automatic retrieval subprocesses may maintain a greater and more prolonged importance in their reading. In a second investigation, Wolf and Goodglass (1986) studied the relationship among confrontation naming accuracy and two types of reading ability, silent comprehension and oral reading in context. They reported that accuracy on confrontation naming tasks (discrete naming) predicted higher forms of reading such as silent comprehension and oral reading in context but not word recognition speed. Integrating the findings of both investigations, it appears that retrieval rate on automatic naming tasks may be used to predict both a child's reading abilities of oral single words and oral context. In contrast, lexical accuracy on confrontation naming tasks appears to be better used to predict reading abilities in oral context and silent comprehension reading.

Shared Processes in Word Finding and Reading

In all, the preceding investigations support a significant relationship between students' word retrieval skills and their reading skills. Proposed models indicate that some processes of reading and word finding intersect, thus sharing parts of the same system.

> [R]eading and picture naming begin with highly similar perceptual operations, are subject to the same or similar information/rate/memory constraints, enter the same percept/concept operation and are then divided by some prelexical categorizing and detector system into separate routes, according to whether the stimuli are automatized (e.g., letters, numbers), linguistic or nonlinguistic. . . .
>
> Naming, with its added categorical requirements would make extensive use of both semantic and phonological processing. Reading, on the other hand, would be trajected along a separate automatic, visual–verbal route to very specified areas of phonological information with immediate projections to specific semantic areas. (Wolf, 1980, pp. 463–464)

Rubin and Liberman (1983) agree that naming and reading processes share the same critical components, that is, accurate phonological representations and short-term memory coding. Relative to word retrieval, routines proceed from the phonological representation of the name to a phonological buffer that holds the representation until the word is articulated. Similarly in reading, the decoded word is translated into its phonological representation and then held in the phonological buffer zone until mapped on its paired entry in the lexicon.

Similarities between word finding and reading processes have been observed clinically in analyses of a student's oral reading errors. Because oral reading errors often indicate that the reader had tacit knowledge of the target word, the errors imply that the reader was able to decode the target word in the text but was unable to encode (retrieve) it orally. This is particularly true when observed reading errors suggest the reader had semantic knowledge (*house* for *home, dog* for *puppy*), or phonemic knowledge (*impeachable* for *impeccable*) of the target word or when the error indicates both semantic and phonemic closeness to the target word (*elevator* for *escalator*). One could hypothesize that these reading errors are the result of word retrieval difficulties during the oral reading task. Rubin and Liberman (1983) reiterate that oral naming errors phonemically close to the target (*propilator* for *propeller*) indicate that the target was identified because the generic phonemic characteristics of the target were retained in the substitution.

Difficulties with oral reading apparently can occur in the presence of adequate reading comprehension. Printed material may be processed before and possibly independently of the oral production of the written word (phonological output lexicon). Practitioners should note that oral reading involves the additional step of verbally retrieving the written word. Therefore, success on oral reading tasks may be confounded by student's word finding abilities. Consequently, teachers might want to minimize oral reading relative to silent reading when programming for students with word finding difficulties.

In summary, numerous investigations have reported a significant relationship between both naming speed on continuous naming tasks and accuracy on discrete (confrontation) naming tasks and reading disabilities. In addition, the impact of word finding abilities on students' reading manifests itself differently depending on the reading process involved and the developmental maturity of students. Additional studies are needed to clarify the nature of word finding difficulties across spoken and written domains. Of interest would be to assess whether noted naming difficulties are part of an overall cognitive/linguistic difficulty in word finding (German, 1986, 1990; Wiig & Semel, 1984) or whether naming difficulties are related more to the subprocesses of reading involving automaticity. If many students with reading difficulties also exhibit word finding difficulties in their oral language, which the research suggests, one might consider these word finding difficulties to be a significant concomitant language difficulty that may be contributing to the child's reading difficulties.

ASSESSMENT

Brief History

Since the early 1970s, the assessment of word finding skills has been of interest to researchers in the fields of adult aphasia, reading, learning disabilities, and speech and language. Each has contributed to the development of assessment measures in this area. For example, The Boston Naming Test (BNT) (Kaplan, Goodglass, & Weintraub, 1976), a test of confrontation naming, emerged from the field of adult aphasia. Although developed initially to identify word finding difficulties in adults, the BNT has been used for children in clinical settings. From research in the reading field, two experimental measures were developed, the RAN (Denckla & Rudel, 1974) and the Rapid Alternating Stimulus (RAS) Test (Wolf, 1986). These research tools measured children's automaticity in naming and were used to differentiate between children with and without reading difficulties. The RAN investigates students' serial naming speed for known objects, colors, numbers, and letters presented by semantic category. The RAS assesses students' naming speed of the same stimuli but in a format that alternates semantic categories (i.e., letter, object, number, color, etc.).

In the fields of learning disabilities and speech and language, both informal and formal measures of word finding emerged. An early measure was the Northwestern Word Latency Test (Rutherford & Telser, 1971). Although developed as an informal research tool designed to differentiate fluency difficulties from word finding difficulties, it was used in some clinical settings. Two subtests, developed as components of a more general language assessment battery, also emerged from these fields. They are the producing words on confrontation and the producing word associations subtests of the Clinical Evaluation of Language Functions (CELF) (Semel & Wiig, 1980). The producing words on confrontation subtest (eliminated from the CELF-Revised [CELF-R], Wiig & Semel, 1984) evaluated students' naming accuracy and speed when naming colored geometric shapes. The producing word associations subtest, included in a modified form in the CELF-R, asks students to retrieve items belonging to a specific category. Information regarding students' word finding abilities has also been gleaned informally from performance on subtests from broad-based cognitive batteries (Kaufman & Kaufman, 1983; Woodcock, 1978) and other expressive vocabulary tests (Gardner, 1981; Jorgensen, Barrett, Huisingh, & Zackman, 1981). These cognitive and expressive vocabulary tests were not specifically designed to assess word finding skills in children, but they put high demands on their retrieval system.

Most recently, three standardized measures of word finding have been designed to assess word finding skills of children, adolescents, and adults. These include the TWF, the TAWF, and the TWFD (German, 1986, 1990, 1991). They are discussed later.

Where to Begin!

An assessment of a student's word finding abilities is primarily an evaluation of student's oral language skills. However, it is critical to differentiate between word finding difficulties that are due to general vocabulary deficits and those that are due to word retrieval problems. Therefore, a measure of a student's word knowledge should be incorporated in the word finding evaluation (Wiig & Becker-Kaplan, 1984). The assessment of a student's word finding abilities should also include both a convergent naming assessment—the ability to retrieve words that satisfy specific semantic constraints imposed by a context (single word naming)—and a divergent naming evaluation—the ability to retrieve a variety of words in response to a stimulus (narrative discourse) (Guilford, 1967). Discussed next are diagnostic models and formal tests for both these assessments.

Assessment in Single Word Retrieval Contexts

Diagnostic Model. One diagnostic model for word finding assessment in single word naming (German, 1989) includes (1) a variety of naming contexts; (2) a comprehension assessment; and (3) specific indices that define word finding difficulties in individuals. Relative to specific indices, the model includes an accuracy score (misnamings, e.g., *tool* for *drill*, would be scored as incorrect); response time (delayed responses, e.g., . . .*chin* for *chin*); substitution types (unique responses, e.g., *shoehorn* for *horseshoe*); and secondary characteristics (gestures or extra verbalizations) (German, 1989) (see Figure 12–9). Practitioners assessing students' word finding skills would want to consider each of the indices indicated. Indeed, intervention would vary depending on student's performance with respect to these measures and observations across contexts (see Silliman & Wilkinson, chaps. 2, 6).

Two instruments that employ the diagnostic model discussed previously are TWF (German, 1986) and the TAWF (German, 1990). These instruments employ several naming contexts, incorporate indices traditionally used to define word finding problems in

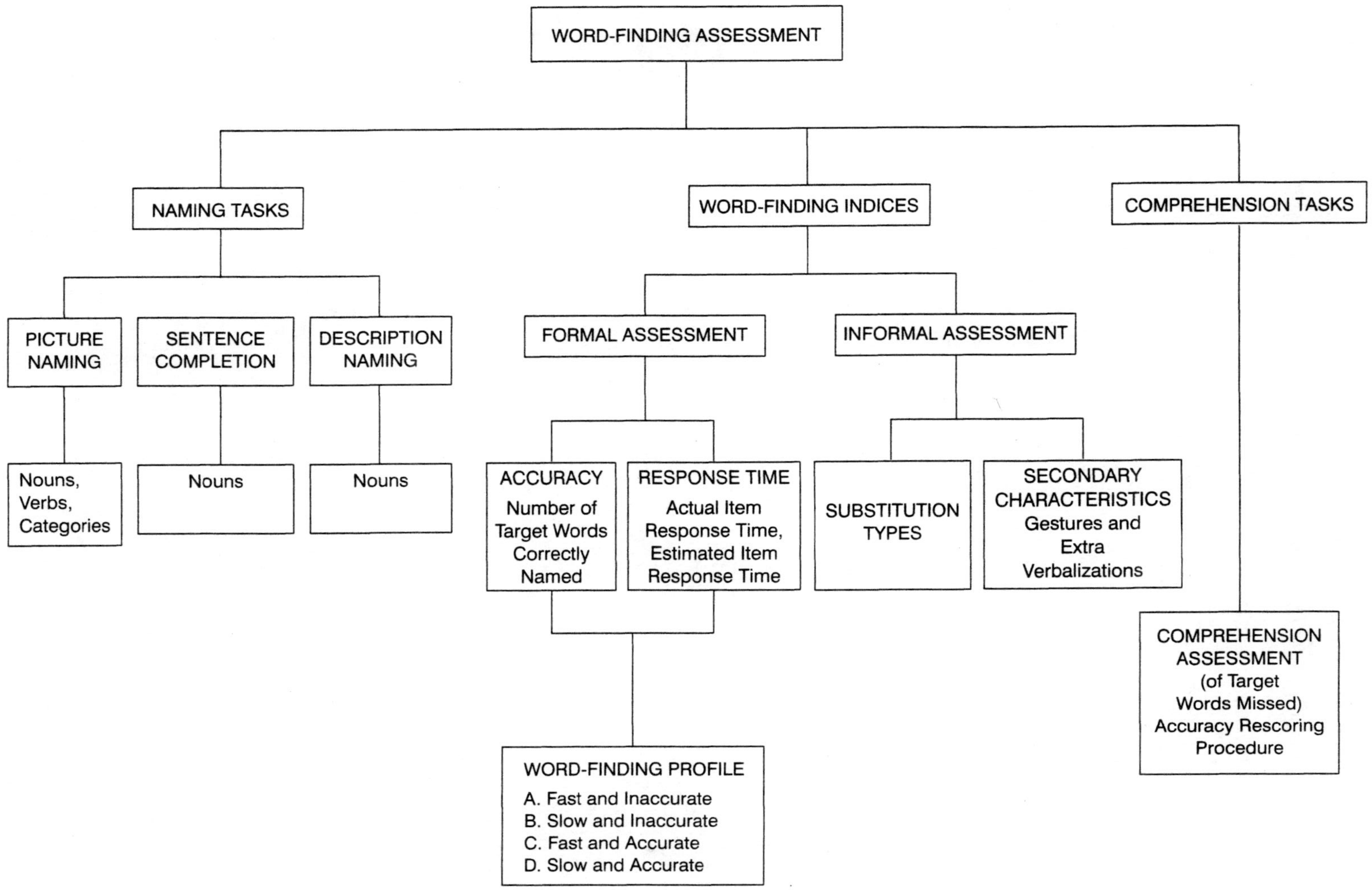

FIGURE 12–9
Diagnostic model for comprehensive assessment for word finding skills

From "Administration, Scoring, and Interpretation Manual—Revised" in *National College of Education Test of Word Finding (TWF)* by D. J. German, 1989, Chicago: Riverside. Copyright 1989 by the Riverside Publishing Company. Reprinted by permission.

children and adults, and provide for a comprehension assessment of target word naming errors. Specifically, both instruments assess word finding skills in picture-naming tasks (picture-naming nouns, verbs, and category words) and in response to open-ended sentences, descriptions, and subordinate words (sentence-completion naming, description naming, and category naming). Both the TWF and the TAWF include a comprehension assessment of all naming errors to help differentiate word finding errors from lack of knowledge errors. The comprehension aspect aids the examiner in differentiating between students whose naming difficulties are due to general vocabulary deficits and those who have word finding problems in the presence of good comprehension of the target word.

Standard scores and percentile ranks are generated to measure students' naming accuracy. Item response times and estimated item response time cutoffs are provided to measure students' naming speed. Informal procedures are provided to categorize a student's unique response substitutions (semantic, phonological, etc.) and use of secondary characteristics (gestures and extra verbalizations). Four word finding profiles, discussed in the section on characteristics, can be identified from the accuracy and response-time evaluations. These profiles are helpful in determining the most appropriate intervention program for students who have difficulty retrieving specific words in single word naming contexts.

Assessment in Discourse

Despite clinical observations of children's word-finding difficulties in spontaneous language (D. Johnson & Myklebust, 1967; German, 1987; Wiig & Semel, 1980), diagnostic models and tests for word finding in discourse are sparse. Rather, word-finding assessment in children has focused, for the most part, on the convergent naming type task (single word naming) (Denckla & Rudel, 1976a, 1976b; Mattis et al., 1975; Rudel, Denckla, & Broman, 1981; Wolf, 1980). Yet the importance of assessing children's word finding skills in narratives and conversations has been documented (Wiig & Semel, 1984). Additionally, characteristics of children's word-finding behavior in discourse and the identification of pragmatic variables that affect naming skills in conversations have been highlighted in the literature, as discussed previously in this chapter (D. Johnson & Myklebust, 1967; Schwartz & Solot, 1980; Wiig & Becker-Caplan, 1984; Wiig & Semel, 1984).

The TWFD (German, 1991) was developed to assess children's word finding skills in narratives. The TWFD requires the examiner to obtain a sample of a student's discourse. Three pictures are provided to elicit the child's narrative: a park scene, a sale scene, and a carnival scene. Probes are recommended for each picture to help students extend their narratives. This instrument is based on two types of analyses: incidence of specific word finding behaviors and language productivity. The three word finding profiles discussed previously that signal word finding difficulties in discourse (German, 1991) can be identified on the TWFD. The profiles include high productivity, but a high incidence of word finding behaviors; low productivity with a high incidence of word finding behaviors; or low productivity with a low incidence of word finding behaviors. Indices used for the assessment of word finding skills in discourse are discussed in the next section.

Incidence of Word Finding Behaviors. The index of the incidence of word finding behaviors focuses on identifying specific word-finding characteristics in children's discourse (German, 1991). This index consists of a global word finding behaviors index and a series of specific word finding behavior indices. Of interest in this analysis is whether students exhibit a high incidence of word finding behaviors in their narratives. The presence of these characteristics in children's discourse has previously been documented to differentiate children with and without word finding problems (German, 1987; Wiig & Semel, 1984). The individual word-finding behaviors include repetitions ("They all, they all are . . ."); reformulations ("They are, she is . . ."); substitutions ("He is catching a bird [butterfly]"); empty words ("You know, the . . ."); delays ("He is looking through the [6 seconds] binoculars"); insertions (metacognitive or metalinguistic comments made during the discourse, e.g., "He is looking through the . . . I can't think of it"); and time fillers ("He is um, going um, uh to . . ."). The high incidence of these word-finding behaviors (in particular, repetitions, word reformulations, substitutions, and insertions) in children's narratives suggests problems in word finding in discourse.

Productivity Index. The productivity index (German, 1991) measures the amount of language a child produces in spontaneous language tasks; that is, it measures the length of a child's discourse. Individual indices that define a student's productivity on the

TWFD include the total number of words and total number of T-units (a main clause plus those subordinate clauses that may be attached to the main clause). Of interest in this analysis is to observe whether the students under study indicate low productivity in their discourse in a decontextualized context. Productivity has been documented to differentiate children with and without word finding problems on other divergent naming tasks, that is, free and controlled association naming tasks. Specifically, Wiig and Semel (1975, 1984) reported that language disordered students manifested low productivity, quickly running out of words to name, on the Detroit Test of Learning Aptitude, free association subtest (Baker & Leland, 1967), and on the fluency of controlled association subtest (Goodglass & Kaplan, 1972).

A statement of caution is needed here relative to the issue of language productivity. Although it is important to look at language productivity when assessing students' word finding skills in discourse, factors other than retrieval skills can impact on students' language productivity, as suggested by several authors of this text (e.g., Scott, chap. 8; Westby, chap. 7). For example, cultural diversity, motivation, emotional stability, metacognitive demands, and contextual variables (stimuli employed, settings, examiners) can all affect children's abilities to produce narratives in decontextualized tasks. Clinicians therefore should clarify test results for those students who indicate low productivity on the TWFD, by observing their word finding skills across school and home situations (as discussed by Silliman and Wilkinson, chap. 6).

Ultimately, a diagnosis of a word finding problem lies with the clinical judgment of the professional involved. Standardized methods for observing student's word finding skills in single word naming tasks and in discourse provide guidelines for observations and bases for age and grade-level comparisons. Test results, however, must be integrated with results from informal observations of language contexts most representative of the discourse demands typically imposed on the child at school and at home (Nelson, chap. 4) and interpreted by professionals who understand the complexity of word finding problems. These informal procedures should include (1) classroom, lunch room, and playground observations of students responses during oral quizzes, classroom discussions, conversations with peers during various activities, and (2) interviews with the student's teachers and parents to verify observations gained on the formal diagnostic measures (German, 1991). One technique developed to help focus clinicians and teachers observations is the Word Finding Referral Checklist (German, 1992). It directs the user to observe students in the classroom or at home with respect to a list of characteristics typically associated with difficulties in word finding. Children manifesting many of the behaviors on the checklist in the classroom and at home are referred for follow-up evaluation.

Comprehensive Test Batteries: Observing Word Finding Difficulties

If they are familiar with the language characteristics that mark difficulties in word finding, examiners can also glean insights about a student's word finding skills on subtests from comprehensive test batteries. For example, expressive vocabulary subtests that ask students to name a picture can be useful in identifying word finding difficulties. The untimed nature of such subtests may draw out response-time delays terminated with the correct response (" . . .airplane"/airplane) or an incorrect response but in the same category ("helicopter"/airplane). The delays may be punctuated with time fillers ("um . . . er . . . ah . . . airplane") or empty words ("that . . . what-cha-ma call-it" for airplane). Such response delays should alert the examiner that the child may be having difficulty retrieving the target word. Students may also describe the object ("oh, it's silver and it flies" for airplane); substitute pronouns ("that flying thing" for airplane); or produce a number of self-corrections ("train, helicopter, no, I mean airplane"). Also, the following errors on digit span subtests may be suggestive of word finding difficulties: (1) a consistent failure to retrieve a particular number (child misses 5 in each sequence); (2) retrieval of a higher for a lower number (15 for 5); (3) self-corrections ("three, no I mean four"); and (4) consistent repetition of age-appropriate number of units, but with number substitutions within the sequence. In all, responses such as those indicated previously might suggest difficulties in word finding and, thus, should be followed up with formal assessments and informal observations of children's word finding skills.

Confounding Effect of Word Finding Difficulties on Valid Assessments

Difficulties in word finding make it difficult to obtain valid assessments of student's cognitive abilities, linguistic skills, and achievement levels. As indicated earlier, students with word finding difficulties sometimes have difficulty retrieving words for spontaneous usage, even though they understand the words they are unable to retrieve. Consequently, they may know answers to test questions but be unable to retrieve the vocabulary necessary to express their answers correctly. This is particularly noticeable on timed tests. The discrepancy between students' understanding of material and their ability to express their knowledge of the material leads to incorrect interpretation of test results. For example, some subtests on widely used intelligence tests put high demands on students' retrieval skills. Even though the main objective of intelligence instruments is to obtain information about students' prior knowledge, test formats that require oral responses more often provide information about a student's ability to express that knowledge. For example, oral vocabulary subtests on many IQ tests often prove difficult for students with word finding difficulties; the subtests require specific responses that must be scored as correct or incorrect by the examiner, who has limited flexibility in scoring. In particular, vocabulary knowledge is frequently assessed through a picture naming task, a task typically used to draw out word finding difficulties in language assessments. As pointed out throughout this chapter, children may demonstrate naming inaccuracies in the presence of understanding the vocabulary being tested. Because of typical scoring procedures, vocabulary items named incorrectly are scored as incorrect. Good alternatives to this one-sided approach would be subtests whose scoring procedures allow credit for responses that reflect understanding of the target word even though the target word is not retrieved (e.g., "write your name" for "pencil" would be scored correct).

Other subtest formats that may be difficult for students with word finding problems include those that require the student to explain why something is important, why something is done, or why something is absurd. Because these tests require the student to provide a short narrative or explanation, students with divergent naming difficulties may have difficulty expressing the answer necessary to receive a correct score.

Inability to differentiate between students' knowledge of answers to test questions and their ability to express those answers on intelligence tests or other test batteries can result in erroneous assessment of students' abilities. Erroneous interpretations often result in inappropriate programming in school. Also, it is important to remember that in addition to the complexity of the knowledge versus expression of knowledge relationship, many tasks on standardized tests require high level metalinguistic processing (see van Kleeck, chap. 3). In all, these confounding variables make it difficult to determine why a student might be having difficulty when he responds incorrectly.

INTERVENTION

"Real-Life"–Based Intervention

Real-life–based intervention for students with word finding difficulties focuses on improving student's word finding skills at home, in school, on the playground, in the neighborhood, and so on. Intervention considers the language demands made on the student's word finding skills at school; across subjects (math, science, social studies, language arts); academic tasks (reading, writing); and assignments (oral reports, cooperative learning groups) (as discussed by Nelson, chap. 4; Ehren, chap. 15) and at home in various family situations (dinner table discourse, sibling and parent conversations); and at play (clubs, sports, and other social activities) (van Kleeck, chap. 3).

Planning Intervention

A first step in planning an intervention program in word finding is to glean from assessment and observation across contexts the source of the student's word finding difficulties. Intervention focused on improving lexical organization and storage is appropriate when there is evidence of significant delays in vocabulary acquisition, concept formation, and semantic hierarchical classification (Wiig & Becker-Caplan, 1984). Intervention of this nature is best matched to students who manifest word finding problems because they have not established elaborate semantic networks for those words (see Milosky, chap. 10; Blachowicz, chap. 11).

It is also appropriate for students who have both underlying comprehension difficulties as well as word finding (word retrieval) difficulties (see discussion of subgroups 2 and 3 earlier in this chapter). Intervention for students who fall in these two groups can take place in collaborative settings. Speech–language pathologists, learning disability teachers, and classroom teachers can join together to identify vocabulary and concepts from students' content areas to serve as the curriculum of the language intervention program (see Blachowicz, chap. 11; Ehren, chap. 15; Nelson, chap. 4). Objectives focus first on establishing a knowledge base for the material under study, followed by activities focused on improving the students' retrieval of that information in class discussion, oral reports, and in cooperative group activities.

For those students with word finding difficulties in the presence of age-appropriate understanding of language (see preceding discussion of subgroup 1), intervention programs specific to improving word retrieval skills are recommended. Students in subgroup 1, for the most part, do not have difficulty understanding and learning concepts and vocabulary presented in class or used in their home and recreational setting; they have difficulty retrieving information for spontaneous usage (see discussion of subgroup 1). Such programs would also be appropriate for students in subgroup 3, as long as the core vocabulary employed consists of words the student understands.

The second step when planning intervention is to determine the nature of students' word finding profile. This involves first determining whether students manifest word finding difficulties in single word retrieval contexts or in discourse. Next, within language contexts, it involves determining whether students are slow or inaccurate namers or manifest a high incidence of word finding behaviors in discourse with high versus low language productivity. Noting students' potential word finding strengths, as well as noting weaknesses, will help in designing an intervention program specific to their needs (see Palincsar, Brown, & Campione, chap. 5).

Efficacy Studies of Intervention

Efficacy studies of word finding treatment procedures have been conducted on adult populations (Howard, Patterson, Franklin, Orchard-Lisle, & Morton, 1985; Huntley, Pindzola, & Weidner, 1986; Wiegel-Crump & Koenigsknecht, 1973). However, only a few investigations contrasting intervention procedures for improving word finding skills in children have been conducted. McGregor and Leonard (1989) contrasted elaboration and retrieval remediation in a study of four children with language and learning difficulties. Elaboration training, both phonemic and semantic, focused on providing children with a richer knowledge of the target words to establish more elaborate representations of words in long-term memory. Retrieval training focused on teaching children to use phonemic, locative, and category retrieval cues. Their findings indicated that a word finding treatment that combined both elaboration training and retrieval strategies was the most effective. Wing (1990) contrasted the effects of three treatment programs on word finding skills: a semantic treatment to improve elaboration and organization of the semantic lexicon; a phonological treatment to increase metalinguistic awareness of phonological structure of words; and a perceptual/imagery treatment that used auditory and visual imagery to cue target word retrieval. Specifically, the semantic treatment focused on activities that enhanced categorization skills, the use of attributes to describe animals and objects, and the use of categories and attributes to define words. In the phonological treatment, children segmented target words into phonemes or syllables, matched rhyming objects and pictures, and provided rhymers for target words similar to some of Blachman's suggestions in Chapter 9. In the imagery activities, children were asked to revisualize target word referents and reauditorize target words to aid retrieval of those words. She reported that subjects receiving the phonological and imagery treatments improved significantly in retrieving untrained targets, while the semantic treatment group made no significant improvement. Together, the findings from these investigations indicate that specific intervention can improve children's word finding skills. However, the apparent overlap in the treatment procedures employed in the two investigations makes generalization difficult. For example, the rhyming type techniques referred to as elaboration training by McGregor and Leonard (1989) were referred to as phonological treatment by Wing (1990). Further category techniques referred to as retrieval strategies by McGregor and Leonard (1989) were employed as semantic elaboration techniques by Wing (1990). Because of this overlap in procedures, readers need to be cautious in concluding from this research that one intervention approach is preferred over another for children with word finding problems.

Approaches to Intervention

Models for word finding intervention in children are sparse. Some authors have recommended clinical models that incorporate strategies typically used with adults be applied to language remediation for children (D. Johnson & Myklebust, 1967; Wiig & Semel, 1980, 1984). Ehren (chap. 15) talks extensively about the importance of strategy training for generalization. Although some materials have been developed to develop word finding skills, they focus primarily on confrontation naming activities (naming to pictures, open-ended sentences, and description). Arbitrary word lists presented in random fashion typically have little relevance for children. They are presented in a test format and are not structured to teach the students how to improve their retrieval skills. It is sometimes assumed that improvement in word finding skills will automatically occur on the presented material and later will generalize to more meaningful contexts (see Silliman & Wilkinson, chap. 2).

A program for word finding intervention has been developed (German, 1993), drawn from the literature in adult aphasia, psychology, and learning disabilities. The primary goal of this program, the Word Finding Intervention Program (WFIP) is to improve the student's word finding skills across contexts. Therefore, inherent in the WFIP is a "real"-life-based perspective. Objectives set, materials employed, and contexts practiced are relevant to the life of the student. Built-in application to school, home, play, and work experiences are incorporated into the program. The word finding intervention model and intervention objectives for each of its components are presented next.

Most approaches to word finding programming have focused on remediation only (Wiig & Semel, 1984). The intervention approach underlying the WFIP involves programming not only in the area of remediation but also in the teaching of self-advocacy and compensatory modification (German, 1993). Although the primary goal of each of the components is to facilitate word retrieval skills across language and situational contexts, each focuses on different aspects of the intervention process. That is, the primary objective of the remedial component is to provide students with word finding strategies and retrieval techniques that will facilitate retrieval in single word naming contexts and/or in discourse. The major objective of compensatory planning is to modify the school and home environment to reduce activities that put high demands on the student's retrieval skills. The purpose of self-advocacy instruction is to "help students develop their executive system around their word-finding abilities" (German, 1992, p. 46). This component of the program helps students develop the following executive functions: (1) awareness of their word finding abilities; (2) self-monitoring skills for ongoing evaluation of their word finding skills; and (3) self-instruction sequences for modification of these target behaviors (Ylvisaker & Szekeres, 1989).

Remediation Objectives. Remediation objectives in the WFIP vary depending on whether the focus is on improving retrieval skills in single word retrieval contexts or in discourse. Objectives for single word retrieval contexts should focus on strategies that improve naming accuracy for the inaccurate namer, or that increase naming speed for the student who is a slow namer. Objectives developed for students who indicate difficulties in both accuracy and speed may focus on strategies in both areas. Strategies for the inaccurate namer may include attribute cuing techniques, rehearsal, metalinguistic reinforcement, cognitive modification, and synonym substituting (Cermak, 1975; Conca, 1989; Huntley et al., 1986; Love & Webb, 1977; Ornstein, Naus, & Liberty, 1975; Wiig & Semel, 1984). Strategies for improving speed in naming in the WFIP may include rapid drill, rehearsal, and synonym substituting (Conca, 1989; Ornstein et al., 1975; Wiegel-Crump & Koenigsknecht, 1973; Wiig & Semel, 1984).

For students who manifest word finding difficulties in discourse, objectives would address (1) activities focused on either reducing or modifying inappropriate word finding behaviors and/or (2) increasing language productivity. Reducing and extinguishing inappropriate word finding behaviors moves from self-identification of behaviors, to external modification of behaviors, to self-instruction to inhibit behaviors. For students with low productivity, German (1991) suggests the application of "ideational scaffolding" to aid retrieval. These activities employ various discourse menus to cue students of discourse components they need to express. These menus provide the student with the narrative schema of the discourse being considered and provide headings to serve as place holders for ideas to be expressed. (See Silliman & Wilkinson, chaps. 2, 6; Blachowicz, chap. 11, for additional ideas on the application of "scaffolding techniques" to aid students' word finding skills.)

Other authors suggest verbal elaboration activities for students with word finding difficulties in discourse. These verbal elaboration activities focus on the ability to retrieve details in response to direct questions: verbal description of pictured objects and familiar events (Wiig & Semel, 1984).

Compensatory Modification. Objectives for compensatory modification in the WFIP (German, 1993) focus on reducing activities that put high demands on the retrieval process in both oral and written language. These objectives are applied to activities in both the in-school and out-of-school curriculum. For example, for the student with word finding difficulties in single word naming, objectives should include modification of the learning environment (i.e., reducing oral questioning by the teacher and written evaluations that require one- or two-word answers, e.g., "In what country did the scientist live?"). Instead, the use of multiple-choice frames ("The scientist lived in (1) Germany, (2) Japan, or (3) the United States?") or find or point to the answer formats is recommended initially. These modifications focus the evaluation on the students' understanding of the information rather than on their ability to express that information. Subsequently, students are asked questions that allow them to elaborate so that they can use the structure of the discourse, that is, a scaffold, to aid retrieval ("Tell me what you know about where the scientist lived"). Conversely, for those who exhibit word finding difficulties in discourse, the clinician would recommend that oral discussions that require expansion or elaboration on a topic ("Tell me what you think will happen next in the story" or "How would you change the ending of the story?") be replaced with oral or written evaluations that use open-ended sentence frames that lead the students to the answer ("The track star will ________") or multiple choice ("A new ending could be (a) the musician plays a solo; (b) the musician chooses a new instrument; or (c) the musician leaves the orchestra"). Additional examples are provided by Blachowicz in Chapter 11.

Self-Advocacy Instruction. The purpose of the self-advocacy component of the WFIP (German, 1993) intervention program is to help students understand the nature of their word finding difficulties by providing them with techniques for self-monitoring and self-instruction. The goal is to help them become their "own best advocate." This is particularly important if students are to be motivated to apply self-cuing and other strategies to improve their retrieval skills and to learn to negotiate necessary compensations in their academic environment to further their learning. These techniques have been recommended in other contexts to facilitate academic instruction for students with learning disabilities (Rooney & Hallahan, 1985). Application of this part of the intervention model, however, will require that students be able to reflect on their linguistic skills (see van Kleeck, chap. 3; Ehren, chap. 15). Practitioners may need to modify objectives for younger students who may not have yet developed the metaskills necessary to apply the cognitive modification techniques discussed next.

Objectives for this part of the WFIP focus on helping those students who can participate become aware of their strengths and weaknesses in retrieval skills. Students are taught self-monitoring techniques to help them identify (1) language contexts (single word or discourse naming) where retrieval is the most difficult versus language contexts that facilitate word retrieval; (2) language activities (group discussion, one on one etc.) that hinder word retrieval skills versus language activities that facilitate word finding skills; and (3) experiences or contexts (classroom, playground, home etc.) that make word retrieval more difficult versus experiences that facilitate retrieval. Other objectives are met through collaborative conferences between the student, the speech-language pathologist, and/or the classroom teacher. These include (4) making teachers and parents aware of student's strengths and weaknesses in retrieval skills; (5) continuously updating students on the remedial objectives of their lessons; (6) consulting with and informing students of the classroom compensations and accommodations being made to aid their retrieval skills; and (7) making students aware of the naming strategies that aid their retrieval.

A final objective involves teaching students self-instruction sequences to help them modify target behaviors. For example, a student who hits the table when experiencing word finding difficulties may be taught to say the following self-instructional sequence to herself: (1) I just hit the table; (2) Next time I will pause; and (3) I will keep my hand to my side. Self-instruction sequences taught are jointly designed by the student and clinician to match student needs.

Curriculum for Intervention

The language curriculum of a real-life–based intervention approach in word finding difficulties needs to be based on language drawn from the student's in-school and out-of-school curriculum (German, 1993). As Nelson (1989; chap. 4) indicates, there is no need to add a separate speech-language curriculum but rather to use the language of the student's classroom curriculum for language intervention. Therefore, random word lists or open-ended sentences are inappropriate content for an intervention plan in word finding difficulties. Rather, the vocabulary chosen and the language content used should emerge from the child's classroom curriculum, daily routine, recreational activities, social life, and home environment. Vocabulary practiced should consist of words drawn from three sources: (1) words that the student had difficulty retrieving; (2) vocabulary drawn from the student's classroom curriculum (reading, science, social studies, etc.); and (3) vocabulary drawn from home or recreational experiences (see Blachowicz, chap. 11). Intervention should be thematic, with vocabulary grouped conceptually (see Silliman & Wilkinson, chaps. 2, 6). For example, lessons may focus on applying strategies to retrieval of computer vocabulary, science vocabulary, social studies vocabulary, and the like. The selection is based on the relevance of the content to a specific student. Vocabulary should initially be practiced in isolation as the student learns to apply appropriate cuing strategies (see Ehren, chap. 15). However, follow-up practice should use scripts that ensure vocabulary retrieval practice in the context of a meaningful discourse. These scripts can be developed jointly by the student and speech-language pathologist. For example, for a student who might be practicing retrieval of sports vocabulary (e.g., basketball), a script representative of events involved in attending a basketball game could be developed. This could include discussing the players' positions, the score, and the plays occurring at a hypothetical game. The student and other members of the language group could rehearse the script, applying the strategies they have learned to aid their retrieval of target words in the script. Computer games that simulate various sports competition could be used to motivate and maintain students' interests. Depending on the size of the group, the speech-language pathologist could participate in the discourse or could serve as a facilitator of the students' conversations (Hoskins, 1987). Intervention directed toward improving word finding skills in discourse would also use language content relevant to either the student's in-school or out-of-school curriculum. The various discourse rehearsed and strategies suggested would be those most immediately applicable to the students' home and learning environments. For example, a student with an upcoming presentation of his life science project at the science fair would apply retrieval strategies to the vocabulary appropriate to his exhibit and rehearse the discourse specific to his presentation. This direct application of retrieval strategies to the student's curriculum will help facilitate carryover of retrieval competencies into the student's daily routine.

SUMMARY

As the previous discussion indicates, a word finding difficulty is a significant language difficulty. First, and most noteworthy, there is a high incidence of word finding difficulties in special populations (German, 1979, 1984; D. Johnson & Myklebust 1967; Smith, 1991; Wiig & Semel, 1984; Wolf, 1980; Wolf et al., 1984). These children are in our schools today. They need ongoing language services. Second, word finding difficulties have a significant impact on academics (Blumenthal, 1980; Rubin & Liberman, 1983). Smith (1991) indicates that word finding problems can be a "lifelong source of reading, learning and expressive difficulties" (p. 162). She indicates that word finding is "one of those slow-maturing skills in which lags get greater through the elementary years, persist into adolescence and are troublesome even in adulthood" (p. 117). Third, based on currently available research, word finding difficulties appear to persist into adulthood, changing, but not disappearing, across time (Wallach & Butler, chap. 1). Fourth, word finding difficulties interfere with interpersonal communication. Clinical experience has indicated that students with this difficulty express fear in being called on in class or having to give oral presentations or reports. One student was heard saying that when the teacher begins oral questioning in class "I hide behind my book and say to myself 'I hope, I hope, I hope, I won't be called on!'" Students with word finding difficulties express frustration with trying to maintain conversations with peers. They may withdraw from quick-paced oral interactions and ultimately choose careers that put minimal demands on their oral language performance. In fact, interviews with students who can reflect on their word finding skills reveal that they believe their word finding difficulties have significantly affected their ability to have successful academic, recreational, and personal lives. Such testimonies impress on the field the need to provide direct programming for students with these difficulties. In summary, the pervasive nature of word finding difficulties, their affect on students' academic learning, and their impact on students' interpersonal skills mark them as an important aspect of the language learning landscape. Therefore, speech-language pathologists and teachers must understand the nature of word finding difficulties and work toward developing appropriate word finding strategies for the children and adolescents in their care.

REFERENCES

Albert, M. S., Heller, H. S., & Milberg, W. (1988). Changes in naming ability with age. *Psychology and Aging, 3*(2), 173–178.

Baker, H. J., & Leland, B. (1967). *Detroit tests of learning aptitude.* Indianapolis: Bobbs-Merrill.

Bjork, R., & Bjork, L. (1992). A new theory of disuse and an old theory of stimulus fluctuation. In Healy, A., Kosslyn, S., & Shiffrin, R. (Eds.), *Learning processes to cognitive processes: Essays in honor of William K. Estes* (Vol. 2, pp. 35–67). Hillsdale, NJ: Lawrence Erlbaum.

Blachman, B. A. (1984). Relationship of rapid naming ability and language analysis skills to kindergarten and first-grade reading achievement. *Journal of Educational Psychology, 76*(4), 610–622.

Blumenthal, S. H. (1980). A study of the relationship between speed of retrieval of verbal information and patterns of oral reading errors. *Journal of Learning Disabilities, 13,* 568–570.

Bowers, P. G., Steffy, R., & Tate, E. (1988). Comparison of the effects of IQ control methods on memory and naming speed predictors of reading disability. *Reading Research Quarterly, 23,* 304–319.

Bryan, T., Donahue, M., & Pearl, R. (1981). Studies of learning disabled children's pragmatic competence. *Journal of Learning Disabilities, 4*(1), 13–22.

Carrow-Woolfolk, E., & Lynch, J. I. (1982). *An integrative approach to language disorders in children.* New York: Grune & Stratton.

Cermak, L. S. (1975). Imagery as an aid to retrieval for Korsakoff patients. *Cortex, 11,* 163–169.

Conca, L. (1989). Strategy choice by LD children with good and poor naming ability in a naturalistic memory situation. *Learning Disability Quarterly, 12,* 97–106.

Denckla, M. B., & Rudel, R. (1974). Rapid automatized naming of pictured objects, colors, letters and numbers by normal children. *Cortex, 10,* 186–202.

Denckla, M. B., & Rudel, R. (1976a). Naming of object drawings by dyslexic and other learning disabled children. *Brian and Language, 3,* 1–16.

Denckla, M. B., & Rudel, R. (1976b). Rapid "automatized" naming (R.A.N.): Dyslexia differentiated from other learning disabilities. *Neuropsychologia, 14,* 471–479.

Donahue, M. (1984). Learning disabled children's conversational competence: An attempt to activate an inactive listener. *Applied Psycholinguistics, 5,* 21–36.

Feagans, L., & McKinney, J. D. (1982, April). *Longitudinal studies of learning disabled children.* Paper presented at the meeting of the Association for Children with Learning Disabilities, Chicago.

Feagans, L., & Short, E. J. (1984). Developmental differences in the comprehension and production of narrative by reading-disabled and normally achieving children. *Child Development, 55,* 1727–1736.

Fried-Oken, M. B. (1982). *Understanding the development of confrontation naming through immediate response corrections.* Paper presented at the Boston University language conference, Boston. (ERIC Document reproduction Service No. ED 227 723)

Fried-Oken, M. B. (1984). *The development of naming skills in normal and language deficient children.* Unpublished doctoral dissertation, Boston University.

Fry, M. A., Johnson, C. S., & Muehl, S. (1970). Oral language production in relation to reading achievement among select second graders. In D. J. Bakker & P. Satz (Eds.), *Specific reading disability* (pp. 123–146). Rotterdam, The Netherlands: Rotterdam University Press.

Gardner, M. F. (1981). *Expressive one-word picture vocabulary test.* Novato, CA: Academic Therapy.

Garnett, K. (1986). Telling tales: Narratives and learning disabled children. *Topics in Language Disorders, 6*(2), 44–56.

German, D. J. (1979). Word-finding skills in children with learning disabilities. *Journal of Learning Disabilities, 12,* 176–181.

German, D. J. (1982). Word-finding substitutions in children with learning disabilities. *Language, Speech, and Hearing Services in Schools, 13,* 223–230.

German, D. J. (1984). Diagnosis of word-finding disorders in children with learning disabilities. *Journal of Learning Disabilities, 17,* 353–358.

German, D. J. (1985). The use of specific semantic word categories in the diagnosis of dysnomic learning disabled children. *British Journal of Disorders of Communication, 20,* 143–154.

German, D. J. (1986). *National College of Education test of word finding (TWF).* Chicago: Riverside.

German, D. J. (1987). Spontaneous language profiles of children with word finding problems. *Language Speech and Hearing Services in Schools, 18,* 217–230.

German, D. J. (1989). Administration, scoring, and interpretation manual—revised. *National College of Education test of word finding (TWF).* Chicago: Riverside.

German, D. J. (1990). *National College of Education test of adolescent/adult word finding skills (TAWF).* Chicago: Riverside.

German, D. J. (1991). *National College of Education test of word finding in discourse (TWFD).* Chicago: Riverside.

German, D. J. (1992) Word finding intervention in children and adolescents. *Topics in Language Disorders, 13*(1), 33–50.

German, D. J. (1993) *Word finding intervention program (WFIP).* Tucson, AZ: Communication Skill Builders.

German, D. J., & Simon, E. (1991). Analysis of children's word finding skills in discourse. *Journal of Speech and Hearing Research, 34,* 309–316.

Goodglass, H., & Kaplan, E. (1972). *The assessment of aphasia and related disorders.* Philadelphia: Lea & Febiger.

Guilford, J. P. (1967). *The nature of human intelligence in language disabilities in children and adolescents.* New York: McGraw-Hill.

Hoskins, B. (1987). *Conversations: Language intervention for adolescents.* Allen, TX: DLM Teaching Resources.

Howard, D., Patterson, K., Franklin, S., Orchard-Lisle, V., & Morton, J. (1985). Treatment of word retrieval deficits in aphasia: A comparison of two therapy methods. *Brain, 108,* 817–829.

Huntley, R. A., Pindzola, R. H., & Weidner W. E. (1986). The effectiveness of simultaneous cues on naming disturbance in aphasia. *Journal of Communication Disorders, 19,* 261–270.

Johnson, A. R., Johnston, E. B., & Weinrich, B. D. (1984). Assessing pragmatic skills in children's language. *Language, Speech, and Hearing Services in the Schools, 15,* 2–9.

Johnson, D., & Myklebust, H. (1967). *Learning disabilities: Educational principles and practices*. New York: Grune & Stratton.

Jorgensen, C., Barrett, M., Huisingh, R., & Zachman, L. (1981). *The word test: A test of expressive vocabulary and semantics*. Moline, IL: Lingui Systems.

Kail, R., Hale, C. A., Leonard, L. B., & Nippold, M. A. (1984). Lexical storage and retrieval in language-impaired children. *Applied Psycholinguistics, 5,* 37–49.

Kaplan, E., Goodglass, H., & Weintraub, S. (1976). *Boston naming test* (experimental ed.). Boston: Veterans Administration Hospital.

Katz, R. B. (1986). Phonological deficiencies in children with reading disabilities: Evidence from an object-naming task. *Cognition, 22,* 225–257.

Kaufman, A., & Kaufman, N. (1983). *Kaufman assessment battery for children, interpretive manual.* Circle Pines, MN: American Guidance Service.

Knight-Arest, I. (1984). Communicative effectiveness of learning disabled and normally achieving 10 to 13 year old boys. *Learning Disability Quarterly, 1,* 237–245.

Kowal, S., O'Connell, D. C., & Sabin, E. J. (1975). Development of temporal patterning and vocal hesitations in spontaneous narratives. *Journal of Psycholinguistic Research*, *4*(3), 195–207.

Lahey, M. (1988). *Language disorders and language development*. New York: Macmillan.

Lerner, J. (1988). *Learning disabilities: Theories, diagnosis, and teaching strategies.* Boston: Houghton Mifflin.

Liberman, I., & Shankweiler, D. (1985). Phonology and the problems of learning to read and write. *Remedial and Special Education, 6*(6), 8–17.

Liles, B. Z., & Purcell, S. (1987). Departures in the spoken narratives of normal and language-disordered children. *Applied Psycholinguistics, 8,* 185–202.

Litowitz, B. E., & German, D. J. (1990). *Speech disruptions in children's narratives: first through sixth grade.* Unpublished manuscript.

Loban, W. (1963). *The language of elementary school children* (NCTE Research Rep. No. 1). Urbana, IL: National Council of Teachers of English.

Love, R. J., & Webb, G. W. (1977). The efficiency of cueing techniques in Broca's Aphasia. *The Journal of Speech and Hearing, 42,* 170–177.

MacLachlan, B. G., & Chapman, R. S. (1988). Communication breakdowns in normal and language learning-disabled children's conversation and narration. *Asha, 53*(1), 2–7.

Mattis, S., French, J., & Rapin, I. (1975). Dyslexia in children and young adults: Three independent neurological syndromes. *Developmental Medicine and Child Neurology, 17,* 150–163.

McCord, J. S., & Haynes, W. O. (1988). Discourse errors in students with learning disabilities and their normally achieving peers: Molar versus molecular views. *Journal of Learning Disabilities, 41,* 237–243.

McGregor, K. K., & Leonard, L. B. (1989). Facilitating word-finding skills of language impaired children. *Journal of Speech and Hearing Disorders, 54,* 141–147.

Murphy, L. A., Pollatsek, A., & Well, A. D. (1988). Developmental dyslexia and word retrieval deficits. *Brain and Language, 35,*(1), 1–23.

Nelson, N. W. (1989). Curriculum-based language assessment and intervention. *Asha, 31,* 170–181.

Nippold, M. (1992) The nature of normal and disordered word finding. *Topics in Language Disorders, 13*(1), 1–15.

Noel, M. M. (1980). Referential communication abilities of learning disabled children. *Learning Disability Quarterly, 3,* 70–75.

Ornstein, P. A., Naus, M. J., & Liberty, C. (1975). Rehearsal and organizational processes in children's memory. *Child Development, 46,* 818–830.

Ripich, D. N., & Griffith, P. L. (1988). Narrative abilities of children with learning disabilities and nondisabled children: Story structure, cohesion, and propositions. *Journal of Learning Disabilities, 21,* 165–173.

Rooney, K. J., & Hallahan, D. P. (1985) Future directions for cognitive behavior modification research: The quest for cognitive change. *RASE—Remedial and Special Education, 6,* 46–51.

Roth, F. P. (1986). Oral narrative abilities of learning-disabled students. *Topics in Language Disorders, 7*(1), 21–30.

Roth, F. P., & Speckman, N. J. (1985, June). *Story grammar analysis of narratives produced by learning disabled and normally achieving students*. Paper presented at the symposium on research in child language disorders, Madison, WI.

Roth, F. P., & Speckman, N. J. (1986). Narrative discourse: Spontaneously generated stories of learning disabled and normal achieving. *Journal of Speech and Hearing Research, 51,* 8–23.

Rubin, H., & Liberman, I. (1983). Exploring the oral and written language errors made by language disabled children. *Annals of Dyslexia, 33,* 11–20.

Rudel, R. G., Denckla, M. B., & Broman, M. (1981). The effect of varying stimulus context on word-finding ability: Dyslexia further differentiated from other learning disabilities. *Brain and Language, 13,* 130–144.

Rudel, R. G., Denckla, M. B., Broman, M., & Hirsch, S. (1980). Word-finding as a function of stimulus context: Children compared with aphasic adults. *Brain and Language, 10,* 111–119.

Rutherford, D., & Telser, E. (1971). *The word latency test.* Paper presented at the meeting of the Association of Children with Learning Disabilities, Chicago.

Schwartz, E. R., & Solot, C. B. (1980). Response patterns characteristic of verbal expressive disorders. *Language, Speech, and Hearing Services in the Schools, 11*(3), 139–144.

Semel, E. M., & Wiig, E. H. (1980). *Clinical evaluation of language functions.* New York: Merrill/Macmillan.

Smiley, S. S., Oakley, D. D., Worthen, D., Campione, J. C., & Brown, A. L. (1977). Recall of thematically relevant materials by adolescent good and poor readers as a function of written vs. oral presentation. *Journal of Educational Psychology, 69,* 381–388.

Smith, C. R. (1991). *Learning disabilities: The interaction of learner, task, and setting.* Boston: Allyn & Bacon.

Spear, L. C., & Sternberg, R. J. (1987). An information processing framework for understanding reading disability. In S. J. Ceci (Ed.), *Handbook of cognitive, social and neuropsychological aspects of learning disabilities* (Vol. 2). Hillsdale, NJ: Lawrence Erlbaum.

Speckman, N. J. (1981). Dyadic verbal communication abilities of learning disabled and normally achieving 4th and 5th grade boys. *Learning Disabilities Quarterly, 4,* 139–151.

Swanson, L. B. (1989). *Analyzing naming speed-reading relationships in children.* Unpublished doctoral dissertation, University of Waterloo, Ontario.

Tuch, S. (1977). The production of coherent narrative texts by older language impaired children. *The South Africa Journal of Communication Disorders, 24,* 42–59.

Weaver, P., & Dickinson, D. (1979). Story comprehension and recall in dyslexia students. *Bulletin of Orton Society, 28,* 157–171.

Westby, C. (1984). Development of narrative language abilities. In G. Wallach & K. Butler (Eds.), *Language and learning disabilities in school-age children* (pp. 103–127). Baltimore, MD: Williams & Wilkins.

Wiegel-Crump, C., & Dennis, M. D. (1986). Development of word finding. *Brain and Language, 27,* 1–23.

Wiegel-Crump, C., & Koenigsknecht, R. (1973). Tapping the lexical story of the adult aphasic: Analysis of the improvement made in verbal retrieval skills. *Cortex, 9*(4), 411–418.

Wiig, E. H., & Becker-Caplan, L. (1984). Linguistic retrieval strategies and word finding difficulties among children with language disabilities. *Topics in Language Disorders, 4*(3), 1–18.

Wiig, E. H., & Semel, E. M. (1975). Productive language abilities in learning disabled adolescents. *Journal of Learning Disabilities, 8,* 578–586.

Wiig, E. H., & Semel, E. M. (1980). *Language assessment and intervention for the learning disabled.* New York: Merrill/Macmillan.

Wiig, E. H., & Semel, E. M. (1984). *Language assessment and intervention for the learning disabled (rev. ed.).* New York: Merrill/Macmillan.

Wing, C. S. (1990). A preliminary investigation of generalization to untrained words following two treatments of children's word-finding problems. *Language, Speech, and Hearing Services in Schools, 21,* 151–156.

Wolf, M. (1980). The word-retrieval process and reading in children and aphasics. *Children's Language, 3,* 437–490.

Wolf, M. (1986). Rapid alternating stimulus naming in the developmental dyslexias. *Brain and Language, 27,* 360–379.

Wolf, M. (1991). Naming speed and reading: The contribution of the cognitive neurosciences. *Reading Research Quarterly, 26,* 123–141.

Wolf, M., Bally, H., & Morris, R. (1984). *Automaticity retrieval processes and reading: A longitudinal study in average and impaired readers.* Unpublished manuscript.

Wolf, M., Bally, H., & Morris, R. (1986). Automaticity, retrieval processes, and reading: A longitudinal study in average and impaired readers. *Child Development, 57*(4), 988–1000.

Wolf, M., & Goodglass, H. (1986). Dyslexia, dysnomia, and lexical retrieval: A longitudinal investigation. *Brain and Language, 28,* 154–168.

Woodcock, R. W. (1978). *Development and standardization of the Woodcock-Johnson Psycho-Educational Battery.* Allen, TX: DLM Teaching Resources.

Ylvisaker, M., & Szekeres, S. (1989) Metacognitive and executive impairments in head-injured children and adults. *Topics in Language Disorders, 9,* 34–39.

REFLECTIONS FOR PART THREE: CHAPTERS 7–12

PULLING THE PIECES TOGETHER FOR STUDENTS IN TROUBLE

Chapters Past and Chapters Future

Chapters 7 to 12—dealing with spoken and written discourse across ages, stages, and language styles and abilities—provide an opportunity to see children in trouble within the context of an educational system in trouble. Researchers and practitioners have long debated whether the "trouble" is within the child or within the educational system, or perhaps, in both. As in many aspects of life, a unidimensional selection of the locus of "trouble" is likely to be incorrect. To say that students struggling with "academic language" are responsible (i.e., the "trouble" is all "inside their heads" rather than "outside their heads") ignores the entirety of the broader educational context (Samuels, 1987). While language specialists have moved away from *less meaningful* types of skill-based learning, as some of the excerpts that follow demonstrate, "failure on the part of the school to teach certain component skills may lead to student failure" (Samuels, 1987, p. 295). Samuels provides an example that relates to learning to read that reminds practitioners that (1) some of the onus for student "failure" must rest with the school, and (2) some skills, or prerequisite abilities, may be more relevant than others. He notes "one of the goals of . . . [reading] instruction is to enable the students to recognize words they have never seen in print before. If beginning readers are given instruction in letter–sound correspondence but not sound blending, many of the students will fail to recognize new words because an essential skill has been omitted" (Samuels, 1987, pp. 295–296).

Blachman (chap. 9) brings "component skills" into a 1990s perspective and demonstrates that phonological awareness is one of the most important pieces of reading and literacy acquisition. She states that overwhelming evidence now suggests that performance on tasks measuring such awareness early in the elementary school years predicts later reading achievement (see also the Part Reflection following chaps. 1 to 3). After reviewing several intervention studies, she also notes that the effectiveness of early and direct instruction in code-based strategies has been heavily documented and adds (emphasis hers): *"It is critical that professionals continue to support the inclusion of these strategies in beginning literacy programs if they hope to reduce the incidence of reading failure."* Thus, it is clear that teachers and clinicians can make a difference in providing such intervention ~~and~~ that what may be perceived as an "inside the head" problem can be solved by an "outside the head" instructional plan.

Less clear-cut are the "student-in-trouble" problems addressed by Westby (chap. 7). She attempts to sort out whether some children from nondominant cultures fail to achieve academic success as a result of their language differences or language disorders. As Westby points out, although language specialists have considerable (but not total) information about the development of language and literacy among middle-class children, there is much less information available to teachers and language specialists regarding the impact of the school culture on children whose cultural and linguistic backgrounds are at variance with these data. A careful reading of Westby's contribution reveals that there may be insufficient tools within the language specialist's armamentarium to make the necessary distinction between language differences and language disabilities. The reader may recall her statement: "Schools walk a tightrope in evaluating and placing students from nondominant cultural groups in programs for the learning disabled." Noting that a primary language activity in one culture may be absent from another, she states that "although it may be impossible to determine which students are 'truly learning disabled' [as opposed to those who are culturally different] it is not impossible to determine which students are not using the social and academic texts of the classroom." Westby also reminds practitioners that older children may have attained some facility with language necessary for classroom success and may be able to cope with early elementary instruction because the variety of text structures needed in the first few grades are relatively limited. However, as children proceed through elementary school into middle and secondary schools, as Scott (chap. 8) also reports, they may lack the variety of text structures needed for comprehending and producing higher level course content or may have less sophisticated strategies. In addition, Westby reminds readers that the importance of schema knowledge and its permeability to language variations also bring controversy to the assessment process. The concepts she discusses relate to many children who have academic and language difficulties, not only children from diverse cultures. Even dynamic assessment may not answer the questions Westby raises, "Do the students lack specific schema knowledge or are they just slow? What strategies do students use to comprehend text and how successful are these strategies? Are ineffective strategies related to cultural styles or metacognitive deficits? Are students' text productions really incoherent, or does the evaluator lack the necessary schema to recognize the coherence in the story?"

Rereading the information on the effect of culture on genre, structure, and style in oral and written texts brings to the fore the difficulties inherent in the accurate evaluation of students in trouble. It is doubtful, given the changing demographics in this country, that any professional will be free of facing these difficulties. Most readers of this text will spend their professional lives interacting with students from multiple cultural and linguistic communities. This calls for in-depth knowledge and appreciation for student differences as well as a commitment to pulling the pieces together in an appropriate fashion. Assisting students from different cultures as well as those with language learning disabilities in the two-tiered task of becoming literate in social and academic language requires a level of skill not previously required. Thus, although it is important to understand "in the child's head" difficulties, it is also necessary to discern what is "inside one's own head" while observing, assessing, and planning intervention. Excerpts from clinical and school reports of recent origin indicate that Individualized Education Plans (IEPs) may still reflect a less than contemporary knowledge base that tends to exclude newer findings:

> "To improve Billy's ability to sequence and to follow instructions, we'll be starting with two- and three-level commands and working up from there."
>
> "Because Don is a visual learner, he should have an easier time making the transition to reading and writing."
>
> "Janice will master fifteen metaphors by December 18th."
>
> "Because Betsy has ADD and possibly ADHD, we cannot decide whether she should be placed in an LD, CD, or BD program."

This brief list easily could continue with additional examples of current statements that one might see in reports about children, their communication problems, and/or academic recommendations. After completing Chapters 7 through 12, and as a preview to the chapters that follow, readers might note that the previous excerpts say less about "the students' problems" and more about the clinician's/educator's frame of reference. Indeed, the statements seem somewhat misplaced, not only in this text but also in terms of the wealth of information accumulated during the 1980s and 1990s alone. Yet, overly simplistic views of language and learning still influence many IEPs and assessment interpretations (Kamhi, 1993).

Although one might argue that the preceding excerpts are taken out of context, most readers have heard similar statements at team meetings, in classes, or at conferences. Many practitioners must wonder about what recommendations would follow. Do these excerpts include any suggestion of the depth of analysis and understanding required and just discussed as per Westby (chap. 7)? Is there a hint of the discourse strategies and patterns outlined by Scott (chap. 8) or Blachowicz (chap. 11)? Does the number of metaphors to be mastered within a given time frame seem to fit the complexity of time and task described by Milosky (chap. 10)? Is the "alphabet game" of diagnosis and placement a reasonable one? The idea that a child might master "two-level commands" or that being a "visual learner" has anything to do with learning to read or becoming literate seems based on inaccurate assumptions about the complexity of discourse processing and literacy acquisition (Kamhi, 1993). Although the paradigm shift for both assessment and intervention, so eloquently discussed by Nelson (chap. 4); Palincsar, Brown, and Campione (chap. 5); Silliman and Wilkinson (chap. 6); and several of the authors in Part 3 gives practitioners some meaningful guidelines, more time may be required before these concepts can be comfortably integrated into practice by most professionals.

Several key concepts weave their way through the chapters in Part 3 and may be critical for moving both theory and practice forward. Blachman (chap. 9) and Scott (chap. 8) define the nature of the oral-to-literate continuum in far different ways from the more simplistic models of auditory-to-visual transfer, as did Silliman and Wilkinson (chap. 2) earlier in the text. Scott (chap. 8) demonstrates beautifully how genre, modality, and purpose interact in interesting ways. She shows how the ability to use high-level discourse styles, such as compare–contrast, grows out of an intricate and complex series of dependencies. Scott also emphasizes that informed language assessment and intervention are not simple tasks but rather require intimate familiarity with the medium of language. She points out that until recently specialists may have been (and may still be) "less knowledgeable about language variables characteristic of older children and adolescents." In approaching the specifics of a discourse continuum within the academic context, Scott provides readers with a "fitting together" of seemingly disparate pieces, noting that the goal is to find better ways of teaching students in trouble. Milosky (chap. 10) and Blachowicz (chap. 11) also show how understanding language comprehension requires understanding its multilayered nature. Milosky (chap. 10) shows readers why nonliterate language comprehension and production are increasingly necessary for academic success as children progress through school. Metaphors, idioms, and irony are very much a natural part of communicating as well as vehicles for a richer understanding of the language in talk and in text. The development of figurative language spans the school years, and therefore its use by language learning disabled (LLD) students should be evaluated and remediated as necessary. Milosky brings relevance to the area by helping readers become more sensitive to the pervasiveness of figurative language and its many faces.

Blachowicz brings readers back to the metacognitive arena when she notes that students with language learning disabilities may have difficulties with problem-solving in the cognitive domain. Indeed, she shows readers how to move from theory to practice in a most eloquent way. Blachowicz clearly has helped many troubled students toward literacy: her chapter may also help readers become models, guides, and scaffolders themselves. German (chap. 12) reveals to readers how word finding difficulties may be interwoven into the fabric of LLD children's discourse. She leads readers through the many steps necessary to understand and alleviate such problems. Certainly, the clinician who teaches students how to recall words to compensate for the loss of other words is engaging in a significant endeavor. As with Blachowicz, German introduces the concept of self-instruction in a carefully defined set of procedures.

As a prelude to the final chapters in Part 4, Lahey and Bloom (chap. 13) provide readers with a widening of the umbrella of word finding and other language abilities as they open up the discussion of information processing in a most provocative way. They remind practitioners to consider the interconnected factors that cause students to "fall apart" on one occasion but not on another. "Knowing" one day, and failing to know on the next is disorienting to parents, child, teacher, and language specialists. As Lahey and Bloom point out, such variability is a problem that one would prefer to ignore. It should give practitioners who use standardized instruments and consider the students' responses to be representative of the totality of their behavior considerable pause. German's (chap. 12) comments about recall and retrieval complement Lahey and Bloom's view of language processing as a limited capacity system. As they so ably note, this view has had limited attention in the speech-language pathology literature. In this, they are joined by Friel-Patti (chap. 14), whose discussion of auditory processing comes from a somewhat similar view of human information processing. Readers will have the opportunity to view Lahey and Bloom's work and that of Friel-Patti's from a fresh perspective as they become more intimately acquainted with the sometimes conflicting and sometimes collaborative notions in the burgeoning field of information processing. Harking back to earlier chapters, including that of Palincsar et al. (chap. 5), readers may begin to see how emerging processes in children, such as self-regulation, early logic, prediction of consequences, and the ability to derive and apply strategies related to both memory and perception (Lidz, 1991) come into normal students' repertoires, and how and why they may be limited or missing within the repertoires of LLD children and adolescents.

As Friel-Patti (chap. 14) points out, we currently lack a coherent theory of how auditory processing relates to language impairment. However, she draws together the most current data from several fields of interrelated research, providing a view of auditory linguistic processing and language learning that links speech perception and language comprehension research. In doing so, her words should lead practitioners to question the basis for children referred for an "auditory processing disorder" without consideration of how the research cited informs language specialists on the intricacies of such a seemingly simple label (reflective of the "alphabet game" in the earlier IEP excerpt). Again, simplicity is not the key, as appealing as that thought might be; it is not simply "listening," just as it is not simply "talking."

Helping practitioners look further across the developmental continuum, Ehren (chap. 15) brings readers' attention to the predominant factors that come into play as LLD students move into secondary school. Her understanding of the needs of such students as they attempt to master an ever-changing curriculum and her ability to articulate strategies to alleviate the curricular stress through enlightened intervention provide a contemporary view of both LLD adolescents in the secondary school context and the massive changes occurring in schools. Ehren provides a forward-looking view of what can be accomplished in those years—the happiest of times and the worst of times, to paraphrase Dickens.

As readers complete the majority of this text, we anticipate that the final chapters will be equally inviting and challenging. We also hope that readers have availed themselves, in the midst of possible information overload, of the underlying pathos and humor apparent in their professional lives. A clinician recently spoke to us about a seven-year-old boy, David, whose speech and language were seriously disordered, but whose personal life was apparently ebullient. Coming, as he did, from a dysfunctional family, his mother was frequently visited by the school nurse, who had continuing concerns about David's safety and well-being. In group therapy for his phonological and language disabilities, he cheerfully commented to the clinician: "Ou mai Dod, tu nurt daim to mai hou . . . for nou doud readon." (Translation: "Oh, my God, the school nurse came to my house . . . for no good reason.") Does not the staunch defense of his home (and his idiomatic use of language) put a smile on our collective faces?

Such statements, with all that they portend, urge readers to be skeptical of neatly packaged "what-to-do's" across language components and modalities. While holding a package in one's hand may seem reassuring, today's trend toward intervention in more naturalistic contexts, while more difficult, is more rewarding for students and teachers alike. Providing appropriate language intervention requires creativity, a knowledge and understanding of current research, and keen observational skills. Creating innovative language programs may seem, to the novice, a very tall order. As one graduate student said to the co-editor, following a three-hour session on the language of children and the language of schools (plaintively), "I *don't* understand it . . . it's just talking, isn't it?" (Butler, 1992). Who's in trouble? The student who exhibits significant "language trouble," who finds "just talking" difficult, or the graduate student (or practitioner) who has yet to see that talking is not a simple, relatively unimportant accompaniment to living and learning?

REFERENCES

Butler, K. G. (1992). It's just talking, isn't it? Foreword. In G. Donahue-Kilburg, *Family-centered early intervention for communication disorders: Prevention and treatment* (pp. xi–xiii). Gaithersburg, MD: Aspen.

Kamhi, A. G. (1993). Assessing complex behaviors: Problems with reification, quantification, and ranking. *Language, Speech, Hearing Services in Schools, 24,* 110–113.

Lidz, D. S. (1991). Dynamic assessment applied to preschool children. In *Practitioner's guide to dynamic assessment* (pp. 32–39). New York: Guilford Press.

Samuels, S. J. (1987). Factors that influence listening and reading comprehension. In R. Horowitz & S. J. Samuels (Eds.), *Comprehending oral and written language* (pp. 295–329). San Diego: Academic Press.

PART FOUR

SPECIAL ISSUES

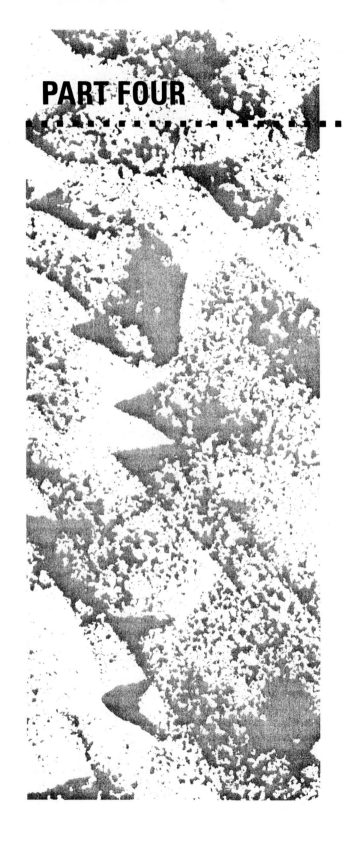

Understanding the Nature of Language Disorders across Tasks and Time

13

VARIABILITY AND LANGUAGE LEARNING DISABILITIES

■ Margaret Lahey
Emerson College
■ Lois Bloom
Teachers College, Columbia University

Information processing has often been used as a theoretical orientation for attempting to understand language learning disabilities. For the most part, the use of this orientation has focused on a search for one aspect of information processing (e.g., memory span, discrimination) that might be defective and the cause of problems with language learning. Such approaches have been criticized by many (e.g., Johnston, 1982; Lahey, 1988; Leonard, 1987; Vellutino, Pruzek, Steger, & Meshoulam, 1973; see also Wallach & Butler, chap. 1). The critiques stress the fact that it is difficult to measure one aspect of processing in isolation from what is being processed. For example, the memory span of language learning disabled (LLD) children in comparison with peers, and of adults in comparison with children, is similar when the material to be recalled is equally familiar (e.g., Case, Kurland, & Goldberg, 1982; Vellutino et al., 1973). Furthermore, the variability among LLD children makes it clear that deficits in one process are unlikely to explain the different manifestations of language problems found among LLD children (Friel-Patti, chap. 14).

Information processing approaches that focus on one deficit as the cause of a student's academic or learning problem are of questionable value (see, e.g., Bloom & Lahey, 1978; Lahey, 1988, for explication of such a specific abilities orientation). The approach presented in this chapter is an alterative information processing approach to language development and disorders and can be applied to identification of LLD children as well as to planning language learning intervention. This approach provides clinicians and teachers with a way of taking into account some of the variability found within a single child's performance as well as some of the variability found among LLD children of similar cultural and linguistic backgrounds. (For a discussion of variability related to cultural and linguistic diversity see Westby, chap. 7; Lahey, 1992; Seymour, 1992.) So often, LLD children perform well at one time but fall apart on a similar task at another time. For example, a child may produce a coherent and cohesive well-developed narrative one day but be dysfluent and incoherent in attempting to produce an apparently comparable narrative the very next day. One is left with the perplexing problem of where to begin language intervention. It is not clear what level of narrative production should be the goal or even that the child needs help with knowledge of narrative structure. In fact, observation of the same child's performance at certain times may lead one to question whether that child has a language learning problem.

Teachers and parents also often report that an LLD child appears to know something one day only to have completely forgotten it the next. This variability has been an enigma to those who try to understand LLD or work with LLD children; it is a problem one would prefer to ignore. One would like to assume that descriptions of a child's performance are a fair indication of the child's knowledge (or competence); professionals hope that they can more readily identify a child who is different from peers and determine what the child needs to learn. However, describing a child's performance in a way that makes possible inferences about knowledge is a difficult task.

The concept of a limited capacity processor as a paradigm for understanding some of the variation observed within and among children is described in this chapter. It is suggested that task analysis of factors that could be competing for limited processing capacity may help to clarify goals and determine intervention procedures in the face of variable performance. This information processing approach focuses on the synergistic interaction of several processes with each other, with context, and with the material to be processed rather than emphasizing a specific ability (see also Silliman & Wilkinson, chap. 2). The view of language processing as a limited capacity system comes from Baddeley (1986), Case (1985), Kahneman (1973), and others.

Integral to the limited capacity processing perspective presented is an important component of language processing that has received little attention in our literature. This component involves constructing and holding in mind the momentary mental representations that underlie the expression and interpretation of language. As discussed later, people can only talk about what they are currently thinking about—the ideas they talk about must be constructed in consciousness based on information from long-term memory and from context (as also discussed by Blachowicz, chap. 11; Milosky, chap. 10, relative to interpreting written language). The concepts presented in this chapter concerning the importance of such mental representations to language processing are based on the works of Bloom (1991, 1993), Bloom and Beckwith (1986), Fauconnier (1985), Johnson-Laird (1983), and others.

A number of assumptions underlie this perspective of language processing as a limited capacity system. These include the following: (1) Language expresses ideas or mental meanings represented in consciousness, and interpreting language involves the construction of ideas in consciousness. (2) One aspect of development is change in the source and an increase in the complexity of the mental representations that can be held in consciousness. (3) The construction of these conscious representations uses the resources of a limited capacity mechanism. (4) The limited capacity mechanism shares resources with other operations that compete with one another for these resources.

These assumptions are discussed briefly in the next sections with a view of how they relate to understanding variability in LLD.

REPRESENTATION OF IDEAS IN CONSCIOUSNESS

Language codes ideas about the world, not actual objects or events (e.g., Bloom, 1974; Bloom & Lahey, 1978). That is, people talk about what they are thinking about. To be expressed intentionally, ideas must be constructed in consciousness. Likewise, in the comprehension of language, listeners and readers construct ideas in consciousness (as discussed relative to reading comprehension by Wallach & Butler, chap. 1; Blachowicz, chap. 11). Ideas are constructed for interpretation and expression by integrating information from the current context with information accessed from memory using language and other contextual cues (Bloom, 1993; Bloom & Beckwith, 1986; Dinsmore, 1987; Fauconnier, 1985; Johnson-Laird, 1983). These points may seem obvious. Of course, people can only talk about what they are thinking about; of course they must construct a representation of the ideas of others in consciousness to comprehend language. But, as obvious as these points seem, professionals rarely take them into account when they are assessing a child or when they are planning intervention (see, however, Blachowicz, chap. 11, as an example of integrating some of these points into practice).

Clinicians and educators frequently try to assess the information that is in a child's knowledge base. For example, educators frequently assess children's knowledge of topics such as science or geography. Less frequently considered are the factors that influence a child's ability to access knowledge to construct the ideas in consciousness that language expresses or sets up in an interpretation. Yet, it is the ideas in consciousness that underlie all intentional actions, including speaking. It is possible to have knowledge about science or geography and be unable to access or represent information from the knowledge base in a way that allows one to act on it. Similarly, because a child demonstrates apparent knowledge of certain vocabulary items or of narrative structure in one or two contexts does not mean the child can access that knowledge in other contexts (e.g., when under time pressure or when attempting to relate a previous novel experience).

The term *consciousness* is used here to refer to the portion of the mind that intervenes between events occurring in the immediate context and the knowledge base stored in memory[1] (Bloom, 1991). All knowledge is represented mentally, although the way it is represented is highly controversial (e.g.,

[1]*Consciousness* as used here does not imply a metalevel. That is, it does not imply that we are necessarily always aware of having an idea in consciousness.

Dell, 1986; Johnson-Laird, 1983; McClelland & Rumelhart, 1985). The representations that are based on past experience and constitute a base of knowledge are not in consciousness but are in what is usually referred to as *long-term memory* (LTM). One cannot act on this stored information until it is brought to some level of consciousness—that is, until one is attending to or thinking about it in some way. Knowledge in LTM can be accessed and brought to consciousness in a number of ways. For example, thoughts of snow skiing can be cued from perceptions in the context (e.g., one sees a pair of skis and thinks of snow and skiing), or it can be cued from language (e.g., in the middle of the summer, one is asked if one has skied at Aspen). To reiterate, this notion is important for understanding LLD students because, as clinicians and educators, professionals try to ascertain whether poor performance is related to insufficient knowledge in LTM, difficulties in accessing that knowledge, or difficulty in constructing and holding ideas in consciousness (perhaps because of competition for cognitive resources).

Terminology used to refer to the mental representations constructed and held in consciousness (in contrast to those in LTM) varies and includes terms such as *mental spaces* (Dinsmore, 1987; Fauconnier, 1985), *intentional states* (e.g., Bloom & Beckwith, 1986; Searle, 1983), *mental plans* (e.g., Miller, Galanter, & Pribram, 1960), and *mental models* (e.g., Johnson-Laird, 1983). The term *mental models*[2] is used in this chapter to refer to the representations or momentary contents of consciousness that underlie intentional actions and interpretations of the actions of others. A mental model is, then, a private representation of an idea constructed out of both knowledge accessed from LTM and the data in perceptions based on the present context. It is fleeting, and its content changes from moment to moment with changes in the context and what is recalled from memory. The content of a mental model occurs with an attitude toward it; these attitudes are the feelings, beliefs, and desires we have about the objects and events represented (Bloom, 1991, 1993; Bloom & Beckwith, 1986). While this constructing process goes on in consciousness and results in the objects of awareness and attention, one is not aware of the process or conscious of it in the metacognitive sense of knowing that one knows (or being conscious of what is in consciousness).

[2]This use of the term *mental models* differs a bit from the use by Johnson-Laird (1983), who distinguishes three types of conscious representations (i.e., images, propositions, and models). The term is used in this chapter to refer to representations that may be eclectic in notation and include images and/or propositions of some sort.

Developmental Changes in Complexity and Source of Mental Models

Mental models are constructed from present perceptions and from a store of knowledge based on past experiences. Developmental differences can be inferred in both the complexity of the models that underlie actions and in the relative influence of present perceptions on the construction of models.

Most clinicians and educators are familiar with the works of Jean Piaget and the concept of representational thinking that develops during the sensorimotor period. Piaget was concerned with the development of the structures of thought that children represent in LTM (e.g., object permanence, means–end relations) and that provide the organization of the knowledge base. He was also concerned with the symbolic process that enables children to form representations in consciousness. The methodology for descriptions of mental models is similar to the methods proposed by Piaget. Both rely on inferences made about what underlies intentional actions.

Mental Models and Play. The actions of the young infant allow one to infer simple mental models. The young infant models are formed primarily from perceptual data. For example, the infant's play with objects can be described in terms of the mental models underlying their actions (Lifter & Bloom, 1989). As described by Lifter and Bloom, the infant, early on, dismantles objects presented in a configuration (e.g., rings on a tower, little people in a bus); the model underlying such intentional behavior can be cued primarily from what the infant sees (i.e., that the objects are separable). Eventually, the infant begins to reconstruct what has been taken apart. Now the mental model includes memory of recent prior experiences with these objects or similar objects. However, immediate perceptions still provide some cues for the reconstruction; the shapes of the objects suggest the intended relations (e.g., the hole in the ring and in the bus). Later, the infant relates two objects together in ways that are not so readily cued by their perceptual shapes, as when the child sits a doll in a truck or puts it in a bed. The mental model underlying such intentional behaviors appears to come primarily from knowledge based on past experiences and includes social and conventional knowledge. Thus, the infant's actions reflect the developing ability to form models with decreasing dependence on context and increasing dependence on memory of past experiences (Bloom, 1991; Lifter & Bloom, 1989). This developmental trend continues and is reflected in language performance into the school years; decreasing dependence on context and increasing dependence on information in LTM is often a goal for the LLD student (Milosky, chap. 10).

Mental Models and Language. Other examples of developmental changes, in both the source of input for the construction of mental models and in the complexity of the models underlying actions, come from descriptions of language development. As noted by Brown (1973), young children talk in the "here and now" and only gradually come to be able to talk about the "there and then." Thus, it seems that the mental models underlying early utterances rely heavily on the data of perception in the here and now for their construction. With development, children increasingly come to use information from past experiences that are stored in memory for constructing mental models that underlie language.

As children move from talking about the relations between objects with single words and simple sentences to talking about relations between events that are expressed in complex sentences, an increase in the complexity of the mental models that they construct can be inferred (Bloom, Lahey, Hood, Lifter, & Feiss, 1980). In the early productions of complex sentences, the relations between the events do not need to be held in consciousness before or while the child speaks. For example, when the child looks at a picture and (as she points to the dog) says "The dog eats" (then pointing to a cat) "and the cat eats," no relation between the events needs to have been constructed in consciousness. The model underlying each utterance could have been independent of the other. Such utterances express additive relations. Likewise, a prior mental model of two events and the relations between them is not necessary to produce utterances chained to actions such as "put it away" (as the child places the book on the shelf) "then get another one" (as the child picks up another book). The child needs only have the model of putting the book away for the first utterance. The model with the desire to get another book could have been cued by seeing the desired book on the shelf as the first book was returned. In contrast, other utterances clearly suggest that complex relations between events are represented in consciousness and being expressed. Consider the utterance "bend him so he can sit" as a child handed her mother a rubber doll. In this instance, the child had represented in consciousness a complex relation between the current state of the doll and an action that would result in a desired change of state. Furthermore, the utterance suggests that the child's mental model included not only a representation of the action necessary for the change of state but also her desires regarding that change and a belief that her mother could accomplish the change.

Eventually, as children produce narratives, expression through language relies on models of the relations among multiple events. Narrative development appears to follow a course of development similar to that for complex sentences in terms of expressing first additive relations followed by temporal and causal relations (for a review, see, e.g., Lahey, 1988). However, the early series of utterances that children produce do not necessarily represent complex models of relations among events, even though they appear to be cohesively tied to one another. For example, early "stories" include strings such as "The dog went on the puppet, the puppet went on the house, the house went on the pigeon" as well as "The monster. The monster ate the house, the monster ate the kids, the monster ate the cat and also the dog . . ." (both from Sutton-Smith, 1981). In these stories, each event could have been represented one at a time; no predetermined temporal or causal relations among the events appear to have been represented in an underlying model. In the second story, the child shows evidence of holding in mind a theme of a monster eating but any relations among the eating events are not obvious. Thus, such narratives are like additive chains of utterances that do not appear to require any more complex mental models than early complex sentences with additive relations. These early narratives also tend to repeat the same verb (as in the preceding *went* or *ate*) over and over (e.g., Botvin & Sutton-Smith, 1977). This reduces the load on lexical and syntactic search and reduces the complexity of the mental model.[3]

Changes in narrative productions that come with increased age include the addition of a main character as agent of the events (e.g., the monster in the

[3]Frequent repetition of the same verb is also found among earliest complex sentences, as in "I sit here and you sit there" (Bloom et al., 1980) and is an important feature in the development of contingent discourse (Bloom, Roscissano, & Hood, 1976).

preceding example) and constraints on the objects acted on (e.g., eating only foods) (see, e.g., Applebee, 1978; Botvin & Sutton-Smith, 1977; Sutton-Smith, 1981). These changes suggest a gradual growth in the complexity of the model that can be constructed and held in mind while the child speaks. With more highly developed narratives, the underlying model is quite complex and the relations among events include cause and effect relations (i.e., narratives with plots). With the production of plots, the child appears to be able to hold in mind some model of the sequence of events including a state of disequilibrium (i.e., a problem), attempts to resolve the problem, and a resolution. By the age of nine or ten, children embed one plot within another, suggesting that an even more complex mental model of relations among events has been constructed in consciousness. Thus, narrative development involves more than knowledge of narrative structure; it involves being able to hold in mind a complex model of relations among events while using language to express these relations. With the assistance of pictorial cues or prompts in constructing and holding in mind mental models, children show evidence of earlier knowledge of plots (e.g., goal, plan, purpose, cause–effect relations) than they do with open-ended elicitation techniques (Trabasso, Stein, Rodkin, Munger, & Baughn, 1992). This finding supports the conclusion discussed later in this chapter concerning the importance of varying elicitation techniques in assessing LLD student's language performance. When assessing or facilitating a child's narrative performance, one needs to consider the complexity of the model that underlies the narrative including factors such as use of evaluations and cohesive devices.

The developmental increase in the use of evaluations in narratives is further evidence of children's increasing ability to construct and hold complex models in mind for narrating events. Evaluations require that the narrator hold in mind both the events and the evaluation of the events. For example, in describing the experience of being in a boat during a storm at sea, one might inject evaluative comments such as "I was so scared! I thought I would die!" The frequency and complexity of such comments increase with age (e.g., Labov, 1972; Peterson & McCabe, 1983). Likewise, the use of certain cohesive devices involves constructing and holding in mind models of more than one event. For example, with the utterances "The boys played ball. When *they* finished _____, *they* went home," the production and interpretation of the anaphoric pronouns "they" and the anaphoric ellipses (i.e., the omission of "playing ball") require reference to the model created by an earlier utterance. The use of such cohesive devices increases with age (e.g., Bartlett, 1982; Bloom, Merkin, & Wooten, 1982). These developmental progressions in the use of cohesive devices provide evidence of the child's increased ability to construct and retain more complex mental models (as well as evidence of other knowledge) (see van Kleeck, chap. 3).

Some of the individual differences in comprehension, inferencing, and reasoning also appear to be related to the ability to construct and hold in mind mental models. Inferences and syllogistic reasoning depend on the creation of mental models that exceed what is coded by language (see Milosky, chap. 10; Blachowicz, chap. 11). After hearing the sentence "Three turtles rested on a floating log, and a fish swam beneath them," subjects will infer that the fish swam beneath the log, although that was not explicitly stated. This inference was based on the mental model they had constructed from world knowledge in LTM—knowledge that was cued by the words in the passage (Bransford, Barclay, & Franks, 1972; and see Milosky, chap. 10, for additional examples).

Reasoning syllogistically also depends on constructing and manipulating mental models (Johnson-Laird, 1983). A model of a first premise (e.g., "*some* of the boats are *sailboats*") is constructed, then information from a second premise (e.g., "*all* of the sailboats have *keels*") is integrated or related to the original model. Finally, a conclusion that is consistent with both premises is drawn (e.g., "*therefore,* some of the boats have *keels*"). The ease with which such reasoning takes place depends on the number of models involved and the ease with which they can be constructed. Even most adults have difficulty drawing the correct conclusion in syllogisms where models are difficult to integrate, such as when each premise involves a distinct model (e.g., "none of B are A, all of B are C, therefore, some of C are not A") (Johnson-Laird, 1983). Furthermore, the order in which the premises are presented and the content of the premises can influence the ease with which an integrated mental model is created and, therefore, the accuracy and speed with which conclusions can be drawn. For example, syllogisms with premises about familiar concepts, such as boats, are easier to resolve than those that refer to abstractions such as group A, B, and C. The relative ease with which mental models are constructed, held in mind, and acted on is related to limited capacity processing, discussed later. The point here is that the construction of mental models is part of the process involved in the comprehension of discourse (Bloom, 1974) and in reasoning (Johnson-Laird, 1983), both of which involve inferencing. Any cues that help us build a mental model (e.g., order and type of information presented, use of cohesive devices, inclusion of a title) aid comprehension and recall (e.g., Bransford et al., 1972; Johnson-Laird, 1983). For some specific examples for intervention, see Blachowicz (chap. 11).

Implications. By examining language performance in terms of the complexity of the mental model (i.e., the mental representation constructed in consciousness) that underlies language performance and in terms of the sources of data used to construct the model, one can observe developmental differences that may have important implications for LLD students. Some of the variability in a child's language performance (including production and comprehension of single sentences or of text, inferencing, and reasoning) may be related to the ease of constructing, or to the complexity of, the mental models that underlie correct performance in each instance.

As an example, consider a child's written or oral narrative productions and the mental models that might be attributed to what is underlying that production. Both the degree of complexity of the model and the ease with which such a model might be formed are schematized in Figure 13–1. Degree of complexity is arranged on the x-axis from least complex on the left to more complex on the right. Least

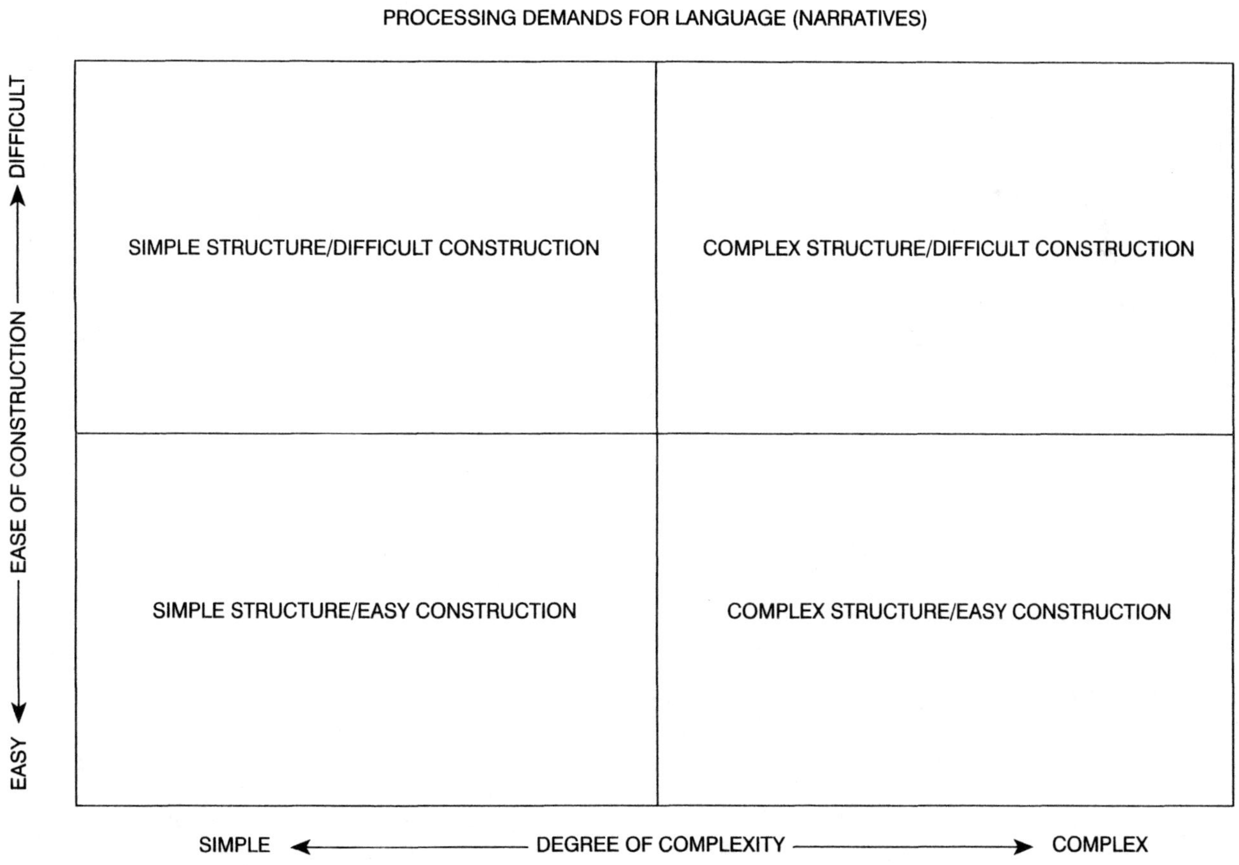

FIGURE 13–1
Evaluation of the mental model underlying an expression or interpretation

complex narratives include chains of utterances that could be produced in any sequence; that is, they are only additive with no logical or temporal connection among them (e.g., the additive chains discussed by Lahey, 1988). These could be descriptive sequences or repeated actions, as in the "monster" example described previously. In these types of productions, mental models might change from sentence to sentence, with perhaps only the topic or main character held in consciousness across the sentences. Increasing complexity, on the right of the grid in Figure 13–1, moves from sentences describing events with sequential relationships between them to the expression of events with causal relationships among them (or simple plots). In addition, the use of elaborated settings, plans, and attempts places a narrative to the right of the grid. At the far right are represented embedded, elaborated causal chains (or plots) with inclusion of information that enables the listener to get the point (as information about the significance of participants) and to understand the narrator's point of view (e.g., evaluations, as discussed earlier). This horizontal axis, therefore, plots a continuum in the varying complexity of the different mental models that narrators construct and hold in mind to successfully produce coherent narratives of increasing complexity. Thus, different narrative productions by the same child are assessed according to the complexity of the mental model that underlies each. An important second step in understanding why variability in performance may exist is to examine the ease with which these models can be constructed.

The ease with which such a model could be constructed, given the individual's context, is arranged on the *y*-axis in Figure 13–1. The lower levels in Figure 13–1 represent models constructed relatively easily because the production of the narrative entails accessing familiar content that has been well practiced in prior experiences and is supported by contextual cues. Contextual support might include visual cues such as the presence of the persons or objects involved as well as linguistic cues including probing comments by the listener or an outline format by the teacher. The upper levels of Figure 13–1 include models that depend more on LTM with little cues from context. Furthermore, these upper levels include the expression or interpretation of less familiar ideas that have not been expressed before. If all other factors are equal, one would expect elicited narratives (i.e., when we ask someone to make up a story or retell a previously heard story) to be higher in difficulty on the chart than spontaneous narratives, because spontaneous narratives express a model the speaker has already constructed in consciousness. For practical necessity, however, most assessment procedures with LLD children involve elicited narratives. To sample varying degrees of complexity in constructing mental models, we must vary the types of elicitation (e.g., retelling, creating, telling from pictures, recalling past experiences) and the use of prompts (e.g., Trabasso et al., 1992), thereby varying the degree of contextual support and familiarity of content.

The important point is that both familiarity of content and the strength of contextual cues influence ease of constructing a mental model. Strength, or usefulness, of contextual cues could also vary with the child (e.g., pictures may help one child but constrain or hinder another, pictures of some content may be easier than those of another). Intuition might suggest that retelling a story would be easier for a child than making up a new story. However, in retelling a story a child must still construct a mental model from the original story to produce a coherent and cohesive retelling (unless the story is short enough to be memorized). The difficulty of retelling will depend on how easy it is for a child to develop a mental model from the original presentation of the story as well as the ease of accessing what is recalled of the original model. For a familiar story, this may be easy, but for an unfamiliar story, it may be a very difficult task.

Degree of complexity of a model (i.e., represented horizontally on Figure 13–1) could fall anywhere on the continuum of ease of access (represented vertically) and vice versa. Some of the variability in a child's performance could be related to the ease with which mental models can be constructed and held in mind. Given familiar material, a child might express complex narratives; given unfamiliar material, the child may well be dysfluent and have difficulty expressing even a simple sequence of relations. Recall your own efforts trying to explain a new concept presented from a lecture to a colleague or friend. At the time you first heard the ideas, you might have understood them well and could relate them to your past experiences. In other words, you found it easy to construct a mental model of the ideas presented as the lecture was presented. But when, in turn, you try to explain them to a friend, you may find it difficult, at first, to do so coherently and cohesively. This difficulty has little to do with your knowledge of language or narrative structure. Rather, you may be having difficulty representing what you remember of the new concept in a mental model for expressing it. Reference to notes might help you reconstruct the lecture by cuing some of the ideas in LTM. Often, after you have attempted this explanation to a few people, it is much easier to construct the model and to express the ideas coherently and cohesively.

Other types of performance (e.g., play behavior, reading comprehension, inferencing) could also be evaluated with a similar grid to evaluate complexity and ease of constructing the underlying mental models. To reiterate: mental models underlie all intentional behavior, and mental models vary in complexity and in the ease with which they can be constructed and held in mind. Consideration of these points may help professionals sort out why some children appear to perform well in one context but not in another. It may explain why some children appear to communicate well with their friends (even relating rather complex narratives) but have considerable difficulty in the classroom. However, ease of constructing mental models by itself will not explain much of the variability in performance that exists within or among children. The ability to construct, retain, and act on mental models is heavily influenced by the limited capacity of working memory (Johnson-Laird, 1983).

A LIMITED CAPACITY SYSTEM

Constructing and holding mental models in mind uses a portion of a limited supply of cognitive resources. This limited supply of resources is shared with other operations. When the system is strained, the operations compete with one another, and tradeoffs can result. Such competition for resources is evident in many aspects of everyday living. For example, in learning to drive a manual shift car, many people have trouble operating the clutch and the accelerator pedals while shifting and steering at the same time. Few novices can do this while carrying on an intense conversation. In time, shifting and steering become automatic; that is, they cease to use as many cognitive resources. After this automatization occurs, people are able to drive while arguing, planning complex affairs, and problem solving. However, some still need to turn down the radio or ask others to be quiet when traffic is heavy, the roads are slippery, or other factors need more of their cognitive resources to manage the car safely. Language processing is also influenced by the competition for the resources that are tied to operations that involve other intentional actions, although the sources of such competition are often more subtle than in learning to drive.

The concept of a limited capacity mechanism being involved in language processing has been postulated by many (e.g., Baddeley, 1986; Bloom, 1993; Bloom, Miller, & Hood, 1975; Case, 1985; Kahneman, 1973; Pascual-Leone, 1970). Baddeley's construct of "working memory" differs from the usual concept of short-term memory in that "working memory" includes processing as well as storage.

Working Memory

According to Baddeley and Hitch, working memory "consists of a limited capacity work *space* that can be divided between storage and control processing demands" (1974, p. 76). A part of the system is allocated to storage and a part to processing. Working memory, therefore, contrasts with the typical view of short-term memory as a limited capacity storage-only mechanism; working memory is an information processing system with limits on both storage and processing capacity.

The storage components are modality specific; there is an auditory store, referred to as the *articulatory loop,* and a visual store, referred to as the *visual-spatial scratch pad* (Baddeley, 1986). The articulatory loop is the storage component for phonological information and is the component of working memory that has been most often studied (usually by measuring the number of items that can be repeated after presentation). A number of studies have demonstrated that memory span for linguistic information is related to phonological and articulatory coding. For example, people can repeat back a longer sequence of short words than long words (e.g., Baddeley, 1986; Hulme, Thomson, Muir, & Lawrence, 1984). Memory span has also been highly correlated with rate of articulation (Case et al., 1982; Hulme et al., 1984). Phonological similarity of stimulus items decreases memory span for these items, at least if the number to be recalled is not near span capacity (Baddeley, 1986; Shankweiler & Liberman, 1976).

Although the storage component in working memory is considered to be dedicated to storage, the processing component, referred to by Baddeley and associates as the *central executor,* is more flexible and can be used for both processing and storage. If the storage component is at capacity, the processing component is also used to store information, and this can result in a decrement in the rate and accuracy of other processes. Even when storage is not at capacity, the processing component is involved in some aspects of storage in that it recodes input, sets rehearsal routines, and retrieves information from storage. In experiments that require subjects to hold in memory a long series of digits while performing other tasks (e.g., semantic categorization, reasoning, or comprehending narratives), accuracy and/or speed in performance are impaired (see, e.g., Baddeley, 1986; Baddeley & Hitch, 1974).

The central executor described by Baddeley (1986) has been likened by him to the supervisory attentional system of Shallice (1982, cited in Baddeley, 1986). This system is used for a wide range of tasks that involve conscious attentional control including planning or decision making, trouble-shooting normally automatic operations, performance of new or poorly learned acts, and blocking strong habitual responses that are not appropriate to the situation. When first learning tasks (e.g., speaking, writing, reading, throwing a ball, typing, driving), efforts to carry them out require conscious attentional control and use the limited resources of the central executor. These resources are, then, not available for other operations such as constructing the complex mental models necessary for problem solving or creative thinking. When, for some reason, people have difficulty carrying out operations that are usually automatic, they also need conscious attentional control. For example, when listeners try to understand someone with an unfamiliar accent or dialect or to understand someone in a noisy environment, they use more processing resources than when listening to familiar speech patterns in a quiet room. Likewise, when trying to construct mental models of unfamiliar content to problem solve in a new situation, one uses considerable processing resources. If speakers try to express ideas with words that they rarely use, perhaps to impress someone or because only those words capture the concept, they may have to consciously search for the words and use extra processing resources. In each of these cases, by using the resources of the central executor, one limits the resources available for other operations. LLD children for whom certain operations (e.g., word retrieval, decoding, writing) may not be as automatic as they are for their peers will use resources that their peers have available for other tasks (e.g., constructing complex mental models).

Many developmental changes in language performance that occur with age (for both young and old) have been related to limitations in "working memory." Reports of decrements in language performance in some elderly suggest that the effective capacity of working memory decreases with advancing age in adulthood. For example, analyses of written diaries indicated a decrease over time in the use of such cohesive devices as anaphoric reference and ellipsis, and in the use of complex sentences (e.g., Kemper, 1990; Lahey, 1984). The appropriate use of cohesive devices in text as well as the use of complex sentences require holding more than one event in mind while processing language. Furthermore, a trade-off in performance found between the complexity of narrative structure and the use of cohesive devices supported the notion that limitations in working memory are involved (Kemper, 1990).

In contrast to what happens during the course of aging in adults, the "effective capacity" of working memory increases as children grow older. For example, older children use more cohesive devices than younger children. Further support for a developmental expansion in the limits of working memory comes from evidence of increased memory span for words (e.g., Case, 1985; Huttenlocher & Burke, 1976), speed of naming objects (Cirrin, 1983; German, chap. 12; Lahey & Edwards, 1991), and speed in making lexical decisions (Edwards & Lahey, in press). Thus, many developmental changes in language performance appear to be related to changes in the effective limits of working memory. As noted early, however, these developmental increases in "effective capacity" are influenced by other factors such as familiarity with the stimuli.

How can one account for the developmental expansion of the limits of a working memory system that includes both storage and processing components? The changes are, no doubt, partially explained by neurological factors. Physical maturation may result in speeded processing and, perhaps, such maturation also increases the absolute capacity limitations of working memory (e.g., Case, 1985). In addition, efficiency in processing appears to have a major influence on the limits of working memory (e.g., Case, 1985). Although increased efficiency and automatization of processes do not increase absolute capacity, they can free resources (or "space") in working memory with a resulting effective increase in capacity. This is an important concept to clinicians and educators, who can do little to directly manipulate neurological development and increase the absolute capacity of working memory. *However, professionals can facilitate increased efficiency and automatization of many aspects of processing and, therefore, effectively increase working memory capacity*. Certainly, one way to help automatize processes involves repeated use or practice. Often, attempts to bring a child's performance up to peers lead professionals to move quickly on to new skills without allowing the child the opportunities to establish some level of automaticity with the old. At times the child is still using so many resources to accomplish what has just been learned that movement forward is thwarted or is limited to very few contexts. Practice does not necessarily mean repetitive production—or what one derisively thinks of as drill—of words or syntactic structures out of context. Practice can be repeated production of language in communicative contexts (i.e., repetition of content–form–use interactions). Providing opportunities for repetitive meaningful contexts is the task for the clinician and educator.

Limitations in working memory could be the result of a number of different problems. In addition to the developmental changes in working memory discussed previously, researchers find differential performance among the components within working memory. As discussed in detail by Blachman (chap. 9), poor readers have difficulty with phonological processing but not visual-spatial processing. Furthermore, some believe that difficulty with phonological processing may be related to speech-motor encoding (Catts, 1989; Kamhi, Catts, Mauer, Apel, & Gentry, 1988; Spring, 1976). Evidence suggests that some reading problems can be a result of a deficit in the articulatory loop or the auditory storage component of working memory (e.g., Baddeley, 1986). In contrast to developmental reading problems, Baddeley suggests that dementia is a deficit in the functioning of the executive processor although the articulatory loop and rehearsal strategies for repetition of presented material apparently function normally. That is, immediate short-term recall (as measured by immediate repetition) is less of a problem than constructing complex mental models from language input and accessing information in LTM. Thus, differential deficits can exist in storage mode and between storage and the central executor. To say the least, statements such as "the student has a memory problem" need further explication to be useful for educational purposes.

Mental Models and Working Memory. One relevant function of working memory is to maintain earlier presented information and to integrate it with new information. This function is an important one for constructing and holding in mind mental models. Mental models use some of the limited capacities of the central executor and storage components of working memory. Some models require more resources than others. If the assumption is made that developmental sequences suggest a continuum of complexity for children (i.e., that what they do first is easier than what they do later), then constructing models based on perceptual evidence is easier than constructing a model from information in LTM. Factors that influence the ease with which models can be constructed from LTM no doubt include how information is organized in LTM (e.g., the type and strength of associative links) as well as the number of times that information has been previously accessed. Complex mental models that involve unfamiliar content and that have little perceptual support (those with difficult access and complex structure, represented in the upper right quadrant of Figure 13–1) would use the most resources. By contrast, simple models based on familiar events with perceptual support to cue necessary information from memory would use the least resources (i.e., those with easy access and simple structure, represented in the lower left quadrant of Figure 13–1). A child might, therefore, produce a fluent complex narrative using complex syntactic structure if the narrative falls in the easy-access/simple-structure quadrant. However, the child may have obvious word finding problems and errors in syntax and may appear to be unaware of the listener's needs when the narrative falls in the difficult-access/complex-structure quadrant or even the difficult-access/simple-structure represented in the upper left quadrant of Figure 13–1. The resources needed to construct and hold the model in mind may be competing with the resources needed to search for lexical or syntactic structures or to adapt presentations to listener needs. The effect of resource competition may be seen in an assessment session. For example, in conversation about a particular baseball game or in retelling a familiar story (e.g., "The Three Bears") from a picture book, the child may be fluent and coherent, expressing cause–effect relations with complex linguistic structures. Yet, the same child may perform more poorly when asked to retell an unfamiliar, and perhaps more complex, story without visual context, or when asked to explain the game of baseball to an unknowledgeable listener.

Language Performance and Working Memory. In addition to the mental representation of ideas and attitudes in consciousness, both the expression and interpretation of language involve accessing knowledge of language form. Knowledge of form includes phonological, morphological, and syntactic information and its relation to content and use. The better developed one's linguistic procedures, and the more experience one has had accessing them, the more automatic the operations become and the less resources one needs to carry them out. Accessing linguistic procedures may use considerable resources if they are not well established and their use has not been fully automatized.

Many of us have studied and gained some degree of proficiency in a foreign language. Yet, when we travel to the country where only that language is spoken, we often find ourselves resorting to single word utterances or stereotyped expressions when communication is urgent; processing the speech of the natives is slow, and they appear to talk very fast. Increased resources are needed to construct mental models, particularly under stress (as with disagreements about the bill or explaining an apparent traffic violation). Similarly, accessing linguistic information uses more of the young child's, or the LLD child's, resources when first learning language; accessing linguistic information uses more of the LLD child's resources continually if the child has word finding problems or problems with other aspects of spoken or written language learning or use. Even small differences in the resources needed to access particular words or structures can have incremental impacts on the production or comprehension of connected discourse. When accessing language is not automatic, resources that could be devoted to constructing complex mental models, taking account of listener needs, or other processes are diverted to the effort of interpreting or producing lexical and syntactic structures. Some monolingual LLD students function in their native language like foreign language students function in their newly acquired language (see Wallach & Butler, chap. 1).

In normal development, the use of "old forms for new functions" (e.g., Bloom, 1970; Slobin, 1973) has been noted and seems related to sharing resources of a limited capacity processor. When talking about new semantic relations, children tend to use familiar forms. For example, "and" is one of the first conjunctions learned. It is used by two-year-olds to code many new semantic relations in complex sentences (e.g., adversative, temporal, causal) (Bloom, Lahey, et al., 1980). LLD children often persist in using "and" in writing for many semantic relations (e.g., Wallach & Butler, chap. 1; Scott, chap. 8; Westby, chap. 7). The use of familiar forms frees resources needed for constructing and holding in mind mental models of new or more complex relations. Likewise, when learning new syntactic forms, children tend to talk about familiar ideas (e.g., the early use of some verb inflections, e.g., *-ing*, redundantly codes the aspect [durative, noncompletive] of the verbs to which it is attached, as with "*playing*"; Bloom, Lifter, & Hafitz, 1980). When added resources are needed to access and produce new linguistic forms, it helps ease the total load if the new forms are used to express models of familiar content. Application of such concepts to learning a new modality of expression such as written language appears promising, as discussed in the next section and by Scott in Chapter 8.

Perceptual-Motor Factors and Working Memory. The motor action involved in expressing ourselves with language (spoken or written) also draws on the limited resources of working memory. Children's rate of articulation and motor responses become more rapid with age (e.g., Abbeduto, 1987; Edwards & Lahey, in press; Lahey & Edwards, 1991). Thus, practitioners assume that older children need fewer cognitive resources than younger children for expressing themselves through speech. Children first learning to talk use a small number of preferred phonemes or phonological shapes for producing many of their new "words" (Ferguson & Farwell, 1975; Ferguson, Peizer, & Weeks, 1973; Ingram, 1976; Lahey, Flax, & Schlisselberg, 1985; Menyuk & Menn, 1979; Schwartz & Leonard, 1982; Schwartz, Leonard, Folger, & Wilcox, 1980; Waterson, 1978); the effect of this is to maximize a child's resources. Moreover, they tend to learn new words faster if the new words conform to those preferences (e.g., Leonard et al., 1982). In children who are just learning to express themselves through written language, the level of language produced is less complex than that used for oral expression (e.g., Lahey & Launer, 1986). As mentioned earlier, the process of writing uses resources that cannot then be devoted to the processes of constructing mental models and accessing linguistic structures (Scott provides many examples in chap. 8).

Even adults devote considerable conscious effort to producing or reading long phonologically complex words that are new in their vocabulary. They may pause and stumble when introducing someone with a foreign name. When typing, adults may quickly gloss over familiar words as if they were one stroke but struggle letter by letter in typing new medical terms, unusual names, or other phonologically unfamiliar words. Individuals with problems in motor planning or execution may require a considerable amount of attentional resources to express themselves through either speech or writing. For such individuals, the act of expressing may use so many resources that it interferes with setting up mental models underlying the expression and with accessing the language to express the ideas.

As noted earlier, some evidence suggests that LLD children have deficiencies in speech-motor planning (e.g., Catts, 1989; Kamhi et al., 1988; P. H. Wolf, Michel, & Ovrut, 1990). For such children, processing at this level may be using resources that could be allocated to constructing mental models and accessing and producing language to express them. It could be, therefore, that problems with oral language expression observed in some LLD children are related to the load placed on working memory by difficulties with aspects of processing required for speaking.

In comprehending either written or spoken language, perceptual processing of the input may also be problematic (particularly if the input is distorted) and may require the use of additional resources. Listeners who are anxious to hear about the stock market or the results of a game played by their favorite football team may find themselves devoting extra resources to processing the signal when the radio is filled with static. This allocation of attention may cause them to have trouble doing other tasks simultaneously. Similarly, when trying to interpret the penmanship of a friend or teacher whose writing is illegible, readers often work so hard to decipher the words that they have few resources left for constructing a mental model to make sense of the entire message. Many people find that they cannot carefully proof work for errors of form (e.g., spelling, verb agreement) at the same time that they read for content of any complexity.

Again, one's attentional resources are taxed so they cannot process the form and construct a mental model of the content at the same time. Similarly, an LLD student who must work extra hard on form may have considerable difficulty constructing and holding in mind complex mental models.

Social-Emotional Factors and Working Memory. Emotional and interpersonal factors can also compete for use of resources that could be used for other operations. Most people have experienced a temporary inability to coherently relate events when talking with particular people (e.g., someone who is extremely critical of them, or someone who has the power to make an important decision based on their performance) or in front of groups (particularly if one has a history of failure in such a context). Indeed, it seems as though one's intentional efforts to do well often have the opposite effect and interfere with successful performance. A person's efforts may be using the resources needed for operations related to the construction of ideas (i.e., mental models) or to accessing and producing the language to express the ideas. At other times emotional concerns may interfere with performance; it is hard to concentrate, that is, to use one's limited resources to construct and express models not related to one's personal concerns.

Some seminal research in the interaction between affective expression and language development supports the view that affective expression can compete with expression through language (Bloom, 1993; Bloom & Beckwith, 1989; Bloom, Beckwith, Capatides, & Hafitz, 1988). Children with high frequency of affective expression spoke their first words later than children with lower levels of affective expression. The infants tended to say their early words while they were expressing neutral affect, and new words continued to be said in neutral affect. Familiar words (i.e., words the infant had used a number of times before) were more likely than unfamiliar words to be spoken in conjunction with positive or negative affect. Furthermore, as children were first learning to say words, there was a drop in affective expression about three to eight seconds before a word was uttered with a rise in affective expression after the word was completed. These findings support the suggestion that children learning language need to allocate considerable cognitive resources for speaking (i.e., constructing and holding a mental model in mind, finding the appropriate lexical item, planning motor response, and executing the motor plan) and that affective expression competes for the same resources. Once a word has become more practiced and automatic, fewer resources are needed for speaking. As a result, resources are then available and can be allocated to affective expression.

The variable language performance often observed in LLD children may be the result of several different factors competing for the limited resources of working memory. A number of processing operations that compete for resources include constructing the mental models underlying expression (including accessing world knowledge); accessing words and linguistic procedures; perceptual-motor processing related to interpreting and expressing messages; and expressing affect. Competition among these operations can explain both the variability seen among children and variability in a particular child's performance at different times (i.e., differential use of resources varies with context).

Implications for Assessment and Intervention

One might ask "so what?" How does this information processing perspective change how language specialists and educators view the LLD child or what they do in assessment or intervention? One possible consequence of using any information processing approach is to consider a task analysis for each child's performance. Task analysis is not new to the field. Task analyses, however, have often focused on looking for weakness in a particular process so that the weak process could be remediated; they have rarely focused on how aspects of the task itself influence performance. For example, a finding that the number of words or numbers that a child can repeat is less than age expectations was often interpreted as evidence of a deficit in short-term memory that needed direct remediation. Rarely was variability in such performance considered. If observed, variable performance was attributed to the child's being tired or "inattentive" rather than being analyzed to see what information it could give about the child's processing.

In the information processing approach to task analysis discussed in this chapter, one might try to understand poor and variable performance by varying elements of the task. For example, one could vary the stimuli and observe the effect. Variations in stimuli used for recall could include length, familiarity, concreteness, phonological structure, and semantic grouping. The child's performance could be compared with achieving students when nonsense words are used as stimuli. It may well be that no differences are found in the number of items recalled and, thus, that the deficit is not in absolute memory capacity. Further variations in the task could include giving the child the opportunity to practice production of the stimuli before recall, or the task could be administered by a different examiner. Finally, the stimuli could be presented more slowly, or a delay could be introduced between input and recall. Thus, a task analysis could look for information on how aspects of the task itself influence performance. Such assessment might lead to a conclusion other than a deficit in memory. The apparent memory deficit may, instead, be related to factors such as retrieval of stimuli, speech-motor planning, interpersonal factors with a given examiner, speed of processing, or phonological processing.

The concept of a limited capacity working memory, as described earlier, suggests a synergistic view of processing components that directly relates to variable performance. A load on one processing operation interferes with the functioning of another. Furthermore, the drain on resources from the process of constructing and holding mental models in mind for expression and interpretation has not generally been recognized in task analyses. A modification of previous task analyses is in order. The modification suggested here attempts to account for variable performance and contributes to understanding how processing can be influenced by a number of factors. Such analysis could lead to conclusions that are quite different from those previously reached about the techniques that may improve language performance. Alternatively, for experienced clinicians, it may simply provide a way to talk about, think about, and perhaps slightly alter, the techniques that they already have found successful.

Assessment. One part of assessment is the identification of children who are having difficulty with oral or written language performance. Some of these children may have the knowledge of language they need but be unable to access that knowledge, whereas others may have limited linguistic knowledge. (See German, chap. 12, for a discussion of this distinction in relation to word finding.) For purposes of identifying students with LLD, diagnosticians are not looking for best performance (or what the child *can* do) but are looking, instead, for what the child does in comparison with what peers usually do when the system is stressed. One assessment implication of the earlier discussion about limited capacity processing and mental models is that assessment procedures be evaluated in terms of the demands that procedures place on working memory. For example, contexts of connected speech (e.g., narrative production or comprehension about unfamiliar past events) will no doubt reveal more problems than tasks requiring single word or single sentence processing (e.g., McLachlin & Chapman, 1988), particularly if the content of the single words or sentences is supported by context. Materials that involve complex mental models and in other ways use considerable cognitive resources should perhaps become a regular part of assessment batteries; reports should describe the influence of different levels of cognitive load on performance.

Moreover, reaction times and timed performance may reveal problems that are not otherwise obvious when time is not an issue. LLD students are often given untimed tests when the purpose of testing is to evaluate what they know. Timed performance reveals accessing problems not always evident in untimed tasks. For example, research suggests that LLD children perform more slowly on rapid automatized naming tasks (Denckla, 1974; Menyuk et al., 1991) and confrontation naming tasks (German, chap. 12; Leonard, Nippold, Kail, & Hale, 1983; M. Wolf, 1982) even though the stimuli are a part of the child's productive vocabulary. In young children, performance on such timed tasks appears to be predictive of future success in learning to read (Menyuk et al., 1991; M. Wolf, 1982). Thus, timed tasks might also be considered as an important part of a protocol designed to identify children who are having, or who are at risk for having, language learning problems. Stressing the system does not have to stress the child. To try to do something "as fast as you can" does not need to be a context for potential failure. Feedback about effort and attention can be given without mention of obtained or desired response time. Timed tasks appear to be most useful when the purpose of assessment is identification of a child as LLD, or as being at risk for having future problems with language, and when other more standard types of assessment have not so identified the child. Slow performance, however, does not explain the totality of an LLD child's problems or lead directly to intervention. That is the next step in assessment.

After a child has been identified as LLD or as being at risk for having language learning problems, assessment is geared toward determining goals and procedures of intervention. At this level of assessment, it is helpful to determine how much of the child's performance is related to deficits in general knowledge versus problems in accessing that knowledge (see also, Milosky, chap. 10; German, chap. 12). Similarly, language performance on any task could be the result of deficits in linguistic knowledge or problems in accessing that knowledge. Problems that appear to be related to access might be related to limitations on working memory caused by the resources needed for other processes. Available resources change from child to child and from time to time. For some children, poor performance may be related to organization or depth of world or linguistic knowledge (as discussed in Milosky, chap. 10). For others, speech-motor encoding and planning may take extra resources. Whereas for still others, social-emotional factors (including cultural factors, as discussed by Westby, chap. 7) may usurp the resources of working memory. The variability among and within children suggests that professionals try to determine how these factors interact in any one child and that professionals plan different goals and procedures of intervention depending on this interaction.

For example, slow performance on confrontation naming tasks may be related to semantic access or word familiarity for some children, as pointed out by German in Chapter 12. For others, slow performance may be related to perceptual encoding of the input or to response encoding (e.g., phonological processing, motor planning, motor execution), as noted by Lahey and Edwards (1991). Assessments that attempt to sort out some of these factors may lead to more efficient treatment strategies. Two treatment strategies for word finding have been tested by Wing (1990). In one, the focus was on perceptual-motor training; in the other, it was on semantic organization. Although the group effect indicated more improvement based on perceptual-motor strategies, individual children no doubt vary in the impact of each. Strategies focused on phonological processing or perceptual processing may not be helpful to the child whose problem is related to semantic organization or limited vocabulary. Likewise, treatment strategies designed to improve semantic organization may not be beneficial to a child whose problem is in response encoding. One might try to assess which is most important to a particular child by comparing a child's performance relative to peers for immediate naming in contrast to naming when the child has looked at the picture for one or more seconds (e.g., Lahey & Edwards, 1991). If differences between the LLD child and peers in the delayed naming task (where plenty of time is available for access) are equal to those in the immediate naming task, one could conclude that response factors rather than semantic organization or access is what differentiates these children. Therefore, intervention would not focus on semantic organization. If intervention was deemed necessary, it might better focus on phonological processing or motor responses. By contrast, if differences between an LLD child and peers on an immediate naming task were eliminated by the delay condition, then intervention might focus on semantic organization and access (see German, chap. 12, for additional information on word finding intervention).

Another example of how tasks can be varied was presented earlier under the discussion of mental models and working memory. The grid in Figure 13–1 schematizes the ease with which mental models underlying performance on a task can be constructed and held in mind. It considers the interaction between the complexity of the model and the ease with which the information necessary to construct the model can be brought to awareness. Assessment tasks could be designed that fall in various quadrants of this grid. For example, tasks involving the retelling of a familiar story or narrating a scripted event may have been so well practiced that the underlying models are easy to construct, even though they may have a rather complex structure. In contrast, retelling a new story or relating a novel event could involve a model of similar complexity but be more difficult to construct because the information cannot be easily accessed from LTM. The tasks where mental models would appear to use the least resources (those in the lower left quadrant) are those for which the child must name an object or express a simple relation with contextual support. If all other factors are equal (e.g., familiarity, affect, social pressures, linguistic complexity), one would expect better performance on tasks that fall to the left of the figure than on the right, and for those closer to the bottom than the top. By varying tasks, diagnosticians and teachers may be able to better understand the degree to which a child's problems are related to language knowledge or model construction and what factors influence expression of those mental models. Holding constant the ease with which mental models can be constructed and varying the load for other processing operations will help us understand the interactions among factors that compete for the limited processing capacity in a particular child.

Assessment of a child's best and worst performance might also reveal information about a child's language knowledge. Concepts such as productivity and achievement are useful in distinguishing various levels of knowledge (see Bloom & Lahey, 1978; Lahey, 1988, for further discussion). Productivity implies the child has some limited knowledge, such as of the interactions of content–form–use in language. Productivity in language has often been inferred when three to five different examples of a behavior are observed in different contexts (e.g., Bloom, 1970; Bloom & Lahey, 1978; Lahey, 1988). By contrast, achievement of a content–form–use interaction implies a more established knowledge and is often inferred when a behavior is observed in 80% to 90% of obligatory contexts (e.g., Brown, 1973; Bloom & Lahey, 1978; Lahey, 1988). Only stressed conditions will give evidence of how automatic that knowledge is. Perceptual processing and motor planning and execution also need to be evaluated. Many measures are in place for evaluating a child's ability to process stimuli, usually under distorted conditions (see, e.g., Keith, 1984). If a child is slower or less accurate than peers on such tasks, one does not have to assume that the child has a perceptual deficit, because familiarity with the stimuli as well as other factors will influence such performance (e.g., Lahey, 1988; Vellutino et al., 1973). However, one may infer from poor performance that the child is more likely straining available resources for processing such input than peers and that stressed conditions could influence that child's language performance. Likewise, measures of rate of articulation or of initiation of motor responses suggest greater use of resources for motor production (with the same caveat as previously).

Emotional factors may be a bit more difficult to manipulate. Social contexts, however, can be varied after discussion with the child and those who know the child. For most children, some interpersonal interactions are more threatening than others. Communication with peers they are trying to impress or who have made fun of them may demand more resources than communication with siblings, younger children, or friends. Furthermore, some contexts are more demanding than others. In contexts where children presume they are being evaluated (e.g., diagnostic sessions or presentations in front of peers), they may pay more attention to the content and form of communication than they do in casual conversations with one or two friends. Information from other professionals and reports as well as direct observations of the child in a number of social contexts could be informative in planning contexts that would exemplify varying pressures for a particular child. When observing the larger social contexts, one might apply Silliman and Wilkinson's "wide-angle" lens (as described in chap. 6).

The important point relative to the information processing perspective presented here is that each child may have some unique complex of factors that interferes with language performance. Whereas researchers tend to look for commonalities among LLD children, clinicians and educators must realize that most group findings are only hypotheses for what to expect in a particular child. Statistically significant findings for a group are not necessarily relevant to any one child. Rather, it is important to examine which factors might be competing for resources in working memory and, therefore, be influencing the level of language performance that is observed in each child.

Intervention. The notion of language being processed by a limited capacity processor suggests that one should be constantly aware of the load being placed on working memory during teaching and intervention sessions. When attempting to facilitate new behaviors, one wants to lighten the use of resources for other behaviors. For example, in teaching a child to write stories, clinicians might consider conditions of low social stress, familiar lexicon, mental models that are easy to construct and not too complex, and use of simple syntactic constructions. Over time, each of these could be independently varied, so eventually the child has practice in more difficult conditions. One might work with descriptions or scripted events and practice these before asking the child to produce plots (i.e., causal chains). When the child is ready to relate less familiar events from LTM, one could at first provide appropriate contextual and linguistic cues to ease access. If accessing knowledge from LTM is often a major problem for a child, the clinician can work on ways to ease that burden, including semantic mapping and the traditional techniques involved in improving semantic organization. Learning new syntactic structures should involve familiar lexical items and those with simple phonological form. When beginning work on inferences or developing reasoning skills, one would use familiar content. Several sequences for written language are described in greater detail by Scott (chap. 8).

Furthermore, language specialists may want to watch how they set the climate for classroom and individual learning. Often, clinicians and educators tend to present and encourage a high level of affect during our sessions to keep the child engaged. Given the suggestion that affective expression uses resources that could be allocated to expression with language, one may need to rethink this style for some children. This is not to say that teachers need to bore them but that they need to allow children more time in a neutral reflective affect when presenting new material. In particular, facilitation of new types of expression or interpretation of language may be more successful with expression of neutral affect.

When the search for lexical and syntactic structures is more automatic, fewer resources are needed for expression and interpretation. Automatization comes from the repetitive use of content–form–use interactions. When clinicians are tempted to move too quickly with the goals of intervention (perhaps because the child seems able to perform in some contexts), they may want to reconsider the resources the child needs in order to use this new knowledge. One argument for following a developmental sequence in setting goals of intervention (e.g., Lahey, 1988) (rather than teaching the skills that are age appropriate) is the need for a degree of practice at earlier levels before some aspects of later levels can be expected. For example, the child who can produce only narratives with additive chains (i.e., sequences of clauses without any sequential or causal relations) may need some practice at this level and with sequential relations before producing the traditional plot narrative, even though the child might be eight or ten years of age.

SUMMARY

Variation in performance among LLD children and within the performance of individual LLD children from time to time is common. Differences in performance observed in LLD children have important implications for both identification and planning goals of intervention. An information processing perspective involving a limited capacity system provides a means of looking at some of the possible sources of variation in a child's performance. One of the processing factors considered was the need to construct and hold in mind the mental models that underlie intentional performance. These models are mental representations in consciousness and were differentiated from representations in LTM. Factors influencing the ease with which they are constructed and held in mind were discussed. Such activity uses some of the limited resources of working memory. In addition, some of the other processes that use the limited resources of working memory were considered, including accessing linguistic knowledge, processing perceptual input, motor programming and execution, and social-emotional factors. Task analysis of the factors that may be competing for working memory may be helpful in planning intervention with LLD children. Some examples of how contexts could be varied to examine the influence of different factors (as a type of task analysis) were presented. Furthermore, some suggestions for taking account of the limited resources in working memory during teaching were discussed.

REFERENCES

Abbeduto, L. (1987). Syntactic, semantic, and rhythmic influences on children's and adults' motor programming of speech. *Journal of Psycholinguistic Research*, *16*(3), 201–221.

Applebee, N. (1978). *The child's concept of story.* Chicago: University of Chicago Press.

Baddeley, A. (1986). *Working memory.* Oxford: Clarendon Press.

Baddeley, A., & Hitch, G. J. (1974). Working memory. In G. Bower (Ed.), *Recent advances in learning and motivation* (Vol. 3, pp. 47–90). New York: Academic Press.

Bartlett, E. (1982). *Anaphoric reference in written narratives of good and poor elementary school writers.* Unpublished manuscript, New York University Medical Center, New York.

Bloom, L. (1970). *Language development: Form and function in emerging grammars.* Cambridge, MA: MIT Press.

Bloom, L. (1974). Talking, understanding and thinking: Developmental relationship between receptive and expressive language. In R. Schiefelbusch & L. Lloyd (Eds.), *Language perspectives—Acquisition, retardation, and intervention* (pp. 285–312). Baltimore: University Park Press.

Bloom, L. (1991). Representation and expression. In N. Krasnegor, D. Rumbaugh, & M. Studdert-Kennedy (Eds.), *Biobehavioral foundations for language development.* Hillsdale, NJ: Lawrence Erlbaum.

Bloom, L. (1993). *The transition from infancy to language: Acquiring the power of expression.* Cambridge, UK: Cambridge University Press.

Bloom, L., & Beckwith, R. (1986). *Intentionality and language development.* Unpublished manuscript, Columbia University, Teachers College, New York.

Bloom, L., & Beckwith, R. (1989). Talking with feeling: Integrating affective and linguistic expression. *Cognition and Emotion, 3,* 313–342.

Bloom, L., Beckwith, R., Capatides, J., & Hafitz, J. (1988). Expression through affect and words in the transition from infancy to language. In P. Baltes, D. Featherman, & R. Lerner (Eds.), *Life-span development and behavior* (Vol. 8, pp. 99–127). Hillsdale, NJ: Lawrence Erlbaum.

Bloom, L., & Lahey, M. (1978). *Language development and language disorders.* New York: Wiley.

Bloom, L., Lahey, M., Hood, L., Lifter, K., & Feiss, K. (1980). Complex sentences: Acquisition of syntactic connectives and the semantic relations they encode. *Journal of Child Language, 7,* 235–261.

Bloom, L., Lifter, K., & Hafitz, J. (1980). Semantics of verbs and the development of verb inflection in child language. *Language, 56,* 386–412.

Bloom, L., Merkin, S., & Wooten, J. (1982). Wh-questions: Linguistic evidence to explain the sequence of acquisition. *Child Development, 53,* 1084–1092.

Bloom, L., Miller, P., & Hood, L. (1975). Variation and reduction as aspects of competence in language development. In A. Pick (Ed.), *Minnesota symposia on child psychology* (Vol. 9, pp. 3–55). Minneapolis: University of Minnesota Press.

Bloom, L., Rocissano, L., & Hood, L. (1976). Adult–child discourse: Developmental interaction between information processing and linguistic knowledge. *Cognitive Psychology, 8,* 521–552.

Botvin, G. J., & Sutton-Smith, B. (1977). The development of structural complexity in children's fantasy narratives. *Developmental Psychology, 13,* 377–388.

Bransford, J. D., Barclay, J. R., & Franks, J. J. (1972). Sentence memory: A constructive versus interpretive approach. *Cognitive Psychology, 3,* 193–209.

Brown, R. (1973). *A first language, the early stages.* Cambridge, MA: Harvard University Press.

Case, R. (1985). *Intellectual development: Birth to adulthood.* New York: Academic Press.

Case, R., Kurland, D. M., & Goldberg, J. (1982). Operational efficiency and the growth of long term memory span. *Journal of Experimental Child Psychology, 33,* 386–404.

Catts, H. P. H. (1989). Speech production deficits in developmental dyslexia. *Journal of Speech and Hearing Disorders, 54,* 422–428.

Cirrin, F. M. (1983). Lexical access in children and adults. *Developmental Psychology, 19*(3), 452–460.

Denckla, M. B. (1974). Rapid 'automatized' naming of pictured objects, colors, letters and numbers by normal children. *Cortex, 10,* 186–202.

Dell, G. S. (1986). A spreading activation theory of retrieval in sentence production. *Psychology Review, 93,* 283–321.

Dinsmore, J. (1987). Mental spaces from a functional perspective. *Cognitive Science, 11,* 1–21.

Edwards, J., & Lahey, M. (in press). Auditory lexical decisions in children and adults: An examination of response factors. *Journal of Speech and Hearing Research.*

Fauconnier, G. (1985). *Mental spaces: Aspects of meaning construction in natural language.* Cambridge, MA: MIT Press.

Ferguson, C., & Farwell, C. B. (1975). Words and sounds in early language acquisition. *Language, 51,* 419–439.

Ferguson, C., Peizer, D., & Weeks, T. (1973). Model-and-replica phonological grammar of a child's first words. *Lingua, 31,* 35–39.

Hulme, C., Thomson, N., Muir, C., & Lawrence, A. (1984). Speech rate and the development of short-term memory span. *Journal of Experimental Child Psychology, 38,* 241–253.

Huttenlocher, J., & Burke, D. (1976). Why does memory span increase with age? *Cognitive Psychology, 8,* 1–31.

Ingram, D. (1976). *Phonological disability in children.* New York: Elsevier.

Johnston, J. (1982). The language disordered child. In N. J. Lass, L. McReynolds, J. Northern, & D. Yoder (Eds.), *Speech, language, and hearing: Vol. 2. Pathologies of speech and language*. Philadelphia: W. B. Saunders.

Johnson-Laird, P. N. (1983). *Mental models.* Cambridge, MA: Harvard University Press.

Kahneman, D. (1973). *Attention and effort.* Englewood Cliffs, NJ: Prentice-Hall.

Kamhi, A., Catts, H., Mauer, D., Apel, K., & Gentry, B. (1988). Phonological and spatial processing abilities in language- and reading-impaired children. *Journal of Speech and Hearing Disorders, 53,* 316–327.

Keith, R. (1984). Central auditory dysfunction: A language disorder? *Topics in Language Disorders, 4,* 48–56.

Kemper, S. (1990). Adult's diaries: Changes made to written narratives across the life span. *Discourse Processes, 13,* 207–223.

Labov, W. (1972). *Language in the inner city.* Philadelphia: University of Pennsylvania Press.

Lahey, M. (1984). The dissolution of text in written language: Evidence toward a continuum of complexity. *Discourse Processes, 7,* 419–445.

Lahey, M. (1988). *Language disorders and language development.* New York: Macmillan.

Lahey, M. (1992). Linguistic and cultural diversity: Further problems for determining "Who shall be called language disordered." *Journal of Speech and Hearing Research, 35,* 638–639.

Lahey, M., & Edwards, J. (1991). *Response factors in confrontation naming of children and adults.* Paper presented at the annual meeting of the American Speech-Language-Hearing Association, Atlanta, Georgia.

Lahey, M., Flax, J., & Schlisselberg, G. (1985). A preliminary investigation of reduplication in children with specific language impairment. *Journal of Speech and Hearing Disorders, 50,* 186–194.

Lahey, M., & Launer, P. (1986). *Unraveled yarns: Narrative development in children.* Paper presented at the meeting of the California Speech-Language-Hearing Association, Monterey, CA.

Leonard, L. (1987). Is specific language impairment a useful construct? In S. Rosenberg (Ed.), *Advances in applied psycholinguistics, Volume 1: Disorders of first language development* (pp. 1–39). New York: Cambridge University Press.

Leonard, L., Nippold, M., Kail, R., & Hale, C. (1983). Picture naming in language impaired children. *Journal of Speech and Hearing Research, 26,* 609–615.

Leonard, L., Schwartz, R., Chapman, K., Rowan, L., Prelock, P., Terrell, B., Weiss, A., & Messick, C. (1982). Early lexical acquisition in children with specific language impairment. *Journal of Speech and Hearing Research, 25,* 554–559.

Lifter, K., & Bloom, L. (1989). Object play and the emergence of language. *Infant Behavior and Development, 12,* 395–423.

McLachlin, B., & Chapman, R. (1988). Communication breakdowns in normal and language learning-disabled children's conversation and narration. *Journal of Speech and Hearing Disorders, 53,* 2–7.

McClelland, J. L., & Rumelhart, D. E. (1985). Distributed memory and the representation of general and specific information. *Journal of Experimental Psychology: General, 114,* 159–188.

Menyuk, P., Chesnick, M., Liebergott, J. W., Korngold, B., D'Agostino, R., & Belanger, A. (1991). Predicting reading problems in at-risk children. *Journal of Speech and Hearing Research, 34,* 893–904.

Menyuk, P., & Menn, L. (1979). Early strategies for the perception and production of words and sounds. In P. Fletcher & M. Garman (Eds.), *Language acquisition* (pp. 49–70). Cambridge, U.K.: Cambridge University Press.

Miller, G., Galanter, E., & Pribram, K. (1960). *Plans and the structure of behavior.* New York: Holt-Dryden.

Pascual-Leone, J. A. (1970). A mathematical model for the transition rule in Piaget's developmental stages. *Acta Psychologica, 32,* 301–345.

Peterson, C., & McCabe, A. (1983). *Developmental psycholinguistics: Three ways of looking at a child's narrative.* New York: Plenum Press.

Schwartz, R., & Leonard, L. (1982). Do children pick and choose? Phonological selection and avoidance in early lexical acquisition. *Journal of Child Language, 9,* 319–336.

Schwartz, R., Leonard, L., Folger, M., & Wilcox, M. J. (1980). Early phonological behavior in normal-speaking and language disordered children: Evidence for a synergistic view of linguistic disorders. *Journal of Speech and Hearing Disorders, 45,* 357–377.

Searle, J. (1983). *Intentionality: An essay in the philosophy of the mind.* Cambridge, U.K.: Cambridge University Press.

Seymour, H. (1992). The invisible children: A reply to Lahey's perspective. *Journal of Speech and Hearing Research, 35,* 640–641.

Shallice, T. (1982). Specific impairments of planning. *Philosophical Transactions of the Royal Society London B, 298,* 199–209.

Shankweiler, D., & Liberman, I. (1976). Exploring the relations between reading and speech. In R. Knights & D. Bakker (Eds.), *The neuropsychology of learning disorders: Theoretical approaches.* Baltimore: University Park Press.

Slobin, D. J. (1973). Cognitive prerequisites for the development of grammar. In C. Ferguson & D. Slobin (Eds.), *Studies of child language development* (pp. 175–208). New York: Holt, Rinehart & Winston.

Spring, C. (1976). Encoding speed and memory span in dyslexic children. *Journal of Special Education, 10,* 35–40.

Sutton-Smith, B. (1981). *The folkstories of children.* Philadelphia: University of Pennsylvania Press.

Trabasso, T., Stein, N. L., Rodkin, P. C., Munger, M. P., & Baughn, C. R. (1992). Knowledge of goals and plans in the on-line narration of events. *Cognitive Development, 7,* 133–170.

Vellutino, F. R., Pruzek, R., Steger, J. A., & Meshoulam, U. (1973). Immediate visual recall in poor and normal readers as a function of orthographic-linguistic familiarity. *Cortex, 9,* 368–384.

Waterson, N. (1978). Growth of complexity in phonological development. In C. Waterson & C. Snow (Eds.), *The development of communication.* Chichester, U.K.: Wiley.

Wing, C. S. (1990). A preliminary investigation of generalization to untrained words following two treatments of children's word-finding problems. *Language, Speech, and Hearing Services in Schools, 21,* 151–156.

Wolf, M. (1982). The word retrieval process and reading in children and aphasics. In K. Nelson (Ed.), *Children's language* (Vol. 3, pp. 437–493). New York: Gardner.

Wolf, P. H., Michel, G. R., & Ovrut, M. (1990). Thi timing os syllable repetitions in developmental dyslexia. *Journal of Speech and Hearing Research, 33,* 281–289.

14

AUDITORY LINGUISTIC PROCESSING AND LANGUAGE LEARNING

■ Sandy Friel-Patti
University of Texas at Dallas

It has been more than twenty years since Norma Rees questioned the contribution of auditory processing factors in language and learning disorders. Rees observed that auditory processing failures were often described as contributing to language disorders in children or adults despite the "relatively limited and weak evidence for such a factor and the inconsistency of this conclusion with current findings in speech perception research" (Rees, 1973, p. 304). The term *auditory processing disorders* lingers in the diagnostic vocabulary of many speech-language pathologists, audiologists, and educators today, even though it continues to be controversial. Auditory processing deficits generally refer to difficulties processing the speech signal in the absence of any permanent peripheral hearing loss, although conductive hearing losses are sometimes thought to be a contributing factor. Much as Rees described in 1973, clinicians and teachers persist in the conviction that such problems are causally linked to language learning and academic difficulties. For most educators, the term *auditory processing problems* is used to describe children who "do not follow directions," who "are not listening," or who seem unable to learn information presented to them auditorially. Much of what happens in a classroom depends on information given orally, and so students who are having difficulty learning auditorially will not achieve much academic success. Teachers often make homework assignments or explain requirements on a particular aspect of the assignment orally; teachers dictate planned and unannounced quizzes to the class; and students give oral presentations of special projects. Certainly, a frequently occurring classroom learning opportunity occurs during question and answer sequences between teachers and students in which clarification of specific information may be critical. In situations such as these, children described as having auditory processing problems are likely to experience distress and possible failure. Because of the potential for interference with classroom success, it is not surprising that concern with auditory processing problems endures.

Evidence gathered over the years has generated confusion about the role of auditory processing factors in language development and disorders. Confusion, in part, is undoubtedly due to the interdisciplinary nature of auditory processing; several disciplines are trying to understand auditory processing disorders from entirely different viewpoints—speech-language pathology, audiology, education, and speech perception (Katz, Stecker, & Henderson, 1992), and these viewpoints have, as yet, not converged. Additionally, special educators and learning disabilities teachers have also become involved, and they bring the perspective of learning differences and special needs to the topic. Misunderstanding arises from differences in meaning when using the same terminology to refer to distinct aspects and levels of speech and language. For example, the assumption that there is a set of subskills that can be identified, measured, and remediated may cause some misconceptions (Keith, 1988; Lahey & Bloom, chap. 13; Rees, 1981). Likewise, failure to recognize the metalinguistic nature of many auditory processing tasks leads to confusion (van Kleeck, chap. 3). Finally and most importantly, the absence of a coherent theory addressing the contribution of auditory processing to language acquisition as well as accounting for difficulties experienced by some language impaired children clearly impairs advancement in this area (Rees, 1973; Rees, 1981).

This chapter reviews several recurring themes of the past two decades regarding the role of auditory processing in language acquisition and disorders. The specific focus of how auditory processing may or may not be a contributor to language learning disabilities in school-age children is achieved in the following ways: (1) reexamination of some fundamental assumptions of current language acquisition theories; (2) examination of recent thinking about speech perception, auditory processing, and language comprehension; and (3) consideration of the ways these issues affect children with language learning differences. The first part of the chapter reviews the broad theoretical framework of language acquisition with particular attention given to the ways in which theoretical assumptions alter interpretation of the role of auditory processing in language development. The next part examines recent thinking about speech perception, auditory processing, and language comprehension. The final section concludes with a discussion of educational principles derived from these issues for learning disabled school-age children. This topic is a critical addition to a text on language, literacy, and academic success because listening, speaking, reading, writing, and spelling are all common processes and interrelated systems that develop through complex social interactions beginning in infancy (Westby, 1990). Difficulty with auditory processing/listening has the potential to pervade all aspects of classroom performance, and so it is important to examine this issue closely.

THEORETICAL FRAMEWORK FOR LANGUAGE ACQUISITION

Although professionals are well versed in theories of language acquisition, these theories are presented here briefly because assumptions about disability models and related intervention programs typically mirror a prevailing theoretical framework. Indeed, commitment to theory is fundamental for building effective and efficient intervention programs (Fey, 1986). Johnston describes theories as "vital tools in our therapeutic enterprise because they make us more creative and flexible clinicians" (1983, p. 56). Even the words used to describe the intervention process often disclose a theoretical bias: clinicians who portray their role as one of *language facilitator* are fundamentally different from those who are concerned with *teaching children to talk.* Whether or not they are acknowledged, such differences in theoretical underpinnings alter treatment options. In this section, some of the assumptions of current theories of language acquisition are considered.

Advances in understanding how children use and comprehend language are abundant since the early work of Roger Brown and colleagues on Adam, Eve, and Sarah (Brown, 1973, 1988). Unfortunately, the development of a unified theory to account for the array of findings has not kept pace with the accumulation of facts (Bohannon, 1993). Proposed theories of language acquisition can be broadly classified as reflecting assumptions about nativist endowment for language, the role of environmental input, and interactionist accounts that view children and their language environments as interdependent dynamic systems. In this section, the major tenets of each of these theoretical positions of language acquisition are reviewed, and several key studies from this literature are cited. This discussion "sets the stage" for following sections, specifically examining the literature on speech perception, auditory processing, and language comprehension.

The Nativist Position

Theorists adhering to the nativist position believe that the language system is innate because it is too complex and is acquired in too short a period of time to be anything other than genetically based. Followers of this position also maintain that language is a species-specific behavior. Arguments offered in support of this view include the observation that patterns of language development are similar across different languages. The Language Acquisition Device (LAD) is suggested as a type of language processor that offers children enough inborn knowledge of language universals to provide them with the capacity to speak any language (Bohannon, 1993; Chomsky, 1965, 1979; McNeill, 1970). Although the exact nature of the LAD is still a matter of great debate, the LAD is assumed to be a physiological part of the brain that is a specialized language processor. The nativist approach limits the role of the environment to one that merely triggers the maturation of the LAD. As such, the LAD sets the parameters for the specific language(s) being acquired and, consequently, environment has minimal impact on the maturation of language.

Specification of the LAD originally focused on linguistic universals with which children are innately equipped. The language learning child is seen as an active learner, well endowed with a predisposition for organizing and analyzing information leading to linguistic rule discovery. This predisposition is thought to be based on some kind of biological structures presumably shared by all normally developing members of the species (Bates, Bretherton, & Snyder, 1988; Bickerton, 1990). Slobin describes the child's natural linguistic tendencies as "operating principles" that function to facilitate the acquisition of grammar. These operating principles aid the child in decoding the relations between what is said (surface structure) and the underlying meaning (deep structure) (Slobin, 1979).

Recent interest in the language faculty involves the notion of modularity. Fodor argues that when a class of signals is important for survival of a species, then the neural analysis of these signals may be modularized. To serve the survival function, the module must be fast acting and error free (Hoffman, Schuckers, & Daniloff, 1989). Modularity for language is generally defined as an informationally encapsulated computational input system consisting of identifiable mechanisms for perceiving and learning a language. Fodor describes these input systems as "hardwired," autonomous, domain specific, and innately specified (Fodor, 1983). According to Fodor, the essence of modularity is in the informational encapsulation of the input systems. In other words, for all the information that might be important in a particular perceptual analysis, only a small portion of that information is considered. Thus, informationally encapsulated input systems achieve speed of processing because they ignore much of the input data. So, for example, the comprehension of a particular utterance involves analyses at several levels of representation including phonetic, phonological, lexical, syntactic, and so forth. The result of the analysis at one level potentially impacts analyses at any of the other levels: that is, feedback from higher level analyses may affect lower level analyses and vice-versa. In addition, understanding the utterance is affected by the listener's judgment of the speaker's intention (i.e., speech act) and the discourse context in which the utterance occurs. Fodor argues that, of all of the information that might bear on a perceptual analysis, only a portion of it is actually considered. This idea is familiar to educators and clinicians as top–down and bottom–up information processing. Consider the example of a student in a busy classroom trying to participate in a small group discussion about Greek mythology. For much of the discussion, the student can ignore or suppress phonetic input because she readily understands what is said through reliance on higher level analyses. The topic itself, however, involves unfamiliar vocabulary and unusual names that may necessitate phonetic analyses of the input stimulus because perception of novel input often depends on such bottom–up analyses.

Others have presented similar arguments in favor of hard-wired perceptual and linguistic modules. For example, Gardner (1983) uses the modularity thesis to explicate his theory of multiple intelligences. Gardner argues for submodules within the language processor and describes the phonological and syntactic processes as special, species specific, and unfolding with relatively little environmental influence; semantic and pragmatics aspects of language are thought to arise from more general information processing mechanisms (Gardner, 1983). Bickerton proposes a language bioprogram hypothesis suggesting that the infrastructure of language is specified as "a series of highly modular task-specific cognitive devices interacting with an equally modular and task-specific processing component which imposes a formal structure on the output of the learner" (1984, p. 187). Bickerton agrees with Chomsky's model of Universal Grammar (Chomsky, 1980) specifying the tacit knowledge of linguistic structure that humans are presumed to have before experience. The Universal Grammar is a set of parameters, and each parameter has a limited number of possible settings; various combinations of these settings, then, are thought to yield all possible core grammars of native language. Young children are said to have these possible grammars latent in their minds, and Bickerton's "bioprogram grammar would simply constitute the list of preferred settings that the child, in the absence of contrary evidence, would assume to be appropriate" (Bickerton, 1984, p. 178). In other words, the bioprogram grammar can be converted to the grammar of any language. While the Universal Grammar suggests that all possible core grammars are latent in the child's mind, various parameters are free to be set by the child's experiences with specific language(s). Bickerton theorizes that the role of the bioprogram is to supply early forms and structures from which children, guided by the input from the target language, can develop more complex forms and structures.

In summary, the main features of the nativist position are that language is species specific, innately endowed, and largely independent of environmental influence other than to set the parameters of the language(s) being acquired. Some form of a physiologically based LAD is presumed to exist, and adherents of the nativist position posit that the environment triggers its maturation. The nativist position presents certain practical concerns for educators and interventionists because of the diminished role of the environment. If one assumes a nativist position, then the feasibility of intervention to facilitate language learning becomes doubtful.

Environmental Input Account

In its most stringent form, the environmental input position affirms that language development is a process of linking environmental stimuli to internal responses and linking the internal responses to overt verbal behavior. Thus, there is a progression from early random vocal behavior to mature communication through both classic and operant conditioning (Bohannon, 1993). In this view, receptive vocabulary is believed to develop through classic conditioning, whereas operant conditioning is seen as responsible for the development of productive speech (Moerk, 1983). Care givers are assumed to "teach" language to their children by providing a model, encouraging imitation, and offering reinforcement for successful imitations. Vocabulary is taught in context-sensitive interactions that are highly referential so that children learn the word *milk* in the presence of milk and the word *dog* in the presence of dogs (Bohannon, 1993). Adherents of this position posit that language develops as a result of training, imitation, and rewards and not because of maturation. Behaviorists typically do not credit children with rule discovery; rather, environmental stimuli are thought to elicit certain responses from the child, and these are directly shaped by contingencies.

Imitation plays an important role in the behaviorist explanation of how children develop increasingly sophisticated language skill. Imitation may be exact or partial, immediate, or delayed; imitation has also been extended to include vicarious experience so that observation of another being rewarded or punished is sufficient for learning without direct consequence to the observer. Whitehurst and colleagues (Whitehurst & Novak, 1973; Whitehurst & Vasta, 1975) have suggested that children acquire grammatical forms from imitation of adult models and that these forms become increasingly complex through a series of successive approximations and shaping of the child's verbal behavior by parents and peers. This view of learning through imitation is a bit more restricted than the kinds of imitation, practice, and scaffolding described by Silliman and Wilkinson (chap. 2) and Palincsar, Brown, and Campione (chap. 5).

The principal features of the environmental input, or behaviorist, account of language acquisition can be summarized as follows: (1) Classical and operant conditioning are responsible for the acquisition of receptive and expressive language. (2) Language is "taught" to children through exposure to adult models, encouragement to imitate, and reinforcement of successive approximations. (3) The sequence of acquisition is determined by salient environmental stimuli and by the child's experience with the stimuli (Bohannon, 1993). In sum, the environmental input account puts all of the emphasis on the environment rather than on biologically endowed innate mechanisms for learning language. Although it was once a popular explanation for language learning, few currently adhere strictly to the environmental input account because the assumption that language is just another behavior that can be shaped through successive approximations and carefully administered reinforcement is questionable. While there does seem to be a role for principles of learning such as imitation and reinforcement, general learning theory does not account for most of what happens as children learn language.

Interactionist Position

Within the interactionist position of language acquisition, descriptions of the complementary interaction between innate capacities and environmental forces replace dichotomized discussions of the nature–nurture controversy. Current interactionist theories of language acquisition acknowledge the biological endowment that makes language possible and that language is a species-unique system (Berko Gleason, 1993); interactionists also credit the role of the environment for producing linguistic structures. Adherents believe the structure of native language is influenced by social-communicative functions of language in social interactions (Bates & MacWhinney, 1982; Bohannon, 1993; Nelson, chap. 4; Palincsar et al., chap. 5). Bates and her colleagues describe the acquisition path through the structural possibilities of natural languages in the following way:

> Hence language acquisition can be viewed as a process of setting successive parameters and living with their preordained consequences. . . . Biology provides the universal parameters; language input triggers a set of constrained choices within that pool of possibilities. (p. 6)

Proponents of the interactionist theory believe that language development is affected by cognitive, social, linguistic, and biological factors; conversely, the process of language acquisition itself modifies these domains of development. In contrast to the explicit bias of vertical boundaries within the language faculty espoused by Fodor (Fodor, 1983), Bates and colleagues (Bates, et al., 1988) have argued for horizontal modules "i.e., component processes that language shares with other aspects of cognition, and processes that grammar shares with phonology, lexical semantics, and pragmatics" (p. 27). Whether the language processor can be characterized as a vertical or a horizontal module and which view offers the better account of the empirical support is still open for considerable debate (Bates, et al., 1988; Liberman, 1992; Liberman & Mattingly, 1985, 1989).

Interactionists are represented by three different perspectives: (1) the Piagetian cognitive approach, (2) the social interactionist approach, and (3) the information processing approach (Bohannon, 1993). Within the Piagetian cognitive approach, language is not considered a separate innate characteristic but is rather thought to be one sort of a general set of cognitive abilities. Piaget theorized that children are biologically driven to adapt to their environment through complementary processes of accommodation and assimilation. Adaptation involves cognitive organization of experience including auditory experience with language; as such, then, language is subsumed under general cognitive development. The desire to specify the relations between cognitive and language development has spawned many investigations. For example, researchers attempting to explicate the mapping of semantic meanings and pragmatic intentions onto language forms have found strong associations between certain cognitive and linguistic achievements (Bates, Benigni, Bretherton, Camaioni, & Volterra, 1977, 1979; Bates et al., 1988; Gopnik & Meltzoff, 1986, 1987). A growing body of findings confirms the correlational hypothesis; that is, specific cognitive achievements correlate with linguistic milestones rather than reflect a causal relationship between cognition and language (Bohannon, 1993; Kamhi, 1992; see van Kleeck, chap. 3, for additional information).

The social interactionists' perspective is a compromise between the two extremes of the nativist and behavioral positions. Like behaviorists, the social interactionists believe the environment plays an important role in producing language structure. Further, they depict, as do several authors of this text, a bidirectional, dynamic interaction between children and their language environments. Like the nativists, they recognize that language is physiologically based and species specific. Interactionists also agree that emergence of some language abilities depends on physiological maturation. Children learn increasingly complex grammatical structures because they have a need to understand and be understood (Brown, 1973, 1977); in this view, language structure is intimately tied to social-communicative functions. Hence, "the innate linguistic predispositions must interact with the environment in order to mature" (Bohannon, 1993, p. 274).

The information processing paradigm assumes that human information processing can be described as a mechanism that encodes and interprets environmental stimuli, stores representations of the stimuli in memory, and permits recall of the information stored (see also Lahey & Bloom, chap. 13). One model of information processing is a parallel-distributed processing (PDP) model of cognition proposed by Rumelhart, McClelland, and the PDP Research Group (Rumelhart, McClelland, & Group, 1986). In this model, knowledge is organized into overlapping processing levels that include, for example, phonemes, syllables, words, propositions, concepts, and meaning. The organization of knowledge in such models is said to be *distributed* because the information exists as a network of relationships among units; it is described as *parallel* because it happens simultaneously at all levels (Hoffman et al., 1989). The processing units at one level exist as connection strengths among more basic levels; they are also connected to higher levels. Thus, the organization of knowledge is interconnected within a particular level and among the other levels. There remains considerable debate surrounding specification of the nature of the communication and integration process among the various components, as Lahey and Bloom also note in Chapter 13. However, a primary assumption is that experience with linguistic evidence from the environment causes changes within processing mechanisms (Nelson, 1993).

One parallel-distributed processing model is the competition model, proposed by Bates and MacWhinney (Bates & MacWhinney, 1987; MacWhinney, 1987). This model delimits a set of processing mechanisms that, at given points in development, can be linked to individual differences in language learning among children. The competition model predicts that children learn from exemplars of speech so that those forms addressed to them most frequently will be among the first learned. Similarly, cues that consistently signal certain meanings will be learned first. The rate at which a specific form is learned is determined by the relationship between form and function in the language and by the manner in which these forms are presented to children. The competition model, therefore, predicts learning based on input with a parallel-distributed processor/learning mechanism as the only innate component posited (Bohannon, 1993). The success of the competition model remains to be demonstrated empirically. Bates and MacWhinney (1987), however, report that results of analyses of several target cues across a number of languages support these predictions. The order of acquisition of language forms is cued by the function of the form itself such that forms that consistently serve the same function are learned first, even if they occur less often in the input. For example, Turkish has an extremely reliable case marking system, and even though word order is often considered an initial strategy, Turkish children learn case marking sooner than they do word order (Slobin & Bever, 1982).

To summarize, the primary components of the interactionist position include (1) acknowledgment of a biological endowment for language learning, (2) recognition of the role of the environment in producing linguistic structures, and (3) affirmation of the influence of social-communicative functions of language in social interactions. Information processing models are examples of the interactionist position because they assume an innate processing mechanism to encode and interpret environmental input, store representations in memory, and recall information stored. The interactionist position is especially intriguing for educators and clinicians because of the balanced emphasis on both physiologically based language processor and environmental input. Within this framework, innate linguistic predispositions interact with the environment and social-communicative functions play an important role in the development of language abilities.

Thus far, this chapter has considered several theories of language acquisition. In particular, it focused readers' attention on the respective role of the environmental input and innately endowed language processor. Speech-language clinicians and educators need to understand the basic assumptions of each of the theories presented as they have an impact on educational practice and intervention planning. Table 14–1 provides a summary of the theories and the assumptions associated with each.

At the heart of the issue of how auditory processing interfaces with language acquisition is the theoretical position one assumes regarding the innateness of language. The interactionist position recognizes the complimentary interaction between innate capacities and environmental input. Because it reflects best what occurs as children learn to talk, this position is the most viable. The environmental input, or behaviorist, model neglects the overwhelming evidence that there are innate neural substrates for language. On the other hand, the nativist position that the child is equipped with some form of a LAD, which is "triggered" by the environment, seems to deny the active role of the child in the development of language. Working from the interactionist perspective, Snow and Tomasello (1989) note that the usability of a particular experience to act as a trigger depends on the child's comprehension and analysis of the situation. That is, before any adult input can act as primary linguistic data for a trigger experience or a parameter-setting mechanism, the child must first derive an appropriate syntactic analysis and real world contextual gloss for the input to be available to the child. How the child goes about accomplishing this uptake hinges on both the cognitive and linguistic developmental stage of the child as well as the social-communicative-interactive context for the use of the adult linguistic forms.

Others have also taken issue with an oversimplified account of parameter setting (Morgan, 1989; Stabler, 1989), because, in so many aspects of language acquisition, children learn by doing. Snow and Tomasello (1989) reject the trigger experience as too limited to reflect accurately the developmental evidence; rather, they propose that Keith Nelson's (1987) rare event model may be more appropriate. The rare event, like a trigger, is a single event that occurs at just the right time in development and can cause a significant change in the child's language system. Snow and Tomasello point out that the difference between the rare event and the trigger is that Nelson's model gives particular attention to the developmental achievements that are prerequisites to the rare event effect. In this sense, therefore, the cognitive-linguistic and social-interactive accomplishments of the child are critical preconditions for the relevant linguistic change to occur.

The interactionist theory challenges educators and speech-language clinicians to develop ecologically and socially valid learning experiences. In fact, language learning must be considered in a broader sense so that the focus is on developing communicative skills in natural, socially mediated interactions. Teachers and clinicians must find ways to capi-

TABLE 14–1
Summary of language acquisition theories and associated assumptions

Language Acquisition Theory	Assumptions
Nativist Position	1. Language is species specific 2. Language processor is innately endowed 3. Language acquisition device (LAD) 4. Environment sets the parameters of language to be acquired 5. Environment triggers maturation of LAD
Environmental Input Position (Behaviorist)	1. Classic and operant conditioning account for language development 2. Language is "taught" by adult models, imitation, reinforcement 3. Sequence of acquisition determined by salient stimuli and child's experience with stimuli
Interactionist Position	1. Complementary interaction between innate capacities and environment 2. Language is species specific 3. Language processor is innately endowed 4. Language processor may be described with parallel-distributed processing model 5. Bidirectional, dynamic interaction with environmental input is needed for producing linguistic structures 6. Language development affected by cognitive, social, linguistic, and biological factors

talize on alterations in input across different conversational partners so that students have multiple opportunities to process, analyze, and consolidate information. Thus, building on existing knowledge, the child takes an active part in processing the input to construct linguistic rules.

SPEECH PERCEPTION, AUDITORY PROCESSING, AND LANGUAGE COMPREHENSION

Before examining recent thinking about speech perception, auditory processing, and language comprehension, it is important to recall the distinction between *input* and *intake.* Not all experiences that a child has are used as a basis for generalization of learning; similarly, not all the sentences a child hears are used as a basis for language acquisition (Snow & Tomasello, 1989). *Input* refers to all of the language to which a child is exposed, whereas *intake* refers to the child's selective use of the input. Input itself is not what is really important for language acquisition; what is important is what children do with the language they hear all around them. *Intake* (sometimes called *uptake*) refers to whether the child notices, hears, and/or listens to the environmental input; what kind of an interpretation the child places on what is heard; and how this instance of language input can be organized and incorporated into existing linguistic knowledge (Kuczaj, 1982). The basic assumption motivating such a distinction is that even simplified input will not facilitate language learning if children do not attend to the information and organize the regularities. As such, children are active participants who bring a set of organizational strategies that permit them to benefit from adults' facilitating behaviors (Friel-Patti & Conti-Ramsden, 1988).

Recall that nativists limit the role of the environment to one of triggering hard-wired perceptual and linguistic modules. From a nativist perspective, this distinction between input and intake is important only insofar as the input is available as a "trigger experience" for the maturation of the LAD and to set the parameters of the specific language(s) being acquired. Lightfoot (1989) argues that the trigger experience is "a subset of a child's total linguistic experience and hence that much of what a child hears has no consequence for the form of the eventual grammar" (p. 321). On the other hand, adherents of the environmental input theory define linguistic input more specifically as language addressed directly to the language learning child. Contrary to the nativist position that children could not possibly derive the rules of language from the degraded input given, the environmental input theorists believe that the language addressed to young children has certain characteristics that could facilitate language learning (Brown, 1977; McDonald & Pien, 1982; Olsen-Fulero, 1982; Olsen-Fulero & Conforti, 1983; Smolak & Weinraub, 1983; Snow, 1977). Analogously, the interactionists maintain that usability of a particular piece of primary linguistic data (input) depends on the child's understanding of the input (i.e., intake) (Snow & Tomasello, 1989). As such, then, in this view, an innate language processor interfaces with the input given to yield intake/uptake. This distinction regarding the child's use of the input (i.e., intake) contributes an important perspective for appreciating individual differences in language development. Two children in the same (or very similar) linguistic environment such as a classroom may well learn language quite differently because of their own prior linguistic experiences, their processing abilities, and organizing strategies. Similarly, the input will be more or less salient to each one depending on its relevance to world knowledge and cognitive preferences. For example, one student may be quite engrossed in a lesson on mollusks because of prior experience with them and a basic interest in learning about creatures from the sea. This student will likely learn names of mollusks, be able to label body parts, and describe preferred habitat after minimal exposure to the facts. Another student in the same lesson may not even attend closely to the unfamiliar names and descriptions, because such concepts are neither salient nor relevant to him. Teachers intuitively know that not all children learn equally well in every situation. Good instruction therefore requires presentation of information in several formats with repetition of details. In this way, teachers adjust the input to maximize intake. This distinction between input and intake will be returned to after a discussion of the literature on speech perception, auditory processing, and language comprehension.

Speech Perception

Concern with the contrast between input and intake leads one to consider the nature of the input and exactly how children are thought to use it as intake. If an innate language processor does exist, then an obvious question is exactly how does the language processor work and how does this species-specific language learning system "know" universals (Pinker, 1979)? A number of proposals have been offered to suggest ways in which systems are pretuned to universals in phonology and syntax, for example. One such theory holds that the processes that mediate phone recognition must have access to the underlying motor gestures of the vocal tract; in this motor theory of speech perception, "the objects of speech perception are the intended phonetic gestures of the speaker, represented in the brain as invariant motor commands that call for movements of the articulators through certain linguistically significant configurations" (Liberman & Mattingly, 1985, p. 2). In effect, then, the motor theory posits that perception of an utterance is perception of a pattern of intended gestures. Evidence for the motor theory comes from investigations primarily done at Haskins Laboratories and suggests that *auditory perception for the speech signal is distinctive and comes into play only when the acoustic signals are utterances; nonspeech signals are processed differently in an auditory mode* (Liberman, Cooper, Shankweiler, & Studdert-Kennedy, 1967). Thus, the mechanisms involved in the perception of speech differ from those that analyze nonspeech auditory input. This domain specificity of the input analyzer is rather remarkable in that it is inflexible: Listeners simply do not hear speech as noise or noise as speech (Best, Hoffman, & Robson, 1981). In part because stimuli heard as speech are judged meaningful while those heard as noise or nonspeech are judged nonmeaningful, it has been suggested that speech perception is quite different from auditory perception in general.

Recently updated to accommodate new findings, the revised motor theory proposes that phonetic information is perceived in a biologically distinct system that is an informationally encapsulated module specialized to detect intended gestures of the speaker (Liberman & Mattingly, 1985). This phonetic module is not unique; it is part of a large class of modules that are biologically based as special neural structures. Liberman and Mattingly (1985) propose that what they have been referring to as a "phonetic module" could more correctly be called a "linguistic module." Modularity of the motor theory is the same concept presented by Fodor, that is "a piece of neural architecture that performs special computations required to provide central cognitive processes with representations of objects or events belonging to a natural class that is ecologically significant for the organism" (Liberman & Mattingly, 1985, p. 27). Thus, the listener does not just perceive a string of sounds, but rather processes higher levels of syllable structure, morphemic units, syntax, and propositions all simultaneously with the lower level processing of phonemes (Hoffman et al., 1989).

It has long been known that auditory feature analysis is important in speech perception. In a now classic study, Miller and Nicely (1955) demonstrated that when adults listened in conditions of increasing background noise, the errors they made were usually only one feature different from the target sound. Similarly, it is understood that the speech signal is cued by multiple features. Slis and Cohen (1969) showed that more than twelve acoustic features were important for the perception of stop consonants. This redundancy of cues was interpreted as facilitative for listeners who might miss a cue as a result of competing signals or poor attention and still successfully perceive the target sound. Therefore, the listener uses available cues to predict intended phonemes rather than needing all of the cues in the signal produced to achieve perception of the intended phonemes. The more information that is available about sentence structure and content, the more readily the listener can predict the missing unit and "fill in" the unit in noisy conditions (Hoffman et al., 1989; Warren, 1970). It should not be surprising, then, that listeners more accurately predict the missing information at the end of a sentence or in longer sentences.

Another phenomenon should be considered in any attempt to understand the role of auditory cues in speech perception. Differences in vocal tract size and shape from speaker to speaker result in different formant frequencies. Listeners are known to normalize this information to account for the differences in acoustic cues. So, listeners do not depend on absolute acoustic cues, but rather, they accommodate these changes in absolute values by normalizing relative cues (Lieberman & Blumstein, 1988).

Categorical perception for speech has been confirmed in adult listeners for many phonetic features (Liberman et al., 1967). The typical result of such studies demonstrates that the listener's response for two sounds given the same phonetic label is near chance level, whereas discrimination of stimuli labeled differently is nearly perfect (Kuhl, 1979). Of critical importance is that the two speech sounds are heard as different only if the listener can categorize them into two different phoneme classes, that is, label them as two different sounds. Initially thought to be a species-specific ability, categorical perception has also been demonstrated in nonhuman listeners, suggesting that categorical perception may be a function of a neural transform by mammalian cochleas (Kuhl, 1981, 1982; Kuhl & Miller, 1975, 1978).

Young infants are sensitive to segmental sound units of speech, and they make exceptionally fine discriminations of sounds in a manner that is linguistically significant; that is, they respond to acoustic differences that make a difference linguistically. Eimas and colleagues found that infants as young as one month of age respond to speech in a manner approximating categorical perception (Eimas, 1975; Eimas, Siqueland, Jusczyk, & Vigorito, 1971). They postulated that this sensitivity hastens the acquisition process and may even make language possible for the child. Because infants can perceive phonetic features, they also possess a means for segmenting a continuous acoustic stream into discrete elements. Eimas (1975) explains:

> That the infant automatically analyzes speech into at least one form of discrete units, that is, phonetic features, would seem to serve well the requirement that the potential language user recognize the discrete nature of language, despite its continuous packaging. Indeed, this form of analysis, in occurring at the very

> beginnings of the language acquisition process, precludes the infant from having to *learn* that language is composed of discrete elements and, as a consequence, must likewise hasten the acquisition process. (p. 227)

Recently, investigators have begun to ask if infants are sensitive to prosodic cues in the native language as well as segmental units of speech. Mehler and associates (Mehler et al., 1988) have shown that four-day-old infants prefer listening to passages of their mothers' native language as opposed to a foreign language. Other work in progress (Jusczyk, 1992) also indicates that infants recognize utterances in their native language based on prosodic cues. So, the apparent trend for both prosodic and phonetic cues is that infants seem to become narrowly tuned to their native language early in life.

Several researchers have developed and tested models of speech perception that posit neural property detectors operating in response to specific acoustic signals. The work of Eimas and others with infants implies that the human brain has a number of property detectors responding selectively to particular types of acoustic signals (Cutting & Eimas, 1975). The motor theory of speech perception corresponds to this idea, because these neural property detectors respond to signals that the human vocal tract makes. That is, the sounds that humans seem uniquely adapted to perceive conform to the sounds that humans can make, and infants are thought to be furnished from birth with neural substrates that readily respond to human speech (Lieberman, 1984; Lieberman & Blumstein, 1988).

It is also known that infants' perception of speech is altered by linguistic experience such that exposure to a certain language results in the reduction of ability to perceive differences that do not differentiate between sounds in that language (Strange & Jenkins, 1978). Studies have suggested that effects of linguistic experience on infants' phonetic perception are evident at one year of age, a time that also coincides with the development of word meanings and first words (Werker & Lalonde, 1988; Werker & Tees, 1984). However, in a recent study of six-month-old infants from the United States and Sweden, phonetic perception had already been altered by exposure to the specific language (Kuhl, Williams, Lacerda, Stevens, & Lindblom, 1992). Kuhl and her colleagues interpret this finding to indicate that a language specific pattern of perception does not depend on an understanding of word meaning and the emergence of a phonological system as previously assumed; rather, the phonetic categories are seen to emerge from the infant's underlying cognitive capacity and from the ability to represent information as a prototype. Thus, Kuhl advances the notion that these phonetic prototypes are in place at the time of early word meanings and first words, suggesting that they are "fundamental perceptual-cognitive building blocks rather than by-products of language acquisition" (Kuhl et al., 1992, p. 608). This evidence has a striking impact on the way in which the biological mechanism and linguistic experience are thought to interface.

From the information presented, it is clear that speech perception in human listeners is a robust phenomenon. Speech processing occurs in parallel such that *multiple levels operate simultaneously.* This redundancy enables the speech processor to be relatively resistant to interference because information "lost" at one level can be predicted from that gained at another. However, the listener does experience more difficulty in noisy backgrounds and especially when presented with novel input in degraded listening conditions. Classrooms frequently are poor listening environments because of the general room acoustics as well as the background noise often present when students are doing seatwork or working in small groups. Classrooms are also learning environments; this means that teachers present novel stimuli as they introduce new concepts and new vocabulary words. Students are often listening to information that may be especially challenging because they have no frame of reference for it, thus reducing accurate prediction and restoration in noise. As with all listeners, students must rely on linguistic competence to build predictions in these situations of auditory demand. Being able to process language in a classroom is vital for academic success because language is used to structure a lesson, deliver a lecture, organize information, build knowledge, clarify specific points of confusion, and direct inquiry, among other functions (Bashir & Scavuzzo, 1992). Children who are having difficulty processing information presented auditorially in a classroom pose a special problem because the curriculum is the medium through which learning is expected to progress. Therefore, *even though there is evidence for neurologically based substrates for speech perception, it must be remembered that the usability of a particular piece of linguistic data depends on the child's understanding of the input.* Once again, the distinction between input and intake is critical: the input to which the student is exposed is varied and challenging; a student's uptake of the information depends on many factors, including ability to perceive speech in degraded listening environments.

Auditory Processing

Definitions of auditory processing vary, but the terminology generally refers to how auditory input is manipulated and used by the central auditory nervous system. Distinction is sometimes made between auditory processing and central auditory processing. The term *auditory processing* is usually reserved for processing of auditory information along the entire auditory pathway, including the external and middle ear; *central auditory processing* is used to refer to auditory processing that begins at the level of the cochlear nuclei in the brain stem, ascending ultimately to the cortex (Katz, et al., 1992; Lasky & Katz, 1983). Often, the two terms are used interchangeably.

Many tests developed to assess the central auditory processing mechanism are behavioral. The specific ones used reflect the disciplinary orientation of the examiner. That is, audiologists choose tests to identify the site of the lesion in the auditory pathway or to evaluate an individual's ability to understand speech in various social interactive situations. Speech-language pathologists, on the other hand, frequently select tests to assess auditory processing abilities in a search for explanations of educational difficulties (Dempsey, 1983). Audiologists work from a lesion-site approach and focus attention on specification of the stimuli used in testing and on the level of the central auditory nervous system being evaluated; speech-language pathologists have adopted an information processing approach and concentrate on task analysis and the interrelatedness of processing at different levels (Matkin & Hook, 1983). In short, the two approaches differ markedly in purpose and specific tests used.

It is beyond the scope of this chapter to review individual auditory processing tests and batteries of tests used in either audiologic or speech-language evaluations. Such information is available to the reader elsewhere (Dempsey, 1983; Matkin & Hook, 1983; Stecker, 1992; Wiig & Semel, 1976). Many of these tests were first developed to detect central auditory nervous system lesions in adults, and others were created to describe auditory function and were modified to capture children's interests. Typically, the stimuli are speech signals, and the testing protocol manipulates the signal under varying conditions with the effect that the listening demand is more difficult. In dichotic listening tasks, signals ranging from nonsense syllables to sentences are presented simultaneously to the two ears. Such tests have been used extensively to study hemispheric dominance as well as central auditory function.

The underlying principle of central auditory testing is one of redundancy. The acoustic properties of speech are redundant, and these redundancies can be reduced and manipulated by filtering, interrupting, time compressing the message, alternating between the two ears, presenting competing noise in the same or opposite ear, or lowering the signal-to-noise ratio. Additionally, the neuroanatomical pathways are characterized as highly redundant and capable of adjusting for degraded speech signals. This redundancy in both language and the neuroanatomy renders the mechanism quite robust to challenge (Keith, 1981, 1988).

Another important assumption of auditory processing tests is that the central auditory system can be thought of as a series of abilities including auditory figure ground, auditory memory, auditory discrimination, auditory closure, and so on. These abilities (or a subset of them) are evaluated using tests of central auditory function (Keith, 1988). Rees (1981) urges caution when using this type of information processing approach, in which auditory abilities are seen as a series of skills and subskills, because such auditory abilities need to be interpreted within the context of language and communication systems (see also Lahey & Bloom, chap. 13). That is, the interaction between perceptual and linguistic factors is critical (Rees, 1981).

In addition to behavioral measures, several methods of noninvasive brain monitoring have been applied to the study of the central auditory nervous system in humans since the 1980s. These techniques include measures of brain structure such as computed tomography (CT) and magnetic resonance imaging (MRI); methods for studying brain function consist of evoked potentials (EPs), quantitative electroencephalograms (EEGs), positron emission tomography (PET), single-photon emission computed tomography (SPECT), and magnetoencephalography (MEG) (Lauter, 1992). Usually, some of these electrophysiologic measures are included in the audiologic evaluation of the central auditory processing when warranted. Recent progress in brain imaging offers means to explore the anatomical and physiological design of the auditory nervous system and to explicate brain and behavior relationships in auditory processing and language (Friel-Patti, 1992). As technological advances continue, the currently indeterminate understanding of auditory processing may be clarified.

Identification and subsequent management of central auditory processing dysfunction (CAPD) in children are controversial issues because, as Keith (1982) has pointed out, identification of lesions of the central auditory pathways is quite different from identification of auditory perceptual difficulties in learning disabled children. Children are referred for central auditory processing evaluations, which include the following behavioral profiles: oral language impairments, phonological disorders, reading disabilities, dyslexia, learning disabilities, and/or poor academic achievement in spite of average or above potential as measured by nonverbal tests of intelligence. Recently, clinical attention has shifted to include measurement and remediation of auditory dysfunction in severely impaired individuals including children with autism or autistic-like behaviors, children with attention deficit disorder (ADD) and attention deficit hyperactivity disorder (ADHD), and children identified as pervasive developmentally delayed (PDD). These are acknowledged heterogenous groups: subject descriptions for many of these clinical groups are not well established, and behavioral profiles often overlap (Gascon, Johnson, & Burd, 1986; Keller, 1992). The value of central auditory processing testing with these populations is questioned because the results are difficult to interpret from an educational/intervention perspective; they simply do not provide insight into educational planning and management.

Controversy surrounds diagnosis of an auditory perceptual processing dysfunction when the relationship of the auditory behaviors tested to speech and language development is largely unknown. Attempts have been made to devise auditory tests that identify children with learning disabilities or that predict which children are likely to develop language learning problems (Martin & Clark, 1977; Stubblefield & Young, 1975). With such an approach, there is the risk of identifying a "problem" based on performance on a set of tests for which we have no data to demonstrate validity of the behaviors measured (Rees, 1981). Confounding this situation is the fact that many children who score poorly on these tests of central auditory processing achieve normally in language, learning, and academic skills (Keith, 1988). "At the heart of the issue is a disagreement among professionals concerning whether disorders of auditory perception *cause* speech and language, reading, or learning disabilities or whether they are just highly correlated" (Keith, 1988, p. 1233). On the other hand, children with learning disabilities may demonstrate disturbances of central auditory function on test procedures, but the results are difficult to interpret because the lesion or cause of the dysfunction is unknown (Pinheiro & Musiek, 1985). Northern and Downs (1991) caution:

> All of these tests diagnose symptoms, not disease. Nowhere can one find a correlation between auditory symptoms and an underlying CNS [central nervous system] disorder such as one finds in the literature on adults or children who have had demonstrable trauma or insult to the brain. . . . In the absence of confirmed lesions in the CNS, there is real doubt as to what is measured in all of the tests for "central auditory processing disorders." . . . Symptom treatment of auditory learning disorders presupposes that the symptoms have caused the language dysfunction and that isolating the symptoms and treating each one will cure the language learning problem. However, from a developmental viewpoint, the specific auditory problems appear to be a result of the language disorder, not a cause of it. (pp. 123–124)

Some investigators have found that children with language impairment and/or learning disability have difficulty with auditory processing of speech (see, e.g., Breedin, Martin, & Jerger, 1989; Ferre & Wilber, 1986; Jerger, Martin, & Jerger, 1987; Watson, & Rastatter, 1985). In a series of studies, Tallal and colleagues, demonstrated that language impaired children were less well able to process short, rapidly sequenced bits of auditory information (Stark & Bernstein, 1984; Tallal, 1978; Tallal & Stark, 1981; Tallal, Stark, Kallman, & Mellits, 1981; Tallal, Stark, & Mellits, 1985). Tallal has advanced the notion that children with language impairment have a specific deficit related to rate of processing of auditory stimuli.

Speech perception has also been investigated in groups of children with phonological disorders (Leonard, 1985; Locke, 1980a, 1980b). Again, the relations among phonological development, disorders, and speech perception are not yet clearly specified, although much has been done in this area since the early 1980s (Leonard, 1992). Recently, Leonard

(1989) hypothesized that specifically language impaired children's serious limitations with grammatical morphemes may be reflections of a limitation in perceiving and testing features with low phonetic substance. Admitting that this hypothesis is at present imprecise, Leonard asserts that specifically language impaired children can be viewed as "normal learners whose input is distorted in principled ways" (1989, p. 198). Leonard believes that the learnability principles assumed in the low phonetic substance contribute to professionals' understanding of language impairment by linking the research in this area with a more comprehensive theory of language acquisition.

The part that does not yet "fit" into a theory of language acquisition is central auditory processing testing. In the absence of a model of the neurophysiological relationships between auditory processing and language, understanding of central auditory processing is markedly hampered. Northern and Downs's (1991) admonition that clinicians are simply measuring symptoms and not identifying disease is serious. Identification of "dysfunction" in the absence of well-developed normative information is misleading at best, if not altogether dangerous. The electrophysiological tests that are beginning to be used to study the neural substrates of auditory processing (brain electrical activity mapping [BEAM], SPECT, EPs, PET, etc.) offer the means to explicate the brain–behavior relationships in adults more precisely. An additional complication with children, of course, is that brain maturation spans a number of years and different areas of the brain mature at different rates. The result is that the age of maturation differs from child to child. This fact poses a considerable difficulty for establishing normative data (Pinheiro & Musiek, 1985).

The absence of a coherent theory of how auditory processing relates to language acquisition and what auditory processing difficulties contribute to the understanding of language impairment delays advancement in this area. Professionals still know relatively little about the neurophysiological relationships between auditory processing and language. Until they do, understanding of central auditory processing will be incomplete. Additionally, the cognitive and linguistic demands imposed by some tests of auditory processing must be more fully explored. As indicated earlier in the chapter, it is likely that some children perform poorly on CAP tests because of metacognitive and metalinguistic problems with the tasks, rather than because they have auditory disorders (see van Kleeck, chap. 3).

Language Comprehension

A consideration of the role of auditory processing in language acquisition would be incomplete without some reflection on what is meant by *language comprehension.* Many studies of language comprehension focus on the process by which meaning is ascribed to the sentence; these studies initially concentrated on single sentences, but currently, the scope has broadened to include comprehension at the discourse level. With this shift to comprehension of sets of sentences in text or discourse came corresponding concerns for the effect of context on comprehension and how individual sentences could be understood as part of a larger context (Cairns, 1984).

Milosky (1992) presents three types of processing models for language comprehension: autonomist (both serial and parallel), interactive, and compromise models. It will be useful to review these current models of language comprehension and to highlight the major theoretical issues in this area of child language.

Autonomist models assume that listeners perform a separate linguistic analysis of the sentence syntax and semantics and then compare the outcome with the context to see if it makes sense within that context. Serial autonomist models describe this process in a linear fashion: The meaning for each word is accessed, the syntax is generated, and the result is compared with context to determine the appropriateness of the derived meaning. Parallel autonomist models hypothesize that several interpretations are generated. The autonomy position posits that a linguistic processing system exists independently of the general cognitive processes. Adherents of this position maintain that the language processor is an autonomous module that is innately specified. Cairns (1984) argued that the linguistic processor comprises a lexical and structural processor to perform all linguistic analyses; further, Cairns theorized that the linguistic processor interfaced with an interpretive processor in which inference and general cognitive operations occurred. A critical distinction between the two processors is that the linguistic processor responded only to linguistic information while the interpretive processor responded to real world knowledge.

Interactionist models propose that comprehension arises from semantic meaning and syntax as well as from information about the context in which the utterance/discourse is occurring. The child talk model proposed by Chapman and colleagues (1992) specifically assumes that linguistic knowledge is developed and embedded in world knowledge. Early linguistic representations include episodic knowledge of situations and procedural knowledge of how to perform in different circumstances. Working from the perspective of the child talk model, Milosky presented the view that the development of language comprehension "is a process of gaining familiarity and experience with increasingly diverse contexts of language use; that context is inherently necessary to the disambiguation of language" (1992, p. 38). The use of context and world knowledge as comprehension strategies can be seen in the following example:

■ Several students are working on a science experiment with yeast cultures. One girl takes off her glasses to look into the microscope. The glasses fall off the lab table, and the student covers her mouth with her hand to suppress a gasp. The teacher walks up at just this moment and says, "Hand me the glasses."

■ The question is: Will the student immediately arrive at the correct interpretation of "glasses" because of the context in which it was said? Or will she gloss the meaning of "glasses" as objects for correcting vision or as containers for liquid and then decide which meaning is intended? The interactionist model predicts that context will cue the intended meaning immediately (Milosky, 1992).

The compromise models propose that lexical and syntactic processors are capable of building all possible interpretations for the constituents of an utterance (Milosky, 1992). In this model, however, after the first constituent generates all possible meaning activations, a central unit with access to contextual knowledge inhibits the generation of multiple interpretations of subsequent constituents. In this model, then, context affects processing indirectly (Sperber & Wilson, 1986).

From this review of models of language comprehension, it is apparent that comprehension is a complex process involving multiple levels of linguistic decoding in combination with real world knowledge (Lahey & Bloom, chap. 13). Once again, one is confronted with the distinction between input and intake. What the child attends to and learns from undoubtedly depends on input that is both salient to the ongoing experience (context) and relevant or important. Milosky (1992) asserts that "Comprehension is maximal when what is most salient is also most relevant" (p. 31). Both salience and relevance are determined from the context and the communicative goal.

Comprehension problems may be of two general types. There are those that result from the lack of an established association between a linguistic form and its meaning. For example, when the input is received, it fails to elicit meaning, either because the relationship between form and meaning has never been established or it has been lost, as in aphasia. The second type of comprehension problem results from a failure in the processing system so that inaccurate or incomplete signals are transmitted. In this instance, the individual may have an adequate association between form and meaning, but may not be able to access it reliably. Obviously, this second type of problem is associated with what is referred to as an *auditory processing problem* (Carrow-Woolfolk, 1985). It is difficult to discern which type of problem a student may have. Standardized testing of language comprehension occurs in very controlled situations with the student and examiner alone in a quiet room, free from distraction. Comprehension in settings such as classrooms, lunchrooms, and family rooms is much more difficult because of the competing signals and multiple sources of distraction. Once again, the condition of a noisy background creates an auditory demand that may precipitate problems.

EDUCATIONAL IMPLICATIONS

Much has been learned since Rees (1973) first cautioned speech-language clinicians about the overuse of the empty diagnostic term *auditory processing disorders*. However, the research that has been reviewed has raised many more questions and added new variables to an already complicated area. The problem is, of course, that educators and clinicians cannot wait for the answers. Their challenge is to bridge the gap between theory and practice now by making sense of the current state of knowledge. While many questions remain, a few principles are apparent from what has been reviewed up to this point.

Children who are described as having auditory processing problems typically have poor language and/or listening skills, although they have average or above-average intelligence. Peripheral hearing is normal for pure tones and speech discrimination. Academic performance is below what would be expected based on intelligence measures. Neurological test results may be unremarkable for some; for others, there are neurological findings. Many of these children seem to do fairly well in one-to-one conversations, but they have much more difficulty in backgrounds with competing noise. The challenge these children present to educators and speech-language clinicians is that their performance varies so that in quiet, structured testing situations, they may do well; however, these test results may not reflect classroom performance. What is not clear from this description is whether the student has a language comprehension problem or whether the problem is difficulty in listening to speech in noise or even is an ADD. Whatever diagnostic label is attributed, several principles will be useful in meeting the educational and language learning needs of these students.

Educational Principles

Principle 1: Confirm the Status of Peripheral Hearing. This discussion began with the statement that auditory processing deficits generally refer to difficulties processing the speech signal in the absence of any permanent peripheral hearing loss. However, many of the behaviors demonstrated by students with auditory processing problems are also seen in children with mild to moderate hearing loss, either conductive or sensorineural. In fact, students with a mild conductive hearing loss are more likely to show inconsistent performance than those with a similar sensorineural hearing loss (Friel-Patti, 1990; Northern & Downs, 1991). Additionally, children with unilateral hearing loss have considerable difficulty in typical classroom settings (Bess, Klee, & Culbertson, 1986; Oyler, Oyler, & Matkin, 1987, 1988). Therefore, the first principle of educational management with children suspected of having auditory processing problems is to confirm that peripheral hearing is indeed normal. The possibility of a mild and/or unilateral hearing loss should not be discounted until a reliable audiogram is obtained.

Principle 2: Observe and Record. Because the performance of these students is inconsistent and may vary considerably from an assessment setting to a more natural setting such as a classroom or multi-speaker conversation, it is important to observe the student in a variety of learning environments and to record error patterns, as Silliman and Wilkinson (chap. 6) also suggest. Clinicians and educators should make note of those situations in which students appear to do well versus those in which the students have difficulty. For example, it is important to know what length of time students attend to auditory information, how well they filter out irrelevant auditory or visual information, and how well and under what conditions they can resist auditory or visual distractions (Butler, 1981, 1983). Most students will be able to contribute to this phase if they are encouraged to reflect on their performance in different settings and if they have the metacognitive skills to do so. Once a baseline record is obtained, it is possible to engage the student in a form of "diagnostic teaching" in which various environments are manipulated and the student's response is noted to see what parameters contribute to better performance.

Principle 3: Analyze Task Demand. It is as yet unclear whether students classified as having auditory processing problems are experiencing difficulty because of auditory demands of a particular task, language/linguistic demands, or short-term memory demands. As clinicians and educators analyze the situations in which students experience success or failure, it is also important to consider task demand. As has been previously suggested, what may be called an auditory processing problem may actually reflect a metalinguistic problem. For example, are students having trouble attaching meaning to linguistic units of increasing complexity? Or having trouble attaching meaning to linguistic units of increasing length? Are students failing to predict or recognize linguistic information from what has already been learned or use cues from the context? Are they having problems responding to new linguistic information such as new vocabulary and unfamiliar concepts? Is this a problem with organizational strategies, including chunking and cross-modal pairing? Is the problem only apparent during competing background noise? Does the level of the noise matter in how well the students cope? Is it a problem of learning how to divide attention between at least two auditory tasks (Butler, 1981)? Are students unable to perform because they do not have a meaning for a particular word? Do the students have subtle expressive language problems, which thus insinuate that problems in comprehension exist? Is this a metacognitive problem? Do the students have adequate metacognitive strategies such as self-assessment, self-instruction, and self-control for learning to occur? What about short-term memory? Are the students using efficient strategies for rehearsal and recall?

Principle 4: Consider Attention. It is impossible to describe the performance of students who are said to have auditory processing problems without referring to poor attention, inattentiveness, or distractibility. Clinicians and educators should be aware of the possibility that students' problems may well be associated with poor attention skills. Some practitioners believe that many children presumed to have auditory processing problems would be better classified and managed as exhibiting ADD (Burd & Fisher, 1986). The relationship between auditory processing disorder and ADD is unclear (i.e., Does one cause the other? Are they simply correlated? Is one a subset of the other?). Nevertheless, it is a good idea for the teacher and speech-language clinician to be aware of the contribution of attention problems to students' performance in tasks requiring both focused attention and divided attention.

Principle 5: Consider Comprehension. There are several levels of comprehension, and students may not operate at the appropriate level for a given situation because of a comprehension deficit. Language comprehension is an extremely difficult and varied process, especially when listening to connected discourse. For example, as indicated earlier, students not only use linguistic rules to understand a story, conversation, or lecture, but they also rely on prior experience, their own knowledge of the topic, and contextual cues. One student may understand the story at a literal level, while another can draw the appropriate inference. Similarly, during a lecture, one student may be able to draw on information learned in a prior class to follow the current discussion, while another is overwhelmed by new vocabulary and fails to do so. Younger students and those with language learning problems often have problems with comprehension because their knowledge of grammar and their strategies for analyzing sentences they hear are not yet well developed (Wallach, 1982). It is important that these differences in comprehension ability not be overlooked before concluding that a child has an auditory processing problem.

Principle 6: Develop Strategies for Effective Learning and Teaching. Every effort should be made to ensure that students understand what is said in the classroom. To accomplish this, both students and teachers/clinicians will have to work to develop strategies that promote effective learning. Teachers and clinicians should provide an adequate auditory stimulus for learning to occur and should be aware of rate and loudness while speaking in class. The input needs to be heard and understood before any learning can take place. Topics need to be introduced in such a way that clear, simple explanations are offered and new vocabulary is defined and spelled on the board so the students do not lose valuable listening time trying to figure out the new word. Repetition should be built into the curriculum, and alternate forms of expressing ideas should be implemented. Students need opportunities to interact with the information in different settings: alone, doing seatwork or library work, in groups, doing collaborative work on a given project or topic. Teachers should offer multiple occasions for students to express their own ideas using their own words, either orally or in writing. Students should be encouraged to reflect on how they learn best so they can employ the strategies that bring success. In particular, students should be encouraged to monitor their own periods of inattention and develop alternate strategies for staying focused on a task until completion (Stark & Bernstein, 1984).

SUMMARY

This chapter has addressed some of the issues and concerns relating to auditory linguistic processing and language learning. A diverse literature on this complex topic has been reviewed, covering areas such as language acquisition, speech perception, auditory processing, and language comprehension. A major problem with working in this area is that few investigators have traversed transdisciplinary space so that findings from one discipline do not always advance research in others. A function of this chapter has been to identify points of convergence as well as those areas in which the findings diverge. While much has been learned about auditory processing of speech and language, it is clear that many questions remain. Notably absent is an accepted model of the brain–behavior relationships in the language processing system that encompasses the complexity of this interdisciplinary topic.

Because of the potential for interference with academic success and the chain of events that result when an individual does not perform to the level of intellectual ability, it is not surprising that concern with auditory processing problems endures. Clinicians and educators have the ability to contribute much to advancement in this area. Explicit discussion of reasons why something did or did not work helps clarify the working hypotheses and governing theory. Practitioners can adopt qualitative approaches to study students identified as having auditory processing problems in naturalistic settings. Such an approach concentrates on hypothesis building rather than hypothesis testing and permits the clinician-researcher to make open-ended observations and watch general patterns emerge (Patton & Westby, 1992). This inductive procedure holds promise for real world situations such as classrooms with socially mediated learning and naturally occurring consequences. Such qualititative research will inform our theories of language acquisition and language intervention and will help researchers ask the appropriate questions. In this way, clinicians and educators can fuse their interests to advance the theory of auditory linguistic processing.

REFERENCES

Bashir, A. S., & Scavuzzo, A. (1992). Children with language disorders: Natural history and academic success. *Journal of Learning Disabilities, 25*(1), 53–65.

Bates, E., Benigni, L., Bretherton, I., Camaioni, L., & Volterra, L. (1977). From gesture to the first word. In M. Lewis & L. Rosenblum (Eds.), *Interaction, conversation and the development of language.* New York: Wiley.

Bates, E., Benigni, L., Bretherton, I., Camaioni, L., & Volterra, V. (1979). *The emergence of symbols: Cognition and communication in infancy*. New York: Academic Press.

Bates, E., Bretherton, I., & Snyder, L. (1988). *From first words to grammar: Individual differences and dissociable mechanisms*. Cambridge: Cambridge University Press.

Bates, E., & MacWhinney, B. (1982). Functionalist approach to grammar. In E. Wanner & L. Gleitman (Eds.), *Language acquisition: The state of the art* (pp. 173–218). New York: Cambridge University Press.

Bates, E., & MacWhinney, B. (1987). Competition, variation, and language learning. In B. MacWhinney (Ed.), *Mechanisms of language acquisition* (pp. 157–193). Hillsdale, NJ: Lawrence Erlbaum.

Berko Gleason, J. (1993). Studying language development: An overview and a preview. In J. B. Gleason (Ed.), *The development of language* (3rd ed., pp. 2–37). New York: Macmillan.

Bess, F. H., Klee, T., & Culbertson, J. L. (1986). Identification, assessment and management of children with unilateral sensorineural hearing loss. *Ear and Hearing, 7,* 43–51.

Best, C., Hoffman, H., & Robson, R. (1981). Perceptual equivalence of acoustic cues in speech and nonspeech perception. *Perception and Psychophysics, 29,* 191–211.

Bickerton, D. (1984). The language bioprogram hypothesis. *The Behavioral and Brain Sciences, 7,* 173–221.

Bickerton, D. (1990). *Language and species.* Chicago: University of Chicago Press.

Bohannon, J. N. (1993). Theoretical approaches to language acquisition. In J. Berko Gleason (Ed.), *The development of language* (pp. 240–297). New York: Macmillan.

Breedin, S. D., Martin, R. C., & Jerger, S. (1989). Distinguishing auditory and speech specific perceptual deficits. *Ear and Hearing, 10,* 311–317.

Brown, R. (1973). *A first language: The early years.* Cambridge, MA: Harvard University Press.

Brown, R. (1977). Introduction. In C. E. Snow & C. A. Ferguson (Eds.), *Talking to children: Language input and acquisition* (pp. 1–27). Cambridge, U.K.: Cambridge University Press.

Brown, R. (1988). Afterword. In F. S. Kessel (Ed.), *The development of language and language researchers: Essays in honor of Roger Brown* (pp. 393–394). Hillsdale, NJ: Lawrence Erlbaum.

Burd, L., & Fisher, W. (1986). Central auditory processing disorder or attention deficit disorder? *Journal of Developmental and Behavioral Pediatrics, 7*(3), 215–216.

Butler, K. G. (1981). Language processing disorders: Factors in diagnosis and remediation. In R. W. Keith (Ed.), *Central auditory and language disorders in children* (pp. 160–174). San Diego: College-Hill Press.

Butler, K. G. (1983). Language processing: Selective attention and mnemonic strategies. In E. Z. Lasky & J. Katz (Eds.), *Central auditory processing disorders: Problems of speech, language, and learning* (pp. 297–315). Austin, TX: Pro-Ed.

Cairns, H. S. (1984). Research in language comprehension. In R. C. Naremore (Ed.), *Language science* (pp. 211–242). San Diego: College-Hill.

Carrow-Woolfolk, E. (1985). *Test for auditory comprehension of language* (rvised ed.). Allen, TX: DLM.

Chapman, R. S., Streim, N. W., Crais, E. R., Salmon, D., Strand, E. A., & Negri, N. A. (1992). Child talk: Assumptions of a developmental process model for early language learning. In R. S. Chapman (Eds.), *Processes in language acquisition and disorders* (pp. 3–19). St. Louis: Mosby Year Book.

Chomsky, N. (1965). *Aspects of a theory of syntax.* Cambridge, MA: MIT Press.

Chomsky, N. (1979). Human language and other semiotic systems. *Semiotica, 25,* 31–44.

Chomsky, N. (1980). *Rules and representations.* New York: Columbia University Press.

Cutting, J. E., & Eimas, P. D. (1975). Phonetic analyzers and processing of speech in infants. In J. F. Kavanagh & J. E.

Cutting (Eds.), *The role of speech in language* (pp. 127–148). Cambridge, MA: MIT Press.

Dempsey, D. (1983). Selecting tests of auditory function in children. In E. Z. Lasky & J. Katz (Eds.), *Central auditory processing disorders: Problems of speech, language, and learning* (pp. 203–221). Austin, TX: Pro-Ed.

Eimas, P. D. (1975). Speech perception in early infancy. In L. B. Cohen & P. Salapatek (Eds.), *Infant perception: From sensation to cognition: Vol. 2. Perception of space, speech, and sound* (pp. 193–231). New York: Academic Press.

Eimas, P. D., Siqueland, E. R., Jusczyk, P., & Vigorito, J. (1971). Speech perception in infants. *Science, 171,* 303–306.

Ferre, J. M., & Wilber, L. A. (1986). Normal and learning disabled children's central auditory processing skills: An experimental test battery. *Ear and Hearing, 7,* 336–343.

Fey, M. (1986). *Language intervention with young children.* San Diego, CA: College-Hill Press.

Fodor, J. A. (1983). *The modularity of mind.* Cambridge, MA: MIT Press.

Friel-Patti, S. (1990). Otitis media with effusion and the development of language: A review of the evidence. *Topics in Language Disorders, 11,* 11–22.

Friel-Patti, S. (1992). Research in child language disorders: What do we know and where are we going? *Folia Phoniatrica, 44*(1), 126–142.

Friel-Patti, S., & Conti-Ramsden, G. (1988). Intervention tactics for learning disabled children with oral language impairments. In D. K. Reid (Ed.), *Teaching the learning disabled: A cognitive developmental approach* (pp. 140–161). Boston: Allyn & Bacon.

Gardner, H. (1983). *Frames of mind: The theory of multiple intelligences.* New York: Basic Books.

Gascon, G. G., Johnson, R., & Burd, L. (1986). Central auditory processing and attention deficit disorders. *Journal of Child Neurology, 1,* 27–33.

Gopnik, A., & Meltzoff, A. (1986). Relations between semantic and cognitive development in the one-word stage: The specificity hypothesis. *Child Development, 57,* 1040–1053.

Gopnik, A., & Meltzoff, A. (1987). The development of categorization in the second year and its relation to other cognitive and linguistic developments. *Journal Verbal Learning and Verbal Behavior, 5,* 492–496.

Hoffman, P. R., Schuckers, G. H., & Daniloff, R. G. (1989). *Children's phonetic disorders: Theory and treatment.* Boston: College-Hill Press.

Jerger, S., Martin, R., & Jerger, J. (1987). Specific auditory perceptual dysfunction in a learning disabled child. *Ear and Hearing, 8,* 78–86.

Johnston, J. (1983). Discussion: Part I: What is language intervention? The role of theory. In J. Miller, D. Yoder, & R. Schiefelbusch (Eds.), *Contemporary issues in language intervention* (pp. 52–57). Rockville, MD: American Speech-Language-Hearing Association.

Jusczyk, P. W. (1992). Developing phonological categories from the speech signal. In C. A. Ferguson, L. Menn, & C. Stoel-Gammon (Eds.), *Phonological development: Models, research, implications* (pp. 17–64). Parkton, MD: York Press.

Kahmi, A. G. (1992). Three perspectives on language processing: Interactionism, modularity, and holism. In R. S. Chapman (Ed.), *Processes in language acquisition and disorders* (pp. 45–64). St. Louis: Mosby Year Book.

Katz, J., Stecker, N., & Henderson, D. (1992). *Central auditory processing: A transdisciplinary view.* St. Louis: Mosby Year Book.

Keith, R. W. (1981). Audiological and auditory-language tests of central auditory function. In R. W. Keith (Ed.), *Central auditory and language disorders in children* (pp. 61–76). San Diego, CA: College-Hill Press.

Keith, R. W. (1988). Central auditory tests. In N. J. Lass, L. V. McReynolds, J. L. Northern, & D. E. Yoder (Eds.), *Speech, language, and hearing: Vol. 3. Hearing disorders* (pp. 1215–1236). Philadelphia: W. B. Saunders.

Keller, W. D. (1992). Auditory processing disorder or attention-deficit disorder? In J. Katz, N. A. Stecker, & D. Henderson (Eds.), *Central auditory processing: A transdisciplinary view* (pp. 107–114). St. Louis: Mosby Year Book.

Kuczaj, S. A. (1982). On the nature of syntactic development. In S. A. Kuczaj (Ed.), *Language development: Vol. 1. Syntax and semantics* (pp. 37–71). Hillsdale, NJ: Lawrence Erlbaum.

Kuhl, P. K. (1979). The perception of speech in early infancy. In N. J. Lass (Ed.), *Speech and language: Advances in basic research and practice* (Vol. 1, pp. 1–47). New York: Academic Press.

Kuhl, P. K. (1981). Discrimination of speech by non-human animals: Basic auditory sensitivities conducive to the perception of speech–sound categories. *Journal of the Acoustical Society of America, 70,* 340–349.

Kuhl, P. K. (1982). Speech perception: An overview of current issues. In N. Lass, L. McReynolds, J. Northern, & D. Yoder (Eds.), *Speech, language, and hearing: Vol. 1. Normal processes* (pp. 286–322). Philadelphia: W. B. Saunders.

Kuhl, P. K., & Miller, J. M. (1975). Speech perception by the chinchilla: Voiced–voiceless distinction in alveolar plosive sonsonants. *Science, 190,* 69–72.

Kuhl, P. K., & Miller, J. M. (1978). Speech perception by the chinchilla: Identification for synthetic VOT stimuli. *Journal of the Acoustical Society of America, 63,* 905–917.

Kuhl, P. K., Williams, K. A., Lacerda, F., Stevens, K. N., & Lindblom, B. (1992). Linguistic experience alters phonetic perception in infants by 6 months of age. *Science, 255,* 606–608.

Lasky, E. Z., & Katz, J. (1983). Perspectives on central auditory processing. In E. Z. Lasky & J. Katz (Eds.), *Central auditory processing disorders: Problems of speech, language, and learning* (pp. 3–9). Austin, TX: Pro-Ed.

Lauter, J. L. (1992). Imaging techniques and auditory processing. In J. Katz, N. Stecker, & D. Henderson (Eds.),

Central auditory processing: A transdisciplinary view (pp. 61–78). St. Louis: Mosby Year Book.

Leonard, L. B. (1985). Unusual and subtle phonological behavior in the speech of phonologically disordered children. *Journal of Speech and Hearing Disorders, 50,* 4–13.

Leonard, L. (1989). Language learnability and specific language impairment in children. *Applied Psycholinguistics, 10,* 179–202.

Leonard, L. B. (1992). Models of phonological development and children with phonological disorders. In C. A. Ferguson, L. Menn, & C. Stoel-Gammon (Eds.), *Phonological development: Models, research, implications* (pp. 495–507). Timonium, MD: York Press.

Liberman, A. M. (1992). Plausibility, parsimony, and theories of speech. *Haskins Laboratories Status Report on Speech Research,* SR-109/110, 109–118.

Liberman, A. M., Cooper, F. S., Shankweiler, D. P., & Studdert-Kennedy, M. (1967). Perception of the speech code. *Psychological Review, 74,* 431–461.

Liberman, A. M., & Mattingly, I. G. (1985). The motor theory of speech perception revised. *Cognition, 21,* 1–36.

Liberman, A. M., & Mattingly, I. G. (1989). A specialization for speech perception. *Science, 243,* 489–494.

Lieberman, P. (1984). *The biology and evolution of language.* Cambridge, MA: Harvard University Press.

Lieberman, P., & Blumstein, S. (1988). *Speech physiology, speech perception, and acoustic phonetics.* NY: Cambridge University Press.

Lightfoot, D. (1989). The child's trigger experience: Degree-0 learnability. *Behavioral and Brain Sciences, 12,* 321–375.

Locke, J. L. (1980a). The inference of speech perception in the phonologically disordered child. Part I: A rationale, some criteria, the conventional tests. *Journal of Speech and Hearing Disorders, 45,* 431–444.

Locke, J. L. (1980b). The inference of speech perception in the phonologically disordered child. Part II: Some clinically novel procedures, their use, some findings. *Journal of Speech and Hearing Disorders, 45,* 445–468.

MacWhinney, B. (1987). The competition model. In B. MacWhinney (Ed.), *Mechanisms of language acquisition* (pp. 249–308). Hillsdale, NJ: Lawrence Erlbaum.

Martin, F. N., & Clark, J. G. (1977). Audiologic detection of auditory processing disorders in children. *Journal of American Audiology Society, 3,* 140–146.

Matkin, N. D., & Hook, P. E. (1983). A multidisciplinary approach to central auditory evaluations. In E. Z. Lasky & J. Katz (Eds.), *Central auditory processing disorders: Problems of speech, language, and learning* (pp. 223–242). Austin, TX: Pro-Ed.

McDonald, L., & Pien, D. (1982). Mother conversational behavior as a function of interaction intent. *Journal of Child Language, 9,* 337–358.

McNeill, D. (1970). *The acquisition of language.* New York: Harper & Row.

Mehler, J., Jusczyk, P. W., Lamgertz, G., Halstead, N., Bertoncini, J., & Amiel-Tison, C. (1988). A precursor of language acquisition in young infants. *Cognition, 29,* 143–178.

Miller, G., & Nicely, P. (1955). An analysis of perceptual confusions among some English consonants. *Journal of the Acoustical Society of America, 27,* 338–352.

Milosky, L. M. (1992). Children listening: The role of world knowledge in language comprehension. In R. S. Chapman (Ed.), *Processes in language acquisition and disorders* (pp. 20–44). St. Louis: Mosby Year Book.

Moerk, E. (1983). *The mother of Eve—As a first language teacher.* Norwood, NJ: Ablex.

Morgan, J. L. (1989). Learnability considerations and the nature of trigger experiences in language acquisition. *Behavioral and Brain Sciences, 12*(2), 352–353.

Nelson, K. (1987). Some observations from the perspective of the rare event cognitive comparison theory of language acquisition. In K. E. Nelson & A. van Kleeck (Eds.), *Children's language* (pp. 289–331). Hillsdale, NJ: Lawrence Erlbaum.

Nelson, N. W. (1993). *Childhood language disorders in context: Infancy through adolescence.* New York: Merrill/Macmillan.

Northern, J. L., & Downs, M. P. (1991). *Hearing in children* (4th ed.). Baltimore: Williams & Wilkins.

Olsen-Fulero, L. (1982). Style and stability in mother conversational behavior: A study of individual differences. *Journal of Child Language, 9,* 543–564.

Olsen-Fulero, L., & Conforti, J. (1983). Child responsiveness to mother questions of varying type and presentation. *Journal of Child Language, 10,* 495–520.

Oyler, R. F., Oyler, A. L., & Matkin, N. D. (1987). Warning: A unilateral hearing loss may be detrimental to a child's academic career. *Hearing Journal, 40*(9), 18–22.

Oyler, R. F., Oyler, A. L., & Matkin, N. D. (1988). Unilateral hearing loss: Demographics and educational impact. *Language, Speech and Hearing Services in Schools, 19,* 201–210.

Patton, M., & Westby, C. (1992). Ethnography and research: A qualitative view. *Topics in Language Disorders, 12*(3), 1–14.

Pinheiro, M. L., & Musiek, F. E. (1985). Special considerations in central auditory evaluation. In M. L. Pinheiro & F. E. Musiek (Eds.), *Assessment of central auditory dysfunction: Foundations and clinical correlates* (pp. 257–265). Baltimore: Williams & Wilkins.

Pinker, S. (1979). Formal model of language learning. *Cognition, 7*(3), 217–283.

Rees, N. (1973). Auditory processing factors in language disorders: The view from Procrustes' bed. *Journal of Speech and Hearing Disorders, 38,* 304–315.

Rees, N. S. (1981). Saying more than we know: Is auditory processing disorder a meaningful concept? In R. W. Keith (Eds.), *Central auditory and language disorders in children* (pp. 94–120). San Diego, CA: College-Hill Press.

Rumelhart, D. E., McClelland, J. L., & Group, P. R. (1986). *Parallel distributed processing: Exploration in the microstructure of cognition: Vol 1. Foundations*. Cambridge, MA: MIT Press.

Slis, I. H., & Cohen, A. (1969). On the complex regulating of the voiced–voiceless distinction. *Language and Speech, 12,* 80–102.

Slobin, D. (1979). *Psycholinguistics* (2nd ed.). Glenview, IL: Scott Foresman.

Slobin, D., & Bever, T. (1982). Children use canonical sentence schemas: A cross-linguistic study of word order and inflections. *Cognition, 12,* 229–265.

Smolak, L., & Weinraub, M. (1983). Maternal speech: strategy or response? *Journal of Child Language, 10,* 369–380.

Snow, C. E. (1977). Mothers' speech research: from input to interaction. In C. E. Snow & C. A. Ferguson (Eds.), *Talking to children: Language input and acquisition* (pp. 31–49). Cambridge, U.K.: Cambridge University Press.

Snow, C., & Tomasello, M. (1989). Data on language input: Incomprehensible omission indeed! *Behavioral and Brain Sciences, 12*(2), 357–358.

Sperber, D., & Wilson, D. (1986). *Relevance: Communication and cognition.* Cambridge, MA: Harvard University Press.

Stabler, E. P. (1989). What's a trigger? *Behavioral and Brain Sciences, 12*(2), 358–360.

Stark, R. E., & Bernstein, L. E. (1984). Evaluating central auditory processing in children. *Topics in Language Disorders, 4,* 57–70.

Stecker, N. A. (1992). Central auditory processing: Implications in audiology. In J. Katz, N. Stecker, & D. Henderson (Eds.), *Central auditory processing: A transdisciplinary view* (pp. 117–127). St. Louis: Mosby Year Book.

Strange, W., & Jenkins, J. (1978). The role of linguistic experience in the perception of speech. In H. L. Pick & R. D. Walk (Eds.), *Perception and experience* (pp. 125–169). New York: Plenum.

Stubblefield, H. H., & Young, C. E. (1975). Central auditory dysfunction in learning disabled children. *Journal of Learning Disabilities, 8,* 89–94.

Tallal, P. (1978). Relation between speech perception, language comprehension, and speech production in children with specific language delay. *Allied Health and Behavioral Sciences, 1*(2), 220–236.

Tallal, P., & Stark, R. E. (1981). Speech acoustic-cue discrimination abilities of normally developing and language-impaired children. *Journal of Acoustical Society of America, 69*(2), 568–574.

Tallal, P., Stark, R., Kallman, C., & Mellits, D. (1981). A reexamination of some nonverbal perceptual abilities of language-impaired and normal children as a function of age and sensory modality. *Journal of Speech and Hearing Research, 24,* 351–357.

Tallal, P., Stark, R. E., & Mellits, E. D. (1985). Identification of language-impaired children on the basis of rapid perception and production skills. *Brain and Language, 25,* 314–322.

Wallach, G. (1982). Language processing and reading deficiencies: Assessment and remediation of children with special learning problems. In N. J. Lass, L. V. McReynolds, J. L. Northern, & D. E. Yoder (Eds.), *Speech, language, and hearing* (pp. 819–838). Philadelphia: W. B. Saunders.

Warren, R. (1970). Perceptual restoration of missing speech sounds. *Science, 167,* 392–393.

Watson, M., & Rastatter, M. (1985). The effects of time compression on the auditory processing abilities of learning disabled children. *The Journal of Auditory Research, 25,* 167–173.

Werker, J. F., & Lalonde, C. E. (1988). Cross-language perception: Initial capabilities and developmental change. *Developmental Psychology, 24,* 672–683.

Werker, J. F., & Tees, R. C. (1984). Cross-language speech perception: Evidence for perceptual reorganization during the first year of life. *Infant Behavior and Development, 7,* 9–64.

Westby, C. (1990). The role of the speech-language pathologist in whole language. *Language, Speech, and Hearing Services in Schools, 21,* 228–237.

Whitehurst, G., & Novak, G. (1973). Modeling, imitation training, and the acquisition of sentence phrases. *Journal of Experimental Child Psychology, 16,* 332–335.

Whitehurst, G., & Vasta R. (1975). Is language acquired through imitation? *Journal of Psycholinguistic Research, 4,* 37–59.

Wiig, E. H., & Semel, E. M. (1976). *Language disabilities in children and adolescents.* New York: Merrill/Macmillan.

15

NEW DIRECTIONS FOR MEETING THE ACADEMIC NEEDS OF ADOLESCENTS WITH LANGUAGE LEARNING DISABILITIES

■ Barbara J. Ehren
The School Board of Palm Beach County, Florida

ACADEMIC NEEDS OF ADOLESCENTS WITH LANGUAGE LEARNING DISABILITIES

When Plato observed that youth is the time for extraordinary toil more than twenty-three centuries ago, he may not have had in mind the adolescent with language learning disabilities. In truth, adolescence is viewed as a time of extraordinary toil and trouble for most youth. For adolescents with language learning disabilities, this may be doubly true. Therefore, professionals working with this population, or planning to do so, need to understand the nature of this group and explore appropriate intervention options. Professionals whose interests lie primarily with younger children might consider this chapter less relevant to them. However, it is important to recognize that (1) children grow up; (2) language problems tend to persist into adolescence and adulthood; and (3) intervention is a continuum whose elements are affected by what has preceded it and what will follow (Wallach & Butler, chap. 1). Therefore, the study of adolescent language is an important component in any comprehensive discussion of language learning disabilities.

This chapter has several objectives, all aimed at identifying students' language learning needs at higher school-age levels and presenting directions for meeting those needs. The first section presents a general description of the population. Three profiles of adolescent students with language learning disabilities illustrate the different ways that language disorders manifest themselves across time. The second section describes language and learning characteristics of the population in greater detail. Three areas are explored: language difficulties at the word, phrase, sentence, and discourse/text levels; classroom performance problems; and characteristics in light of secondary school setting demands—academic, social, motivational, and executive. These areas provide information basic to considering programming options. The third section discusses historical perspectives as a framework for understanding present issues and exploring future directions. The remaining sections deal with the nature of services provided. The discussions cover key concepts in provision of services, identification principles, and principles of language intervention. Finally, an intervention paradigm is presented at the end of the chapter as an example of conceptualizing a total approach.

THE POPULATION: STUDENTS WITH LANGUAGE LEARNING DISABILITIES IN ADOLESCENCE

The Language–Learning Disabilities Connection Revisited

"Of all the problems experienced by students with learning disabilities, language may be the most pervasive" (Wiig & Semel, 1984). By the time students reach adolescence, however, language and its disorders frequently become a neglected area, as McKinley and Lord-Larson (1985) have pointed out. This trend persists despite ample evidence to substantiate the existence of language disorders in adolescents with learning disabilities (Bashir & Scavuzzo, 1992; Donahue & Bryan, 1984; Jones, 1984; Klecan-Aker, 1985; Nelson, chap. 4; Wiig, Becker-Redding, & Semel, 1983; Wiig & Fleischmann, 1980; Wiig, Lapointe, & Semel, 1977; Wiig & Roach, 1975; Wiig & Semel, 1974, 1975; Wiig, Semel, & Abele, 1981). Additionally, and as discussed throughout this text, much evidence demonstrates the impact of language disorders on academic and social performance throughout the stages of development and learning (Bashir, Kuban, Kleinman, & Scavuzzo, 1983; Vellutino, 1977; Wallach & Butler, 1984; Wiig & Semel, 1984).

Although prevalence studies for adolescents with language disorders are limited at this time, clinical and educational data suggest that a significant number of students who are described as "learning disabled" have language difficulties that have persisted throughout their school careers (ASHA, 1982; Bashir & Scavuzzo, 1992; see Wallach & Butler, chap. 1). Case studies, such as those presented by Nelson (chap. 4), offer additional insight into the ways in which language disorders manifest themselves as children grow into adolescence.

The problems with standardized tests notwithstanding, some information may be gleaned by interpreting results of such testing on large numbers of adolescents with learning disabilities. For example, when eighty-two randomly selected middle school students with learning disabilities were administered the Clinical Evaluation of Language Functions (CELF)—Advanced Level Screening Test (Semel & Wiig, 1980a), 79% of these students failed. A follow-up evaluation using the CELF Diagnostic Battery (Semel & Wiig, 1980b) indicated that all these students failed at least one subtest and 81% failed three or more subtests. The most frequently failed subtests were producing word series (65%), requiring recitation of the days of the week and months of the year, and processing word classes (61%), requiring a semantic categorization task (Florida Department of Education, 1983).

Although professionals could take issue with the CELF and other tests like it, these results along with longitudinal research appear to reiterate the ongoing nature of language disorders. In light of the available data, it seems counterproductive to deemphasize or ignore language as an area of intervention for adolescents with learning disabilities. Indeed, it should be a core consideration when trying to understand academic failure. The language factor takes on added significance when noting that adolescents often perform poorly on academic measures after years of previous intervention in programs for the learning disabled (Deshler, Schumaker, Alley, Warner, & Clark, 1982; Sinclair & Ghory, 1987). Clearly, there is much to learn about the continuum of language disorders and the specific ways language difficulties interface with the demands of secondary level curricula and school success. Consideration of some of the patterns of performance in individual students may provide insights into the nature of language learning disabilities in adolescents.

Identification Profiles

Three major patterns emerge when studying adolescents with learning disabilities. The first subgroup's background includes significant language disorders at early ages. The second subgroup has a history of academic difficulties not attributed to underlying language difficulties. The third subgroup appears to encounter language-related academic problems only in adolescence. The following cases illustrate each of these profiles.

Case 1: Amanda. This case illustrates the first subgroup: students who have a history of language disorders that have persisted into adolescence. Although many of these students have been identified as language disordered during the preschool years, others may have been identified during the elementary school years.

Amanda is a fifteen-year-old beginning high school student. Her language disorder was identified in preschool at the age of three, when her family became concerned that she could not communicate as well as her older siblings at her age. She has had language intervention continuously since that time. She has also been served in programs for the learning disabled. When she was young, she had overt oral language difficulties, including deficient vocabulary, severely restricted syntax, pragmatic language difficulties, and phonological problems, which were dealt with as "articulation" problems. Her current problems differ significantly from those she had in the preschool period, because the symptomatology of her language disorder changed over time. Her use of vocabulary and syntax is adequate for conversation but inadequate for written expression (see Scott, chap. 8). When writing, she displays a narrow repertoire of word usage and typically uses simple sentences without clauses. Conversational interchanges reveal pragmatic difficulties that are more subtle than in the preschool years but that interfere significantly with her social effectiveness. Although she can converse on a topic, she does not always provide topic transitions, leaving her communication partner with questions as to the relatedness of some of her statements. "Articulation" problems do not exist presently, but her previous difficulties with phonology are reflected in continuing problems in decoding written text and in spelling. In general, Amanda has serious problems coping with the academic demands of high school. In particular, she has difficulty with reading and writing requirements and in following complex oral and written directions given in her classes.

Case 2: Joshua. This case illustrates the second subgroup: students with a history of academic difficulties whose school progress deteriorates in secondary settings but whose problems have *not* been attributed to linguistic difficulties. The language disorders of this group appear to have manifested themselves in more subtle ways when the students were younger. For example, their conversational skills may never have been a problem; reading decoding skills may be adequate, and reading comprehension tasks at lower grade levels involving simple recall and response to factual questions may have been intact. However, reading comprehension tasks, requiring more semantic manipulation such as inferencing and prediction, may have posed difficulties. For students in this subgroup, language difficulties begin to interfere seriously with academic success only as the academic school demands required a greater degree of language competence. In some cases their language problems may have been missed entirely when they were younger.

Joshua is a fourteen-year-old seventh grader in middle school. He never had an easy time succeeding in school but "squeaked by." He was retained once in elementary school (third grade) and was referred in fourth grade for possible special education services. He passed his speech and language screening and did not qualify for any special programs. Joshua demonstrated increasing difficulty as the academic demands increased through the grades. For example, he barely met requirements for promotion from fifth grade to sixth grade in middle school and entered middle school reading at a third-grade level. Reading comprehension, involving such skills as understanding inferences and predicting outcomes, became a major problem for Joshua. In seventh grade, the quantity and complexity of the curriculum, especially in social studies, is now more than he can handle. He is failing social studies and language arts and doing poorly in science. Computational math is a strength, whereas math problem solving poses difficulties for him. Unfortunately, Joshua is beginning to hate school and talks about dropping out when he turns sixteen. After a team evaluation, which focused on analysis of language use in relevant contexts, including classroom performance, Josh was diagnosed for the first time as having a language disorder, predominantly in higher level semantics. Skills involving verbal problem solving, inferencing, and comparisons and contrasts are difficult for him. Had a more thorough evaluation been completed when he was in fourth grade, or preferably earlier, the language difficulties underlying his academic difficulties may have been understood and appropriate intervention implemented.

Case 3: Scott. This case illustrates the third subgroup: students who have no history of academic failure but who experience difficulty coping with complex metacognitive and metalinguistic demands as these increase after elementary school. For these students, secondary school is significantly more difficult than their earlier academic careers.

Scott is a twelve-year-old sixth grader beginning middle school. He has never excelled in school but has never had significant difficulties. He had to work harder than most of his peers to achieve academically. It typically took him longer to do his work than his classmates; he spent more time at home studying. His organizational skills were never strong. His grades started to drop at the end of fifth grade, but he managed to obtain passing grades. However, he failed two classes in the first semester of middle school (language arts and social studies). When Scott had to cope with the new setting demands of middle school, including a variety of teaching styles, less structure, and greater demands for independence, his performance deteriorated. He was always more successful with hands-on learning and multisensory presentations, but these have not been part of the presentation mode in the two classes he failed. Scott's language difficulties are more covert because his language skills for interpersonal communication are good. In fact, interpersonal communication has always been his strength. He likes to talk and has been considered by teachers to be a "verbal" child. On evaluation, it was discovered that Scott has difficulty processing and producing complex text structures in written language. Further, his metacognitive skills were found to be deficient. He was not aware of his own thinking processes and did not approach tasks in a planful way. For example, he could not explain to teachers how he approached an assignment. Further observation revealed that Scott did not generate strategies for acquiring and manipulating information. He failed to use past experiences to build a repertoire of effective and efficient approaches to tasks. He tended to make the same mistakes over and over again.

ADOLESCENT CHARACTERISTICS

Although every adolescent with learning disabilities will present a unique profile of strengths and weaknesses, as the cases outlined earlier demonstrate, some commonalities across language and school culture characteristics are likely to occur. The following areas are discussed in the section that follows: (1) specific language difficulties; (2) classroom performance problems; and (3) characteristics vis-à-vis setting demands.

Language Characteristics

Several paradigms can be used to discuss the language characteristics of adolescents. For example, Chappell (1985) adapted Guilford's structure of the intellect model and offered five levels of linguistic information to describe the language difficulties of junior high school students: basic vocabulary, classification, language system, information transformation, and information implication. Larson and McKinley (1987) described expectations and problems in the following areas: cognition, comprehension and production of linguistic features, discourse, nonverbal communication, and what they call "survival" language.

Some of the predominant language characteristics are covered next. They are categorized by language complexity levels: word level, phrase/sentence level, and discourse/text level. These difficulties may be evident in both oral and written language, although the demand for formal written language, especially expository text, tends to increase the task complexity and, therefore, the likelihood of breakdown (Scott, chap. 8).

Word Meaning and Relationship Difficulties

■ Gaps in vocabulary, either in recognition and/or use, for content that adolescents should typically know greatly interferes with acquisition of academic information, because learning in academic areas relies on a strong word knowledge foundation. (Wallach and Butler talk about cultural literacy in chap. 1. They refer to aspects of basic vocabulary knowledge as being related to understanding the events of one's world. The notion that adolescents do not have a strong cultural literacy base may relate to this vocabulary gap.) As noted throughout this text, the interaction between print literacy, prior knowledge and experience, and word/vocabulary gaps requires careful scrutiny and additional research.

■ Lack of flexibility in interpreting multiple-meaning words can create misunderstanding in interpersonal communication and confusion in deciphering subject information (see Milosky, chap. 10).

■ Mismatch of responses to information requested (e.g., supplying a *when* answer to a *where* question or giving a statement when a description is called for) often results in incorrect responses when the student is asked to explain, describe, or compare information orally or in writing.

■ Imprecise relationships among categories and the inability to use language to elucidate similarities, differences, and distinguishing features of concepts interferes with learning of subject area content.

■ Difficulty defining words (e.g., may be able to use the words correctly and provide information about their meaning but cannot give a definition) negatively affects performance on vocabulary definition assignments.

Word Structure

■ Lack of morphological markers that denote differences in use (e.g., tense markers on verbs, plural and possessive on nouns, *-er* or *-or* on verbs to make them nouns, etc.) may result in reading comprehension problems. The student may not use the markers, especially in writing, or may fail to attend to them when reading words.

■ Imprecise use of word forms (e.g., the "democracy/democratic government") interferes with communicating through written expression.

■ Misunderstanding of words used may involve misdiscrimination of sounds and may be at the root of incorrect word use described previously. It may adversely affect vocabulary acquisition and understanding of lecture material.

■ Lack of segmentation rule knowledge for analysis of words results in a corresponding difficulty with reading decoding (see Blachman, chap. 9) and spelling.

Word Retrieval

■ Trouble calling forth the exact word needed may be related to ineffective storage of information or difficulty accessing a specific word at a given time. It may be exhibited as use of overly general words, circumlocution, or neologisms in oral or written forms and can affect performance in classroom participation activities (see German, chap. 12, for an in-depth discussion).

Phrase Structure

■ Lack of implicit or explicit knowledge of noun and verb phrase structure rules may result in an inability to make predictions, which can impair reading fluency. It may also result in an inability to use linguistic context for interpreting information, thus interfering with understanding classroom instruction or obtaining meaning from written text.

■ The tendency to "lose" small or structural words in phrases, leading to misinterpretation of discourse/text, adversely affects learning of academic content through lecture or reading (see Scott, chap. 8).

Sentence Structure

■ Difficulty with comprehension of clauses, especially embedded clauses hinders interpretation and manipulation of complex thoughts necessary for subject area learning (recall Silliman and Wilkinson's discussion of "problems of orality" in the population with language learning disabilities in chap. 2).

■ Use of simple constructions, especially in written work, reflects difficulty using constructions to combine thoughts (as Scott points out in chap. 8 and as Wallach and Butler discuss in chap. 1). This interferes with expression of complex thoughts, which are required in many academic assignments (e.g., end-of-chapter questions, essay tests, and report writing).

■ Inflexibility in constructions (e.g., difficulty expressing an idea in more than one way and in paraphrasing). This inflexibility is typically related to problems in doing research and report writing when reference material is copied verbatim, sometimes without regard to information relevance.

■ Lack of comprehension of metaphors and idioms interferes with understanding of subject area content via textbook reading (see also Milosky, chap. 10).

Discourse/Text

■ The tendency to process ambiguities at the sentence level only and difficulty using context to decode ambiguities typically results in misinterpretations of lecture or textbook material (van Kleeck, chap. 3).

■ Lack of flexibility in interpretation (only one interpretation given; literal interpretation anticipated; cannot make inferences consistently; Milosky, chap. 10) may cause difficulties in problem solving in science, explaining cause and effect relationships in social studies, and interpreting literature in English.

■ Difficulty synthesizing information to obtain central message (e.g., may attend to details as opposed to global meaning; may use the main idea in lecture or textbook content) results in learning relatively unimportant information as opposed to key concepts.

■ Poor expressive fluency; for example, failure to elaborate on a topic typically results in short answers to teachers' questions, oral or written, and restricted oral presentations or written assignments.

■ Poor topic maintenance (e.g., discourse or text containing off-target elements) may interfere with social interaction because communication partners cannot follow discourse or may interfere with academic performance when written products fail to communicate a cohesive message.

■ Inadequate information is supplied to the listener/audience to promote understanding of the speaker's message. Communication partners may have the impression that a story has been started in the middle. Readers of written products may lack sufficient information to understand content or context.

This summary is far from an exhaustive list of all the language difficulties encountered by adolescents. However, it provides an overview that should contribute to an understanding of adolescent needs. And although it is common to address language in terms of the subsystems of pragmatics, semantics, syntax, morphology, and phonology for ease of discussion, it is impossible to separate these elements in terms of how they interrelate for communication effectiveness in the adolescent. The interactions among the systems are multiple and often subtle. Scott's framework (see chap. 8), which considers the discourse continuum from several perspectives, offers innovative and integrated ways of looking at spoken and written communication.

Bashir and Scavuzzo (1992) apply the notion of *reciprocal causation,* when speaking of the complex interrelationship among and between language, socialization, and academic learning. Indeed, persistent language disorders can have an effect on self-concept, motivation, and cumulative learning in school. Further, achievements in reading, writing, and content learning can affect the development of later language learning. As Wallach and Butler (chap. 1) note, the literate styles of language, which tend to be more complex and which appear most commonly in print, are not easily learned without access to the written word. This reciprocity between oral and read language presents greater difficulty to adolescents with reading problems, confounding their acquisition of more complex language and academic content. The end result can be a progressive and escalating pattern of failure in secondary school.

Classroom Performance

Another perspective in identifying adolescent needs is classroom performance. It is an understatement to say that adolescents with language learning disabilities encounter difficulty in their classes. From both identification and intervention standpoints, what goes on in the subject area classrooms (i.e., language arts, social studies, science, etc.) is key to dealing with this population, as Nelson (chap. 4) also suggests. The following are classroom performance characteristics of adolescents with language learning disabilities (Ehren, 1987). This list may help professionals to focus their attention on an appropriate outcome orientation for both identification and programming.

Classroom Performance Characteristics of the LLD Adolescent

- Does not meet minimum performance standards for the class.
- Exhibits a negative approach to learning.
- Does not seem to listen to teacher-directed lessons or participate in lessons.
- Does not follow directions, within academic ability, without further prompting.
- Does not participate appropriately in other instructional settings such as physical education or elective classes.
- Does not organize and express ideas in a logical order.
- Does not recall information presented to the group during a lesson.
- Asks irrelevant questions on content.
- Defines words poorly or uses them inappropriately.
- Fails to learn from questions asked by other students (e.g., asks a question just answered).
- Does not complete work without repetition or delay.
- Answers are irrelevant to questions asked.
- Has difficulty demonstrating knowledge on written tests.
- Does not work independently in class.
- Completes class assignments late, if at all.
- Does not organize work and materials.
- Does not come prepared to class (materials, homework).
- Does not participate in group discussions.
- Relates poorly to authority figures.
- Gets along poorly with other students.
- Interacts in an irrelevant way in conversations with peers and adults.
- Does not use the social rules of conversation (turn taking, entry, and exit).

Whereas language difficulties are frequently at the root of the problems listed previously, it must be noted that these behaviors may have other causes. For example, students who have adequate language abilities but who may be disinterested in school or have emotional problems unrelated to language may perform poorly in class and fail to participate. Ineffective teaching may result in students' inability to work independently in class. Students with conduct disorders may relate poorly to authority figures. As Silliman and Wilkinson (chap. 6) remind professionals, there are many "lenses" one should use when observing students in trouble.

Characteristics and Setting Demands

Ehren and Lenz (1989) maintain that productive views of adolescent needs come from an understanding of secondary school (including middle/junior and senior high school) setting demands. A setting demand is simply a requirement of a specific environment. School levels (i.e., elementary, middle/junior, and senior high school) have different setting demands, as do different teachers within the schools. For example, elementary students are not usually required to take notes from lecture, although this is often a setting demand of some, but not all high school teachers. The performance of adolescents is viewed as a function of the interaction between the individual and the environment. Information on intrinsic characteristics becomes useful only when it is accompanied by information about the demands of the settings in which students must succeed.

Since the early 1980s, the relationship between adolescent characteristics and setting demands has been explored (Lenz, Clark, Deshler, & Schumaker, 1989). In general, a major shift in setting demands occurs between elementary and secondary school years. Elementary school students are expected to acquire basic academic skills; secondary school students are required to demonstrate independent mastery of secondary school content. As students progress from elementary to middle/junior to senior high school, progress is increasingly measured in terms of their ability to express knowledge across a wide variety of disciplines and, as Scott (chap. 8) points out, through written text. At the senior high school level, mastery of the school curriculum is based primarily on the number of Carnegie units or credits earned (i.e., courses for which a passing grade has been received) and completion of prescribed course work. Uniform standards for secondary courses within school systems increases the rigor of requirements, often with less flexibility permitted in adapting the curriculum to the students' needs. There is no doubt that among the environments in which adolescents must succeed, the secondary school setting offers major challenges to adolescents with language learning disabilities. Compounding the problem for adolescents is the fact that language learning competence is needed in increasing depth as the student progresses through middle, junior, and senior high school (Nelson, chap. 4). Curriculum content becomes more difficult, and mastery becomes more reliant on intact language skills. In general, the language of textbooks and teachers' instruction places greater demand on linguistic functioning (see Nelson, chap. 4; Scott, chap. 8).

A number of specific secondary setting demands have been identified by Lenz, Clark, et al. (1989) in the following categories: academic demands, social demands, motivational demands, and executive demands. The ability to predict how adolescents with learning disabilities will fare with secondary school demands is helpful to professionals seeking to meet their needs. The general characteristics of the population, which have emerged since the early 1970s, can be viewed in light of setting demand categories. The descriptions presented in Table 15–1 juxtapose setting demands and characteristics of adolescents with learning disabilities to permit comparison.

When comparing the list of setting demands with the list of student characteristics, professionals might ask themselves whether students with language learning disabilities have the skills necessary to meet the demands of the secondary school setting.

HISTORICAL PERSPECTIVES

While the descriptions in the previous sections help practitioners to understand the nature of adolescents with language learning disabilities, it is helpful to consider past influences when attempting to understand present issues and proposed directions for language intervention with adolescents. History frequently puts into perspective current situations (Bashir & Scavuzzo, 1992). There has certainly been some improvement in language services to adolescents since 1985, when McKinley and Lord-Larson described these students as the neglected population. However, if the type and number of services available are part of the criterion for judging perceived importance, adolescents with language learning disabilities are still a low priority in many places. Consider the contributing factors discussed in the following sections.

Hope of Early Cure

In the recent past, professionals expected early identification to be the key to the remediation of language learning disabilities. "Find them when they're young, and fix them" was often the operative principle. As longitudinal research accumulated during the 1970s and 1980s, it became apparent that despite early efforts, language disorders persisted into adolescence and beyond (Aram, Ekelman, & Nation, 1984; Aram & Nation, 1980; Hall & Tomblin, 1978; King, Jones, & Lasky, 1982; Strominger & Bashir, 1977; Weiner, 1974). A growing body of evidence supported the notion that symptomatology of language disorders changes over time, as the cases presented earlier illustrate, with older children experiencing difficulty with later developing skills, especially those necessary for reading and writing competence (Maxwell & Wallach, 1984). As Bashir and Scavuzzo (1992) point out, "It is not simply a matter of providing more time or early treatment so that a child with a language disorder will eventually 'catch

TABLE 15–1
Academic setting demands and characteristics of adolescents with learning disabilities

Demands	Characteristics
Academic demands: Expectations of the student that relate to passing secondary coursework.	Academic characteristics
Gain information from materials written at the secondary level, not modified or adapted. Gain a significant amount of information from lectures without teacher assistance. Demonstrate learning primarily through objective tests. Write mostly short answers. However, when more lengthy responses are required, correct spelling and complex sentence structure are criteria in their grading.	LD adolescents appear to reach an achievement plateau by tenth grade. On the average, LD tenth graders write at approximately a fifth- to sixth-grade level and read at the fourth- to fifth-grade level, as measured by the Woodcock-Johnson Psychoeducational Battery. They do not use effective or efficient study routines. They have difficulty completing assignments. They frequently have difficulty distinguishing the important from the unimportant. They do not organize information appropriately for study.
Social demands: Expectations of the student that relate to peer and adult interactions and relationships.	Social characteristics
Follow rules and instructions. Participate in social activities. Participate in discussions and conversations with both peers and adults. Accept criticism and help. Recruit assistance when help is needed. Resist inappropriate peer pressure. Be pleasant across social interactions.	Adolescents with learning disabilities have difficulty resisting peer pressure. They do not participate in discussions. They often demonstrate rule-breaking behaviors. They are often less active in school and out-of-school activities. They do not recognize opportunities to use social skills, even when they can demonstrate the same skills in isolation.

up' with age peers" (p. 57). Language disorders persist throughout life. It is likely that during adolescence, and even early adulthood, many of these individuals may need intervention that deals directly with language and communication. To say the least, while research and educational practice suggest otherwise, vestiges of the notions of both "catch up" and "cure" for early language disabilities linger in some education circles.

Failure to Conceptualize Problems as Language Related

While educators recognize the existence of learning and behavior problems in adolescents, attribution of

Demands	Characteristics
Motivation demands: Expectations on the student that relate to overt demonstrations of effort.	Motivation characteristics
Plan and complete tasks on time.	LD adolescents often fail to see the relationship between appropriate effort and success.
Demonstrate a proactive approach to life.	They often do not see the benefits of staying in school.
Set short, intermediate, and long-term goals.	They have difficulty making a commitment to learn or perform.
Put forth maximum and appropriate effort to achieve goals.	They have few goals or plans for the future.
Complete educational programs.	They have trouble setting and attaining goals.
Executive demands: Expectations on the student that relate to self-reliance and efficient use of cognitive resources.	Executive characteristics
Work independently with little feedback.	LD adolescents often do not invent appropriate strategies or approaches that lead to successful task completion.
Apply knowledge across the content areas.	They have difficulty learning how to solve problems.
Solve problems on their own.	They often do not generalize what they learned.
Organize information and a variety of resources independently to solve problems.	They often fail to take advantage of prior knowledge when facing new problems.

these difficulties to underlying linguistic or metalinguistic problems has not always been a serious consideration. Educators may fail to understand the role of language in social or academic skill acquisition, as discussed in this text. Only recently have professionals focused on the language of curriculum and instruction to provide clues to school failure in the middle, junior, and high school population (see Nelson, chap. 4). Language specialists have just begun to come to terms with written language as a language disorder (e.g., Wallach & Butler, chap. 1; Scott, chap. 8).

A related issue is the approach of parsing out language disabilities and learning disabilities as separate entities in investigating school-related problems. In the past it would also have been common for practitioners to speak in terms of adolescents with learning disabilities and those with language disorders, as if they were distinct populations. As the fields of language, reading, and learning disabilities come to appreciate the degree to which underlying linguistic and metalinguistic difficulties contribute to the overall profiles of adolescents with learning disabilities, programming may begin to change. However, as Wallach and Butler (chap. 1) note, practice may not always reflect what is "known." Even today, intervention programs for adolescents with learning disabilities often omit specific attention to the language component.

Inappropriate Screening Procedures

In addition to the problems related to standardized tests in general, noted throughout this text, screening practices tend to be ineffective in identifying students with learning disabilities who have language-based problems. Often, these students have sufficient social use of language to handle the type of language screenings they encounter, although they may lack the necessary linguistic base on which to build complex academic skills (Nelson, chap. 4; Scott, chap. 8; Westby, chap. 7). Consequently, if these students are screened as adolescents, or if they have been screened in earlier years and have more subtle language deficits, the existence of language disorders may be missed.

Inadequate Diagnostic Tools

It has been difficult for practitioners to document language disorders in adolescents until recently. Before the early 1980s, most instruments were normed on young children. Standardized tests, even when they are normed on adolescents, often measure discrete skills in limited or absent contexts. For example, the Peabody Picture Vocabulary Test—Revised, although standardized through adult ages, involves a decontextualized receptive language task at the word level. This task may have little or no relationship to the task demands for the language processing and production that adolescents encounter in school. More complex discourse and text-level skills and strategies are not routinely measured on most instruments available currently.

Although it is recognized that formal, standardized tests tap only small samples of language, cognitive, and metalinguistic abilities, their absence in the past hampered identification efforts at adolescent levels, especially because most public school systems had and still have eligibility requirements involving the use of normative data. With all their pitfalls, tests such as the CELF (Semel & Wiig, 1980a, 1980b) and the Test of Adolescent Language (TOAL) (Hammill, Brown, Larson, & Wiederholt, 1980) were among the first widely used tools that provided practitioners with some assistance in the identification process. Currently, other standardized instruments appropriate for adolescents are available (see the identification section in this chapter). Fortunately, as diagnosticians move toward some of the innovative assessment techniques described by Nelson (chap. 4); Palincsar, Brown, and Campione (chap. 5); and Silliman and Wilkinson (chap. 6), their understanding of adolescents with language learning disabilities will be enhanced.

Limited Prevalence Data

Even when the existence of language disorders in adolescents is acknowledged, the lack of prevalence data specific to this population, as mentioned earlier, has thwarted efforts in program planning. It is difficult to advocate for attention to a population when one is unable to articulate the predominance of language disorders within the population. School administrators, in particular, worry about opening Pandora's box in terms of designing and implementing programs for adolescents, when they are unsure of the numbers of students who may require them (Wallach & Butler, chap. 1). If too many students are identified, think administrators, then the school district may deplete already limited financial resources. Consequently, they may be left in the bind of providing services to some but not all students in need, thus creating legal problems for the school district in terms of equal access to services.

Paucity of Intervention Research

The number of empirically based studies of language intervention efficacy is limited. Paucity of intervention research makes it difficult for practitioners who recognize the existence of adolescent language disorders and who would like to take positive action to design programs and then "sell" them to administrators. Additionally, trial and error approaches to language intervention at this age level, or any age level, contribute to difficulties in program implementation. When programs are ineffective in meeting student needs, and when they fail to contribute to academic success, the movement to conceptualize language intervention as an important component in educating the adolescent with language learning disabilities loses ground.

Service Delivery Models Imported from Elementary Schools

The pervasive nature of language disorders in adolescents and the failure of students to outgrow their learning disabilities have challenged professionals to meet these students' needs. In an effort to provide appropriate programming, educators and clinicians looked to known service delivery models to serve adolescents' school needs. As a result, the popular "resource room" construct for special education services and "pull-out" models for speech-language pathologists were brought to middle, junior, and high schools. These "borrowed," traditional approaches are still being used with questionable success in some places, even though alternative models and programming approaches exist, such as those described in this chapter and by Nelson (chap. 4) and others in this text.

Funding Priorities

With the passage of Public Law (PL) 99–457, the nation has focused its attention and resources on meeting the mandate to serve three- to five-year-olds with disabilities, as well as to provide early intervention initiatives for infants and toddlers (zero to three years). In an economic environment with seriously constrained financial resources for education, the momentum gained in advocacy for improved services to adolescents may have dissipated in some school systems with the increased pressure to meet the new early childhood mandate.

Frustration

Many language specialists find adolescents a difficult group with whom to work. All the normal uneasiness of that age period applies, coupled with the baggage associated with history of school failure. For speech-language pathologists, and other specialists, in particular, it has always been an uphill battle to motivate this age group to attend language intervention and "special help" sessions, especially in pull-out models.

It is important to acknowledge these factors when considering directions in meeting the needs of adolescents with language learning disorders.

GUIDELINES FOR PROVISION OF SERVICES

As professionals seek to address the needs of adolescents with language learning disabilities, several concepts should guide service provision.

Reconceptualize language screening as a process involving several components and different professionals to promote more accurate identification. Professionals must not assume that a "passing" score on standardized screening instruments precludes the possibility that a language learning disability exists. Conversely, teachers should be encouraged to look for signs of language problems in classroom performance. Psychologists and educational diagnosticians should analyze their evaluation results in light of language factors. The following markers may help to identify an initial pool of students for whom more specific attention to language variables as a predominant aspect of their school-related problems may be warranted:

- Academic difficulties
- History of prior language intervention
- Present label of "learning disabilities"
- Referral for special education services at some point in their school career
- Participation in remedial, compensatory, or dropout programs
- Exhibit average nonverbal intelligence

Figure 15–1 presents a checklist of "red-flag" behaviors. This checklist may be used with teachers to seek their assistance in identifying adolescents whose academic failure may be related to language factors.

A note of caution is warranted here: It is important to acknowledge that some learning and behavior problems in school exist apart from language disability as a cause. Practitioners need to balance their attention to the language component with an understanding of other factors related to school difficulties, such as motivation, home influences, emotional problems, substance abuse, and teaching effectiveness, among other influences.

Include language evaluations for students with learning disabilities at all ages. The speech-language pathologist should be a member of the multidisciplinary team responsible for evaluating students suspected of learning disabilities at all age levels. Although it is now understood that early intervention

FIGURE 15–1
Checklist of classroom behaviors of adolescents with language learning disabilities
From *Contextualized Adolescent Language Learning* by B. J. Ehren, 1987, unpublished curriculum.

Frequently uses gestures, not words
Uses "quips" (short, rapid-fire utterances)
Speaks in choppy sentences
Mispronounces words
Gives "ballpark" responses (answers that are related, but not quite correct)
Uses overly general words
Frequently cannot call forth exact words, when vocabulary is known
Asks for repetitions
Complains that teachers talk too fast
Rarely asks questions
Does not participate in class discussions
Does assignments incorrectly, or not at all

does not translate into early cure, intervention geared to underlying language factors that influence school learning may help children with language disorders in preschool and elementary settings make smoother transitions to literacy and academic learning (Wallach & Butler, chap. 1). Further, in the event that language problems were missed in early grades or that problems with higher level language emerge in adolescence, the practice of evaluating language in adolescents with learning disabilities is warranted.

Evaluation procedures may include the use of the following instruments to assess the presence of a language disorder when standardized tests must be used: Clinical Evaluation of Language Fundamentals—Revised (CELF-R) (Semel, Wiig, & Secord, 1987); Test of Adolescent Language—Second Edition (TOAL-2) (Hammill, Brown, Larson, & Wiederholt, 1987); Test of Language Competence (TLC)—Expanded (Wiig & Secord, 1989); Test of Problem Solving (TOPS)—Adolescent Test (Zachman, Barrett, Huisingh, Orman, & Blagden, 1991); Test of Word Knowledge (TOWK) (Wiig & Secord, 1992); Test of Written Language—Second Edition (TOWL-2) (Hammill & Larson, 1988); the WORD Test—Adolescent (Zachman, Huisingh, Barrett, Orman, & Blagden, 1989). Evaluation procedures that furnish alternatives to standardized, norm-referenced testing (which are described in detail by Nelson, Palincsar et al., and Silliman and Wilkinson, chaps. 4 to 6, respectively) should also be incorporated. Specifically, as part of the evaluation process, it is important to include performance on tasks related to setting demands. For example, how well does the student paraphrase written material for report writing, if that is a requirement of the setting? Can the student structure answers to end-of-chapter questions assigned in subject area classes? Evaluation of language strategies in addition to skills is essential. For example, does the student have a planned approach for organizing new vocabulary to promote comprehension of academic subject matter?

Recognize that secondary settings differ from elementary settings and that adolescents have unique needs. The mistakes of the past—including importing elementary models to secondary levels, irrespective of setting demands and characteristics of adolescents—can be avoided. Delivery models and intervention approaches should be designed specifically for adolescents. Several school districts have designed secondary models for language intervention (Comkowycz, Ehren, & Hayes, 1991; Silliman, Wilkinson, & Hoffman, 1993; Work, Ehren, & Cline, 1993).

Recognize that middle or junior high school is different from high school. A single secondary delivery model will be inadequate. Because the nature and structure of middle/junior and senior high schools differ, intervention approaches should be designed to address the specific setting demands at the different school levels as well as the changing needs of the students as they get older.

Plan for transition from elementary to middle (or junior) and middle (or junior) to high school. Although specific planning for postsecondary transition is now required by federal mandate, attention to interschool transitions is sometimes minimal. Students can easily get lost in the shuffle of moving from one school setting to another. As students progress through school levels, careful consideration should be given to changing needs, as parents, professionals, and students develop individualized education programs. Professionals from the sending and receiving schools should collaborate in drafting goals and objectives and in discussing program options.

Use innovative service delivery models. "Just say, 'No' to pull-out!" (Ehren & Wallach, 1990) is a motto that should direct professionals' thinking about the provision of language services at the secondary level. The traditional pull-out delivery model falls far short of meeting the myriad academic and social needs of adolescents for a variety of reasons: (1) It is disruptive to the school day. (2) It is inconsistent with the organizational structure of middle/junior and high schools, which are organized by designated class periods. (3) It calls too much attention to the adolescent during a period of his life when blending into the crowd is a top priority. (4) There is generally no consequence for student nonparticipation or cooperation. (5) Students miss sessions frequently. Professionals must think beyond traditionally defined service delivery and explore alternative models that meet the requirements found in Table 15–2.

Design and implement language intervention programs that follow the criteria listed next. These criteria have been derived from principles of language and its disorders developed throughout this text as well as from information on specific language difficulties, classroom performance problems, and student characteristics in light of setting demands presented earlier in this chapter.

PRINCIPLES OF LANGUAGE INTERVENTION FOR ADOLESCENTS

Contextualize Language in Terms of Other Curricular Areas

As emphasized throughout this text, language intervention should not have its own agenda. Because language needs are embedded within curriculum and instruction, language intervention work should be conceptualized and implemented within the framework of curricula. For example, mastery of social studies curricular objectives will involve understanding textbook information. Comprehension of new social studies concepts requires understanding complex syntactic and semantic forms, which may be a problem for adolescents with language learning disabilities. Language intervention should target manipulation of the kinds of language present in that textbook. Table 15–3 provides a tool for analyzing

TABLE 15–2
Program design for adolescents with language learning disabilities: Self-evaluation checklist
Data from *Contextualized Adolescent Language Learning* by B. J. Ehren, 1987, unpublished curriculum.

Characteristics of the Language Intervention Program	Yes	No
Is palatable to the adolescent		
Makes the adolescent accountable		
Evidences direct applicability to academic and social skill learning		
Is integrated within the curriculum		
Targets objectives related to a selected curriculum not as isolated skills or strategies		
Includes spoken and written language		
Teaches linguistic underpinnings of academic content		
Facilitates content acquisition but does not provide tutoring in subject areas		
Teaches skill prerequisite to other strategies		
Promotes collaboration among professionals		

TABLE 15–3
Language requirements in the secondary curriculum
Data from *Contextualized Adolescent Language Learning* by B. J. Ehren, 1987, unpublished curriculum.

Requirements	Spoken	Written
Comprehend word meanings		
Retrieve specific words		
Pronounce words precisely (phonological accuracy)		
Note linguistic detail		
Formulate complex sentences		
Elaborate on a topic		
Answer questions with precision and accuracy		
Semantically on target (content is in correct class)		
Syntactically correct (structure is sufficiently complex)		
Define terms		
Explain concepts		
Summarize and state conclusions		
Describe events and situations clearly		
Use a variety of complex linguistic forms		
Vary communicative style based on situation and context		
Use appropriate mechanical production skills		
Self-monitor		

specific language requirements of the secondary curriculum.

Reflect Academic Content Areas

Secondary students take a variety of subject classes that can provide a context for targeting language intervention goals and objectives. However, *tutoring* in academic subjects is an inappropriate language intervention approach. A distinction must be made between mastery of academic content and use of academic subjects as context for therapeutic language intervention goals. In tutoring, one teaches the content of subjects such as math, science, and social studies; in therapeutic language intervention, the content provides *a reference point* for teaching the language skills and strategies needed to deal with the content. Language arts and English classes provide unique opportunities for integrating language intervention, which will be discussed later in this chapter. Although materials that incorporate academically relevant topics and concepts can be used, as can textbooks, a focus on completion of classroom assignments and tasks should be avoided. Rather, the academically related materials may be used as a springboard for the facilitation of language skills and strategies. Therapeutic language intervention involves more than doing the academic work. For example, a chapter of the earth science textbook can be used to teach students how to analyze text cues available for identifying important information. The object of language intervention would not be to teach students the concepts contained in the chapter but to help them become familiar with expository text and its structure.

Include Pragmatic Language Work for Some Students

Some adolescents have difficulties with verbal and nonverbal aspects of social communication, as many researchers have suggested (Boucher, 1984; Wiig & Harris, 1974). Practitioners will encounter students who need help with the conversational skills necessary for establishing relationships with peers and adults outside of the classroom context. It is also important, however, to focus on the discourse abilities needed for teaching–learning exchanges in the classroom, including appropriate questioning, group turn taking, and providing appropriate information

(Nelson, chap. 4; Ripich, 1989; Ripich & Spinelli, 1985; Scott, chap. 8).

Attend to Setting Demands

The specific language skills and strategies that students need to survive in their classes as well as social discourse situations should be the focus of language intervention. Things that may be important to know at a later date should be left for another time. For example, although taking notes from lectures may be useful to a student at some point, until a specific teacher requires this activity, the student (1) will not likely be motivated to learn this task and (2) will not have a practical opportunity to generalize this activity to the classroom setting. The fact that setting demands may vary from class to class and from day to day should also be considered.

Integrate Spoken and Written Language Systems

Listening, speaking, reading, and writing should be packaged together in language intervention programs. Although some adolescents may not exhibit oral language problems, program designs should include all language elements. Following this line of thinking, excluding written language from the role of speech-language pathologists should be challenged as inappropriate in this context. The notion of reciprocal causation, noted previously, and the corresponding importance of print in the academic world of secondary school students provide a strong rationale for integrating written and spoken language components. To reiterate a suggestion made in other chapters of this text (e.g., Wallach & Butler, chap. 1; Blachowicz, chap. 11), graphic organizers may be used for both listening and reading comprehension improvement.

Include a Strategy for Academic Performance and Social Interaction

Traditionally, the focus of language intervention has been on the development and facilitation of language *skills.* More recent metacognitive approaches highlight the development and facilitation of *strategies* (Brown, 1978; Brown & Palincsar, 1982; Palincsar, 1986; Palincsar & Brown, 1987; Palincsar & Ransom, 1988). An individual's approach to a task is called a *strategy;* it includes how a person thinks and acts when planning, executing, and evaluating performance on a task and its outcomes (Lenz, Clark, et al., 1989; Mayer, 1987). Instruction in strategy use should be applied to language intervention, as encouraged by Palincsar and her colleagues (chap. 5), among other authors including Chabon and Prelock (1989) and Wiig (1984). Planned approaches to oral and written language tasks that focus on the "how to's" need to be taught directly to adolescents as language strategies. In fact, certain types of language disabilities may be more responsive to a strategic orientation. For example, for adolescents experiencing difficulty with acquiring the vocabulary germane to an academic subject, learning an effective and efficient vocabulary acquisition strategy that can be applied across settings will be more helpful than vocabulary skill instruction focusing on learning individual content words. Rather than drill and practice with specific new vocabulary words in all subjects, one would teach the adolescent a strategy for learning new words when they are encountered in a variety of academic classes. The LINCS strategy, a "starter" strategy for vocabulary learning (Ellis, 1992), might be taught in this context. Pragmatic language competencies required for effective social interaction also need to be viewed within the context of strategy acquisition.

Teach Skills Prerequisite to Strategy Acquisition

Certain skills may be basic to a strategic orientation to learning. Clinical experience with adolescents reveals that skills such as paraphrasing, task analysis, visualization, subordination, and superordination are required for the acquisition and use of many strategies. Programs should incorporate these prerequisites into their sequences for individual students who require instruction in these areas.

Target Generalization Specifically

Evidence from several sources suggests the need for promoting generalization in a planned, directed way as an intrinsic part of intervention (Ellis, Lenz, & Sabornie, 1987; Hughes, 1985, 1989). Practitioners cannot expect to teach skills and strategies and hope for their transfer to other situations and settings. Every intervention activity should contain the seeds of generalization; that is, learning should be contextualized, relevant to an academic, social, emotional, or vocational need and immediately useful to the student across situations and settings. Three points should be noted: (1) Adolescents need to be instructed on how and when to generalize. (2) Classroom teachers need to be engaged in providing cues in their environments for generalization. (3) A system for self-monitoring skill and strategy use should be developed.

Promote Student Accountability

Research on motivation in adolescents supports the need to promote ownership of outcomes through student self-management approaches (Deci, 1992; Lenz, Ehren, & Smiley, 1989; Tollefson, Tracy, Johnsen, Buenning, & Farmer, 1981; Van Reusen & Boss, 1990). Students at a minimum should (1) participate in the development of their Individualized Education Plan (IEP); (2) participate in development of instructional plans to implement the IEP; (3) record evaluation results for IEP objectives; (4) keep track of daily and weekly progress; (5) self-monitor performance in specific target areas, such as the use of specific strategies across settings.

Facilitate Strategy Acquisition

In addition to teaching language-specific strategies, programs concerned with school success should include strategies that facilitate academic learning, motivation, and executive and transition strategies. All professionals working with adolescents with language learning disabilities should attend to these broader metacognitive aspects of intervention, perhaps with varying degrees of responsibility. The likelihood that language problems may interfere with the learning and use of broader cognitive strategies provides a rationale for language specialists to analyze possible language factors that may interfere with strategy acquisition and use.

Involve Collaboration among Professionals

In the complex world of secondary settings within different organizational patterns of service delivery, many professionals may be involved in the education of adolescents with language learning disabilities. Regardless of the specific role delineations in intervention, components must be coordinated among specialists. Specialists, in turn, must actively engage general educators in the process of meeting the students' needs. Specifically, specialists should assist classroom teachers in making reasonable accommodations in the curriculum and instruction to facilitate student success in regular classes.

Practitioners wishing to design and implement language intervention programs incorporating these principles may find the self-evaluation checklist found in Table 15–2 (p. 405) to be helpful in this endeavor. This checklist highlights the critical features described in the previous section.

A PARADIGM FOR CONCEPTUALIZING A TOTAL APPROACH

There are many ways to design programs incorporating the principles outlined in the preceding section. The paradigm described in this section is an example of a total approach to meeting the needs of adolescents with language learning disabilities. This paradigm can serve as a basis for designing program delivery models at both middle/junior and high school levels.

When conceptualizing an intervention approach, it is important to project a desired outcome for the students served. In planning for and with adolescents with language learning disabilities, the following outcomes represent an appropriate focus: (1) to function successfully in the school and in the community with the necessary communication competencies and (2) to graduate from high school with the necessary skills and strategies to hold a job or participate in postsecondary programs. To achieve these outcomes, intervention should be conceptualized as a shared responsibility involving multiple and interrelated components. Collaboration among professionals is essential, as is student ownership of outcomes and self-management of progress. Figure 15–2 depicts a format for conceptualizing a program development paradigm for secondary school students. The content of the circles will depend on several factors: severity of the language learning disabilities encountered, configurations of school districts, resources available, role definition of professionals, existing delivery model components, and opportunity to create new delivery models.

Application of the Paradigm to the Design of Middle School Delivery Systems

The paradigm just described may serve as a context for designing middle/junior high school intervention programs. Figure 15–3 demonstrates a specific application of the paradigm. This model has served as a basis for developing a comprehensive middle school delivery model for regular diploma-seeking adolescents with language learning disabilities for the School Board of Palm Beach County, Florida. The components revolve around a partnership among speech-language pathologists, learning disabilities teachers, and subject area teachers in regular classes. Therapeutic language arts is the combined language therapy and language arts teaching component provided by the speech-language pathologist in the Adolescent Language Program (ALP) using the Contextualized Adolescent Language Learning

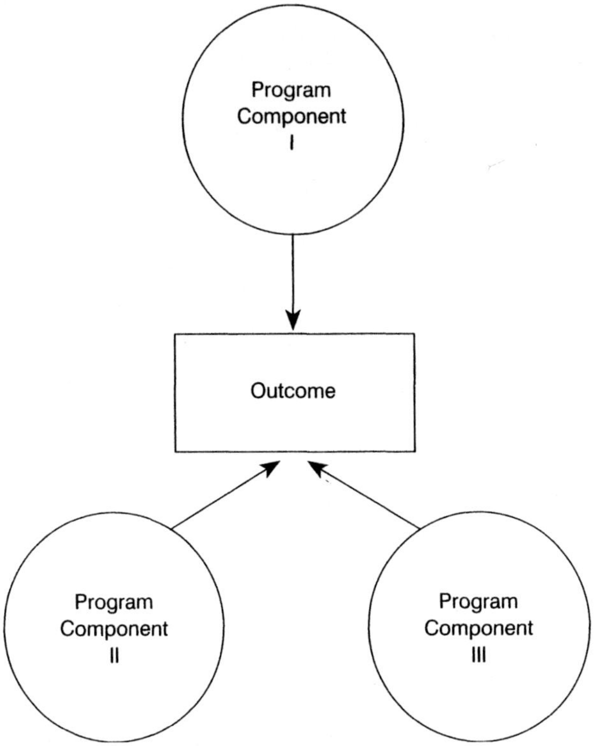

FIGURE 15–2
Total intervention approach paradigm

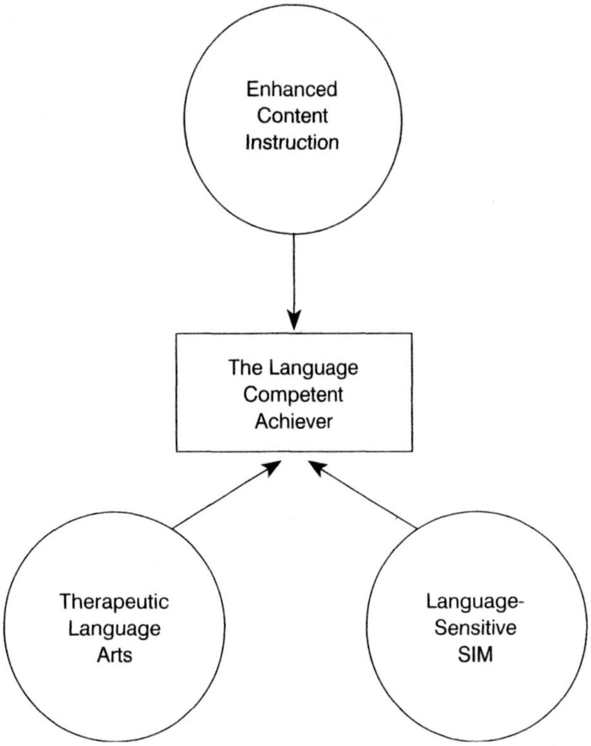

FIGURE 15–3
Total intervention approach for middle school. SIM, strategies intervention model.

(CALL) curriculum (Ehren, 1987). Language-sensitive SIM is the learning strategy instructional model, based on the strategies intervention model (SIM) developed by researchers at the University of Kansas Institute for Research in Learning Disabilities (Deshler & Schumaker, 1986). Classes are taught by a learning disabilities teacher, specially trained as a strategist. Enhanced content instruction is provided by classroom teachers of academic content areas. They use general content enhancement procedures for teaching their classes, which facilitates learning for all students. All the components contribute to the desired outcome of middle school students becoming "language-competent achievers." A more detailed description of the components follows.

Therapeutic Language Arts Component (Academic Strand)

Purpose. To teach outcomes and standards of the regular language arts curricula in grades six to eight with greater emphasis on the linguistic underpinnings at the root of these skills.

Rationale. Language learning disabled adolescents who are regular diploma-seeking students must acquire the skills of the regular curriculum. Those skills, however, require further task analysis because of the language difficulties encountered by adolescents with learning disabilities. Thus, both the methodology for teaching and the curricular design must be adjusted.

Content. Curriculum standards are identified from sixth-, seventh-, and eighth-grade language arts classes based on state-mandated curriculum frameworks. These skills are analyzed for their linguistic underpinnings, essential to acquisition for language disordered students. The following areas in which language disordered students typically experience difficulty are highlighted within the context of the language arts performance standards and outcomes specified for the grade:

Vocabulary
Word analysis
Linguistic precision
Semantic clarification
Elaboration
Problem solving
Memory storage/retrieval
Formulation/presentation

The following additional content area is taken from ESE language arts: six to eight targets in social competence.

Pragmatics. The curriculum targets spoken and written language objectives in an integrated manner and incorporates listening, speaking, reading, and writing activities. A teaching sequence centered around a theme or topic taken from subject-matter classes, either one that is yet to be presented in another academic class or one already introduced, provides the framework for the curriculum. Specific skills and strategies are introduced, and they are appropriately integrated into this context. A major component of the curriculum is the teaching of what are called "ministrategies." Ministrategies can complement or provide alternatives to the complex strategy systems taught in SIM (discussed later). Figure 15–4 provides a list of targets for which ministrategies may be developed.

Curricular Characteristics. The following elements are present within the curriculum:

1. Is sensitive to the language disorders of adolescents with language learning disabilities.
2. Targets skills of a regular language arts curriculum but presents skills in a modified manner.
3. Teaches skills in a more holistic context of spoken and communication, not as splinter skills.
4. Integrates curriculum in various academic areas.
5. Is responsive to immediate setting demands.
6. Includes spoken and written language.
7. Teaches skills needed for strategy use.
8. Teaches ministrategies and facilitates complex strategy system acquisition.
9. Promotes generalization of language skills and strategies to other settings.
10. Motivates the student.

As part of the ALP delivery model, of which therapeutic language arts is a part, speech-language pathologists also consult with regular and special education teachers to facilitate success of students in those classes.

Language-Sensitive Strategies Instruction Model

The SIM is perhaps the most fully researched and developed approach to strategy training available to date. SIM focuses on teaching students how-to-learn approaches that will enable them to meet a variety of setting demands independently. It was developed specifically to address the needs of adolescents with learning disabilities and includes several components. The curriculum component offers learning strategies, social skill strategies, motivation strategies, and executive strategies that have been or are being developed and validated. Learning strategy interventions designed to assist students in meeting the academic demands of a setting are the most fully developed set of strategies in SIM. These packaged curricular materials offer training in complex strategy systems for the purpose of acquiring, manipulating, or expressing information. Strategies related to paraphrasing, self-questioning, interpreting visual aids, error monitoring, sentence writing, paragraph writing, test taking, and first-letter mnemonics, among others, have been designed.

SIM also includes an instructional component that focuses on effective methodology for delivery strategy content in a manner that will facilitate the understanding, remembering, and transfer of strategies across settings. These instructional procedures have been specifically designed to promote the acquisition and generalization of strategies. In the Palm Beach County Schools, either separate learning strategy classes, using SIM, are taught as part of the middle school curriculum for adolescents with learning disabilities, or SIM training is incorporated within other classes for students with specific learning disabilities. Many students with language learning disabilities may receive SIM training. This model has been implemented since the early 1980s. Although it offers a promising alternative to traditional skill-oriented or content-oriented approaches for adolescents with learning disabilities, greater attention to the language variables inherent in the approach is warranted.

Toward this end, training is provided for Palm Beach County School strategy teachers in the following areas: (1) the relationship between language and learning disabilities; (2) the nature of language and its disorders in adolescents with language learning disabilities; (3) the language–learning strategies connection; and (4) language-sensitive, learning strategy instruction. In the last area, information is provided relating to the general requirements of language processing and production present across SIM strate-

FIGURE 15–4
Areas for ministrategy development
From B. J. Ehren, 1993.

I. Using appropriate behavior during class
   A. Engaging in activities
   B. Responding when called on in class
   C. Volunteering responses in class
   D. Requesting the teacher's assistance

II. Completing tasks
   A. Analysis tasks
   B. Organizing tasks
      1. Organizing and using a notebook
      2. Maintaining a calendar
      3. Formatting assignments
   C. Prioritizing tasks
      1. Scheduling tasks
      2. Managing time (completion within time limits)
   D. Evaluating/monitoring performance (accuracy)
   E. Completing at appropriate level of independence

III. Doing homework
   A. Recording homework
   B. Organizing homework
   C. Completing homework
   D. Checking homework
   E. Submitting homework

IV. Working on a project with others

V. Deriving meaning from text
   A. Using parts of a book (table of contents, glossary, index, title page, headers)
   B. Using emphasis cues
   C. Using graphic organizers
   D. Paraphrasing
   E. Acquiring new vocabulary

gies, language demands inherent in the strategy teaching methodology, and language demands inherent in the content of specific SIM strategies. For adolescents with language learning disabilities to succeed in acquiring SIM learning strategies, teachers must adapt their instruction using a more language-sensitive SIM approach. Therefore, this component is essential in conceptualizing a total approach to meeting adolescent needs.

Enhanced Content Instruction

The component provided by general education teachers is, of course, crucial to the overall success of students in reaching the desired outcome. Unless adolescents perform satisfactorily in subject area classes, special intervention approaches are for naught. Therefore, it is important to focus on instructional approaches used in content-area subjects.

Practitioners report some resistance from secondary teachers to making individual accommodations for students experiencing academic difficulties. From the content teacher's perspective, spending an inordinate amount of time attending specifically to a few students when serving perhaps 150 students, which for some secondary teachers is a typical teaching load, is an unrealistic expectation. Teachers

FIGURE 15–4, *continued.*

VI. Using a subject area textbook
   A. Previewing chapter content
   B. Answering textbook questions
   C. Using contextual clues (direct definition, restatement, contrast, inferences, examples)

VII. Reading and interpreting graphs (pictographs, pie graphs, vertical bar graphs, line graphs, horizontal bar graphs, tables)

VIII. Comparing information from different types of graphs

IX. Studying material
   A. Two-, three-, four-column notes
   B. Paraphrasing
   C. Using story grammars
   D. DRTA (preparing, previewing and purpose setting, guided silent reading, discussing and rereading, doing extension activities)

X. Making oral presentations
   A. Preparing
   B. Presenting

XI. Taking notes
   A. Taking notes from written material
      1. Paraphrasing
   B. Taking notes from oral material (messages, news broadcasts, lectures)
      1. Paraphrasing

must use techniques that are powerful, yet require little energy to use. Techniques that can be implemented on an individual basis without preparing special materials before delivering the content and that can be readily integrated into traditional approaches to teaching content are the ones most likely to be used (Lenz, Bulgren & Hudson, 1991).

To address the concerns for effective content instruction, researchers at the University of Kansas Institute for Research in Learning Disabilities developed the content enhancement model. The content enhancement model is defined as

> the process of teaching scientific or cultural knowledge to a heterogeneous group of students in which: (a) group and individual learning needs both are met; (b) integrity of the context is maintained; (c) critical features of the content are selected, organized, manipulated, and complemented in a manner that promotes effective and efficient information processing; and (d) the content is delivered in a partnership with students in a manner that facilitates and enriches learning for all students. (Lenz, Bulgren & Hudson, 1991; p. 123)

Critical features of the model include the actual content enhancement options available to teachers

FIGURE 15–4, *continued.*

XII. Researching a topic
- A. Selecting the appropriate reference source
- B. Using reference books for information
  - 1. Alphabetizing
  - 2. Dictionary
    - a. Locating words quickly in a dictionary
    - b. Reading and interpreting dictionary entries
  - 3. Encyclopedia
    - a. Locating entries in an encyclopedia
    - b. Locating information in encyclopedia entries
  - 4. Atlas
- C. Organizing information

XIII. Writing text
- A. Using spool papers
- B. Using framed paragraphs
- C. Proofreading assignments
  - 1. Using spellcheck programs to identify correct spelling

XIV. Taking tests
- A. Using format-specific strategies (multiple choice, true–false, short answer, essay)
- B. Organizing and managing time

XV. Attaining goals
- A. Setting
- B. Analyzing
- C. Implementing
- D. Evaluating

in the form of routines and devices. Content enhancement routines include (1) orientation routines such as the advance organizer, the postorganizer, and the chapter survey; (2) understanding routines such as concept teaching, semantic mapping, semantic feature analysis, concept generalization, concept exploration, and process explanation; and (3) activation routines such as assignment construction, assignment instruction, and assignment completion. Content enhancement devices include (1) devices for understanding (e.g., examples, comparisons, and cause and consequence); (2) devices for remembering (e.g., "big picture," mental image, familiar association, key word, rhyming, method of loci, and first-letter mnemonic); and (3) devices for organizing (e.g., use of guides, verbal cues, and illustrators).

All of these teaching techniques would benefit entire classes of students, not just students with language learning disabilities. This is perhaps their greatest selling point to harried secondary teachers. They do not have to devote time and energy to learning specific techniques that may apply to few students. Rather, content enhancement routines and devices, when learned, can be readily incorporated as a part of daily instruction while promoting greater teacher satisfaction with instruction effectiveness. As a way of training teachers in these techniques, some schools are implementing collaborative teaching models wherein special education specialists team teach with regular content area teachers, providing a way to model use of the approach.

Application of the Paradigm to the Design of High School Delivery Systems

Another application of the basic paradigm represented by Figure 15–2 is presented in Figure 15–5 with postsecondary success as an outcome for high school students. Components are similar, but the demands of the high school, especially with regard to earning credits toward graduation, require a different conceptualization. Pivotal to this paradigm are the services offered by the speech-language pathologist in the Palm Beach County Schools in what is called the *high school menu model*. In this model, several components are designed in a choice format, similar to a menu. Specific components are selected for use by particular high schools to meet their unique needs.

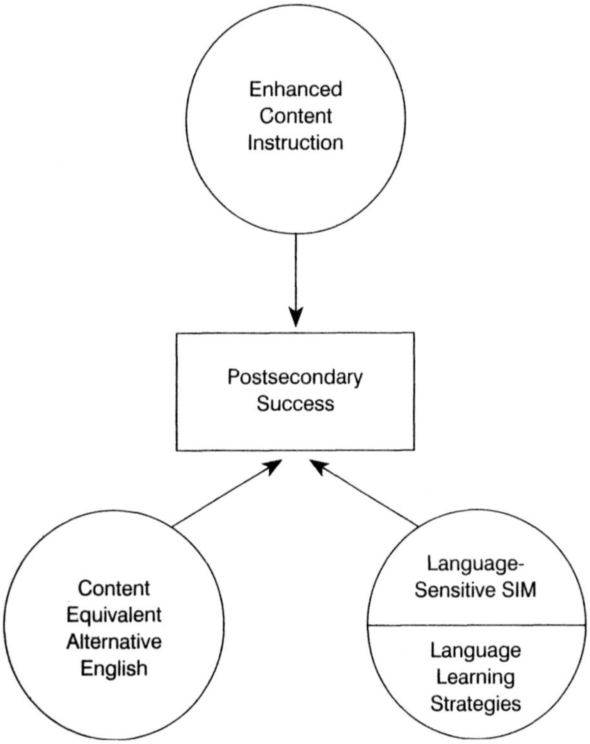

FIGURE 15–5
Total intervention approach for high school: SIM, strategies intervention model

The enhanced content instruction component previously described in the middle school application remains the same in the high school model. However, language-sensitive SIM may or may not be involved. In high school, the existence of separate SIM courses is more widespread than in middle school. SIM courses are used for elective credit toward graduation in high school. Those students who are able to handle the SIM curriculum are usually placed in SIM classes with the speech-language pathologist working closely with the learning disability teacher who teaches the learning strategies class. For those students needing an alternative strategy approach, a language learning strategy course is provided by the speech-language pathologist as part of the high school menu model. For example, in the Palm Beach program, the speech-language pathologists observed that many adolescents with language learning disabilities were unsuccessful in learning complex strategy systems. Many of them seemed to need a ministrategy approach, at least in ninth and tenth grades.

Several options are available in the high school menu model. Students who are able to cope with the structure of a regular English course take required English classes in general education. Similar to the system described with the SIM classes, those who need a different approach leading to the same curriculum performance standards as required by the state for Carnegie units or credits take content-equivalent alternative English. This required course is co-taught by a speech-language pathologist and a learning disabilities teacher with the speech-language pathologist sharing instructional duties three days a week. The high school menu model also includes time for the speech-language pathologist to consult with regular and special education teachers.

SUMMARY

As discussed throughout this chapter and throughout the entire book, professionals working with students with language learning disabilities can reasonably expect to find language problems in the adolescent population. It is hoped that professionals reading this chapter are well versed in the role of language proficiency in school success. Consequently, they understand that a core consideration in programming for adolescents with learning disabilities is specific attention to the language component of their education. The multidimensional view of characteristics presented in this chapter, together with information gleaned from historical perspectives, provide a base for some future directions professionals may take. The suggested directions focused on reconceptualizing the screening and evaluation process, designing programs that are appropriate to the settings of middle/junior and high schools and using innovative delivery models. Specific principles of language intervention included contextualized language intervention to deal with academic and social discourse requirements of adolescents; integration of spoken and written language; a strategic orientation to language intervention, including generalization; student accountability; and collaboration among professionals. The key notion in the paradigm presented is that intervention should be conceptualized as a multifaceted endeavor, driven by a common outcome. The middle school and high school models described were offered as exemplars of the paradigm. Readers are challenged to consider their own setting demands and constraints and to identify appropriate directions for meeting the learning needs of adolescents with language learning disabilities within their communities.

REFERENCES

American Speech-Language-Hearing Association. (1982). Position statement on language learning disorders. *Asha, 24,* 937–944.

Aram, D., Ekelman, B., & Nation, J. (1984). Preschoolers with language disorders: 10 years later. *Journal of Speech and Hearing Research, 27,* 232–244.

Aram, D., & Nation, J. (1980). Preschool language disorders and subsequent language and academic difficulties. *Journal of Communication Disorders, 13,* 159–170.

Bashir, A., Kuban, K., Kleinman, S., & Scavuzzo A. (1983). Issues in language disorders: Considerations of cause, maintenance, and change. In Miller, J., Yoder, D., & Schieflebush, R. (Eds.), *ASHA report* No. 12, 92–106.

Bashir, A. S., & Scavuzzo, A. (1992). Children with language disorders: Natural history and academic success. *Journal of Learning Disabilities, 25*(1), 53–65.

Boucher, C. R. (1984). Pragmatics: The verbal language of learning disabled and nondisabled boys. *Learning Disability Quarterly, 7,* 271–286.

Brown, A. L. (1978). Knowing when, where and how to remember: A problem of metacognition. In R. Glaser (Ed.), *Advances in instructional psychology.* Hillsdale, NJ: Lawrence Erlbaum.

Brown, A. L., & Palincsar, A. (1982). Inducing strategic learning from texts by means of informed, self-control training. *Topics in Learning and Learning Disabilities, 2,* 1–17.

Chabon, S. A., & Prelock, P. A. (1989). Strategies of a different stripe: Our response to a zebra question about language and its relevance to the school curriculum. *Seminars in Speech and Language, 10*(3), 241–251.

Chappell, G. (1985). Description and assessment of language disabilities of junior high school students. In C. Simon (Ed.) *Communication skills and classroom success: Assessment of language learning disabled students* (pp. 207–242). San Diego, CA: College-Hill Press, 207–242.

Comkowycz, S., Ehren, B., & Hayes, N. (1987). Meeting classroom needs of language disordered students in middle and junior high schools: A program model. *Journal of Childhood Communication Disorders, 11,* 199–208.

Deci, E. L. (1992). Autonomy and competence as motivational factors in students with learning disabilities and emotional handicaps. *Journal of Learning Disabilities, 25*(7), 457–471.

Deshler, D., & Schumaker, J. (1986). Learning strategies: An instructional alternative for low-achieving adolescents. *Exceptional Children, 52,* 583–590.

Deshler, D., Schumaker, J., Alley, G., Warner, S., & Clark, F. (1982). Learning disabilities in adolescent and young adult populations: Research implications. *Focus on Exceptional Children, 15,* 1–11.

Donahue, M., & Bryan, T. (1984). Communicative skills and peer relations of learning disabled adolescents. *Topics in Language Disorders, 4,* 10–21.

Ehren, B. J. (1987). *Contextualized adolescent language learning.* Unpublished curriculum.

Ehren, B. J., & Lenz, B. K. (1989). Adolescents with language disorders: Special considerations in providing academically relevant language intervention. *Seminars in Speech and Language, 10,* 192–205.

Ehren, B. J., & Wallach, G. (1990). *ASHA teleconference.* Rockville Park, MD: American Speech-Language-Hearing Association.

Ellis, E. S. (1992). *LINCS: A starter strategy for vocabulary learning.* Lawrence, KS: Edge Enterprises.

Ellis, E. S., Lenz, B. K., & Sabornie, E. (1987). Generalization and adaptation of learning strategies to natural environment. Part I: Critical agents. *Remedial and Special Education, 8,* 6–20.

Florida Department of Education. (1983). *Project Adolang, identification of adolescent language problems and implications for education.* Tallahassee, FL: Bureau of Education for Exceptional Students.

Hall, P., & Tomblin, J. (1978). A follow-up study of children with articulation and language disorders. *Journal of Speech and Hearing Disorders, 43,* 227–241.

Hammill, D., Brown, V., Larson, S., & Wiederholt, J. (1980). *Test of adolescent language: A multidimensional approach to assessment.* Austin, TX: Pro-Ed.

Hammill, D., Brown, V., Larson, S., & Wiederholt, J. (1987). *Test of adolescent language—second edition* (TOAL-2). Austin, TX: Pro-Ed.

Hammill, D., & Larson, S. (1988). *Test of written language—second edition* (TOWL-2). Austin, TX: Pro-Ed.

Hughes, D. L. (1985). *Language treatment and generalization: A clinician's handbook.* San Diego, CA: College-Hill Press.

Hughes, D. L. (1989). Generalization from language therapy to classroom academics. *Seminars in Speech and Language, 10,* 218–230.

Jones, J. (1984). Comprehension of perceptual and psychological metaphors by language learning disabled and normally achieving adolescents. *Dissertation Abstracts International, 45,* 2065A.

King, R., Jones, C., & Lasky, E. (1982). In retrospect: A fifteen-year follow-up report of speech-language-disordered children. *Language, Speech and Hearing Services in Schools, 13,* 24–32.

Klecan-Aker, J. (1985). Syntactic abilities in normal and language deficient middle school children. *Topics in Language Disorders, 5,* 46–54.

Larson, V. L., & McKinley, N. L. (1985). General intervention principles with language impaired adolescents. *Topics in Language Disorders, 5,* 70–77.

Larson, V., & McKinley, N. (1987). *Communication assessment and intervention strategies for adolescents.* Eau Clair, WI: Thinking Publishers.

Lenz, B. K., Bulgren, J., & Hudson, P. (1990). Content enhancement: A model for promoting the acquisition of content by individuals with learning disabilities. In E. E. Scruggs & B. L. Wong (Eds.), *Intervention research in learning disabilities* (pp. 122–165). New York: Springer-Verlag.

Lenz, B. K., Clark, F. L., Deshler, D. D., & Schumaker, J. B. (1989). *The strategies instructional approach: A training package.* Lawrence, KS: University of Kansas, Institute for Research in Learning Disabilities.

Lenz, B. K., Ehren, B. J., & Smiley, L. R. (1989). A goal attainment approach to improve completion of project-type assignments by learning disabled adolescents. *Learning Disabilities Focus, 6*(1).

Maxwell, S., & Wallach, G. P. (1984). The language–LD connection: Symptoms of language disability change over time. In G. P. Wallach & K. G. Butler (Eds.), *Language learning disabilities in school-age children.* Baltimore, MD: Williams & Wilkins.

Mayer, R. E. (1987). *Educational psychology: A cognitive approach.* Boston: Little, Brown.

McKinley, N., & Lord-Larson, V. (1985). Neglected language-disordered adolescent: A delivery model. *Language, Speech and Hearing Services in Schools, 16,* 2–15.

Palincsar, A. S. (1986). Metacognitive strategy instruction. *Exceptional Children, 53,* 118–124.

Palincsar, A. S., & Brown, D. (1987). Enhancing instructional time through attention to metacognition. *Journal of Learning Disabilities, 20,* 66–75.

Palincsar, A. S., & Ransom, K. (1988). From mystery spot to the thoughtful spot: The instruction of metacognitive strategies. *The Reading Teacher, 41,* 784–789.

Ripich, D. (1989). Building classroom communication competence: A case for a multiperpective approach. *Seminars in Speech and Language, 10*(3), 231–240.

Ripich, D., & Spinelli, F. (1985). *School discourse problems.* San Diego, CA: College Hill Press.

Semel, E., & Wiig, E. (1980a). *Clinical evaluation of language functions (CELF)—Advanced level screening test.* New York: Merrill/Macmillan.

Semel, E., & Wiig, E. (1980b). *Clinical evaluation of language functions (CELF)—Diagnostic battery.* New York: Merrill/Macmillan.

Semel, E., Wiig, E., & Secord, W. (1987). *Clinical evaluation of language fundamentals—Revised (CELF-R).* San Antonio, TX: Psychological Corporation.

Silliman, E. R., Wilkinson, L. C., & Hoffman, L. P. (1993). Documenting authentic progress in language and literacy learning. Collaborative assessment in the classroom. *Topics in Language Disorders, 14*(1).

Sinclair, R. L., & Ghory, W. J. (1987). *Reaching marginal students: A primary concern for school renewal.* Chicago: McCutchan.

Strominger, A., & Bashir, A. (1977). *A nine-year follow-up of language-delayed children.* Paper presented at the annual convention of the American Speech-Language-Hearing Association, Chicago.

Tollefson, N., Tracy, D. B., Johnsen, E. P., Buenning, M., & Farner, A. (1981). *Implementing goal setting activities with LD adolescents* (Research Report No. 48). Lawrence, KS: The University of Kansas Institute for Research in Learning Disabilities.

Van Reusen, A. K., & Boss, C. S. (1990). I PLAN: Helping students communicate in planning conferences. *Teaching Exceptional Children, 22*(4), 30–32.

Vellutino, F. (1977). Alternative conceptualization of dyslexia: Evidence in support of a verbal-deficit hypothesis. *Harvard Educational Review, 47,* 334–354.

Wallach, G. P., & Butler, K. G. (1984). *Language learning disabilities in school-age children.* Baltimore, MD: Williams & Wilkins.

Weiner, P. (1974). A language-delayed child at adolescence. *Journal of Speech and Hearing Disorders, 39j,* 202–212.

Wiig, E. H. (1984). Language disabilities in adolescents: A question of cognitive strategies. *Topics in Language Disorders, 4,* 41–58.

Wiig, E., Becker-Redding, U., & Semel, E. (1983). A cross-cultural, cross-linguistic comparison of language abilities of 7 to 8 and 12 to 13 year old children with learning disabilities. *Journal of Learning Disabilities, 16,* 576–585.

Wiig, E., & Fleischmann, N. (1980). Knowledge of pronominalization, reflexivation, and relativization by learning disabled college students. *Journal of Learning Disabilities, 13,* 571–576.

Wiig, E. H., & Harris, S. P. (1974). Perception and interpretation of nonverbally expressed emotions by adolescents with learning disabilities. *Perceptual and Motor Skills, 38,* 239–245.

Wiig, E., Lapointe, C., & Semel, E. (1977). Relationships among language processing and production abilities of learning disabled adolescents. *Journal of Learning Disabilities, 10,* 292–299.

Wiig, E., & Roach, M. (1975). Immediate recall of semantically varied "sentences" by learning disabled adolescents. *Perceptual and Motor Skills, 40,* 119–125.

Wiig, E., & Secord, W. (1989). *Test of language competence (TLC)—Expanded.* San Antonio, TX: Psychological Corporation.

Wiig, E., & Secord, W. (1992). *Test of word knowledge (TOWK).* San Antonio, TX: Psychological Corporation.

Wiig, E., & Semel, E. (1974). Logico-grammatical sentence comprehension by learning disabled adolescents. *Perceptual and Motor Skills, 8,* 1331–1334.

Wiig, E., & Semel, E. (1975). Productive language abilities in learning disabled adolescents. *Journal of Learning Disabilities, 8,* 578–586.

Wiig, E., & Semel, E. (1984). *Language assessment and intervention for the learning disabled* (2nd ed.). New York: Merrill/Macmillan.

Wiig, E., Semel, E., & Abele, E. (1981). Perception and interpretation of ambiguous sentences by learning disabled twelve year olds. *Learning Disabilities Quarterly, 4,* 3–12.

Work, R., Ehren, B., & Cline, J. (1993). Adolescent language programs. *Language, Speech and Hearing Services in the Schools, 24,* 43–53.

Zachman, L., Barrett, M., Huisingh, R., Orman, J., & Blagden, C. (1991). *TOPS—Adolescent test (test of problem solving).* East Moline, IL: Linguisystems.

Zachman, L., Huisingh, R., Barrett, M., Orman, J., & Blagden, C. (1989). *The WORD test—adolescent.* East Moline, IL: Linguisystems.

16

KEEPING ON TRACK TO THE TWENTY-FIRST CENTURY

■ Katharine G. Butler
Syracuse University
■ Geraldine P. Wallach
Emerson College Los Angeles Center

As theory and practice undergo a paradigm shift in the 1990s and beyond, practitioners may be asking themselves how this text has relevance—relevance in terms of the school reforms of the present and near future (the year 2000) that will affect both students and the professionals who serve them. As "inclusion"[1] looms on the horizon, readers will note several concepts from this text that provide a strong knowledge base to reflect on as we all face the challenges outlined in Chapter 1. As a result of the changing paradigms of the 1990s, the questions raised about "why children are in trouble" will continue to be broader than in the past. Questions that have a narrow or vague focus, such as whether children are "visual" or "auditory" learners or whether they can "sequence," are left behind us as assessment and observational lenses are widened to include more sophisticated views of discourse, literacy, and processing discussed throughout this volume. The development of keener observational skills will be critical to understanding the "special" student in the "regular" classroom (recall Silliman & Wilkinson's discussion in chap. 6). The importance of understanding learner potential and the potential role of both oral and print scaffolds in the enhancement of that potential should not be underestimated. The interwoven yet distinct natures of oral and written language and their influence on a set, created, or modified curriculum must be well understood.

Indeed, there is much to think and *do* about the educational and social changes that surround us. In this, the final word, the co-editors pause to consider a number of questions. We have asked some of our colleagues to join us by responding to queries emanating from the construction of this text. In reflecting on the status of both the study of language and the potential of school reform and on their possible status in the year 2000 and beyond, we concede that the wheels of progress grind slowly. Part of the slow pace of change comes from the reality that theoretical constructs and experimental studies are usually the forerunners of change, followed by a lengthy incubation period while the outcomes of the first studies are either verified or derivations on the theme rendered. Another contribution to the slow-change mode is fear of change, even when considerable justification and previous research support a change. For example, dynamic procedures have been under development for well over fifteen years, but they are just now becoming accepted alternatives. And, last, it is worth noting that although language has "been around" for centuries, we have been slow to understand how we acquire it and how language disabilities may occur and be remedied. Only in the twentieth century have we begun to construct the scientific base on which to build our knowledge and skills. Recognizing that language study is a relatively new discipline, we can see why speech-language pathology and related educational and clinical professions have their own "trickle-down" theory that accounts in some degree for the lengthy time span from research to practice. Each generation of students-in-training go out into the field with minds stuffed with research paradigms, but without the "real-world" experience needed to build on theoretical perspectives in assessment and treatment. On the other side of the coin, clinicians

[1]"Inclusion is a process whereby exceptional students are educated in neighborhood schools in age-appropriate classroom settings with nonexceptional peers and are provided with services and programs based on their individual strengths and needs using appropriate instructional strategies" (Crawford & Porter, 1992, quoted in Hoffman, 1993a). Inclusion, as a value, supports the right of all children, regardless of their diverse abilities, to participate actively in natural settings within their communities (DEC Position Statement, 1993).

and educators who have developed "hands-on" expertise find themselves buffeted by circumstances well beyond the research laboratory, the university classroom, and clinic. The requirements of various work settings may make the introduction of new precepts and new procedures difficult. Conversely, clinicians and educators may be expected to adopt new, and at times, relatively untried or documented approaches to reforms—"whole language" and "inclusion" to name only two. In the hurly-burly that is the typical milieu of the practicing professional, there may be few opportunities to analyze and reflect on "what works" and *why* it may work as the theory–practice gap remains an ongoing reality (Kamhi, 1993; Wallach, 1993). The questions asked of Launer, Paratore, Catts, and Hoffman are a mere sample of so many questions one could raise as we "stop to think" about some of the most-discussed issues of the day. And while frustrations may abound, some real progress has been made since the 1970s; some of that progress is reflected in the depth and scope of information we now have about language and literacy learning, including some "what-to-do's" for children and adolescents in trouble. Our colleagues share some of that collective knowledge next.

Question: Professionals will argue that they need tests to get children into programs, measure progress, and provide accountability. In your view, what is the greatest misunderstanding professionals have about the "power" of standardized language tests? How does one move away from using standardized tests (and move toward more innovative observation and dynamic assessment procedures covered in this text) when pressure from state, federal, and local sources suggests otherwise?

Answer by Patricia B. Launer
San Diego State University

In the past decade, there have been numerous attacks on the appropriateness of norm-referenced tests for meeting any of our multiple objectives of assessment. Nonetheless, these tests continue to be used, and in some cases, they are demanded by districts, states, and other funding sources. Two of the most profound pitfalls in the use of these standardized measurements are irresponsible consumerism and inaccurate interpretation.

We are all buzzword junkies. We comb the professional literature, scanning the ads for the word-of-the-week. We skipped blithely from *pragmatics* to *narrative* to *emergent literacy* to *whole language* to *phonological awareness* to *collaborative consultation*. If we're hip, we're hopping to buy test materials that promote the latest linguistic lingo. But as the old Latin saying goes, caveat emptor, let the buyer beware.

With the ever-increasing refinement of desktop publishing and the decreased professional publishing-house competition (the big fish have swallowed up most of the little fish), almost anything can be put out there in the marketplace, slickly packaged and advertised, without so much as a glance by another professional, let alone a formal peer review. Take a couple of kids into your basement, whip a few tasks by them, and voila! A test is born. (Granted, readers will recognize the preceding as an "overstatement"; however, it makes the point that healthy skepticism is warranted every time we walk into the exhibitor's area at national, state, and local conferences. Caveat emptor must remain in effect.)

For years, I have taught a class in diagnostic methods in speech-language pathology. Besides bemoaning and abhorring the course title (I do not feel that our job is to diagnose; it is to describe, assess, and evaluate), I have focused a good deal of attention on informed consumerism. No matter what I say, however, those graduate students are just itching to get out there and try those myriad standardized tests, old and new. The best I can do is to expose them to alternate ways to obtain and evaluate information and to make them better buyers of the products that are available.

Outside our safe, academic, ivory-tower walls, the people in the trenches are struggling every day, fighting for services for our language learning disabled (LLD) students. To justify their needs and requests, they are using these myriad tests with gay abandon, and often without full understanding.

First, when perusing any standardized test, or even an ad for such a test, one must closely examine the statistical validity and reliability of the tool. If these data are not reported (especially in the ad), they probably do not exist or are not worth reporting. We need to look for numbers (usually, reliability coefficients) relating to construct validity, concurrent validity, predictive validity, test–retest reliability and interexaminer reliability. We need to inspect the normative sample and the materials themselves; with our increasingly diverse student population, some of these tests are less relevant than ever.

We also need to evaluate the kinds of derived scores used. The most popular possibilities are age-equivalent scores, percentile ranks, and standard scores. These differ in the degree to which they make use of information about the central tendency and variability of scores obtained by the normative sample.

Although age scores are most easily understood by parents, teachers, and even speech-language pathologists, they should be avoided at all costs. As the American Psychological Association (APA) put it back in 1974, developmental/equivalence scores are often difficult to interpret and "lend themselves to gross misinterpretation" (APA, 1974, p. 23). More important, for those of us who see ourselves as the staunchest of child advocates, age scores give no leeway, no range of normality to the child. He is either fifteen days within chronological age or there is some delay, but how much of a discrepancy constitutes a delay is extremely difficult to determine and varies with the age of the child. Furthermore, because the age score is often merely an average of the age of all children who received a certain raw score on a given test, it is entirely possible that not even *one* child at the derived age actually achieved that score. In 1990, Lahey wisely called for "a moratorium on the use of all equivalence measures in our journals and other official publications, and their use should be discouraged in our clinic and school reports" (p. 615).

Percentile ranks make it easier to compare the test taker with the normative group (by means of relative standing), and in recent years, they have been embraced by speech-language pathologists. Percentile ranks, however, have their own disadvantages, such as the fact that small differences in rankings at the high or low end of the percentile scale often reflect very big differences in raw scores, because most scores tend to cluster around the mean, and the relative scores are not at equal intervals.

Standard scores are considered by some to be the most satisfactory kind of derived score (Anastasi, 1988), even though they are slightly more difficult to understand, calculate, and interpret than percentiles or age-equivalent scores. Their calculation, however, uses information about the average score and variability of scores obtained by the normative sample, which makes them more statistically robust and more flexibly applied. They can be used to estimate the position of a test taker's score relative to the scores obtained by the normative sample, to compare scores on two different tests, and to compare one person's score to someone else's in a meaningful way (McCauley & Swisher, 1984a). Some speech-language pathologists are taking the great leap into the statistical abyss and beginning to look for the standard error of measurement, which, when reported in a test manual, provides a confidence interval or range of performance within which an individual child's true score probably falls, rather than assigning just one specific, absolute value to test performance.

If you have not been in school for some time, and all this sounds vaguely foreign and frightening, but you know in your clinical gut that it makes all the sense in the world, consult McCauley and Swisher (1984a), who have set down ten criteria for evaluating any norm-referenced test, clearly describing each of the psychometric criteria, and specifying the consequences if each is unmet. They have, in fact applied them to fifty-eight of our commonly used language and articulation tests.

Now, all that said, we have to address the notion of weaning ourselves away from overreliance on norm-referenced tests, for any number of reasons: (1) Tests do not reflect actual communicative abilities and take little account of pragmatics or the use of language. (2) Tests only tap very specific skills in very specific ways. (3) Tests are anxiety producing and may not elicit optimal performance. (4) Tests are not interactive; one person asks questions, the other is required to answer, so there is communicative asymmetry and the student is seen only as responder, never as initiator. (5) Tests rarely allow for creative responses or flexibility in scoring and interpretation. (6) Tests do not reflect communication in the context of the classroom. (7) Tests are often culturally biased and may not reflect in any way the enormously growing diversity in our clinical population. We have to fight for more informal formal assessments to be acceptable to "the powers that be." In most school settings, we have won the battle for language sampling, and informal narrative analysis is next. We need to push on, to fight even harder.

In terms of culturally and linguistically diverse students, assessment is generally more valid and accurate if data collection and analysis are conducted within the framework of a collaborative model, and this fits right in with current trends in schools. The collaborative context, with its emphasis on more frequent and diverse behavioral sampling, increases the ecological validity of our assessments.

Damico (1990) recommends a bi-level analysis paradigm: "descriptive analysis" and "explanatory analysis." Explanatory analysis entails a team approach to determining whether the communicative difficulties noted at the descriptive level are a result of external factors such as cultural or linguistic diversity, or whether these problems reflect an actual language learning impairment. The assessment process includes pre-referral assessment (which elicits suggestions for alternative classroom instructional or supportive strategies); task analysis based on real-life situations (most likely narrative analysis and language sampling); direct observation (best for obtaining ecologically valid data); curriculum-based assessment (which includes probe activities, observation, artifact analysis, interviewing and direct assessment to determine the language demands of the curriculum and how well the student handles those demands); contextual analysis (which may focus on the context of the classroom, the home, or specific tasks such as assessment); and ethnographic assessment (the application of anthropological methodologies to obtain relevant data from multiple perspectives, focusing on detailed behavioral description of the student's communicative ability and the various contextual and cultural factors that have an impact on this ability).

Read that paragraph over again. If you can justify it for culturally diverse populations, doesn't it make sense to apply it to *all* our LLD students? We have got to get tough, aggressive, and proactive. We have got to make a strong case for alternative assessments and back it up with the "big guns" of literature support and "what other schools/districts/states are doing."

The psychobabble buzzwords of the day are *self-esteem, self-actualization,* and *empowerment.* Go for it. But this time, jump on a bandwagon bound for glory. Empower your profession, your students, and yourself by justifying the need for nonstandardized assessments and becoming more proficient at using and interpreting them. Get fire in your belly and fight for what you know is right.

Question: Recently, heated arguments about which reading approaches are "best" have resurfaced, with particular emphasis on "whole language" vs. "direct instruction" or "basal reading approaches." What is your opinion about the usefulness of having such arguments about "best program" or "approach"?

Answer by Jeanne R. Paratore
Boston University

I do not believe that the debate that has centered on "whole language" versus "direct instruction" or "whole language" versus "the basal reader" has been useful in advancing our understanding of the conditions under which children learn best. We seem to have become lost in labels and materials, at the expense of developing a shared understanding of the basis for success in reading and writing. In addition, advocates on both sides of the debate seem to subscribe to a belief that a single approach or program is best for all children at all stages of learning. Important questions need to be asked and answered about whether or not different approaches are more or less effective at different levels of literacy development (Stahl & Miller, 1989). As well, questions need to be asked and answered about the ways different approaches lead us to communicate with children and whether such modes of communication are uniformly successful with all children (Delpit, 1993). We need to have a more reasoned exploration of how children with differing levels of performance and diverse instructional needs respond to different approaches. Finally, we need to remember that throughout the history of reading research, the evidence has been strong that in the final analysis, it is the teacher, not the approach, that makes the difference (Dykstra, 1968). We must be more vigilant about helping teachers to become knowledgeable about the theoretical underpinnings of effective instruction, about valid assessment, and about the connections between assessment and instruction.

Question: Children and adolescents with language learning disabilities have been known to have difficulties "processing, retaining," and "comprehending" both spoken and written text. What are some selected strategies professionals might consider when attempting to improve children's understanding of oral and written text?

Answer by Jeanne R. Paratore
Boston University

Several strategies have proven to be successful for children who have been identified as having language learning disabilities. These can be framed within the three parts of a typical reading lesson: before reading activities, during reading activities, and after reading activities. Before reading, it is important to engage students in tasks and activities that will help them to access and relate their own background knowledge and to build the knowledge that is lacking. Several strategies have been found to be helpful, including learning to survey the text and accompanying illustrations to make predictions and to pose questions about the text. One practice has proven to be especially useful. Semantic mapping, a strategy for categorizing words and ideas in the text, helps students to organize information before they read. When used effectively, it incorporates students' own knowledge and the key words that are necessary for them to know before reading to comprehend the text (Johnson, Pittelman, & Heimlich, 1986). During reading, students who have language processing difficulties often need help knowing where to focus attention and how to sort out important versus unimportant details. Providing them with graphic organizers that visually represent the important ideas in the text helps them to identify and recall important information (Taylor, 1992). Sometimes graphic organizers or "maps" may be used as simple visual reminders. Other times students may benefit from using them as note-taking guides. After reading, students will benefit from having some way to check their own understanding and to fix up when they do not understand. A practice known as *reciprocal teaching* has been found to be especially beneficial in teaching both ways to self-question and ways to fix up (Palincsar & Brown, 1984; Palincsar, Brown, & Campione, chap. 5).

Question: Several authors of this text, notably Blachman (chap. 9) and van Kleeck (chap. 3), discussed the importance of phonemic awareness in the acquisition and development of reading and writing. How do you respond to reading specialists who propose that "children do not need to be taught phonemic awareness, they will simply grow into it"?

Answer by Hugh W. Catts
University of Kansas, Lawrence

I have sometimes heard similar statements in discussions of meaning-based or whole language approaches to teaching reading. Some argue that phonemic awareness is not a precursor of reading but rather one of the numerous abilities that emerge as children are exposed to and interact with print in a meaningful manner. Such statements strike me as a rather shortsighted view of phonemic awareness and its relationship to reading.

Phonemic awareness refers to one's conscious awareness of speech sounds. It is the ability to reflect on the phonemic structure of words separately from the meanings of words. Two general types of phonemic awareness have often been considered (Morais, 1991). The first is a holistic and nonanalytical awareness of phonemes. This awareness allows one to make judgments about the similarities and differences in the phonemes of words. For example, it is the awareness that words may rhyme or begin with the same sound segment. Such rhyme or alliteration awareness does not necessarily require explicit knowledge of phonemes (Morais, 1991). This latter awareness represents a second type of phonemic knowledge. This explicit phonemic awareness is more analytical in nature and enables one to segment words into phonemes, count the phonemes in words, or isolate and manipulate phonemic segments.

The question of whether or not children need to be taught phonemic awareness depends on which type of phonemic awareness is considered. Research suggests that the ability to reflect on and/or make judgments about rhyme and phonological similarity may emerge naturally during development. On the other hand, the more analytical knowledge necessary to explicitly segment words into phonemes (e.g., explicit phonemic awareness) may require specific instruction or attention (Morais, 1991).

Children's awareness of the phonemes in words emerges gradually during the preschool years. Two factors seem to play a major role in the emergence of early phonemic awareness. These are cognitive-linguistic development and literacy experience. Phonemic awareness appears to rest in part on the maturation of a specific cognitive-linguistic ability. This ability, which is somewhat independent of intelligence, allows children to bring their unconscious knowledge of speech to a conscious level. Early literacy experiences may also promote phonemic awareness. Several researchers have shown that early experiences with nursery rhymes and other literacy materials may heighten young children's awareness of speech sounds (e.g., Bryant, Bradley, Maclean, & Crossland, 1989).

As a result of cognitive-linguistic development and early literacy experiences, most children enter school with some rudimentary awareness of the phonemes in words. Most children, however, do not enter school with explicit phonemic awareness. The ability to explicitly segment words into phonemes does not appear to emerge naturally during the preschool years. Spoken words are not composed of discrete phoneme-sized segments. Rather, the information corresponding to phonemes in words is spread across the entire syllable. As a result, phonemes are not perceptually distinct units. They are, in fact, extremely difficult for listeners to isolate or segment. Nonetheless, children can learn to divide words into phonemes. Most children learn to do this while learning the alphabet and its use in reading and spelling. To help children understand how the alphabet works, educators have often explicitly taught children to divide words into phonemes. With this directed attention to phonemes, most children acquire explicit awareness of the phonemic segments in words and can use this knowledge to learn to read and spell. Individuals who have not, however, had this experience will not acquire explicit awareness of phonemes. Research demonstrates that preschoolers, illiterates, and adult readers of a nonalphabetic language generally are not explicitly aware of phonemic units and cannot isolate, count, or manipulate the phonemes in words (see Catts, 1989).

We still might ask if children can acquire explicit phonemic awareness from indirect as opposed to direct alphabetic instruction. In other words, do children learn to segment words into phonemes when taught to read using a meaning-based approach, which does not directly teach alphabetic reading? Some children no doubt may be able to acquire explicit phonemic awareness from mere exposure to an alphabetic language. Many children, however, do not easily come to appreciate the individual phonemes in words and how the alphabet represents those phonemes (Alegria, Pignot, & Morais, 1982). In fact, the preponderance of evidence indicates that children who are provided with explicit instruction in alphabetic reading (including explicit phonemic awareness) get off to a much better start in learning to read than do those who have not been provided with this instruction (see Adams, 1990; Vellutino, 1991). Explicit instruction concerning the phonemes in words appears to be particularly important for children who are at risk for reading disabilities. Research conclusively documents that deficiencies in phonemic awareness underlie many of the difficulties of poor readers (see Catts, 1989). Furthermore, training studies have shown that phonemic awareness can be taught to poor readers (or children at risk for reading problems) and that such training has a significant effect on their reading achievement (e.g., Alexander, Andersen, Heilman, Voeller, & Torgesen, 1991; Ball & Blachman, 1988).

In summary, some aspects of phonemic awareness appear to be acquired naturally during the preschool years. Other aspects, specifically, explicit awareness of phonemes, require experience with an alphabetic language. Teaching children the alphabet and how it works directs children's attention to the phonemes in words. In turn, this explicit awareness of phonemes can have a significant effect on how quickly and easily children learn to read.

Question: How have collaborative/consultative models worked in your setting?

Answer by Lauren P. Hoffman
South Metropolitan Association for Low-Incidence Handicapped, Flossmoor, IL

Collaborative consultation models have been used within the south Metropolitan Association for Low-Incidence Handicapped (SMA) in an effort to serve students in both special education and in general education. The first model described here focuses on students in a self-contained special education program; the second model is geared toward working with staff and students in general education.

The Communication Development Program, a self-contained special education program, is committed to the concept of transdisciplinary collaborative teamwork. In this setting, speech-language pathologists function on transdisciplinary teams consisting of an educator, a social worker, and a teaching assistant. The speech-language pathologist has a significantly expanded role and is equally responsible for all aspects of classroom instruction and management. All team members, with the leadership of the speech-language pathologist, provide communication-based instruction by integrating the student's speech and language goals and objectives into the curriculum. This requires ongoing training, communication among the team members, and a willingness to expand their knowledge and expertise by crossing disciplinary boundaries. Team members incorporate a problem-solving attitude as they work closely with each other and recognize that obtaining multiple perspectives is critical in comprehensively understanding the students' diverse learning needs. This type of collaborative teamwork requires additional time and must be supported by the school administration to succeed. Training and staff development is an integral factor in implementing this model effectively. Team members need to develop new competencies as they assume new roles and responsibilities.

To maintain students in general education within their home school (as inclusion philosophies suggest), another collaborative model has been developed for students with severe speech and language disabilities. In this model, the consulting speech-language pathologist teams with the general classroom teacher and the district speech-language pathologist in the school where the student is placed. The consulting speech-language pathologist functions as a problem solver, collaborator, and resource person. Although the consulting speech-language pathologist readily shares her expertise, developing an equal and open relationship is of prime importance. This collaborative role may include some aspects of the preceding model such as crossing disciplinary boundaries and adapting curriculum. This model, however, does not include direct classroom instruction as a primary role for the consulting speech-language pathologist. Although there may be some co-teaching for purposes of assessment and demonstration, the main focus of this role is to assist the teacher and the district speech-language pathologist in implementing the type of speech and language support necessary for a particular student. In this model, the consulting speech-language pathologist has less direct control over the actual implementation of the instruction and must demonstrate superior follow-up and monitoring abilities. When everyone works together with a similar focus, this model can be extremely effective.

Question: What guidelines would you offer professionals who might be involved in the start-up phases of incorporating a collaborative consultation model?

Answer by Lauren P. Hoffman
South Metropolitan Association for Low-Incidence Handicapped, Flossmoor, IL

The first question to ask is "Why do we want to incorporate collaborative consultation, and how will this model assist in better meeting the needs of the students?" Collaborative consultation models, and any type of program development, should be directly linked to one's philosophy and principles of language and learning development. If one understands the rationale underlying the model, the practice and procedural issues will more quickly and easily fall into place.

The next question to ask is "What kind of training is necessary for staff to implement a collaborative consultation model successfully?" It is clear that staff need ongoing training in literacy development and in understanding the connections between language and learning, in addition to training in the "how to's" of collaboration. Both content and process need to be addressed to maximize the potential success of the collaborative effort.

A question that comes later is "How should we start?" Starting small and starting with colleagues who are interested and enthusiastic may be a key in creating a positive and accepted collaborative model and/or program. We need to build on the successes and share our experiences with others so that everyone begins to learn about the impact of the model. Staff will require more support during the initial phases of the transition as they will be required to expand their competencies, along with changing their roles and responsibilities.

SUMMARY

Our colleagues leave us much to think about while providing us with provocative, challenging, and realistic answers. And although we may have a tendency to become overwhelmed by the infusion of information and the quest for change, we might stop to think about how far we have come as a perspective check on how far we may have to go; we might also note how the past sometimes foreshadows the future (Stark, 1993). We might think back to a time, although few may recall it, in speech-language pathology (then known as speech correction) when speech correction services were provided only through "regular education" and service to special education students was forbidden in many states, as a colleague who has been in the profession for fifty years reminded us, rather sardonically. Parents of the retarded pleaded with clinicians to help their children by providing them with language instruction. Under state regulations, however, it was often impossible to accede to those requests. Many clinicians today, those who entered the field from the mid-1970s onward—have grown accustomed to the differences that were created when Public Law 94–142 was passed in the mid-1970s and their services were subsumed in large measure under its regulations. Caseloads in schools dropped precipitously from 250 to 500 or more "regular education" students, to 40 or 50 students with "special needs." However, while the caseloads were declining, the tasks faced by the clinicians in terms of level of service and the level of severity were rising. Itinerant clinicians were less peripatetic, dropping from five, or twenty-five schools, to perhaps only one or two. Speech improvement programs that flourished in the 1950s disappeared, only to be reborn in the 1990s as a collaborative model of service delivery. Indeed, the rationale for speech improvement in the 1950s was to provide classroom-based instruction to whole classrooms at the elementary school level and to acquaint classroom teachers with techniques that they might use in developing the expressive skills of all children, including the "speech-defective" child's use of speech and language (Van Riper & Butler, 1956). Foreshadowing the efforts of speech-language pathologists in the 1990s, but using the terminology of the times, the recommendation to conduct speech programs in the classroom included goals such as

> to help the child identify and recognize the characteristics of speech sounds, a goal which pays dividends not only in terms of better speech but in improving other basic skills needed in school . . . and . . . to improve the child's vocal phonics so that he cannot only learn new pronunciations easily but also through the analysis and synthesis training come to attain the phonic skills necessary in reading and spelling. (Butler, 1956, p. 2)

One can see an interesting 1950s prelude to today's terms and phrases such as phonology, metaphonology, phonological awareness, and its role in lexical access (Swank, in press), phonological output disorders, communicative competence, and intelligibility, among others. Although it is evident that in the 1950s clinicians had begun to suspect that there was a connection between spoken language, reading, writing, and spelling, it was not yet a fully realized belief. Indeed, echoing thoughts about the newness of language study, it has only been since the early to mid-1980s years that multiple studies from around the world have confirmed that phonological awareness plays a causal role in early reading difficulty, again as noted throughout this text. Such understanding has been more than thirty years in coming.

Indeed, concepts such as *communicative competence, input and uptake,* and *scaffolding,* among many others were unknown to the "speech-teach" of the early 1960s. Even terms such as *discourse,* called "running speech" (which sounded a little peculiar even in those days), were yet to come. In fact, language disorders themselves were primarily classified as "delayed speech," which was defined as difficulties in speaking that ranged from baby talk to speech retardation to mutism, all thought to be caused by low intelligence, hearing defects, poor coordination, illness, lack of motivation, poor speech standards, shift of handedness, bilingual conflicts, emotional shocks, accidents and/or conflicts, poor auditory memory span, and aphasia (Van Riper, 1947). Because these terms may seem strange to readers in the 1990s, it should be remembered that there was no clear demarcation between speech and language. Moreover, we had not yet recognized that *language* would be considered a system in which phonology, morphology, syntax, semantics, and pragmatics were embedded subsystems. In fact, the American Speech and Hearing Association did not concede to changing its name until late in the 1970s to the American Speech-Language-Hearing Association. *Speech pathologist* became *speech-language pathologist* at about the same period. So, we have come a long way.

As we think back on the content of this text, which encourages the integration of services, it becomes interesting to reflect on the separation of services that existed (and sometimes still exists) between speech-language programming and reading programming. One might recall that most speech clinicians had little interaction with reading teachers over the years, although this was perhaps more by happenstance than design. In more traditional service delivery models of the past, reading researchers and speech clinicians both tended to be itinerants, moving from school to school and perhaps sharing broom closets, nurse's rooms, or the cafeteria during quiet time. They were seldom in the same school on the same day. Moreover, in a not-so-rare display of the isolation of training in the various disciplines, few regular and special education classroom teachers recognized that the "specialists" shared children, sometimes replicating services, to an unknown degree. While split and replicated services may continue to thwart progress toward more collaborative programming today, heightened awareness of and training in some of the oral-to-literate connections discussed throughout this text can only help to prevent making "inclusion" another exercise in "exclusion" for children and adolescents in trouble.

The work in sociolinguistics in the 1960s and 1970s laid the research base for much of today's knowledge of language differences as contrasted to language disorders. Chall, Jacobs, and Baldwin (1990) remind readers (as did Butler and Wallach in their reflection following Part 3) that the "blame" for language difficulties cannot always be "inside the child's head." While we talk about "oral and literate language styles" in this text, sociolinguists of the 1960s such as Basil Bernstein (discussed in Chall et al., 1990) talked about "restricted" and "elaborated" language codes. Bernstein believed that some children from lower-class homes, for example, may have had little or no opportunity to *practice with* the "more exact, more abstract communication" of elaborated language codes. Consequently, they came to school, perhaps using restricted codes, which are reserved for face-to-face and informal interactions, ill equipped to deal with the elaborated codes required for reading and academic learning. Sound familiar?

Other research of the 1960s and 1970s influenced today's practice in very positive ways. Labov's work (discussed by Chall et al., 1990) on the differences between Black and Standard English riveted the field and demonstrated the linguistic integrity of Black English, which made it a separate code variety of English. During the same time period, Bereiter and Englemann (1966) published their reading and language program, providing "scripts" and materials for teachers' use in the classroom. A highly structured program, it was used by educators and speech-language pathologists and continues in use in some places to this day. Chall (1983) has debated its merits in her seminal work, *Learning to Read: The Great Debate.* No doubt, this debate will continue as long as there are books and children who learn to read them.

As researchers have moved toward anthropology and ethnography, the work of Shirley Brice Heath in the 1980s attracted the attention of those who worked with minority and culturally different children with and without speech and language impairments, although her points have relevance for all children. Her approach to narrative across cultures (Heath, 1986) revealed not only the variation in narrative genres, use, and learning but has also made us aware of the ethnocentricity that may underpin a number of current approaches to narrative discourse. Heath (1986) summarizes her well-made points:

> Academic success depends not on the specific language or languages children know, but on the ways of using language that they know. This is a simple point but one that teachers and testers find incompatible with customary ways of assessing children in school . . . researchers and evaluators (test makers as well as test administrators) must find ways of working together to use what children do with language in their homes and communities to extend and enrich the school's repertoire of narrative genre. (p. 93)

The 1980s and 1990s paradigm shift to assessment and remediation "in context" calls for all professionals to increase their understanding of naturalistic contexts and their contribution to the success or failure of intervention attempts. As Westby (1992) notes:

> The validity and reliability of qualitative data depend to a great extent on the methodologic skill, sensitivity and integrity of the researcher, teacher or clinician. Systematic and rigorous observation involves far more than just being present and looking around. Skillful interviewing involves much more than just asking questions. Content analysis requires considerably more than just reading to see what is there. Generating useful and credible qualitative findings through observation, interview, and content analysis requires discipline, knowledge, training, practice, creativity, and hard work. (p. 13)

The co-editors concur, as do the authors throughout the text. In the preceding chapters, readers undoubtedly have caught the implicit message: serving the LLD student has not been easy over the past decades, and there is no sign that this will change in the immediate future. Indeed, while knowledge, training, practice, creativity, and hard work may help us meet the challenge signaled by Hoffman's final words in the question and answer section about "expanding competencies" and "changing roles and responsibilities," implementing new and innovative programming will require administrative, financial, and staff support. We might keep in mind the recent Council for Exceptional Children's (CEC) policy statement and recognize that we are not alone: Inclusive education must be "supported by an infusion of especially trained personnel and other appropriate supportive practices according to individual needs of the child" (Division of Early Childhood of the CEC, 1993).

As we move toward new and innovative practices, we move toward implementing Launer's challenge to "get fire in our bellies and fight for what we know is right," Paratore's encouragement to look beyond a program's promise, and Catts's research-based approach for early and proficient reading. Success will follow if the settings in which we practice and the professionals with whom we practice meet us half-way.

We began the introductory section to this chapter by setting the stage for the questions we have asked our colleagues to address. We have also asked ourselves how we have come to arrive within the shadow of the year 2000 by looking back over the past four or five decades. In so doing, we provided examples of how theories, concepts, and clinical activities have been modified over time to fit the ever-changing social and political climates of a society that is evolving from one that attempted to "Americanize" all comers to a society that, we hope, continues to value diversity within a democratic framework. We have noted the currents and cross-currents in the world of the schools, where a majority of the professionals in speech-language pathology, reading, and other related disciplines gather. We have recognized the shadow of school reform as a challenging and at the same time frightening prospect. We have noted the emergence of "language" in its broadest context as significantly modifying the role of language specialists in the schools. Hoffman (1993b) eloquently reminds us, as we search for answers in the midst of a changing world:

> The bottom line is doing what's best for kids. Different situations will present different obstacles and the answers may be different depending on the variables. Let's hope that by the year 2000 we'll figure it all out. (p. 18)

REFERENCES

Adams, M. (1990). *Beginning to read.* Cambridge, MA: MIT Press.

Alegria, J., Pignot, E., & Morais, J. (1982). Phonetic analysis of speech and memory codes in beginning readers. *Memory and Cognition, 10,* 451–456.

Alexander, A., Andersen, H., Heilman, P., Voeller, K., & Torgesen, J. (1991). Phonological awareness training and the remediation of analytic decoding deficits in a group of severe dyslexics. *Annals of Dyslexia, 41,* 193–207.

American Psychological Association. (1974). *Standards for educational and standards for educational and psychological tests.* Washington, DC: Author.

Anastasi, A. (1988). *Psychological testing* (6th ed.). New York: Macmillan.

Ball, E., & Blachman, B. (1988). Phoneme segmentation training: Effect on reading readiness. *Annals of Dyslexia, 38,* 208–225.

Bereiter, C., & Englemann, S. (1966). *Teaching disadvantaged children in the pre-school.* Englewood Cliffs, NJ: Prentice-Hall.

Butler, K. G. (1956). Even the stalwart stumble. *Education, 77*(2), 1–4.

Bryant, P., Bradley, L., Maclean, M., & Crossland, J. (1989). Nursery rhymes, phonological skills, and reading. *Journal of Child Language, 16,* 407–428.

Catts, H. (1989). Phonological processing deficits and reading disabilities. In A. Kamhi & H. Catts (Eds.) *Reading disabilities: A developmental language perspective* (pp. 101–132). Boston: Allyn & Bacon.

Council for Exceptional Children. (1993, May). CEC policy on inclusive schools and community settings [Special issue]. *Teaching Exceptional Children, 25*(Suppl.), 4.

Chall, J. S. (1983). *Learning to read: The great debate, updated edition.* New York: McGraw-Hill.

Chall, J. S., Jacobs, V. A., & Baldwin, L. E. (1990). Literacy and language among low-income children. In J. S. Chall, V. A. Jacobs, & L. E. Baldwin (Eds.), *The reading crisis: Why poor children fall behind* (pp. 1–19). Cambridge, MA: Harvard University Press.

Crawford, C., & Porter, G. (1992). *How it happens: A look at inclusive educational practice in Canada for children and youth with disabilities.* Submitted by the Reoher Institute to National Welfare Grants Health and Welfare, Canada.

Damico, J. S. (1990). Descriptive assessment of communicative ability in limited English proficient students. In E. V. Hamayan & J. S. Damico (Eds.), *Limiting bias in the assessment of bilingual students* (pp. 157–218). Austin, TX: PRO-ED.

Delpit, L. (1993). The silenced dialogue: Power and pedagogy in educating other people's children. In L. Weis & M. Fine (Eds.), *Beyond silenced voices: Class, race and gender in United States schools* (pp. 19–142). Albany, NY: State University of New York Press.

Division of Early Childhood (DEC) of the Council for Exceptional Children. (1993, April). *Position statement on inclusion.* Presented at the annual business meeting of the Council for Exceptional Children, San Antonio, TX.

Dykstra, R. (1968). Summary of the second-grade phase of the cooperative research program. *Reading Research Quarterly, 4,* 49–70.

Heath, S. B. (1986). Taking a cross-cultural look at narratives. *Topics in Language Disorders, 7*(1), 84–95.

Hoffman, L. P. (1993a, April). *Language and literacy programming across the educational continuum: From inclusive to self-contained settings.* Workshop presented at the Emerson Language Learning Disabilities Institute, Willowbrook, IL.

Hoffman, L. P. (1993b). Language in the school context: What is least restrictive? *Special Interest Division 10 Newsletter: Language Learning and Education, 3*(1), 1–18.

Johnson, D. D., Pittelman, S. D., & Heimlich, J. E. (1986). Semantic mapping. *The Reading Teacher, 39,* 778–783.

Kamhi, A. (1993). Some problems with the marriage between theory and clinical practice. *Language, Speech, and Hearing Services in Schools, 24,* 57–60.

Lahey, M. (1990). Who shall be called language disordered? Some reflections and one perspective. *Journal of Speech and Hearing Disorders, 55*(4), 612–620.

McCauley, R. J., & Swisher, L. (1984a). Psychometric review of language and articulation tests for preschool children. *Journal of Speech and Hearing Disorders, 49,* 34–42.

McCauley, R. J., & Swisher, L. (1984b). Use and misuse of norm-referenced tests. *Journal of Speech and Hearing Disorders, 49,* 338–348.

Morais, J. (1991). Phonological awareness: A bridge between language and literacy. In D. Sawyer & B. Fox (Eds.), *Phonological awareness in reading, The evolution of our current perspectives (31–71).* New York: Springer-Verlag.

Palincsar, A. S., & Brown, A. L. (1984). Reciprocal teaching of comprehension-fostering and comprehension-monitoring activities. *Cognition and Instruction, 1,* 117–175.

Stahl, S. A., & Miller, P. A. (1989). Whole language and language experience approaches for beginning reading: A quantitative research synthesis. *Review of Educational Research, 59,* 87–116.

Stark, J. (1993, June). *I don't care who said it or what it means, just tell me what to do.* Panel discussion at the Emerson College Language Learning Disabilities Institute, Boston.

Swank, L. K. (in press). Assessing phonological-coding abilities related to reading. *Topics in Language Disorders, 14,* 2.

Taylor, B. M. (1992). Text structure, comprehension, and recall. In S. J. Samuels & A. E. Farstrup (Eds.), *What research has to say about reading instruction* (2nd ed., pp. 220–235). Newark, DE: International Reading Association.

Van Riper, C. (1947). *Speech correction: Principles and methods* (2nd ed). Englewood Cliffs, NJ: Prentice-Hall.

Van Riper, C., & Butler, K. G. (1956). *Speech in the elementary classroom.* New York: Harper & Row.

Vellutino, F. (1991). Introduction to three studies on reading acquisition: Convergent findings on theoretical foundations of code-oriented versus whole-language approaches to reading instruction. *Journal of Education Psychology, 83,* 437–443.

Wallach, G. P. (1993, June). *I don't care who said it or what it means, just tell me what to do.* Panel discussion at the Emerson College Language Learning Disabilities Institute, Boston.

Westby, C. (1992). Ethnography and research: A qualitative view. *Topics in Language Disorders, 12*(3), 1–14.

AUTHOR INDEX

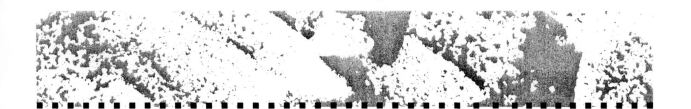

SUBJECT INDEX